Corporate Social Res|

Strategy, Communication, Governance

This upper-level textbook offers an original and up-to-date introduction to issues in corporate social responsibility (CSR) from a global perspective. Written by an international team of experts, it guides students through key themes in CSR including strategy, communication, regulation and governance. Balancing critiques of CSR with a discussion of the opportunities it creates, it includes chapters devoted to critical issues such as human rights, anti-corruption, labour rights and the environment.

Pedagogical features include customised case studies, study questions, key term highlighting, practitioner pieces and suggestions for further resources. The book is also complemented by a companion website featuring adaptable lecture slides, teaching notes for cases and links to related resources. Tailored for upper-level undergraduate and postgraduate courses on corporate social responsibility, sustainability and business ethics, it is also relevant to non-business courses in political science, international relations and communications.

Andreas Rasche is Professor of Business in Society at the Centre for Corporate Social Responsibility at Copenhagen Business School. He has published more than fifty academic articles and cases as well as four books, and is Associate Editor of *Business Ethics Quarterly*.

Mette Morsing is Professor and Co-Director of the Sustainability Platform at Copenhagen Business School. She was a Founding Member of the Academy of Business in Society (ABIS) in Brussels, and was Associate Editor of *Scandinavian Journal of Management*.

Jeremy Moon is Velux Professor of Corporate Sustainability at Copenhagen Business School. He is the co-author of *Corporations and Citizenship* (with Andrew Crane and Dirk Matten, 2008) and author of *A Very Short Introduction to Corporate Social Responsibility* (2014).

CORPORATE SOCIAL RESPONSIBILITY

Strategy, Communication, Governance

ANDREAS RASCHE

Copenhagen Business School

METTE MORSING

Copenhagen Business School and
Stockholm School of Economics

JEREMY MOON

Copenhagen Business School

CAMBRIDGE
UNIVERSITY PRESS

CAMBRIDGE
UNIVERSITY PRESS

University Printing House, Cambridge CB2 8BS, United Kingdom

One Liberty Plaza, 20th Floor, New York, NY 10006, USA

477 Williamstown Road, Port Melbourne, VIC 3207, Australia

314-321, 3rd Floor, Plot 3, Splendor Forum, Jasola District Centre, New Delhi – 110025, India

79 Anson Road, #06-04/06, Singapore 079906

Cambridge University Press is part of the University of Cambridge.

It furthers the University's mission by disseminating knowledge in the pursuit of
education, learning, and research at the highest international levels of excellence.

www.cambridge.org
Information on this title: www.cambridge.org/9781107114876
10.1017/9781316335529

First published 2017
Reprinted 2018

Printed in the United Kingdom by Clays, St Ives plc

A catalogue record for this publication is available from the British Library.

Library of Congress Cataloging-in-Publication Data
Names: Rasche, Andreas, editor. | Morsing, Mette, editor. | Moon, Jeremy, 1955- editor.
Title: Corporate social responsibility : strategy, communication, governance
/ [edited by] Andreas Rasche, Copenhagen Business School, Mette Morsing,
Copenhagen Business School, Jeremy Moon, Copenhagen Business School.
Description: Cambridge, United Kingdom : Cambridge University Press, 2016.
| Includes bibliographical references and index.
Identifiers: LCCN 2016036438| ISBN 9781107114876 (hardback) | ISBN 9781107535398 (pbk.)
Subjects: LCSH: Social responsibility of business. | Corporate governance.
Classification: LCC HD60 .C6954 2016 | DDC 658.4/08–dc23 LC record available at https://lccn.loc.gov/2016036438

ISBN 978-1-107-11487-6 Hardback
ISBN 978-1-107-53539-8 Paperback

Cambridge University Press has no responsibility for the persistence or accuracy
of URLs for external or third-party Internet Web sites referred to in this publication
and does not guarantee that any content on such Web sites is, or will remain,
accurate or appropriate.

Table of Contents

List of Figures

List of Tables

List of Boxes

List of Contributors

Karin Buhmann is Professor of Corporate Social Responsibility, Sustainability and Public-Private Regulation at Copenhagen Business School. She is also a member of the Danish National Contact Point under OECD's Guidelines for Multinational Enterprises. Her research and teaching focus on regulatory governance aspects of corporate social responsibility and business and human rights. Buhmann has published widely on these issues.

Lars Thøger Christensen is Professor of Communication and Organization at Copenhagen Business School. His research interests include issues of organisational identity, corporate communication, autocommunication, CSR, transparency and accountability, which he approaches from critical and postmodern perspectives. For further information: http://tinyurl.com/CBS-Christensen.

W. Timothy Coombs is Professor in the Department of Communication Studies at Texas A&M University. His primary area of research is crisis communication and how it intersects with elements of strategic communication. He is a member of the Arthur Page Society and an Honorary Professor in the Department of Business Communication at Aarhus University.

Joep Cornelissen is Professor of Corporate Communication and Management at the Rotterdam School of Management, Erasmus University. The main focus of his research involves studies of the role of corporate and managerial communication in the context of innovation, entrepreneurship and change, and of social evaluations of the legitimacy and reputation of start-up and established firms. He also has an interest in questions of scientific reasoning and theory development in management and organisation theory.

Frank de Bakker is Professor at the Department of Management at IÉSEG School of Management (CNRS-LEM), Lille, France. His research focuses on the intersection of institutional theory, stakeholder management and social movement theory, specifically concerning interactions between NGOs and firms. More information is available at: www.frankdebakker.nl.

Frank den Hond is the Ehrnrooth Professor of Management and Organization in the Department of Management and Organization at Hanken School of

Economics, and Editor of FT50-listed journal 'Organization Studies' (2013–2017). He has a secondary affiliation with the Department of Organization Sciences at VU University Amsterdam. In his research he seeks to develop an organisational understanding of social movements and their interaction with companies.

Sergiy Dmytriyev is pursuing a Doctorate in Management at the Darden School of Business at the University of Virginia. He also holds an MBA from IESE Business School in Barcelona, Spain. His research interests include supererogation in business, stakeholder responsibility, stakeholder engagement, defining company success, creating value from disagreements, and the meaning of life. Prior to Darden, Sergiy worked at different levels for Proctor & Gamble, Bain & Company and Monsanto in Eastern Europe.

R. Edward Freeman is University Professor, Elis and Signe Olsson Professor, Academic Director of the Institute for Business in Society, and Senior Fellow of the Olsson Center for Applied Ethics at the University of Virginia Darden School of Business. His latest book *Bridging the Values Gap* (with Ellen Auster) was published by Barrett Koehler in July 2015. He has received honorary doctorates (Doctor Honoris Causa) from Radboud University Nijmegen, Universidad Pontificia Comillas in Spain, and the Hanken School of Economics in Finland for his work on stakeholder theory and business ethics. He is a lifelong student of philosophy, martial arts and the blues. Freeman is a founding member of Red Goat Records (redgoatrecords.com), bringing the joy of original soul and rhythm and blues music into the twenty-first century.

Dirk Ulrich Gilbert is a Professor of Business Ethics and Associate Dean at the University of Hamburg, Germany. His most recent research focuses on management education, international accountability standards, deliberative democracy and regional strategies of multinational corporations.

Jean-Pascal Gond is a Professor of Corporate Social Responsibility at Cass Business School, City University London. Before coming to Cass in 2012 he held various academic positions at HEC Montréal (University of Montréal, Canada) and at the International Centre for Corporate Social Responsibility at Nottingham University Business School. His research mobilises organisation theory and economic sociology to investigate corporate social responsibility. For further details, see http://bunhill.city.ac.uk/research/cassexperts.nsf/(smar turl)/J.Gond.

Jonas Haertle is Head of Principles for Responsible Management Education (PRME) secretariat and Global Compact Academic Affairs at the UN Global Compact Office, New York. He is responsible for driving the mission of the

PRME initiative, a global business school network, and bringing together good practice of PRME and the UN Global Compact, the world's largest corporate responsibility initiative. He holds graduate degrees from Hamburg University in Germany and Rutgers University in the USA, and is currently pursuing a PhD in Business Administration at Nottingham Trent University Business School, UK.

Hans Krause Hansen is Professor of Governance and Culture Studies at Copenhagen Business School. His current research revolves around the emergence of new modes of governance, corruption and corruption control, transparency and surveillance regimes. His publications include anthologies, volume chapters, journal special issues and articles in journals across several disciplines, including international political economy, international political sociology, criminology, and organisation and communication studies.

Christian Herzig is Professor of Management in the International Food Industry at the University of Kassel. His research interest lies in accounting and control for sustainability, social and environmental accountability and strategy as well as discourses on corporate social ir/responsibility. He is author of the book *Environmental Management Accounting* (Routledge). More information is available at: www.uni-kassel.de/go/mifi/staff.

Kristin Huber is pursuing a PhD in Business Ethics at the University of Hamburg, Germany. Her research focuses on corporate social responsibility, multi-stakeholder governance, and the theory and practice of deliberative democracy.

Jette Steen Knudsen is Shelby Cullom Davis Chair in International Business, and focuses on sustainability at the Fletcher School of Law and Diplomacy, Tufts University. Her research centres on the interface between government regulation and business actions. She is currently studying the ability of governments in economically advanced industrialised nations to promote social change through the regulation of social practices of home country multinationals in developing countries.

Anna-Lena Kühn is Postdoctoral Researcher at the University of Kassel's Management in the International Food Industry unit. Her current research focuses on CSR reporting and comparative CSR in emerging economies. More information is available at: www.uni-kassel.de/go/mifi/staff.

Jane Lister is Senior Research Fellow and Associate Director of the Centre for Transportation Studies at the Sauder School of Business at the University of British Columbia. Her research focuses on the business and politics of corporate sustainability.

Daniel Mittler is the Political Director of Greenpeace International. Based in Berlin, he leads a global team of specialists advising Greenpeace on political and corporate strategies. He has led Greenpeace delegations to many global forums – from the Global Compact to the World Trade Organization and Rio+20. He is a co-founder of CorA – Germany's corporate accountability network, and from 2000 to 2002 led Friends of the Earth International's 'Don't let big business rule the world' campaign, advocating 'Global rules for global players' at the Johannesburg World Summit on Sustainable Development. He writes mainly on NGO strategy, climate politics and corporate accountability. His writings can be found at www.greendaniel.blogspot.com.

Mark Moody-Stuart is Chairman of Hermes Equity Ownership Services. He was previously chairman of the Royal Dutch/Shell Group and of Anglo American, and has served on many public boards, including HSBC, Accenture and Saudi Aramco. He has a long-term interest in the contribution of business to development globally and has been involved in the UN Global Compact since its inception. He is Chairman of the Global Compact Foundation.

Jeremy Moon is Velux Professor of Corporate Sustainability at the Centre for Corporate Social Responsibility at Copenhagen Business School. His research focuses on comparative CSR, business and governance, and corporate citizenship. He is the author of *Corporate Social Responsibility: A Very Short Introduction* (Oxford University Press). For further details see http://tinyurl.com/CBS-JMoon.

Mette Morsing is Professor and MISTRA Chair of Sustainable Markets at Stockholm School of Economics and Professor at and founder of the Centre for Corporate Social Responsibility at Copenhagen Business School. Her research focuses on CSR and sustainability mobilising organisation theory, communication studies and management research.

Luisa Murphy is PhD Fellow in Corporate Sustainability at Copenhagen Business School (CBS). She was formerly Research Assistant and Project Manager at CBS. She holds an MSc from the University of Oxford. Her research examines corporate social responsibility and sustainability through communication, governance, organisational, development studies and human rights perspectives. Prior work includes three years at the Department of Justice, USA.

Mads Øvlisen has been Chairman of the Board of Directors of LEGO A/S since 1996, after becoming a Board member in 1990. He was president and CEO of Novo Industri A/S from 1981 to 1989, then of Novo Nordisk A/S from 1989 to 2000. He was also a member of The United Nations Global Compact Board from 2006 to 2012, and is now special advisor to the Global Compact on supply chain sustainability. In addition, he holds the position of Adjunct Professor of Corporate Social Responsibility at Copenhagen Business School.

Stefano Ponte is Professor of International Political Economy in the Department of Business and Politics at Copenhagen Business School. His research examines how the global economy is governed and how developing countries fare in it. His work is informed by global value chain analysis and convention theory, and explores the overlaps and tensions between private governance and public regulation, especially in relation to sustainability issues.

René Taudal Poulsen is Associate Professor at the Department of Innovation and Organizational Economics at Copenhagen Business School. He has carried out research on overfishing in a historical perspective, and is now focusing on sustainability and environmental governance in the shipping industry.

Andreas Rasche is Professor of Business in Society at the Centre for Corporate Social Responsibility at Copenhagen Business School and Research Director of the CBS World-Class Research Environment on 'Governing Responsible Business'. His research focuses on corporate responsibility standards (particularly the UN Global Compact), the political role of corporations in transnational governance, and the governance of global supply networks. More information is available at: www.arasche.com.

Dennis Schoeneborn is Professor of Communication, Organization, and Corporate Social Responsibility at Copenhagen Business School. He also serves as main coordinator of the Standing Working Group 'Organization as Communication' at the European Group of Organizational Studies (EGOS). His research focuses on organisation theory, organisational communication, CSR communication, social media and new forms of organising. For further information see: www.cbs.dk/en/staff/dscikl.

Clare Short is a former UK Member of Parliament and was Secretary of State for International Development from 1997 to 2003. She was chair of the international board of the Extractive Industries Transparency Initiative from 2011 to 2016. She is also senior policy advisor to Cities Alliance, a global partnership focused on urban poverty, and a trustee of Hope, an organisation which provides housing and support for destitute asylum seekers in Birmingham.

Laura J. Spence is Professor of Business Ethics and Co-Director of the Centre for Research into Sustainability at Royal Holloway, University of London. Her research is on critical, social and ethical perspectives of business practice. Recent co-edited books include *CSR: Readings and Cases in A Global Context* (Routledge) and *Small Business Social Responsibility: Global Perspectives* (Edward Elgar). She is a Trustee of the Institute of Business Ethics. For further information, see www.royalholloway/CRIS.

Robert Strand is Executive Director of the Center for Responsible Business and member of the faculty at the University of California-Berkeley, Haas School of Business. He is also Assistant Professor of Leadership and Sustainability at the Centre for Corporate Social Responsibility at Copenhagen Business School. His research and teaching focuses on the strategic aspects of corporate social responsibility and sustainability that includes the role and effects of formalised organisational structures dedicated to CSR and sustainability.

Mike Valente is an Associate Professor in Organization Studies and Sustainability at Schulich School of Business, York University, Canada. His research examines the interaction between business strategy and society. He is interested in the typology of organisational responses to social, ecological and economic issues, including those responses that represent a paradigmatic difference from mainstream business models and result in systems-level change.

Steen Vallentin is Associate Professor at the Department of Management, Politics and Philosophy, Director of the Centre for Corporate Social Responsibility and Coordinator of CBS Sustainability at Copenhagen Business School. His research interests are centred on corporate social responsibility as a social and political phenomenon in the broadest sense, including studies of the role of government and of the political-ideological side of corporate responsibility. He regularly contributes to international journals in his field of study.

Sandra Waddock is Galligan Chair of Strategy, Carroll School Scholar of Corporate Responsibility, and Professor of Management at Boston College's Carroll School of Management. Her research focuses on large system change, intellectual shamans, corporate responsibility, wisdom and management education, among other areas. Her latest book is *Intellectual Shamans: Management Academics Making a Difference* (Cambridge University Press, 2015).

Jim P. Walsh is a long-time professor at the University of Michigan's Ross School of Business. His research explores the purpose, accountability and control of the firm and even more generally, business itself in society. Engaging his students with these kinds of questions, he does his best to prepare the next generation to lead both in and for society. Jim served as the 65th president of the Academy of Management. See http://jamespwalsh.com/ for a more comprehensive look at his commitments.

Florian Wettstein is Professor and Chair of Business Ethics and Director of the Institute for Business Ethics at University of St Gallen in Switzerland. His research focuses on business and human rights, the political role and responsibility of multinational corporations, normative theory and business ethics.

He is the author of *Multinational Corporations and Global Justice: Human Rights Obligations of a Quasi-Governmental Institution* (Stanford University Press, 2009) and Editor-in-Chief of the *Business and Human Rights Journal* (BHRJ), published by Cambridge University Press.

Glen Whelan is Marie-Curie Intra-European Research Fellow at Copenhagen Business School, and a member of the CBS World-Class Research Environment on 'Governing Responsible Business.' His research focuses on how corporations and other organisations influence, and are influenced by, moral and political norms and structures.

Christopher Wickert is an Assistant Professor of Management and Organisation at VU University Amsterdam, The Netherlands. His research interests include corporate social responsibility, organisation and institutional theory, critical management studies, social entrepreneurship and business ethics. He has published several book chapters and articles in international journals. For further details, see http://tinyurl.com/VU-Wickert.

Preface

The significance of **corporate social responsibility** (CSR) for business, society and governance is now undisputed. It is even discussed at length by its traditional critics, ranging from neo-liberal economists to anti-corporate campaigners and scholars. Yet, it is also a contested concept, not only by its critics, but also by those who claim to work for it. Our aim is to clarify understanding of CSR and the nature of and reasons for the contestation.

This textbook joins a growing number of texts and other resources on CSR. It is designed for advanced undergraduate and postgraduate students, although no prerequisite knowledge is assumed. But, what you are holding in your hands (or viewing on your hard-drive) differs in many ways from other textbooks on CSR and such related concepts as business and society and **corporate sustainability**. This is for five main reasons: its conceptual ambition; its focus on issues; its critical awareness; its integration of expertise; and its attention to how you learn from it, or pedagogy.

First, this book is unique in bringing together *three indispensable conceptual perspectives on CSR*: strategy, governance (including regulation) and communication. Like most other CSR textbooks, we address strategic approaches to CSR in our book (Part I). However, we bring new perspectives on these, including critical and developing country viewpoints. We also examine the role of governance in CSR because so much of CSR now pertains to socio-economic governance and the political nature of corporations' responsibilities. This book helps students to explore how CSR itself is regulated (Part II), and the role that corporations play in new governance arrangements (e.g. multi-stakeholder initiatives (MSIs) or public–private partnerships – Part IV). As much of CSR is about communicating firms' social and environmental responsibilities, we invite students to think about how communication is formative of CSR actions (Part III). We explore the significance of CSR communication in different contexts, such as crises, transparency and reputation management.

Second, while other CSR texts are structured around stakeholders or management issues, they often give rather selective attention to the *issues that CSR practitioners are concerned with*. We have provided chapters that allow students to gain knowledge about four core CSR issue areas: human rights, labour rights, environmental issues and corruption. The chapters offer an accessible and clear introduction to these issues and show students why these areas matter, what firms can do to improve their social performance, and what voluntary (and legal) frameworks have influenced firms' practices over time.

This will help students to understand what exactly is at stake when we talk about firms having responsibilities towards society.

Third, other CSR textbooks tend to take a relatively uncritical stance on CSR, offer a standalone critical chapter or are single-mindedly critical. We asked authors throughout the book to engage in *critical reflection* – i.e., to reflect on the concepts, theories and frameworks used in their chapter in a way that explores their limits and hence challenges students to 'think ahead'. All three of us share a deep desire to have challenging conversations in the classroom, and this book is designed to help instructors create such conversations by making readers aware of critical as well as positive insights into CSR.

Fourth, while most textbooks are authored, we offer an edited guide to CSR. Given the multifaceted and dynamic nature of CSR, we have brought together *leading experts to write chapters* on the topics of their established scholarly reputations. So while the structure, character and themes of the text reflect our own editorial thinking, the individual chapters reflect knowledge and insights of subject specialists in our international networks. We have taken a lot of care to avoid redundancies across chapters and also to make chapters comparable in terms of style, pedagogical features and length.

Finally, this book offers more than the text. It presents eighteen chapters which both link to one another and can be used in a standalone fashion. These scholarly contributions are *supplemented by a variety of other resources*, including: reflection pieces by well-known practitioners on the four major themes; case studies at the end of each chapter to enable students to critically reflect on CSR opportunities, challenges and dilemmas; and access to the slides that have been prepared in collaboration with the chapter authors.

Many people have contributed to make this book a success. We would particularly like to thank Luisa Murphy and Helene Morissette at Copenhagen Business School who assisted us in coordinating with authors and preparing the final manuscript. Paula Parish and Rosemary Crawley supported this project at Cambridge University Press and gave many helpful comments while finalising the book. We want to thank the VILLUM Foundation, the Governing Responsible Business (GRB) research environment at CBS, and the CBS Sustainability Platform for their financial support of this project. Materials for this book were also produced with funds from the Carlsberg Foundation and the International Network Programme (INP) under the Danish Social Science Council. Most of all we need to thank all those who contributed to the book. We appreciate their patience and openness to adapt their texts during the editing phase, so that we all can enjoy a book that is filled with exciting content!

Much like the man on this book cover, who overlooks a city with its busy social and economic life, studying CSR is about standing back for a moment and reflecting on the purpose of business. We hope that this book serves this purpose.

Andreas Rasche
Mette Morsing
Jeremy Moon

List of Abbreviations

AA1000	AccountAbility Standards Series
ACC	Aquaculture Certification Council
ACTA	Alien Tort Claims Act
API	American Petroleum Institute
ASC	Aquaculture Stewardship Council
B2B	Business to Business
BCI	Better Cotton Initiative
BHR	Business and Human Rights
BSCI	Business Social Compliance Initiative
CCC	Clean Clothes Campaign
CCWG	Clean Cargo Working Group
CDM	Clean Development Mechanism
CDP	Carbon Disclosure Project
CEO	Chief Executive Officer
CFP	Corporate Financial Performance
CER	Corporate Environment Responsibility
CITES	The Convention on International Trade in Endangered Species
CO2	Carbon Dioxide
COO	Chief Operating Officer
COP	Communication on Progress
CPA	Corporate Political Activity
CPG	Consumer-Packaged Goods Companies
CPI	Corruption Perception Indices
CRRep	Corporate Responsibility Reporting
CSO	Civil Society Organisation
CSP	Corporate Social Performance
CSIR	Corporate Social Irresponsibility
CSR	Corporate Social Responsibility
CSV	Creating Shared Value
ECOSOC	United Nations Economic and Social Council
EEDI	Energy Efficiency Design Index
EGS	Environmental Goods and Services
EITI	Extractive Industries Transparency Initiative
EMAS	European Union Eco-Management and Audit Scheme
EP	Equator Principles
EPA	Environmental Protection Agency

ERM	Enterprise Risk Management
ESI	Environmental Ship Index
ETI	Ethical Trading Initiative
EU	European Union
FCCC	Framework Convention on Climate Change
FCPA	US Foreign Corrupt Practices Act
FDA	Food and Drug Administration
FDI	Foreign Direct Investment
FLA	Fair Labor Association
FSC	Forest Stewardship Council
FSG	Foundation Strategy Group
FWF	Fair Wear Foundation
GDP	Gross Domestic Product
GHG	Greenhouse Gas
GMO	Genetically Modified Organism
GRI	Global Reporting Initiative
GVC	Global Value Chain
HRDD	Human Rights Due Diligence
IATI	International Aid Transparency Initiative
ICC	International Chamber of Commerce
ICCPR	International Covenant on Civil and Political Rights
ICCT	International Council on Clean Transportation
ICESCR	International Covenant on Economic, Social and Cultural Rights
ICT	Information and Communication Technology
IIRC	International Integrated Reporting Council
ILO	International Labour Organization
ILRF	International Labour Rights Forum
IMO	United Nations' International Maritime Organization
INGO	International Non-Governmental Organisation
IPF	International Project Finance
IRS	Internal Revenue Service
IRT	Image Repair Theory
ISAE	International Standard on Assurance Engagement
ISCC	International Sustainability and Carbon Certification
ISEAL	International Social and Environmental Labelling Alliance
ISO	International Organization for Standardization
ITTO	International Tropical Timber Organization
LEED	Leadership in Energy and Environmental Design
LETS	Local Exchange Trading Systems
MACN	Maritime Anti-Corruption Network
MARPOL	IMO's International Convention for the Prevention of Pollution from Ships
MEA	Multilateral Environmental Agreement
MeTA	Medicines Transparency Alliance

MNC	Multinational Corporation/Companies
MNE	Multinational Enterprises
MRV	A mandatory scheme for Monitoring, Reporting and Verification
MSC	Marine Stewardship Council
MSI	Multi-Stakeholder Initiative
NAFTA	North American Free Trade Agreement
NCP	National Contact Point
NGO	Non-governmental Organisation
NHRI	National Human Rights Institutions
NOx	Nitrogen oxides
NPO	Non-profit Organisation
OECD	Organisation for Economic Cooperation and Development
OSH	Occupational Safety and Health
PACI	Partnering Against Corruption Initiative
PEFC	Programme for the Endorsement of Forest Certification
PPP	Public Private Partnership
PRME	Principles of Sustainable Management Education
PWYP	Publish What You Pay
RED	Renewable Energy Directive
RSB	Roundtable for Sustainable Biomaterials
RSPO	Roundtable on Sustainable Palm Oil
RTRS	Roundtable on Responsible Soy
SA 8000	Social Accountability 8000
SBR	Sustainable Beef Roundtable
SCCT	Situational Crisis Communication Theory
SDG	Sustainable Development Goals
SEC	Securities and Exchange Commission
SEEMP	Ship Energy Efficiency Management Plan
SME	Small and Medium-Sized Enterprise
SOE	State-Owned Enterprise
SRI	Socially Responsible Investment
SRSG	Special Representative of the Secretary-General
SSE	Sustainable Stock Exchanges
SSI	Sustainable Shipping Initiative
TEG	Transnational Environmental Governance
TI	Transparency International
TNC	Transnational Corporations
UDHR	Universal Declaration of Human Rights
UN	United Nations
UNCAC	United Nations Convention against Corruption
UNCED	United Nations Conference on Environment and Development
UNCTC	United Nations Centre on Transnational Corporations
UNDP	United Nations Development Programme
UNEP	United Nations Environment Programme

UNFCCC	UN Framework Convention on Climate Change
UNGC	United Nations Global Compact
UNGP	United Nations Guiding Principles
UNODC	United Nations Office for Drugs and Crime
VP	Vice-President
WCED	World Commission on Environment and Development
WEF	World Economic Forum
WPCI	World Ports Climate Initiative
WTO	World Trade Organization
WWF	World Wide Fund for Nature

List of Case Studies

Prologue

JAMES P. WALSH

Andreas Rasche, Mette Morsing and Jeremy Moon have edited and authored a very important book here. CSR, as they define it, may be the most important issue we as a people confront in the decades ahead. We face it with a mix of appreciation and apprehension. While we have debated the proper place of the firm in society since the dawn of commerce (Avi-Yonah, 2005), the power and reach of the modern firm raises the stakes in this debate. Now living in what Perrow (1991) calls 'a society of organizations,' we live in a world where commerce is global and corporate control is local. Spanning nation states, transnational firms can operate in most all of them and at the same time, be bound by none of them. While firms can affect life on the entire planet, there is nothing resembling a planetary governance system to control them. And so, the way we conceive and control business enterprises' responsibility to humanity carries with it enormous consequences. Business leaders and citizens of the world alike must understand these issues. Our challenge is to find a way to embrace the prosperity that private enterprise generates, while at the same time guarding against its excesses or worse. We learn here that no less than our human rights and the sustainability of the planet hang in the balance.

Open this book to learn why business plays such a central role in our lives these days. With both a historical appreciation for 'Business and Society' scholarship and and evaluation of the changing nature of business activity through the years, we learn what society now wants from business (in the areas of human rights, labour rights and environmental sustainability). We also learn what we do not want from business (corruption). We then learn about the nature of accountability, from both the firm and society's point of view. Communication and transparency are crucial: control is a knotty issue. Readers will come away with a considered understanding of the range of control mechanisms now available. They range from business **self-regulation** to government regulation, with non-governmental organisations (**NGOs**) and

---

We decided to invite Jim Walsh for the opening reflections on the importance of understanding CSR for students in view of his passion for making students aware of how they may influence the world as future leaders. Since 1991 Jim Walsh has been Professor at the Stephen Ross School of Business at University of Michigan, and he has influentially set CSR on the agenda in the world's leading scholarly network, Academy of Management, where he served as President (2011). Today he serves on the Editorial Boards of some of the world's leading management journals.

activists of various kinds operating in the voids. All the while, the authors are quick to point out the promise and peril in every domain. This book aims not just to communicate knowledge about these important issues but also to cultivate wisdom. We will certainly need this wisdom as we manage and navigate a world so marked by immense corporate power and influence.

Ultimately, this book raises questions about how we may best live. Focusing on the many complexities attendant to the place of business in our lives, readers in the end may find themselves questioning an even broader dynamic in play here. After all, any business' attention to human rights and environmental sustainability must commingle with its quest to generate sustained competitive advantage and shareholder value. A firm cannot exist for long without profit. High CSR aspirations notwithstanding, corporate leaders can be tempted to put profits before people. In such times, business no longer serves humanity; humanity serves business. Perhaps universal values should guide our business activity. Donaldson and Walsh (2015) recently made a case for dignity. At minimum, they argue, we should prohibit any indignity committed in the name of business to humans, animals and the Earth itself.

Absent consensus about values, one wonders if our planet can withstand a life so shaped by business activity. Questioning the quality of a life marked by consumerism and consumption, Pope Francis (2015) recently wondered aloud if the planet itself could long sustain such life choices. In the end, readers of this book will better understand our social, environmental, ethical and philanthropic responsibilities towards society, both mediated by business activity and not mediated by such activity. Such insight is as important to living a good life as it is to sustaining life on the planet itself.

1 The Changing Role of Business in Global Society: CSR and Beyond

ANDREAS RASCHE, METTE MORSING AND JEREMY MOON

Learning Objectives

- Understand how globalisation has impacted corporate social responsibility (CSR).
- Explain and criticise the concept of CSR.
- Reflect on the implications of different CSR approaches.
- Differentiate CSR from other related concepts (e.g. sustainability).
- Understand different motivations that firms have to adopting CSR.

1.1 The Corporation in Society: Shifting Perspectives

Consider the following three facts: The revenue of the largest corporation in the world, Wal-mart Stores ($482 billion in 2014), is worth more than the gross domestic product (GDP) of all but twenty-seven of the world's economies. The world's largest asset management firm, a New York-based company called Black Rock, currently manages $4.5 trillion of assets and thus invests more money than the total monetary reserves of any country in the world (China having the largest reserves with $3.9 trillion in 2015). The Bill and Melinda Gates Foundation, a private philanthropic organisation, spends about $3.9 billion annually on healthcare and development work, about the same amount as is spent by the World Health Organization (see also Rothkopf, 2012). What do these three facts suggest? They show that the relationship between public and private authority has taken an interesting turn in recent years. Globalisation together with an emerging privatisation of public goods/services has given rise to a situation where the state has withdrawn from many areas where it traditionally exercised a regulatory monopoly, such as in many Western countries. Nowadays corporations provide goods such as water, transport, education and healthcare. Private firms even run prisons, provide security and have become important actors in the conduct of war. In short, corporations are increasingly critical to a number of aspects of society, including many which are fundamental to security and welfare. As a result, they have become more powerful actors and often assume a political role, either directly or indirectly. This shift in power has important implications for how we understand and manage firms' responsibilities towards society.

Due to their increased size and reach, corporations contribute significantly to some of the world's most vital social and environmental problems, such as overfishing of the oceans, water scarcity, violation of human rights, corruption and deforestation. While business activity is at the heart of these (and other) problems, private businesses are also increasingly seen as part of the solution. The United Nations (UN) Sustainable Development Goals, launched in 2015, which cover key targets such as ending poverty, safeguarding gender equality and ensuring sustainable management of natural resources, emphasise the importance of capacity-building through the private sector. Corporations are increasingly seen as reliable partners that mobilise resources and voluntarily comply with new standards. But the hope that corporations can help to solve some of today's biggest problems also creates risk. For instance, it furthers our dependence on corporations as the dominant institution in modern life. For example, Enron, which proved a fundamentally fraudulent company, was once a key player in the US energy market. Reliance on corporations to solve public problems also creates trade-offs that are sometimes difficult to judge. In 2015, Facebook's Mark Zuckerberg announced that he would donate 99 per cent of his Facebook stock (currently worth around $45 billion) to advance the public good. Critics pointed out that this would lead to enormous tax advantages for him, as a donor receives a charitable contribution deduction when donating stock.

The relationship between corporations and (global) society has also shifted because of the rise of the digital economy. We are increasingly living in a 'datafied' society, and this has significant consequences for the responsibilities of corporations. To 'datafy' something implies to put it into a quantified format so that it can be analysed through digital means (Mayer-Schönberger and Cukier, 2013). Google datafies an enormous amount of books through its Google Books project, Facebook datafies friendships through 'like' buttons and LinkedIn datafies human resources through online CVs. This datafication impacts corporations' responsibilities in numerous ways. On the one hand, it increases public scrutiny and makes responsible as well as irresponsible corporate conduct more transparent. Datafication has increased the connectivity of people who share more content in faster ways (e.g. stories about corporate misconduct). Some apps even give consumers direct access to a product's responsibility score, while other apps measure air pollution and allow for tracking deforestation. On the other hand, datafication has created new powerful corporations with a new set of responsibilities. Tech giants like Apple, Google, Microsoft and Facebook belong to the most valuable corporations in the world (when comparing the market capitalisation of all public traded companies). These firms impact peoples' rights in new and often unforeseen ways. In early

2006, Google announced that it would censor the Chinese version of its search engine upon request by the Chinese government. Similarly, Yahoo was asked to disclose information on at least two email customers to the Chinese government. Both customers, who were known to be government critics, were later jailed for revealing state secrets.

This book takes you on a journey to study CSR against the background of the changing role of business in global society. The blurring of boundaries between the public and private, and the rise of the digital economy are just two important examples of how the roles and responsibilities of corporations in global society are changing. Throughout the book we will touch upon many debates, which extend this picture. This introductory chapter will first look at how globalisation has impacted CSR. We then discuss how best to frame CSR in conceptual terms and how to understand its relationship to other (partly competing) concepts, such as **corporate citizenship** and sustainability. The next section debates why firms engage in CSR, especially when considering the changing context of doing business that we discussed above. Finally, we will look at the three main conceptual pillars of this textbook: strategy, communication and **governance**. We show why these topics matter when it comes to CSR and how the book is organised around them.

1.2 Globalisation and CSR

The regulation of global business activity remains a challenge. There is an imbalance between the flexibility of multinational corporations (MNCs) to spread their value chain activities across different countries and the limited capacity of civil societies and nation states to adequately regulate corporate conduct across borders. Scherer and Palazzo call this the 'regulatory vacuum effect' (Scherer and Palazzo, 2008a). Such a vacuum exists because the sovereignty of political authorities is greatest within their national borders and more tenuous outside them, while businesses have become transnational actors. This makes it difficult for the governments of individual countries to address social and environmental problems that reach beyond single state boundaries. The failure to address global warming is a case in point. MNCs also have the chance to arbitrate among alternative regulations; i.e., they escape strict regulations by moving their operations or supply activities to countries with rather low standards (e.g. to lower their tax burden or cost of production). All of this has led to a 'globalisation of responsibility' and calls for alternative ways to regulate global business activity.

Existing political institutions, which reach beyond individual nation states (e.g. the UN system or the World Bank), lack the formal powers or political support to develop and enforce any binding rules or even sanction corporate misconduct. The UN system was mostly designed for state actors, and falls short when it comes to regulating non-state actors. International law and UN-based treaties and conventions have been designed as a legal framework to direct the behaviour of nation states. It is rarely possible to apply these legal frameworks *directly* to corporations, especially when it comes to regulating their impact on social and environmental issues. In principle it is technically possible to craft legally binding international frameworks applying to corporations, but political interests and business lobbying have curtailed such efforts until now.

While the UN has been successful in developing, and winning support for, norms of responsible business, investment and business education, through the UN Global Compact (see Chapter 7), attempts by intergovernmental institutions to design more binding rules to control the obligations of private actors have so far failed. In 2004, the UN Commission on Human Rights rejected a proposal for human rights norms (officially called 'UN Norms on the Responsibilities of Transnational Corporations and Other Enterprises with Regard to Human Rights'), which might have developed into binding rules. One argument leading to the rejection of the Draft Norms was that they would place state-like obligations on non-state actors. That argument was raised by states who had been lobbied by some powerful business associations that felt they had been excluded from the process leading to the text of the Norms. In 2011, the UN Human Rights Council adopted the UN Guiding Principles on Business and Human Rights, which were developed with broad stakeholder involvement (see Chapter 15).

Some have argued that the missing direct applicability of international law to corporations can at least partly be compensated by stronger **extraterritorial regulation**. Extraterritorial jurisdiction refers 'to the ability of a state, via various legal, regulatory and judicial institutions, to exercise its authority over actors and activities outside its own territory' (Zerk, 2010: 13). Put differently, states can apply certain domestic legal instruments beyond their own territory and hence can regulate the activities of corporate actors 'abroad'. Although the application of extraterritorial law has given rise to tensions between nation states, which see their sovereignty endangered, the use of such legal instruments is commonplace in a few areas relevant to the CSR debate. For instance, the US Foreign Corrupt Practices Act allows the US government to sue corporations (even non-US ones) for offering or accepting bribes in another country (see Chapter 16). The UK Bribery Act, which was launched in 2011, can also be applied as extraterritorial jurisdiction. Even though the extraterritorial nature of certain domestic laws has helped to better regulate anti-corruption, it has not much affected other areas relevant to the CSR debate. In 2013, the US Supreme Court rolled back the impact of the Alien Tort Claims Act (ATCA), which allowed the prosecution of human rights violations by corporate actors in other countries. Many proceedings under ATCA were objected, based on the argument that the cases raise 'political questions', and that judicial action by a US court in this area would interfere with 'foreign policy interests' (Zerk, 2010: 152). Overall, we can state that extraterritorial law has improved the regulation of global business activity in some selected areas, but it has not sufficiently closed the general 'regulatory vacuum' that surrounds the conduct of MNCs.

CSR is often conceptualised as an alternative and more pragmatic way to regulate the conduct of private actors in a global economy, especially as national and international legal frameworks remain limited in many respects. Although CSR remains primarily a voluntary construct, focused on self-regulation or on regulation that is exercised by multiple **stakeholders**, it offers a point of orientation for companies when thinking about their social and environmental responsibilities. Such orientation is needed as corporations increasingly operate in a global playing field that is characterised by a hetero-geneous set of norms, values and interests. Moreover, for the many millions of citizens who do not live in democratic political systems, business organisations may sometimes prove more responsive to their values and interests than are their governments. The pluralisation of modern societies, which we can under-stand as an ongoing process of increasing individualisation, the devaluation of traditions and the globalisation of society, has increased the cultural heterogen-eity that corporate actors in general, and MNCs in particular, have to cope with (Scherer and Palazzo, 2008a). What is a fair wage in Vietnam? Can petty bribes be culturally accepted? Do we need to support collective bargaining even though national legislation does not require it? Corporations need to find convincing answers to these (and other) questions while at the same time acknowledging that such answers are not defined once and for all. CSR is a concept in 'ongoing emergence' and managers need to develop an alert 'sensory apparatus' to understand how best to navigate. If exercised in the right way, CSR can help to develop a moral compass for firms to operate in a changing global society.

1.3 CSR: Framing the Debate

1.3.1 What is CSR?

Defining CSR is not a simple task. There are at least three reasons for this (Matten and Moon, 2008: 405). First, CSR is a contested concept that is defined (and applied) differently by different groups of people. We could even argue that this ambiguity is part of the reason why CSR has been so successful; under the label of CSR yet across a variety of (often disagreeing) stakeholders, people have for decades agreed on the importance of debating the role of business in society. However, this ambiguity has also caused criticism.

If the meaning of CSR cannot be agreed upon and specified precisely, corporations can easily exploit the concept by selectively applying the concept to those issue areas they can conveniently address. Second, CSR overlaps with other conceptions that describe business–society relations (e.g. business ethics, sustainability, accountability). Finally, like forms of business organisation and governance, CSR is a dynamic phenomenon. What counts as an issue relevant to the CSR debate changes over time, as new problems emerge and formerly novel practices become routine.

Despite these challenges we need a working definition for CSR. The term 'CSR' is used as follows throughout this book, even though some individual chapters have a more particular focus:

> CSR refers to the integration of an enterprise's social, environmental, ethical and philanthropic responsibilities towards society into its operations, processes and core business strategy in cooperation with relevant stakeholders.

This definition emphasises a number of important aspects of CSR. It stresses that CSR is not entirely about **philanthropy** (e.g. companies' charitable donations). While a firm's CSR strategy can include philanthropic activities, and may have been built on these, it is much more than that. Well-designed CSR goes into the very core of a corporation; it influences its everyday practices and business processes, and is aligned with its overall business strategy. Corporate philanthropy is sometimes detached from a firm's core activities, while CSR is about reflecting on the social, environmental and ethical impact of these activities. This is not to say that CSR always has to be 'strategic' (a term that is often used as a synonym for 'being profitable'; Porter and Kramer, 2006). Rather, it means that CSR should be embedded into what a firm does on a day-to-day basis, and it should also be reflected upon when deciding upon a firm's strategic direction (e.g. which markets or regions it wants to enter).

It is also important to note what the definition does *not* mention. The definition does not explicitly indicate that CSR is a voluntary concept. We believe it would be misleading to exclusively conceptualise CSR in this way. Social and environmental responsibility is a de facto requirement among larger firms in some industries and countries. It is hard to find firms in the automotive or extractive industries without any CSR activities, because their sectors have developed industry-wide standards. In many business systems, companies observe 'implicit' obligations to undertake certain responsibilities simply by virtue of being members of those societies, as Matten and Moon revealed in their comparison of US and European CSR (Matten and Moon, 2008). Also, some governments have started to incentivise or even regulate CSR-related activities (e.g. the disclosure of relevant non-financial information; see Chapter 8). This has pushed the CSR debate beyond talking about purely voluntary actions.

It would also be misleading to define CSR as a completely voluntary concept, as a company's responsibilities towards society also include its legal obligations (Carroll, 1979, 1991). Sometimes meeting this legal minimum already is a challenge, especially as the regulatory environment is in a constant state of flux. One of the reasons for Siemens' large-scale corruption scandal, which started to unfold in 2006, was that the company underestimated the changing nature of the legal environment. Until 1999, it was legal in Germany to pay bribes abroad (it was even possible for firms to deduct bribes from their taxable income). Siemens found it hard to break the habit when German legislators changed relevant laws.

We explicitly use the term 'enterprise' in our definition. With this we want to highlight that CSR is not only a concept that is relevant for larger (multi-national) corporations, but that discussing businesses' responsibilities towards society also includes small and medium-sized enterprises (SMEs). SMEs are defined as firms with fewer than 250 employees. They make up the vast majority of businesses in an economy and provide the most jobs. The CSR activities of SMEs differ in a number of ways from those of larger firms (Baumann-Pauly, Wickert, Spence and Scherer, 2013). Often, the main motivation to integrate CSR is influenced by the personal beliefs and values of the founder (who in many cases is also the owner and manager of the firm). By contrast, CSR in larger firms is more driven by the hope that responsible business practices will yield some positive financial return and hence satisfy shareholder interests. SME's activities in the area of CSR are also more connected to the specific needs of the local communities in which they are embedded, while larger firms usually operate a portfolio of social and environmental practices that cut across different geographic contexts. Although there are significant differences in the way CSR is understood and operationalised in SMEs and larger corporations, there are also similarities. Most importantly, the issue areas relevant to the CSR debate rest on the same basic principles. For instance, human rights rest on universal principles, which equally apply to all corporations regardless of their size or the geographic location of their activities.

Our definition also emphasises that CSR is a multidimensional construct. Despite the term 'corporate *social* responsibility', CSR also includes discussions about firms' environmental footprint. The discussions throughout this book follow the internationally agreed view that CSR encompasses corporate responsibilities in at least four key issue areas: human rights (as agreed upon in the Universal Declaration of Human Rights), labour rights (as agreed upon in the International Labour Organization's Declaration on Fundamental Principles and Rights at Work), environmental principles (as fixed in the Rio Declaration on Environment and Development), as well as anti-corruption (as stated in the UN Convention Against Corruption). These four issue areas should not be seen as an exhaustive and definite list of responsibilities. They form a moral compass, outlining a minimum standard when discussing what should be

expected from corporations. One advantage of this textbook is that it introduces you directly to debates and principles in these four areas (see Chapters
15–18). We do not want to treat CSR as an abstract concept. CSR comes to life
and is filled with practical meaning when we start to discuss how firms address
specific problems in the four issue areas.

There is no one-size-fits-all approach towards CSR. Discussing a firm's
social, environmental, ethical and philanthropic responsibilities is contextually
dependent and multidimensional by nature. It depends, among other things, on
what kind of firm is being analysed (e.g. its size and ownership structure), what
sector the firm operates in, and the location of relevant business activities.
Contexts and events matter when it comes to CSR and that is why general
recipes need to be treated with care (see Chapter 2)!

1.3.2 Other CSR Definitions

While our definition highlights certain aspects of CSR, other definitions
describe the phenomenon differently. We offer an overview of five conceptualisations of CSR (although we do not claim this to be exhaustive). The existing
range of definitions reflects the ambiguous, dynamic and contested nature of
CSR. We group existing definitions into five main clusters (see similar Garriga
and Melé, 2004), keeping in mind that these clusters reflect analytical distinctions and that most CSR definitions possess elements of more than one cluster.

Some scholars have emphasised the *normative dimension* of CSR. Their
definitions usually highlight CSR's ethical foundations. Firms need to accept
their social and environmental responsibilities because it is their ethical obligation to align their activities with the values of society. For instance, Bowen
defined CSR as referring 'to the obligations of businessmen to pursue those
policies, to make those decisions, or to follow those lines of actions which are
desirable in terms of the objectives and values of our society' (Bowen, 1953: 6).
Of course, one can use different ethical principles to evaluate how managers
ought to act. Some have emphasised the universal nature of rights underlying
CSR (reflecting a Kantian perspective), while others have suggested that
businesses, like other societal actors, have to contribute to 'the common good'
of society (reflecting an Aristotelian perspective). Chapter 2 presents ethical
underpinnings of CSR from a variety of cultures.

Another group of scholars has stressed that firms *integrate social and
environmental demands* via CSR practices (Garriga and Melé, 2004). Such
an integrative view highlights that corporations depend on society for their
existence; CSR then is a way to integrate different societal demands into
business operations. Carroll's classic definition of CSR reflects this perspective: 'The social responsibility of business encompasses the economic, legal,
ethical, and discretionary expectations that society has of organisations at a
given point in time.' (Carroll, 1979: 500) CSR is here defined with regard to

the different kind of expectations that society has vis-à-vis a corporation. Instead of looking at the generic responsiveness to certain expectations, some scholars have emphasised integrating the demands of those who have a legitimate stake in a firm (i.e. its stakeholders; see Chapter 5). Campbell, for instance, views 'corporations as acting in socially responsible ways if they do two things. First, they must not knowingly do anything that could harm their stakeholders. Second, if they do harm to stakeholders, then they must rectify it whenever it is discovered and brought to their attention' (Campbell, 2006: 928).

Some of the literature on CSR adopts an *instrumental perspective* (see also Chapter 3). Definitions in this direction emphasise an economic approach to business responsibility. CSR becomes a means to an end, a strategic tool to achieve competitive advantage. Although CSR is rarely defined in a purely economic fashion (for an exception see Friedman, 1970, 1987), many scholars have emphasised its instrumental character. McWilliams and Siegel (2001: 119), for example, state that 'CSR can be viewed as a form of investment' and that managers need to 'determine the appropriate level of CSR investment' (118). Understanding CSR in this way stresses that a firm should only accept responsibilities if this advances its economic self-interest. The assumption behind this type of thinking is that managers are legally obliged to fulfil their fiduciary duties (i.e. to protect the investment of shareholders). A number of scholars have challenged this perspective by highlighting that managers also bear a fiduciary relationship to other stakeholders (Freeman, 1984).

Increasingly, definitions of CSR that highlight its *political nature* have gained prominence (see also Chapter 6). There has been a long-standing, if often understated, political theme in CSR, as evidenced by Bowen's (1953) references to CSR as being a delegated power directed at social welfare. In part, **political CSR** has been explored under the aegis of 'corporate constitutionalism', 'integrative social contract theory' and 'corporate citizenship' (Garriga and Melé, 2004: 55–57). We can add the contribution of CSR scholars investigating 'public responsibility', by which they meant 'not only the literal text of law and regulation but also the broad pattern of social direction reflected in public opinion, emerging issues, formal legal requirements and enforcement or implementation practices' (Preston and Post, 1981: 57). A more recent version of political CSR suggests that CSR 'entails those responsible business activities that turn corporations into providers of public goods in cases where public authorities are unable or unwilling to fulfil this role' (Scherer, Rasche, Palazzo and Spicer 2016: 3). This definition emphasises that corporations are often entering the political sphere, as they directly or indirectly become involved in the regulation of social and environmental problems (e.g. by joining voluntary multi-stakeholder initiatives (MSIs)). Such a view of CSR presupposes a new understanding of global politics and the role of business in society. Rather than only focusing on the interaction of governmental actors, business firms and civil society actors become active participants in the regulation of market transactions.

Finally, we present an *emergent perspective* on CSR in which the flux and changing nature of CSR is emphasised. According to this perspective, CSR is best described as 'a permanent issue and an area of debates in management theory and practice, rather than a well stabilized construct with a clear and constant operationalization' (Gond and Moon, 2011: 4). Across practice and theory there is a general agreement that no single authoritative concept has succeeded in defining the field. In fact, some scholars have argued that it makes 'little sense to talk about CSR as if it possessed a definition that is stable and fixed and only has to be discovered and applied' (Cantó-Milà and Lozano, 2009: 158). Others have proposed that knowledge about CSR is in a 'continuing state of emergence' (Lockett, Moon and Visser, 2006: 133), and that CSR accordingly is an essentially contested concept (Gond and Moon, 2011). Such acknowledgment of the ambiguous and evolving nature of CSR has caused considerable confusion and concern across practitioners and scholars who have agreed that a clear and consistent definition on CSR is needed to gain influence and impact across a wide range of stakeholders. However, it is also acknowledged that CSR needs to conform to culturally and contextually bound ambiguities that change over time. Rather than agonising over the lack of consistency, scholars have started to inquire to what extent the discursive openness of CSR may be an advantage for firms but also importantly for society. From this perspective, it is suggested that CSR is 'best understood not as a clear or consistent agenda, but rather as a forum for sensemaking, diversity of opinion, and debate over the conflicting social norms and expectations attached to corporate activity' (Guthey and Morsing, 2014: 555). CSR becomes an undisputed yet contested precondition for business development, where managers need to proactively engage rather than respond.

Table 1.1 summarises the five perspectives on CSR. Whatever definition one might adopt, CSR needs to be distinguished from corporate social irresponsibility (CSIR). CSIR is more than the failure of a firm to perform CSR. Corporations can deliberately decide to become engaged in CSIR (e.g. when paying bribes), but firms can also 'stumble into' acts of irresponsible behaviour without any direct intention (e.g. when underestimating business risks). We refer to CSIR as corporate activity that 'negatively affects an identifiable social stakeholder's legitimate claims (in the long run)' (Strike, Gao and Bansal, 2006: 852). Some would argue that CSR and CSIR are extreme ends on a continuum and thus mutually exclusive. This, however, neglects that CSR and CSIR can exist simultaneously in a corporation. Kotchen and Moon find in a study of 3,000 publicly traded companies that firms that do more 'harm' (CSIR) also do more 'good' (CSR) (Kotchen and Moon, 2012). In other words, firms often invest in CSR to compensate for past, present or anticipated irresponsible acts. For instance, the US supermarket chain Whole Foods is often praised for its proactive CSR behaviour, while it also neglects unions and

Table 1.1 Five perspectives on CSR

	Normative perspective	Integration perspective	Instrumental perspective	Political perspective	Emergent perspective
Definition	CSR as 'the obligations of businessmen to pursue those policies, to make those decisions, or to follow those lines of actions which are desirable in terms of the objectives and values of our society.' (Bowen, 1953: 6)	'The social responsibility of business encompasses the economic, legal, ethical, and discretionary expectations that society has of organizations at a given point in time.' (Carroll 1979: 500)	'CSR can be viewed as a form of investment' and managers need to 'determine the appropriate level of CSR investment' (McWilliams and Siegel, 2001: 119)	CSR 'entails those responsible business activities that turn corporations into providers of public goods in cases where public authorities are unable or unwilling to fulfil this role.' (Scherer et al. 2016: 3)	CSR 'as a permanent issue and an area of debates in management theory and practice, rather than a well stabilized construct with a clear and constant operationalization.' (Gond and Moon, 2013: 4)
Motivation to adopt CSR	CSR is an ethical obligation for a firm, often driven by leaders' personal values and integrity, to serve society.	Firms are faced with certain economic, environmental and social expectations from society and have to integrate these expectations into their business.	CSR advances the economic self-interest of firms.	Firms turn into political actors and hence have to manage a new set of responsibilities.	CSR engagement is an undisputed yet contested precondition for ongoing business development.
Implications for the firm	Firms and their managers base their decisions and actions on societal well-being as the firm's ultimate goal.	Firms and their managers are primarily concerned with CSR as a means to appear legitimate vis-à-vis significant stakeholders.	Firms and their managers focus on how CSR may increase company profits.	Firms and their managers are expected to serve as political actors with political responsibilities.	Firms and their managers engage proactively in the ongoing debate on CSR.

the right to collective bargaining. In some cases firms may also be in a situation where they cause harm while working to do good. When H&M is working to improve its CSR engagement in Bangladesh by requesting suppliers to improve labour conditions (for example, by establishing more ventilation and sanitary facilities for women workers), such engagement may easily be critiqued for not being enough. As a profitable and resourceful multinational company, H&M is expected to do more, and the company may be seen as irresponsible for not pushing suppliers further. However, H&M's engagement may simultaneously be seen as an act of responsible behaviour. Rather than disengaging with the supplier and leaving workers in a status quo, H&M strives to push the boundaries and improve working conditions in small steps in a political and cultural context that is not easily influenced and changed. The definition of responsible versus irresponsible behaviour is not always straightforward and most often paved with many shades of grey.

1.3.3 CSR as a Dynamic Concept

As we have seen, defining CSR is a challenging task. One of the reasons why it is so difficult to define CSR is that what counts as responsible corporate conduct changes over time. What we consider to reflect responsible behaviour not only depends on the relevant business context but also on temporal dynamics (Rivoli and Waddock, 2011). A number of factors influence these dynamics:

1. Broader public expectations shift as novel scientific research, the media and other groups show the relevance of new problems and solutions.
2. Expectations can institutionalise into behavioural norms and thus turn formerly disregarded practices into de facto requirements.
3. Regulators can turn a previously neglected issue into a required one.
4. Companies can innovate around CSR in order to secure competitive advantage and thereby set new standards of CSR.

In other words, there is no generalisable agenda of CSR issues that is valid independent of these time-context dynamics. These dynamics also impact whether or not responsible corporate behaviour 'pays off' in financial terms. If more firms in an industry adopt a certain responsible business practice, industry-wide capabilities and institutions are developed. This lowers the overall costs of adopting the new practice. Also, with the emergence of new regulations laggards are often penalised for not meeting relevant standards.

Rivoli and Waddock suggest that the time-context dynamic underlying CSR resembles the public issue life cycle (Rivoli and Waddock, 2011). The life cycle describes how CSR issues emerge and become institutionalised, and how resulting widespread changes in corporate conduct occur (see Figure 1.1).

Figure 1.1

Public issue life cycle

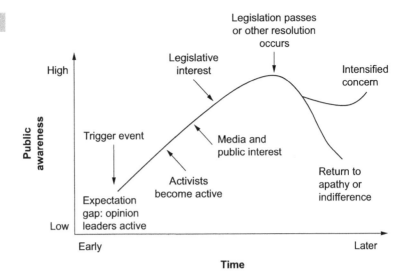

Source: adapted and modified from Mahon and Waddock, 1992: 23.

Before the life cycle even starts there are often some pioneering activists who see a gap between desirable and actual corporate behaviour. Corporations usually ignore these activists, as the identified gap is not widely acknowledged by other stakeholders. The life cycle is usually started by a 'trigger event', that is, an event that draws widespread public attention to a CSR issue (e.g. Nike's problems with **sweatshop** labour in the 1990s). Such trigger events change public perception of an issue and also alter expectations towards firms. Ignoring is no longer an alternative. Instead, corporations respond by arguing that the requested behaviour would harm business activities and hence create negative consequences for society (e.g. job losses). In the resulting debate, activists and corporations usually 'frame' the same CSR issue in different ways, although some proactive firms start to accept their responsibility. For instance, Exxon-Mobil denied climate change for a long time, while many of its competitors accepted their responsibility. Finally, potential CSR practices may become fully institutionalised because they turn into accepted and expected behaviour, even though there is no legal requirement. Some CSR practices may also become a legal requirement, often after there has been widespread voluntary acceptance for a while. In some cases, a potential CSR issue can also disappear again, such as when it neither is institutionalised nor becomes part of the legal system.

1.4 CSR and Beyond: Related Concepts and Debates

Often, there is confusion around what terminology is used when talking about business' role in and relationship to society. Part of this confusion comes from academic work using concepts/terms in different ways, as well as differences in the language used by practitioners and academics. Some of the confusion is also due to CSR overlapping with related concepts, such as, but not limited to: corporate sustainability, **corporate accountability**, corporate citizenship and **business ethics**.

In recent years, the term '(corporate) sustainability' has increasingly been used to supplement the CSR debate. Some firms have even started to completely relabel their social and environmental activities as being about corporate sustainability, often without changing the substance of these activities. Discussions around corporate sustainability are usually based on and relate to the popular notion of **sustainable development**. The World Commission on Environment and Development (WCED) defined such development in a much-cited report as being about meeting 'the needs of the present without compromising the ability of future generations to meet their own needs' (World Commission on Environment and Development, 1987: 54). This definition highlights two key concepts:

1. the concept of 'needs', especially when considering the developing countries and world's poor, and
2. the idea of 'limitations' that are imposed on the environment's capacity to satisfy present and future needs.

Sustainable development as such is *not* centred on the role of organisations or even corporations. It is, as the name indicates, focused on the development of entire societies and hence adopts a macro-level perspective. Some have seen the concepts as different but related, such that CSR can be regarded as the contributions of businesses to sustainable development.

In the 1990s, several researchers used the term 'corporate sustainability' in an ecological sense. The focus was predominantly on discussing business' impact on the natural environment and opportunities resulting from innovation and eco-efficient production (Shrivastava, 1995). More recent definitions have emphasised a triple bottom line perspective, discussing corporate sustainability as an approach that balances economic responsibility, social equity and environmental integrity (Bansal, 2005). As many scholars conceptualise CSR in a similar way, one can say that the theory and practice of corporate sustainability and CSR are converging. Differences mostly relate to the assumed level of integration and connectedness between social, environmental and economic issues. While the corporate sustainability debate emphasises the need for systems-level change in the sense that the economy is embedded into society, which in turn is part of a larger ecological system, CSR-related discussions are often more focused on relevant management practices within corporations. CSR does not neglect the connected nature of social, environmental and economic aspects, but its main focus is on how to manage these aspects in a corporate context. Corporate sustainability, on the other hand, puts more emphasis on how changes made by an individual corporation connect and contribute to larger systems-level change (Montiel, 2008). Although these differences still exist, there is also significant convergence between the corporate sustainability and CSR discourse.

Corporate accountability is another concept that has attracted much attention in recent years, especially from **civil society organisations** and activists. Generally speaking, accountability implies the exchange of reasons for behaviour; 'to account' for something means that actions and omissions are explained and justified (Messner, 2009). Corporate accountability is about a firm's ability to be answerable for what it did or did not do. Many argue that corporate accountability is a 'stronger' concept than CSR (Utting, 2008). While a firm can assume responsibility for a number of things, being accountable means informing relevant stakeholders about specific practices that enact this responsibility. In practice, firms can work towards increased accountability through various means, including the provision of mechanisms that allow external stakeholders to raise complaints against a firm's actions. Corporate accountability can also be strengthened through rigorous **CSR reporting**. A major criticism here, however, is that some corporations appear to prioritise their reporting methods over the conduct of their responsibilities. While some CSR reports remain superficial and are mostly a window-dressing exercise, some firms have succeeded in creating reports that importantly serve to generate attention and changed behaviour among employees while also informing stakeholders about relevant actions and omissions.

Corporate citizenship is a concept that shares many insights with the political perspective on CSR. Most obviously it denotes the political implications of CSR and forms of corporate political involvement related to CSR (Moon, Crane and Matten 2004). Matten and Crane have distinguished three different views of corporate citizenship (Matten and Crane, 2005). In the limited view, corporate citizenship is used as a way to describe firms' philanthropic activities (e.g. charitable donations and other types of community action). This view reflects the early usage of the term and comes close to a philanthropic understanding of CSR. In the equivalent view, corporate citizenship becomes another way to describe firms' CSR activities, but without defining any new relationship between business and society. Finally, the extended view of corporate citizenship assumes that corporations start to protect, facilitate and enable citizens' rights whenever governments are not willing or not able to do this. This makes corporate citizenship a concept that is concerned with how businesses affect and are affected by social, civil and political rights. Many discussions throughout this book focus on the political nature of CSR and hence include discussions of corporate citizenship.

We view business ethics as a foundation for all discussions about CSR. While CSR has a stronger focus on management practices, business ethics is more generally concerned with questions of 'right' and 'wrong' in the context of business situations (Crane and Matten, 2007: 5). 'Right' and 'wrong' can be assessed from a number of different perspectives (e.g. something can be financially 'right'). Business ethics focuses exclusively on moral judgements. Such judgements are usually informed by a certain moral point of view, such as different philosophical, social or religious perspectives. Ethical reflection goes beyond the law. In fact, it is particularly concerned with those areas that are not clearly covered by the law. Although the law embodies ethical norms, it cannot regulate all possible business situations. There are always loopholes, and managers have a certain degree of interpretive flexibility, that is, they need to reflect on how to best comply with the law (e.g. when paying taxes). Business ethics is also concerned with those situations where values are in conflict or tension and ethical dilemmas occur as a result. For instance, managers may wonder whether or not to blow the whistle when suspecting misconduct by one of their peers. We view business ethics as an analytical lens to reflect on the values that should guide corporate conduct, while CSR is about the managerial practices that translate these values into tangible actions.

1.5 Why Do Corporations Engage in CSR?

Firms engage in CSR for a number of reasons. The most widely mentioned (and also most debated) reason for engaging in CSR is the so-called **business case**. Some corporations create CSR policies and practices because they believe that it positively influences their financial bottom line. There is no definitive (generalisable) link between firms' financial and their social/environmental performance; much depends on the context in which the business operates (e.g. its exposure to certain risks). CSR can influence existing key business metrics, such as return on capital employed (ROCE) or economic value added (EVA), in a number of ways. There are a number of practical difficulties when trying to measure the impact of CSR on financial performance. Some CSR initiatives are so embedded in a firm's overall operations that it is difficult to isolate their effects on financial measures. Also, while it is often possible to link broad-based measures with regard to a firm's overall financial performance and its social/environmental activities, it is much harder to see specific ties between relevant CSR practices and selected financial metrics. The UN Global Compact and the Principles for Responsible Investment (2013) have suggested discussing the financial impact of CSR with regard to three components: *revenue growth, productivity improvement* and *risk minimisation* (see Table 1.2).

Some firms profit from CSR financially because their social and environmental activities result in innovative products and services, which in turn improve *revenue growth*. In some cases firms are able to expand their market share and customer base for existing products based on enhancing these with social and environmental features (e.g. when offering fair trade coffee).

Table 1.2 The value driver model

Value driver category	Value driver	Example
Revenue growth	New markets and geographies	Gain access to new markets and geographies through CSR strategies (e.g. bottom of the pyramid (BOP) markets).
	New customers and market share	Use CSR to engage customers and build knowledge and expectations.
	Product and service innovation	Develop innovative products and services addressing unmet social or environmental needs.
Productivity improvements	Operational efficiency	Enable bottom line cost-savings through environmental operations and practices (e.g. energy, water, waste).
	Human capital management	Attract and retain better and highly motivated employees by positioning company as CSR leader.
	Reputation pricing power	Develop brand loyalty and reputation through CSR efforts that garners customers' willingness to pay price premium.
Risk minimization	Operational and regulatory risk	Mitigate risks by complying with regulatory requirements and industry standards, ensuring uninterrupted operations.
	Reputational risk	Facilitate operations and entry in new markets through community dialogue and engaging citizens.
	Supply chain risk	Secure consistent and long-term access to high-quality raw materials.

Source: UN Global Compact and Principles for Responsible Investment, 2013.

Revenue growth can also come from entering new geographic markets with CSR-related products, particularly if social and environmental product attributes act as differentiators. Well-managed CSR practices can also lead to *productivity improvements*. For instance, environmental management practices can lead to operational efficiencies and result in cost-savings (e.g. through reduced wastes and better use of natural resources). Productivity gains can also result from better human resources management, such as when firms are able to attract and retain talent as a result of their CSR commitment or when workers become more productive due to improved health and safety policies. Finally, CSR can enable companies to minimise business risks and hence better connect with investors. *Risk minimisation* can occur in different areas, such as regulatory risks (e.g. when emerging regulations could constrain resource use), supply chain risks (e.g. when noncompliant suppliers could lead to business interruptions) and reputational risks (e.g. when activists initiate boycotts or public shaming campaigns).

CSR commitments do not always pay off in financial terms, and it is important to understand that CSR is often most needed when there are no financial gains to be realised. Some firms engage in CSR because it is quite simply the 'right thing to do'. We call this motivation the moral case for CSR. The moral case is prevalent in business settings where, for example, a family or a manager owns the firm. Research has pointed at how this is most often the case in SMEs. They are often managed by an owner-manager with strong personal values and integrity to 'do the right thing' vis-à-vis his or her stakeholders – sometimes irrespective of 'the right thing' being less profitable in a short-term economic calculation (Spence and Rutherford, 2003). While this may seem the exception in a world driven by economic growth, Spence and Rutherford remind us that 99 per cent of all businesses in Europe are SMEs, and that in fact, the small company is the dominant way of organising.

Institutional theorists have also identified reasons why firms become engaged in CSR. Explanations reaching in this direction focus on the institutional environment that corporations are faced with. Firms often adopt CSR because other firms have done exactly the same. Such imitative (or mimetic) behaviour is particularly relevant if corporations are faced with a high degree of uncertainty (e.g. when there is uncertainty around future regulations). Firms often look at their competitors when deciding whether or not to adopt new management practices, especially as these practices are usually diffused either intentionally through industry associations or unintentionally through employee transfer or turnover. Campbell discusses a number of other institutional factors that influence whether or not firms adopt CSR (Campbell, 2007). Firms from unhealthy economic environments (e.g. characterised by high inflation and weak consumer confidence) cannot be expected to embrace CSR closely, as these firms have fewer resources to spare. This argument assumes that CSR engagement requires upfront investments that corporations may not recoup. Corporations are also more likely to engage in CSR activities if strong and well-enforced legal regulations are already in place. **Compliance** with existing regulations (e.g. on health and safety) can lower the implementation costs for CSR and hence lower the 'financial hurdles' that firms need to overcome. Some firms are also motivated to join CSR efforts because certain actors constantly monitor their behaviour (e.g. non-governmental organisations (NGOs), the media, investors). This applies mostly to larger companies that need to protect the reputation of their brand name or their portfolio of consumer brands.

1.6 CSR: Strategy, Communication and Governance

This book explores CSR in the context of three conceptual frameworks: *strategy*, *communication* and *governance*. Part I of the book focuses on the intersection of strategy and CSR. Part II is about how CSR is regulated (and what this means for socio-economic governance), while Part III discusses the relationship between communication and CSR. Finally, Part IV explores how corporations have become an important player in the governance of global CSR issues (e.g. labour rights). The discussion of the three conceptual frameworks is not limited to the respective parts of the book. For instance, the role of strategy is also debated in Parts II and IV, but in a less explicit way. We ask you to think of strategy, communication and governance as three debates that run through this book and its discussions.

When writing about strategy, we mostly refer to a corporation's strategy. While strategy has turned into a buzzword that is often simply used to designate that something is important, it is crucial to look for a minimal definition of the phenomenon. As with CSR, there are many perspectives on corporate strategy. Most definitions highlight that strategy is about creating potentials for future success by telling firms what they can, want to and should do (Rasche, 2008). Advocates of the market-based view on corporate strategy have argued that firms achieve competitive advantage by analysing their environment in a way that allows them to achieve a superior position on the market (e.g. by being a cost leader or offering differentiated products). Advocates of the resource-based view on corporate strategy have suggested that firms gain a competitive advantage if they possess unique and non-imitable resources. Whatever point of departure we may take to define a firm's strategy, it is important to realise that the chosen strategic direction of a firm can have a significant impact on its responsibilities. For instance, strategic decisions such as outsourcing production to manufacturers in countries with low labour costs or entering a new market in a country with a poor human rights record inevitably raise CSR-related discussions.

Analysing the strategic context of a firm requires looking at its stakeholders, as these either affect a firm's strategic direction (e.g. regulators) or are affected by certain strategic decisions (e.g. workers). Chapter 5 introduces stakeholder theory and shows its relevance for discussing the responsibilities of corporations, especially when considering the rise of the digital economy. Chapters 3 and 4 look at how CSR itself can be understood as a strategic concept and what the limits of such a strategic understanding might be. Some authors (e.g. Porter and Kramer, 2006) have argued that many CSR activities remain unconnected to a firm's strategic direction setting. They argue that CSR needs to be done 'strategically' – that is, CSR should only be undertaken in those cases where it allows firms to reap a competitive advantage. Chapter 3 reviews this debate and criticises its underlying logic. Chapter 4 shows how firms can manage for CSR in a strategic way by rethinking their existing business models. Finally, Chapter 6 discusses the link between corporations' responsibility and their role as political actors. This perspective on 'political CSR' extends the traditional instrumental understanding of **strategic CSR** in various ways, and shows how corporations' role as political actors can shape the direction of future business activities.

While there has been a significant debate on CSR, the literature on CSR communication has remained relatively limited. In fact, much of the CSR literature has demonstrated a certain disdain for CSR communication. It is often stated that CSR communication is superficial, that it is 'just public relations' and an 'empty expression of pious wishes' (Roberts, 2003: 263). *The Economist* once said that CSR communication, such as CSR reporting, is 'a license to obfuscate' (Crook, 2005: 2). Such a view on CSR communication builds on an assumption of consistency: that firms communicate – and should only communicate – what they already do (Christensen, Morsing and Thyssen, 2013). This view on CSR communication has primarily dominated the inquiry among marketing scholars (with a focus on branding, reputation and public relations) and accounting experts (with a focus on reporting, rankings and measurement metrics). It builds on the assumption that firms must practise what they preach (Ciulla, 2005). In this 'transmission view' (Schoeneborn and Trittin, 2013), firms may improve their **legitimacy** and stakeholder relations by *improving* their CSR communication. This type of CSR communication is embedded in Chapters 12 and 13 on respectively the role of crisis communication and reputation.

While there is indeed sufficient reason to remain alert and sceptical to the corporate CSR statements in an era rich with corporate scandals, such critique misses one important point: CSR communication is formative of CSR action. This observation is also noted in Chapters 12 and 13, and it is what Schoeneborn and Trittin label the 'constitutive view' on CSR communication. This view is unfolded in Chapter 11 where three views on CSR communication are discussed. Here it is argued that we should be careful not to discount too easily gaps between CSR talk and CSR communication, as it is through talk, discussion and **deliberation** that decisions are made and consensus achieved that lead to changes in behaviour. It is through the spoken or written word that firms commit themselves to a path of action (Christensen et al., 2013). Moreover, social technologies have made it possible for a variety of stakeholders to engage in the CSR debate as they request more transparency from companies, as discussed in Chapter 14.

The significance of the concept of governance for CSR has long been underestimated, mostly because governance in the business context was often exclusively associated with **corporate governance**. Defining governance is not an easy task, as the concept has become fashionable over the past several decades and hence many different conceptions of governance exist. As with CSR, the ambiguity of the concept is one reason for its success. Generally speaking, governance refers to the 'processes and institutions, both formal and informal, that guide and restrain the collective activities of a group' (Keohane and Nye, 2000: 12). Governance is about the creation of 'ordered rule'; or as Lynn puts it, governance reflects 'the action or manner of governing – that is, of directing, guiding, or regulating individuals, organisations, or nations in conduct or actions' (Lynn, 2010: 671). Governance is different from government. Government reflects just one possible way to exercise governance. Different actors can exercise governance, ranging from individuals (e.g. the Board of Directors) to organisations (e.g. when a firm develops a **code of conduct** for its suppliers) and networks (e.g. when NGOs and businesses develop common standards). Informal actors such as street gangs or the mafia also exercise governance, while we can also think of more abstract creations like 'the market' as a mode of governance. In the end, governance is much about the steering of behaviour and the coordination of actions based on institutionalised rule systems (Benz, 2004).

The concept of governance is significant for CSR in a number of ways. CSR is an attempt to govern – that is, to steer and coordinate the behaviour of businesses (and other actors) in a way that basic principles, norms, standards and laws are met. More specifically, we can understand CSR as one way to produce governance. Firms, NGOs, unions, business associations, international organisations, governmental agencies and other actors can become *'governance-makers'* through their engagement in CSR. For instance, some firms are active in so-called MSIs. They define and enforce rules that other actors can voluntarily adopt and hence exercise governance. Some businesses also define codes of conduct that are relevant for their business partners. These codes coordinate the behaviour among multiple actors and thus govern economic and social interactions. But we can also understand CSR as a way to consume governance. Firms and other actors can also adapt to existing principles, norms, standards and laws and thus become *'governance-takers'*. CSR is an attempt to disseminate and institutionalise rule systems related to social, environmental and ethical corporate behaviour. Finally, CSR also deals with those cases where firms and individuals disregard these systems of rule, where voluntary standards or even legal frameworks are ignored or even deliberately circumvented. This turns relevant actors into *'governance-breakers'* and describes cases of irresponsibility.

Thinking of the relationship between governance and CSR in terms of the making-taking-breaking framework is helpful, as it organises our discussion. We can look at governance-making, -taking and -breaking from different levels of analysis (Table 1.3). Some discussions throughout this book adopt a macro-level perspective and discuss how new organisational forms for governing CSR-related issues have emerged (governance-making), how these new forms were diffused and adopted by business and non-business actors (governance-taking), and why some business actors sidestepped these governance arrangements (governance-breaking) (see e.g. Chapters 7, 8, 10, 16, 17 and 18). Other discussions are more centred on the organisational (meso) level and thus debate what kind of dynamics unfold within these new organisational forms (governance-making), what change processes are needed within adopting firms (governance-taking) and how some businesses resist these change processes (governance-breaking) (see e.g. Chapters 4, 5, 9, 12, 13, 15 and 18). Some contributors focus their discussion on the role of individuals and hence the

Table 1.3 The relationship between governance and CSR

	'Governance-making' (Production of governance for CSR)	'Governance-taking' (Adoption of governance for CSR)	'Governance- breaking' (Circumventing governance for CSR)
Societal level (Macro-level)	Design of new forms of governance for responsible business / emergence of new organisational forms (e.g. MSIs).	Uptake of standards/ policies for responsible business on country/ sector level / new forms of legislation and action plans on national level.	Circumvention or avoidance of new governance arrangements by groups of actors (e.g. coalitions of businesses).
Organisational level (Meso-level)	Organisational dynamics within new organisational forms (e.g. UN reform, NGO-business partnerships) / resistance and control within/by organisations.	Organisational change processes when adopting new standards for responsible business / resistance against new standards by adopting organisations.	Organisations circumventing existing voluntary or mandatory governance arrangements for CSR / cases of corporate irresponsibility.
Individual level (Micro-level)	Individual leadership/ resistance in organisational and institutional change processes while 'producing' governance for CSR.	Impact of governance arrangements on individuals (e.g. consumers) / role of individual leadership in adoption processes (e.g. micro-politics).	Role of individuals in cases of corporate misconduct (e.g. leaders assisting, benefiting or tolerating irresponsible behaviour).

micro-level. They discuss in what ways individuals in these new governance arrangements promote stakeholder dialogue (governance-making), how leaders in corporations promote the adoption of new CSR policies (governance-taking) and how some managers disregard legal and voluntary modes of governance (governance-breaking) (see e.g. Chapters 4, 6 and 9).

1.7 Case Study: Volkswagen: Engineering the Truth

Volkswagen became the world's largest carmaker in July 2015 after selling 5.04 million vehicles in the first six months of the year, thereby surpassing Toyota, which sold 5.02 million cars. Although the title 'largest automaker in the world' has only symbolic value, its achievement fulfilled a long-held objective of the company. Only two months later, on 18 September 2015, the

US Environmental Protection Agency (EPA) publicly issued a notice of violation of the US Clean Air Act to Volkswagen, as investigations revealed that some of their cars exceeded legal emission limits.

The EPA found that Volkswagen sold diesel cars on the US market that had special engine software installed – a so-called 'defeat device'. This software allowed diesel engines to automatically detect whenever they were being tested for emissions. The defeat device recognised test conditions (e.g. the speedometer and steering wheel sensors detected whether their inputs matched those of typical test situations) and then switched the engine into a special anti-pollution mode that minimised emissions. The defeat device makes use of the fact that carmakers know how governmental agencies, such as the EPA, carry out emission tests; they do not perform on-road tests but usually put tested cars on rollers that run at a certain speed for a certain amount of time (Topham, Clarke, Levett, Scruton and Fidler, 2015). While the EPA issued the notice of violation of the Clean Air Act, the actual cheating was discovered by an NGO, the International Council on Clean Transportation (ICCT). The ICCT performed on-road emission tests of several cars (including VW and BMW). It realised that VW cars emitted between twenty and forty times the amount of nitrogen oxides (NOx) when comparing the on-road test results with those under lab conditions.

The EPA recalled 482,000 cars in the US because of the manipulated engine software. Shortly after the EPA revelations, VW admitted that about 11 million cars worldwide were fitted with the defeat device between 2008 and 2015. Given that VW sold around 9.7 million cars overall in 2013, this number seems very high. Some argued that only a small group of rogue engineers were responsible for the manipulation. However, as the scandal unfolded there was a growing belief that a large number of people must have known about the cheating. Max Warburton, an analyst at Bernstein Research, commented in the *Financial Times*: 'Given the complexity of modern cars and the number of engineers involved in developing products, I have argued from the start that we must be talking about hundreds of people.' (Sharman and Brunsden, 2015)

Investigations by VW itself revealed that engineers started to develop the defeat device as early as 2005, mostly because they were unable to find a technical solution to US emission standards within the given timeframe and budget (Rising and Sopke, 2015). The cheating was seen as a solution to fulfil the high (and partly unrealistic) goals that VW engineers had to meet – that is, producing a car which meets high emission standards, while at the same time having a powerful engine that is cheap to produce. Some critics even argued that a 'polluted' corporate culture at Volkswagen and an aggressive management style had an impact on the cheating. Martin Winterkorn, the CEO of Volkswagen from 2008 until September 2015, was known to be a demanding boss. Former managers described the management style under Mr Winterkorn as creating 'a climate of fear, an authoritarianism that went unchecked' (Cremer and Bergin, 2015). Germany's *Süddeutsche Zeitung* reported that this authoritarian corporate culture also played a role when one of VW's senior executives disregarded a warning by an engineer over 'possibly illegal' practices in 2011 (Fromm, Hägler and Ott, 2015).

VW responded to the scandal in multiple ways. Mr Winterkorn said: 'I personally am deeply sorry that we have broken the trust of our customers and the public.' (Volkswagen AG, 2015a) While he initially resisted stepping down, as he attributed the scandal to the wrongdoing of a few individuals, he resigned as CEO on 23 September 2015 after the scale of the scandal had increased. In his resignation statement, he stated: 'As CEO I accept responsibility for the irregularities. I am doing this in the interest of the company even though I am not aware of any wrongdoing on my part.' (Volkswagen AG, 2015b) Others in the company were more direct in responding to the scandal. VW Group of America CEO, Michael Horn, stated: 'Our company was dishonest with the EPA, and the California Air Resources Board and with all of you, and in my German words: we have totally screwed up.' (Ruddick, 2015) During a US congressional hearing, Mr Horn even said: 'This company has to bloody learn and use this opportunity in order to get their act together, and 600,000 people worldwide have to be managed in a different way.' (Cremer and Bergin, 2015) Some even argued that VW needs a new corporate culture. The chief of the VW works council, who represents employees on the board, argued: 'We need in future a climate in which problems aren't hidden but can be openly communicated to superiors . . . We need a culture in which it is possible and permissible to argue with your superior about the best way to go.' (Cremer and Bergin, 2015)

While VW originally assumed that there was no knowledge of the deception among members of the supervisory and management boards, investigations revealed that Mr Winterkorn received two memos in 2014 that highlighted irregularities with the emissions of some vehicles. One memo, which was sent to Mr Winterkorn on 23 May 2014, even mentioned a study by the ICCT. The memo concluded that VW is not able to say why these irregularities occurred, but that the existence of defeat devices was a possibility. The memo was part of Mr Winterkorn's extensive 'weekend mail' and hence it is unclear whether he read it. However, in July 2015, Mr Winterkorn together with other top managers attended a meeting that explicitly discussed the 'diesel issue'. One analyst commented in the *Financial Times*: 'This is either gross incompetence, or extreme arrogance.' (McGee and Wright, 2016)

Financially speaking, the company set aside €6.7 billion to cover the costs of cleaning up the scandal (e.g. recalling millions of cars). VW reported a quarterly loss of €2.5 billion in late October 2015. However, the scandal's financial impact goes further than this. In the US alone, the EPA could fine VW about $18 billion for breaching its standards. VW stock price was significantly affected by the scandal. A number of other governments have taken action against Volkswagen, including German prosecutors who raided VW headquarters on 8 October 2015. In the UK, which is the second worst affected country in the EU, the government announced that it would look into options to put financial penalties on the company. On 21 September 2015, the first day of trading after the EPA announced the violation of the Clean Air Act, VW's stock fell 20 per cent on the Frankfurt Stock Exchange. So far, VW's share price has dropped around 40 per cent ever since the crisis unfolded (data as of January 2015).

Despite the scandal, VW's reputation among German consumers seems not to have suffered much. According to a poll by Prophet, a management consultancy, two-thirds of Germans think that the scandal has been exaggerated and that VW still builds excellent cars. The majority of Germans believes that the entire scandal will be forgotten within a year (Löhr, 2015). However, VW's reputation seems to have taken a hit in other countries. AutoPacific, a market research firm, found that 64 per cent of car owners in the US do not trust VW any more (Isidore, 2015). This reputation damage is not very surprising, as prior to the scandal VW positioned itself as producing 'Clean Diesel' cars in the North American market.

VW's newly appointed CEO, Matthias Müller, promised to be 'ruthless in punishing those involved' (Kollewe, 2015). Nevertheless, some investors expressed discomfort with VW's personal decisions after the scandal. Mr Müller, who used to be the CEO of Porsche (a brand belonging to the VW family), was seen as an insider. In a similar vein, the newly appointed chairman of the supervisory board, Hans Dieter Pötsch, used to be the finance director of the company. Investors urged VW to appoint fresh people in the management and supervisory board to regain trust from capital markets. The seventy-seven-year-old company faced a number of significant challenges, although some analysts cautioned that the company's cheating was not unique. In 2014, Hyundai and Kia were fined $300 million by the EPA for inflating gas mileage claims. Many argued that the VW scandal simply showed again that few test results in the car industry matched real-life situations.

Questions for Discussion

1. Smith (2015) shows the importance of rationalisations that VW employees might use to justify the misconduct to themselves and also in front of others. For instance, some may say, 'Everybody is doing it', pointing out that other firms have also been caught cheating when it comes to fuel consumption tests (e.g. Hyundai and Kia). Why might VW employees use such rationalisations? What other justifications might they present?
2. Who is responsible for the misconduct when looking at the scandal through the CSR lens? Is it VW as a whole? Is it senior management who set very ambitious targets for the company? Is it the engineers who performed the

actual manipulation of the software? Which criteria would you use to judge whether someone is responsible?

3. Do you share the discomfort expressed by some investors that VW's new CEO, Matthias Müller, was a wrong appointment, as he came from inside the company? What would be your concerns if you were Matthias Müller and had just accepted the position as VW CEO?

1.8 Chapter Summary

This chapter introduced you to the concept of CSR against the background of larger societal changes and trends (e.g. digitalisation). We discussed globalisation as an important factor that influences CSR, especially as national governments increasingly struggle to regulate the operations of multinational businesses. We outlined different elements of a definition of CSR and showed that there is often disagreement about what exactly is included in the concept. Our discussion distinguished different perspectives on CSR, including a normative, integrative, instrumental, political and energent understanding of the concept. It is important to realise that a lack of CSR does not necessarily lead to corporate irresponsibility. Some companies may lack explicit CSR policies and practices, but they still may not show irresponsible behaviour. We also discussed in what ways CSR relates to other concepts, such as corporate sustainability, corporate citizenship, corporate accountability and business ethics. Without doubt, there is overlap among these concepts but there are also important differences (some of which are disregarded in practice). Finally, we reviewed some of the key motivations for firms to adopt CSR. Our discussion showed that many refer to the 'business case' as being the most important explanation for firms' interest in CSR. However, we also demonstrated that the 'moral case' should not be underestimated in the context of SMEs and family-owned businesses.

Chapter Questions

1. Why does the globalisation of business activities call for more attention towards CSR?
2. What motivates firms to engage in CSR?
3. Outline different perspectives on CSR. Do you see overlap between the perspectives?
4. How far is CSR different from related concepts such as corporate sustainability, corporate citizenship, corporate accountability and business ethics?

FURTHER RESOURCES

Moon, J. (2015). *Corporate Social Responsibility: A Very Short Introduction*. Oxford: Oxford University Press.
A concise introduction to CSR, reviewing arguments for and against CSR and also discussing how CSR is exercised in different national contexts.

Waddock, S. and Rasche, A. (2012). *Building the Responsible Enterprise: Where Visions and Values Add Value*. Palo Alto, CA: Stanford University Press.
A book written for those who focus on the implementation of CSR. The book explains how visions and corporate values can shape CSR, and which management systems need to be adjusted when turning promises into actions.

Margolis, J. D. and Walsh, J. P. (2003). Misery Loves Companies: Rethinking Social Initiatives by Business. *Administrative Science Quarterly*, 48(2), 268–305.
Reviews the discussion around the business case for CSR, and proposes an alternative approach that takes the tension between societal objectives and economic thinking as a starting point.

Ihlen, Ø., Bartlett, J. and May, S. (Eds.) (2011). *The Handbook of Communication and Corporate Social Responsibility*. Oxford: Wiley-Blackwell.
This book provides the most up-to-date and comprehensive overview of CSR communication. It contains a number of communication theories, and discusses their contributions to CSR.

Schwartz, M. S. and Carroll, A. B. (2008). Integrating and Unifying Competing and Complementary Frameworks, The Search for a Common Core in the Business and Society Field. *Business and Society*, 47(2), 148–186.
Discusses commonalities and differences between key concepts relevant to the business and society field, such as business ethics, CSR, sustainability and corporate citizenship.

The UN Sustainable Development Goals (SDGs), https://sustainabledevelopment.un.org
Launched in 2015, the SDGs consist of seventeen key goals that represent the 2030 agenda of the UN (and its partners) with regard to sustainable development. The goals include vital aspects such as: poverty reduction, gender equality and action on climate change.

Ethical Corporation, www.ethicalcorp.com
Ethical Corporation is the leading monthly magazine on issues related to CSR and sustainability.

The Business of Society (BOS) Blog, www.bos-cbscsr.dk
> The BOS Blog is devoted to CSR, sustainability and related debates. BOS is edited by Andreas Rasche, Mette Morsing and Jeremy Moon. Check this blog for the latest updates on responsible business practices.

ICCSR, www.nottingham.ac.uk/business/ICCSR/resources.php
> The International Centre for Corporate Social Responsibility (ICCSR) at Nottingham University Business School offers a list of resources related to CSR and sustainability, including: research papers, interviews, and notes on conferences and workshops.

The Aspen Institute's CasePlace, www.caseplace.org
> This platform offers students and faculties a selection of materials (e.g. cases and interviews) focused on the role of business in society.

PART I

STRATEGY AND CSR

Introduction from the Editors

The first part of the book discusses the link between corporate strategy and CSR. This link has been subject to much debate among academics and practitioners. Some believe that CSR should always be well aligned with a firm's strategic direction, which means that responsibility needs to pay off for corporations, and that it has to support firms' long-term objectives and strategic positioning on the market. Others do not necessarily fully reject the importance of such a strategic alignment, but they emphasise that firms' engagement in CSR should not be limited to such a strategic understanding. After all, CSR is often needed in precisely those situations where strategic fit is missing.

The chapters in this section show that CSR and strategy can be related in different ways. Business strategy can be used as a justification for CSR ('You only do CSR because it serves your business.'); it can be seen as part of the rationale for CSR ('You do CSR and it serves your business, but it is not the only reason to engage in it.'); and it can be seen as one way to conduct CSR ('You do CSR and you do it in a strategic way.').

Jeremy Moon, Luisa Murphy and Jean-Pascal Gond (Chapter 2) start us off with a journey back in time to explore how CSR has changed throughout history. This discussion shows that the 'strategic' nature of CSR is by no means a given. The chapter frames business–society–government relations as a context for understanding different CSR issues, norms and rationales. If we want to understand how firms have linked strategy and responsible business, we have to appreciate the meaning of CSR in different contexts and at different points in time. Steen Vallentin and Laura Spence build on these remarks in Chapter 3, introducing different arguments that can be made for and against a strategic understanding of CSR. They show how strategic CSR itself went through different phases of development, from early discussions of a strategic view on philanthropy to more recent discussions on **creating shared value** (CSV). They also debate the limits and inherent contradictions of a strategic view on CSR.

Mike Valente (Chapter 4) discusses the full continuum of possible interactions between CSR and strategy. On the one end of the continuum, there are firms that believe CSR is irrelevant to their strategic orientation. This leads them to view responsible business as a purely philanthropic activity without any concern for their core competences. On the other end of the continuum, there are firms that deeply embed CSR into their strategic orientation and hence make changes to their competitive environment. This more active orientation towards the environment is also reflected in Glen Whelan's chapter on the political nature of CSR (Chapter 6). He shows how firms' products and services can have political impact, especially when looking into the activities of high-tech companies. He also discusses ways in which firms use CSR to strategically influence their non-market environment; for instance, when they interact with NGOs and governments. All of this turns firms into political actors that behave in strategic ways.

Chapter 5 by Ed Freeman, Sergiy Dmytriyev, and Robert Strand introduces you to stakeholder thinking. Any discussion of the link between strategy and CSR rests on an analysis of a firm's stakeholders. Freeman and colleagues show how company–stakeholder relations can be managed and what opportunities and risks this creates. They demonstrate how digitalisation is affected by and affects stakeholder engagement, and what we can learn from this when thinking about CSR. Digitalisation is a key issue when it comes to stakeholder thinking, as it introduces new (virtual) stakeholders and also changes the way we think about firms' responsibilities towards society.

2

Historical Perspectives on Corporate Social Responsibility

JEREMY MOON, LUISA MURPHY AND JEAN-PASCAL GOND

Learning Objectives

- Understand corporate social responsibility (CSR) history in terms of key phenomena: issues, modes, rationales.
- Understand CSR history as a feature of key relationships between society, business and government.
- Apply these understandings in three key phases: industrialisation; the rise of the modern corporation; internationalisation.
- Understand the dynamics of CSR: its contexts, what motivates it and how it changes.

2.1 Introduction

As history is about the past, and concerns with CSR are very present, why look backwards? As Henry Ford is thought to have said, 'History is more or less bunk'. Others contend that history enables lessons about CSR which can be applied today, warning that: 'those who cannot remember the past are condemned to repeat it' (Santayana, 1905: 284). History also gives insights into 'path dependencies' whereby today's CSR is informed not just by today's agendas, but also by inherited assumptions and approaches. Moreover, an understanding of CSR in history enables you to better distinguish what is recurrent and what is novel, and to understand the significance of its different contexts.

CSR is a moving target. Over the last four millennia it has developed from its ethical underpinnings in the norms of ancient societies and religions governing the behaviour of people engaged in commerce and with wealth. Over the last two hundred years it has developed from industrial philanthropy and **paternalism** to more integration in the business. In the last hundred years or so it has emerged as a corporate practice, rather than leadership characteristic. Since the beginning of the twenty-first century, it has become internationalised, and responsibility has extended to issues beyond the corporation's workforce and immediate community, throughout their value chains. But the changes in business social responsibility (which we retrospectively call, CSR) over these years, decades and centuries have played out very differently in different places: CSR has a history of uneven development.

So any aspect of history could only offer a limited account of the unfolding and recursions of CSR. Hence, we offer two *perspectives* on how to conceptualise historical and comparative CSR. The first perspective addresses the 'what', 'how' and 'why' questions about CSR. Thus, we discuss its phenomena: 'issues', 'modes of practice' and 'underlying rationales'. Second, we discuss the 'who' questions of CSR, focusing on the key types of CSR actor: society, business and governmental. We then use these conceptualisations of CSR 'phenomena' and CSR 'actors' to investigate the 'when' question and provide insights into three key historical phases of CSR:

1. *industrialisation*, occurring in 'Western' systems in the late eighteenth and nineteenth centuries;
2. *the rise of the modern corporation*, which corresponds to the development of 'managerial capitalism' in the late nineteenth and twentieth centuries; and
3. the period of rapid *internationalisation* in the late twentieth and early twenty-first centuries that also corresponds to the emergence of more financialised forms of capitalism.

These two perspectives on CSR history – the phenomenological and the actor-orientated – enable an understanding of the different contexts for CSR strategies.

2.2 CSR Phenomena: Issues, Modes and Rationales

When asked to describe CSR, experts, supporters and critics of CSR – sometimes after a pause – may refer to CSR issues, modes and rationales. These three types of CSR phenomena can be understood as answers to the following key questions about CSR:

1. 'In *what* ways has CSR changed?' Answer: 'It has changed in terms of the *issues* addressed (e.g. community development, ecological diversity, employee volunteering).'
2. 'Are there changes in *how* CSR is enacted?' Answer: 'Changes in the way CSR is conducted are evident in particular CSR *modes* (e.g. foundations, corporate codes, cause-related marketing).'
3. 'Are there changes in *why* companies engage in CSR?' Answer: 'These changes in explanation for CSR can be found in some underlying *rationales*'. CSR rationales combine principles (e.g. customary ethics) and strategies (e.g. the business case).

We continue by examining these phenomena more closely.

2.2.1 CSR Issues

CSR *issues* are the causes to which CSR is invoked or addressed. These issues often reflect key items in business – societal, and sometimes governmental agendas. It can also refer to certain underlying *trends* which are beyond single issues, such as climate change or loss of ecological diversity. It can also refer to *events* which trigger new responsibility agendas that companies have to face. For example, the 1984 Bhopal gas leak at the Union Carbide India Limited pesticide plant killed over 2,000 people immediately, with catastrophic long-term implications for the health and welfare of over half a million residents (all figures related to the disaster's impacts are vigorously disputed). The event and the question of the company's responsibility continued to dog the company, and several of its senior employees, for decades thereafter. It also highlighted the issues of responsibility and risk outside a company's own country (Chapter 13 discusses the BP Deepwater Horizon disaster in 2010).

CSR issues have shifted in several main ways. First, there have been changes in the welfare element of CSR. It was often originally associated with support for communities and other forms of charitable action; later with responsibilities for the welfare of businesses' own workers and their families; and subsequently to responsibility for the welfare of workers and their families in companies' supply chains. Second, the adage that 'whereas CSR was once about what companies did with their profits, it is now as much about how they make their profits' exemplifies another change. Namely, this captures a shift to include concern for the social, economic and environmental impacts of the production and commercial processes of the respective companies.

Third, CSR issues now reflect quite specific consumer or investor social preferences, as represented for example by the fair trade movement. Fourth, many companies are also being asked to address through CSR what might have appeared to them as relatively core governance issues, including the provision of physical infrastructure, education, security and the administration of labour rights, particularly for their own workers and families (Matten and Crane 2005; Crane, Matten and Moon, 2008: Chapter 3). Finally, CSR has been increasingly attached to wider agendas of business-society relations, such as responsibility for the financial crisis, and for their taxation payments (see Chapter 16).

2.2.2 CSR Modes

Historical change in CSR has also been reflected in its *modes* or its organisational and regulatory forms (the 'how' questions). The modes of CSR have developed from discretion on the part of individual business owners to the 'complete' organisation of CSR at the company level, for example in the form of the application of corporate governance and company codes of conduct to CSR issues. Corporate foundations have emerged as a common mode of CSR. This has often been assisted by donor tax exemptions granted by governments since the English Charitable Uses Act 1601, adopted and adapted through much of the British colonial system and more widely. Many of the famous foundations – such as the Carnegie, Ford and Gates in the USA, Leverhulme and Nuffield in the UK and the Sir Ratan Tata Trust in India – operate externally to their founding firms. But in the Danish cases, Foundations (e.g. Carlsberg, Novo Nordisk, Velux) often operate as major shareholders of the companies.

There has been a general historical development of CSR modes, specifically with the shift *from* CSR being organised entirely in and by the corporations themselves *to* reflecting shared organisation with other actors. This is a shift from 'complete organisation' of CSR, where all its organisational 'elements' (i.e. 'membership, hierarchy, rules, monitoring and sanctioning' – Ahrne and Brunsson, 2011) are provided by the corporation itself. Instead, CSR increasingly reflects 'partial' organisation by the corporation in conjunction with some organisational elements provided by and with other actors (Rasche, de Bakker, and Moon, 2013). The corporations, in whose name the CSR is enacted and communicated, are no longer its sole organisers.

Thus the modes of CSR represented by **partnerships** (Seitanidi and Crane, 2009); CSR associations (Grayson and Nelson, 2013), standards (see Chapter 7) and systems of social reporting, **transparency** (see Chapter 8) and management control (see Gond, Grubnic, Herzig and Moon, 2012) are modes of organising CSR which extend CSR from complete organisation in and by the corporation. They reflect wider membership (e.g. of other businesses, civil society, governmental agencies, international governmental organisations – respectively), which in turn brings usually very flat systems, rather than corporate style hierarchies, as well as shared involvement in setting and monitoring the rules. The specification and execution of sanctions are also partial to the corporation, and as a result often symbolic and 'last resort' (e.g. exclusion from the UNGC for non-submission of periodic progress reports). While losing complete ability to organise their CSR, corporations gain much greater ability to deal with complexity as a result of the confluence of expertise that these new organisational approaches bring, as well as much greater legitimacy for their involvement in social agendas.

2.2.3 Rationales for CSR

The changes in CSR among companies and business systems have been about the underlying *rationales* of CSR that businesses offer, or which are attributed to them (the 'why' questions). These changes in rationale combine principle and strategy, and often reflect ideological perspectives on the sociability of business.

Table 2.1 Rationales for responsible business

Rationale	Illustration
The social responsibility of business is to create wealth	'To say then, that a man is entitled to a living wage is absurd... if you take from the strong and give to the weak you encourage weakness; let men reap what they and their progenitors sow.' (Charles Elliot Perkins)
The social responsibility of business is to use wealth for social ends	'Great wealth should be administered for the common good ... the man of wealth thus becoming a mere agent and trustee for his poorer brethren.' (Andrew Carnegie)
Business should be a vehicle for social responsibility	'The help that nourishes civilization is ... the investment of effort or time or money ... to the power of employing people at a remunerative wage, to expand and develop the resources at hand, and to give opportunity for progress and healthful labor.' (John D. Rockefeller)
CSR legitimises business to society and government	'The continuing socio-institutional influences were, if anything, more important than those influencing the businessmen's earlier lives.' (Jonathan Boswell)
CSR as a vehicle for wealth creation	'[Robert Owen] argued that fair treatment of workers could result in a return equal to 50 percent to 100 percent on money invested.' (Husted, 2014)
CSR as a form of governance	'The growth of American CSR in schools represents a re-appraisal of the connections between the education system and broader economic and social well-being.' (Amitai Etzioni)

Six recurring underlying rationales of CSR are presented in Table 2.1. Of course, more negative rationales are also attributed to CSR, such as: managers' exploitation of company resources for their personal interest; **greenwashing** of less responsible business practices; and thus that CSR deflects from issues of wider corporate reform (see Moon, 2014: Chapter 6).

2.2.3.1 The Social Responsibility of Business Is to Create Wealth

This first rationale – to create wealth – in some ways sits oddly in this context, as many regarded it as a legitimisation of corporate social *ir*responsibility. Yet, it does not strictly offer a manifesto for greed and social negligence. From a Social Darwinist perspective, there is a public interest in growth, and this is best achieved by a laissez-faire approach, as illustrated by railway entrepreneur, Charles Elliot Perkins (Table 2.1, quoted in Husted, 2015: 130). From the perspective of Milton Friedman (Friedman, 1970), greater societal benefits are available if business leaders focus on building profitable companies which pay taxes, employ workers, and provide goods and services that customers and societies desire.

2.2.3.2 To Use Wealth Created by Business for Social Ends

This more familiar rationale for CSR is rooted in social norms of philanthropy which were initially applied to wealthy citizens, then to business leaders, and latterly to corporations (Heald, 1970; Table 2.1; Table 2.2). It may be considered as a foundational idea of CSR, East and West. It has been associated with the idea of stewardship of wealth by business leaders, whether on behalf of a deity or humanity. It has been criticised for focusing on what is done with the profits of a company (which could be made irresponsibly) rather than on creating wealth in a responsible way. In other words, it is less about responsible business and more about the distribution of wealth. The case for wealth redistribution was made most famously by Andrew Carnegie, a Scottish immigrant to the USA who became one of the richest men of his time, only to discover – and inspire – the 'Gospel of Wealth' (see Table 2.1, quoted in Husted, 2015: 129).

2.2.3.3 Business as a Vehicle for Social Responsibility

Whereas the previous rationale for CSR is predicated on business as a creator of surplus wealth, this rationale is based on the idea that the very activity of business is itself an opportunity for social responsibility. This view is illustrated by companies like Ben & Jerry's and The Body Shop, which were used by their founding owners as means of addressing social agendas as well as creating wealth. It is also reflected in the many social enterprises, including cooperatives, which aspire to use business to trade in the interests of their members. An early version is captured by John D. Rockefeller (Table 2.1, quoted in Husted, 2015: 129) whereby the provision of employment inside the company is regarded as a social investment.

2.2.3.4 CSR Legitimises Business to Society and Government

Many accounts of CSR point to the rationale of legitimacy. Accordingly, it is assumed that CSR is as much a reflection of social expectations as the inspiration of business leaders and innovative companies. Accordingly, business, individually and collectively, acquires a social licence to operate comparable to the various legal licences that they also require. Alone, the legitimacy model can be criticised for encouraging compliance, rather than innovation. The details of what is legitimised reflect the variation of social expectations of business across sector and country as well as era; see Table 2.1 for an elaboration by Boswell (Boswell, 1983: 242).

2.2.3.5 CSR is a Vehicle for Wealth Creation

This rationale is also known as the 'business case for CSR' (Carroll and Shabanna, 2010), and is most famously epitomised by Porter and Kramer's concept of Creating Shared Value (Porter and Kramer, 2011; see Chapter 3). However, this idea is as old as CSR (Bowen, 1953). Robert Owen, known for his blending of business with social innovation in the early 1800s through model communities (New Lanark Mill, New Harmony), introduced company level rules for schools for workers' children, and rules on maximum working hours and against hiring young children. But he nevertheless indicated that this approach combined social and business benefits (Table 2.1 quoted in Husted, 2015: 127). This rationale is also evident in the stakeholder approach to CSR (see Chapter 5) as well as such CSR strategies as 'the bottom of the pyramid' by which means companies can serve the poor through enlightened business models (Prahalad and Hart, 2002; see information on Boots and Tata below).

2.2.3.6 CSR Is a Form of Governance

CSR has also been understood as a business contribution to societal governance, and has been observed throughout CSR's history. These contributions are normally in the form of provision of services and infrastructure, and in the administration of rights, through **private regulation**. These contributions to governance can take place in the absence of government provision as illustrated in pre-welfare state European CSR, in various developing country contexts and in cross-border contexts where no single national government has authority (e.g. in responsible supply chain initiatives – Moon, 2002; Matten and Crane, 2005; Scherer and Palazzo, 2011).

They are also increasingly illustrated in partnership where companies operate with, rather than in place of, governments. In undertaking such roles, business thereby contributes to the wider social and economic environment as Amitai Etzioni observes (Table 2.1 quoted in Moon, 2002: 407). Businesses also often regard these roles as providing the social and economic conditions for their own prosperity (Moon, 2001). From the governmental side, it is also illustrated by injunctions via various governmental ministers for business to join them in addressing problems such as mass unemployment, in view of the distinctive resources and capabilities that they can bring to such tasks (Moon and Richardson, 1985; Moon, 2002). This rationale points to the common root of corporate governance and CSR concepts in early scholarly debates

(Berle and Means, 1932; Bowen, 1953), and is now closely associated with corporate citizenship and political CSR perspectives (see Chapter 6).

We have seen how change in CSR history can be understood in terms of: the issues for which businesses are expected to take responsibility (the 'what'); the modes by which they conduct this responsibility (the 'how'); and the underlying rationales for this behaviour (the 'why'). However, there is little sense of linear development in these CSR phenomena. Rather, the picture is one of recurrence of issues, modes and rationales but always in different contexts which reflect changing relationships between and among the key CSR actors: society, business and government.

2.3 CSR Actors: Society, Business and Government

We now turn to investigating how society, business and government roles in CSR can reflect and shape issue agendas, the organising effect of its modes and the imperatives of changing rationales. As with the CSR phenomena discussed above, CSR actors are also central to the discussion of some key CSR questions, such as:

1. 'Who is supposed to be the key beneficiary of CSR?' Answer: 'Society'. But other questions then arise, such as: 'What does society expect of business?' 'How does society ensure that business reflects its expectations?'
2. 'Who is primarily responsible for CSR?' Answer: 'Business'. But this prompts further questions, such as: 'How does business enact this responsibility?' 'How does CSR impact the operational and commercial success of business?'
3. 'Which actor can represent societies' expectations of business and devise solutions to business's collective action problems in pursing social expectations?' Answer: 'Government'. But other questions then arise, such as: 'Do governmental roles in CSR undermine "corporate responsibility"?' 'How does business know about societal expectations in the absence of democratic government?'

CSR, then, primarily reflects the relationships and interactions between these three actors: society, business and government.

2.3.1 Society Actors

Society is the ostensible core context of CSR. Societies have expectations of business and certain powers over business, particularly concerning legitimacy (Aguilera, Rupp, Williams and Ganapathi, 2007; Carroll, 1979; Davis, 1960).

These expectations are sometimes conveyed directly to business, but otherwise societies use governmental authority to regulate business. This reflects the business responsive element of CSR. But these expectations can also reflect societies' experience of the effects of business, including its irresponsibility.

Societies are made up of people whose political status may vary from being 'subjects' of others (e.g. sovereigns, chiefs, landowners) to being citizens (in which the people have some rights of protection and powers over formal authority holders). People also vary in their context (e.g. communal, family or individual living) and wealth, and in their relationships to business (e.g. in stakeholder terms of being employees, shareholders, customers). Societies also develop as institutionalised systems, with regular habits of interaction and norms of acceptable and appropriate behaviour. They also develop organisational forms, which enable the development of social identities and points of solidarity, and the representation of the respective parts of society, which are collectively known as 'civil society'.

From ancient times, societies have developed ethics, based either on religion or other forms of cultural organisation and belief, and these have been applied to business activities and the uses of wealth. About half of the Code of Hammurabi, a Babylonian legal code dating back to about 1700 BC, is devoted to matters of labour and consumer contract, and the corresponding responsibilities. Subsequent civilisations also recorded norms and codes to give guidance to wealthy people and those engaged in commerce, as presented in Table 2.2. Many of these norms have been adapted to contemporary CSR.

A number of key themes emerge (Kim and Moon, 2015: 363–365). First, many of the norms are assumed to apply principally to people, and in more modern times they have been extended to apply to business organisations, and corporations in particular (Heald, 1970). Second and relatedly, in their time, these ethics simply accompanied daily life, thus the distinctions between society, business and government may have been rather blurred. Moreover, in many contemporary societies, particularly in Asia, these ethical framings are reflected in everyday religiosity and are therefore very much part of the conduct, or at least legitimisation, of business life. Even in Western societies, more imbued with enlightenment and post-enlightenment, the concepts of charity and stewardship have both an everyday meaning and thought, and are invoked in CSR (Bowen, 1953: Chapters 5 and 6). Third, different CSR systems are not simply reflections of respective nation states, but also of the variety of cultural mores within a single country, as in Malaysia with distinct Malay, Indian and Chinese business cultures. Certainly, however, modernity has seen the erosion of some religiously inspired ethical expectations of business and the emergence of more secular ones. This in part reflects changing social structures, social classes and other political identities based on language, region and gender, for example. These have

Table 2.2 Ethical foundations of business responsibility

Religion/ society	Keyword	Definition	CSR concept
Ancient Greece / Rome			
	Paternalism	'As if by a father to children'	Care of employees
	Philanthropy	'Love of humanity'	Giving (wealth/profits) to the needy
Buddhism			
	Dāna	'Giving'	Charity/justice
	Dharma	'Duty'	Righteousness
	Karuṇā	'Compassion'	Compassion for others
	Mettā	'Benevolence'	Good will
	Sila	'Ethics'	Ethical conduct
Christianity			
	Charity	'Benevolence'	Community/public service
	Stewardship	'Responsibility to the world God created'	Care of resources in trust
Confucianism			
	Li	'Good manners'	Ethical conduct
	Ren	'Benevolence'	Altruism
	Shu	'Reciprocity'	Reciprocity
	Xiao	'Obedience/filial piety'	Responsibility
	Xin	'Sincerity'	Integrity
	Yi	'Righteousness'	Righteousness
	Zhong	'Loyalty'	Responsibility/duty
Hinduism			
	Dāna	'Giving' as a duty	Charity/justice
	Dharma	'Righteousness'	Duty
	Karma	'Sum of actions'	Consequences of action
	Sanatana dharma	'Eternal order'	Unity
	Sarva loka hitam	'Well-being of others'	Philanthropy
Islam			
	Adalah	'Justice'	Justice
	Amanah	'Trust'	Integrity
	Khalifah	'Trusteeship'	Stewardship

Table 2.2 (*cont.*)

Religion/ society	Keyword	Definition	CSR concept
	Riba	'Usury'/ non-exploitative commercial relationships	Fairness
	Sadaqah	'Voluntary charity'	Charity/philanthropy
	Tawhid	'Oneness' e.g. profits are in union with moral action	Unity
	Ummah	'Community' e.g. wealth sharing	Unity/justice
	Waqf	'Voluntary endowment' e.g. A building for charity	Charity/philanthropy
	Zakat	One of the five pillars of Islam. Purification through the mandatory alms of 2.5% to the poor	Charity/philanthropy
Japanese			
	Keiei	'Governing the world in harmony while bringing about the well-being of the people'	Management
	Keiretsu gaisha	'Affiliates'	Ethical business conduct with suppliers
	Kigyo jokamachi	'Company town'	Community involvement
	Shogai koyo	'Life-time employment'	Employee welfare
	Asha	'Truth'	Righteousness
Judaism			
	Bal tashchit	'Do not destroy'	Environmental responsibility
	Chesed	'Kindness' or 'love'	Voluntary charity
	Tikkun olam	'Repairing the world'	Philanthropy
	Tzedakah	'Obligation to be just'	Charity/stewardship
Taoism			
	Chi'i	'Natural energy'	Unity
	De	'Virtue'	Integrity
	Wu wei	'Non-action'	Non-obstruction
	Yin yang	Harmony	Balance

Adapted from Kim and Moon (2015); see Kim and Moon's Appendix 1 for Asian Sources; and Ray et al., 2014.

informed expectations and CSR agendas around diversity and equality, for example. Environmental expectations of business responsibility were historically defined around the use and management of natural resources, particularly water and the effects of industry on air pollution. In the last few decades, however, planetary concerns of global warming and ecological diversity have emerged.

The sources of social expectations of business behaviour have become increasingly plural following waves of communications revolutions, from the use of paper through to the invention of the printing press, the telegraph, radio and television, to contemporary information and communication technology (Castells, 2000). During the nineteenth century, mass campaigns took place on social issues such as slavery, working conditions, employee rights and remuneration which sometimes addressed the culpability of business. But some businesses also aligned themselves with these societal campaigns (e.g. the Wedgwood company created products in support of anti-slavery). In the early twentieth century, the use of mass circulation printed media by 'muckraker' journalists emerged to reveal and shame business irresponsibility, particularly in the new oil, gas and railway corporations. Consumer leagues also emerged such as the *Ligue Sociale d'Acheteurs* in France, whose (mainly female) members promoted more ethical consumption by publicising shops in whose supply chains working conditions were deemed appropriate. In the twenty-first century, social media has been extensively used both by non-governmental organisations (NGOs) and other civil society organisations to mobilise support for campaigns against corporations' roles in such issues as de-forestation (e.g. Greenpeace attacks on Nestlé's sourcing of palm oil) (Castelló, Etter and Nielsen 2016; Whelan, Moon and Grant 2013).

Of course, society has also internationalised as reflected in migration patterns and revolutions in communication technologies, leading some authors to speak of a cosmopolitan society (Habermas, 1998). This is illustrated in a CSR context by the international spread of the Occupy Wall Street movement and of forms of **activism** against the oil and gas industry, with the diffusion of anti-fracking activism from the US to Québec and France.

Certainly, as Carroll, Lipartito, Post and Werhane (2012) observe of America, through CSR, business 'has sought and secured public acceptance, endorsement, and support – in other words, *social legitimacy*' (2012: 1). Thus to an extent, it can be argued that CSR issues, modes and rationales simply reflect the expectations that society makes clear. At various points in history, the significance of societal expectations has been raised to a higher level than customary practices, often because of perceived unethical, irresponsible or unsustainable business behaviour, such that these expectations have become more closely applied, made more explicit and even extended. But the mechanisms by which this happens tend to be society- and period-specific.

2.3.3 Business Actors

Having described society as the context for CSR, business is the main actor. It is the business's responsibility that is in focus in CSR. While societal expectations may shape CSR and its evaluation, it is business choices that give it substance and shape.

Business is, of course, in society. The wider effects of business are experienced by members of societies (owners, investors, managers, employees, and customers and consumers) as well as by other species and the natural environment. Moreover, social organisations also develop distinctive forms of business (e.g. cooperatives, social enterprises – see Chapter 9). However, business is also a distinct part of society, being made up of organisations, which are designed to sell goods, and services. And these roles have changed dramatically according to unfolding business purposes and organisation.

Although the precise purposes of business vary, throughout history there is a central expectation that the sale of goods and services will not only meet the costs of running the business, but also yield profits which will provide means of living for the owners and their families, or, in the corporate context, rewards (known as dividends) for their shareholders. Historically, many businesses have combined these purposes with social objectives. These have included doing business in a particular way (e.g. not employing children), sourcing products with socially-valued attributes (e.g. organic food), serving particular social groups (ethnically or otherwise defined) or meeting the needs of the vulnerable (e.g. the poor). In many US states, a new form of business incorporation, 'B Corps', has been introduced to legally distinguish companies with these mixed profit and social objectives (Rawhouser, Cummings and Crane, 2015), but the model itself is as old as business.

The nature of business organisations varies from the sole trader, through partnerships, small and medium-sized enterprises (SMEs), corporations and multinational corporations (MNCs), and the balance of these has also varied historically. Corporations have long existed for special licensed purposes (Avi-Yonah, 2005) and while some of them have had huge impacts (e.g. the British East India Company – Banerjee, 2008), they did not loom large until the second half of the nineteenth century (Chandler, 1984). MNCs, mainly creatures of the late twentieth century, are few in number but large, with commensurately huge impacts on other businesses from which they buy and sell goods and services. Historically, most businesses have been owned by those who also managed them, but with the emergence of corporations, owners increasingly employed professional managers (see section 2.4.2). Cooperatives are owned by consumers and employees. Most businesses are privately owned, whether by individuals, families, banks and private equity funds, and by more dispersed shareholders. Some are owned or part-owned by governments, particularly in socialist systems like China, and historically in Western countries.

So businesses have been infused with social characteristics and criteria for acting in sociable ways, in which CSR may only be 'implicit'. However, the recent emergence of business organisations for CSR has contributed to CSR becoming more 'explicit' (Matten and Moon, 2008).

While most CSR, implicit and explicit, has reflected the relationships of individual companies with society, businesses have also developed collective approaches to CSR. Historically this was through business guilds (often trade- or sector-based) and associations (e.g. chambers of commerce). However, there has been a recent growth of CSR-specific business associations. These can be: national (e.g. the UK's Business in the Community; Singapore Global Compact); international (e.g. ASEAN CSR, World Business Council for Sustainable Development); issue-based (e.g. the Business Coalition for HIV AIDS); or sectoral (e.g. the Electronics Industry Citizenship Coalition).

These organisational developments of CSR remind us that business is not simply a cipher enabling societal values and expectations to be translated into CSR as the compliance and legitimacy models alone would suggest. Business has also shaped CSR agendas in order to win legitimacy, innovate, attract new customers, motivate employees and make efficiency savings. Some have even argued that business organisations have been instrumental in shaping CSR for their own ends (Kaplan, 2015).

2.3.4 Governmental Actors

If society has offered the context for CSR and businesses have been the key actor type, then governments have been the key rule-makers and institutional shapers for business responsibility (see Moon, Kang and Gond, 2010: Chapter 10). As governments possess unique regulatory resources, societies expect them to curb business excesses to ensure that corporations serve the public. In the light of governments' regulatory power, business has also sought to influence how this power is used, by providing direct support or simply lobbying governments.

The role of government in shaping CSR goes back to the fundamental issue of its role in regulating the corporate form. This covers issues such as membership and the development of legal personality; the ability of corporations to operate for profit; share ownership; and the emergence of the global firm (Avi-Yonah, 2005). Increases in government welfare provision can lead to the substitution of CSR activities (e.g. as company-owned schools were replaced by local authority schools in much of Europe around the turn of the twentieth century). Governments can also discredit CSR provision (e.g. in the 1930s New Deal era in the USA).

Aside from these indirect roles, governments have also made regulations that directly impact on CSR. These include the creation of incentives for philanthropy (e.g. the English Charities Act 1601) or for the provision of insurance (e.g. in USA health and retirement plans); subsidies for CSR activities or organisations (e.g. as directed by the Thatcher government to companies and CSR associations and partnerships in the early 1980s); the introduction of CSR-type criteria for public procurement (e.g. the adoption of fair trade or sustainable product requirements by public agencies); and 'soft rules' to encourage CSR (e.g. the requirements for various forms of social reporting in countries from Denmark to India; and in stock exchanges from the USA to China).

Notwithstanding the internationalisation of CSR (Section 2.4.3), national governments have mediated its spread within their own jurisdictions (see Chapter 10). This first reflects both the established regulatory settings and the roles of governments. But second, this also reflects the contemporary agendas that face governments, and the uses that they have for CSR therein. Some governments have encouraged CSR to complement their public welfare policies, particularly in periods of high unemployment (e.g. the UK, Australia, Denmark). Other governments have used CSR to stimulate competitiveness (e.g. the UK in the 2000s). The Chinese government has used CSR to win legitimacy for Chinese exports in the twenty-first century.

International governmental organisations have also emerged which, to varying degrees, bring the collective authority of their national members to bear. At one extreme is the United Nations (UN), which includes virtually all national governments. While its effective authority is limited, its significance in endorsing, facilitating and partnering CSR through the UN Global Compact and related initiatives is highly significant. The Organisation for Economic Cooperation and Development (OECD) has been an author of guidelines for responsible behaviour by MNCs (OECD, 2011). The European Commission of the European Union has also been a source for a great deal of CSR guidance (see e.g. Commission of the European Communities 2002; 2006; 2011 and European Commission Multi Stakeholder Forum on Corporate Social Responsibility (2015)).

This actor-based historical perspective has presented CSR as reflecting interactions between social expectations of business, business actions to meet these through CSR and governmental regulation of social responsibility. We will now illustrate these relationships in three phases of CSR.

2.4 Three Phases of CSR Development

There are three phases of CSR development: industrialisation, the rise of the modern corporation and internationalisation. *Industrialisation* commenced in the UK in the late eighteenth century, emerged in much of Western Europe and North America in the nineteenth century, in other parts of the world in the twentieth or even twenty-first century experience (e.g. East Asia), and is yet to occur in some countries. The *modern corporation* also emerged in different ways, reflecting the respective national regulations for ownership and control, ownership spread, liability, management techniques and corporate governance systems. *Internationalisation,* although a recurring feature of history, has proceeded at a dramatic pace since the late twentieth century, including some transnational and even global features (Rosenau, 1990), closely related to the recent processes of financialisation (Davis, 2009).

The following sections present CSR developments in these three contexts, illustrated with reference to CSR issues, modes and rationales, and their respective society–business–government contexts. Each section also contains snapshots of two long-standing companies, the UK company Boots, and the Indian company Tata. Boots and Tata both originated as family-run companies in the nineteenth century and championed responsible business conduct from their inception.

Boots began as a pharmaceutical retailer in 1848, and was the UK market leader for much of the twentieth century when it expanded its product range to include household goods, photography and electricals. In the twenty-first century it was acquired by a private equity fund alongside other European pharmaceutical companies to form Alliance Boots (2006), which in turn has merged with US pharmaceutical retailer, Walgreens, to form Walgreens Boots Alliance (2014). (The three Boots' 'snapshots' draw upon the following references: Blythe, 2011; The Boots Company 2015a, 2015b, 2016.)

Tata commenced as a trading company in 1868 and soon expanded, first into cotton mills, then into iron and steel, electricity generation and diverse other businesses. During the twentieth century it grew to become India's largest conglomerate with companies, often part-owned by Indian public authorities, in such sectors as electricity, steel and aviation. In the twenty-first century it embarked on an internationalisation strategy, including through acquisitions in the European steel and motor manufacturing sectors, and through the spread of its consultancy business, particularly in Asia. (The three Tata 'snapshots' draw upon the following references: Tata Sons Ltd 2008, 2015, 2016a, 2016b.)

2.4.1 Industrialisation

As noted above (section 2.3.1), business responsibility was a clear societal expectation well before industrialisation. In medieval Europe, more distinctive forms of organising and regulating responsible business emerged, ranging from the obligations that attended being accorded corporate status, to the collective social duties – often in codes of conduct – that went with membership of guilds of trade (Caulfield, 2013: 223–226). There were also vigorous debates about

Social responsibilities of medieval guilds	Social responsibilities of the Elizabethan merchants	Social responsibilities of the early industrialists	Strategic CSR practice
Establish apprenticeships and fund secular education (1460)	Large-scale support for education and health (1600)	Efforts to attract, train, and retain employees (1812)	Secure business inputs
Negotiate charters to protect monopolies (1480)	Government intervention to codify charitable causes (1601)	Established improvements to working conditions (1802)	Improve governance of competition
Act to create and enforce quality standards (assize) (1491)		Highly public use of propaganda (1813)	Increase demand potential
		Interventions to provide housing and other services (1851)	Ensure supply conditions
Use of endowments to fund philanthropy (1332)	Use of endowments and gifts in kind (1630)	Capital accumulation for public works (1840)	Leverage capabilities

Figure 2.1

Evolution of strategic CSR
Source: Caulfield, 2013.

the roles and responsibilities of business in the eighteenth and nineteenth centuries, over the principle of joint stock ownership following the South Sea Bubble (1720) and over the alleged abuses of power by the British East India Company (in the late 1700s). Moreover, pre-industrial CSR issues, modes and strategic practices also informed their industrial successors. (Figure 2.1).

However, industrialisation constituted a systemic change in business – society relations, all of which made for recalibrations of earlier forms of CSR. This is because societies became reshaped by the exodus from agricultural production to industrial production in cities. The emptying of English villages and the growth of new centres such as Manchester, Leeds and Birmingham were echoed in much of the Western world, and latterly in parts of South and East, notably in China, the new 'workshop of the world'. Moreover, the labour conditions of industrialisation raised questions of responsibility, as did those of the working week and remuneration. In most cases, the rise of industrialisation was accompanied by the rise of movements for unionisation and labour rights. Increases in literacy and improvements in communications publicised critical images of industrialisation, popularised in the writings of Charles Dickens and Emile Zola in the nineteenth century.

New industrial businesses brought concentrations of wealth and power, but also social challenges of securing workforces and achieving legitimate reputations with society and regulators. Key CSR issues often centred on communities where workers were located, and included the living and recreational conditions of workers and their families. Issues of health and safety at work, the length of the working week, remuneration and pensions loomed large for many of the CSR leaders.

There were examples of parallel government regulation, but often these followed, or were in tandem with, company initiatives. The main CSR modes for addressing these issues were philanthropy in the form of charitable giving for communities broadly, popularised by Andrew Carnegie, but also throughout Europe and parts of Asia (notably India), including through tax incentives. Paternalism addressed the circumstances of workers and their families. A common mode was the model village and other forms of housing provision for workers, pioneered by Robert Owen's New Lanark Mill in Scotland, but emulated, including by Lever Brothers' Port Sunlight and Cadbury's Bourneville in England, the Pullman company town outside Chicago and Godin's *familistère* (Social Palace) in Guise, France. Even where companies did not create whole communities, many nonetheless invested heavily in employee housing (including for retirees), schools, hospitals and even recreation through swimming pools, pubs and casinos.

Company-based regulation for working conditions often preceded legislation, including limits on the working day and on child labour, and higher than market rate wages (e.g. Owen's New Lanark), health insurance (e.g. Krupp in Germany), pension schemes (e.g. London and North West Railway) and profit-sharing (e.g. Lever Brothers). In Japan, this extended to lifelong employment in many companies.

Turning to the environment, while many industrialists viewed 'smoke as prosperity' (quoted in Husted, 2015: 130), others used self-restraint and investment in 'clean technology and methods' to moderate their adverse environmental impact. Some of the worker communities were designed to provide a good living environment for workers and communities. In Germany, the Hamburg Chamber of Commerce led a collective initiative to lower smoke pollution which was complemented by relaxation of taxes – an early example of governmental rewards for self-regulation.

Rationales for responsible business vary enormously across the range presented in Table 2.1. Many leading figures appear to combine rationales, particularly that business should be a vehicle for social responsibility, that responsible business legitimises business to society and government, and that it is also a vehicle for wealth creation. Even Robert Owen was very clear that treating workers fairly resulted in better business returns.

In the mid-nineteenth century when medicine was expensive, Boots provided low-cost drugs to the poor, combining mass production techniques and a network of retail outlets. This was reflected in the company's initial slogan of 'health for a shilling' – an early version of the 'bottom of the pyramid' business model (Prahalad and Hart, 2002). This strategy was complemented by such social investments as a lending library service through the shops. Boots created numerous staff welfare initiatives (e.g. five-day working week, social and athletic clubs) and free education programmes and schools around the Boots factory. Boots thus undertook neo-governmental roles by providing social services that were later assumed within the welfare state (Matten and Crane, 2005; Crane et al., 2008: Chapter 3).

Box 2.1	Boots: CSR in industrialisation

Motto: 'We declare - For Pure Drugs For Qualified Assistants For First-class Shops For Reasonable Prices For your Good Health For our Moderate Profits. We minister to the comfort of the community in a hundred ways.' (Jesse Boot, son of Boots founder, 1897)

Issues: health, poverty, community, employee welfare and accountability.

Modes: paternalism (e.g. schools around factory); philanthropy; transparency (e.g. minutes at first meeting of the Directors of Boots, 1888, twenty years before legal requirement); pricing (e.g. subsidised pharmaceuticals for the poor in 1894, over a decade prior to UK National Insurance Act 1911).

Rationale: health for the poor as a business model.

Like Boots, the Tata Company displayed an early and distinctive dedication to social purpose and identity. This has been partly associated with ethical assumptions that Parsees should be especially charitable in foreign places. Thus, the company founder, Jamsetji Nusserwanji Tata, created the JN Endowment (1892) to encourage young Indians to study.

Box 2.2	Tata: CSR in industrialisation

Motto: 'In a free enterprise, the community is not just another stakeholder in business, but is in fact the very purpose of its existence.' (Tata Group founder, Jamsetji Tata, 1868)

Issue: community.

Modes: philanthropy (e.g. JN Tata Endowment, 1892: education trust for higher education studies); ownership transferred to charitable trusts.

Rationale: stakeholder orientation in the community as a business model.

2.4.2 The Rise of the Modern Corporation

While business in general, and corporations in particular, have long been associated with the distinctive resources and powers they can mobilise for private and societal ends, this feature became ever more apparent in the late nineteenth and early twentieth centuries, preoccupying socialists, liberals and conservatives alike (albeit for different reasons). In the USA, anxieties about the power of the new corporations, and its anti-social purposes, were illustrated in the work of the 'muckrakers' such as Upton Sinclair's (1927) book, *Oil!* (which inspired the acclaimed film, *There Will Be Blood*). This presented corporations with the challenge of being seen as sociable. Some corporations invested in their own image, illustrated by telephone monopoly AT&T's efforts to present itself as a person in its marketing 'to make people understand and love the company' (Bakan, 2004: 17).

The rise of the modern corporation marked several new departures for CSR, because the separation between ownership and control gave rise to a new class of business professionals who were thought better able to reflect on society's needs and goals than the increasingly dispersed shareholders. Indeed the 'doctrine of social responsibility' was seen by managers as a way to justify their legitimacy (Bowen, 1953: 84–106). Thus, the separation between ownership and control made the development of an ideology of social responsibility both *possible* and *desirable* in the eyes of the new business professionals. This brought in new discussions not only about their governance but also about their responsibilities to society, captured in Clark's (Clark, 1916) seminal paper, *The Changing Basis of Economic Responsibility*. Illustrative of the place of responsible business in the managerialism of the new corporations, Henry Gantt, famous for his eponymous chart, contended that 'the business system must accept its social responsibility and devote itself primarily to service, or the community will ultimately make the attempt to take it over in order to operate it in its own interest' (1919 – quoted in Husted, 2015: 125).

It is no coincidence that the developments cited above were in the USA. This is where the emergence of the modern corporation appeared most dramatic and where, compared to other democracies, its responsibilities tended to be more lightly regulated by government. While CSR dipped out of favour during the Roosevelt New Deal in the 1930s, it reemerged stronger in the post-war period. The newly emerging PR industry assisted corporations in adopting such rhetorical terms as business 'considerations of the public' and 'ethical awakening' to describe their responsibilities, and the modes of corporate–community relations and corporate philanthropy were institutionalised at the heart of American CSR (Kaplan, 2015).

Hence, twentieth century *corporate* social responsibility is regarded as essentially an American management concept. It was taken for granted by Nobel Economists Arrow and Galbraith, and, though famously challenged by their colleague, Friedman (Friedman, 1970), has remained a feature of the American corporation. CSR became theorised as a concept corresponding to a third way between governmental regulation and pure laissez-faire (Heald, 1970). Hence CSR's US character reflected a balance between the corporate governance obligations to profit-seeking shareholders and the judicial toleration of community-giving (Stout, 2012).

Box 2.3	Boots: CSR and the modern corporation

Motto: 'When we build factories in which it is a joy to work, when we establish pension funds which relieve our workers of fears for their old age, when we reduce the number of working days in the week, or give long holidays with pay to our retail assistant, we are setting a standard which Governments in due time will be able to make universal.' (John Boot, 1938)

Issues: workplace and public community development.

Modes: first full-time welfare staff appointed (1911); Boots Day Continuation School for younger employee education (1920); recycling machinery (1930s); five-day work week (1934); bottle recycling (1940s); 24-hour opening times; Boots Charitable Trust (1970); Environment Manager hire (1972); Social Responsibilities booklet (1977).

Rationale: workplace and public community development as a business model.

In Europe, however, the welfare state emerged as a relatively consensual feature of government until near the end of the twentieth century. So many corporations reduced their community level CSR (e.g. the provision of schools, cultural activities). However, during the last two decades of the twentieth century, CSR was emphasised more strongly on European shores, and subsequently there were greater parallels in approach related to the legitimisation of the modern corporation, particularly regarding issues of social deprivation and environmental costs. European CSR adopted various American modes, such as employee volunteering and the orientation of wider CSR activities to winning the loyalty and commitment of employees. This combined rationalisations of CSR as legitimisation and as a vehicle for wealth creation.

By the end of the twentieth century, on both sides of the Atlantic, CSR reflected organisational features of the modern corporation, namely functional specialisation (e.g. the growth of CSR organisational units) and professionalisation (e.g. CSR professional networks; inclusion in business school accreditation systems). Finally, CSR has emerged as a focus of business for specialised and general consultants.

Over the twentieth century, Boots evolved from a family firm with a narrow focus on pharmaceuticals to having a dispersed public ownership and a much wider product range (e.g. cosmetics, home electricals). A summary of its CSR issues, modes and rationalisation is presented in Box 2.3 which can be compared with Box 2.1 and considered in the light of the emergence of the modern corporation discussed above.

Like Boots, Tata grew enormously in the twentieth century. It became a conglomerate of enterprises, many of which acquired or spawned subsidiaries. The ownership structures vary among the enterprises, but have all included dispersed ownership through stock exchange listing and in some cases joint ownership with state and national governments. Tata emphasised employee

Box 2.4	Tata: CSR and the modern corporation

Motto: 'Be sure to lay wide streets planted with shady trees, every other of a quick-growing variety. Be sure that there is plenty of space for lawns and gardens. Reserve large areas for football, hockey and parks. Earmark areas for Hindu temples, Mohammedan mosques and Christian churches.' (Jamsetji Tata, 1902)

Issues: workplace and public community development.

Modes: The Indian Institute of Science for Advanced Studies, Bangalore (1911); eight-hour work days (1912); Tata provident fund (1920) thirty-two years' ahead of government regulation; Tata townships for employees.

Rationale: workplace and public community development as a business model.

welfare with the introduction of eight-hour working days in 1912, the development and funding of townships and the introduction of the Tata Provident Scheme in 1920. Reflecting its developing country status and unusual size and reach in this context, Tata's CSR reflected a continuing engagement with wider governance issues in its own communities and value chain throughout the century, whereas this was diminished for the middle section of the century for Boots, given the increased role of the welfare state in this period.

2.4.3 Internationalisation

Internationalisation is distinguished by the increase in: the volume of goods traded internationally; the movement of people; information and communication technologies; the extension of corporations' value chains across borders; the development of global financial markets; and the increasing power of international commercial and financial institutions. In some countries and regions, particularly in Asia, industrialisation, the modern corporation and internationalisation have occurred in different sequences, or, as is the case in China, almost simultaneously.

All of these trends have had immense implications for CSR in the early twenty-first century. Moreover, CSR has also acquired a much more global and commodified character. Contemporary approaches to CSR issues tend to approach the issues as universal and have encouraged the commodification of CSR through the 'business case'. Likewise CSR modes have become more international as transnational CSR organisations have emerged to develop shared norms, practices and evaluative systems.

Although local CSR issues remain central, especially in the context of developing countries, MNCs' CSR agendas increasingly focus on social and environmental issues that are 'global' in nature or because of systemic inter-actions between nation states. Climate change is one such issue, as it is planetary by definition, intergovernmental in institutionalisation, of growing concern to business (e.g. following the Stern Review Report in 2006) and an issue of widespread social awareness (e.g. as popularised in Al Gore's book, *An Inconvenient Truth* and Naomi Klein's *This Changes Everything*). The UN Millennium Development Goals, and their recent successor, the Sustainable Development Goals (SDGs), present a unified framework, which has become a convenient reference point for many organisations to evaluate and communi-cate their CSR.

Despite some of the sceptical prognoses that CSR would remain only in 'niche markets' (Vogel, 2005), CSR has endured serious challenges to its legitimacy in this context of internationalisation. In stark contrast with the post-1929 Great Crash, the 2008 financial crisis has not led to CSR disappear-ance to the niches. Rather, organisational CSR practices have been refocused towards the search of economic performance (Herzig and Moon, 2013; see Chapters 3 and 4). It is significant in this light that international institutional financial actors, for so long regarded as barriers to CSR, have encouraged such approaches as the integration of environmental, social and governance issues in investment processes. More generally, numerous institutional investors tend to regard responsible investment as a relevant and long-term risk management strategy, promoting the adoption of CSR practices by MNCs. These trends have also been encouraged by governance initiatives by national (e.g. the UK Stewardship Code) and international agencies (e.g. the UN-backed Principles for Responsible Investment).

Since 2008, investment in some CSR programmes appears to have increased, resulting in CSR and sustainability-related functions becoming more strongly institutionalised. The industries of CSR consultancy, teaching, certifi-cation, investing, marketing and auditing seem more resilient than expected, and the breed of new CSR professionals are now forming CSR professional associations.

The theme of the internationalisation of CSR is also reflected in the emer-gence and development of new modes of transnational governance that still involve the nation state government yet in a distinct capacity (Djelic and Sahlin-Andersson, 2006). A growing number of intergovernmental organisa-tions on regional and international levels have stepped into the CSR sphere, contributing to a 'globalised' and 'trans-nationalised' concept of CSR itself as well as to its management. The International Organization for Standardization (ISO) has recently produced a new norm defining how CSR can be managed for the benefit of any type of organisation (ISO 26000). Multiple similar 'private' CSR standards have emerged since the beginning of the century, forming a 'soft' law that interacts with governmental attempts at regulating local CSR initiatives in ways that are heterogeneous and have yet to be clarified. The diffusion of CSR standards and practices by MNCs to their local

Box 2.5	Boots: CSR and internationalisation

Motto: 'Our CSR mission and purpose "To be the UK's most socially responsible retailer in the health and beauty market." We will do this by: improving the health of our customers and their communities, protecting the environment, leading the development of sustainable products, placing our customers and colleagues at the heart of our business.' (Corporate Social Responsibility – Boots, *our approach*, website)

Issues: stakeholder orientation in community, environment, marketplace and workplace.

Modes: fundraising and volunteering: e.g. Boots Charitable Trust (1970), BBC Children in Need (2003), Macmillan Cancer Support; Safety of Chemicals Committee (2003), Waste Resources Action Programme (WRAP), Logistics Carbon Reduction Scheme (LCRS), Carbon Trust Standard; Boots 'Code of Conduct for Ethical Trading' (2002); 'Dignity at Work' diversity policy (2012); employment schemes, Big Tick award from Business in the Community for 'Inspiring Young Talent' (2014), website.

Rationale: CSR as a business model.

subsidiaries is also one of the processes by which CSR has become 'transnationalised' across the globe (see Chapter 7).

As noted above, Boots has illustrated two features of internationalisation: international mergers and private equity buy-out. These developments have led to some criticisms of Boots' social responsibility, notably regarding the relocation of the Head Office to Switzerland, resulting in a loss to the UK economy of Boots' corporate tax payments (see www.theguardian.com/news/2016/apr/13/how-boots-went-rogue for a wider critique of Boots' CSR).

Box 2.5 indicates that Boots continues to focus on the community and workplace issues, but it has also expanded its efforts to emphasise the environment and the marketplace. Also new CSR corporate governance mechanisms have been introduced (e.g. the Boots UK Executive Team, the Walgreens Boots Alliance Social Responsibilities Committee Code of Conduct) further institutionalising CSR within the company and further rationalising CSR for the company's successful business endeavours of the future.

Like Boots, Tata's CSR reputation has been somewhat tarnished through internationalisation, particularly as a result of the downsizing and withdrawal from UK steel industry acquisitions (see www.theguardian.com/business/2016/mar/29/tata-set-to-announce-sale-of-uk-steel-business-port-talbot). As Box 2.6 shows, Tata's CSR retains a stakeholder orientation with a focus on the community, workplace, marketplace and environment. And it governs its activities through the Tata Code of Conduct, in-house organisations (e.g. Tata Steel, Tata Tea and Tata Chemicals) and other governance modes. So, CSR has also been professionalised and institutionalised in the Tata Group, as well as rationalised as a successful business model of the past and future.

Box 2.6

Box 2.6	Tata: CSR and internationalisation

Motto: 'At the Tata group we are committed to integrating environmental, social and ethical principles into our core business, thereby enhancing long term stakeholder value and touching the lives of over a quarter of the world's population. That is our guiding philosophy that ensures we remain an employer of choice, a partner of choice and a neighbour of choice.' (Tata Sustainability Group, *About Tata Sustainability Group*, website)

Issues: stakeholder orientation in community, environment, marketplace and workplace.

Modes: volunteering: 'Tata Engage'; training: 'Tata Strive', disaster response; 'Climate Change Champions Programme', 'Water Champions Programme'; Tata Affirmative Action Programme (TAAP) (2007); Tata Index for Sustainable Human Development Taxonomy (2012); Tata Sustainable Group (2014); Tata Global Beverages' 100% sustainable sourcing by 2020, website.

Rationale: CSR as a business model.

2.5 Case Study: Marks and Spencer's CSR: From Community to Global Responsibility?[1]

Marks and Spencer (M&S) is a household name in UK garment and food shopping, reflecting its longevity in multiple high street locations, successfully branded products (e.g. St Michael underwear), and high profile marketing campaigns featuring top models and media personalities (e.g. Twiggy in the 1960s and more recently, actress Dame Helen Mirren, Olympic gold-winning boxer Nicola Adams and pop singer Ellie Goulding). M&S also has an international profile both in its sourcing and retail activities. It has been a CSR leader in various phases, but has also faced serious challenges to its responsible business reputation.

M&S is a listed company on the London Stock Exchange, and part of the FTSE 100 Index with a market value of £350 billion. M&S has 900 stores in the United Kingdom and nearly 500 international stores in over 50 different European, Middle Eastern and Asian countries. The majority (90 per cent) of its international suppliers are located in South Asia (India, Sri Lanka, Bangladesh). The company employs 80,000 staff. M&S's total revenue for 2016 was over £10 billion, 90 per cent of which was generated in the UK. M&S holds an 11 per cent share of the UK menswear market and 9 per cent of the UK womenswear market (2015).

---

[1] This Marks and Spencer's case study draws upon the following references: Boswell 1983; Elman et al 2012; Hamed 2013; Statista 2016; Marks and Spencer Company 2016a, 2016b, 2016c, 2016d, 2016e.

2.5.1 Foundations and the First Century

M&S was founded in 1884 when Michael Marks, a Polish refugee, set up a market stall to sell garments in Leeds, northern England. The company slogan was 'Don't ask the price, it's a penny.' M&S's founding business model was a precursor to the 'bottom of the pyramid' strategy: that the poor constitute an under-served market. This business strategy has been complemented by a commitment to, first, the company's communities and, subsequently, to wider communities throughout its value chain. This case study details the place of CSR in M&S's business model for its first hundred years, and then identifies two challenges: one of the late twentieth century, the internationalisation imperative; and the second, of the early twenty-first century, the ambition of sustainability as M&S's core strategy.

A decade after Marks had established his market stall, he went into partnership with Thomas Spencer, and in 1904 they opened their first shop in Leeds. Their business really took off in the inter-war period, when M&S adopted what was a revolutionary strategy of buying direct from suppliers. This enabled the company to burgeon, symbolised by the opening of a store in Marble Arch, London, and the expansion of the business to include food products. Although M&S became a public company in 1928, a family board presence stretched from the foundation to the twenty-first century to the retirement of Michael Marks' great-grandson, Sir David Sieff, in 2001.

Following public listing, the company invested more substantially in its own value chain, including creating its own fabrics research laboratory. But M&S also invested heavily in staff welfare, including pensions, subsidised canteens, health and dental services, hairdressing and recreation opportunities. In this period the 'Buy British' sourcing policy was adopted.

Boswell (1983) explains that M&S's interest in 'relevant public interests' was not only personally derived but also structured by the business model of social proximity and public visibility, given their high street locations; the familiarity of the goods sold; the frequency of purchases; and the transparency of employee working conditions. As a result of this and the company's public profile as a multiple chain store, its operations were very visible and thus subject to considerable informal social control.

The post-war period started with more of the same: greater investment in its own research department, broadening of the food range (e.g. Indian and Chinese food, wine), and the opening of more stores, including in Canada, Belgium and France. However, the UK economic downturn of the late 1970s and early 1980s brought the challenges of mass unemployment, urban decay and alienation. This prompted a renewed vigour in M&S's community engagement, with an additional £1.25 million investment in community work and charities in 1981 alone, and a wave of secondments of senior managers to local enterprise agencies and other new organisations to address the problems. *The*

Economist observed that M&S was 'making a sensible long-term investment in its marketplace. If urban disorders become a regular fact of life, many of its 260 stores would not survive' (Moon and Richardson, 1985: 136). It was said at the time, though we know of no documentation, that M&S shops were spared the damage inflicted on other high street premises in the urban riots of 1981. M&S was also one of the first companies to join and encourage others to join the new association 'Business in the Community', and David Seiff was its first Deputy Chairman.

For the rest of the twentieth century, M&S experienced highs and lows in economic performance and the challenges of operating stores outside the UK. It experimented with various new product lines, retail models and marketing campaigns, and it suffered boardroom turmoil. But the greatest challenge to M&S's community credentials was the demise of the 'Buy British' garments policy.

2.5.2 The challenge of internationalisation

The 'Buy British' garments policy ensured that M&S purchased 90 per cent of its merchandise from British producers. This policy was pursued by M&S for some seventy years, because it not only reduced supply chains but also made its brand synonymous with quality. It also benefited a number of British producers (over 800 at one point) and ensured a constant stream of UK employment.

M&S's commitment to 'Buy British', founded on its overall community orientation, slowed the company's adaptation to the competitive pressures of internationalisation from the 1980s. Whereas competitors were increasingly supplied from cheap labour factories around the globe, M&S officially refused to abandon its 'Buy British' policy, and encouraged suppliers to open up new plants in Britain. But as imported products became cheaper, M&S suffered financial losses and responded by periodically cutting UK suppliers' profits. Matters came to a head in 1999, when M&S ended its relationships with a number of home suppliers, with immediate effects on business and reputation. Long-term and loyal suppliers themselves elected not to renew contracts with M&S, fearful that their contracts would not be honoured nor profitable, and in some cases sued the company for damages. The company simultaneously suffered reputational damage for being a late mover in international sourcing. For example, a 1996 BBC *World in Action* programme accused M&S of condoning child labour in a Moroccan factory supplier.

As the turn of the century approached, the company accepted that an active change was needed in its business model and approach, to reflect the realities of the global marketplace.

2.5.3 Taking Sustainability Seriously

M&S's purchase of British-made clothing dropped from 87 per cent in 1988 to a mere 10 per cent by 2004. In light of the realities of its new internationalisation strategy, M&S began to develop new CSR commitments, informed not least by market research evidence of its customers' preference for ethical and environmental products and sourcing. It published its *Global Sourcing Principles* and joined the Ethical Trading Initiative (ETI) in 1999. It integrated its CSR in various ways through its first *Corporate Social Responsibility Review* in 2003, and through marketing its wider commitments (e.g. the 2006 *Look Behind the Label* campaign signalled its ethical and sustainable production and sourcing methods, and Fairtrade products).

However, the most conspicuous move to integration of its sustainability came as the M&S leadership turned to position sustainability at the core of the company's business strategy, with the launch of 'Plan A' in January 2007. Echoing the company's unwavering commitment to this sustainability strategy, Chief Executive Sir Stuart Rose explained categorically that 'there is no Plan B'.

Essentially, Plan A encompassed five pillars: climate change, waste, fair partnership, natural resource, and health and well-being, together containing a hundred sustainability commitments, which M&S aspired to achieve in five years. With an initial investment of £200 million, the company enjoyed the fruits of its commitment, with a reported savings of £320 million in 2014. The company also met its primary goal to make the UK business carbon neutral.

M&S inaugurated 'Plan A 2020' in 2014 which contained a hundred new and amended commitments, including the company's zealous aspiration to be the 'world's most sustainable major retailer'.

The hallmark of M&S's overall vision has been sourcing responsibly and thereby protecting the planet, reducing waste and helping communities as well as the accompanying professionalisation of these activities. M&S prides itself on issues such as central coordination, local ownership, engaging stakeholders, building capacity, reporting and standards to meet its intertwining sustainability and business objectives. Clearly, the business has taken radical steps to identify and correct its earlier mistakes. However, 'Plan A' might not be so far from M&S's origins as a community and employee welfare-focused company. In M&S's words, 'we believe a successful business must also be environmentally and socially sustainable. This belief isn't new. We've always maintained that business practices that benefit society improve our long-term performance.' (Our approach, M&S website)

Yet, 'Plan A' has not remained immune from challenges nor criticisms. Shareholders and pundits have criticised the large investment poured into Plan A and the risks of the ambitious 'all or nothing' sustainability approach. The Global Head of Plan A delivery, Adam Elman, has noted that one of Plan A's key challenges (apart from the built environment, legislation and policy) is stakeholder engagement, including with its internal business and operations stakeholders. Another challenge for consistent implementation of Plan A's operations goals results from the mixed ownership models of its stores, with some franchised and others fully owned. M&S has also continued to struggle to manage its supply chains. For example, challenges have been encountered in relation to the sustainable sourcing of natural resources to its food suppliers. The implementation of some sustainability initiatives in country-specific political and social landscapes has also posed difficulties. Elman cited the company's well-known and successful 'Shwopping' initiative, which facilitates clothing recycling in the UK as an example. Such a concept is not transferable to other countries where M&S is present, e.g. in India, as there is no established practice of throwaway textiles.

Clearly, the introduction and implementation of 'Plan A' has not been without its challenges. Yet, as a company that has survived and fought for its existence and relevance for over a century, its goal of being the world's most sustainable retailer may yet be within its reach.

Questions for Discussion

1. In what ways did the social responsibility issues, modes and rationales undertaken by M&S complement its wider business model?
2. Why did M&S invest so heavily in CSR during the early 1980s?
3. What else could M&S have done in response to the 'internationalisation imperative'?
4. What sort of risks and benefits do you envisage for M&S being a first mover in sustainability strategy?

2.6 Chapter Summary

This chapter has first adopted a phenomenological perspective on CSR history. This has enabled illustration of changes in CSR in terms of: the issues addressed (to answer the question 'what' is CSR?); the modes deployed for CSR (to answer the question 'how is CSR performed'?); and the rationales offered for CSR, particularly by business and business observers (to answer the question 'why CSR'?). Second, it has taken an actor-orientated perspective, which has enabled examination of how CSR has reflected different society–business–government relationships. These two perspectives have been illustrated in three key historical stages: industrialisation, the emergence of the modern corporation, and late twentieth and early twenty-first century globalisation. Further, they have been more closely examined in the parallel mini-cases of Boots and Tata, and in the fuller case study of M&S.

Certainly, we have seen that concern with business responsibility has been long-standing, particularly as articulated in societal values. Equally there is long-standing evidence of cases of business responsibility, as illustrated from medieval Europe. Third, we have seen long-standing government ambition to encourage business responsibility (e.g. since the early seventeenth century introduction of charities laws). And that is leaving aside longer-standing government roles in shaping this through wider regulation (e.g. of the corporate form) and regulating against business irresponsibility (e.g. against various manifestations of fraud).

However, it is harder to be conclusive about a dominant CSR trajectory. There have been patterns of *continuity*, as in the case of the prominence of community in most phases of CSR. One exception was in Europe during the periods of strong welfare states, but even here, community concerns have reemerged on CSR agendas with elements of the welfare state shrinking (e.g. in the UK), and as European companies have acquired international value chains, entailing developing countries.

There is also evidence of *development*, as illustrated in the case of CSR issues. First, there is a continuing shift from the prioritisation of community alone to issues of the products and processes entailed in business. Second, while the environment has been a continuing theme in debates about business responsibility, it has now become a much more accepted responsibility among businesses and in their CSR agendas. Third, there has been a development from concerns in the immediate value chain of companies to collective social, economic and environmental issues. As a result it could be contended that business responsibility is now much more about business roles in societal governance. There has also been *development* in the prevalent *modes* of CSR. The most obvious shifts are from company/business leader-based philanthropy and paternalism, first to company level foundations and codes (all evident in the nineteenth century but flowering subsequently), and then to the adoption of collective business and multi-stakeholder partnerships and standards, introducing the theme of a shift from the 'complete to the partial organisation of CSR' (Rasche et al., 2013).

Third, there have been CSR *recursions* whereby themes that were once extant are forgotten and then reinvented. This is probably most evident in the recurring rationalisations offered for CSR (Table 2.1), illustrated in Figure 2.1. A more recent example is Porter and Kramer's shared value (CSV) concept reflecting the views of Robert Owen (Table 2.1), regarding the social and economic value that can be simultaneously added.

These CSR continuities, developments and recursions take place in the very different contexts of national business systems, sectors and companies, which in turn reflect their own dynamic society–business–governmental relationships. A few general observations can be made here. The first is of the abiding significance of the national contexts of these relationships (Matten and Moon, 2008). It was also illustrated in the abiding importance of community as an issue, and ethical norms as a regulatory mode in much Asian CSR (Kim and Moon, 2015). The second observation is that nevertheless, society, business and governmental actors are more likely to operate in partnerships, reflecting the observation about 'partial organisation'. Third, all three actor types have also internationalised in the last few decades, and in many cases have done so collaboratively in cross-sector partnerships and multi-stakeholder initiatives (MSIs).

As you continue to read subsequent chapters of this book, you can employ these perspectives to engage in your own contemporary history analysis. You can identify: first, the nature of the key CSR issues, modes and rationales; and, second, the key CSR relationships between society, business and governmental actors. In each case, you can also ask whether these are stable or in flux, and whether they are contested or consensually valued.

Chapter Questions

1. What CSR issues, modes and rationales seem prevalent in your country? Have these changed recently? Do they vary by sector? And what role does path dependency exhibit in these issues, modes and rationales?
2. What are the CSR relationships between society, business and government in your country? Have these changed recently? To what extent do you think these CSR relationships will change in the future?
3. As you read each chapter in the book, can you identify the nature of the key CSR issues, modes and rationales? Are these stable or in flux? Are they contested?
4. As you read each chapter in the book, can you identify the key CSR relationships between society, business and government? Are these stable or in flux? Are they contested?
5. What CSR issues, modes and rationales characterised Boots, Tata and M&S's CSR over the three periods? What are the differences and/or similarities? What explains these patterns?

FURTHER RESOURCES

Bakan, J. (2004). *The Corporation: The Pathological Pursuit of Profit and Power*. New York, Free Press.

This book brings two themes together, a relatively crisp and even-handed history of the corporation, particularly in the UK and the USA (particularly Chapters 1–3), and a more focused critical perspective of the corporation as a psychopath (particularly Chapters 4–6).

Boswell, J. (1983). The Informal Social Control of Business in Britain: 1880–1939. *Business History Review*, 57(2), 237–257.
This paper presents a historical account of the social institutions which shaped responsible business in the UK, 1880–1939.

Gond, J-P., Kang, N. and Moon, J. (2011). The Government of Self-Regulation: On the Comparative Dynamics of Corporate Social Responsibility. *Economy and Society*, 40(4), 640–671.
This paper focuses on the role of government in regulating CSR, and offers a comparative analysis to shed light on different national experiences.

Husted, B. W. (2015). Corporate Social Responsibility Practice from 1800–1914: Past Initiatives and Current Debates. *Business Ethics Quarterly*, 25(1), 125–141.
This paper presents a comparative history of CSR in the nineteenth century, exploring its relevance for contemporary CSR.

Kaplan, R. (2015). Who Has Been Regulating Whom, Business or Society? The Mid-20th Century Institutionalisation of 'Corporate Responsibility' in the USA. *Socio-Economic Review*, 13(1), 125–155.
This paper presents a historical account of CSR in post-war USA as business-led.

The Corporation (Documentary)
The Corporation is based on Bakan (Bakan, 2004 – see above), and includes interviews with some of CSR's leading advocates (e.g. Ray Anderson, founder of Interface) and long-standing critics (e.g. Milton Friedman, Noam Chomsky). Edited versions of this rather long documentary are available online.

3

Strategic CSR: Ambitions and Critiques

STEEN VALLENTIN AND LAURA J. SPENCE

Learning Objectives

- Assess the strengths, weaknesses and practical implications of strategic CSR within the wider CSR field.
- Understand the different types of arguments – theoretical, empirical and normative – that can be used in support of a strategic understanding of CSR.
- Distinguish between different ways of arguing for the strategic value of CSR, including corporate social responsiveness and the business case, and to be able to reflect on their respective strengths and weaknesses and how they can be combined.
- Understand why and how it is useful to consider Porter and Kramer's notion of shared value not as a standalone concept, but one that should be combined with other perspectives in order to get a fuller picture of corporate responsibility.

3.1 The Strategic Turn in CSR

Since the early 2000s, the discourse on corporate social responsibility has taken what might be called a *strategic* turn. Not only 'the usual CSR supporters' but also some former believers in the neoclassical dictum that 'the business of business is business' have started to embrace the positive, productive, innovative, value-creating aspects of social responsibility. In the wake of insidious corporate scandals – ranging from Enron in 2001 to Volkswagen in 2015 – and, in particular, the events surrounding the global financial crisis of 2008 and beyond, the proposition that we can rely on the 'invisible hand' of the market to secure beneficial outcomes for society does not seem very comforting to many. In 2005 it was famously declared in a critical survey in *The Economist* that the advocates of CSR seemed to have won 'the battle of ideas' (Crook, 2005), and it has been suggested that we have reached a point where it is no longer a matter of *whether* but only of *how* companies are to engage in social responsibility (Smith, 2003). These conditions would seem to call for new, more accommodating economic approaches to CSR. It is in this context that strategic CSR has emerged.

Although Baron (2001) is reputedly the first to have made use of the term 'strategic' to capture CSR as value creation for the firm within the resource-based view of the firm (McWilliams and Siegel, 2011), and although we can point to a number of important contributions to the strategic turn, our treatment of strategic CSR in this chapter will in particular draw out the work of esteemed Harvard Business School professor Michael Porter and his co-author and business partner Mark Kramer. Porter and Kramer's strategic approach to CSR and CSV (creating shared value) has had considerable traction among business leaders as well as public policy-makers, and *shared value* is arguably emerging as a dominant mindset within instrumental views of corporate responsibility. Therefore it is imperative to understand the strengths as well as the weaknesses of their proposed contribution – and how it can be combined with other perspectives. To put their contribution in perspective, however, we start with a discussion of the antecedents of strategic CSR, with a particular focus on the notion of corporate social responsiveness and the business case for CSR. This is followed by a brief exposé of how Porter and Kramer's understanding of CSR has evolved over the course of their three essential papers on the topic (Porter and Kramer, 2002, 2006, 2011), leading to their novel concept of CSV. Next, we discuss arguments *for* and *against* strategic CSR as presented by Porter and Kramer. These discussions are wrapped up in a section focusing on the need to combine perspectives. No single perspective has all the answers – a point that is clearly reflected in the remainder of this book. In the case study we explore how the multinational conglomerate Maersk Group is working with shared value.

3.2 Antecedents of Strategic CSR

Etymologically, 'strategy' comes from the Greek *stratēgía*, meaning 'office or command of a general'. If you look in the dictionary, the adjective 'strategic' means something that is designed or planned to seek a particular purpose, or, in parallel, something that is related to the identification of long-term or overall goals and interests and the means of achieving them. The purposes, goals and interest of private businesses are usually centred on economic gain in one form or another. Speaking of 'strategic CSR', then, is a matter of attributing an economic purpose or quality to responsibility, that is, a purpose or quality above and beyond doing good for the sake of doing good. This implies a foregrounding of extrinsic (as opposed to intrinsic) motivations for acting responsibly.

The purposeful, strategic mindset has played an important part in the CSR literature for decades and is by no means monopolised by Porter and Kramer. William C. Frederick has contended that 'CSR, whatever form it takes, *serves* corporate interest and goals – and has been intended to do so since its inception around the turn of the 20th century' (Frederick, 2006: 7). The starting point of the classical literature on CSR was thus liberal capitalism and the free enterprise system. The fundamental idea was that businesses within such a system, apart from their economic, technical and legal responsibilities, have an obligation to work for social betterment, and that it is in their own best interest to do so – on a voluntary basis. Apart from variations on the general theme of enlightened self-interest of business, the strategic mindset had its major breakthrough with the coming of the notion of *corporate social responsiveness* in the 1970s (Frederick, 1978/1994).

3.2.1 Corporate Social Responsiveness

According to Frederick's seminal 1978 working paper, corporate social responsiveness refers to the capacities of companies to respond to social pressures. In contrast to the elusive principles and philosophical overtones often characterising the normative debate over corporate social responsibility, the focus on responsiveness indicates a more pragmatic and/or managerial take on how companies can respond 'to tangible forces in the surrounding environment' (Frederick, 1978/1994: 155). Responsiveness does not depend on the social conscience of the CEO or C-level management, but looks instead to institutionalised company policies for successful implementation. It gives weight to corporate strategy and strategising as it replaces questions of *why* with questions of *how* to be responsible in the smartest possible way. It is assumed that the central question of *whether* companies should respond to social pressures 'has already been answered affirmatively by general public opinion and a host of government social regulations and that the important task for business now is to learn *how* to respond in fruitful, humane, and practical ways' (ibid.: 156). Corporate social responsiveness has, however, been considered an unsatisfactory replacement for responsibility because it fails to give proper guidance in terms of positive values. Self-interested responsiveness is not necessarily synonymous with (other-regarding) responsible behaviour as seen from a stakeholder or societal perspective.

The answer to this challenge in the CSR literature was to argue that responsiveness only forms part of a larger whole and needs to be embedded in the broader, more holistic conception of **corporate social performance** (CSP): *processes* of responsiveness can then be accounted for alongside *principles* of responsibility and *results* relating to social responsibility (Wood, 1991). A strategic view of responsibility also figures prominently in the stakeholder management literature as it promotes value creation with and for stakeholders, and acknowledges that instrumentalism can provide the motivational basis for stakeholder engagement (Freeman, Harrison, Wicks, Palmar and de Colle, 2010). Another important antecedent to strategic CSR is the extensive literature on the business case for CSR.

3.2.2. The Business Case for CSR

As mentioned, CSP originated as a holistic concept that was meant to capture normative and instrumental aspects of corporate responsibility alongside concrete outcomes. However, the concept (with its 'performance' component) has in recent years been captured by a research agenda that is preoccupied with the measurement of particular CSR metrics and tends to provide anything but a holistic view of corporate responsibilities. In the words of Vogel, 'Oceans of ink have flowed to support the claim that corporate virtue delivers financial rewards' (Vogel, 2005: 11). In a review paper, Peloza counts no fewer than 159 studies examining the business case for CSP, the first of which was published in 1972 (Peloza, 2009). The majority of these studies (63 per cent) show a positive relationship between CSP and financial performance, some studies (15 per cent) report a negative relationship, while others (22 per cent) indicate a neutral or mixed relationship. This is similar to the findings of other meta-reviews. Apart from the mixed findings, there are a number of well-documented problems with such studies. One problem has to do with the lack of proper theoretical underpinning: 96 per cent of the studies mentioned by Peloza examine the value of CSP empirically, with only a few including financial metrics in efforts to theorise corporate responsibility. As noted by Perrini, Russo, Tencati and Vurro, 'most of the existing studies share the often-unstated assumption that the stronger a firm's involvement in CSR activities and programs is, the higher the economic and financial value firms will be able to obtain' (Perrini, Russo, Tencati and Vurro, 2011: 60). In attempts to defend the alignment of CSR with profit maximisation objectives, studies have been 'trying to demonstrate the theoretical superiority of CSR in terms of its positive correlations with economic and financial performance measures' (ibid.: 60). The lack of more rigorous theorising does, however, turn out to be a problem as correlations drawn from cross-sectional data cannot establish the direction of causality (Vogel, 2005). This leaves us with the problem of figuring out whether it is CSP that leads to better financial performance or vice versa. What causes what? CSP research has failed to provide a satisfactory answer to this question.

Another vital concern is that the studies measure different things. A total of thirty-nine unique measures of CSP were used to examine relationships between CSP and financial performance, with the most popular metric (pollution control or output) being used in only 18 per cent of the studies. Moreover, 82 per cent of the studies made use of a single measure only. This highlights a tremendous inconsistency and, if you will, arbitrariness in extant research. Similarly, thirty-six unique measures were used to capture financial performance. These included marked based metrics (such as share price), accounting metrics (such as Return on Assets or Return on Equity) and perceptual metrics (such as rankings and surveys). Peloza refers to these as 'end state metrics' and argues that they are appealing because they reflect the overall financial health of the firm. They are, however, inappropriate measures for managers whose CSR initiatives only make a small contribution to, for instance, share price movements. While end state metrics can 'provide a certain elegance and finality to the business case' (Peloza, 2009: 1524), they often provide little meaningful guidance for managers trying to measure the returns from CSR. This problem is exacerbated by the fact that CSP is most often examined at a cross-industry level, with the sample data not being specific to any particular sector(s) of the economy. Hence, this research tends to operate at the macro level rather than at the level of particular CSR initiatives. As a result, it fails to address firm-specific issues and provides little concrete guidance for managers wanting to assess the impact of CSR within their own firms. Against this, Peloza argues for the need to also make use of mediating metrics (related to, for instance, stakeholder relations) and intermediate metrics (related to particular revenue- or cost-based outcomes) – and thus for the value of measuring performance as close to concrete CSR initiatives as possible.

This is also the message of Perrini and colleagues, who see a need to venture beyond simplistic linear assumptions and aggregate measures when speaking of the business case (Perrini et al., 2011). They argue for the value of a multilevel framework that distinguishes between CSR efforts related to particular stakeholders or stakeholder groups (internal organisation; customers; supply chain; society; natural environment; corporate governance), drivers of performance in regard to these particular efforts, and performance related to revenue- or cost-related outcomes. This effort to make the business case a more tangible and less generic concern is also reflected at the level of corporate practice where many companies are using impact assessment tools, including key performance indicators, to assess the value of particular CSR initiatives.

Perrini et al. suggest that the quantitative studies of the CSP–CFP (Corporate Financial Performance) relationship 'substantially share the same view of CSR as a strategic and profit-driven corporate response to social and environmental pressures placed on firms by many different actors' (Perrini et al., 2011: 60–61). On the one hand, the normative implication of such studies is that they, for better or worse, subject CSR to economic measures of worth. On the other, the instrumentalism brought forward by this research is often not an end in itself, but a means to an end. This is well expressed by Vogel in his critical exposé of the business case and its promoters: 'The reason they have placed so much importance on "proving" that CSR pays is because they want to demonstrate, first, that behaving more responsibly is in the interest of *all* firms, and second, that CSR always makes business sense' (Vogel, 2005: 34). The business case is used pragmatically, as a tool to convince naysayers about the salience of CSR and bring disbelievers onboard. Ultimately, however, this research makes an ambiguous and vague contribution to our understanding of strategic CSR. The underlying assumption is that strategic benefits accrue to CSR in general, i.e., that CSR as practised by companies and reflected in various metrics is somehow inherently strategic.

3.3 From Strategic Philanthropy to CSV

Porter and Kramer provide an important corrective to such an understanding. They argue that conventional notions of CSR fail to qualify as being properly strategic, and that a new way of thinking about responsibility is required for a proper integration of CSR and corporate strategy to take place. Instead of being preoccupied with past performance, we should focus on creating value going forward. Their message is that strategic CSR needs to venture beyond responsiveness and should be guided by instrumental rather than normative concerns. As they write in a repartee with some of their critics in *California Management Review*: 'using the profit motive and the tools of corporate strategy to address social problems ... can contribute greatly both to the redemption of business and to a better world' (Porter and Kramer, 2014: 150). They make it clear that strategic CSR is not about personal values (Porter and Kramer, 2011), nor about doing good. It is fundamentally about business and economic value creation (Porter interviewed in Driver, 2012). The underlying idea is that capitalism can encompass all the necessary tools that businesses need to address social problems in the smartest and most efficient way. In an interview, Porter talks about 'the ability to use the core of the power of the capitalist system' in order to create shared value (Driver, 2012: 423), and Porter and Kramer adamantly do not identify with the social values espoused by the CSR movement.

Their three essential *Harvard Business Review* papers on CSR (2002, 2006, 2011) can be read as a three-step neoclassical reconfiguration of this concept. In the first paper from 2002 they provide a critique of the narrow definition of CSR as corporate philanthropy and argue for the superiority of *strategic philanthropy*, i.e., corporate giving that creates value for business as well as for society/ beneficiaries. In 2006 this idea is extended to the field of CSR more broadly. Here, they aim to show that strategic CSR is superior to conventional approaches and make their case in opposition to what they refer to as the prevailing justifications for CSR: moral obligation, sustainability, licence to operate (in relation to stakeholders) and reputation. As they see it, all these approaches suffer from the same weakness in that they focus on (negative) tensions between business and society as opposed to (positive) interdependencies. Another shortcoming is that they create a generic rationale as opposed to one that is operational from the point of view of business and strategy. Consequently, they are insufficient when it comes to helping companies identify, prioritise and address the most important social issues, i.e., the ones in regard to which they can make the largest impact. And this is supposedly why we are seeing so many corporate efforts being fragmented and more concerned with style (i.e. glossy reporting) over substance.

Strategic CSR, in contrast, is a means of prioritising social issues. The purpose of prioritising issues is 'to create an explicit and affirmative corporate social agenda' (Porter and Kramer, 2006: 85), and the message is that such an agenda must be responsive to stakeholder expectations, but that truly strategic CSR goes beyond responsiveness. Although companies must work to mitigate harm from their activities, this is considered more as a routine, operational challenge. Strategy is about finding ways to transform value chain activities and use strategic philanthropy as a lever to improve salient areas of the competitive context – and this is where the greatest potential for social impact and business benefits is to be found. According to Porter and Kramer, while responsive CSR is about 'being a good corporate citizen and addressing every social harm the business creates, strategic CSR is far more selective'; it is about mounting 'a small number of initiatives whose social and business benefits are large and distinctive' (ibid.: 88). The shared value mindset they promote is about finding the points of intersection, the sweet spots where companies can create value for themselves as well as for society. Instead of seeing CSR as a cost or focusing on trade-offs between doing good and doing well, responsibility is considered an opportunity and an investment that can benefit business and society at the same time.

In 2011, they take a step further and propose to use CSV as a conceptual alternative that is free of the wishful thinking and ineffective legacy of CSR. Here, they address the failure of neoclassical economics to incorporate a broader view of the business environment, and the way in which companies remain stuck in a narrow and outdated approach to value creation that tends to focus too much on industry-specific concerns and the short term while overlooking opportunities to meet fundamental societal needs in the long term. Yet, they maintain that this problem can best be taken care of within the system – through the use of the powers of capitalism, not by resorting to extra-economic means. They write: 'Our field of vision has simply been too narrow ... Companies have failed to grasp the importance of the broader business environment surrounding their major operations' (Porter and Kramer, 2011: 67). Thus: 'The purpose of the corporation must be redefined as creating shared value, not just profit per se' (ibid.: 64). They define shared value as 'policies and operating practices that enhance the competitiveness of a company while simultaneously advancing the economic and social conditions in the communities in which it operates' (ibid.: 66). Value is identified as benefit relative to cost, and three basic ways of CSV are outlined: re-conceiving products and

Table 3.1 The practicalities of CSV

How to create shared value	Key question	Example
Re-conceive products and markets	Is our product good for our customers?	Vodafone's M-PESA mobile banking service in Kenya with 10 million customers in 3 years representing 11% of gross domestic product (GDP).
Redefine productivity in the value chain, e.g. in terms of energy use and logistics; resource use; procurement; distribution; employee productivity; location	How can externalities be addressed to create social value and avoid economic cost?	Hindustan Unilever's direct-to-home distribution system, run by underprivileged female entrepreneurs, supported by microcredit and training provided by Unilever. Accounts for 5% of the company's revenue in India.
Enable local cluster development	How can addressing gaps in a cluster's framework conditions improve productivity?	Yara, the fertiliser company, invested $60 million into transport infrastructure improvements in Mozambique and Tanzania. Yara and the agricultural sector benefit from business growth via easier access to supply (e.g. of fertiliser) and distribution.

Source: Developed from Porter and Kramer (2011).

markets, redefining productivity in the value chain, and enabling local cluster development. These are summarised below and in Table 3.1 with illustrative examples.

The starting point for the first kind of shared value is 'to identify all the societal needs, benefits and harms that are or could be embodied in the firm's products' (ibid: 68). Productivity in the value chain is related to social issues such as natural resource and water usage, health and safety and working conditions in general. It is emphasised that opportunities to create shared value arise because social and environmental problems can create economic costs for companies (ibid: 69). Local cluster development is about engaging in collective/collaborative action with other societal actors in order to provide better framework conditions (institutions, infrastructure, etc.) and thus support the competitive context. They claim that CSV 'presumes compliance with the law and ethical standards, as well as mitigating any harm caused by the business, but goes far beyond that' (ibid.: 75).

While Porter and Kramer acknowledge in 2011 that there is something wrong with capitalism as we have known it, they consider this to be an economic problem rather than a moral one – making it amenable to economic solutions. They write: 'Not all profit is equal, an idea that has been lost in the narrow, short-term focus of financial markets and in much management thinking. Profits involving a social purpose represents a higher form of capitalism' (ibid.: 75). What defines this elevated form is not, however, personal values or altruism, but a utilitarian principle related to social impact as the ultimate measure of worth. According to Porter and Kramer, a higher and more sophisticated form of capitalism is 'one that will enable society to advance more rapidly while allowing companies to grow even more' (ibid.: 75). Indeed, they propose that CSV be considered as 'a broader conception of Adam Smith's invisible hand ... It is not philanthropy but self-interested behaviour to create economic value by creating social value' (ibid.: 77).

We would argue that to date, CSV may not be universally admired but has certainly gained a dominant position within the strategic CSR subfield. We will now go on to unfold a more detailed analysis of its strengths and weaknesses as the front-runner in the strategic CSR debate.

3.4 Arguments *for* Strategic CSR

The arguments *for* strategic CSR are to a large extent built into the models and the mindset presented by Porter and Kramer. It is, however, worth briefly summarising the strong points and the general arguments that can be made in favour of their approach.

In an interview, Porter expresses his view of the predicament of the modern corporate executive:

> I think that business as usual has become less satisfying for many CEOs, frankly, and for many employees and many of the graduates of this school [Harvard Business School] and other business schools ... many of the leaders I interact with feel trapped in the system as it is defined today and they feel like they are having ridiculously short time horizons and I think they feel uncomfortable about CSR because of the impact they did not see. (Driver, 2012: 426)

In light of the practical failure of CSR, what is called for is a hard-nosed, no-nonsense approach that is able to bridge competitiveness and value creation with the social needs of the communities that companies operate in. Whereas CSR often turns into a sideshow, the strategic CSR/CSV mindset is much better aligned with the core competencies and the concrete strategic outlook and challenges of individual businesses, in their particular settings. It ensures that economic rationality and economic measures of worth hold sway over proceedings, and not fleeting ethical, social or environmental sentiments (as promoted by more or less knowledgeable and qualified stakeholders). According to Porter and Kramer, lofty, wishful thinking

> has led to so many corporate responsibility and sustainability arguments falling on deaf corporate ears, by insisting that profit-seeking enterprises need to abandon their core purpose for the sake of the greater good. Such a perspective merely drives further the wedge between society and business, to the detriment of both. (Porter and Kramer, 2014: 150)

Shared value represents an internally driven, positive and innovative mindset in regard to addressing social problems and needs in ways that are also beneficial for the company. Therefore it has much better prospects of motivating corporate action and creating a lasting, and thus sustainable, drive for development.

Although this mindset purports to be well aligned with the fiduciary duty of managers, the creation of shared value will often be a matter of making medium- or long-term strategic investments. Porter and Kramer acknowledge that this can be in conflict with the short-termism perpetuated by financial markets: 'Capital markets will undoubtedly continue to pressure companies to generate short-term profits, and some companies will surely continue to reap profits at the expense of societal needs. But such profits will often prove to be short-lived, and far greater opportunities will be missed' (Porter and Kramer, 2011: 77). Thus, CSV is an important step beyond business as usual and a corrective to the short-term orientation of many corporate executives. This step does not come with promises (or threats) of more radical reform of businesses, but that is exactly its strength. There is no need for radical transformation, but for bold yet realistic visions of how we can move beyond the status quo within capitalism.

3.5 Arguments *against* Strategic CSR

After this summary of the espoused strong points of Porter and Kramer's conception, we will proceed with a critical discussion of some of its shortcomings and the questions it leaves unanswered. Thus, we need to examine not only what it highlights or foregrounds, but also what it hides or can be used to hide (Aakhus and Bzdak, 2012). Apart from exclusions and blind spots, we also want to point to some of the internal tensions and contradictions in their reasoning and the implications such tensions and contradictions can have for the clarity and usefulness of the CSV framework. We turn first to the matter of CSV as a provider of corporate legitimacy.

3.5.1 Legitimacy Issues

Porter and Kramer have argued that their approach is about substance (social impact) over style. Therefore it is perhaps surprising how strongly they emphasise that CSV can help businesses earn the respect of society and serve to reshape capitalism's relationship to society. They write: 'Perhaps most important of all, learning how to create shared value is our best chance to legitimize business again' (Porter and Kramer, 2011: 64). In their recent rebuttal to Crane, Palazzo, Spence and Matter (2014), they argue that, even if it must be acknowledged that not all businesses are good for society and that shared value cannot eliminate all injustice, 'using the profit motive and the tools of corporate strategy to address social problems, a practice that is growing rapidly in part motivated by the shared value concept, can contribute greatly both to the redemption of business and to a better world' (Porter and Kramer, 2014: 150). In an interview in 2003, Porter's major criticism towards the field of CSR was that it had 'become a religion filled with priests, in which there is no need for evidence or theory' (Morsing, 2003), and it is perhaps surprising that he would use theological terms to encapsulate his own work. Interestingly, Porter and Kramer associate redemption not with doing good (altruism, philanthropy), nor with the atonement of past sins (acceptance of guilt for wrongdoing), but with economic success (doing well in terms of value creation) – and they do not question the sanctity of corporate self-interest (Crane et al., 2014).

This focus on legitimacy and impression management as foremost concerns can arouse suspicion. Is public image more important than performance after all? Do appearances matter more than actual results? Instead of being redeemers and social innovators, are Porter and Kramer rather to be seen as veiled reactionaries standing in the way of more fundamental reform of the capitalist system? They insist that not only can corporate capitalism be a force for social good, it can have a greater impact on social good than other institutions, but this is *only provided that businesses apply the right strategic mindset*. Is shared value, then, merely a reflection of business as usual flying under a new flag, adapting to new societal conditions and market opportunities while undermining more far-reaching notions of social responsibility? For critical commentators, of course, this type of critique applies to all forms of instrumental thinking in regard to CSR (Vallentin, 2015).

Although Porter and Kramer contend that the shared value mindset can and should be applied to all corporate decisions, the empirical support they provide (see below) focuses mostly on singular projects and product innovations while saying nothing about how the activities in question relate to overall CSP. This suggests that capitalism can be reformed one activity, project or product at a time, without, again, any need for a more fundamental overhaul of the system. The limitations of this brand of reform, not to mention its redeeming qualities, are made abundantly clear by Porter himself in a recent interview. Here, he clarifies that the discussion of CSV

> presumes meeting the letter and the spirit of the law and that companies and managers operate ethically. Obviously we are not there. I mean there are a lot of corporations that do not operate ethically and there are some that fudge the law, cut corners, and break the law. That is a different problem. That is a problem we have to continue to address. That is kind of a foundational problem. (Driver, 2012: 426).

Here is an admission that the legitimacy problem may be important, but that their proposed solution is dealing with symptoms rather than root causes. CSV does not deal with fundamental, systemic problems of corporate irresponsibility (we return to the matter of compliance below). Such matters are beyond its scope of action. Should we expect creation of shared value to be a redeeming force for capitalism if we are continually exposed to corporate scandals like the one that Volkswagen has recently been involved in (regarding fraud in testing of automobile emissions)? Do cases such as this not reflect an ongoing need to address the systemic imbalances that lead to unethical and harmful behaviour in business? This leads us to our second point of contention.

3.5.2 Value Blindness and Conceptual Confusion

Porter and Kramer make it clear that CSV is not about personal values (Porter and Kramer, 2011). It is about 'creating economic value in a way that *also* creates value for society by addressing its needs and challenges' (Porter and Kramer, 2006: 64). The shared value mindset is not, according to a *New York Times* article, a moral stance. Kramer is here quoted as saying 'this is not about companies being good or bad ... It's about galvanizing companies to exploit the market in addressing social problems' (Lohr, 2011). As we saw, they consider CSV as a broader conception of Adam Smith's notion of 'the invisible hand' (of the market) instead of calling more explicitly for the visible hands of management to make a difference. They are indeed promoting creation of shared value, not shared *values* (which, economic theory will tell us, are not required in market exchange). However, as Ghoshal informs us, all theories of social phenomena are, and have to be, if not ideologically motivated then certainly reflective of underlying values. This goes for economic theories as well as other theories. Ghoshal writes:

> Despite the pretense to be values-free, no social theory can be values-free. And, while no social science discipline makes a stronger claim to objectivity than economics, no domain of the social sciences is more values-laden in both its assumptions and its language than economics and all its derivatives, including much of modern finance and management theories. (Ghoshal, 2005: 83)

To argue that we should leave personal values aside in dealing with matters of social responsibility is in itself a strong value proposition reflecting an ideological standpoint. This is important because it can help to explain Porter and Kramer's urge to distance themselves from conventional notions of CSR.

In 2011 they wrote: 'Shared value is not social responsibility, philanthropy or even sustainability, but a new way to achieve economic success' (Porter and Kramer, 2011: 64). This statement suggests either that CSV is different from those other concepts or that it can serve as an actual replacement. Either way, this and other statements show an unwillingness to yield any ground to or accommodate any insights provided by conventional CSR pundits that would seem to be rooted in the ideological predispositions of the neoclassical paradigm. While Porter has acknowledged that the solutions offered by the model of shared value are highly insufficient when it comes to alleviating capitalism's own, internal problems of irresponsibility, the work of Porter and Kramer does not in any way recognise that conventional CSR can have a positive role to play in addressing and correcting these maladies. Instead they proceed to give economic value creation, growth and corporate self-determination precedence over social and democratic values in a broader sense. Their vision of a 'better' world is first and foremost one wherein there are better opportunities for economic growth and prosperity.

Apart from the knee-jerk critique that they hereby downplay or ignore tensions between business and society and ultimately provide a shallow understanding of the corporation's role in society (Crane et al., 2014), their dismissal of conventional CSR leads to unnecessary conceptual confusion. Hence, Porter and Kramer confuse matters by arguing that CSV is superior to CSR and different from CSR while at the same time defining it so that it assumes and thus includes responsive behaviours (compliance with the law and ethical standards) that we normally associate with CSR – thus acknowledging that companies do need to engage in such behaviours. CSV is different, but also, partly, the same. Theoretically, their argument would seem to be logically inconsistent. On a practical level, this leads to a certain confusion regarding the identification of CSV as opposed to CSR. As Crane et al. argue, there is, apart from the labels used, no realistic way to distinguish a CSV initiative from other CSR activities as there is no conceptual distinctiveness to CSV as a specific corporate practice (Crane et al., 2014). Apart from its symbolic significance, does the choice of preferred term/label involve any substantial difference, and how can this be determined? And when do corporate activities taken together qualify as being more one thing than the other? Perhaps more importantly: how are companies to reconcile the strategic call for a small number of focused activities with the need to address all the social harms their business creates? Porter and Kramer arguably fail to provide concise answers to such questions, but perhaps their recommendation boils down to a relative prioritisation of value-creating as opposed to responsive activities, however vague that may seem. We return to this issue in our case study of Maersk.

Finally, while Porter and Kramer claim greater concept clarity for CSV compared to CSR, more effort is needed to clarify the boundaries of the former. As reflected in some empirical studies, just about any product or service can be said to create value for a company while also serving some social need (Bertini and Gourville, 2012). This can lead to over-inclusiveness in the sense that most market exchanges can be seen to reflect creation of shared value. Where to draw the line, then? What social needs qualify as representing enough of a problem or concern to be deemed worthy of inclusion in CSV?

3.5.3 Measures of Value and Social Impact

Then there is the matter of how to measure or assess the value of shared value. As pointed out by Dembek, Singh and Bakhoo (Dembek et al., 2015), the lack of clarity and precision in definition is also reflected in problems with the operationalisation and measurement of the concept, in spite of the implied economic rigour. Research has pointed to a number of problems. To begin with fundamentals: there is no agreed-upon way to measure shared value at this time (Pfitzer, Bockstette and Stamp, 2013). Research has provided assessment frameworks, but no specific measurement tools or metrics. Moreover, the cases used by Porter and Kramer and others tend to focus on the corporate 'win' rather than on social benefits. Hence, there is a bias towards the achievement of economic success for business. The costs and broader impacts of organisational actions are largely neglected, and most cases and examples are brief and lack the detailed information and data that would be required to properly support the author's arguments (Dembek et al., 2015). Hence, the CSV concept rests on anecdotal evidence – with many of the examples cited by Porter and Kramer being clients of FSG (consulting firm Foundation Strategy Group) or affiliated with Harvard Business School (Aakhus and Bzdak, 2012). Furthermore, CSV is primarily analysed at the level of singular initiatives, projects and products, which begs the question of whether or how it can be applied to the organisational level of analysis (Dembek et al., 2015). Crane et al. speak of CSV's myopic focus on new projects and products (Crane et al., 2014).

Ultimately, Porter and Kramer's pivotal measure of worth, social impact, would seem to provide less rigour and direction than promised. Indeed, with their corporate-centric point of departure they fail to make it clear what they mean by *social* impact, simply because they have not properly addressed the wants and needs of those social groups that belong to the other side of the CSV equation. Although they do extol the value of joint initiatives and collaboration (across profit/non-profit and private/public boundaries) (2011), what they present is an asymmetrical and unbalanced approach to 'sharing'. This absence of multiple perspectives can be considered as a critical shortcoming (Dembek et al., 2015), and it is symptomatic of an approach that puts corporate interests before social concerns. We are told that CSV is about creating economic value through the creation of social value and about enhancing competitiveness while simultaneously advancing economic and social conditions in surrounding communities. CSV is not about redistributing value, but about 'expanding the total pool of economic and social value' (Porter and Kramer, 2011: 65). However, Porter and Kramer fail to provide a clear definition of what they actually mean by, again, *social* value. It is suggested that social value is something 'of value' to people in need within a cost-benefit framework, but so far none of the cases and examples provided by the literature on CSV has considered the degree to which such needs are actually satisfied (Dembek et al., 2015). Following from this: who is to determine what social value is for particular beneficiaries/stakeholders? The company or those stakeholders? Is it possible or meaningful to speak of value creation as something shared without actively engaging the societal side in some form of dialogue or deliberation? Dembek et al. suggest that there needs to be more focus on the *means*, *resulting outcomes* and *beneficiaries of the outcomes* of CSV (Dembek et al., 2015), and we would likewise argue that a meaningful measure of the value of shared value must embrace the notion of social value in a more inclusive manner.

Perhaps a recent article on shared value indicates a turn in this direction. In 'The Ecosystem of Shared Value', Mark Kramer and Marc Pfitzer argue for the value of the notion of 'collective impact', and make the case for companies to engage in trust-building and mutually reinforcing partnerships with non-governmental organisations (NGOs), governments and competing businesses as this will provide the strongest basis for dealing effectively with social problems and create shared value. The authors even concede that companies cannot be the backbone of such projects as they are not neutral players; instead, a separate and independently funded staff is called for. Indeed, collective impact calls for a new brand of leadership – 'system leadership' – that involves multiple individuals from different constituencies leading together (Kramer and Pfitzer, 2016). It remains to be seen whether this article (which comes without the Porter imprint) will have an impact comparable to the ones we have already discussed. Its opening towards a more inclusive and democratic approach to responsibility is interesting considering the starting point, but is lacking in originality with regard to actual content.

3.5.4 Compliance and the Big Picture

Porter and Kramer strongly advocate companies to go beyond compliance. This is nothing new in CSR. One of the classical contributors to the early CSR literature, Keith Davis, argued that a firm 'is not being socially responsible if it merely complies with the minimum requirements of the law, because this is what any good citizen would do' (Davis, 1973: 313). Whereas Davis makes a moral argument, Porter and Kramer, as we have seen, simply presume compliance with the law and ethical standards. They are effectively reducing conventional CSR efforts to unadventurous, responsive, routine, largely compliance-driven activities, while the most promising prospects of corporate action are taken out of this realm. Although there is some strength to this, there are also some obvious shortcomings, some of which have to do with the questions they hereby leave unanswered. By taking compliance for granted they tend to grossly underestimate the complexity of corporate supply chains and the ongoing challenges that are involved in securing compliance with rules and regulations in different social settings (Crane et al., 2014). By the same token, and by focusing almost exclusively on the positive, value-creating side of responsibility, they downplay issues related to risk and risk management and how such considerations can have strategic value, vis-à-vis the **materiality** assessments used by many companies. Porter and Kramer are silent on the matter of how the broad accountability perspective of CSR can or should be aligned with the more focused agenda of CSV. Hence, they fail to capture the bigger picture of corporate responsibility. As mentioned, this problem is a result of their preferred level of analysis, which is the individual project or product rather than the overall corporate strategy or the organisation as such. This leads us to our final point of contention.

3.5.5 Delivering on Integration

The shared value mindset comes with promises of integration, of operating (unlike CSR) close to the core of the business. However, CSV has been accused of simply providing a recipe for cherry-picking activities that can fit neatly within a win-win framework – allowing corporations to engage in those activities that suit them while ignoring other pressing social issues that have less direct financial benefit and may involve difficult dilemmas or trade-offs. Although Porter and Kramer are sceptical about glossy sustainability reporting, they have come up with a concept that lends itself extremely well to such reporting and to positive storytelling in other forms of corporate communication. While Porter and Kramer have made an undeniable difference when it comes to defining the *how* of CSR, there is little evidence suggesting that they have been even remotely successful in their endeavour to redefine the *how* of capitalism. CSV has become a preferred way for some companies to select, frame and communicate their social responsibility efforts, in whole or in part, but has so far gained little ground when it comes to being fully integrated into corporate strategies and value propositions of companies. We are not yet seeing the realignment of entire corporate budgets in accordance with shared value that they are advocating. As we have shown, Porter and Kramer fail (along with, admittedly, many other contributions to the CSR literature) to provide concrete recommendations on how integration is to be achieved in organisational and thus more holistic or systemic terms (Dembek et al., 2015). What they propose instead is an integrated mindset. They emphasise that CSV is integral to competing and to profit maximisation, while also being company-specific and internally driven (Porter and Kramer, 2011). When all is said and done, however, they remain rather vague about the social implications of CSV – both in terms of the meaning of social value (externally) and in terms of the social organisation/implementation of this mindset (internally). As a result, shared value activities can be practised by companies that are simultaneously involved in irresponsible activities – without Porter and Kramer apparently having much to say about this. In the words of Crane et al., 'CSV may lead to islands of win-win projects in an ocean of unsolved environmental and social conflicts' (Crane et al., 2014: 139).

3.6 Combining Perspectives

Based on an extensive literature review, Dembek et al. conclude that shared value is at a nascent stage as a theoretical concept and more resembles a management buzzword (Dembek et al., 2015). Buzzwords are characterised by being overused while their meaning often gets distorted and overextended (ibid.). One recurrent critique of Porter and Kramer's work in this field is that it lacks originality and even, in some respects, borders on intellectual piracy – because they fail to acknowledge how other researchers have come up with ideas similar to their own (Crane et al., 2014). Apart from the antecedents already mentioned, the familiarity with concepts such as conscious capitalism, sustainable value creation, blended value, mutual benefit, social innovation/ entrepreneurship and base of the pyramid has also been highlighted (Crane et al., 2014; Dembek et al., 2015). Part of the critique levelled against Porter and Kramer for being unoriginal can, to some extent, be due to others' broad uses of the concept and their own use of cases and examples that stretch the concept (as they have defined it). The buzz around the concept can, however, be interpreted in both a positive and a negative way. In the negative take, shared value floats around as a loosely defined signifier that adds to the conceptual confusion surrounding CSR instead of contributing to an economic consolidation of the field. The positive take presents a pragmatic overall assessment of how shared value has contributed – and is contributing – to the development of corporate responsibility. All ideological concerns aside, the value of shared value must ultimately be considered in terms of the practical difference it makes in the world. Porter and Kramer's contribution to this stretches beyond their academic publications. To bolster support, the shared value mindset is also promoted through the consultancy arm of the Porter and Kramer enterprise, the FSG consulting firm, and networks such as the Shared Value Initiative, which, apart from Nestlé – a company with which they have had a close collaboration on developing shared value – counts big multinationals such as Chevron, Coca-Cola, Deloitte, Hewlett-Packard, Intel, Novartis and Verizon among its strategic partners.

Not only businesses but also governments and other organisations are making use of the concept of shared value, but most often without buying into the whole package, so to speak. That is, without identifying with the neoclassical underpinnings of Porter and Kramer's argument and without necessarily putting the interests of business before those of society in the way that they propose. Even corporate uses of the concept, as we shall see in the case of Maersk Group, tend to translate or adapt it rather than slavishly follow the prescriptions given. For instance, many companies, such as Maersk, have a strong focus on compliance and risk management, and would not want to reduce the handling of such matters to bland routine bereft of strategic value. Governments and NGOs may use the concept to lend an air of economic credibility to responsibility or development efforts – using shared value to signify win-win while balancing the interests of business and its stakeholders more evenly. Hence, we may speak of the relational value of the concept and how it can serve as a lever for development in more ways – and according to more agendas – than the one envisioned by Porter and Kramer.

As we have shown, shared value has primarily been used at the level of new projects and products, not to capture responsibility or value creation at the organisational level. It refers to parts rather than the whole, whether we are talking corporate responsibility efforts or corporate strategy more broadly. Instead of seeing it as a standalone concept or as a replacement for conventional CSR, we think that it makes more sense to see it as a supplement and argue for the need to combine perspectives and come up with hybrid forms of responsibility. Even if we acknowledge that the cost-benefit mindset of shared value is an important contribution to CSR, we still, in the words of Hartman and Werhane, need moral imagination as well. As they put it: '"Shared value" is just one of the many viable means to reconstruct a corporate worldview to tackle new-world social, environmental and economic problems' (Hartman and Werhane, 2013: 42).

3.7 Case Study: Maersk Group and Shared Value

To illustrate and elaborate some of our points on strategic CSR, we turn to the case of the multinational conglomerate A.P. Møller – Mærsk (hereafter Maersk Group). The core business of Maersk Group is shipping and energy: oil and gas. Its four core business units are Maersk Line (the world's largest container shipping company), APM Terminals, Maersk Oil and Maersk Drilling. It is the largest company in Denmark based on total revenue and #240 on the Forbes

Global 500 (list of 2016). The Maersk Group signed up to the UN Global Compact in 2009, and in 2011 became one of approximately fifty members of UN Global Compact LEAD: a platform designed to challenge highly engaged companies to experiment, innovate and share knowledge and learning – with the overall aim of leading new efforts to raise sustainability performance. In a recent survey by KPMG, Maersk was singled out as one of ten companies from the Global Fortune 250 to score more than ninety points out of a hundred on CSR reporting quality (KPMG, 2013). In 2015 Maersk Group also joined the Shared Value Initiative, which is a global community operated by Porter and Kramer's consultancy FSG and consists of leaders 'who find business opportunities in societal challenges' (Shared Value Initiative, 2016). Maersk is thus a global leader in sustainability that has made an explicit commitment to the shared value agenda. In order to reflect on the practical ramifications of this commitment we will focus here on Maersk Group's overall CSR policy and range of engagements as reflected in its sustainability reporting.

Maersk Group's 2014–18 sustainability strategy articulates a vision of unlocking growth for society and Maersk Group by focusing on three key priority areas: *enabling trade, investing in education* and *energy efficiency* (A.P. Møller – Mærsk Group, 2015). The new strategy was approved in 2013 and launched in 2014. Its formulation was inspired by the focused approach of Porter and Kramer and the Maersk Group CSR department's desire to obtain a mandate to work with sustainability issues in a more forward-looking, business development- and innovation-orientated way. The strategy came into being through a development process involving workshops and brainstorms with business units, and its content reflects the concrete commercial and societal challenges that Maersk business units are facing. The focus on education, for instance, addresses the difficulties of finding qualified personnel in the energy sector. In many developing countries, companies such as Maersk Drilling are faced with local content policies aiming to protect domestic economic, labour and business interests in dealings with the oil and gas industry. In a potential growth market like Angola, for instance, local content rules broadly aim to promote Angolan employment and ownership of businesses along with Angolan industry, production and services – in order to avoid unfair exploitation. Oil and gas companies operating in Angola are required to have a work force consisting of 70 per cent Angolan nationals (and no more than 30 per cent expats). This is referred to as *Angolanization*, and companies are obliged to be in compliance within three years of signing a private investment contract with government. To be in compliance with this rule requires education and training of locals, as safety is imperative. Investment in education can provide value for society by raising the level of qualifications among the populace and value for the business by making a scarce resource (skilled labour) less scarce, and thus less expensive, and perhaps more importantly by helping to build goodwill with government, which may give Maersk a competitive edge in bids for future contracts.

Whether this should be considered as strategic CSR or smart compliance is another matter.

Overall, the new strategy focuses on ways to boost corporate performance by strengthening competitive context and reducing costs. However, these focus areas by no means capture the full range of the company's current sustainability commitments and how it is held accountable by its stakeholders. This is reflected in its award-winning sustainability reporting, which provides a much broader view of the company's social engagement. Maersk Group's latest sustainability report covers a wide range of topics, most of which are related to compliance and/or responsive CSR. These include integration of human rights, safety, diversity, global labour relations, reduction of environmental impacts, mitigating oil spills, fighting corruption and a responsible approach to tax payments (A.P. Møller – Mærsk A/S, 2015).

Maersk Group's turn to strategic CSR has to be seen as part of a process. Its first sustainability strategy, which ran from 2010–2014, was to integrate sustainability into business processes and make it a competitive advantage. The goal was to achieve full business integration by 2013. Integration was measured in terms of business units following group standards and sustainability being integrated into management systems and metrics of performance management. The first part of the process was meant to establish a strong basis for responsibility in the classical CSR sense, meaning that the focus was on compliance, transparency and minimum standards for proper behaviour. These basics had to be in place, otherwise a turn to a more strategic and innovative approach would not seem credible and could too easily be perceived as cherry-picking. In this sense, the turn to a more strategic approach can be seen as a sign of maturity (although the old strategy is still very much alive alongside the new one). It implies a shift from mitigating the negative to accelerating the positive impacts of responsibility, and it is inspired by Porter and Kramer's idea of seeing societal needs as opportunities to create value for the business (and society) while focusing efforts on a few select areas instead of going off in all directions. However, Maersk Group's CSR department very consciously does not make use of the term 'shared value' in the new strategy. The feeling is that if they use the term, they will have to buy into everything that Porter and Kramer are saying (or would signal that they do). Instead they prefer to be able to pick the parts they find useful and define the rest themselves. As indicated, they do for instance attribute a higher value to responsive CSR activities than Porter and Kramer tend to do. Joining the Shared Value Initiative is thus seen as much less of a commitment and as having much less of an overall impact than the membership of UN Global Compact and LEAD. The new strategy, after all, is also a reflection of the **triple bottom line**, covering economic (enabling trade), social (investing in education) and environmental (energy efficiency) aspects of corporate performance.

Although Maersk Group maintains a strong focus on mitigating negative impacts, the new strategy is indeed meant to accelerate efforts in the area of positive impacts, meaning that relatively more resources at Group level will be devoted to the three areas identified in the new strategy – and that recommendations for the business units will be centred on these areas. A distinction is made between operational (i.e., responsive) and strategic activities, and the hope is that it will be possible to free up more resources for long-term exploration of new strategic opportunities. This in turn calls for more traditional competencies being required (as opposed to CSR specialisation) when things are really moving. However, development of the new strategy is still at an early stage. The Maersk Group CSR department has a mandate from top management to proceed with the new strategy, but, at time of writing, it is still at the level of pilot projects, mapping of opportunities (e.g. in the area of education) and providing general recommendations for development. Indicators and targets – and thus the ambition level – of the strategy still need to be set, and it remains to be seen how much and how many it will involve and what will come out of it.

Questions for Discussion

1. What does the Maersk Group case tell us about the practical implementation of strategic CSR/CSV?
2. What are some of the possible weaknesses of the new Maersk Group sustainability strategy?
3. What does the Maersk Group case tell us about the limitations of strategic CSR in general?

3.8 Chapter Summary

In this chapter we have presented the popular notion of strategic CSR/CSV, and provided a discussion of its theoretical and practical strengths and weaknesses. Overall, mainstream perspectives in the broad field of CSR have, albeit with considerable reservation, engaged with the instrumentalism evident in strategic CSR, while simultaneously issuing warnings about the negative effects it may have if the strategic mindset is not somehow curbed or kept in check by extra-economic (social, moral) values. Nevertheless, it cannot be ignored that strategic CSR has gained considerable traction in business, and this is not surprising considering its corporate-centric design and pro-business stance.

However, our section focusing on the arguments against strategic CSR highlighted the dangers of accepting what seems to be an ideal solution to social problems at face value. Those who believe that business and capitalism need to undergo more fundamental reform to be sustainable need to look elsewhere for viable solutions. Even Michael Porter has acknowledged that the shared value mindset is incapable of addressing issues of corporate irresponsibility properly, but instead of throwing the baby out with the bathwater, we have acknowledged the motivational strengths of this mindset and argued for the value of combining strategic CSR with other perspectives in order to more fully address and help companies deal with the challenges of responsibility they are facing. Our Maersk case study illustrates the complexity of strategic CSR and how one corporation has sought to find a balance between their commercial and social goals.

Chapter Questions

1. Does it matter *why* corporations are socially responsible? What are the implications if they practise CSR for *instrumental* reasons only?
2. Porter and Kramer have been accused of making a straw man out of conventional CSR. Do you agree with this critique? Why/why not?
3. Should corporations ever invest in a social project which has limited or indiscernible financial reward attached to it? What about vice versa?
4. Is there a role for CSR in changing capitalist economy and society?
5. What values might enhance strategic CSR's legitimacy?

FURTHER RESOURCES

Crane, A., Palazzo, G., Spence, L. J. and Matten, D. (2014). Contesting the Value of 'Creating Shared Value'. *California Management Review*, 56(2), 130–153.
   This paper provides a wide-ranging and very direct critique of Porter and Kramer's work and contribution to the field of CSR, with a particular focus on the 2011 paper. The paper is followed by a lively exchange between the protagonists.
Dembek, K., Singh, P. and Bhakoo, V. (2015). Literature Review of Shared Value: A Theoretical Concept or a Management Buzzword? *Journal of Business Ethics*, DOI 10.1007/s10551-015-2554-z.
   This literature review provides a good – and critical – overview of theoretical and empirical development in shared value so far.

Perrini, F., Russo, A., Tencati, A. and Vurro, C. (2011). Deconstructing the
Relationship Between Corporate Social and Financial Performance.
Journal of Business Ethics, 102(Supplement 1), 59–76.
This paper provides a useful framework for making the business case more
strategic and attuned to the particular circumstances of individual
companies.

Shared Value Initiative, http://sharedvalue.org/
This is the primary website for promoting the CSV approach. It is led by
FSG, Porter and Kramer's consultancy, and features many contributions
and testimonials from supporting companies.

Nestlé Creating Shared Value, www.nestle.com/csv
Nestlé co-created the CSV approach with Porter and Kramer. This is their
wide-ranging CSV website.

4

Corporate Responsibility Strategies for Sustainability

MIKE VALENTE

Learning Objectives

- Understand that there is wide variation in the strategies which companies use to engage in responsible business practices or sustainability.
- One of the ways to distinguish strategies for responsible business practices is to ascertain how well companies adopt three principles of sustainability.
- Apply conventional notions of strategy to the three principles of sustainability to unveil five distinct strategies for sustainability adoption.
- Within each of these strategies, identify some of the key mechanisms that explain their adoption.

4.1 Introduction

The term 'corporate sustainability' has grown increasingly prevalent in corporate boardrooms and on executive agendas. In a study of 766 CEOs worldwide, it was concluded 'that sustainability is truly top-of-mind for CEOs around the world' (Lacy, Cooper, Haywood and Neuberger, 2010: 10). Growing pressure to respond to issues of climate change, the financial crisis, environmental degradation and increasing social inequality have precipitated the diffusion of sustainability in internal business text, company websites, CEO speeches and company reporting (KPMG, 2008, 2011; Lacy et al., 2010). CEO action on sustainability issues has shifted from being a discretionary choice to a corporate priority, with 93 per cent of executives claiming that sustainability issues will be critical to the future success of their business and 80 per cent saying that in fifteen years a majority of companies globally will have incorporated sustainability (Lacy et al., 2010). In a recent study, McKinsey concluded that 'the choice for companies today is not if, but how, they should manage their sustainability activities' (Bonini, 2011), with 96 per cent of CEOs believing that sustainability issues should be fully integrated into the strategy and operations of a company.

CEOs themselves regularly tout their efforts to 'embed' or 'weave' sustainability into their operations and culture as the ultimate commitment while scholars and practitioners have offered a number of prescriptions to achieve this objective (e.g. Andersson, Shivarajan and Blau, 2005; Aragon-Correa, Martin-Tapia and Hurtado-Torres, 2013; Benn, Dunphy and Griffiths, 2014; Ethical Corporation, 2009; Haugh and Talwar, 2010; Willard, 2009). Yet despite the prevalence of sustainability, there is tremendous variation in how companies have responded. Part of this variation can be explained by enormous ambiguity around what sustainability actually means, leaving the term open to various managerial interpretations that translate into diverse actions at the firm level. The purpose of this chapter is to define what we mean by sustainability and then to develop a typology of business strategies for sustainability. This chapter builds on an article published in *Organization Studies* which set out to understand more progressive adoption levels of sustainability based on the term's original application to business in the mid-1990s that was overlooked empirically (Valente, 2012).

4.2 What Does Sustainability Mean?

As discussed in Chapter 1, the past decade or so has seen a convergence of the terms corporate social responsibility (CSR) and sustainability. Even though many public companies today reporting on non-economic performance tend to use the term 'sustainability' rather than 'corporate social responsibility', the nature of what they report on could be labelled either one of these two terms. Thus, although this chapter uses sustainability as its central term, the concepts and arguments put forward are equally relevant to CSR.

Although sustainability originally embodied environmental issues exclusively, the term today is often synonymous with the triple bottom line, where a firm is measured across social, economic and environmental performance indicators. Gladwin and colleagues (Gladwin et al., 1995) introduced the notion of sustaincentrism, where human behaviour is guided by constraints imposed by the ecological environment and a moral compass meant to preserve spirituality and cultural values within and across generations. Although an agreed-upon definition of sustaincentrism (and its root word sustainability) has eluded scholars for decades, there is some consensus on some of its underlying principles (Gladwin et al., 1995; Starik and Rands, 1995). Reviewing existing research from a wide range of scholarly sources, one can create an inventory of definitions and properties of the sustainability concept to tease out similarities and differences from which to categorise terms and phrases. A condensed version of this process is presented in Table 4.1 and revealed three principles of sustainability.

Table 4.1 Sustainability principles (adapted from Valente, 2012)

1st Order	2nd Order	3rd Order	Principle
• Environmental integrity and ecological sustainability. • Maintain, preserve, or restore the health of habitats and ecosystems as a basis for human life. • Avoiding the erosion of the Earth's land, air and water resources, consider limited regenerative capabilities and carrying capacity; and avoid launching toxins and waste into the biosphere.	Ecological systems: Ability of one or more entities to exist and flourish (Bansal, 2005; Gladwin et al., 1995; Sharma and Henriques, 2005; Shrivastava, 1995; Starik and Rands, 1995)	Broader systemic viewpoint; multiple systems considered (Hoffman, 2003)	Inclusiveness
• Social justice. • Social and political aspects of systems (Hoffman, 2003). • Developing and maintaining desired 'social values, institutions, cultures, or other social characteristics'. • Social justice, the distribution of wealth and power, and society–nature relations. • Civic participation in how sustainability is defined.	Social systems: Intra- and inter-generational equity; All members of society (Baker, 2007; Barbier, 1987; Bebbington, 2001; Carvalho, 2001; Fergus and Rowney, 2005; Klostermann and Cramer, 2006)		
• Economic responsibility. • Productive capacity of organisations and individuals. • Creation and distribution of goods and services that raise the standard of living (Bansal, 2005). • Open, competitive and international markets that encourage innovation, efficiency and wealth creation. • Development is not exclusively economic-based, and economic growth is not a means to an ends.	Economic systems: Critical as part of a broader definition of development (progressive transformation of economy and society) (Bansal, 2005; Gladwin et al., 1995; Holliday, Schmidheiny and Watts, 2002; Stubbs and Cocklin, 2008)	Inclusion as a philosophical base for social advancement	
• Question dominance of instrumental rational paradigm to include intuition, subjectivity and experience. • Reflective communicative rationality versus blinkered self-reinforcing instrumental rationality. • Democratic processes of social learning, cultural politics and new institutional arrangements. • Including all factions of society in decision-making processes on development.	Open, critical, democratic, integrated discourse based on an ethic of values and diversity (Alvesson, 1996; Fergus and Rowney, 2005; Milanez and Buhrs, 2007; Mol and Spaargaren, 2000; Scherer and Palazzo, 2008b)		

Interconnectedness			
	Nested	Economy is part of society, which is part of the larger ecological system (Bateson, 1972; Golley, 1993; Montiel, 2008; Odum, 1975; Rolston, 1994)	• Nested in biological ecosystems and interconnected with biogeochemical cycles. • Viewed as part of rather than in opposition to the socio-ecological environment. • The focus on ecosystem health in this paradigm is not simply to preserve wilderness by attempting to outlaw culture from the perimeters of nature. Modern culture is also a part of nature. • Human beings and organisations are members of ecosystems. • Attempts to use a reductionist approach where individual systems are considered independently is counterproductive. • Human freedom and rights to self-determination remain intact so long as the actions deriving from these freedoms and rights do not destroy the life-support systems upon which such human autonomy depends. • Self-interested individual and organisations are more likely to pursue an economically advantageous course of action when confronted with a choice between environmental preservation or economic development.
	Integrated	Social, environmental and economic responsibilities are complementary (Axelrod, 1984; Bansal, 2005) Sustainable development requires integration across multiple systems (Fergus and Rowney, 2005; Starik and Rands, 1995)	• Integration as a philosophical base for social advancement. • Integrating the four entities of society, government, environment, and business in a common process of development. • Integration and broadening in an inclusive manner. • Integration and coordination are systemic elements that are fundamental to understanding the ecological sustainability of organisations.
	Complexity	Appreciation of the complexity of social, ecological and economic processes (Carson, 1962; Leopold, 1970)	• The recognition of such complexity means that one could never know with complete certainty what effects the manipulation of individual components within an ecosystem would have on the ecosystem as a whole. • The most cost-effective solution to dump toxic waste chemicals into a watershed may benefit the individual firm, but places the surrounding ecosystem at risk, as toxic chemicals find their way into the biological food chain.

Table 4.1 (*cont.*)

1st Order	2nd Order	3rd Order	Principle
• All members of society have equal access to resources, opportunities and basic needs (food, clothing and shelter).	Universal access to basic needs and opportunities (Bansal, 2005)	All systems have equal rights	Equity
• Future generations have access to basic rights and resources.			
• Local rural communities receive similar privileges as global industrialised regions.			
• Humans are equal to nature.			
• Well-being of other species is as important as human welfare.	There is no power imbalance where one system of interests dominates over another (Banerjee, 2003; Fergus and Rowney, 2005)		
• Mitigating poverty does not require natural ecosystem exploitation.			
• Social, ecological and economic systems must be given equal priority.			
• Diversity of cultures is preserved and given equal standing.	All systems have equal intrinsic value (Montiel, 2008)	There are no trade-offs between systems	
• The natural environment is not seen as a resource to be mastered and deployed.			
• Economic growth does not trump environmental preservation and nature has inherent worth.			

The first principle requires the inclusion of multiple systems (Alvesson, 1993; Bansal, 2005; Fergus and Rowney, 2005; Hoffman, 2003; Purser, Park and Montuori, 1995). As Gladwin and colleagues explained, moral monism is rejected in favour of moral pluralism where sustainability actively embraces the full conceptualisation of political, civil, social, ecological and economic rights and systems (Gladwin et al., 1995). Ecological systems might include water systems, the climate system, biodiversity or species reproduction. Economic systems might encompass the global financial system, income equality, the free flow of goods and services while social systems might include things like the proper functioning of civil society, low poverty rates, the education or health systems, social justice or the food system. Second, inclusivity is insufficient unless firms acknowledge how these systems are interconnected as parts of a broader system of activity (Hoffman, 2003; Montiel, 2008; Shrivastava, 1994; Starik and Rands, 1995). Unlike a reductionist approach where issues are considered independently, sustainability requires the mastery of understanding interrelationships of causality and predicting the diverse effects of decisions on ecological cycles, socio-cultural ways of life (Hart, 2005; Hawken, 2007; Shrivastava, 1995; Starik and Rands, 1995), and economic systems. As an example, Hoffman explained that environmental management initiatives by firms, however proactive, tend to involve technical equations and numerical analyses that neglect social aspects of transformational change such as community acceptance of a new industrial facility (Hoffman, 2003). Finally, including social, ecological and economic objectives in an interconnected way is insufficient unless they are incorporated equitably. The equity principle replaces any position of privilege afforded to certain objectives (Livesey, 2002) with equality through the fair distribution of resources, opportunities, basic needs and property rights (Bansal, 2005; Gladwin et al., 1995) within the limits of Earth's carrying capacity (Bansal, 2005; Gladwin et al., 1995; Stubbs and Cocklin, 2008).

What does this definition mean for the way in which firms develop strategies for sustainability? Almost all public companies and most non-public companies lay claim to the notion that they are doing something to preserve these systems either by minimising harm (i.e. negative externalities) or finding ways to reinvigorate and improve them. But because there is extreme variation in how companies respond, it is important to clarify the different strategies companies can adopt. One of the ways to do this is to consider the extent to which these principles are incorporated into the core strategy and operations of the firm. When you want to know what makes a business tick, you typically turn to its strategy. A firm's strategy can be determined using three factors: (1) its positioning in the marketplace relative to competitors, (2) its core competencies that differentiate it from those competitors, and (3) its underlying culture that clarifies to employees the underlying purpose and identity of the organisation, supported by structures, processes and policies. First, positioning goes beyond marketing and represents a unique value proposition to consumers that distinguishes the firm from its competition. Wal-Mart's positioning is the low-cost leader, while Apple's positioning is innovativeness and high quality. Marketing is important in conveying this image to outside actors but positioning is supported by strong evidence that supports these claims (e.g. Wal-Mart's low prices). Second, strategy is very much about what the company does really well that is valuable and unique (its core competencies) that competitors find very difficult to imitate or find substitutes for. This might include particular individuals employed by the firm (e.g. Steve Jobs at Apple), specific decision-making processes, unique products, a strong brand, innovation practices, intellectual property, highly valuable machinery or low-cost operations. Finally, external positioning and internal competencies must be supported by an organisation's culture and identity that transcends the worldviews of employees to the point where they see the relevance of the firm's strategy to their daily activities, making it feel like employees live this strategy on a daily basis. On what employees are rewarded, how they are trained, how decisions are made, and company policies and mission statements all support culture.

With the above in mind, it is possible to categorise companies into one of five business strategies for sustainability, beginning on the one hand with businesses that separate sustainability principles from strategy and ending on the other hand where sustainability principles defines their strategy. These five strategies are illustrated in Figure 4.1.

4.3 Strategy #1: Denial Strategy

In the first case, denial, sustainability and CSR are highly irrelevant to the firm's overall strategy. Any involvement in social or ecological issues is relegated to philanthropic contributions that have very little to do with the firm's core operations. Here the purpose is often to build social goodwill to combat any negative publicity that might be associated with their core operations. Any public criticism of the firm is deflected as managers vehemently deny any wrongdoing or responsibility. For many years, the tobacco industry denied any responsibility for the link between their products and various forms of cancer, in the same way that many actors in the food industry today deny responsibility for obesity and other related health issues associated with food. Associations representing restaurants or food production companies are often heard arguing that the unprecedented growth of food-related health problems is hardly a problem of the food itself but much more a problem of personal responsibility and a deficit in exercise. Unrelated to food health, the association representing fast food restaurants (National Restaurant Association) launched

Figure 4.1

Business strategies for sustainability

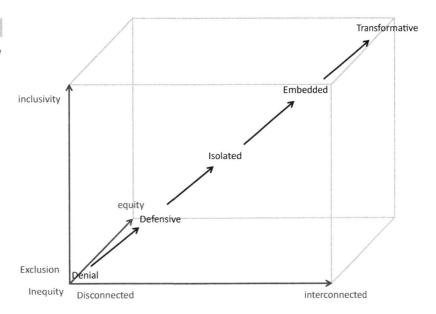

an advertisement in Times Square during 2013 and 2014, denying any responsibility for the growing dependence of their own employees on government assistance, and arguing against any need on their part to increase employee pay to a living wage because these employees have no skill or experience and are often lazy. Nike in the 1990s denied responsibility for the growing instances of labour issues in developing countries because the suppliers making their products were distinct entities and therefore not under the responsibility of Nike. Ultimately, companies will often say that nothing they are doing is against the law and so they are doing nothing wrong.

The denial strategy omits any use of sustainability or CSR in its competitive positioning, and at most would rely on its disconnected philanthropic contributions as part of their marketing strategy to suggest that the company is a good corporate citizen. In fact, companies adopting this approach are often heavily reliant for their success on practices that are particularly corrosive to social, ecological and economic systems. Although growing more rare, companies may actually promote this positioning, as did low-end burger chains such as Harvey's or A&W that chose a positioning that countered any need for healthy food by allowing consumers to indulge, to avoid any compromise on taste. More common is a particular positioning that very much relies on the erosion of social or ecological systems, where denial of responsibility is often the only option. Ashley Madison, an American dating agency for 'discreet encounters', is an organisation whose fundamental premise is based on a service that most people would argue erodes social systems. Payday loan retailers can be classified under this strategy as well because their positioning as a source of capital for those consumers typically unable to get credit naturally positions the firm as an exploiter of vulnerable consumers. Big banks often try to avoid this low-end market because, although it is legal, they do not want to position themselves in such a way that leads to outcomes that can be perceived by many as exploitative.

The companies in this category are therefore dependent on unrelated philanthropic initiatives that aim to distract stakeholders from the impact of their core operations. In the context of sustainability principles, firms using a denial strategy are inclusive to a limited number of unrelated social, economic or ecological efforts, yet do so in a reductionist way ignorant of the complexity of any of these issues while giving these efforts low priority over other firm objectives. McDonald's children's charity has attracted substantial criticism due to the claims it makes for improving the lives of children while ignoring the health impacts of their products and the marketing tactics that have historically targeted children. A bank's anti-cancer initiatives, although a worthy cause, might ignore how everyday decisions associated with capital lending might actually be greasing the wheels of those companies making products that have shown linkages to cancer. Virtually all companies today claim to be inclusive of some social or ecological objective, including those using a denial strategy. But what typically guides their choice of issue to address is public relations, rather than a comprehensive attempt to respond to the complexities that define the issue.

From an internal competence perspective, what distinguishes the firm from its competitors has virtually nothing to do with sustainability. In fact, their source of distinction represents a key erosion of social, ecological and economic systems. Consider gun manufacturers, tobacco companies and weapons manufacturers, all of whom have developed strong competencies related to their products whether it be design innovation, the manufacturing process or logistics. But what is unique and difficult to imitate in these organisations are the very things that contribute to system erosion. Culturally, employees often see virtually no relevance of sustainability to their daily operations and tend, at most, to consider the company's identity to revolve around some philanthropic endeavours. Internal processes, reward systems, performance evaluation, and employee skill and training have virtually nothing to do with sustainability.

4.4 Strategy #2: Defensive Strategy

In the second strategy, companies have moved beyond denial of responsibility and have begun to admit that they are partly responsible for the erosion of certain social, economic and ecological systems. Unlike the previous strategy where companies feel that there is no need to adjust operations, the companies in this strategy work to lower their impact incrementally but avoid any serious reconsideration of their strategy. The overarching objective here is to continue with business as usual but with some minor adjustments to respond to upcoming regulation or consumer pressure. In other words, companies are starting to lose the argument that they are not responsible for system degradation, and so want to show that they are responding to pressures of stakeholders, especially consumers.

One response is to engage in philanthropic activities that are more associated with the impacts of their operations. This helps them defend their operations because they can lay claim to the fact that they are at least redistributing some of the profit associated with these operations to various causes that work to stem their effects. Canada's coffee chain Tim Hortons recently did this. One has to have a sense of humour not to baulk at the company's initiative to raise money for child nutritional education by selling sugar-laden cookies through their Smile Cookie Program. This is an excellent example of avoiding changes to their core operations of food and instead launching philanthropic initiatives to show that they care about these issues. Oil and gas companies have also undergone tremendous criticism for touting their commitment to reducing climate change but have invested substantial resources in lobbying against policies that would support renewable energies such as wind and solar. *The Guardian* reported that the European Commission's outlawing of subsidies for clean energy were largely requested by BP, Shell, Statoil and Total, and by trade associations representing oil and gas companies (Macalister, 2015).

Another very common response in the defensive strategy is for companies to aim for the low hanging fruit; a common expression that refers to those initiatives that represent relatively easy changes that at the same time make obvious business sense. The most common initiatives are related to reductions in energy and fuel use in manufacturing processes, or a reduction in waste through an increase in resource efficiency coupled with an increase in recycling efforts. Mining companies, for instance, have begun to tout 'green mining' to represent incremental improvements in power and fuel use along with reductions in toxicity, emissions and water use. Thinking beyond just the ecological dimension, an investment bank might indicate that they have reduced their portfolio of subprime loans from 60 per cent to 40 per cent or a fast food chain might announce that they are reducing sugar and salt content of existing products by 15 per cent over the next few years. Companies claim that they are working to reduce the impact of their existing operations, products and services on systems, but the fundamental business practices have not changed. They have merely become more efficient or incrementally 'less unsustainable'.

Internally, core competencies remain associated with practices that are associated with system degradation. That said, some companies might develop competencies in their brand as stakeholders perceive a certain company as a leader in making incremental improvements to their impact. Other companies may develop expertise associated with resource efficiency that competitors have been unable to replicate. Culturally, employees are likely to be unaware of any positioning around sustainability and are more likely to understand any improvements as a reflection of their business improvement. So whereas the company may be successful in creating a responsible image to broader society through philanthropic contributions, its identity internally does not at all reflect sustainability. Performance evaluations are tied to cost reductions efforts that just so happen to be associated with environmental system improvements for instance, but there is very little in the way of accountability towards social and ecological goals across levels of the business.

From the perspective of inclusivity, interconnectedness and equity, defensive firms, like their denial strategy counterparts, are including more social and ecological objectives. But because these are rather more related to their core operations, they demonstrate a deeper understanding of the interconnectedness of these social and ecological objectives with their traditional financial object-ives. That said, these philanthropic endeavours remain a low priority outside marketing and public relations because they warrant little or no strategic attention.

4.5 Strategy #3: Isolated Strategy

The third strategy is one where sustainability begins to make substantial inroads into the firm's strategy and operations. This typically involves an entire department or product line being positioned according to sustainability. Elem-ents of more radical changes to sustainability begin to emerge, such as Nike's green shoe initiative where consumers can design their own shoes using environmentally benign materials. Other examples might be a manufacturing firm's use of a new technology that cuts emissions by 90 per cent, such as Vale Inco's supposed plans to use a carbon sequestration scheme that would replace smokestacks; or a retail company's efforts to fuel half of the energy required to operate its stores using renewable energy sources such as wind and solar.

The important difference from the defensive strategy is that the company has begun to innovate in ways that have revolutionised a particular product or process, resulting in a substantial reduction in social, ecological or economic system degradation that goes well beyond incremental improvements. Under the defensive strategy, improvements are limited by an 'improvement ceiling' because the process or product itself is often inherently unsustainable. The isolated strategy questions the fundamental design of the product/service or the process of interest, thereby avoiding the ceiling. Clorox, the consumer-packaged goods company, launched a highly popular Greenworks line which represents an isolated brand in the minds of consumers. In this example, the product category is not associated with Clorox perceptively but nevertheless represents an important strategic endeavour by the firm. We can see similar types of initiatives in the social realm as well. Food manufacturers have either developed their own highly sustainable products or they might purchase healthy brands, such as PepsiCo's purchase of Naked Juice. A mining company, as another example, might take a much more comprehensive approach to community development surrounding one or two of their mines but relies predominantly on donations and philanthropy on the remainder of their mines. Alternatively, they might introduce a technology that dramatically reduces the use of water. An oil and gas company might have a fully fledged renewable energy programme, staffed within a legitimate department such as BP that is distinct from its core operations of oil and gas exploration and production which can still result in catastrophic environmental damage. Finally, Toyota introduced a vehicle part that removed completely the need for a particular toxic mineral.

A firm's positioning in the marketplace then represents somewhat of a contradiction because on the one hand, a part of their operations or a small section of their product line exemplifies sustainability principles, but on the other hand, the remainder of their operations is non-sustainable or continues to be criticised as such. As a result, companies adopting the isolated strategy will not necessarily lay claim that their positioning embodies sustainability, but they will tout their efforts to make this a core part of their strategy by reflecting on the resources allocated to efforts to challenge certain sections of their products/ services and operations. When attempting to distinguish a firm between defensive and isolated strategies, you need to examine to what extent these initiatives represent a substantial part of their strategy or, as the defensive strategy described, if they instead represent a means to mask the system degradation of their traditional operations. In other words, do these initiatives represent a substantial business endeavour that generates (or could eventually generate) a sizeable portion of revenue that positions them relative to competitors (beyond marketing)? If genuine, managers may position the firm as a leader in sustainability innovation but the innovation, while noteworthy if not groundbreaking, represents a small part of the firm rather than, as will be described in Strategy 4, a key part of the firm's DNA. Incidentally, many firms do well with this strategy partly because of a number of third-party ranking bodies that tend to be more attracted to key initiatives undertaken by the firm, in contrast to the extent to which the firm lives and breathes sustainability. From the perspectives of the three sustainability principles, inclusivity remains unchanged from the previous two strategies, but the extent to which the firm incorporates the equity of social and ecological systems increases. This is because the strategic merits of the endeavour increase its prioritisation relative to other traditional firm endeavours that are less sustainable.

Internally then, firms adopting an isolated strategy demonstrate isolated yet highly lucrative competencies that are more typically found in pockets of the firm. They may have a particular product that is so revolutionary in its benefit for the environment or consumer health that, despite their other operations, represents a highly innovative capability that could be replicated internally in the firm but is hard to replicate by competitors. When Toyota came out with the Prius as the first hybrid vehicle, they demonstrated a highly lucrative core competency that competitors could not duplicate for quite some time. The process behind the development of this technology was highly valuable for the firm. Often companies, in the absence of core competencies in the area of sustainability, will acquire firms that have these competencies with the alleged intent to slowly integrate this way of thinking into its mainstream product lines (more often than not, this does not actually happen). Common across the 'acquisition versus greenfield' approach to sustainability is that there is potential, however remote, for these initiatives to gain greater traction in the organisation. Thus, while the core competencies associated with sustainability might be isolated from other competencies that conflict with sustainability, this strategy is the first of the five to show strategic relevance of sustainability.

From the perspective of employees, an isolated strategy represents a bizarre identity as they might find it difficult to pinpoint just who they are and who they are not. If sustainability exists in an isolated department, employees not in this department often consider sustainability to be irrelevant to their daily operations. In fact, the existence of a sustainability department has been found to give employees a licence to continue with business as usual or, in some cases, to operate even more egregiously in their degradation of social, ecological and economic systems. Business schools themselves have fallen victim to this problem as core business courses were given a licence to 'stick to the basics', because new departments operating under the labels 'corporate social responsibility' and 'corporate sustainability' were meant to sensitise future managers to some of the complications arising from putting these core courses into practice. This is textbook isolated strategy. Ironically, the influx of specialisations in sustainability in business schools inadvertently pushed mainstream professors and lecturers to avoid thinking more critically about how their course might be partly responsible for some system-level issues.

Other businesses may simply consider sustainability to be one of the many things that they do, and do not hide the fact that there is a contradiction because, in their mind, they are simply responding to the highly diverse set of demands in the marketplace at the time. From a systems and process perspective, there are probably job descriptions that relate directly to sustainability initiatives. This can go as high up as a Vice-President (VP), as in the case of Centerra Gold where there is a VP for Sustainability and Environment. But in most cases, the highest position tends to be at the director role, as is the case at grocery chain Loblaw Companies. From a performance appraisal point of view, only a selected group of employees, managers and directors would be held accountable for performance indicators related to sustainability. Decision-making at the organisation, at most, will have sustainability as one of its key decision criteria but more often will not consider sustainability in its decisions because, again, a department or group of employees and managers is doing that for them.

4.6 Strategy #4: Embedded Strategy

Because existing approaches to business tend to be exclusive in their endeavours, reductionist in their approach, and inequitable in their prioritisation of objectives, management scholars have argued that any serious adoption of sustainable business practices requires firms to undergo a deep-seated transition in culture or paradigm shift (Gladwin et al., 1995; Hart, 2005; Hoffman and Sandelands, 2005; Waddock and McIntosh, 2009). In the embedded strategy, sustainability is infiltrated throughout the firm where, unlike the previous strategy, sustainability is no longer relegated to a particular department among some isolated die-hard employees or reflected in one or two product lines, but is instead present in all aspects of the business across all products and services and among most, if not all, employees. From a competitive positioning standpoint, sustainability represents *the* key differentiating factor among competitors. While there might be other factors that differentiate the firm in the marketplace (e.g. customer service), stakeholders consider the firm's primary value proposition to be related to its commitment to sustainability. That is, consumers are loyal to the company because they can count on the fact that all products and services, and the operations used to support the design, manufacturing and distribution of those products and services, reflect sustainability principles.

Many companies adopting this strategy tend to be relatively small, simply because the market is not large enough to support the business. That said, those consumers who are supportive of these businesses, however niche in nature, are more willing to pay premium prices that support the extra costs that often come with these practices. The value these businesses create for consumers above and beyond the alternative include health and safety, poverty reduction, the responsibility that comes with environmental conservation and, perhaps less intuitively, a desire to be associated with a company or brand that aligns with their values. This latter, rather less studied, reason has important implications for competitive positioning because it offers consumers an opportunity to be activists through their purchasing power, a strategy pioneered by The Body Shop. Patagonia, a textile and garment retailer, is a good example of a company that has clearly differentiated itself from competitors such as North Face or Timberwolf. They command a premium price for their products, but the philosophical value alignment they facilitate for their consumers justifies the price increase. Other examples include Ben and Jerry's, Interface Carpets and Level Ground Trading.

On the surface, companies adopting the embedded strategy possess similar capabilities to those companies adopting the third strategy. That is, their unique products and services might be difficult for competitors to replicate, or the processes behind the creation and delivery of these products and services might be inimitable. But the fourth strategy reveals additional competencies that are higher in levels of complexity. Complexity is high when there is a large number of interdependent parts or actors that collectively create an unpredictable pattern of behaviour as they respond dynamically to their respective local environments. Complexity is important when considering internal competencies because the higher the complexity of a given competence, the more difficult it is for a competitor to copy or substitute it. In fact, the company itself struggles to work out how they were able to develop these competencies. One common source of competitive advantage for companies adopting an embedded strategy is its culture. Culture is often defined as a set of values and belief systems that guide individuals in a particular group or organisation. Often, companies that embed sustainability have a very strong culture where employees, feeling that they are part of something that aligns closely with their values, are more productive and committed to their work. These companies often refer to how close they are to their fellow employees, how collaborative they are in their work, and how rarely politics erodes workplace performance. Unlike companies adopting the third strategy where sustainability-related capabilities are confined to one department or small group of employees, capabilities are often at the firm level, crossing functional areas as employees interact daily in ways that create innovative forms of value for consumers and other stakeholders.

What is interesting about this strategy is that, when asked about what they do in their job that demonstrates their commitment to sustainability, employees of these companies struggle to answer the question because they do not see sustainability as distinct from their daily routines and activities. This is an important paradigm shift from the first three strategies because employees of the company struggle to understand how the business could exist without sustainability filtered through their daily activities; in the same way, employees of the denial, defensive and isolated strategies struggle to understand how sustainability could at all be relevant to their daily operations. Employees of firms using this strategy engage in sustainability activities as part of their daily routines (Annandale, Morrison-Saunders and Bouna, 2004) and are therefore well versed in social and ecological issues. The identity associated with businesses adopting this strategy tends to revolve around a sustainability leader, consciously distinct from companies that do not take sustainability seriously. Most, if not all, levels of the organisation have performance indicators related to sustainability, and decision-making processes incorporate social and ecological indicators.

As a consequence, companies adopting an embedded strategy are highly inclusive in the consideration of multiple social and ecological objectives, and they consider these objectives equitably and as much of a priority as traditional financial objectives. What is more, firms systematically respond to issues not through independent initiatives but holistically as a central and enduring attribute of the firm. Grameen Bank's business model is predicated on the inclusion rather than exclusion of multiple social objectives, including women, aspiring entrepreneurs and individuals who lack collateral for credit. They also consider the interconnectedness of economic and social objectives through a business model that builds economic welfare of its consumers through the integrity of surrounding social systems. So rather than considering social issues as separate from the core business as is the case with philanthropic initiatives of big banks, Grameen Bank addresses major social issues directly through a business model that commands economic sustainability.

4.7 Strategy #5: Transformational Strategy

The fifth and final strategy is called transformational because companies adopting this strategy make substantial changes to the external environment in which they operate. The external environment can be defined here as an industry, supply chain, local community or even broader society in which the company operates. Unlike the previous strategy where the focus was on diffusing sustainability within the firm, the focus in this strategy is facilitating more sustainable practices outside the firm. Recently, scholars have discussed the role of markets in facilitating social movements to more sustainable consumption habits (Rao, 2009), implying that firms can benefit from and help ignite social movements. Garment brand Veja has been an important spark in building awareness about the possibilities associated with sustainable practices in the garment supply chain, while TerraCycle is working on facilitating a no-waste movement.

Many scholars and practitioners alike have come to the realisation that no organisation can single-handedly make substantive strides to sustainable practices. Wal-Mart, McDonald's, Starbucks and Google, no matter how genuine they might be or how embedded sustainability might be internally, can only push the envelope on sustainability if they facilitate change among multiple, highly interconnected actors in their supply chain and industry. Interface Carpets is a US-based carpet company that has pioneered a number of technologies that have revolutionised the once very toxic carpet industry. But a key difference from the fourth strategy is that their focus was not just on embedding sustainability, it was about rewriting the norms associated with the carpet industry by demonstrating that more sustainable modes of manufacturing carpet were possible. That is, the mainstream market, which consisted of large industry government facilities purchasing industrial carpet, now expected that Interface competitors offer a similar portfolio of sustainable products.

When done successfully, the strategic benefits become quite lucrative for businesses that adopt this strategy. Competitive positioning becomes one of leadership, where competitors look to the company for the next wave of technological innovation that they too need to adopt or, at least, be mindful of the market's response to what the company is doing. Even more lucrative is when government, always uneasy about setting harsh social and environmental regulation that might stifle growth and job creation, establishes regulation that is based on what the company has in fact proven to be possible, without the economic costs governments want to avoid. SEKEM is an organic conglomerate located just outside Cairo, Egypt that specialises in agricultural commodities for a wide range of industries. Established in the late 1970s, the company was so transformative in its business model that it single-handedly convinced over 800 Egyptian farmers to change their practices to organic cultivation in exchange for guaranteed access to the European market. SEKEM's own 'mother farm' was so advanced in its agricultural practices environmentally and socially that the Egyptian government established regulatory policies in the agriculture sector based partly on what SEKEM proved was possible. Imagine that – organic farming in the middle of the desert.

Another interesting dynamic associated with competitive positioning for this strategy is that the rivalry among competitors that typically exists in strategies 1–4 is much lower. Rivalry is lower because for any transformation to take place in an industry, it is easier to have competitors on board for the change. This sounds counter-intuitive because competitors are supposed to 'compete'. But evidence in the last decade suggests otherwise. Open source innovation is a relatively new practice where multiple competitors join forces to innovate in ways that no individual company could possibly innovate. This requires the sharing of important intellectual capital. Patagonia's business model is predicated on the notion that it is meant to share any of the new innovations it encounters in the development of more environmentally sustainable garments. Similarly, leading CEOs, such as Tesla's CEO, Elon Musk, have been quoted as saying that trying to establish a monopoly in their industry is counter to the goals of sustainability because it delays the establishment of a much needed industry standard all competitors can adopt to move forward and leave less sustainable practices behind. Think about the old BETA/VHS war (for those who are old enough) or the more recent HD-DVD/Blu-Ray war, where the supply chain had to wait to find out which standard would become dominant. Companies in the transformational strategy want to avoid these stand-offs and establish a common standard that competitors can use as well. Leading electric car companies could have put forth separate and technologically-specific charging facilities in the hope of being the VHS or Blu-Ray winner. But at least two leading CEOs have instructed governments in the jurisdiction that they were considering entering that any charging infrastructure must be universal and therefore usable by competing electric car companies. Another reason why rivalry must be lower is that companies need to collaborate to avoid the tragedy of the commons. In the absence of government regulation, natural resources such as a fish species, water or clean air would be depleted if companies behaved independently. Transforming an entire industry away from unsustainable practices, such as fishing for a threatened species, requires collaboration among large groups of fishing companies.

The transformational strategy then can only be transformational if networks of actors are created. In addition to combining forces to innovate, competitors, customers and suppliers along the supply chain often come together to self-regulate in ways that governments have struggled. Consider the diamond mining industry where several leading companies partnered to impose peer pressure on their industry to stem conflict diamond mining. The Equator Principles is a similar platform through which major global banks agreed to prohibit any loaning of capital to projects in developing countries of the world that carry substantial social or environmental risks to its citizens. In the absence of any governing body with the power to develop and enforce such a policy, these banks, through peer pressure, have pushed the industry in a direction that fosters more sustainable lending practices.

Stakeholders outside the firm therefore represent critical actors or partners, either in the execution of the business model itself or in support of core activities for the business model. Extending the notion of shared value (Porter and Kramer, 2011), this suggests that stakeholders do not simply acquiesce to company initiatives but are instead critical actors in building value for the firm in the same way that the firm is critical in helping to build value for the stakeholder. Similar to how firms recognise the pivotal role of the stakeholder in the execution of their core operations, the stakeholder recognises the pivotal role of the firm in the execution of their objectives. Recent research has shown that while past studies have focused predominantly on the firm when understanding how stakeholders influence and assist the firm in their social and ecological aspirations (Hart and Sharma, 2004; Sharma and Vredenburg, 1998), a transformational strategy demonstrates the reciprocal recognition by the stakeholder and the firm of the importance of the other in the achievement of their own objectives. The expertise and resources provided by the firm and its stakeholders make up a portfolio of complementary capabilities where the total value created by the network of actors exceeds the independent sum of these capabilities.

The common thread of interdependence just described suggests that while the embedded firm and its stakeholders are independently concerned about their own welfare, those engaged in transformational strategies believe that these objectives would be better served by operating as a network or system of actors working collaboratively to develop responses to complex problems. With this in mind, boundaries that separate roles and responsibilities of the firm and outside actors are lowered, which allows for a more collective response to a common objective. Firms adopting a transformational strategy are therefore adept at fostering a network of actors who relax the institutional-ised practices of their respective organisational fields to achieve a common objective. So long as the balance of power is shared among actors, interaction between the firm and stakeholders plays an important role in infusing alterna-tive frames of reference, which enables firms and their stakeholders to better acknowledge and incorporate multiple issues equitably (Scherer and Palazzo, 2008b).

A critical source of competitive advantage for companies adopting a trans-formational strategy is their ability to foster relationships with key actors in its external environment. If the company is going to revolutionise practices in its supply chain effectively, its industry or even great society, it is going to require a very strong trusting relationship with key players that want to take the leap to more sustainable practices. More importantly, these companies need to under-stand how to develop a network or ecosystem of actors that is connected and interact in ways that can create the necessary creative destruction that warrant changes in behaviour among all these actors. Any innovation developed in the transformational strategy is often less valuable than the processes that created the innovation.

The organisation itself starts to be redefined in the transformational strategy as the lines that once separated its own boundaries from external stakeholders become blurred. That is, in the context of sustainability, thinking of the company as a distinct organisation is unhelpful. A more accurate term to define what is needed for a transformational strategy is a meta-organisation. Meta-organisations are unique networks of organisations in that they organise actions around a system-level goal but are not bound by formal authority relations. Meta-organisations typically possess lead organisations that use their promin-ence or power to take on a leadership role in pulling together the dispersed resources and capabilities of potential meta-organisation participants. The innovativeness of meta-organisations as alternative forms of organisation to traditional hierarchical organisations bestows on them an advantage in coping with the complexity of sustainability. Meta-organisations are effective at rec-ognising opportunities through previously unimagined or unavailable partici-pant connections. The Fair Labour Association, The Kimberley Process and Wal-Mart Labs are examples here. The organisations involved range from businesses, to non-governmental organisations (NGOs) to community-based organisations and even governmental bodies.

Culturally, employees view the organisation as one piece of a larger puzzle of organisations who collectively work to achieve sustainability goals. The identity of the organisation is largely tied to the connections it has with key participants of the meta-organisation as employees feel that they are part of something much bigger than their own organisation can accomplish independently. In addition to performance appraisal mechanisms of Strategy 4, managers may also be accountable to the networks they create with other participants while decision-making processes within the firm encompass a wide range of external actors.

The fifth and final strategy most exemplifies the three principles of sustainability. But most important here is the principle of interconnectedness. By going beyond the boundaries of the firm in the embedded strategy, the transformational strategy bridges the many interconnected parts of a system of activity that facilitates unsustainable practices. Companies using this strategy are working to reconfigure entire supply chains and industry practices, and need to understand how the pieces fit together to change the system in order to do so.

4.8 Case Study: Terracycle

TerraCycle[2] is a privately owned small business with its headquarters in Trenton, New Jersey that offers recycling services to a wide variety of customers. The idea for TerraCycle came in 2001, when founder Tom Szaky was in his first year at Princeton University. Visiting friends in Montreal, Tom noticed that they were feeding food scraps to worms and using the resulting excrement as fertiliser to feed indoor plants. Using waste (food scraps) as a valuable resource to make a high-quality product (fertiliser) inspired Tom to start TerraCycle, based on the concept of upcycling.

Building on what he saw in Montreal, Tom's first product for TerraCycle was a worm excrement fertiliser sold in reusable plastic soda bottles. The use of reusable plastic bottles (e.g. Coca-Cola bottles) was important because it inspired an emerging TerraCycle philosophy that all of its products' components should be made up of waste materials. Unlike recycling which uses energy in ways that erodes the value of the waste (e.g. plastic bottle is broken down into pellets), upcycling adds value to waste (e.g. worm excrement converted into a household fertiliser). This fundamental premise underlies the TerraCycle model.

But to challenge the highly institutionalised linear consumption system, TerraCycle needed help. The company launched the 'Bottle Brigade', which was an initiative in which TerraCycle partnered with schools where children

---

[2] Information for this case was gathered from www.terracycle.ca/en-CA/histories.

collected reusable plastic bottles and received a nominal fee from TerraCycle per bottle collected. With this support, the fertiliser product was placed in a wide range of major retail outlets including Wal-Mart and Home Depot, and today represents a competitive alternative to the conventional and often highly toxic chemical fertilisers on the market. By 2006, TerraCycle had sold over $1 million in fertiliser products in reused soda bottles.

By 2007, Tom took the notion of upcycling to the next level by expanding its product portfolio to related products such as concentrated fertilisers, seed starters and potting mix. Then, TerraCycle took things a step further by expanding to unrelated product categories including backpacks and pencil cases. In 2008, TerraCycle partnered with Target and ran a campaign on the cover of Newsweek's Green Issue, convincing almost 50,000 readers to send in their plastic Target bags to TerraCycle to be upcycled into the world's first reusable tote bag made from plastic bags. By this point, the company had the support of over 5,000 participating schools, collecting not only used soda bottles but also drink pouches, yogurt cups and energy bar wrappers. By 2010 the drink pouch brigade had collected and recycled over 50 million drink pouches, resulting in the payment of over $1 million to schools and NGOs in the process.

By 2012, TerraCycle not only expanded their product portfolio but they also expanded operations to dozens of countries around the world. Revenue growth between 2004 and 2010 was explosive. The brigade programmes expanded beyond schools as well. TerraCycle joined forces with consumer-packaged goods companies (CPGs) such as Kraft, that sponsored the collection and shipping of the waste coming from their products in exchange for placing the TerraCycle logo on their products. The CPG companies pay TerraCycle an annual fee as well as a variable shipping fee for each shipment of waste recovered. TerraCycle then commits to reuse, upcycle or recycle all collections from the CPG companies. This allows CPG companies to demonstrate to their waste-conscious consumers efforts to reduce waste of their products going to landfills. Similar to the brigade programme, the Zero Waste Box initiative allows end consumers and small businesses to purchase a box from TerraCycle that they can fill and return when full. TerraCycle then commits to reuse, upcycle or recycle whatever comes in the box. Material which cannot be reused or upcycled is sold to a materials buyer to make recycled products.

By 2015, TerraCycle operates in twenty countries around the world, has strong partnerships with many retail brands and CPG companies, has donated millions of dollars to over 100 brigade programmes, and convinced many consumers to rethink the idea of waste. TerraCycle has attracted much media attention as a result of its revolutionary business model. It won the United Nations Leader of Social Change award in 2012, and Brand Packaging named Tom Szaky the Brand Innovator of the Year in 2008.

Questions for Discussion

1. Which of the five strategies is TerraCycle employing with regards to their adoption of sustainability? Why?
2. How would you articulate their positioning in the marketplace? What are their (intended) core competencies?
3. Do you think TerraCycle will continue to be successful?

4.9 Chapter Summary

Research has shown that companies respond to pressures for sustainable business practices in very different ways according to how many issues they consider, whether they consider those issues in an interconnected manner, and whether they respond to them equitably. One of the ways to understand these differences is to consider them in the context of strategic adoption levels where sustainability in the firm varies according to its role in positioning the company in the marketplace, representing lucrative competencies that are difficult to imitate, and creating a particular culture and identity that aligns with sustainability. It is important to note that companies will exhibit behaviours that span some of these strategies. For instance a company might engage in philanthropic activities that are both related (defensive) and unrelated (denial) to their operations, or they might both defend the impact of their operations while still having a department that contradicts the seemingly careless operations of other departments (isolated). It is the job of the analyst to put these initiatives together to create an overarching strategy that defines their positioning, core competencies and internal culture and identity.

Chapter Questions

1. What is a fundamental difference between the denial and defensive strategy?
2. How does a company's adoption of the principles of sustainability vary across the five strategies for sustainability?
3. Why is a transformational strategy considered more advanced than an embedded strategy for sustainability?

4. At what level of sustainability adoption does the strategic relevance of sustainability begin to emerge? Why?
5. Which strategy contains as a core competence a firm's ability to create relationships with stakeholders? Why is this competence important for this strategy?

FURTHER RESOURCES

Benn, S., Dunphy, D. and Griffiths, A. (2014). *Organizational Change for Corporate Sustainability*. London, UK: Routledge.
This book provides a very detailed overview of how organisations facilitate change to more sustainable practices. In the context of this chapter, Benn and colleagues flesh out some of the internal organisational changes that must take place to achieve an embedded strategy of sustainability.

KPMG (2011). *KPMG International Survey of Corporate Responsibility Reporting*. KPMG International Cooperative: www.kpmg.com.
This article provides insight into the latest trends in corporate responsibility reporting. Like all objectives in business, it is imperative that executives find the appropriate measures to manage progress and to develop targets. In the context of this chapter, this article provides some of the latest statistics on the extent to which companies are reporting and thus measuring their sustainability strategies.

Lacy, P., Cooper, T., Haywood, R. and Neuberger, L. (2010). *A New Era of Sustainability: UN Global Compact-Accenture CEO Study*. New York: UN Global Compact-Accenture.
This article provides the results of a survey conducted across a wide range of CEOs of public companies to understand their views on sustainability. The results demonstrate that CEOs of the largest global companies consider sustainability to be a strategic issue and critical for future success. In the context of this chapter, the article provides some important signals to managers that denial and defensive strategies are unlikely to have a place in the business environment in the future.

Porter, M. and Kramer, M. (2011). Creating Shared Value. *Harvard Business Review* (January–February), 63–77.
Because sustainability ultimately comes down to finding ways to optimise value for multiple stakeholders, this article provides a framework through which to achieve this end. The notion of creating shared value suggests that rather than assume a zero-sum game between profitability and social value, companies should create additional value for all stakeholders, including the firm. In the context of this chapter, it provides an idea of how

companies can aim to achieve an isolated sustainability strategy but falls short in explaining how companies can achieve an embedded one.

Willard, B. (2009). *The Sustainability Champion's Guidebook*. Gabriola Island, BC: New Society Publishers.

Like the Benn et al. book (2011) listed above, Bob Willard's book provides some important advice for managers on how to embed sustainability into their corporation.

5   Managing for Stakeholders in the Digital Age

R. EDWARD FREEMAN, SERGIY DMYTRIYEV AND ROBERT G. STRAND

Learning Objectives

- Identify the core principles of stakeholder theory.
- Understand why and how stakeholder theory pioneered and developed in the Scandinavian context.
- Understand company-stakeholder relationships in the age of technology.
- Analyse the Monsanto case study, illustrating the challenges behind managing for stakeholders in the twenty-first century.

5.1 Introduction

At the beginning of the 1990s, Jack Smith, the General Motors (GM) CEO, brought Jose Ignacio Lopez, who had previously served as the successful GM head of purchasing in Europe, to purchasing operations at Detroit. The objective was clear: to stop the automaker's losses by cutting costs. Often described as a fanatically dedicated and hard-working manager, Lopez became a GM hero by ripping up long-standing contracts with dedicated suppliers and demanding lower prices. Within his first year in Detroit, Lopez achieved an astounding $1.1 billion of savings in purchasing and identified another $2.4 billion in savings for the next year, which made Jack Smith acknowledge that Lopez had 'stopped the bleeding' at GM (Kurylko and Crate, 2006).

Was Lopez successful in his managerial position with the cost-cutting strategy he was using? For those who consider maximising financial returns as the primary objective of any business, it is only logical to answer 'yes'. The rationality behind this train of thought runs, generally speaking, in the following way: shareholders own the company and their primary objective is to maximise a company's financial returns within legal boundaries; shareholders hire an executive manager to run the company and serve their interests in the best possible way; the hired executive will be rewarded, both financially and career-wise, based on his/her success in serving shareholders' interests; thus, keeping shareholders happy, within legal boundaries, is the executive's primary responsibility, and the interests of all other parties in the business are secondary.

Lopez was certainly successful in keeping his shareholders happy. However, this GM story does not end happily: Lopez's deeds significantly undermined the level of trust between GM and its long-time suppliers. Over time this strategy of constantly squeezing suppliers turned out to be less productive compared to the trusting long-term relationship built by Japanese car produ-cers. The lesson behind the story is self-evident. Maximising immediate profits at the expense of ruining relationships with a stakeholder holds the company back. Lopez's success was more than dubious. The tension with suppliers, along with other mistakes in managerial practices, contributed to the deterior-ation of GM's position in the automobile industry over the next decade (Helper and Henderson, 2014). GM's market share in the US decreased from 35 per cent to 28 per cent (WardsAuto, 2015), while the rival Japanese car-makers steadily increased their presence in the American market with Toyota and Honda taking over GM's customers. The effect is indeed long-lasting: a survey conducted among automobile supplier companies in the USA in 2014 revealed that GM was considered the worst company to work with, while Toyota and Honda were in the lead (PR Newswire, 2014).

So is business simply a way to increase wealth for shareholders because a company owes its existence to its founders and owners? Some management scholars and business leaders intuitively feel that a company should be doing more than just serving the interests of its shareholders even if the law does not require more; something that feels as important as fiduciary duty for share-holders. These ideas found their way into Freeman's work on an alternative, more sustainable and more ethical view of business, known as stakeholder theory (Freeman, 1984).

The initial ideas about stakeholder theory have been further developed by many management scholars, so that stakeholder theory has become more comprehensive and applies to numerous industries and settings. Yet, the core principles of stakeholder theory have remained the same over all this time, and the first section of this chapter covers the fundamental ideas of stakeholder theory. The second section illustrates stakeholder model development in busi-ness settings over time, as well as the influence of the cultural context, such as the one found in Scandinavia, to foster a stakeholder mindset in business. The third section analyses the impact of the rapid technological progress, especially in social communication tools, on business practices in view of stakeholder theory. The last section provides a business case of Monsanto as an illustrative example of how neglecting some stakeholders can have a long-lasting effect on the company.

5.2 Stakeholder Theory in Brief

5.2.1 Business as Relationships Among Stakeholders

Stakeholder theory[3] has been developed over the last thirty or so years by an interdisciplinary group of scholars from the management disciplines of strategy and ethics to finance and accounting. The basic idea is that businesses, and the executives who manage them, actually do and should create value for customers, suppliers, employees, communities and financiers (or shareholders). And, that we need to pay careful attention to how these relationships are managed and how value becomes created for these stakeholders. Stakeholder theory has been developed to solve three main problems (Freeman, Harrison, Wicks, Palmar and De Colle, 2010). First, how is value creation and trade possible in fast-changing environments that have little stability? Second, how do we understand the ethics of capitalism, and how can we put capitalism on firmer ethical ground? And, third, what should we teach in business schools?

Stakeholder theory in part grew out of dissatisfaction with the current ideology of business in the West; namely, that shareholders were the only group who should have managerial priority. The scholars who developed the idea of corporate social responsibility (CSR) were instrumental in supporting the development of the stakeholder idea, as a more precise and managerially relevant way to talk about the social responsibility of business. Freeman et al. argue that in fact stakeholder theory can replace the idea of CSR by substituting 'Stakeholder' for 'Social' in the definition of CSR (Freeman et al., 2010). Furthermore, such a substitution redefines the very nature of business. Let us be a bit more specific.

The basic idea of stakeholder theory or 'managing for stakeholders' is quite simple. Business can be understood as a set of relationships among groups that have a stake in the activities that make up the business. Business is about how customers, suppliers, employees, financiers (stockholders, bondholders, banks, etc.), communities and managers interact and create value. To understand a business is to know how these relationships work. And, the executive's or entrepreneur's job is to manage and shape these relationships, and keep them working together in some kind of harmony.

Figure 5.1 depicts the idea of 'managing for stakeholders' in a variation of the classic 'wheel and spoke' diagram. However, it is important to note that the stakeholder idea is perfectly general. Corporations are not the centre of the universe, and there are many possible pictures. One might put customers in the

---

[3] This section draws heavily on 'Managing for Stakeholders' by R. E. Freeman (2008), in *Ethical Theory and Business*, 8th edition, edited by T. L. Beauchamp, N. E. Bowie, and D. G. Arnold, Pearson Prentice Hall. Passages are reprinted here with permission of the copyright holder.

Figure 5.1

Creating value for stakeholders

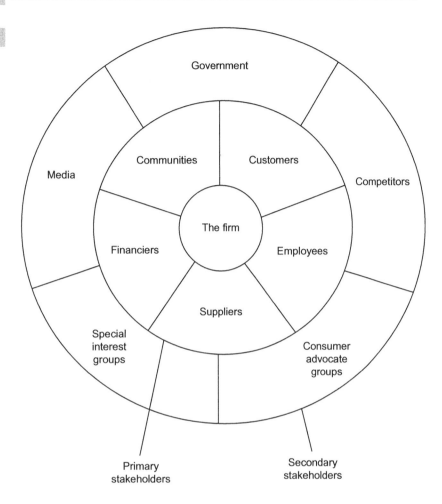

centre to signal that a company regards customers as the key priority. Another might put employees in the centre and link them to customers and shareholders. We prefer the generic diagram because it suggests, pictorially, that 'managing for stakeholders' is a theory about management and business; hence, managers and companies are in the centre. But, there is no larger metaphysical claim here.

Owners or financiers (a better term) clearly have a financial stake in the business in the form of stocks, bonds, and so on, and they expect some kind of financial return from them. Of course, the stakes of financiers will differ by type of owner, preferences for money, moral preferences, and so on, as well as by type of firm. The shareholders of Google may well want returns as well as be supportive of Google's articulated purpose of 'Do No Evil'. To the extent that it makes sense to talk about the financiers 'owning the firm', they have a concomitant responsibility for the uses of their property (Stout, 2012).

Employees have their jobs and usually their livelihood at stake; they often have specialised skills for which there is usually no perfectly elastic market. In return for their labour, they expect security, wages, benefits and meaningful work. Often, employees are expected to participate in the decision-making of the organisation, and if the employees are management or senior executives, they often shoulder a great deal of responsibility for the conduct of the organisation as a whole. And, employees are sometimes financiers as well, since many companies have stock ownership plans, and loyal employees who believe in the future of their companies often voluntarily invest. One way to think about the employee relationship is in terms of contracts. Customers and suppliers exchange resources for the products and services of the firm and in return receive the benefits of the products and services. As with financiers and employees, the customer and supplier relationships are enmeshed in ethics. Companies make promises to customers via their advertising, and when products or services do not deliver on these promises then management has a responsibility to rectify the situation. It is also important to have suppliers who are committed to making a company better. If suppliers find a better, faster and cheaper way of making critical parts or services, then both supplier and company can win. Of course, some suppliers simply compete on price, but even so, there is a moral element of fairness and transparency to the supplier relationship.

Finally, the local community grants the firm the right to build facilities, and in turn, it benefits from the tax base and economic and social contributions of the firm. Companies have a real impact on communities, and being located in a welcoming community helps a company to create value for its other stakeholders. In return for the provision of local services, companies are expected to be good citizens, as is any individual person. It should not expose the community to unreasonable hazards in the form of pollution, toxic waste, etc. It should keep whatever commitments it makes to the community, and operate in a transparent manner as far as possible. Of course, companies do not have perfect knowledge, but when management discovers some danger or runs afoul of new competition, it is expected to inform and work with local communities to mitigate any negative effects, as far as possible.

While any business must consist of financiers, customers, suppliers, employees and communities, it is possible to think about other stakeholders as well. We can define 'stakeholder' in a number of ways. First of all, we could define the term fairly narrowly to capture the idea that any business, large or small, is about creating value for those groups without whose support the business would cease to be viable. The inner circle of Figure 5.1 depicts this view. Almost every business is concerned at some level with relationships among financiers, customers, suppliers, employees and communities. We might call these groups 'primary' or 'definitional'. However, it should be noted that as a business starts up, sometimes one particular stakeholder is more important than another. In a new business start-up, sometimes there are no suppliers, and paying lots of attention to one or two key customers, as well as to the venture capitalist (financier), is the right approach.

There is also a somewhat broader definition that captures the idea that if a group or individual can affect a business, then the executives must take that group into consideration in thinking about how to create value. Or, a stakeholder is any group or individual that can affect or be affected by the realisation of an organisation's purpose. At a minimum some groups affect primary stakeholders, and we might see these as stakeholders in the outer ring of Figure 5.1 and call them 'secondary' or 'instrumental'.

There are other definitions that have emerged during the last thirty years, some based on risks and rewards and others based on mutuality of interests. The debate over finding the one 'true definition' of 'stakeholder' is not likely to end. We prefer a more pragmatist approach of being clear of the purpose of using any of the proposed definitions. Business is a fascinating field of study. There are very few principles and definitions that apply to all businesses all over the world. Furthermore, there are many different ways to run a successful business, or 'managing for stakeholders'. We see limited usefulness in trying to define one model of business, either based on the shareholder or stakeholder view, which works for all businesses everywhere. We see much value to be gained in examining how the stakes work in the value creation process, and the role of the executive.

Executives play a special role in the activity of the business enterprise. On the one hand, they have a stake like every other employee in terms of an actual or implied employment contract. And, that stake is linked to the stakes of financiers, customers, suppliers, communities and other employees. In addition, executives are expected to look after the health of the overall enterprise, to keep the varied stakes moving in roughly the same direction, and to keep them in balance.

5.2.2 The Jointness of Stakeholder Interests

No stakeholder stands alone in the process of value creation. The stakes of each stakeholder group are multifaceted, and inherently connected to each other. How could a bondholder recognise any returns without management paying attention to the stakes of customers or employees? How could customers get the products and services they need without employees and suppliers? How could employees have a decent place to live without communities? Many thinkers see the dominant problem of 'managing for stakeholders' as how to solve the priority problem, or 'which stakeholders are more important?' or 'how do we make trade-offs among stakeholders?' We see this as a secondary issue.

First and foremost, we need to see stakeholder interests as joint, as inherently tied together. Seeing stakeholder interests as 'joint' rather than opposed is difficult. It is not always easy to find a way to accommodate all stakeholder interests. It is easier to trade off one versus another. Why not delay spending on new products for customers in order to keep earnings a bit higher? Why not cut employee medical benefits in order to invest in a new inventory control system?

Managing for stakeholders suggests that executives try to reframe the questions. How can we invest in new products and create higher earnings? How can we be sure that our employees are healthy, happy and able to work creatively so that we can capture the benefits of new information technology such as inventory control systems? In a book reflecting on his experience as CEO of Medtronic, Bill George (2004) summarised the managing for stakeholders mindset:

> Serving all your stakeholders is the best way to produce long term results and create a growing, prosperous company ... Let me be very clear about this: there is no conflict between serving all your stakeholders and providing excellent returns for shareholders. In the long term it is impossible to have one without the other. However, serving all these stakeholder groups requires discipline, vision, and committed leadership.

The primary responsibility of the executive is to create as much value as possible for stakeholders. Where stakeholder interests conflict, the executive must find a way to rethink the problems so that these interests can go together, so that even more value can be created for each. If trade-offs have to be made, as often happens in the real world, then the executive must figure out how to make the trade-offs, and immediately begin improving the trade-offs for all sides. Managing for stakeholders is about creating as much value as possible for stakeholders, without resorting to trade-offs.

5.3 Cultural Context and Historic Development of Stakeholder Models

In no way does stakeholder theory deny the relevance and importance of the economic success of a firm. What stakeholder theory rejects is a narrowly economic view which focuses solely on financial returns. Instead, stakeholder theory posits that value creation for a broader range of stakeholders (including shareholders) should be the primary objective of a company.

Managing for stakeholders requires a certain type of managerial mindset. This stakeholder mindset can develop easier in cultures which go beyond a narrowly economic view of the firm and value a more society-orientated business approach. In this regard the Scandinavian context can be of great interest. According to Geert Hofstede, the founder of the cultural dimension theory, Scandinavian culture can be described as the most feminine in the world. As opposed to masculine cultures, such as the USA or Japan, feminine cultures can be characterised as societies driven by care for others rather than competition and achievement. In feminine cultures, 'An effective manager is supportive to his/her people, and decision making is achieved through involvement. Managers strive for consensus and people value equality, solidarity and quality in their working lives' (The Hofstede Centre, 2016).

Strand and Freeman (2015) summarised previous academic works on the Scandinavian context to show that its dominant cultural norms and institutional structures encourage engagement between companies and their stakeholders (see Strand, Freeman and Hockerts, 2015 for further elaborations on the Scandinavian context). Norms and structures in Scandinavia include a general tendency to embrace and promote participatory leadership, rejection of self-protective (i.e. 'face-saving') leadership that entails engagement with critical voices, reflection by practitioners, flatter organisational hierarchies and corresponding high degree of employee involvement, egalitarianism, democratic principles, peace, consensus-building and cooperation, embeddedness of economic interests within broader societal interests, strong regulatory bodies and active non-governmental organisations (NGOs), employee representation on boards of directors and a general stakeholder orientation to corporate governance, and concentrated company ownership with comparatively high levels of ownership of public companies by the state, by foundations and by families. In the Scandinavian context, 'shareholders are less likely to behave as a disparate assemblage of faceless entities with a lone objective of short-term share price maximization' (Strand and Freeman, 2015: 75).

These cultural norms and institutional structures were reflected in the works of Scandinavian management scholars led by the Swedish academician Eric Rhenman. In particular, he developed many ideas (Rhenman, 1968) akin to stakeholder theory in parallel to the work going on in the United States at that time. All this contributed to Scandinavian companies pioneering stakeholder engagement in business.

The example of Danish Novo Nordisk is a great illustration of stakeholder engagement dynamics over time. Figure 5.2 shows stakeholder maps developed at Novo Nordisk starting as early as 1970 and finally moving into the twenty-first century. First, we can observe that the sheer number of stakeholders has increased dramatically over time. In the 1970s the company was primarily concerned with the interests of those groups who had a very direct tangible impact on the company activities. Satisfying the needs of customers, investors and regulators was vital for the company existence. To a certain degree this initial map corresponds to the curtailed inner circle on Freeman's stakeholder map. Twenty years onwards, the initial stakeholder list saw a considerable expansion that among other things reflected Novo Nordisk's strong commitment to CSR (adding local community as a

Figure 5.2

Evolution of stakeholder
engagement at Novo Nordisk

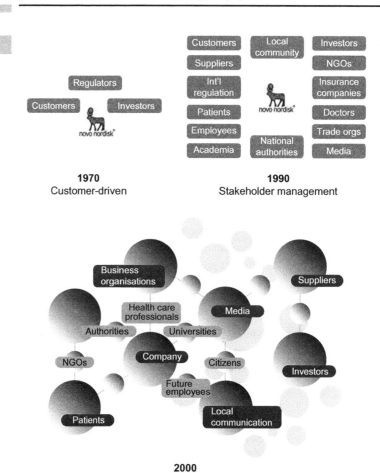

1970
Customer-driven

1990
Stakeholder management

2000
Stakeholder engagement

stakeholder), sustainability (NGOs, academia, community) and transparency (media). By the end of the 1990s, Novo Nordisk took to the idea that a company itself did not need to be at the very centre of a stakeholder map. Rather, the entire business environment could be treated as a constellation with multiple stakeholder-players constantly interconnecting and co-influencing each other.

Over time we have been seeing a growing trend of applying the stakeholder approach by many businesses across the globe. Today for any Scandinavian company engaged in managing for stakeholders such as H&M, IKEA, Novo Nordisk, Novozymes, Norsk Hydro and Statoil (Strand and Freeman, 2015), there will be numerous US counterparts such as DuPont, Nike, Nordstrom, Panera Bread, Southwest Airlines, The Container Store and Whole Foods Markets. These companies give due respect to all their stakeholders and try to create value for all of them.

Driven by the best practices in managing for stakeholders, many companies have committed to the common trend of writing a stakeholder engagement chapter when it comes to company mission and values. Nowadays, in the oil and gas industry for example (apart from Statoil), there are many other major players, such as Exxon Mobil, ConocoPhillips, BP and others, who talk about focusing on stakeholder engagement on their website front pages. There may be criticism that it is easier to write about it than to implement 'managing for stakeholders' in practice, but recognising stakeholder engagement as a priority for a company can definitely be viewed as moving in the right direction. The growing pressure for implementing the stakeholder approach in business is also stipulated by the rapid advancements in technology that we all experience nowadays, and the next section looks at the relationship between technological progress and 'managing for stakeholders' in more detail.

5.4 Stakeholder Theory in the Age of Technology

5.4.1 Advancements in Technology Call for a Stakeholder Approach

In the 1990s, the ubiquitous introduction of new communication channels such as faxes, voice-mails, emails and company webpages transformed the previously cumbersome and slow information exchange between a company and its stakeholders. Inasmuch as this transformation expedited the very process of communication, it did not affect the dyadic character of a relationship between a company and its stakeholders, nor did it directly influence the proximity/ remoteness between the two. As we entered the digital age at the beginning of the twenty-first century, new technologies extended communication between companies and their stakeholders to include writing in public forums, posting in social media (such as Facebook and Twitter), sharing personal blogs, providing reader comments for online articles, following online postings of opinion leaders, joining online groups of interests, and more. If previously it took days and weeks for stakeholders to reach company managers, now, due to the development of new technologies, information reaches managers immediately. The information exchange between the organisation and its stakeholders became instantaneous, dynamic and open to a broad public.

What do these dramatic advancements in technology mean for the stakeholder theory? The cornerstone of stakeholder theory lies in 'creating as much value as possible for stakeholders, without resorting to trade-offs' (Freeman et al., 2010: 28). Stakeholder theory also aims at integrating business and ethical components in managerial decision-making (the integration thesis) and 'as such, matters of ethics are routine when one takes a "managing for stakeholders" approach' (ibid.: 29). Rapid technology developments have amplified the role of stakeholders and made it obvious that a stakeholder approach is both a necessary condition for any business to remain successful and an ethical approach of simply doing the right thing. Here we analyse how recent advancements in technology have moved stakeholder theory to the very front page of the managerial agenda.

5.4.2 Organised Groups – Stronger Voices

New communication technologies make stakeholder groups more organised, so their role in a firm's success becomes even more salient. Previously, in the case of a negative experience with a product or service, customers had to deal with a company on their own and the success of separate actions was limited. The lack of individual stakeholders' influence in traditional media allowed some companies to neglect the interest of certain stakeholder groups. However, new technologies enable individual stakeholders to act as organised stakeholder groups, and their opinions, whether it is customer feedback or employee experience-sharing, quickly spread across the market and become a tangible thing that the company has to deal with. Social media makes millions of previously disconnected individual stakeholders unite under common ideas, and their voices become stronger.

Stronger stakeholder voices, empowered by the technological progress, make stakeholders noticeable even for those practitioners who did not previously recognise a stakeholder approach. It does not surprise anyone these days if a CEO refers to a particular customer feedback from an online source during a leadership team meeting. Understanding the growing importance of new communication technologies, many companies started actively working with their stakeholders in this direction. The KLM Airline's website offers a prompt response through social media: 'Contact us 24/7 via our social networks in Twitter, Facebook and LinkedIn. Our social media teams ... will always try to respond within the hour.' However, not all stakeholder groups manage to benefit from the age of technology in the context of their relationship with the companies. While customers, employees and communities increasingly use technology with regard to companies, there are still untapped opportunities for investors and suppliers, who have not been leveraging social media as much so far.

5.4.3 Names and Faces – Emotional Bond

Technological progress makes it possible to apply a names-and-face approach as a part of efficient stakeholder management. This approach, proposed by McVea and Freeman (2005), argues that it is easier for managers to make decisions within a stakeholder mindset if they think about stakeholders not as generic groups but as individuals with names and faces. The problem is that '[w]hen stakeholders are thought of in terms of their generic roles rather than as individuals of moral worth, it is much easier to formulate strategies that are not only inhuman and unethical but also counter to the long-term interests of the firm' (ibid: 60). This view resonates with the importance of proximity for ethical behaviour. Jones argued that moral considerations increase with the level of perceived moral intensity which is driven by the degree of proximity the manager feels towards the object of her action (Jones, 1991). The feeling of proximity to other people can relate not only to physical distance as such but also to the way we think about those people.

McVea and Freeman claim that 'generic thinking dulls our sense of proximity to stakeholders' and it becomes easier for managers to ignore moral responsibility for some stakeholder groups (McVea and Freeman, 2005: 63). The effects of discriminating decisions towards particular stakeholders are discounted by managers when they have taken this generic perspective. It is easier to squeeze suppliers that managers have never met, neglect the facts of causing pollution in the communities the managers have never visited or underpay employees they have never worked with. However, the digital age eliminates the distance effect in such a way that even remote stakeholders can potentially obtain names and faces, and become salient during the managerial decision-making. Discriminated suppliers located in other regions can arrange a video conference call with a CEO to demonstrate real faces behind their work; members of polluted communities can share online real time measurements of pollution indicators in their neighbourhood with people walking on those street; and underpaid employees in a remote office can express their feelings during annual corporate surveys, and share the survey results with the headquarters to complement happy customer feedback and visual demonstrations of productive employee–customer joint work.

New technologies make it possible to regularly remind managing practitioners that their business decisions affect or are affected by people who have names, faces, families, feelings and aspirations. Remote and long-forgotten stakeholders become conspicuous. Using the names-and-faces approach, it has become easier to avoid managerial decisions involving taking from one group of stakeholders and giving to another that managers probably have higher proximity with. Stakeholder theory considers firms as 'a tool to achieve morally rich human ends – including financial sustainability, human thriving and the pursuit of the firm's specific value proposition' (Freeman et al., 2010). By reminding managers about the individuality of each person, the names-and-faces approach contributes to the fulfilment of the moral components of stakeholder theory.

5.4.4 High Transparency – Always in the Spotlight

New communication technologies mean that companies are constantly in the public eye which, among other things, entails making it much harder for a company to hide any corporate misconduct. Company activities are documented in digital forms, such as computer files, and from time to time those fall into the hands of and are scrutinised by company stakeholders. What is done by night appears by day. Stakeholders can easily access company financial reporting and managerial presentations, as well as lots of different communications shared by individuals affected by the company. Firms are expected, and even forced, to be more open and transparent with their stakeholders, and higher transparency should inevitably lead to higher levels of responsibility. Under higher transparency, managerial thinking may exhibit the following logical pattern: if I am not responsible enough for my actions, my mistakes can be exposed to the company stakeholders much easier than ever before. With modern technologies at hand, odds are high that this may happen and if it does, my company reputation will be seriously affected. Therefore, I should be more responsible for my decision-making.

With higher transparency, company reputational issues become much more acute (see also Chapter 14). Not only do stakeholders gain access to information regarding company wrongdoing, but this access is often instantaneous. On top of that, the history of a company is easy to trace and this makes it much harder for a company to repair its reputation after a transgression. Articles published in the digital world are stored by online search engines, and even if the original article is deleted in the venue of its appearance, it will continue popping up in relevant online searches. Thus, unprecedentedly high transparency of company activities further increases companies' responsibility to act in the interests of all stakeholders.

5.4.5 Dispersed Interactions – Blurred Boundaries

The Internet, and social networks in particular, activate interactions among different stakeholder groups. Previously, all company-related communication was run by stakeholders through the company; stakeholder groups did not communicate among themselves and were not much aware of processes taking place outside their areas. The Internet enabled interactions among different stakeholder groups, not only through the organisation as the centre of the communication flow but also directly with one another. Different stakeholders can now engage in company-related discussions without soliciting any permission from the company itself. Thus a lot of communication and business activity can happen in a 'behind the backs' mode. What are the implications for the company? It would seem quite challenging to keep track of all of these interactions between stakeholders. One cannot simply control and in fact does not need to control all these multiple activities and communication. Instead, demonstrating responsible behaviour towards all stakeholders at all times will help the company successfully manage those interactions of which it is aware, and preclude any possible negative information flow into those it cannot follow. Prevention rather than reparation of failure would be the preferred strategy.

In 2010, Nestlé S.A., one of the largest global food processing companies, found itself in the midst of the online war over the use of palm oil purchased from a supplier whose irresponsible actions led to mass deforestation of orangutan habitat in Indonesia. Ignoring the letter from Greenpeace asking to cut off any business relationships with the irresponsible supplier, Nestlé miscalculated the possibility of the forthcoming outburst of negativity which would eventually damage the company's reputation. Without any official response from Nestlé, Greenpeace embarked on a massive online strike, attracting millions of consumers along the way. The NGO directed the battle, soliciting help and cooperation from the Internet users. Specifically, Greenpeace encouraged consumers to bring their protesting to Nestlé's official Facebook page, create and post subject-related videos and write letters of protest to the Nestlé CEO. The fight driven by Greenpeace was complete with successful strategy and communication flow between the two stakeholder groups: the NGO and the consumers. Nestlé's response was extremely unprofessional: the company engaged in taking down videos, deleting unpleasant remarks and posting rude, inappropriate retorts to its Facebook account page. Rather than embracing its stakeholders' concerns and satisfying their requests through meaningful and respectful conversation, Nestlé chose to resort to an aggressive type of self-defence. Quickly the battlefield migrated from online social media to major publications such as the *New York Times* and the *Wall Street Journal*. Finally, Nestlé had no other option but to officially apologise, cut its ties with the supplier and commit itself to sustainable practices in palm oil purchasing (Chaudhari and Purkayastha, 2011).

Inter-stakeholder communication stipulates more responsible ethical behaviour on the part of the company, as such communication blurs the boundaries among stakeholder groups and they start understanding each other better. As a result, it becomes harder for a company to make trade-offs among stakeholders, as the discriminated stakeholder can easily reach the other stakeholder groups and discredit company reputation. The communication flow has changed its direction and it is 'no longer unidirectional, and as stakeholders increasingly communicate with each other … this communication becomes infinitely more complex' (Van der Merwe, Pitt and Abratt, 2005: 40). In the digital age, stakeholders speak to companies much more often than companies do to stakeholders. Millions of individual stakeholders share their experiences, opinions and ideas about companies, thus shifting the focus of stakeholder management in organisations from *speaking* to stakeholders to *listening* to stakeholders.

5.4.6 New Stakeholder Emerges – Virtual Stakeholder

The creation of the Internet expanded the arena of company activities into new areas. Companies can use the Internet as a key element of their business model – a platform for selling products or services, or as a tool for exchanging information with their stakeholders (customers, employees, suppliers, communities and financiers). However, a new class of stakeholder has emerged that is affected and affects company performance – virtual stakeholders. These individuals are not necessarily customers of the company but they choose to actively follow the company news and business activities in social media by providing comments, opinions and engaging in discussions. These followers create hype around the company, and their activities may have an indirect impact on other company stakeholders as well as create certain repercussions for the company reputation.

As of 2015, the Facebook page of elite car-maker Porsche has almost 10 million people who regularly follow it. Those people are not necessarily company customers or community members, but they are interested in following the development of Porsche models and they share their opinions on Porsche's Facebook page from time to time. Many of these people have never owned a Porsche car, but they are car fans who promote it among their friends and acquaintances, on their Facebook pages and personal blogs. Should the company treat this large group of 10 million followers as company stakeholders? According to Freeman, stakeholders are groups that the firm needs in order to exist and without their support it would fail (Dunham, Freeman and Liedtka, 2006). According to Porsche's annual report (Porsche, 2014: 46), 'With 189,849 new vehicles delivered, financial year 2014 was the most successful year in Porsche's history thus far. This represents a 17-percent increase on the prior year, which had also been a strong year.' Would Porsche generate a two-digit growing sales per year without all the hype generated around Porsche by its fans, especially by its 10 million virtual stakeholder group?

Another example is that of Blue Origin, a private company building space ships for orbital tours around the Earth. The company activities were kept confidential during a research phase, but soon after a test flight of its suborbital spacecraft New Shepard in April 2015, Blue Origin opened a Facebook page and attracted over 500 followers in its first few days. Half a year later, the page had attracted more than 5,500 virtual supporters. These people, who follow the Blue Origin web page, support it in public forums and write personal blogs about them, and as such can potentially exert a direct impact on the company as well as affect it through virtual communication with other company stakeholders. Smart stakeholder-minded company management will definitely keep track of its virtual stakeholder space, understanding that virtual stakeholder effects can have quite real-life positive and negative spill-outs and as such are important for the success of the whole venture. It may seem that a virtual stakeholder is only a secondary stakeholder (Figure 5.3), but the importance of this group has been gaining in salience with the pervasive development of social networks, and managers

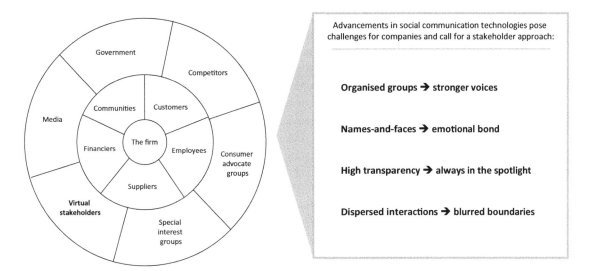

Figure 5.3

Stakeholder map, including virtual stakeholders, and challenges posed by advancements in social communication technologies

should not underestimate the importance of this stakeholder. The case study offered later in this chapter provides a relevant example of the 'physical reality' of a virtual stakeholder.

Figure 5.3 summarises key challenges imposed on companies by the recent major progress in social media. The call for a stakeholder approach in business becomes even stronger, as managing for stakeholders can help the business cope with these contemporary challenges.

5.4.7 'Yes, and ...' – the Epitome of Stakeholder Thinking

Technological progress gave birth to a new business model – open sourcing – which has a very different set of stakeholders. For example, the R software for statistical computing and graphics is created and maintained by its users. The interesting part of this model is that all stakeholders, who are typically represented by different groups of people, are now blended in one person. This person is a customer, since she uses R in her work; an employee, since she constantly works on improving the R software; a supplier, since all necessary materials for producing the product (like a computer and printer) are provided by this person; a community member, since this person works from her home; a financier, since this person decides on resources to be allocated to the project; a virtual stakeholder, as she typically follows and shares news about the R software. While open sourcing is typically employed in the software industry, we can see this business model migrate to other domains, beyond software development. For instance, Opensource-solar project is built around the idea of free sharing of information and designs to build a solar power system (Opensource-solar, 2015). Anyone can share and modify the already available designs and eventually build their own systems. Again, we see that each Opensource-solar user is considered a service provider, a customer and a supplier at the same time.

Merging all stakeholder manifestations into one takes away the difficulty of prioritising one stakeholder group over another. Yet, for this model to work the basic expectation is that each stakeholder, who now combines all previous stakeholder types (employee, supplier, etc.) into herself, respects and interacts with other similar-type stakeholders like herself.

This new open sourcing model is, in a way, the epitome of stakeholder thinking. Each player has to recognise not only what she can contribute, but what others can as well. Here we can borrow from theatrical discipline. One of the key elements of improvisational comedy is a 'Yes, and ...' approach, which dictates that each actor should try to consider what another actor is doing. Rather than disagreeing with her actions or words, one has to accept the scenario given to her and then add to it. For stakeholder theory it translates into accepting what one stakeholder does and adding value to it, thus ultimately increasing the total value received by stakeholders. This is illustrated in Figure 5.4.

Figure 5.4

The epitome of stakeholder thinking

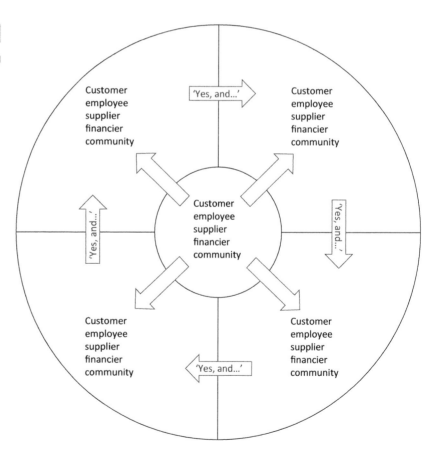

5.5 Case Study: Monsanto

This case aims to analyse the root causes of Monsanto's controversial reputation associated with its biotech development. It shows how we can use stakeholder theory as an appropriate approach to understand the problems which the company faces. It should be noted that this study is not in any way about metaphysical aspects of applying biotechnologies in the life of humanity. It is mainly concerned with finding appropriate solutions to business situations.

5.5.1 Company History: Success Driven by Innovation

Monsanto was established in Missouri in 1901 to produce food additives, such as the first artificial sweetener saccharin. The company quickly grew, and by the 1940s it expanded its business to industrial and agricultural chemicals such as plastics and herbicides, as well as to pharmaceutical products such as aspirin.

Since acquiring Thomas and Hochwalt Laboratories in 1936, Monsanto has always had a strong focus on research. Monsanto innovations included the development of the first industrial process to synthesise L-dopa, which is currently the main drug used to treat Parkinson's disease (Yun, 2005), and William Knowles who led the team at Monsanto was later awarded a Nobel Prize. Monsanto scientists also developed 'the Monsanto process' for making acetic acid, which became the most common method for making industrial chemicals. During that time the company tried to enter different areas of production, and among many innovative solutions created at Monsanto was the development of Astro Turf, a surface of synthetic fibres looking like natural grass which has been widely used in numerous sport arenas around the world. The company also developed a laundry detergent which was later sold to Unilever. Another important phase in the history of Monsanto was becoming the first company to start mass production of LEDs (light emitting diodes), which significantly boosted company revenues.

The company entrepreneurial spirit showed itself in the agriculture division established at Monsanto in the 1960s. In the mid-1970s the cell biology research programme brought to the market Roundup, a glyphosate herbicide that is widely used by farmers even in modern times. In 1981 a molecular biology group was set up and, according to the company website, since then biotechnology has become 'firmly established as Monsanto's strategic research focus'. Monsanto scientists were the first to genetically modify a plant cell in 1982, and by the end of that decade Monsanto conducted the first field trials with biotechnology traits in the US.

During the 1980s and 1990s, in parallel with the successful research with cells, Monsanto entered corn, soybeans, cotton and canola seed markets by acquiring several companies producing conventional (non-genetically modified organism (GMO)) seeds. At the end of the 1990s, after receiving approval from the US regulatory body, Monsanto launched the first genetically modified products with in-seed tolerance to Roundup and in-seed protection against insects.

By that time, Monsanto operated three standalone businesses: an agricultural products business (the Ag Business), a pharmaceutical and nutrition business (the Pharmaceuticals Business) and a chemical products business (the Chemicals Business). According to the Monsanto website:

> former Monsanto is … known as Pharmacia LLC. Pharmacia is now a wholly owned subsidiary of Pfizer Inc., which operates the Pharmaceuticals Business. Solutia [the company created by Monsanto to consolidate its chemicals business] … is now a wholly-owned subsidiary of Eastman Chemical Company, which operates the Chemicals Business. Today's Monsanto includes the operations, assets and liabilities that were previously the Ag Business.

So the current Monsanto is the continuation of the agriculture division of the previous large chemicals-pharmaceutical-agriculture conglomerate.

5.5.2 Controversial Company Reputation: Biotech Move Did Not Help

The history of Monsanto was full of innovative solutions that advanced technological progress and human well-being. However, some of its innovations caused reputational concerns for the company. As Rhodes mentioned,

> In the 1960s it [Monsanto] was notorious as a large producer of PCBs – a chemical compound used for lubricants, coolants and waterproofing – which were discovered to be carcinogenic and subsequently banned. It was also the largest producer of Agent Orange, the toxin used by the American forces to defoliate the rainforests of Southeast Asia during the Vietnam war. (Rhodes, 1999)

In 1999 Hugh Grant (who would become the CEO of the company in 2003, until the present day), recollected in his interview that the move to biotechnology (a term used by professionals for GMOs) was seen by the company management as a step to mitigate some previous negative reputation issues associated with certain industrial chemical products. Grant thought that while working for Monsanto, he would be 'helping to transform the company from a controversial industrial chemical business into an ecologically minded concern that promotes the most sophisticated advances in biological science' (Rhodes, 1999). However, Grant 'never imagined that what he saw as progress could be viewed with such suspicion'. As Grant recollects, it was a complete eye-opener for him, when having his hair trimmed in a barber shop in London and replying to the barber's inquiry into his occupation which was running the agriculture division at Monsanto, he was suddenly confronted with a sharp retort before even finishing his sentence: 'You're responsible for that Frankenfood that's killing us all.'

The US Food and Drug Administration (FDA), being responsible for protecting the public health and regulating foods and food ingredients introduced into or offered for sale in the country, did not find negative outcomes of using biotech products. In its Guidance for Industry (FDA, 2000), representing 'FDA's current thinking on voluntary labelling of foods indicating whether foods have or have not been developed using bioengineering', FDA stated that 'FDA has no basis for concluding that bioengineered foods differ from other foods in any meaningful or uniform way, or that, as a class, foods developed by the new techniques present any different or greater safety concern than foods developed by traditional plant breeding.' FDA also noted that the arguments used by the opponents of biotechnology

> were mainly expressions of concern about the unknown. The agency is still not aware of any data or other information that would form a basis for concluding that the fact that a food or its ingredients was produced using bioengineering is a material fact that must be disclosed under sections 403(a) and 201(n) of the act.

As a result, FDA allowed the commercialisation of biotech products and made a decision 'to not require special labelling of all bioengineered foods'.

Farmers liked the biotech products introduced by Monsanto in corn, soybeans, cotton and canola as they could receive a higher income due to a significant increase in yields. Also, the biotech seeds, due to in-seed protection to insects and diseases, allowed farmers to considerably decrease expenses on agriculture chemicals which were a large portion of crop-growing costs. Though there were no negative consequences observed with the introduction of biotech products and the advantages for farming, including higher yields and lower production inputs, were considerable (USDA, 2014), the move from industrial chemicals to biotechnology, that could become as groundbreaking as space exploration or nanotechnologies, did not create a positive image for Monsanto. Biotechnology is a part of human technological progress and it is widely used in the pharmaceutical industry with a wide acceptance in our society. However, biotech development associated with Monsanto became highly controversial, and this issue is hotly debated by some of the company's important stakeholders.

5.5.3 Strong Support from some Stakeholder Groups

Traditionally Monsanto focused on three major stakeholders: investors, customers (farmers) and employees. Active engagement with these three groups was beneficial for the company in many ways.

Monsanto was repeatedly named as one of the best companies to work for in the USA and worldwide. In 2014 Monsanto was ranked #8 in the list of the twenty-five world's best multinational workplaces. Locally, Monsanto is highly recognised as an employer in almost every location the firm has its offices. Thus, Monsanto India was awarded the 'Top 50 Employer in India' in 2003, 2008, 2009 and 2010. Monsanto Brazil was selected as 'One of the best companies to work for in Brazil' for fifteen consecutive years, starting in 1999. Monsanto Argentina was named one of the best employers in the country for nine consecutive years in 2014 (Monsanto, 2015a). The company has also been recognised as one of the best workplaces for women and the LGBT community. One can easily find solid confirmation of Monsanto's well-considered relationship-building with its employees on popular websites where any person can rank and review their current workplace. As an example, Monsanto scores 4.5 (out of 5) based on 283 reviews on www.indeed.com website. Among other things, current employees stress that they enjoy the relaxed environment, friendly management, supporting and helping co-workers, and multiple learning opportunities. One of the virtual reviewers summed it up that 'Contrary to popular belief, Monsanto is not an evil corporation filled with greedy businessmen, but rather is one of the best companies to work for in the world (Top 100 according to Fortune) filled with inspired scientists interested in cutting-edge agricultural biotechnology' (Indeed, 2015).

5.5.4 Neglecting Communities Negatively Affected Business

Focusing on customers, employees and shareholders but ignoring other stake-holder groups such as communities turned out to be problematic for the company. In 2013 Monsanto announced its intention to invest $300 million into constructing a seed plant in Ukraine. This seed plant was supposed to be the biggest of its kind in Europe, focusing solely on processing conventional (non-GMO) seed for the Ukrainian market. From Monsanto's point of view, the project was beneficial for the local community in terms of value creation as it was meant to bring great employment opportunities as well as significant investment into local infrastructure. Moreover, it came at a time when due to an unstable political situation Ukraine was extremely low on capital investment and desperately needed foreign capital. However, when Monsanto was very close to signing an agreement with the Vinnytsia City Mayor and the City Council to buy 200 acres at the city boundary, the project was diverted by the community leaders as they feared their status might be put in jeopardy in case they 'hosted' a company with questionable global reputation. Monsanto's arguments that it was forbidden by law to cultivate biotech crops in Europe, including Ukraine, and thus the plant would be processing only conventional seeds, did not help.

A similar situation occurred in Argentina at about the same time. Monsanto was going to expand its production facilities there, but soon after its announcement, protests started near the Monsanto production facilities which impeded its expansion. Experiencing resistance by local communities in Ukraine and Argentina because of the company's global reputation was another important stepping stone for Monsanto's management, helping them to realise that they could not afford to ignore certain stakeholder groups any more.

5.5.5 Ignoring Virtual Stakeholders Created Protests Against the Company

While Monsanto was doing a great job in engaging with employees, customers and investors, it left out another important stakeholder group – the virtual stakeholders. This miscalculation in strategy had serious repercussions. With the rise of the digital age, Monsanto's business activities were easily followed by people all over the world and, if before these remote communities could not come together in their protests because they were disparate points scattered across the globe, nowadays social networks serve as powerful tools which can unite these communities in a flick of a second. Tami Canal, the founder of the March-against-Monsanto project, began her campaign on her Facebook page on February 2013 in response to the California legislators who voted against a mandatory labelling of biotech products. Only three months later, her Facebook page had attracted 85,000 followers (Utiger, 2013) with nearly 110,000 'likes' and about 40,000 visitors a day (Case, 2013). That was not just a virtual adventure: four days later, many of these people marched into the streets to protest against GMO foods and Monsanto in particular. By October 2015, Canal's page accumulated 940,000 likes, with an approximate 2 per cent monthly increase in the number of people who support the project.

5.5.6 Monsanto Changes its Strategy and Starts a Dialogue with Communities

According to Monsanto's webpage, the company has a strong focus on the sustainable development of communities. However, this strong formal emphasis on the development of relationships with communities did not start till 2011. That was the time when the company set up stakeholder engagement exercises through which it heard a clear message: 'Do a better job at opening up and engaging society' (Monsanto, 2015b).

The same year, Monsanto published its annual Corporate Social Responsibility and Sustainability report in which it once again listed its major values under the title of Monsanto Pledge (Monsanto, 2015c). Among other values, the company claimed dialogue to be one of its main values, stating that they 'will listen carefully to diverse points of view and engage in thoughtful dialogue', and that they 'will broaden [their] understanding of issues in order to better address the needs and concerns of society and each other'. In the same report. for the first time Monsanto gave an exhaustive list of its valued stakeholders which among others included 'residential and commercial communities in areas where Monsanto has facilities and trade interests and non-governmental organisations and community groups'. With this new perspective, it seemed the company took a sharp turn in its stakeholder strategy, repenting its previous blunders. Former Monsanto CEO Robert Shapiro (Samuelson and Birchard, 2003) in one of his interviews stated,

> If there was a next time, I'd have much earlier dialogue with a wide range of interested parties in the scientific, academic, governmental, and NGO communities ... It would have taken unusually candid and innovative discussions between ourselves and Greenpeace to create a win/win, but that might not have been impossible.

Monsanto spent too much time isolating itself from the community, when these valuable years could have been spent educating the public about the company innovations and engaging in productive dialogues to solve common problems.

Monsanto came to value dialogue with one of its most important stakeholders – communities – through a series of painful lessons. Nowadays, the company is consistent with its determination to openly participate in a dialogue with all of its stakeholders. In January 2015, Monsanto's CEO, Hugh Grant, opened up the company annual shareholder meeting to the broad audience, including public activists, community leaders and journalists. The heated discussion filled with accusations reveals the fact that the problem is still there: farmers and employees who have both been the long-cherished company stakeholders had to stand in defence of the Monsanto image against community representatives (Bunge, 2015).

Questions for Discussion

1. In which ways, if any, do Monsanto's stakeholders create value for the company? Do trade-offs exist?
2. Will Monsanto be able to recover from its somewhat tarnished image, given the fact that it changed its stakeholder perspective in 2011?

3. What would be different for Monsanto now if it had started the dialogue with its major stakeholders earlier?

5.6 Chapter Summary

As Freeman et al. mentioned, stakeholder theory is 'first, and most fundamentally, a moral theory that specifies the obligations that companies have to their stakeholders' (Freeman et al., 2010: 212). A company should bear responsibility to every stakeholder it has in a manner that does not allow any trade-offs. Customers, employees, financiers, suppliers and communities should all matter. Moreover, as it turns out, treating all stakeholders equally puts everyone in a win-win situation because stakeholder theory is also about 'value creation and trade and how to manage a business effectively' (ibid: 9). Overall, managers should be guided in their work by the principles of stakeholder theory because it provides 'a better way to live, it allows us to be authentic, and it enables cooperation with other stakeholders such that, over time, everybody wins' (ibid: 215).

The digital age makes the stakeholder mindset a necessity for every company aiming to build a successful business. The development of social networks makes individual stakeholders more organised and amplifies the magnitude of their voices, so it becomes difficult to ignore certain stakeholder groups. Technological progress enables high transparency in the business environment so that company activities can be clearly viewed by its stakeholders. Company reputational concerns have become crucial as never before, because corporate wrongdoing, even if it took place a long time ago, can be easily revealed through digital public sources. Furthermore, different stakeholder groups can communicate to each other without any moderation from the company, thus creating direct routes for information flow from one stakeholder to another.

Living in the age of technology does not only place higher expectations on companies, it also provides them with better tools for implementing the stakeholder approach. New technologies make it possible to put names and faces behind generic stakeholder groups and increase the emotional bond between the management of the company and its stakeholders. The digital age created a new type of stakeholders – virtual stakeholders. These people, sometimes reaching in size of tens of millions, follow company activities, express their opinion and help create hype about company products and promote it among other stakeholders. The advancements in technology also enable the creation of new business models where the differences among stakeholders have been flattened. Programmers who develop software applications in an open source environment are stakeholders in one place. Working with a 'Yes, and ...' attitude allows the acceptance of what one stakeholder does and then adds value to it, thus benefiting all parties.

Chapter Questions

1. Why is it important to create as much value as possible for stakeholders without resorting to trade-offs?
2. How does the digital age help avoid trade-offs among stakeholders?
3. How can the Monsanto case study help other companies with regard to stakeholder theory?
4. What is the relationship between stakeholder theory and CSR?

FURTHER RESOURCES

Freeman, R. E., Harrison, J. S. and Wicks, A. C. (2007). *Managing for Stakeholders: Survival, Reputation, and Success*. New Haven: Yale University Press.
This book aims to explore the question of how we can develop a 'managing for stakeholders' mindset and create as much value as possible for all stakeholders. The authors propose ten specific principles and seven techniques for managing stakeholder relationships.

Harrison, J. S., Bosse, D. A. and Phillips, R. A. (2010). Managing for Stakeholders, Stakeholder Utility Functions, and Competitive Advantage. *Strategic Management Journal*, 31(1), 58–74.
The article explains how building trusting relationships with stakeholders, based on principles of justice, leads to a firm's increased competitive advantage.

Parmar, B. L., Freeman, R. E., Harrison, J. S., Wicks, A. C., Purnell, L. and de Colle, S. (2010). Stakeholder Theory: The State of the Art. *The Academy of Management Annals*, 4(1), 403–445.
This book constitutes a major summary work on stakeholder theory literature, looking at what problems it tries to solve and reviewing misunderstandings and misuses of stakeholder theory. The book also analyses the relationship between stakeholder theory and business ethics and CSR, and examines the implications of stakeholder theory for capitalism, arguing for a new narrative for business.

Phillips, R. (2003). *Stakeholder Theory and Organizational Ethics*. San Francisco: Berrett-Koehler Publishers, Inc.

Rob Phillips analyses shortcomings of stakeholder theory and proposes ways to overcome them. He introduces a principle of stakeholder fairness and discusses shareholder legitimacy, stakeholder identity and stakeholder theory in practice.

The Masters Seminars in Business Ethics video series produced by Business Roundtable Institute for Corporate Ethics, www.corporate-ethics.org/videos/

In these videos, prominent management scholars and business leaders, including Norman Bowie, Thomas Donaldson, Ed Freeman, Edwin Hartman, John Mackey, Joshua Margolis, Rajendra Sisodia, Linda Trevino, Patricia Werhane, Andy Wicks and others, talk about various aspects of ethical behaviour in business, including the role of stakeholder theory.

Political CSR: The Corporation as a Political Actor

GLEN WHELAN

Learning Objectives

- Develop insight into the role of corporations in **global governance** and multi-stakeholder initiatives (MSIs).
- Highlight the importance of corporate relations with non-government organisations (NGOs) and state organisations.
- Recognise the political impact of corporate products and services.

6.1 Introduction

How do corporations influence international politics and global governance? Can the products and services they produce transform political realities? The recognition and understanding of such questions is important for future managers because they encourage the proactive management of social pressures associated with direct and indirect corporate impacts on political goods of fundamental importance (e.g. democracy, liberty). In light of such, this chapter first provides you with a brief review of how the 'political' corporate social responsibility (CSR) literature has conceived the role that corporations play in MSIs and global governance more generally. Following this, the role that corporations play in international politics is outlined with reference to the corporate political activity literature, among others. In recognising the currently broadening interest in corporations, politics and responsibility, and in explicitly acknowledging the significance of ongoing developments in high-technology (e.g. the Internet, robotics), we then explore how corporate products and services can also impact on political considerations in fundamental ways.

To better illustrate such transformative potential, David Eggers' fictional work 'The Circle' is used to help construct a case study on how Google Glass might transform political transparency. Moreover, the case reveals that Google itself is commonly accused of lacking transparency with regard to its political contributions, and with regards to its own products and services. In this fashion, the case suggests that while the political impact of corporations can be complex, and even revolutionary, they are also generally informed by base motivations and practices.

By the end of the chapter, you will be able to identify literature most closely connected with corporations, politics and responsibility, to make clear sense of why corporate relations with non-governmental and state organisations are important, and to discuss how corporate products and services can influence political matters. More generally, you will be better able to understand the ways in which corporations influence matters of political importance in multifaceted ways.

6.2 'Political' CSR: Governance Gaps, MSIs and Democracy

The idea of 'political' CSR (Scherer and Palazzo, 2007), and the closely associated idea of corporate citizenship (Matten and Crane, 2005), has recently enjoyed a prominent status within the management and organisation studies literature. By and large, these concepts emphasise that corporations, and multinational corporations (MNCs) in particular, do and increasingly should play a key role in the provision of global public goods, given the presupposition that globalisation results in states (national governments) suffering a loss of power. Furthermore, these writings have tended to emphasise that corporations often can, and once again should, participate within MSIs or international accountability standards so as to better ensure that their policies and practices are democratically legitimate (Rasche, 2012). While a key point of this chapter is that the literature on political CSR is increasingly characterised by a diversity of normative orientations and empirical concerns, it is emphasised that what Whelan specifically labels the 'political' CSR literature (Whelan, 2012) (e.g. Matten and Crane, 2005; Scherer and Palazzo, 2007) has provided the catalyst for much of this present interest. Accordingly, the present section outlines three aspects of the 'political' CSR literature that are widely considered of central importance thereto (e.g. Frynas and Stephens, 2014; Whelan, 2012).

6.2.1 Governance Gaps

'Embedded liberalism' is a term coined by John Ruggie in a 1982 article for *International Organization*. In this article – entitled 'International Regimes, Transactions, and Change: Embedded Liberalism in the Post-War Economic Order' – Ruggie built upon what he described as Karl Polanyi's 'magisterial' 1944 work, *The Great Transformation*, to characterise the post-World War II order as one in which states agreed (with significant directive advice from the United States) to enable global market forces while simultaneously subjecting them to domestic (national) controls. As financial markets and production chains have become increasingly global, however, and as global production chains have become increasingly internalised within the institutional form of MNCs, Ruggie has suggested that the embedded liberal compromise is under threat. In particular, he has proposed that we now live in a world characterised by 'governance gaps ... between the scope and impact of economic forces and actors, and the capacity of societies to manage their adverse consequences' (Ruggie, 2008, para. 3).

The idea of 'governance gaps' has played a key role in the 'political' CSR literature because it suggests the need for MNCs to increasingly provide for a variety of (global) public goods (e.g. basic human rights; rules of governance) that have predominantly been associated with states since World War II. Although this idea can be overstated – in that powerful states such as China and the United States will often be in a position to close governance gaps within specific regions as and when they desire – it points towards a more general consideration of importance. Namely, the notion of governance gaps, or 'regulatory vacuums' (e.g. Matten and Crane, 2005: 172), quickly reveals that MNC policies and practices are often not immediately subject to any sort of meaningful regulation or democratic legitimation.

As the idea of governance gaps has a helpful conceptual role to play in the analysis of global governance matters, it should be distinguished from the 'race to the bottom' thesis it is often related to (e.g. Matten and Crane, 2005: 173). The reason being that, the race to the bottom thesis – which amounts to the suggestion that governments are actively competing with each other to attract MNC investment through the (significant) lowering of environmental standards, occupational health and safety standards, and so on – is undermined by evidence throughout the social sciences (e.g. Whelan, 2012: 712–715). Accordingly, and given that the interest of 'political' CSR scholars in MSIs, and democracy more generally, need not rest on this controversial thesis, it is proposed that the notion of governance gaps be taken as providing the general context within which 'political' CSR has emerged.

6.2.2 MSIs

Although 'political' CSR writings are associated with other empirical phenomena – such as the (unilateral) provision of various citizenship rights (Matten and Crane, 2005) – they are most closely associated with MSIs. MSIs are generally conceived as voluntary, self-regulatory and cross-sector governance structures that 'address a variety of social and environmental problems by bringing together corporations and civil society organizations as well as, in some cases, governments, labour organizations, and academia'

(Rasche, 2012: 679–680). In contrast to states (national governments), whose influence is underpinned by coercive capacities (e.g. the police and military), MSIs are generally conceived as governing without the threat of force or violence. Rather, they make use of standards, principles, organisational learning, certification mechanisms, verification mechanisms and so on, to regulate and improve the performance of corporations, and firms more generally, with regard to concerns regarding human rights, sustainability, deforestation and so on.

The United Nations Global Compact is perhaps the most prominent MSI. First proposed at the World Economic Forum in Davos on 31 January 1999, the United Nations Global Compact was formally launched on 26 July 2000. The Global Compact's board is comprised of four constituency groups: business, civil society, labour and the United Nations. Nevertheless, it is primarily concerned with improving the performance of just one of these constituents, business. In particular, the Global Compact seeks to promote organisational learning among the business and MNC community with regards to their better discharging responsibilities relating to human rights, labour, the environment and anti-corruption. To this end, the Global Compact requires participant companies to submit an annual 'Communication on Progress' with regards to one or more of its ten principles (e.g. principle 5: the effective abolition of child labour), and encourages businesses to participate in its global and local learning networks (Rasche, 2012).

While the merits of the Global Compact and other MSIs are the subject of considerable debate (see below), they are not without their supporters. Indeed, the Global Compact, which aspires to be the world's most inclusive voluntary corporate citizenship initiative, currently has over 10,000 participants. It is thus halfway towards achieving the goal of 20,000 participants set by the United Nations General Secretary in 2013.

Another MSI to have enjoyed some success is the Forest Stewardship Council. Following 'the failure of governments at the 1992 United Nations Conference on Environment and Development (UNCED) to develop shared standards and activities for the protection of forests worldwide ... a group of NGOs and corporations' decided to address this governance gap by creating the Forest Stewardship Council in 1993 (Scherer and Palazzo, 2007: 1110). More structurally:

> The General Assembly, as the highest decision-making body of the FSC [Forest Stewardship Council], is organized into three membership chambers – environmental, social, and economic – for balancing the voting power of its diverse members. On the basis of its principles and criteria, the FSC has developed a certification for timber and timber products that is approved by independent bodies. The certification process itself contains rigorous standards and independent monitoring procedures, which lead to a broad acceptance of the council among critical civil society organizations. (ibid.)

With more than 80 million hectares of certified forest in Europe alone, and given its 'state of the art' organisational structures and certification mechanisms, Scherer and Palazzo's suggestion (ibid.) that the FSC is a standout example of 'political' CSR is reasonable. Nevertheless, they also recognise that the FSC, like MSIs more generally, has its critics (ibid.). While recognising that the criticisms made are often complex and multifaceted, it will suffice to mention three interrelated points with regard to MSIs here.

First, and in line with the negative perspective of 'consensual' CSR more generally, MSIs are often charged with enabling MNCs to avoid or escape meaningful responsibility for any social good concerns they are directed towards. This charge relates to the recognition that corporations are profit-focused actors who control resources that can commonly enable them to co-opt civil society voices by making the smallest of compromises, and to the recognition that the consensual orientation of MSIs acts to prevent relevant critical and dissenting voices being heard (e.g. Levy, 2008).

The second and related criticism often made of MSIs is that they are both limited by, and enabling of, a neo-liberal (rather than embedded liberal) global order more generally. Representatives of developing countries, for example, make use of such neo-liberal limitations when they argue that MSIs, or developments in global governance more generally, should not be used as a trade barrier by the developed world. In reversing this point, both champions (Ruggie, 2008: para. 12) and critics (Moog, Spicer and Bohm, 2014) of MSIs have suggested that existing neo-liberal trade regimes should not be allowed to limit the advance and adoption of progressive, multi-stakeholder-led developments. On the other hand, critics have also suggested that MSIs are enabling of a neo-liberal global order of trade and finance. Thus, and in mirroring the suggestion that individual corporations can benefit from the ceremonial and co-optation opportunities that MSIs provide, critics suggest that global capitalism as a whole can benefit from MSIs that reduce the perceived need for more coercive, state-enforced rules and regulations (e.g. Levy, 2008).

Third, many of the main criticisms of MSIs relate to the existence of different theoretical interpretations and orientations. Thus, and in addition to the above-mentioned critical management scholars, who, in being informed by the likes of Gramsci, can be situated within the Marxist tradition (e.g. Levy, 2008; Moog et al., 2014); there are many other commentators cited throughout the paper that are influenced by a variety of theoretical perspectives, and not located within a 'tradition' as such, who suggest that the merits of MSIs, 'political' CSR, and 'consensual' CSR more generally, should be open to contestation.

6.2.3 Democracy

Many of the most interesting debates that the 'political' CSR literature is subject to revolve around democracy: a fundamental political good within liberal- and social-democratic societies. To immediately constrain a discussion that could easily fill an entire book, it is here simply noted that many of these debates relate to the actuality, possibility and desirability of democratic corporate governance.

A key purpose of MSIs is to establish some sort of increasingly democratic governance of MNCs. Nevertheless, and as even the most vocal supporters of 'political' CSR recognise, the democratic possibilities inherent to MSIs are limited by the impossibility of all individuals interested in the activities of a large MNC participating (directly) in all of its decision-making processes. Indeed, it is for this very reason that supporters of 'political' CSR propose that MSIs should be populated by a variety of formal organisational actors – e.g. environmental and human rights NGOs – who indirectly represent a diversity of social voices more generally (Scherer and Palazzo, 2007). But as more critical voices have argued, the fact that MNCs commonly possess far more resources (e.g. lawyers and money) than all the other participants (combined) (e.g. Moog et al., 2014), and the fact that corporations, NGOs and various other organisations involved in MSIs have significant vested interests that act to prevent them seeing eye to eye on many issues, can result in even the 'sub-ideal' of 'deliberative democracy' being un-actualised. Petroleum corporations such as Shell and 'deep' green environmental organisations such as Greenpeace that are opposed to the petroleum industry, for example, have long seemed more interested in opposing, rather than reaching agreement with each other, in democratic forums.

One key way by which this 'under-democratised' status of MSIs and corporate decision-making could be addressed is through the development of more directly democratic corporate governance structures. In addition to its having been suggested by key advocates of 'political' CSR (e.g. Scherer and Palazzo, 2007), the need to democratise corporate governance structures is suggested by influential scholars in other disciplines such as social and environmental accounting (Cooper and Owen, 2007). The possibility of this occurring 'across the board', however, seems low. The reason why is that private investors generally provide capital in the hope of generating (more or less significant) financial returns. Thus – and given that the actualisation of democratic corporate governance structures are proposed to result in managers *not* being instrumentally concerned to generate significant financial returns, but rather, to provide for the (less profitable) social good (Scherer and Palazzo, 2007) – it is to be presumed that many private investors would choose to invest their monies elsewhere. Moreover, the fact that powerful non-democratic states such as China and Russia are also major financiers (and controllers) of corporations – e.g. Sinopec, Gazprom – suggests that the possibility of states providing finances that are enabling of increasingly democratic corporate governance structures should not be overstated either.

While the above concerns regarding the actualisation and possibility of democratic corporate governance structures are very real, they are by no means insurmountable. The next question that must be raised, then, is: *should* democratic corporate governance structures be developed? While an answer to this question cannot be here provided, it is possible to quickly identify a number of points that have informed prior considerations of it.

In the first instance then, it is noted that the vast bulk of work in 'political' CSR (implicitly) suggests that, in addition to helping 'fill' existing governance gaps, the democratisation of corporate governance structures could have the benefit of positively enabling a cosmopolitan citizenry worldwide. That is, the 'political' CSR literature tends to suggest that the democratisation of MNC governance structures in particular, can potentially enable 'citizens of the world' to transcend national boundaries and participate, more or less directly, in the democratic determination of the policies and practices of globally influential corporate actors.

In contrast, the work of the influential German philosopher Jürgen Habermas suggests that the democratisation of corporate governance structures would undermine the functional differentiation of contemporary, modern Western societies, and that any potentially actualised democratisation of corporate governance would pale in comparison to the (cosmopolitan) democracy enabled by existing liberal- and social-democratic state institutions. Much like Habermas, the work of the (equally influential) American philosopher John Rawls suggests that – because markets have efficiency benefits, and given the presumed importance of free association among individuals of diverse 'comprehensive' beliefs (e.g. different religious beliefs) – the broad principles of political justice that apply to democratic state organisations should not be directly applied to all organisations (e.g. business corporations). Where Rawls' work departs from Habermas, however, is in its suggestion that a more or less pluralistic global political order is desirable. Among other things, then, Rawls' work appears to suggest that MSIs founded on deliberative democratic principles may not be consistent with, and thus legitimately rejected by, 'decent hierarchical peoples' whose political traditions do not emphasise the importance of (thoroughgoing) democratic participation.

On a much more radical tip, various writers from a diverse range of scholarly traditions – e.g. Alberto Melucci's work on social movements; Arne Næsse's work on deep ecology – suggest that rather than asking questions about corporate democracy, what we should really be asking is: should large-scale MNCs even exist? In suggesting that the answer might be no, such radical authors come into fundamental conflict with other important contributions. For example, they conflict with leading business ethicist Tom Donaldson, who used his 1982 book *Corporations and Morality* to argue that the reason corporations and markets exist is because they help societies to solve a whole host of political-economic problems that would otherwise be found in a state of nature characterised by the frightening prospect of a Hobbesian war of all against all.

6.3 Corporations and International Politics

In bringing the above discussed points on governance gaps, MSIs and democracy to the attention of the broader management and organisation studies literature, 'political' CSR writings have had a major and positive impact. Nevertheless, the labelling of 'political' CSR has also been criticised for 'appropriat[ing] the meaning of the term "political CSR" for a narrow research agenda' (Frynas and Stephens, 2014: 3). Put more positively, it has been suggested that there is a need to move away from 'political' CSR and towards political CSRs (Whelan, 2012), or what amounts to 'a more inclusive pluralist research agenda' (Frynas and Stephens, 2014: 3). Accordingly, and given the continuing importance of state actors noted above, the present section highlights that corporate–state relations are at least as important as corporate and NGO relations, and thus suggest that our understanding of political CSR needs to explicitly include relations with governmental actors as well.

6.3.1 National politics

The subject matter of the corporate political activity and strategy literature is generally 'defined as corporate attempts to shape government policy in ways favourable to the firm' (Lawton, McGuire and Rajwani, 2012: 87). Whereas writings on CSR and corporate political economy have commonly been under-pinned by a normative agenda – i.e. the concern to identify what it is that corporations morally should or should not do – writings on corporate political activity have generally sought to 'mirror the natural and formal sciences and [have thus] relegate[d] ethics and (irrational) human behaviour to matters of secondary importance' (ibid.). For this reason, 'political' CSR scholarship appears to have largely ignored the corporate political activity literature, and vice versa (Rasche, 2014).

When one looks to the broader CSR, management and politics literatures, however, the possibility of bridging this existing divide becomes readily apparent. The extensive literature on corporate lobbying (e.g. Lawton et al., 2012) raises questions as to whether or not the liberal notions of citizenship that underpin self-interested practices are justified. Indeed, corporations often promote legislation that clearly benefits themselves and not society, and often prove capable of capturing governmental bodies (e.g. regulators) for their own purposes. This highlights the fact that powerful corporate lobbying entails significant moral and political concerns. Accordingly, it seems that such activities should be considered a part of any meaningful definition of CSR more generally, and political CSR in particular.

In addition to such formalised and legal attempts at influencing national governments, it would seem that discussions of political CSR also need to include more informal, and sometimes illegal, governmental relations. In contrast to writings on corporate government relations in Western democracies, which often emphasise publicly observable lobbying practices, writings on corporate government relations in non-Western countries commonly focus on the importance of more discreet and informal (friendly or familial) networks. Indeed, scholars speculate that

> for many emerging economies, CPA [corporate political activity] essentially involves corruption, or at least the extensive use of connections. The kind of structured CPA known in developed states has been largely presumed not to exist. What takes the place of legitimate CPA in many contexts is corruption or cronyism.
> (Lawton et al., 2012: 92)

Given that the extent to which bribery and corruption exists varies from country to country, it is generally recognised that such (illegal) practices are shaped by a given country's domestic political structure and culture. Moreover, the comparative analysis of foreign direct investment (FDI) suggests that multi-corporate willingness to engage in corrupt practices abroad increases along with the extent of corruption found within its home country (Cuervo-Cazurra, 2006). In addition to being concerned with how corporations seek to influence national governmental actors, then, political CSR should also consider how corporations are shaped by their political environments at 'home' and abroad.

6.3.2 International politics

National and international political matters often overlap in complicated, international, ways. The Siemens bribery scandal of 2008, for example, involved employees within the German engineering giant reportedly paying in the realms of US$1.4 billion in bribes to win contracts in many countries around the world. Further to raising the ire of people globally, and further to other penalties in other countries having to be paid, these bribes resulted in the German company reaching a settlement with the US Securities and Exchange Commission in which the company agreed to disgorge $350 million, and in which they paid a $450 million fine to the US Department of Justice to settle criminal charges.

Despite what such complicated cases suggest, it is still helpful to analytically differentiate between national and international politics. In the present chapter, then, it is suggested that corporate political relations can be said to occur at the national level when they are focused on shaping political environments within discrete state borders (e.g. Siemen's bribing of Greek officials to win contracts within Greece), and at the international level when they are focused on the efforts that corporations make to influence international organisations, international treaties, directives and so on. Moreover, and as summarised in

Table 6.1 Corporate national, international and global governance relations

	Scope	Actors related to	Subject matter
National	Within state boundaries	Mainly national governments	National legislation and regulation
International	Multi-state through global	Mainly national governments and international organisations (e.g. the United Nations, the European Union)	International directives and treaties
Global governance	Regional through global	Mainly NGOs (e.g. those affiliated with the FSC)	International accountability standards

Table 6.1 above, it is suggested that international politics and global governance, while obviously overlapping, can also be distinguished on the basis of the actors that corporations relate to and the subject matter of concern.

Levy and Egan (1998) provide a good illustration of international political corporate relations when they document the multitudinous efforts that corporations made to influence climate change negotiations at the afore-mentioned 1992 UNCED in Rio de Janeiro. In particular, they note that – with 'Maurice Strong, head of the Canadian electric utility Ontario Hydro . . . appointed to the position of secretary general of the conference', and with Strong appointing 'as his principal adviser the Swiss industrialist and multimillionaire Stephan Schmidheiny, who organized' the (World) Business Council for Sustainable Development, 'a group of industrialists representing forty-eight of the world's largest multinational corporations' – corporate interests were better able to 'ensure that the Framework Convention on Climate Change (FCCC) agreed to at the conference contained little commitment to concrete action' (Levy and Egan, 1998: 343). More recently, Banerjee (2012) tells a similar story with regard to the role of industry at the United Nations Durban Climate Change Conference in 2011. In particular, he suggests that the 'Platform for Enhanced Action' that emerged from the conference was a non-binding agreement to reach an agreement at some time in the future, and that this flexible arrangement was more or less consistent with corporate interests at the conference, who tended to argue that:

> emissions reductions would be too costly and would erode the profitability of firms, lead to increased prices for consumers, slow economic recovery, [and] give polluting competitors in developing countries an unfair advantage resulting in the closing down or relocation of plants. (Banerjee, 2012: 1774)

As critical management scholars (e.g. Banerjee, 2012; Levy and Egan, 1998) tend to highlight the efforts that corporations make to block or 'slow down' the development of international standards, it is important to note that corporations can also try to speed them up. Thus, and while it remains an open question as to the genuineness of their claims, it is interesting to note that corporate members of the Business Leaders Initiative on Human Rights (and Global Business Initiative on Human Rights) profess to support the John Ruggie-authored UN *Guiding Principles on Business and Human Rights*. Accordingly, they appear to implicitly support Ruggie's position, which pragmatically emphasises that many international treaties already require government signatories to strengthen the regulative and legislative measures they can use to protect citizens from corporate-related human rights abuses.

6.4 The Political Importance of Products and Services

The preceding two sections have emphasised the various ways in which corporations relate to non-governmental and governmental actors in an effort to shape their political environments at the national and global level. In the present section, by way of contrast, the more immediate and direct political importance of corporations is emphasised. Following on from the views of such famous historical figures as Karl Marx, the political importance of corporate products and services has recently been suggested by social scientists and philosophers focused on the study of science, technology, and information and communication technologies (e.g. Italian philosopher Luciano Floridi, Spanish sociologist Manuel Castells). While the importance of such developments is conceivable in multiple ways, commentators often focus on the (overlapping) political changes, both positive and negative, that high-technology contributes to at the individual and societal levels.

At the individual level, for example, there is significant concern regarding the now 'extensive evidence documenting a relationship between depression and excessive texting, viewing video clips, video gaming, chatting, e-mailing, listening to music and other media uses' (Rosen, Whaling, Rab, Carrier and Cheever, 2013: 1244). More dynamically, there is evidence of a 'relatively new phenomenon, "phantom vibration syndrome" – perceived vibration from a cell phone that is not vibrating – [that] has been reported to occur with large numbers of people' (Rosen et al., 2013: 1245). Furthermore, there is concern that:

> narcissism is exacerbated, and even encouraged, by social
> networking sites ... that encourage users to post status updates and
> photos and comment on others' posts and photos. For example, on
> these sites, people often report the existence of superficial friendships,

self-promotion by way of customizable pages, and vanity by way
of photo albums capable of carrying thousands of pictures.
(Rosen et al., 2013: 1244)

Although these sorts of developments may appear of more moral than political
concern, the fact that they are largely the result of commercially sold products and
services quickly raises questions about who is, or should be, held (morally and
politically) responsible. Is it, for example, the responsibility of governments to
regulate and legislate, and provide education and health services that seek to
address the (potential) problems associated with such psychological changes and
mental health problems? Or is it the corporations who provide them? If it is the
job of corporations, then do they need to be made the subject of some sort of
democratic oversight, or part of some sort of MSI, that can better ensure accountability and legitimacy? While answers to such questions cannot be provided in
the present chapter, the simple raising of them suffices to highlight how the
development of products and services is very quickly perceived as political.

In a more immediately political fashion, there is also evidence to suggest that
use of social media or network sites for news is positively related to social
capital, civic participation, political participation offline and political participation online (Gil de Zúñiga, 2013). As such evidence begins to suggest, there is a
growing recognition that while the Internet and social media may not necessarily result in an increasingly democratic or liberal world, they are at the very
least changing political relations. With specific regard to issues of corporate
citizenship and social responsibility, Whelan, Moon and Grant have argued that
the Internet and social media contribute to significant alterations in the arenas
within which corporations and citizens can interact with, and seek to influence,
each other (e.g. on Twitter, Facebook and so on) (Whelan, Moon and Grant,
2013). More pointedly, they suggest that whereas prior understandings of
corporate citizenship have, in being influenced by stakeholder thinking, tended
to emphasise the importance of corporations engaging with formally and
functionally organised stakeholder groups (e.g., consumer protection organisations, environmental NGOs), the emergence of online networking technologies
suggests that corporations will also have to increasingly engage with individual
citizens, and loose collections or movements thereof. Additionally, they suggest
that because corporations such as Google, Facebook and Twitter control
hitherto unforeseen networking and informational resources (that can be used
for good or bad, by themselves and others), they are becoming corporate
citizens of some significant capacity. Thus, the question as to what sort of
'corporate citizens' these organisations currently are, or what sort of corporate
citizens they should become, is likely to prove of increasing importance.

Further to their contributing to transformations in political and social
communications, the ongoing revolution in information and communications
technologies is contributing to developments in high-technology that are having
a significant impact on political relations – e.g. violent political relations – more

generally. Most significantly for this chapter, leading corporations such as Google are playing an increasing role in such transformative developments, often as a result of purchases they have recently made. It is thus interesting to note that in 2013, Google bought the robotics company Boston Dynamics. Boston Dynamics is a 1992 spin-off from the world-leading technological university MIT (Massachusetts Institute of Technology), has close links to the US military, and builds animal-like and humanoid robots. As noted on their website, one of Boston Dynamics's products, LS3 (Legged Squat Support Systems):

> is a rough-terrain robot designed to go anywhere Marines and Soldiers go on foot, helping carry their load. Each LS3 carries up to 400 lbs of gear and enough fuel for a 20-mile mission lasting 24 hours. LS3 automatically follows its leader using computer vision, so it does not need a dedicated driver. It also travels to designated locations using terrain sensing and GPS. LS3 began a 2-year field testing phase in 2012.

And in referring back to the sorts of concerns that underpinned the nineteenth-century analysis of Marx and Engels, it should also be highlighted that in buying a multitude of other robotics companies – e.g. Google has bought Meka and Redwood Robotics, who make humanoid robots and robot arms in San Francisco, and have also bought Bot and Dolly, a maker of robotic camera systems that are used in films, advertisements and so on – it appears that Google's products also have the capacity to transform relations between labour and capital. Indeed, Frey and Osborne (see annotated list of readings) have recently predicted that advances in fields relating to machine learning, artificial intelligence and mobile robotics (MR) have the potential to make 47 per cent of total US employment automatable within the next couple of decades. As a result, it seems that such corporate enabled high-technology transformations should be accounted for by any meaningful conception of political CSR.

6.5 Case Study: Google Glass – The Future of Political Transparency?

ALL THAT HAPPENS MUST BE KNOWN
                              (The Circle's Mission, in Eggers, 2013: 67)

Google's mission is to organize the world's information and make it universally accessible and useful.

                              (Google Mission Statement)

In a 2013 work, David Eggers conceives of a company known as 'The Circle' that has encompassed all the large social media and search companies of today, and has thus succeeded in becoming a veritable corporate behemoth. In one part of the book, the story is told of a Circle employee named 'Stewart, the Transparent Man', who records (all of) his life for five years with something like a telephoto lens that he had hung round his neck (Eggers, 2013: 205). More specifically, the story is told of a Congresswoman Olivia Santos, the (fictional) representative for the Circle's own area, District 14, who decides to follow Stewart's lead, and who – in speaking to 'Circlers' in the Circle's 'Great Hall' on the Circle's 'campus' – states that:

> We've all wanted and expected transparency from our elected leaders, but the technology wasn't there to make it fully possible. But now it is . . . So I intend to follow Stewart on his path of illumination. And along the way, I intend to show how democracy can and should be: entirely open, entirely transparent. Starting today, I will be wearing the same device that Stewart wears. My every meeting, movement, my every word, will be available to all my constituents and to the world . . . [And as for those who want to meet with me but do not want to be broadcast] Well, then they will not meet with me . . . You're either transparent or you're not. You're either accountable or you're not. What would anyone have to say to me that couldn't be said in public? What part of representing the people should not be known by the very people I'm representing? (Eggers, 2013: 208–209)

While this fictional quest for 'total transparency' may have once seemed fanciful, the development of 'Google Glass' suggests it is now a very real possibility. The (still in development) Google Glass (digitised glasses) can be used to record events and interactions experienced by their wearer, and that, with the aid of apps such as Livestream, can be used to broadcast live events (and seemingly meetings or experiences more generally). It is thus not much of a jump to expect that politicians will soon use Google Glass or something very similar to it (albeit not all the time as with Egger's fictional Congresswoman Santos). Indeed, in May 2013, almost half a year before Egger's fictional work *The Circle* was even released (on 8 October 2013), former Republican Congresswoman and current member of the US House of Representatives, Michele Bachmann:

> was among those who tried on a pair of the new glasses. In an email, a representative for Bachmann told ABC News that the congresswoman enjoyed trying on Google Glass because she 'likes being ahead of the curve when it comes to innovative technology' and believes 'it is a testament to just how much the industry has evolved.' (Wiersema, 2013)

Further to such political 'try outs', Red Edge, a digital advocacy firm in the US with conservative (republican) allegiances, has developed an 'augmented advocacy' app for Google Glass that is contextually aware in that it alerts the wearer to information when they are in a specific place. For example, the app would alert the wearer to how 'massive' government spending is by displaying information regarding the total spending of the Internal Revenue Service (IRS) as and when the wearer walks past the IRS building in Washington DC. Or, it would reveal the cost of a government-sponsored infrastructure project, museum, bridge, etc. In doing so, the Red Edge development team have the professed aim of increasing transparency.

As these ongoing developments indicate, it is clear that products and services from a company such as Google can transform, potentially significantly, key political concerns such as transparency. Nevertheless, it is important to remember that corporations such as Google, no matter how transformative and unexpected their products and services may be, often act in predictable and rather basic ways. In the present context, then, it is of specific interest to refer to a May 2014 article in which Lisa Gilbert and Sam Jeweler suggest that while Google can see our 'Internet searches, our inboxes, our contacts, our instant messages, our use of maps to get around, our shared documents, and more', we know little 'about what the tech giant is spending to influence' the US government. More specifically, they write that:

> The CPA-Zicklin Index of the Center for Political Accountability rates Google's disclosure policy at 51.4 percent – decidedly average among a class of Fortune 500 companies with voluntary disclosure policies.
> Though Google isn't the worst of the worst, it claims transparency and good corporate citizenship while trailing peers like Ebay (64.3 percent), Hewlett-Packard (67.1 percent), Dell (77.1 percent), Intel (88.6 percent) and Microsoft (92.9 percent) on the index.

In short, Gilbert and Jeweler suggest that while a great many of us are (increasingly) transparent to a company like Google, Google is, in terms of its political relations, far from transparent to us (Gilbert and Jeweler, 2014). Furthermore, that fact that the 'core' algorithm(s) behind Google's Internet search business is a (fairly well-kept) trade secret, quickly highlights that effectively all of us are completely 'in the dark' when it comes to Google's otherwise 'illuminating' search function. And, when this darkness is combined with the seeming lack of light currently cast on just who it is that can and cannot access the information that a company such as Google gathers – as the Prism scandal actualised by Edward Snowden clearly indicates – the fact that corporate products, services and relations can all be of overlapping importance for our conception of political CSR seems clear.

Questions for Discussion

1. What is 'total transparency'? Is it desirable?
2. Are users of Google products transparent to Google?
3. Is Google transparent to its users?

6.6 Chapter Summary

This chapter began by introducing you to the 'political' CSR literature. In particular, it was noted that the 'political' CSR literature is notable for the emphasis it has placed on 'governance gaps' or 'regulatory vacuums', for its proposing that MSIs (such as the United Nations Global Compact) do and should play a key role in addressing such 'gaps' or 'vacuums', and for its more general concern with 'democratising' MNCs. Given these discussions, and the critically informed literature thereon, it was then proposed that political CSR should be conceived more capaciously, so that in addition to global governance matters, it should also include matters of international politics: e.g. corporate lobbying and corruption, corporate pressure on international organisations and treaties.

Following this, discussions of high-technology were used to illustrate the need for political CSR to be conceived as also including the direct political importance of corporate products and services. In particular, reference was made to the manner in which developments in social media can impact on an individual level (e.g. mental health, narcissism) and more social level (e.g. political participation) considerations. Additionally, it was noted that through producing technologies of war, and through transforming means of production, the products and services of high-technology corporations can significantly impact on political concerns of widespread importance. Finally, the chapter provided a case study in which David Egger's fictional work *The Circle* was used to introduce and contextualise the potential political importance of a product such as Google Glass, and its impact on transparency considerations in particular.

As these summarising remarks indicate, the general thrust of this chapter is to encourage you to recognise that corporations are indeed political bodies. Further to recognising the relations they form with both NGOs and governmental/state actors then (which are exhaustively discussed throughout the CSR and CPA literatures respectively), you are encouraged to recognise that what corporations do on a daily basis by 'themselves' – i.e. create and try to sell products and services – can often be conceived in political terms. Thus, our understanding of political CSR needs to inform our understanding of corporate relations *and* corporate creations.

Chapter Questions

1. What are 'governance gaps', and how do they relate to 'political' CSR?
2. Are MSIs democratic?
3. Should corporate governance structures be democratic?

4. How can corporations seek to influence national governmental actors in legal and illegal ways?
5. How can corporate national and international political relations be distinguished?
6. Can you provide an example of corporations influencing international standards?
7. How can high-technology products and services impact on mental health and self-identity?
8. How do high-technology products and services change political communicative interactions?
9. Can high-technology corporations help revolutionise modern warfare? If so, how?

FURTHER RESOURCES

Epstein, E. J. (1996). *Dossier: The Secret History of Armand Hammer.* New York: Carrol and Graf.

For a real-life story of corporations and politics you couldn't make up, Epstein's story of Armand Hammer is hard to beat. Epstein reveals that Hammer – the key player in the emergence of the still existent Occidental Petroleum Corporation; a significant benefactor to the arts; and self-proclaimed champion of world peace – had (covert) links to the Soviet Union throughout much of his career, and played a seemingly key role in changing the nature of oil geopolitics. For a primer on the importance and vanity of corporate political relations, this book is hard to beat.

Frey, C. B. and Osborne, M. A. (2013). The Future of Employment: How Susceptible are Jobs to Computerization? *Oxford Martin School Working Paper.* September 2013. Oxford: Oxford Martin School, University of Oxford.

Although currently a working paper, Frey and Osborne's piece on how computerisation is changing the nature of employment makes interesting reading. While not altogether surprising, their findings that jobs requiring knowledge of human heuristics (judgement and decision-making), and jobs involving the development of novel ideas and artefacts (e.g. products), are at lowest risk of computerisation, seems important for students concerned to 'future-proof' their careers.

Gibson, W. (2014). *The Peripheral.* London: Viking.

Almost any part of Gibson's seminal body of work could be referred to here. Nevertheless, his latest work *The Peripheral* is intriguing for its parallel world storyline, and the role that (shady) corporate interests play therein. High-tech throughout – the book's title refers to the possibility of individuals in one world 'inhabiting' androids or robots in another – Gibson's work provides a very clear illustration of the ways in which high-technology corporations can transform political realities (or even multiply them).

Schmidt, E. and Cohen, J. (2010). The Digital Disruption. *Foreign Affairs*, 89(6), 75–85.
Eric Schmidt, Executive Chairman of Google, and Jared Cohen, head of Google's think/do tank Google Ideas, use their *Foreign Affairs* article to discuss the political importance of Internet and social media technologies. Among other things, they suggest that democratic states around the world should link up with information and communication technology corporations, as well as civil society actors, to form a 'coalition of the connected' that will promote democracy worldwide. In doing so, they provide Google's view of the need to link corporate relational and productive political capacities.

Personal Reflection by *Mads Øvlisen*

Doing the Right Thing is not an Option. It is a Must

A reflection on CSR must necessarily be a reflection on my work at NOVO. I cannot point to any particular incident that made us sit down and decide 'we must become socially responsible'. CSR was not another tool which was added to our strategic armoury.

CSR was just our way of doing business; we believed it was the right way to do business.

I have, basically, spent my entire working life with NOVO. It was Novo Therapeutic Laboratory A/S when I started in 1972, then became Novo Nordisk upon the merger in 1989 with Nordisk Gentofte A/S, and finally, Novo Nordisk and Novozymes in 2000 when we split the businesses and I retired as CEO to become chairman of the new Novo Nordisk A/S.

I had not planned to work at NOVO: the company was founded by my wife's grandfather and his brother. My father-in-law was the CEO, and vanity dictated me to make it outside the family company. Yet, I was recruited for a one-year term to prepare the company's IPO, i.e. Initial Public Offering, which was the first sale of stock by Novo to the public. That one year gradually became 34 years! What made me stay that long? The challenging prospect of being part of a team committed to unlocking what we believed was a great global growth potential AND the company's culture of social responsibility.

NOVO was owned by an industrial foundation, the NOVO foundation, to which the founders in 1952 had transferred the dominant voting power to secure – as they said at the time – the future of the company 'and of those who had tied their destiny to the company'. The founders' offspring received shares with little voting influence: the brothers did not believe that ownership equalled leadership, hence the voting power to the independent foundation. For many years no dividends were paid and all earnings were ploughed back into the business.

We decided to invite Mads Øvlisen for his reflection on management motivations and strategies in view of his lifelong experience as CEO (1981–2000) and Chairman (2000–2006) of Novo Nordisk A/S. In this capacity Mr Øvlisen took an early leadership in promoting the importance of CSR for other business managers in Denmark and internationally. He was Chair for the Danish Government's Council for Corporate Social Responsibility, and today he is a Senior Advisor for UN Global Compact and was recently appointed as Chair of the National OECD Contact Point for Mediation and Complaints.

This concern for employees was always the backbone of NOVO and today still reflects the caring culture of the company. Employees received several benefits from the company (which only later were provided by the Danish welfare state): economic help, extra time off, milk money and other help to new mothers, better sick leave and pay schemes than in most other organisations. The employees, said founders Harald and Thorvald Pedersen, invested themselves in the company, which in return should invest in them.

'Who says that you at your own discretion can start a business, recruit society's brightest, use public services and infrastructure without having an obligation to pay back?', my CEO father-in-law, K. Hallas-Møller, asked.

In 1979, I accepted an invitation to make a presentation on 'The Role of Business in Society' to a group of very senior Danish executives who had heard about our business goals and priorities, and they were particularly interested to know about our values-based management and our engagement with society. My talk insisted that the business of business was more than maximising shareholder wealth through profit maximisation.

As a business we depend on society in many regards, and we had to take a wide range of shareholder interests into consideration if the company was to be successful. NOVO's success depended not only on an inflow of share capital, but also importantly on our ability to attract talented young people, to achieve a license to conduct our research and development (including the novel genetic engineering), in a way that the public trusted. For example we had to conduct experiments in such a way that animal welfare groups did not block our gates, i.e. we had to conduct our business in a way that took the concerns and demands of several stakeholders into consideration, even though it might reduce short-term profitability. True, this was to some extent driven by a sense of utility, but overriding was a sense of decency. I never did a financial calculation. It was not a 'quid pro quo'. It was simply, morally the 'RIGHT' way to do business.

In 1976, something happened that influenced me and my colleagues for the rest of our professional lives. One of NOVO's commercially most important products was an oral contraceptive. Unfinished animal experiments indicated that there was a risk of cancer connected with the active ingredient in the pill. Hallas-Møller immediately called a meeting of the six person executive management team; four of us were aged between thirty-two and thirty-six years old. We discussed the preliminary findings, which were indeed preliminary, but Hallas was in no doubt that we had to discontinue this product line, not only in sales, but also in R&D. There was no official demand to do so, but how could a company dedicated to improving people's health bring a product that might not be safe to market? The decision was implemented forthwith. Considerable loss of revenue followed and several jobs were lost. But not one person was dismissed. Job sharing and other initiatives were put into place until our other business areas had brought full employment back. Further research did not confirm the health risk. But we, the 'aspiring eagles', had learned an important lesson about never compromising ethical values for business opportunities.

I was influenced not only by company culture, but also later by discussions I had with Professor of Business Ethics Peter Pruzan and Professor of Philosophy Ole Thyssen at Copenhagen Business School. In the 1980s they were frontrunners in the development of green accounts, and our discussions about stakeholder interests were an important source of inspiration. Being green and having a sustainability agenda was not only a matter of a reporting principle; the challenge was to make sustainability or CSR a business principle. We wanted CSR to be something that continuously guided our business decisions and behaviour, not only how we might split costs and expenses into, for example, environmental investments ex post. Or put differently: CSR is not just about how you spend your money, it is very much a question of how you earn it.

When I was hired, the company had a staff of 1,200 and DKK 1 million in net profit. In 1981, when I became CEO, we had grown to 3,700 employees and a net profit of DKK 365 million. The NOVO ambition that I shared with my colleagues was to become 'a respected company'. Respected for our results and, not the least, for the way in which they were achieved. The financial bottom line alone was not what drove us. It was critically important as a means to an end, but not as an end in itself. And I never imagined that the talent we wanted to attract would find it meaningful to go to work with an exclusive focus on a financial bottom line. People want goals and values they can identify with and personally work and stand for.

Growing globally we established affiliates in many markets, sales offices, labs and production facilities. This brought us into direct contact with persons and communities with basic development needs, which we had to take into consideration, not as charity, but as our way of doing business guided by our values. Our actions were watched carefully not only by NGOs, but also by Novo Nordisk people, who would not have accepted double standards. They would have criticised management if we had made plant location decisions based on lax environmental demands, and would have felt that we betrayed those values, which they identified with and gave them a sense of pride. So a corporate shared conscience of universally 'walking the talk' was an important monitor of responsible corporate behaviour.

We of course had to make investors aware of our priorities. In the 1970s, this was quite an educational task. When we were listed at NYSE, we stated our goals as being 'Best in our businesses and a challenging place to work'. We were in business to do well by outcompeting competition, and social responsibility, using our core competences to address needs in society, was a key part of our competitiveness. Our employees were challenged to take such issues into consideration as an integrated part of every business decision.

In the mid-1990s we realised that we had to be able to document that we did indeed live our values. We had grown considerably, globally, and had to be certain that our claims were not hot air. 'Trust us' had been replaced by the critical stakeholder demand 'Show us'. We therefore initiated a 'Values in Action' programme, where Novo Nordisk people all over the world were asked to report on attitudes and activities which were in conflict with our values and to recommend corrective actions. The results were encouraging and covered a wide range of issues – from how to balance a dominant foundation ownership with good corporate governance to a review of the safety of the already publicly approved use of spent biomass as fertiliser. These were recommendations that we followed and which left us well prepared for later discussions with stakeholders.

In 2001, Novo Nordisk was confronted with criticism from NGOs, as we were part of a pharmaceutical industry association that was accused of giving priority to profits at the expense of improving health for less advantaged people in South Africa. We decided to respond immediately to this concern, and we engaged in many dialogues with NGOs and other relevant stakeholders. This led to our defining a new pricing policy but also importantly a new policy to strengthen our presence and development of medicines to combat diabetes in developing countries.

That same year, shareholders decided to vote for a proposal from executive management to allocate part of the company's income to establish and initially fund 'The World Diabetes Foundation'. The foundation's aim is 'to alleviate human suffering related to diabetes and its complications among those least able to withstand the burden of the disease'. This decision was made in the context of our learnings from South Africa, but also the alarming rise of diabetes in developing countries came more broadly to our attention. Till then it was a fact that was grossly neglected, mainly due to other health priorities. The World Diabetes Foundation reports that it today has grown into a leading international funding agency, supporting grassroots initiatives in the area of diabetes prevention and care.

And, yet, I felt a need to be more explicit. Realising that quite a few financial analysts made their buy/sell recommendations on financial analysis alone, I suggested to our shareholders that we amended the company's Articles of Association (i.e. the bylaws) to include a sentence in the clause 'objects' to state that 'The Company strives to conduct its business activities in a financially, environmentally, and socially responsible way.' Not a single, but a triple bottom line was institutionalised by this change. This was approved at the Annual General Meeting of shareholders in 2004.

I expected my successors, Lars Rebien Sørensen, Novo Nordisk and Steen Riisgaard, Novozymes, to be pleased with this 'Shareholders, be forewarned: here is a company that may forego short-term profits for long-term survival and impact' statement. But no. Lars said, 'Mads, you were right, it is the RIGHT way to do business, but it is also a GOOD way of doing business so we don't need your disclaimer.'

Dialogue is a cornerstone for the culture of NOVO. In the NOVO family group we established our CSR goals in close dialogue with each other.

Becoming aware of issues in society that might need our attention, we would first discuss them internally, often based upon an analysis by external experts, with employee groups and develop a strategy. We would then discuss it with stakeholders; first of all, with NGOs. Many NGOs have highly educated staff members with such backgrounds in the sciences that they can challenge our assumptions and plans. So either you improve your arguments or modify your strategy.

In the beginning, NGOs found it problematic to attend. They did understandably not want to risk being taken hostage by a company. But John Elkington, author and founder of Sustainability in London, helped us make it happen. The meetings took several hours, sometimes more than a day, and the NGO representatives were invited to discuss concerns directly with the responsible Novo Nordisk people.

I firmly believe that such dialogues are essential not only to your CSR activities, but to your overall business success. You cannot create your social goals in a vacuum. The internal dialogue and commitment from employees are critical in creating ownership and supportive action. The external dialogue establishes relevance and priorities. This is where the company confronts its values-based actions with the values of other stakeholders. And in my view the whole discussion is one of understanding each other's values with the purpose of sharing 'values', rather than, as Vallentin and Spence point out in Chapter 3, sharing 'value'. The dialogue with stakeholders will often inspire you to different ways of conducting your business and thus contribute to a broader business renewal. Honest and transparent reporting on progress and setbacks relative to CSR and sustainability goals is of course crucial for this dialogue, which must be anchored in and encouraged by the top executive.

Has it been worth it? Has it been worth getting involved in 'society's business', the realm of politicians and civil servants? This question implies a choice; a choice I do not believe you have.

CSR is in the domain of **soft law**, and many people are tempted to consider it a voluntary concept. I disagree. Just because CSR is considered a soft law does not mean that you can act as you please. A social responsibility is much more than a voluntary act. To me it has been a personal privilege to do business in a way that enriches not only the company, but also society at large.

In my role as an Advisor to the United Nations Global Compact (UNGC), the strength of soft law has become even clearer to me. The UNGC has had implications for how decisions are gradually shaped and made in the global community of UNGC signatory companies. There is no easy or straightforward pathway to join forces and agree on a shared commitment to improve social and environmental impact among companies across the world, but it is indeed a much needed effort. I know that the UNGC goals are continuously critiqued for being 'only words on paper', but today we have many examples of how such 'soft words' become very 'hard' and 'material', when they are translated into practice by multinational companies with the resources and the desire to do better.

And I am convinced that the Sustainable Development Goals agreed upon in 2015 will prove the basis for new impactful concerted action.

So, once more, was it worth it? Wrong question, as this in my view is the only way. And it has been extremely rewarding. My biggest personal reward was the pride the many people who *are* Novo Nordisk and Novozymes feel when they themselves identify with a company that is doing well by doing right. All over the world NOVO family members have testified to this by voting their company the best place to work, pointing to the values of the company and its social responsibility commitment. I take that as a strong indication of Novo Nordisk's commitment to CSR. Because employees will be the first to know if a company does not try to live up to its CSR commitment.

PART II   THE REGULATORY DYNAMICS OF CSR

Introduction from the Editors

Part I focused on how business organisations themselves engage in CSR, including how their approaches have long reflected societal, governmental and stakeholder expectations and institutionalising pressures. But CSR is also regulated by actors and mechanisms outside the company. This is the focus of Part II. The chapters examine more specific forms of regulation shaping contemporary CSR, reflecting CSR's shift from 'complete to partial organisation', and its internationalisation which brings new forms of institutionalisation beyond its national configurations. These forms of regulation vary in nature: from NGO threats to corporate reputation and legitimacy; through forms of partnerships that businesses enter with other businesses, NGOs and governments (including for standards and non-financial reporting systems); to incentives and rules devised by governments to encourage and shape CSR.

Andreas Rasche and Sandra Waddock (Chapter 7) introduce CSR standards which are designed to specify particular principles, enable certification, require some form of reporting and evaluate processes of CSR. Rasche and Waddock indicate how CSR standards have proliferated and strengthened, including through interaction with governmental regulation. They consider their legitimacy and wider impact on firms, consumers and the issues the CSR standards address. Finally, Rasche and Waddock weigh up some of the criticisms of CSR standards as a form of business regulation.

In Chapter 8 Christian Herzig and Anna-Lena Kühn present an overview of the development and main forms of non-financial reporting. They detail how companies have shown a great interest in this form of reporting, and the different national and sector approaches that have emerged. Herzig and Kühn investigate the underlying involvement with stakeholders, the significance of the Internet as the medium for reporting, the implications of the limited assurance and wider critiques of non-financial reporting.

Frank G. A. de Bakker and Frank den Hond present what is often a more unwelcome form of regulation than detailed in Chapters 7 and 8, namely NGO activism (Chapter 9). They introduce different forms of NGO activism, its impacts on corporations and how corporations respond. De Bakker and den Hond also reveal how NGOs can adopt less hostile strategies to regulate firms through partnerships, and how other NGOs develop their own business models to advance their social objectives.

In Chapter 10, Jette Steen Knudsen explores the development of regulation of CSR by and with governments. She presents evidence of the growth of government policies for CSR, and outlines their issue focus and regulatory form. A clear picture arises both of governments regulating or structuring the conditions in which CSR takes place, and of making policies directly to turn CSR to the respective governments' own specific objectives. Knudsen explores this theme with particular reference to national governmental regulation for international CSR issues.

7

Standards for CSR: Legitimacy, Impact and Critique

ANDREAS RASCHE AND SANDRA WADDOCK

Learning Objectives

- Understand what different types of CSR standards exist.
- Explain how to judge the democratic legitimacy of CSR standards.
- Discuss in what ways CSR standards can impact firms and consumers.
- Distinguish different types of critique raised against CSR standards.
- Understand the problems and benefits created by the UN Global Compact.

7.1 Introduction: The Emergence of Private Regulation

In the 1980s, a number of non-governmental organisations (NGOs) organised consumer boycotts against major retailers that were selling products based on tropical woods. The main goal was to tackle deforestation and associated problems (e.g. carbon sequestration). Some NGOs, such as Friends of the Earth, even started to introduce their own labelling and certification schemes. However, as the sourcing of tropical woods is based on long and complex commodity chains, these first attempts to regulate deforestation through voluntary measures remained without much impact. NGOs were convinced that intergovernmental action was needed; they lobbied the International Tropical Timber Organization (ITTO) to adopt a legally binding and government-sanctioned certification scheme. Some hoped that negotiations at the 1992 Earth Summit in Rio de Janeiro would produce such an intergovernmental agreement. Yet, governments showed little interest in adopting a legally binding forest convention that would have helped to tackle the negative effects of deforestation (Gulbrandsen, 2012). As a response, some environmental NGOs (most notably World Wide Fund for Nature (WWF)) were convinced that without the voluntary participation of major industry players (e.g. retailers and manufacturers), a wide-ranging certification programme could not be established. In 1993, a number of parties, including social and environmental NGOs, industry representatives and auditors, met in Toronto to launch the first voluntary certification standard to regulate deforestation: the Forest Steward-ship Council (FSC) was born.

The FSC example points to one consequence of the globalisation of business activity. While companies can split their value chain activities across countries (e.g. to reap the benefits of low wages and access to natural resources), governmental regulation is often still bound to national borders, impeding the effective regulation of transnational social and environmental problems. The emergence of such governance gaps (i.e. areas in which governments and intergovernmental institutions do not contribute much, if at all, to problem solutions) has spurred the proliferation of private global business regulation. Such regulation is usually based on the adoption of voluntary CSR standards, including principles, certification, reporting and process standards, which firms voluntarily join. Unlike other forms of regulation, governmental actors do not have the capacity today to enforce such standards through legal requirements or sanctions. Businesses have different motivations for joining CSR standards, ranging from providing a response to activism by civil society actors to avoiding future legal regulations and gaining market share (e.g. by selling certified products).

This chapter discusses the nature, origins and impacts of CSR standards. Section 7.2 develops a definition of CSR standards and distinguishes four different types. This discussion shows that while standardisation in the field of CSR has grown in recent years, existing initiatives differ in a number of important ways. Section 7.3 discusses how the democratic legitimacy of CSR standards can be assessed. We differentiate between standards' input and output legitimacy. Section 7.4 shows the impact which CSR standards can potentially have on adopting firms, end consumers and the regulated issue area. The next section takes a detailed look at the critique that has been raised against selected standards (e.g. the coexistence of multiple standards with a similar purpose), and the final section develops a case study around one specific initiative: the UN Global Compact.

7.2 CSR Standards: What's in a Name?

7.2.1 Standardising CSR

In their most general sense, standards can be defined as 'rules[s] for common and voluntary use, decided by one or several people or organizations' (Brunsson, Rasche and Seidl, 2012: 616). Standards represent specific types of rules and hence have a regulative capacity. They reflect one specific type of soft law, because they are voluntary for potential adopters and do not rely on legal mandate or sanctioning mechanisms. Legal theory distinguishes between harder and softer forms of law. While hard law is expressed as binding rules (*jus congens*) and usually more precisely formulated, softer forms of law reflect non-mandated norms and expectations that are often framed more vaguely (Abbott, Keohane, Moravcsik, Slaughter and Snidal, 2000). Because soft law does not rest on the authority of states to enforce its rules, it is the various initiatives' perceived legitimacy and, in some cases, pressure by third parties that influence the underlying capacity to regulate.

'CSR standards' is an umbrella term to describe those forms of soft law that promulgate predefined rules and/or procedures to guide, assess, measure, verify and/or communicate the social and environmental performance of firms (Gilbert, Rasche and Waddock, 2011). Unlike company codes of conduct, which are internally generated, firms adopting CSR standards cannot completely define the content of initiatives; CSR standards are decided 'outside' individual firms by coalitions of engaged stakeholders. While internal codes of conduct are developed by individual companies and hence are only applicable within the scope of a firm's activities (e.g. to govern their supply chain; see Chapter 18), most CSR standards are governed as multi-stakeholder initiatives (MSIs). They have governance bodies in which the voices of different groups (e.g. NGOs, firms, unions) are heard. These governance bodies regulate essential decisions such as the nature and content of standards, who is able to join, and which complaint and dispute resolution mechanisms exist. Some standards do not follow the multi-stakeholder format and are designed as exclusive alliances among business actors (e.g. the Business Social Compliance Initiative).

7.2.2 Types of CSR Standard

CSR standards differ along a number of dimensions. We cluster existing initiatives along four categories (see also Gilbert et al., 2011). *Principle-based standards* reflect broadly defined guidelines to steer participants' behaviour on social and environmental issues. Well-known examples include the UN Global Compact, the Organisation for Economic Cooperation and Development (OECD) Guidelines for Multinational Enterprises, the Principles for Responsible Investment and the Equator Principles. These standards reflect a baseline of foundational values and guidelines that businesses can use as a starting point for initiating actions around CSR. For instance, the Equator Principles represent a framework for financial institutions to determine the social and environmental risks involved in project financing (e.g. for large-scale projects such as the construction of river dams or power plants). In some cases, the underlying principles act as a framework for dialogue, learning and the exchange of best practices among participants. Most firms use principle-based standards as a baseline to develop their own internal policies and management processes around CSR. Although principle-based standards do not include verification mechanisms, they try to identify noncompliant participants through other, usually 'softer', means. For example, the UN Global Compact and the Equator Principles force their participants to report on implementation progress, while the OECD Guidelines for Multinational Enterprises contain National Contact Points that are supposed to mediate when an external party raises concerns regarding a firm's behaviour.

Certification standards are more focused on compliance with a set of expected practices, behaviours or principles. Verification rests on certification procedures in which auditors assess practices in factories or farms. Many standards define performance criteria for an industry or set of companies, for example, to ensure decent workplace conditions (e.g. the Fair Labor Association (FLA) or Social Accountability 8000) or they specify certain targets in terms of environmentally friendly management (e.g. the FSC or the Marine Stewardship Council). Some initiatives also require that adopters integrate the specifications of the standard into their management systems (e.g. human resource or supply chain management). Producers that pass the audit are awarded a seal of approval for a specified period of time. Often, such seals act as a precondition to enter into contractual relationships with multinational corporations (MNCs). Noncompliant producers are asked to correct their practices within a specified timeframe, while in serious cases it is also possible to completely revoke a certificate. Some MNCs drop noncompliant suppliers, farms or factories. The standard-setting bodies usually do not perform any audits themselves. Rather, they have rules for accrediting external parties ('certification bodies'), which are then allowed to carry out inspections. A number of standards contain tracking requirements for tracing products from certified production facilities through to the end consumer.

Reporting standards offer frameworks for transparency, that is, disclosing information on a firm's social, environmental and economic performance. Although some firms reported non-financial information in the 1980s and 1990s, comparing the content of these reports and benchmark companies was difficult. Because reporting was not standardised, businesses disclosed whatever information they felt was appropriate. In 2000, the Global Reporting Initiative (GRI) released its first standard to harmonise the disclosure of non-financial or ESG (environmental, social and governance) information (see also Chapter 8). Although other specialised reporting frameworks exist (e.g. Carbon Disclosure Project), the GRI quickly emerged as the de facto global standard for communicating around CSR-related issues (Etzion and Ferraro, 2010). Most reporting standards consist of predefined standard disclosures (telling adopters what information to report) and reporting principles (advising adopters how to manage the reporting process). Recently, some businesses have moved towards adopting a new framework on **integrated reporting** launched by the International Integrated Reporting Council (IIRC). Integrated reporting overcomes the tension between financial and non-financial reporting, and is instead focused on how different types of capital (e.g. human, financial, social, natural) interact and create value for an organisation and society.

Whereas principle-based and certification standards set certain performance requirements that adopters have to meet, *process standards* do not outline any performance criteria. Rather, these standards give guidance on how to understand key terms that relate to the CSR debate and outline management processes in relation to activities which have an impact on social and environmental issues. Well-known examples of process standards include ISO 14001 as well as ISO 26000. Launched in 2010, ISO 26000 defines key terms that are fundamental to understanding an organisation's social responsibility (e.g. accountability and transparency) and describes processes that need to be managed during implementation (e.g. building competency and communicating results). ISO 14001 is more narrowly focused on those processes that are needed to build an environmental management system. The standard is not focused on the product or service that a firm produces, but focuses entirely on the environmental impact of those organisational processes that are needed for value creation. For instance, ISO 14001 asks adopters to assess the direct environmental impact of manufacturing processes and also the more indirect impact of raw material sourcing. The AA1000 standard series reflects another well-known set of process standards. The AA1000 Stakeholder Engagement Standard defines key terms related to stakeholder engagement and outlines an organisational framework to manage relevant processes (e.g. identifying stakeholders).

Although the four categories of CSR standards help us to navigate the landscape of initiatives (for an overview, see Table 7.1), there is overlap among the categories, and a single standard may exhibit features of more than one category. For instance, ISO 14001 is not only a process standard but also contains elements of a certification standard. Certifications are performed by third-party organisations and not ISO itself. By contrast, ISO 26000 is not designed for certification and hence cannot be used in this way. Some certification standards also define relevant management processes. SA 8000, for example, not only sets performance criteria with regard to working conditions but also outlines a number of management processes that impact whether labour rights are lived in a factory. It is hard to standardise the field of CSR standards, and we need to keep its heterogeneous nature in mind.

7.2.3 Interactions of CSR Standards with Government-Based Regulation

CSR standards do not work in isolation. Often, they interact with other forms of regulation, most of all with the work of public regulatory agencies. It is possible to distinguish three types of interactions among standards and government-based regulation (Steering Committee of the State-of-Knowledge Assessment of Standards and Certification, 2012). In some cases, governments have *superseded* CSR standards, for instance when state-based actors start to

Table 7.1 Overview of different types of CSR standards

	Principle-based standards	Certification standards	Reporting standards	Process standards
Description	Broadly defined guidelines to steer participants' behaviour with regard to social and environmental issues; foundational values and guidelines that businesses can use as a starting point for initiating actions around CSR.	Focused on verified compliance; verification rests on certification procedures in which auditors assess a single factory or farm; producers that pass the audit are awarded a seal of approval for a specified period of time.	Frameworks for disclosing information on a firm's social, environmental, and economic performance; reports are usually not verified by standard-setters.	Give guidance on how to understand key terms that relate to CSR; outline management processes in relation to activities that impact social or environmental issues; some standards allow for certification.
Exemplary CSR standards	• UN Global Compact • OECD Guidelines for Multinational Enterprises • Principles for Responsible Investment • Equator Principles • Caux Round Table Principles • Global Sullivan Principles	• Forest Stewardship Council • Marine Stewardship Council • Social Accountability 8000 • Fair Labor Association • Fairtrade • Rainforest Alliance • Ethical Trading Initiative • Worker Rights Consortium • Clean Clothes Campaign	• Global Reporting Initiative • Carbon Disclosure Project • International Integrated Reporting Framework • Greenhouse Gas Protocol	• ISO 14001 • ISO 26000 • AA1000 Stakeholder Engagement Framework • AA1000 Assurance Standard

require or incentivise practices that were originally established by standards. The Leadership in Energy and Environmental Design (LEED) certification standard started out as a purely voluntary initiative. It quickly grew into a widely used standard for construction projects; particularly in the US, LEED-certified buildings demonstrated a number of environmental and economic benefits (e.g. reduced energy use). Regulators in the US noted these benefits, and started to incorporate some elements of LEED into building regulations and incentivise builders to consider other elements (e.g. via lower fees or tax credits).

Governmental regulators thus 'took over' parts of the LEED standard and moved the underlying practices into the domain of hard law.

Governments and CSR standards can also interact in a more *symbiotic* way. In this case, governments and standard-setters reinforce each other's actions, with both maintaining full autonomy. When having symbiotic interactions, state regulators do not integrate the content of a standard into hard law. Rather, CSR standards 'fill gaps' in existing legislation and hence supplement legally binding measures. This type of interaction is particularly relevant when considering the incomplete nature of intergovernmental agreements. For instance, the Clean Development Mechanism (CDM) Gold Standard was established to fill gaps in an existing intergovernmental agreement. The CDM, which was originally established as part of the Kyoto Protocol (defined in Article 12) in 1998, was criticised for multiple shortcomings. This weakened its credibility and undercut trust by multiple stakeholders. In 2002, the WWF launched the CDM Gold Standard as a voluntary certification scheme. The Gold Standard reached beyond the original CDM and certified emission-reduction projects. The CDM and the CDM Gold Standard were symbiotic. The Gold Standard addressed some of the deficits of the original CDM and thus made it more attractive. On the other hand, the CDM managed to become more attractive to investors and thus also increased the popularity of the Gold Standard (for more details see Levin, Cashore, and Koppell, 2009).

Finally, there can be *hybrid* interactions between CSR standards and governments. In this case, governmental actors and standard-setters share the work of regulation (either explicitly or implicitly), such as when a CSR standard specifies state-based regulations or when it ensures compliance with these regulations. For instance, while national law does usually not require GRI reporting, some countries have recommended that firms refer to the GRI in order to produce more specific CSR reports. The Danish Financial Statements Act requires CSR reporting for larger businesses; the explanatory notes and guidance documents to the Act encourage the use of the GRI Guidelines. Such hybrid interactions show that there can be many synergies between regulation by state actors and private regulation.

7.3 The Democratic Legitimacy of CSR Standards

The proliferation of CSR standards has created concerns around the level of democratic legitimacy attached to this type of 'privatised' regulation. Government-based regulation through hard law is ideally embedded into some sort of democratic system, in which those who make political decisions are elected to do so. Regulation through CSR standards does not rest on such democratic mechanisms, as we do not elect those who set voluntary standards.

How, then, do CSR standards establish a level of democratic legitimacy that convinces potential adopters, consumers and other parties (e.g. NGOs) that the underlying rules are appropriate?

A regulator's democratic legitimacy refers to the socially shared *belief* that there is a normative obligation to voluntarily comply with rules of governing authority (Scharpf, 2009). Such beliefs are important as they increase the societal acceptance of CSR standards in the absence of electoral democratic mechanisms. The legitimacy demands on CSR standards are more complex than those on governmental regulation, because such standards operate across national borders and hence function against a background of heterogeneous cultural values and traditions. Two different types of legitimacy need to be distinguished. Input legitimacy refers to the belief that 'decisions are derived from the preferences of the population in a chain of accountability linking those governing to those governed' (Mayntz, 2010: 10). In other words, input legitimacy deals mainly with questions of stakeholder involvement in the process of formulating a CSR standard. Output legitimacy, in turn, is 'derived from the capacity of a government or institution to solve collective problems and to meet the expectations of the governed citizens' (ibid.: 10). The output legitimacy of CSR standards depends on their capacity to provide an effective solution to the policy issues that are being addressed.

7.3.1 Input Legitimacy

The level of a standard's input legitimacy can be judged by four factors (Mena and Palazzo, 2012). First, it is influenced by the degree of *inclusion* of diverse stakeholder representatives in a standard's governance structures. Ideally, representatives of all stakeholders affected by the rules of a standard should also be included into its governance. For instance, the FSC includes stakeholders from the social and environmental domain (e.g. relevant NGOs) as well as the economic domain (e.g. companies in the forest and timber industries) in its decision-making structures. Stakeholders from these three sectors are further divided into sub-sectors according to whether they represent the global North or South. Second, a standard's input legitimacy also depends on whether included stakeholders can actually influence relevant decisions. Even though stakeholders can be formally included into governance structures, they do not necessarily need to be given the right to impact decisions. A standard's level of *procedural fairness* reflects whether stakeholders are given a voice and whether power differences among them are neutralised as far as possible.

Third, input legitimacy is influenced by whether the included stakeholders are willing and able to change their positions if others present convincing reasons. CSR standards that are dominated by one particular group (such as business-driven initiatives) are usually less prepared to adopt such a consensual orientation. By contrast, standards with a high *consensual orientation* often have formal dispute settlement processes in place. Finally, input legitimacy also depends on whether stakeholders affected by a CSR standard can evaluate its actions and decisions. Such external evaluation can only take place if standards are *transparent* about how decisions are reached and the performance level of participating companies. The legitimacy of a particular initiative will be higher if it discloses relevant information (e.g. voting procedures, implementation progress).

7.3.2 Output Legitimacy

The level of rule *enforcement* particularly impacts the output legitimacy of CSR standards (Mena and Palazzo, 2012). In what ways do standard-setters ensure that adopters implement their rules? Certification standards usually enjoy higher degrees of output legitimacy, as they involve monitoring procedures to verify compliance with their rules and sanction noncompliant participants. However, the stringency of the underlying rules and the quality of monitoring vary significantly. Business-driven standards are often criticised for relying on less stringent rules, which shield participants from high implementation costs (Auld, 2014). The output legitimacy of CSR standards is also influenced by their *coverage* – i.e. the number of firms that implement the underlying rules. If more firms participate in a standard and obey its rules, then the underlying social or environmental problem can be better addressed. The number of participants is often driven by the so-called 'bandwagon effect'. The more firms participate in a specific initiative, the higher the competitive bandwagon pressure for non-participants, because there is a threat of lost competitive advantage.

Finally, a standard's output legitimacy is also impacted by the fit of its rules to the underlying problem (i.e. its *efficacy*). Some CSR standards have been criticised for issuing rules that are either too general to be implemented in any meaningful way or formulated in ways that do not require significant and costly changes in corporate behaviour. Rules can also be inefficacious with regard to the nature of potential adopters. The rules underlying many CSR standards are written for large (often Western) firms, while the specific problems of smaller companies (in the developing world) are not much considered.

The factors influencing the input and output legitimacy of CSR standards (see Table 7.2 for an overview) are sometimes hard to change because they are subject to differences in power as well as what has happened in the past. In particular, unequal power among actors involved in standards' governance can impede change. Further, once a certain set of actors dominates decision-making, it is difficult to introduce fundamental modifications despite criticism. For instance, the Business Social Compliance Initiative (BSCI), which is governed exclusively by member companies and national trade associations,

Table 7.2 Criteria for input and output legitimacy of CSR standards (adapted from Mena and Palazzo, 2012: 537)

Dimension	Criterion	Definition	Key questions
Input legitimacy	Inclusion	Involvement of stakeholders affected by the issue in the structures and processes of the standard.	Are the involved stakeholders representative for the issue at stake? Are important stakeholders excluded from the process?
	Procedural fairness	Neutralisation of power differences in decision-making structures.	Does each of these categories of stakeholder have a valid voice in decision-making processes?
	Consensual orientation	Culture of cooperation and reasonable disagreement.	To what extent does the standard promote mutual agreement among participants?
	Transparency	Transparency of structures, processes and results.	To what extent are decision-making and standard-setting processes transparent? To what extent are the performance of the participating corporations and the evaluation of that performance transparent?
Output legitimacy	Coverage	Number of rule-targets following the rules.	How many rule-targets are complying with the rules?
	Efficacy	Fit of the rules to the issue.	To what extent do the rules address the issue at hand?
	Enforcement	Practical implementation of the rules and their verification procedures.	Is compliance verified and non-compliance sanctioned?

has been continuously criticised for low levels of transparency. However, the initiative still does not publicly disclose information on factory locations or social audits.

7.4 The Impact of CSR Standards: Greenwash or Transformative Change?

Can voluntary standards effectively discipline the behaviour of firms? Do standards really help to solve the social and environmental problems they are claiming to address? Answers to these questions are context-bound – i.e. they depend on what dimension of impact we study and what type of CSR standard we analyse.

7.4.1 Impact on Adopting Firms

The most widely discussed dimension of impact is whether adopters really implement standards' content. The implementation quality of principle-based initiatives is difficult to evaluate, as there is no clearly defined baseline against which to measure compliance. While these standards can have a high number of participants, their level of compliance often varies significantly (see case study on the UN Global Compact). Hence, we need to distinguish between impact through standards' *diffusion* and impact through standards' *compliance*. CSR standards can be widely diffused and can have many adopters in quantitative terms. However, when the quality of implementation is low, there will only be limited overall impact on firm behaviour.

The diffusion of some CSR standards is impacted by the bilateral foreign direct investment (FDI) activities between two countries. Often, home countries, whose firms operate under a specific standard, 'export' this standard via FDIs into host countries. MNCs' subsidiaries may adopt CSR standards that are also used in their country of origin. It is also possible that CSR standards diffuse in host countries because subsidiaries can create externalities that impact local firms (e.g. when local suppliers are asked to adopt a certain standard). Such FDI-based effects were shown to be relevant in the context of ISO 14001 (Prakash and Potoski, 2007). Trade can also be a driver of standard diffusion. Importing countries' standards are often de facto requirements for firms based in exporting nations. This effect is particularly observable in industries where global brand name companies push certification standards through their supply chain, as in the case of the garment industry. Given that most exports from developing nations are motivated by trade relationships with firms from developed countries, trade often creates incentives to ratchet up social and environmental standards in developing countries.

The strength of a country's regulatory environment and its attitude towards international treaties also affect the diffusion of CSR standards. Firms operating in countries with more stringent social and environmental regulations usually show higher adoption rates. Joining CSR standards helps businesses to comply with existing regulations and to better anticipate the development of the regulatory environment. For example, the UN Global Compact's tenth principle on anti-corruption paved the way for discussions within firms on how best to cope with newly arising extraterritorial law in this area (e.g. the UK Bribery Act). Some governments have also tied public procurement decisions to the fulfilment of social and environmental criteria. CSR standards are often accepted as evidence that these criteria are met. For instance, the diffusion of the FSC in the UK was supported by the results of a public comparative evaluation of different certification standards. The UK procurement office concluded from this study that the FSC met the highest standards, and that competing initiatives (e.g. the Programme for the Endorsement of Forest Certification) failed on a number of points.

The impact of CSR standards also depends on whether adopters comply with the underlying rules. Standards are only effective tools for regulation if they really improve the social and environmental performance of firms. Although firms cannot freely choose their level of compliance (e.g. because some standardisers enforce rules via inspections), many standards allow for variations in implementation quality. Often, there is a gap between firms' level of compliance and their positive communication about the resulting social and environmental performance, causing claims that businesses 'greenwash' their operations. What, then, influences firms' level of compliance vis-à-vis a CSR standard?

Economic incentives play an important role in this context. Firms usually choose a level of compliance that matches their perceived benefits and costs. High-quality implementation can be costly. For instance, full compliance with ISO 14001 requires maintaining different aspects of an environmental management system, including costs for training personnel, adjusting business processes and documenting outcomes. The exact amount of costs is influenced by the fit of existing corporate practices with the content of a standard. Firms from regions with tight social and environmental regulations often face lower implementation costs and can reach higher levels of compliance without much difficulty. Also, larger firms are usually better equipped to cover implementation costs, as they already have relevant management systems in place and hence face lower costs for corrective actions.

Firms balance costs against the perceived benefits of standard implementation. Market demand is one important consideration in this context. Large corporate buyers often require certain certifications from their suppliers and thus offer them incentives to justify higher costs of compliance. Christmann and Taylor (2006) found that the importance that buyers place on the issue addressed by a standard influences the quality of implementation by suppliers. Suppliers were willing to invest more in implementation and go beyond what is minimally required if buyers perceived the regulated issue as important. The costs attached to finding alternative suppliers also influence the quality of standard implementation. If buyers face high switching costs when replacing existing suppliers (e.g. in case of non-compliance), they are less likely to punish low levels of compliance. A high level of compliance can also result from the need to manage reputational risks. Larger (multinational) firms, which have public images and brand reputations to defend, are especially vulnerable to activism that criticises low levels of compliance. For instance, Greenpeace criticised Nestlé in 2010 for ignoring its commitment to the Roundtable on Sustainable Palm Oil (RSPO). After an extensive public shaming campaign, the company agreed to more ambitious targets when it comes to fighting mass deforestation.

7.4.2 Impact on Consumers

Consumer behaviour is mostly shaped by certification standards that have visible product labels attached (e.g. Fairtrade or FSC), while corporate participation in other types of CSR standards remains unknown to most end consumers. Product labels are one way to overcome information asymmetries in markets. Such asymmetries exist because consumers cannot directly observe the social or environmental characteristics of a good or most companies' production processes. The production of sustainable goods relates to internal business processes (e.g. sourcing), which cannot be observed by individual consumers. Labels transform the unobservable credence attributes of goods (i.e. attributes that need to be taken on faith) into observable search attributes (i.e. attributes that can be assessed prior to purchase). Labels emit market signals and communicate to consumers that a product conforms to the codified requirements of a specific standard. This lowers consumers' search costs, as it helps to compare products and to identify those goods with special social or environmental features. However, product labels are only successful if consumers really alter their purchasing behaviour. Do consumers prefer labelled over non-labelled products, and are they willing to pay price premiums for labelled goods?

A number of studies have shown that a subset of consumers is willing to pay price premiums for labelled products. For instance, Loureiro and Lotade found that consumers were willing to pay a price premium for Fairtrade-labelled coffee (Loureiro and Lotade, 2005). More generally speaking, there are four consumer segments on the CSR spectrum (BBMG, GlobeScan and Sustain-Ability, 2013). The smallest group of consumers (14 per cent) are so-called *advocates* – i.e. individuals who are willing to pay price premiums for social or environmental product features. Advocates believe that responsible consumption is the 'right thing to do'. The largest segment consists of *aspirational* consumers (37 per cent). These consumers are materialistically orientated and care deeply about style and brands. They aim to act in a responsible way, but need to be convinced by firms that including social or environmental aspects into their purchasing decisions is the 'better thing to do'. Labels can activate consumers in this segment, who can be persuaded that labelled products perform comparable and/or better than non-labelled brands. Next, 34 per cent of consumers are *practicals*. These consumers are laggards when it comes to responsible purchasing decisions. They are price-sensitive and view social and environmental product features as an add-on. While practicals are not opposed to responsible consumption, they are also not actively seeking relevant products. Around 16 per cent of consumers are sceptical about including social and environmental criteria into their purchasing decisions. These consumers, called *indifferents*, do not trust relevant labels and believe that consumption by individuals does not make much of a difference.

The impact of product labels on consumer choice is often overestimated, because there is an observed gap between consumers' intention to pay premiums for labelled products and their actual purchasing behaviour. Research in this area often suffers from a so-called social desirability bias – that is, consumers publicly declare that they prefer labelled products (because they consider this answer to be the most socially accepted), while they act in a different way when faced with an actual purchasing decision. Studies just looking at the intention of consumers to purchase labelled goods show a support rate of up to 80 per cent, while studies measuring actual consumer choice typically find that only 10–15 per cent of people really alter their shopping behaviour. This is not to say that product labels and their certification standards are without impact. Rather, consumer reactions to labels are heterogeneous and influenced by a number of factors, such as: the label itself and consumers' trust in it, consumers' interest in and understanding of the regulated issue, and the geographic context of consumption. For instance, the input legitimacy of the standard-setting organisation can influence shopping behaviour. Consumers are often suspicious of standards that are sponsored by industry groups, even when such standards are widely known (Teisl, Peavey, Newman, Buono and Hermann, 2002). Consumers' reaction to labels also depends on the product itself and whether they believe that there is a connection between their usage of the product and the underlying social or environmental problem. Some problem areas are very complex, and consumers need to be educated about the impact of their purchasing behaviour (e.g. the link between palm oil, deforestation and the loss in biodiversity).

7.4.3 Impact on Regulated Issues

Does the adoption of environmental certifications reduce pollution? Do workers really benefit from labour standards? These questions are essential, as it would be possible that a CSR standard impacts firm behaviour and consumer choice, but remains without much influence on the actual social or environmental issue (e.g. because the standard does not raise the bar very much). Methodologically speaking, it is difficult to establish a causal link between the adoption/diffusion of a standard and its social and environmental impacts. Direct measures of gains do not exist in all cases (and hence proxy measures need to be used). Even if gains can be measured directly, it is difficult to correctly 'isolate' the effects of a certain standard, because social or environmental improvements can also be caused by other factors (e.g. better enforcement of hard law). Isolating the correct effects of standards is particularly challenging in the context of principle-based initiatives. As principles are by definition rather broad, firms operate a portfolio of activities in support of the regulated issue area (e.g. protecting human rights). Which of these activities was directly impacted by the adoption of a standard is typically difficult to find out.

Most initiatives address a number of different policy areas. For instance, the scope of the FSC criteria is rather broad, including workers' rights, indigenous peoples' rights and a number of environmental conditions. In many cases, the impact of a standard on its portfolio of issues is uneven. Barrientos and Smith's assessment of corporate codes of labour practice, which were aligned with the

Ethical Trading Initiative (ETI) Base Code, is a case in point (Barrientos and Smith, 2007). Their study showed that the ETI had an effect on outcome standards, that is, those labour standards that are either negotiated or the product of legislated entitlements. Workers benefited from improved health and safety provisions and reduced working hours. However, the study also revealed that the ETI had little or no effect on workers' process rights, that is, those rights that regulate whether and how employees are incorporated into negotiations around labour conditions (e.g. the right to collective bargaining). Such selective impact was also shown for ISO 14001. While higher levels of standard adoption led to reductions in air emissions (sulphur dioxide, SO_2), there was no relationship between adoption levels and changes in water pollution (biochemical oxygen demand). The impact of ISO 14001 was therefore stronger for the issue that was more visible to the public and hence received more policy attention (Potoski and Prakash, 2013). Air pollution is frequently mentioned as an important environmental issue, while, relatively speaking, water pollution is less visible and partially hidden.

7.5 Critique of CSR Standards

7.5.1 The Multiplicity of CSR Standards

The coexistence of multiple CSR standards with a similar purpose is often seen as a challenge to the evolution of effective private regulation. Such standard multiplicity has been observed in some industries. Certification standards in the global coffee industry (e.g. Fairtrade, Utz Kapeh, Rainforest Alliance, the Common Code for the Coffee Community (4C)) partially overlap and serve a similar purpose. A similar situation occurs when looking at the garments industry (e.g. the FLA, Fair Wear Foundation, SA 8000, Clean Clothes Campaign, Worker Rights Consortium). While these standards differ with regard to some dimensions (e.g. their historic roots and level of diffusion), there are also considerable similarities among them (e.g. the criteria used for certification).

Standards multiplicity creates a number of problems. It confuses suppliers, who often have to comply with multiple certifications at the same time (e.g. when supplying buyers who have subscribed to different initiatives). Gaining multiple certifications can also incur substantial costs on the side of suppliers. Standards multiplicity also puzzles consumers, who find it difficult to compare different product labels. Similar standards can also lead to competition for business participants among standard-setters. Such competition is likely to have negative effects, as it can lead to a regulatory 'race to the bottom', that is, initiatives try to attract participants by deliberately watering down their standards. Despite efforts to enhance collaboration among standard-setters (e.g. through the Joint Initiative on Accountability and Workers' Rights, JO-IN, in the garments industry), there are no signs of convergence. Why do CSR standards that serve a similar purpose not converge?

One answer to this question relates to the fact that the proliferation of standards has created a market for responsible goods in some industries (e.g. coffee, tea, garment). This market offers standard-setters a competitive space within which they can coexist through differentiation strategies (Reinecke, Manning and von Hagen, 2012). This differentiation is partly driven by the wish of standard-setters (e.g. NGOs, firms, trade unions) to preserve their identity and autonomy. Standards within one industry often position themselves differently on the market. For instance, some standards in the global coffee industry emphasise social justice and price premium for small-scale producers (e.g. Fairtrade), while others highlight biodiversity conservation (e.g. Rainforest Alliance) and superior coffee quality (e.g. Nespresso AAA). Differentiation also occurs because standards stress different levels of stringency, ranging from initiatives with very strict requirements and implementation procedures (e.g. Fairtrade) to standards with relatively low entry barriers (e.g. 4C). Hence, standards can coexist because they focus on a particular niche in the market and are reluctant to give up what they perceive to be their added value, making consolidation and rationalisation of existing standards difficult at best.

7.5.2 Lack of Inclusiveness in Standard Governance

Many CSR standards are explicitly designed as MSIs. This puts much emphasis on the engagement with stakeholder groups while developing and governing standards, not least because the involvement of different spheres of society is perceived as increasing the independence of standard-setters. While all individual stakeholder groups reflect a certain interest, and are therefore not neutral per se, the combination of different interests can lead to an image of independence (Boström, 2006). The inclusiveness of CSR standards is therefore important. Inclusiveness can refer to the scope of included stakeholders in terms of involving different types of parties (e.g. representing business, civil society and government) and in terms of engaging with parties from different geographic origins. It can also refer to the quality of participation, that is, how stakeholders are involved in decision-making processes relevant to a standard (Schouten, Leroy and Glasbergen, 2012). Critics point out that while many standards claim to be MSIs, in practice there are significant variations in terms of the scope of stakeholder involvement and the quality of participation.

Fransen and Kolk differentiate two types of CSR standards, which represent extreme ends on a continuum of inclusiveness (Fransen and Kolk, 2007). On the one hand, there are standards that follow a strategy of broad inclusiveness and active stakeholder involvement. These initiatives have a balanced representation of different stakeholder interests in their governance bodies (e.g. the FSC). On the other hand, there are CSR standards that follow a narrower approach based on consultation of interested parties (but not active engagement). Stakeholder consultation is mostly found in business-driven standards where non-business stakeholders often just have an advisory function but no formal voting rights (e.g. the BSCI). Such initiatives mostly engage with stakeholders from developed countries, while only having indirect links to representatives from the developing world. Within business-driven standards, the demand for inclusiveness usually conflicts with the aspiration of industry players to have a high degree of control over standard development and governance.

Inclusiveness is only useful for standard-setters when power asymmetries between participants are reduced. Such asymmetries increase if participants are very dissimilar in terms of their size and their control of financial and non-financial resources. Most CSR standards face a dilemma: the more stakeholders are involved in standard-setting, the more likely will be the existence of power asymmetries among participants, which, in turn, impedes the management of the standard and the creation of legitimacy. Completely avoiding 'capture' by one group of stakeholders is difficult. Most of all, it requires a careful design of the formal structures within the standard-setting organisation. For instance, the above-mentioned three-chamber system of the FSC allows the organisation to balance different interests without allowing one particular group to exert too much influence on decisions.

7.5.3 The Limits of Certification

One of the most common critiques of CSR standards is that participating companies do not walk their talk – that is, standards do not influence the everyday practices in corporations. This critique is particularly raised against principle-based CSR standards, which do not contain any monitoring mechanisms and hence cannot verify whether adopters really change their practices. However, it would be misleading to believe that monitoring processes always ensure full compliance. Boiral's study of nine ISO 14001 certified organisations shows that managers adopted different strategies to resolve the tension between the need to appear legitimate to external audiences and the need to protect internal efficiency (Boiral, 2007). One strategy was to adopt the standard only superficially. Managers documented and classified existing practices for environmental protection to come into compliance with ISO 14001, but they hardly launched any new activities or substantive corrective actions. In the end, the documented practices were hardly consulted by employees and the adopting organisations only created an internal rhetoric of success around the effective implementation of ISO 14001.

Monitoring of corporate practices remains a challenge in the context of certification and process standards. One widely documented problem is that auditors are usually paid directly by the brands or factories being monitored. This undercuts their neutrality, as auditing firms have an incentive to 'soften' their monitoring practices in order to retain client relationships. Another problem relates to the fact that audits are often announced and hence give factories sufficient time to cover up problems. The FLA has responded to these criticisms and installed a mechanism, which uses unannounced audits and does not allow firms to pay auditors directly. Long and flexible supply chains makes monitoring a challenging task. MNCs can usually move production quickly to other factories or even countries, and multiple layers of ownership at supply factories make systematic and continuous monitoring difficult. Many standards only cover first-tier suppliers, whereas social and environmental problems are often found further down the supply chain, in the informal sector or in the context of home-based work. Despite all these criticisms, monitoring has raised compliance levels at some factories, especially when it is not used as a standalone strategy but combined with other efforts (e.g. better scheduling of work in global supply chains).

7.6 Case Study: The UN Global Compact: Bluewashing Corporate Practices?

The UN Global Compact (www.unglobalcompact.org) is a principle-based CSR standard. Set up in 2000 by former UN Secretary-General Kofi Annan, the Compact positions itself as a framework that corporations can adopt to align their strategies and operations with ten universal principles as well as the Sustainable Development Goals (SDGs). The ten principles are broadly formulated and cover human rights, labour rights, the environment and anti-corruption (see Table 7.3). The initiative is *not* designed as a tool to monitor corporate behaviour. Rather, participating companies are expected to implement the ten principles and SDGs in their sphere of influence, to share best practices with other stakeholders, and to enter into partnerships with other participants (e.g. UN agencies or NGOs). Hence, the main emphasis of the Compact is offering guidance to participants and providing a platform for mutual learning around social and environmental challenges. The initiative focuses on the idea of 'continuous improvement'. Firms are not necessarily asked to comply with all ten principles at the time of joining, but they are expected to work towards implementation over time.

Historically speaking, the UN Global Compact is not the first attempt of the UN to deal with MNCs. In the 1970s, as FDI activity was increasing throughout the globe, the UN saw businesses mostly as a reason for concern. The belief was that cross-border economic transactions were mostly benefiting developed nations, but created many social and environmental problems in

Table 7.3 The ten principles of the UN Global Compact

1	Human rights	Businesses should support and respect the protection of internationally proclaimed human rights; and
2		make sure that they are not complicit in human rights abuses.
3	Labour	Businesses should uphold the freedom of association and the effective recognition of the right to collective bargaining;
4		the elimination of all forms of forced and compulsory labour;
5		the effective abolition of child labour; and
6		the elimination of discrimination in respect of employment and occupation.
7	Environment	Businesses should support a precautionary approach to environmental challenges;
8		undertake initiatives to promote greater environmental responsibility; and
9		encourage the development and diffusion of environmentally friendly technologies.
10	Anti-corruption	Businesses should work against corruption in all its forms, including extortion and bribery.

the developing world. To overcome these problems, the United Nations Economic and Social Council (ECOSOC) formed a Centre on Transnational Corporations (UNCTC) in 1974. At this time, the UN was openly hostile against 'big corporations' and hence one key task of the Centre was to develop a regulatory, and legally binding, code of conduct to police corporate behaviour. However, conflicting political interests slowed down the development of the code. The United States argued against the binding nature of the code, while many developing countries insisted on legal enforceability by home and host countries. It was also unclear whether the UN itself should be given the authority to implement the code. The code was finally rejected by the General Assembly in 1992, and the UNCTC was dissolved in 1993.

By the end of the 1990s, the UN started to engage more proactively with the private sector. This shift in attitude was driven by then Secretary-General Kofi Annan, who saw business as part of the solution to global problems. Businesses were also welcomed as a partner, because the UN was seeking new ways of financing its operations, especially since there was a lack of sufficient funding from member states. There was an ideological shift under way – from the view that market actors in the global economy need strict regulation to a perspective that favours voluntary partnership. The creation of the UN Global Compact in 2000 was the practical consequence of this shift.

As of September 2015, the Compact has more than 8,300 active business participants and 4,800 non-business participants (mostly global and local NGOs as well as business associations). The barriers to entry are very low. Companies can join the Compact by issuing a 'letter of commitment' to the UN Secretary-General. The letter needs to be signed by the CEO (in order to ensure that there is top-management support for the initiative with the participating firm). Participation is open to companies from any industry, except firms that are involved in the manufacturing or sale of selected weapons and those companies that have been blacklisted by UN Procurement for ethical reasons. The initiative actively discourages tobacco companies from participating, but cannot prevent them from joining for legal reasons. So far, the Compact has active participants in around 170 countries. Participants in around 100 countries are organised in local networks. These networks are local participant clusters that facilitate partnerships and organise learning and dialogue events.

Although the Compact is not designed to monitor or measure participants' performance, it has installed certain 'integrity measures' that are supposed to provide transparency and public accountability. The most important measure is the so-called Communication on Progress (COP) policy. The initiative requires participating businesses to issue a public report on an annual basis. This report is available via the UN Global Compact website and describes what the firm has done to implement the ten principles and support the SDGs. Firms have a lot of flexibility when writing the report, as there are only three minimal content requirements (i.e. the report needs to contain a CEO statement, it needs to describe practical actions, and it needs to measure outcomes in some way). Participants who fail to submit a report on an annual basis are delisted from the initiative. The Compact has expelled more than 5,700 businesses for failure to meet the reporting requirement (as of September 2015). This number is surprisingly high, and critics argue that it shows that many participants are not serious about their engagement. Over half of all delisted firms (58 per cent) are small and medium-sized enterprises (SMEs) – that is, firms with fewer than 250 employees. Larger firms have a reputation to defend and thus are more careful when non-reporting could result in public delisting. Also, larger firms usually have more financial and non-financial resources to produce the required COP report. Most large companies produce CSR reports and hence gather the relevant data anyway. Some use their CSR (or sustainability) reports as their COP.

The Compact is funded through public and private sources. A number of donor governments contribute about 20 per cent of the overall income, while the remaining 80 per cent come from voluntary donations by participating businesses (as of 2013). The UN itself does not directly fund the initiative. Critics argue that the significant involvement of business participants in funding the initiative undercuts its independence. Although the Compact positions itself as an MSI, some critics have also argued that there is an imbalance between business and non-business representatives when looking at the governance of the initiative. Currently, the Global Compact Board, which is the primary forum to make relevant decisions, consists of four representatives from civil society organisations, four representatives from labour organisations and business associations, and seventeen representatives from participating companies. This makes the Compact more of a business-led initiative than a true multi-stakeholder forum.

There is an intense debate around the UN Global Compact, both in academia and practice. Critics have raised various points against the Compact, while advocates have tried to defend the initiative (Rasche, 2009). Various NGOs, labour organisations and also some academics have argued that the Compact has 'no teeth' and hence reflects an insufficient tool to advance corporate responsibility. They suggest that some corporations misuse the initiative as a public relations smokescreen and thus 'bluewash' their operations (i.e. attach their dirty image to the blue UN logo). As the UN enjoys high degrees of legitimacy in most parts of the world, corporations profit from their participation in the Compact even if they do not implement the ten principles. Critics assert that the Compact cannot do much about these free riders as long as companies submit the required annual reports. What is needed, according to the critics, are better mechanisms to control participants' behaviour and more stringent procedures to sanction companies that break any of the ten principles. Advocates, on the other hand, claim that the initiative was never designed as a regulatory standard that monitors and sanctions corporations' behaviour. They suggest that the Compact neither has the financial resources nor the political mandate to regulate (multinational) corporations.

To date, it is unclear whether the UN Global Compact really has a lasting impact on the way firms manage their social and environmental responsibilities. The initiative clearly has helped to shape the public discourse around corporations' changing role in global society. However, some have argued that without proof that the Compact significantly shapes corporate practices on the ground, there is good reason to question whether the initiative's emphasis on 'guidance' and 'learning' (instead of more rigorous sanctioning) pays off. Some argue to simply accept the Compact as the UN's historically grown way of engaging in the CSR debate – for a lack of anything better ...

Questions for Discussion

1. Do you agree with the critics who argue that participants in the UN Global Compact tend to 'bluewash' their corporate image?
2. How can the UN Global Compact tackle the problem of having a high rate of delistings?

3. Should the UN Global Compact focus on quantitative growth (i.e. attract more participants by keeping entry barriers low) or qualitative growth (i.e. keep only high performing firms and delist the rest)?
4. Do you believe that the UN needs to partner with businesses in order to attract sufficient resources for fulfilling its mandate?

7.7 Chapter Summary

This chapter looked at CSR standards as one way to practically implement corporations' social and environmental responsibilities. We showed that CSR standards are part and parcel of a recent move towards global business regulation through soft law. While this does not mean that intergovernmental regulation is not needed, soft law offers a practical alternative to address those problems where governments could not yet agree on any binding rules. We discussed the heterogeneous nature of CSR standards, differentiating between principle-based initiatives as well as reporting, certification and process standards. The discussion showed that CSR standards often struggle with positioning themselves as legitimate alternatives to other forms of regulation, especially when considering their input and output legitimacy.

Our assessment of standards' impact revealed that some firms show rigorous compliance with standards because there are economic benefits of implementation (e.g. eco-efficiency through process improvements). However, these benefits can usually only be activated when firms reach beyond superficial adoption. It would be misleading to limit the discussion of CSR standards' benefits to things like an increase in reputation and new market opportunities; many standards create indirect effects that often remain unacknowledged (e.g. they generate barriers for new market entrants). We also showed that labels such as Fairtrade or the FSC have helped to create a (small but growing) market for sustainable goods in some industries (e.g. paper and coffee). Our discussion also revealed that standardisation in the field of CSR is often criticised, especially for the coexistence of too many initiatives with a similar purpose, lacking inclusiveness in standard development, and the unreliability of auditing mechanisms. While CSR standards face many challenges, it is clear that they are here to stay.

Chapter Questions

1. In what ways, if any, do principle-based standards and certification standards differ with regard to their level of input and output legitimacy?

2. What benefits can firms reap from adopting CSR standards? Do these benefits differ when looking at different types of CSR standards?
3. Are CSR standards an appropriate way to regulate those global problem areas where intergovernmental agreements do not yet exist? Why/why not?
4. How would you criticise CSR standards? Do you think that there are any remedies to address your points of critique?

FURTHER RESOURCES

Vogel, D. (2010). The Private Regulation of Global Corporate Conduct: Achievements and Limitations. *Business and Society*, 49(1), 68–87.
Gives an overview of the debate around private regulation (including some remarks on the history of non-state regulation). The article argues that private regulation cannot be seen as a substitute for more stringent regulation by governments and intergovernmental authorities.

Bernstein, S. and Cashore, B. (2007). Can Non-State Global Governance Be Legitimate? An Analytical Framework. *Regulation and Governance*, 1(4), 347–371.
Discusses the legitimacy of certification standards in more depth. It identifies a three-phase process through which standards could achieve legitimacy, also highlighting the dynamic nature of standards' legitimacy.

Rasche, A. (2012). Global Policies and Local Practice: Loose and Tight Couplings in Multi-Stakeholder Initiatives. *Business Ethics Quarterly*, 22(4), 679–670.
Discusses the multilevel nature of CSR standards and shows how such initiatives have developed organisational structures on the global and local level. The article shows that while actors on the global level are loosely connected, actors on the local level are more tightly linked.

Fransen, L. (2011). Why Do Private Governance Organizations Not Converge? A Political-Institutional Analysis of Transnational Labor Standards Regulation. *Governance*, 24(2), 359–387.
Discusses the multiplicity of certification standards in more depth with a focus on the garments industry. The article shows how competition among standard-setters has negative consequences, and it discusses why convergence of standards is unlikely in the future.

Waddock, S. (2008). Building a New Institutional Infrastructure for Corporate Responsibility. *Academy of Management Perspectives*, 22(3), 87–108.
Gives an overview of existing CSR standards (including principles, certifications, reporting and process initiatives) and discusses the opportunities and problems attached to these voluntary initiatives.

The Ecolabel Index, www.ecolabelindex.com
>   The Ecolabel index, providing an overview of product labels in the area of CSR.

UN Global Compact YouTube Channel, www.youtube.com/user/TheUNGlobalCompact.

The ISEAL Alliance, www.isealalliance.org
>   A global association for standard-setters in the CSR domain.

| 8 | **Corporate Responsibility Reporting** |

CHRISTIAN HERZIG AND ANNA-LENA KÜHN

Learning Objectives

- Enhance appreciation of corporate responsibility reporting (CRRep), its historical development and the different forms it can take.
- Raise critical awareness of rationales advanced to explain the phenomenon of CRRep.
- Impart awareness of possible problems and challenges involved in CRRep.
- Develop knowledge of guidelines and regulatory frameworks which govern CRRep and enable you to critically evaluate their effectiveness in enhancing transparency and accountability.
- Foster understanding of country- and industry-specific developments in CRRep.

8.1 Introduction

Corporate social responsibility refers to the expectation that business is responsible for its impact on society and the environment. Society expects companies to take responsibility for avoiding, reducing or, at best, compensating for negative externalities as well as contributing to social welfare, while also being accountable for these impacts and explaining them in a transparent manner. However, such responsibility is articulated through a complex set of means and is constantly changing. The importance of understanding these complexities and dynamics and the need for transparency and accountability – whether for social responsibility or sustainability – has invited considerable interest in the field of CRRep, the subject of this chapter. CRRep in essence reflects a company's claim to portray – in printed reports or on corporate websites – an account of its ecological, social and economic performance and impacts, and to inform its stakeholders as to what extent and how it can contribute to sustainable development. The number of companies which claim their responsibilities through a dedicated corporate responsibility report has increased considerably in recent decades – as has the criticism of the reluctance and/or incapability of some companies to provide a full and fair account of their performance and impact on society and their stakeholders. This debate reflects the different approaches to regulating CRRep and the roles that society and stakeholders might play in enhanced engagement in and quality of CRRep.

The chapter will be organised as follows: it begins with a general definition of CRRep, an overview of its historic development and the various forms it can take. Then, rationales for and challenges to companies' engagement in CRRep are outlined. At its core, different alternatives for governing CRRep are explored, distinguishing voluntary standards (e.g. the Global Reporting Initiative (GRI) guidelines) from legally binding measures introduced by governments (e.g. disclosure regulations in European and other countries) and stock exchanges. Countries and industries in which reporting has turned into a more institutionalised practice are described in more detail, before presenting a case study on the GRI.

8.2 Definition, Development and Assurance

8.2.1 What is Corporate Responsibility Reporting?

With corporate responsibility reports, companies endeavour to demonstrate their wider responsibility to society and to inform stakeholders as to what extent and how they might contribute to sustainable development. There are various rationales which serve to provide an explanation for a company's engagement in CRRep (see section 8.3.1). Most generally, the demand for transparency and reliable and accountable forms of socially responsible business have notably and globally increased in the past decades due to increased stakeholder activism, growing media coverage, numerous business scandals and various corporate governance failures. Large and multinational companies have become particularly vulnerable to public pressure by consumers, social and environmental activists and other groups interested in responsible and sustainable business. Thus they have engaged in communicating the social and environmental effects of their economic actions to particular interest groups in society and to society at large, thereby claiming that in corporate responsibility reports an overall picture of their ecological, social and economic activities and performance is drawn.

However, as the concept of CRRep is primarily of a voluntary nature, it remains as vague, ambiguous and contested as the entire CSR concept (Gond and Moon, 2011). In particular, the meaning of corporate responsibility can vary according to the context in which businesses operate, and is dynamic in that its meaning, application and use has changed over time. This makes recording and reporting on corporate responsibility difficult. The overlapping nature of the concept with those such as 'sustainability' or 'corporate citizenship' adds to this complexity, and the fairly fast and often changing terminology applied to non- or extra-financial reporting initiatives is just as unhelpful. Currently, there exists a plethora of labels for non-financial reports (e.g. corporate social responsibility report, sustainability report, corporate citizenship report, sustainable development report and integrated report). For the sake of clarity, this chapter refers to 'corporate responsibility reports' and 'corporate responsibility reporting' (CRRep is used as an abbreviation for this term) when addressing any form of company's self-presentation which goes beyond the traditional role of providing financial accounts to the owners of capital.

To get a better sense of what constitutes CRRep, two further basic characteristics and developments need to be examined: its discursive formation within the process of stakeholder engagement and its increased embeddedness in a new public sphere, the virtual reality created by the Internet. Starting with the former, there is general recognition of the vital importance of stakeholder engagement and dialogue and their place within the context of the overall CRRep process through which companies decide on how and what to disclose in their reports (Rinaldi, Unerman and Tilt, 2014). This is reflected in various reporting principles, most prominently laid down perhaps in guidelines and standards published by the GRI and AccountAbility (see Table 8.1 and section 8.4.1). According to these frameworks, a corporate report should cover a company's significant economic, environmental and social impacts which are most relevant to stakeholders and society and substantial to their assessment of the company's performance. Besides these principles of materiality and completeness, there is also a strong expectation that a company explains and reflects on how it identifies and engages with stakeholders and responds to their reasonable expectations and interests (stakeholder inclusiveness and responsiveness). The latter also illustrates and is discussed within the context of institutional reform designed to improve the structure within which CRRep takes place and stakeholders are empowered through greater participation (Cooper and Owen, 2007; Gray, Adams and Owen, 2014). Such institutional reform goes beyond what is understood as 'administrative' (or technical) reform which primarily looks at how CRRep is practised to enhance the level of transparency. With regard to guidelines, standards and regulations, this administrative reform is often expressed in form both of a comprehensive set of environmental, social and economic indicators framing the content of reports, and of guidance provided on technical topics in measuring and reporting on issues related to corporate responsibility. The possible tension which can emerge from different motives for and levels of stakeholder engagement and dialogue as well as their influence on the potential power of CRRep to serve as an accountability mechanism will be discussed below. Rinaldi et al. and Gray et al. provide a comprehensive overview of different forms of engaging with stakeholders in

Table 8.1 Overview of selected voluntary frameworks for corporate responsibility reporting

Initiative (launch year)	Focus of reporting	Description	Core subjects	Application and further information
Eco-Management and Audit Scheme / EMAS (1993) European Union regulation	• Management process • Reporting content (mainly themes but also indicators)	• Represents a European standard to establish a certifiable environmental management system and related reporting scheme ('environmental statement'). • Requires regular environmental reporting (every 3–4 years depending on size) on specific themes and based upon some general types of indicators (more specified through sector guidance documents). • Addresses reporting principles (e.g. comparability through benchmarking) but does not specify them.	• The environment (water, energy efficiency, material efficiency, biodiversity, waste, emissions) • Environmental policy and management system • Environmental programme and objectives • Environmental performance and compliance with legal obligations	• 4,600 organisations and 7,900 sites in Europe • All types of organisations across sectors • Additional sector-specific guidance documents Further information: www.emas.eu
AccountAbility: The AA1000 Series of Standards (1995) Global, not-for-profit organisation governed by multi-stakeholder network	• Management process • Reporting quality (principles)	• Principle-based standards to develop a sustainable business model and strategy, actively engage with stakeholders and foster public disclosure. • World's first sustainability assurance standard. • Publishes guidance notes, offers training and consulting.	• Strategy and governance • Stakeholder management • Corporate responsibility reporting • Performance management system • Programme management	• North America, European Union, Latin America, Middle East, Southern Africa, and developing world • All types of organisations • Sectors: financial services, energy and extractives, consumer goods, pharmaceuticals Further information: www.accountability.org

Global Reporting Initiative / GRI (1997) Global, not-for-profit organisation governed by multi-stakeholder network	• Reporting content (indicators) • Reporting quality (principles) • Management process	• Details reporting principles and entails standard disclosures and specific standard disclosures across four dimensions (management approach, economic, environmental, social category). • Provides an implementation manual, a sustainability disclosure database, a support suite and training programme.	• Organisational governance • Human rights • Labour practices • The environment • Fair operating practices • Consumer issues • Community involvement and development • Stakeholder engagement	• 8,492 organisations in 90 countries • All types of organisations across sectors • Additional sector disclosure guidance Further information: www.globalreporting.org
The Greenhouse Gas Protocol (1998) Global NGO-business partnership	• Reporting content (indicators) • Reporting quality (measurement and partly principles) • Management process	• Supplies the most widely used international accounting standards for companies to measure, manage and report on greenhouse gas emissions (GHG). • Standards cover GHG inventories including emissions from throughout a company's value chain, emissions from a product's full life cycle and from climate change mitigation projects. • Develops also guidance documents (e.g. how to engage with suppliers) which sometimes include reporting principles.	• The environment (climate change)	• More than 430 members globally, within developed and developing countries • All types of organisations across sectors • Additional sector-specific tools Further information: www.ghgprotocol.org

Table 8.1 (*cont.*)

Initiative (launch year)	Focus of reporting	Description	Core subjects	Application and further information
Carbon Disclosure Project / CDP (2000) Investor-led, UK-based, not-for-profit initiative	• Reporting content (indicators)	• Enhances disclosure of environmental information in order to accelerate carbon reduction and protect natural resources. • Provides access to supplementary analytical tools and best disclosure practices.	• The environment (climate change, water, forest, environmental risks in supply chains)	• More than 2,500 organisations globally, within developed and developing countries • All types of organisations (except not-for-profit) across sectors Further information: www.cdproject.net
Organisation for Economic Cooperation and Development / OECD (2006)	• Management process	• The risk awareness tool for multinational enterprises in weak governance zones helps multinationals to identify risks and ethical issues. • Complements the 'OECD Guidelines for Multinational Enterprises'.	• Organisational governance • Human rights • Labour practices • Fair operating practices • Community involvement and development	• 34 member countries including advanced and emerging countries • All types of organisations across sectors Further information: www.oecd.org
United Nations Global Compact / UNGC (2009) UN initiative and global company-based network	• Reporting content (themes)	• Requires participating companies to comply with ten UNGC Principles and produce an annual Communication on Progress (COP) report to inform stakeholders on companies' efforts to uphold the Principles. • Provides guidance on developing COP reports (including software tools), policy documents, overview of COP trends and list of active UNGC reporters.	• Human rights • Labour practices • The environment • Anti-corruption	• More than 13,000 corporate participants in over 130 countries • All types of organisations across sectors Further information: www.unglobalcompact.org

ISO 26000 (2010) International standard-setting body	• Management process	• The non-certifiable standard provides organisations with guidance on how social responsibility can be integrated throughout an organisation based on seven principles, seven core subjects and stakeholder engagement. • Addresses the need for communicating commitments and performance but works together with other reporting initiatives (such as the GRI) to specify concrete links between the initiatives.	• Organisational governance • Human rights • Labour practices • The environment • Fair operating practices • Consumer issues • Community involvement and development	• Members from 163 countries • All types of public, private and non-profit organisations across sectors Further information: www.iso.org/iso
International Integrated Reporting Council / IIRC (2011) Global coalition of regulators, investors, companies, and accounting bodies	• Reporting content (themes) • Reporting quality (principles) • Management process	• Framework describes the process of how value can be created, governed and reported, details reporting principles, and process of engaging with stakeholders. • Provides an examples database, various guidance documents, and various networks.	• Organisational governance • Human rights • Labour practices • The environment • Fair operating practices • Consumer issues • Community involvement and development	• 750 members globally • All types of organisations across sectors Further information: www.theiirc.org

Notes: Reporting content: defines the content of CRRep (themes only or detailing indicators).

Reporting quality: defines how to attain a standard quality for CRRep (principles for the way of reporting and/or measuring).

Management process: guidance on how to design management processes underlying CRRep.

practice and key issues in the implementation of stakeholder engagement and dialogue processes (Rinaldi et al., 2014; Gray et al., 2014).

A related and emerging element of CRRep is the use of the Internet for disclosing information on and engaging with stakeholders about corporate responsibility. Greater use of the Internet for CRRep promises advantages in information provision, accessibility and comprehensibility. This is due to its manifold advantages in providing access to a large quantity of information, presenting an integrated view of different aspects of sustainability through links to other information sources related to the company or other organisations, 'customising' reporting through individual access for stakeholders, and using a combination of different media elements (e.g. audio, images or videos). Thus, the Internet can support the reporting process in various ways to overcome such problems as information overload or lack of target group orientation (see section 8.3.2). Hence, in practice and in spite of disadvantages to using the Internet (e.g. the exclusion of some stakeholders from the reporting process due to limited web accessibility or the difficulties in assuring web content), the combined use of printed reports and online reporting has become the primary means of CRRep. Some companies have even abandoned printed reports completely and now solely focus on Internet-based CRRep.

Advantages attributed to Internet-supported CRRep also include a range of communication possibilities to engaging and communicating with stakeholders. In practice, an increasing number of companies have started to interact with stakeholders on sustainability issues through blogs or discussion forums and more synchronous forms of dialogue such as chats. However, dialogue-based online relationships set up and largely influenced by companies have also been criticised as being a public relations exercise rather than a means through which the role of stakeholders in corporate decision-making and reporting can meaningfully be extended. The concern over deficiencies in stakeholder engagement and reporting processes in the critical accounting community will be referred to below (section 8.3.2) but it is worth noting here that the emancipatory power of the Internet has paved the way to some other form of reporting, the so-called 'counter' or 'shadow' accounting, which usually challenges in particular those companies which provide a high level of self-presentation on corporate responsibility.

Having looked at one of the most recent developments in CRRep, the use of the Internet, the next section will explore the historical development of CRRep (an enlightening historical review is given by Owen and O'Dwyer, 2008; see also Buhr, Gray and Milne, 2014; Herzig and Schaltegger, 2011).

8.2.2 How has Corporate Responsibility Reporting Evolved?

Although companies already disclosed social (in particular employee and community-related) information in earlier decades of the twentieth century, considerable interest in non-financial reporting among practitioners and researchers did not arise before the 1970s. At that time, changing societal expectations and needs imposed new demands on companies and sparked a debate on companies' responsibilities towards the well-being of society. To counter public and governmental criticism, a number of large US and Western European companies started publishing social reports. With these reports, companies informed their stakeholders about the company's activities, products and services, and related positive and negative social impacts. This type of report also included new social accounting techniques such as the value added statement which presents the added value generated by an organisation and its source and distribution among the contributors of the value (e.g. to the state via taxes and duties, to employees via salary and benefits, and to shareholders via dividends). Social reports served to show how company value was created and attributed to a larger number of stakeholders rather than just the shareholders. The emergence of these new forms of accounting and reporting can be seen in the light of rising income levels which shifted the focus of society and politics to objectives such as quality of life. However, by the end of the 1970s, social reporting was already in decline again. Among the reasons for the decline were inadequate target group orientation, a mismatch between the information interests of most stakeholders, social reports often being scientifically designed and remote from the reality of most people's lives, a misuse of social reporting as a public relations tool, which reduced its reliability and credibility, an insufficient integration of social and financial reporting, and the positive economic and political development of Europe, with job movements to the services sector and improved working conditions (Herzig and Schaltegger, 2011).

During the late 1980s and 1990s, non-financial reporting regained its importance. However, the focus shifted from social to environmental issues due to various environmental incidents and catastrophes (e.g. Bhopal, India; Schweizerhalle, Switzerland; and Hoechst AG, Germany). Companies were viewed as being responsible for the consequences of these environmental disasters. In response to the increased pressure for greater transparency and accountability, companies, in particular those operating within environmentally sensitive industries, started to publish environmental reports to inform stakeholders about organisational activities' impacts on the natural environment (through air and water emissions, types and amounts of wastes, etc.) and the use of approaches to managing environmental issues and impacts. These environmental reporting activities were partly forced by new laws (compulsory reporting) and partly voluntary. Succeeding years saw different attempts to integrate environmental and social issues within corporate reporting (e.g. safety, health and the environment reports). Overall, environmental reporting began to supersede the early social reporting activities of companies. Until the end of the last century, the number of environmental reports and the attention they received in the media and society increased considerably. Meanwhile, their average quality improved from being primarily green glossaries and one-off reports, to emerging as more comprehensive environmental reports published on a regular (e.g. annual) basis. An example of a voluntary approach to environmental reporting is the European Union Eco-Management and Audit Scheme (EMAS; see Table 8.1).

From the mid-1990s, the attention shifted towards sustainability reports and 'multi-issue reporting' (Kolk, 2004). Sustainability reports reflect companies' claims to depict an overall picture of their ecological, social and economic sustainability activities and performance, and to inform stakeholders as to what extent and how companies contribute to sustainable development (Herzig and Ghosh, 2014). One of the earlier examples is the so-called 'Triple P-Report' (People, Planet and Profits) of Shell, published in the late 1990s, whose title already indicates the multiple dimensional reporting style. Compared with social reporting in the 1970s (where emphasis was placed on employee-related issues and value creation for various stakeholders), social aspects within sustainability reports are nowadays more of global importance and are more comprehensively dealt with, in terms of moral and ethical questions of sustainable development (e.g. child labour in the supply chain, human rights, poverty alleviation, gender issues and trading relationships). However, while generally integrative in nature, these reports do not necessarily address financial figures or performance measures in a comprehensive way but often concentrate on corporate ecological and social strategy and performance.

Companies vary in their approach to reporting extra-financial issues. While some companies integrate all information in one report, other companies opt for publishing either only individual reports (e.g. environmental, social, community or ethical supply chain reports) or a combination of these reports (but still as separate documents). Such reports are heterogeneous with respect to their title, length, content, standard and external assurance applied. As a whole though, there is a continuous increase in numbers: between 2008 and 2015, the percentage of the world's largest 250 corporations which provided some sort of a standalone corporate responsibility report increased from 80 per cent to 92 per cent (KPMG, 2015).

Besides these developments in extra-financial reporting, environmental and social information has also increasingly been integrated in primarily financially orientated reports. Two main development paths include the extension of annual reports and the rise of the integrated reporting concept. In many countries, companies are required by law or by the respective stock market to produce and publish an annual financial report. The annual report is regarded as the most formal corporate reporting document and traditionally focuses on companies' key financial and performance figures. However, mostly driven by the increasing interest of investors, analysts, and regulatory requirements, there has been an increased focus on selected environmental and social aspects of corporate performance in financial reports in recent years. In Europe, the implementation of the EU Accounts Modernisation Directive with the reformed law regulating the balance sheet (European Parliament and European Council, 2004) has forced shareholder companies to include non-financial performance indicators, specifically environmental and labour-related indicators, in the prognosis reports included in their annual reports. This extension of an annual report has been taken further in various ways and to different extents in individual countries. The coverage of issues related to corporate responsibility in annual reports has increased worldwide from 4 per cent of the top 100 companies in 2008 (22 countries), over 20 per cent in 2011 (34 countries) to 56 per cent in 2015 (45 countries) (KPMG, 2015). The extent to which companies' annual reports address financial, governance, social and environmental performance and corporate responsibility evaluations, however, still varies.

There is the expectation by some (in particular by professional accounting bodies, consultancies, regulators and corporations) that a more consistent approach to reporting can be promoted through the most recent CRRep initiative: integrated reporting. Integrated reports are based on the idea of reporting on the relationship between companies' financial results and sustainability impacts in the form of one 'holistic' and complete report. According to the International Integrated Reporting Council (IIRC), an integrated report is 'a concise communication about how an organization's strategy, governance, performance and prospects, in the context of its external environment, lead to the creation of value in the short, medium and long term' (IIRC, 2013: 7). By effectively linking these often isolated aspects, companies are seen to be able to provide disclosure on past performance and comment on their long-term perspective of future value generation. Moreover, according to the IIRC's Integrated Reporting Framework, released in December 2013, an integrated report aims to elucidate how the company impacts on the communities in which it operates, and how it intends to strengthen its positive impacts and eliminate or mitigate its negative impacts.

Despite the rapid development in integrated reporting policy, integrated reporting is still at an early stage if compared with the historical evolution of other forms of CRRep. The impact it will have on the reporting environment and the extent to which it will serve various stakeholders and contribute to sustainable development is unclear as yet. Initial insights into integrated reporting practice were gained from a case study-based pilot phase (with about a hundred companies in various parts of the world) and a consultation phase aimed at enhanced understanding of the experience and views of those affected by the new reporting framework and involved in its implementation. There is a notable number of scholars and practitioners who also evaluate this most recent reporting initiative critically, especially with respect to its objective and practicability (Villiers, Rinaldi and Unerman, 2014). There seems to be variety in the ways in which integrated reporting is understood and enacted within institutions, difficulties in the implementation of the new framework (e.g. with regard to selecting and linking non-financial with financial key performance indicators) and concern expressed about whether the initiative is managerially captured by mostly financially interested stakeholders.

8.2.3 How can Corporate Responsibility Reports be Externally Assured?

Notable developments have not only been evident in the changing forms and rising numbers of reports but also in the number of reports assured by external bodies. As stakeholders expect companies to publish accurate, reliable and credible corporate responsibility reports, companies face a dilemma: CRRep is mostly voluntary and thus demands a reliable external source which assesses the credibility of the reporting. Moreover, the non-availability of one universal reporting standard puts the validity, reliability and comparability of the reports into question. Accordingly, and in line with the GRI's recommendations to externally assure the reliability of CRRep, an increase in external assurance statements has been observed in recent years. Whereas only 30 per cent of the top 250 companies from the Global Fortune 500 conducted assurance on their corporate responsibility reports in 2005, 46 per cent made use of third-party assurance in 2011 and as many as 63 per cent in 2015 (KPMG, 2015).

To facilitate the assurance of corporate responsibility reports, there are two main standards: the International Standard on Assurance Engagement (ISAE) 3000 and the AA1000 Assurance Standard (AA1000AS). The ISAE 3000 was initiated by the International Auditing and Assurance Standards Board in 2003 and is primarily used by accounting firms. The AA1000AS was proposed in 2003 and updated in 2008 by AccountAbility and is used by assurers other than accountants. Whereas the ISAE 3000 relies on fixed assurance procedures to provide a certain extent of security to the profession, the AA1000AS concentrates on the quality of the reporting process and leaves room for more individual adjustments. Hence, the ISAE 3000 and AA1000AS can be regarded as complements rather than substitutes, and are often simultaneously obtained by companies.

External assurance is generally viewed as enhancing the credibility and quality of the report, the related reporting process and companies' operations and risk management. However, in practice, concern is raised about the effectiveness of current assurance practices. As the GRI and all other reporting standards do not prescribe the extent of the examination, the external assurance varies considerably among companies. Evidence on which to base conclusions from the review of corporate responsibility information is also often restricted, i.e. a limited assurance engagement is often used in preference to the more comprehensive reasonable assurance. Further concerns emerge from ambiguities and inconsistencies in current approaches to sustainability assurance such as independence and degree of thoroughness of audits (Owen and O'Dwyer, 2008).

8.3 Rationales, Problems and Challenges

8.3.1 Why Do or Should Companies Engage in Corporate Responsibility Reporting?

Rationales advanced to explain the existence of CRRep are numerous (for a comprehensive review see Gray et al., 2014). The phenomenon has been looked at from a meta/meso or systems perspective (e.g. political economy and critical theory), an organisational perspective (e.g. resource dependency and organisational change theory) and an individual perspective (e.g. psychology and anthropology). At each level, CRRep has been theorised to provide complementary and overlapping explanations, albeit much more emphasis has been placed upon the first two perspectives. As is the nature of theory, some theoretical lenses have proven to be helpful in exploring and enhancing understanding of CRRep at more than one level. For example, discourse theory has been used to explore both organisational transformation towards sustainable development through text or visual analysis of corporate responsibility reports (intra-organisational perspective) and the advance of local democracy and moral consensus in the light of certain corporate responsibility practices (meta perspective). Viewing the various theories as overlapping and closely interlinked concepts rather than in isolation facilitates a fuller understanding of the phenomenon of CRRep. A joint consideration is also often suggested for three of the most commonly employed theories in CRRep literature: legitimacy theory, stakeholder theory and institutional theory. These three theoretical lenses are placed at the intersection of the organisational and the meso/sub-system levels, and their explanatory power for CRRep will be briefly explained.

From the perspective of institutional theory, institutional pressures create a specific institutional environment within which companies make decisions regarding what to disclose and how (Higgins and Larrinaga, 2014). These external pressures can be coercive (e.g., mandatory CRRep; see section 8.4.2), mimetic (e.g. following reporting practices of competitors), and normative (e.g. fulfilling professional expectations such as compliance with reporting standards and guidelines published by professional accounting bodies; see section 8.4.1). Legitimacy theory, in contrast, builds on the idea that there is an implicit social contract between companies and society. Hence, society grants legitimacy to companies as long as they comply with societal norms and expectations, and CRRep corresponds with actual corporate activities and performance. So while institutional theory discusses more broadly how reporting practices and changes therein bring legitimacy to a company, legitimacy theory investigates how a company mobilises its reporting to legitimise its relationship with society and how CRRep assists a company in managing threats to its organisational legitimacy (Beddewela and Herzig, 2013). However, this corporate legitimacy is put into question if the corporate and societal value systems diverge. Companies have, for example, been accused of pursuing strategies to change perceptions of responsibility without changing actual behaviour, deflecting attention in reporting onto other issues or even seeking to change external expectations of performance through reporting. Overall, strategies to manage threats to organisational legitimacy and establish, maintain or repair legitimacy through CRRep have been investigated in a large body of accounting research (an overview is given by Deegan, 2014).

Stakeholder theory also views companies as embedded within a business environment, which is composed of a diverse range of stakeholders (interest groups and individuals) who – directly or indirectly – can affect or are affected by companies' business operations (Freeman, 1984). Companies are thus considered to be bound by various social contracts with divergent stakeholders. Those stakeholders not only hold different perspectives on corporate business conduct but also vary in their ability to impact on corporate activities and corporate legitimacy. Examples of stakeholders threatening companies' licence to operate or legitimacy include consumers boycotting products and services and employees withholding their loyalty, while governments may impose fines or legal restrictions on the company.

Depending on the level of the importance assigned to stakeholder engagement, two competing perspectives on CRRep – stakeholder accountability and the business case – have increasingly been distinguished from each other because their power to enhance the accountability of organisational activities and impact is seen to differ considerably (Brown and Fraser, 2006; Gray et al., 2014). Stakeholder accountability focuses on increasing the transparency and accountability of companies to their stakeholders. Assuming that companies do have wider responsibilities than simply to generate money for their shareholders, the accountability of companies is extended here beyond the traditional role of providing financial accounts to the owner of capitals. CRRep thus serves the process of communicating the social and environmental effects of companies' economic actions to stakeholders to enable them to meaningfully participate in corporate decision-making and reporting. This is based upon the assumption that in a democratic society, stakeholders have certain information rights, which need to be protected against abuses of corporate power, and that enhanced accountability of companies encourages wider democratic processes of discourse and decision-making. The meaningful engagement with relevant stakeholders through reporting (irrespective of the power they might possess) approximates to what various scholars view as 'true', 'real' or the normative approach to accountability.

This contrasts with the second variant of stakeholder engagement and reporting where stakeholders are consulted or managed by companies through and around reporting processes to gain their support and approval. Here, engagement with CRRep takes place only when benefits are created for both wider stakeholders and the business itself ('win-win paradigm'). The range of reasons for businesses to produce corporate reports includes the creation of competitive advantage through the development and penetration of new market segments, creating financial value through, for example, business efficiency or the identification of possible cost-savings, and motivating and raising awareness among staff. Reasons also relate closely to the above-mentioned three theoretical lenses: using CRRep as a means for companies to legitimise their activities and impacts, and to manage their relationships with stakeholders to further their own interests. Employing stakeholder theory and reporting in such an organisation-centred way resonates in the production of corporate responsibility reports for reasons of reputation, impression and risk management.

The business case for corporate responsibility is, overall, a widely recognised motive underlying CRRep. From the perspective of stakeholder accountability proponents, however, using CRRep as a tool to primarily look after its powerful (i.e. often financially orientated) stakeholders and to report to the extent that it benefits the company's profits only leads to 'soft' accountability and does not promote participatory governance.

8.3.2 What are the Problems and Challenges of Corporate Responsibility Reporting?

A key problem following from the above discussion is the concern that the predominance of the business case perspective in practice deflects attention from social change and current problems to be addressed in corporate responsibility reports. There is criticism that companies may take the role of powerful 'elites' that steer society in a direction that reinforces their own dominance without making sufficient contributions to a sustainable development (Brown and Fraser, 2006; Cooper and Owen, 2007). This concern is manifested in the so-called 'performance–portrayal gap' (Adams, 2004) which reflects the view that reports often convey a favourable rather than a representative picture of the company and fail to establish relationships between environmental and social disclosure and actual performance. Corporate responsibility reports are thus often accused of assisting management in controlling the perceptions of stakeholders and seeking legitimacy and/or reputation rather than enhancing stakeholder accountability for the real impact of companies' activities on society.

To confront managerial capture of the social and environmental agenda and to reveal possible contradictions between a company's self-presentation, on the one hand, and stakeholder perspectives, on the other, the concept of shadow reporting has been put forward. Shadow reporting can be viewed as a technology that collects and compiles, makes visible, represents and communicates evidence from external sources, including newspaper articles, NGO reports, direct testaments from workers, ex-employees, trade unions, suppliers and public pollution registers (Dey, 2007). The purpose of these 'external' accounts (also referred to as 'anti-report', 'counter accounts' or 'social audits') is to reveal contradictions between what companies disclose in their corporate reports and what they suppress, in order to reveal problems with companies' activities and provide additional insights into environmental and social impacts associated with these activities. Overall, shadow reporting can be understood as an attempt to challenge CRRep and move away from an organisation-centred perspective of reporting through the use of independent but not necessarily objective sources (Dey, Russell and Thomson, 2011).

Wider criticism of CRRep includes concerns as to whether the legal company might be the wrong boundary to report on sustainability and demonstrate accountability for material social and environmental impacts. As Gray states: 'Sustainability is a planetary, perhaps regional, certainly spatial concept and its application at the organisational level is difficult at best' (Gray, 2006: 73). Another criticism is that CRRep tends to be non-specific, aiming at a diffuse and excessively wide group of potential readers. Besides uncertainties in boundary setting, this may be due to its dominantly voluntary nature and the somewhat overwhelming range of reporting guide-lines and standards (despite some notable tendencies of convergence – see section 8.4.1). A lack of target group orientation is also associated with the risk of creating an information overload. In particular in the 1990s and early 2000s, some companies tended to 'flood' their readers with increasingly extensive corporate responsibility reports. While this problem has generally diminished with the increased use of online reporting, the quality of reports leaves a lot to be desired at times. Companies are being criticised for putting incorrect and irrelevant data in corporate responsibility reports and considering environmental, social and economic aspects of organisational activities in an additive rather than integrative manner. They thereby fail to recognise and mention possible and actual conflicts and challenges embodied in companies' approach to sustainability.

Overall, it seems there is considerable scope for improvement with regard to the level of accountability provided by corporate responsibility reports, the quality of their content, the stakeholder engagement process and practices of external assurance. While there is a growing number of large, typically multinational companies producing corporate responsibility reports, it appears that many small- and medium-sized enterprises (SMEs) and family companies still do not engage with this topic to a great extent, although they play a significant role in markets, communities and society. Some reasons for this lack of engagement are the high and disproportionate costs associated with the production of reports and the inadequateness of reporting schemes for addressing companies' needs for and routines of managing their relationships with local customers and communities. However, the knowledge about whether and how these companies practise reporting and discharge accountability is rather limited as most research and publications (including texts such as this one) concentrate on the impacts and the role of large and multinational companies in governing sustainability issues at global level.

8.4 Approaches to Governing Corporate Responsibility Reporting

The rise in CRRep can, to a large extent, be attributed to the continuous development of guidelines, standards and regulations. They provide guidance to companies in the development of reports and aim at governing and spreading CRRep within and across countries and sectors. Guidelines are non-binding and often used as a basis for the voluntary development of corporate responsibility reports. They reflect practical experiences encountered by companies and other organisations and institutions. Organisations engaged in the development of these guidelines are governmental (both national and supranational) as well as non-governmental (e.g. industry associations, multi-stakeholder initiatives (MSIs) or research institutions). These guidelines have been followed by the development of standards for reporting and assurance and by the introduction of new regulations (mandatory reporting). Standards are issued by standardisation organisations and often form a basis for certification processes. By contrast, regulations on various forms of CRRep have a binding character and have been enforced by associations and ministries in various parts of the world.

The following section explores voluntary and mandatory frameworks for CRRep and critically reflects on their role in disseminating CRRep and enhancing transparency and accountability.

8.4.1 Voluntary Corporate Responsibility Reporting

A growing body of national and international guidelines for CRRep has evolved in the last two decades to support companies in developing reports and externally communicating their social, ecological and economic performance to satisfy the information needs of different stakeholder groups. A review of forty-five countries identified approximately fifty voluntary standards, codes and guidelines for CRRep (UNEP, KPMG Advisory, GRI and Unit for Corporate Governance in Africa, 2013). Table 8.1 portrays a selection of key voluntary frameworks for CRRep including their most important characteristics (see Chapter 7). As summarised in Table 8.1, the GRI, UN Global Compact (UNGC), EMAS and Carbon Disclosure Project (CDP) are among the most widely used voluntary reporting frameworks. These guidelines address different aspects of corporate responsibility, differ with regard to the sector and the size of companies they can be applied to, and vary in that some of them focus on the reporting content (themes and/or indicators), the reporting quality (formulating principles for the way of reporting and/or measuring) or the management process (providing guidance on how to design management processes underlying CRRep), and some others address all.

These guidelines and standards reflect increasingly mature but still diverse international frameworks for CRRep. In recent years, heightened attention has been given to strengthening the synergies and complementarities and avoiding conflicts or even competition between the initiatives (particularly regarding the largest and most commonly used ones). Closer collaboration between standard- or guideline-setting bodies and attempts to utilise synergies and to work towards convergence and harmonisation of the current reporting standards are, for example, reflected in the production and publication of linkage documents and mutual participation in development processes.

Associated with the enhanced convergence and harmonisation of the numerous reporting schemes is the expectation that this will further strengthen their adoption and implementation. The GRI appears to play a key role in achieving a convergence of the various approaches. The strategic alliance of the GRI and the UNGC was one of the first initiatives to reduce the complexity of reporting practices. Since 2010, the UNGC has encouraged its participants to use the GRI guidelines when demonstrating progress towards attainment of the ten principles of the UNGC within their annual Communication on Progress reports. Easier understanding of the multitude of reporting schemes is especially facilitated by the complementary character of the GRI's guidelines, the UNGC principles, the OECD Guidelines and the ISO 26000 norm, which has crystallised in the GRI G4 guidelines (see case study below).

Despite these convergences and clarifications of the relationships between the various initiatives, concern has been raised about the effectiveness of voluntary frameworks for CRRep in enhancing transparency and accountability, as will be discussed in the following section.

8.4.2 Mandatory Corporate Responsibility Reporting

For many years, there has been a lively debate concerning the role which governments should play in CRRep. Some researchers have called for governments to enact at least a minimal regulatory framework to overcome the incompleteness of voluntary non-financial reporting and the reluctance of a vast majority of companies to make any kind of CRRep. Mandatory reporting, it is argued, would prevent companies from conveying a misleading view of their activities and seeking to manage public impressions in their own interest through the provision of false or incomplete information (Adams and Narayan, 2007). By generating a more balanced CRRep, mandatory reporting is further assumed to foster the quality and hence the credibility of the information disclosed. Moreover, it is expected to provide a more consistent disclosure, thereby enabling a year-on-year comparison of corporate non-financial performance against set objectives and among various companies (Cowan and Gadenne, 2005).

However, concerns have been raised about relying on government regulations to prevent all the shortcomings of voluntary disclosure (Larrinaga,

Carrasco, Correa, Llena and Moneva, 2002). Sceptics question whether regulations (alone) can have a significant impact on both corporate accountability and the quality of CRRep (Cooper and Owen, 2007). It is also stressed that command and control regulation may not only be costly but also stifle innovation. In addition, mandatory reporting: might remove any corporate incentives to do more than necessary; is too inflexible to adjust to changes in the complex business environment; and generally contradicts the voluntary nature of corporate responsibilities. Table 8.2 summarises the advantages and disadvantages of voluntary and mandatory approaches to CRRep as discussed in literature.

In spite of the controversial debate about the role of mandatory frameworks for enhanced transparency and accountability, corporate responsibility issues have become the subject of a growing body of regulations. According to a study by UNEP et al., 72 per cent (or 130 policies) out of 180 CRRep frameworks identified in 45 selected countries can be classified as (at least partially) mandatory (UNEP et al., 2013).

Table 8.3 presents global CRRep initiatives in various countries and regions, most of which are mandatory, although each country and individual legislation concentrate on different issues with varying scopes of application

Table 8.2 Advantages and disadvantages of voluntary and mandatory corporate responsibility reporting

	Voluntary CRRep	Mandatory CRRep
Disadvantages	• Incomplete reporting • Reluctance in reporting behaviour • Focus on positive content • Less transparency • Less credible disclosure • Fewer comparable reports	• No empirical evidence that mandatory reporting significantly impacts corporate accountability and the quality of corporate responsibility reports • High cost of command and control regulation • Stifles innovation, which might limit innovation and creativity in reporting • Inflexible to changes in business environment • Contrary to the idea that corporate responsibilities are voluntary
Advantages	• Coincides with the idea that corporate responsibilities are voluntary • More creative reporting • More adaptable to changes in business environment	• Holistic reporting of positive and negative content • More balanced reporting • Higher quality of reporting • More credible disclosure • More consistent disclosure • Better year-on-year comparison of sustainability performance against set objectives • Better comparability of reports among companies

Table 8.3 Global efforts by governments and stock exchanges to foster corporate responsibility reporting

Country	Government disclosure efforts				Stock exchange disclosure efforts				
	Type of initiative	Policy type	Scope of subject matter	Scope of application	Type of initiative	Policy type	Scope of subject matter	Scope of application	Separate CSR index
Argentina	Regulation	Mandatory	ESG	> 300 employees	–	–	–	–	–
Australia	Regulation	Mandatory	ESG	All issuers of financial products	Regulation	Mandatory	ESG	Companies with exposure to social and environmental risks	–
Austria	Guidance	Voluntary	ESG	All companies	–	–	–	–	–
Belgium	Regulation	Mandatory	ESG	Pension fund managers	–	–	–	–	–
Brazil	–	–	–	–	'Comply with or explain' recommendations	Voluntary	ESG	All listed companies	Corporate governance index
Canada	Regulation	Mandatory	ESG	Pension plan administrators	–	–	–	–	Social venture exchange
China	Guidance (SASAC)	Binding	ESG	State-owned enterprises	Regulation (SSE and SZSE)	Mandatory	ESG	All listed companies	–
	Regulation 'GreenIPO'	Mandatory	Environment	All listed companies	Guidance	Voluntary	ESG	All listed companies	–
Denmark	Regulation	Mandatory	ESG	State-owned companies > 250 employees	–	–	–	–	–
Ecuador	Regulation	Mandatory	Environment	Companies with mining rights and causing emissions or spills	–	–	–	–	–
Finland	Guidance	Voluntary	ESG	Non-listed state-owned and state majority-owned companies	–	–	–	–	–
France	Regulation	Mandatory	ESG	> 500 employees	–	–	–	–	–

Country									
Germany	Guidance (GCSD)	Voluntary	ESG	All companies	–	–	–	–	Alternative energy index
	Regulation (BilReg)	Mandatory	ESG	Companies materially affected by ESG indicators	–	–	–	–	DAXglobal Sarasin sustainability index
Greece	Regulation	Mandatory	ESG	EU Modernisation directive	–	–	–	–	–
Hong Kong	–	–	–	–	Regulation	Mandatory	ESG	All listed companies	–
Hungary	Regulation	Mandatory	ESG	EU Modernisation directive	–	–	–	–	–
India	Regulation	Mandatory	ESG	Net worth > Rs 500 crore	Regulation	Mandatory	ESG	Top 100 companies	CSR exchange
Indonesia	'Comply or explain' regulation	Mandatory	Society and environment	Companies that manage or utilise natural resources	–	–	–	–	–
Ireland	Regulation	Mandatory	ESG	All financial institutions supported by gov. guarantee scheme	–	–	–	–	–
Italy	Guidance	Voluntary	ESG	EU Modernisation directive	–	–	–	–	–
Japan	Regulation	Mandatory	Environment	Specified companies and government agencies	–	–	–	–	Emissions trading exchange
Malaysia	Regulation	Mandatory	ESG	All listed companies	Regulation	Mandatory	Governance	All listed companies	–
Mexico	Guidance	Voluntary	Environment	All companies	–	–	–	–	–
The Netherlands	Regulation	Mandatory	Environment	All companies	–	–	–	–	–
Nigeria	–	–	–	–	–	–	–	–	Governance rating system
Norway	Regulation	Mandatory	ESG	All large companies	–	–	–	–	–
Pakistan	Guidance	Voluntary	ESG	All companies	–	–	–	–	–

Table 8.3 (*cont.*)

Country	Government disclosure efforts				Stock exchange disclosure efforts				
	Type of initiative	*Policy type*	*Scope of subject matter*	*Scope of application*	*Type of initiative*	*Policy type*	*Scope of subject matter*	*Scope of application*	*Separate CSR index*
Philippines	Guidance	Voluntary	ESG	All companies	'Comply or explain' recommendations	Voluntary	Governance	All listed companies	–
Saudi Arabia	Guidance	Voluntary	ESG	All companies	–	–	–	–	–
South Korea	Regulation	Mandatory	Society	Insurance companies	Regulation	Mandatory	Environment	All listed companies	–
Singapore	Regulation	Mandatory	Governance	All companies	Regulation	Mandatory	ESG	All listed companies	–
South Africa	–	–	–	–	Regulation	Mandatory	ESG, integrated reporting	All listed companies	Socially responsible index
Spain	Guidance	Binding	ESG	Government-sponsored commercial companies and state-owned business enterprises	–	–	–		–
Sweden	Regulation	Mandatory	ESG	All state-owned companies	–	–			–
Taiwan	Guidance	Voluntary	ESG	All companies	Regulation	Mandatory	ESG	All listed companies	–
Thailand	–	–	–		Regulation	Mandatory	Governance	All listed companies	–
Turkey	Guidance	Voluntary	ESG	All companies	–	–	–	–	Social stock exchange
United Kingdom	Regulation (FRC)	Mandatory	Environment, social and diversity	All companies	Regulation	Mandatory	Environment	All listed companies	–
United States	Regulation (40 CFR)	Mandatory	Environment	Large emitters of GHG	Regulation	Mandatory	Governance ethics	All listed companies	Dow Jones sustainability index
European Union	Regulation	Mandatory	ESG and diversity	Large companies > 500 employees	–	–	–	–	–

Adapted from: The Hauser Institute for Civil Society, 2014.

(see section 8.5.1). Besides governments and other regulatory bodies, the overview illustrates that stock exchanges have become another key player in actively fostering CRRep in various countries.

Europe's role as a pioneer of legislation on CRRep should be noted, even though the translation of European Directives into national laws has produced mixed results. Among the key developments at the European level has been the implementation of the EU Accounts Modernisation Directive with the reformed law regulating the balance sheet (European Parliament and European Council, 2004) which has forced shareholder companies to include non-financial performance indicators, specifically environmental and labour-related indicators, in the prognosis reports included in their annual reports. In 2014, the European Parliament and European Council enacted mandatory disclosure of a larger range of non-financial information by large companies. As a consequence, several thousand European companies will be required to report on their corporate responsibility policies, the associated results and risks, and risk management in their annual reports from 2017 (European Parliament and European Council, 2014). To date, some European countries (e.g. Germany, the UK) have kept the translation of the basic requirements of the European Directive into national laws to a minimum, while other countries have developed more comprehensive mandatory frameworks (often starting to engage in this topic before the European Directive was developed). France required listed companies to publish integrated annual reports incorporating approximately thirty topics on environmental, social and governance disclosures from 2001 to 2012, and as many as forty-two topics since 2013. The most recent revision of the regulatory framework will extend the applicability to large private French companies or subsidiaries of foreign companies and add new requirements of third-party verification. As a result, by January 2016 all unlisted companies with an annual revenue of more than €100 million and staff of more than 500 will be affected by what is one of the strongest stances yet taken by any national government to enhance transparency on environmental, social and governance issues in annual reports.

With regard to developing countries, South Africa represents a pioneer in CRRep. According to the King III Code on Corporate Governance, companies listed on the Johannesburg Stock Exchange have been required to produce a report which integrates financial and sustainability performance since 2010. This is one of many examples of stock exchanges taking responsibility for encouraging CRRep (Table 8.3). The Sustainable Stock Exchanges (SSE) Initiative is based on cooperation among investors, regulators and companies, and aims at enhancing corporate transparency. Over one-third of the fifty-five participating exchanges offer either CRRep guidance or training to their listed companies. Twelve of the fifty-five exchanges require aspects of environmental and/or social reporting for at least some of their companies, with seven of those exchanges requesting such reporting for all listed companies (e.g. Johannesburg Stock Exchange, Shanghai Stock Exchange, Shenzhen Stock Exchange,

Taiwan Stock Exchange), and five exchanges require such reporting for companies of a specific size or industry (SSE, 2014).

The developments in setting up new or extended mandatory frameworks for CRRep are characterised by two key features. First, while most CRRep regulations had long been limited to a small number of companies of a certain (usually large) size, recent developments have seen state-owned or listed companies, or companies that are significant emitters of pollution required to report. Second, the 'comply or explain' principle has become a common feature of new CRRep frameworks, for example, of the new European Directive on non-financial reporting (2014) or regulations at national levels (e.g. Denmark, South Africa). Based on this principle, companies can decide to comply, and thus disclose non-financial information, or to explain the reasons for not disclosing.

8.5 Country and Sector Developments

Although CRRep is a worldwide phenomenon, there are various regional and sectoral differences as regards its maturity. In this section, differences in the dissemination of CRRep across countries and regions as well as industry sectors are outlined.

8.5.1 How has Corporate Responsibility Reporting Developed in Countries and Regions?

CRRep has steadily increased in various parts of the world. Table 8.4 gives an overview of the progress in the publication of reports in forty-five countries from 1996 until 2015. Not only has the number of countries featuring CRRep considerably increased but so too has the percentage of the largest companies producing reports in every country. Whereas on average 18 per cent of all 100 largest companies surveyed by KPMG in 1996 engaged in CRRep, this percentage increased significantly to an average of 73 per cent in 2015.

Institutional and legitimacy theories were introduced earlier to explain the phenomenon of CRRep. They might also serve as an explanation of the country-level differences in reporting which can be observed in Table 8.4. Those countries that achieve the highest reporting frequencies all enforced regulations on mandatory CRRep either by government regulation or listing requirements of stock markets (or both). Moreover, companies from more developed countries also seem to provide higher reporting rates than companies from developing countries. This is commonly explained by the weak institutional frameworks of developing countries, low stakeholder pressures (consumers, legislators and society at large) and lack of resources and capacities, all leading to a low take-up of corporate responsibility initiatives and

Table 8.4 Two decades of corporate responsibility reporting: developments in selected countries
(Percentage of the largest 100 companies producing corporate responsibility reports)

Country	1996	1999	2002	2005	2008	2011	2013	2015
India	–	–	–	–	–	20	73	100
Indonesia	–	–	–	–	–	–	95	99
Malaysia	–	–	–	–	–	–	98	99
South Africa	–	–	1	18	45	97	98	99
United Kingdom	27	32	49	71	91	100	91	98
France	4*	4	21	40	59	94	99	97
Japan	–	21*	72	80	93	99	98	97
Denmark	10*	29	20	22	24	91	99	94
Norway	26*	31	30	15	37	–	73	90
Sweden	36*	34	26	20	60	72	79	87
United States	44	30	36	32	74	83	86	86
Brazil	–	–	–	–	78	88	78	85
Nigeria	–	–	–	–	–	68	82	85
Hungary	–	–	–	–	26	70	78	84
Singapore	–	–	–	–	–	43	80	84
Spain	-	-	11	25	63	88	81	84
Australia	5*	15	14	23	45	57	82	81
Canada	34*	–	19	41	62	79	83	81
Portugal	–	–	–	–	52	69	71	81
Chile	–	–	–	–	–	27	73	80
The Netherlands	31*	25	26	29	63	82	82	80
Italy	–	2*	12	31	59	74	77	79
China	–	–	–	–	–	59	75	78
Colombia	–	–	–	–	–	–	77	78
Taiwan	–	–	–	–	–	37	56	77
Switzerland	19*	–	–	–	39	64	67	75
Finland	7*	15	32	31	44	85	81	73
South Korea	–	–	–	–	42	48	49	73
Ireland	–	–	–	–	–	–	–	70
Germany	34*	38	32	36	–	62	67	69
Peru	–	–	–	–	–	–	–	69
Romania	–	–	–	–	23	54	69	68
Russia	–	–	–	–	–	58	57	66

Table 8.4 *(cont.)*

Country	1996	1999	2002	2005	2008	2011	2013	2015
Belgium	27*	16	11	9	–	–	68	59
Mexico	–	–	–	–	17	66	56	58
Poland	–	–	–	–	–	–	55	54
New Zealand	0*	–	–	–	–	43	47	52
Slovakia	–	–	–	–	–	63	57	48
Greece	–	–	–	–	–	33	43	46
Czech Republic	–	–	–	–	14	–	–	43
Oman	–	–	–	–	–	–	–	37
UAE	–	–	–	–	–	–	22	36
Angola	–	–	–	–	–	–	40	34
Israel	–	–	–	–	–	18	19	28
Kazakhstan	–	–	–	–	–	–	25	23
Bulgaria	–	–	–	–	–	54	–	–
Ukraine	–	–	–	–	–	53	–	–
N 100 that report (average in %)	**18**	**24**	**28**	**41**	**53**	**64**	**71**	**73**
Number of countries surveyed	**13**	**11**	**19**	**16**	**22**	**34**	**41**	**45**
Global 250 that report (average in %)	**–**	**35**	**45**	**64**	**83**	**95**	**93**	**92**

Notes: * Fewer than 100 countries surveyed.
Adapted from: Buhr et al., 2014; KPMG, 1996, 1999, 2002, 2005, 2008, 2011, 2013, 2015.

accountability measures. Furthermore, whereas Asian countries are well presented in KPMG's review of CRRep and in extant literature, knowledge about CRRep in Latin American countries (except for Mexico and Brazil) and sub-Saharan African countries (excluding South Africa) is as yet very limited. Some studies though indicate that the concept of socially responsible business and related reporting activities are more extensive in these countries than commonly perceived (Fifka, 2013).

8.5.2 How has Corporate Responsibility Reporting Developed in Sectors?

Industry affiliation is another institutional determinant assumed to impact CRRep. Research suggests that sectors which involve more direct risks to

Table 8.5 Two decades of corporate responsibility reporting: sectoral developments

(Percentage of the largest 100 companies producing corporate responsibility reports)

Sector	1996	1999	2002	2005	2008	2011	2013	2015
Mining	25	45	36	52	67	84	84	84
Utilities	40	55	50	61	62	71	79	82
Electronics and computers	33	30	24	35	58	69	78	79
Automotive	–	38	28	32	49	78	77	77
Oil and gas	43	53	39	52	59	69	72	76
Food and beverage	17	22	26	29	47	67	72	76
Financial services, securities and insurance	5	8	12	31	49	61	70	76
Personal and household goods	–	–	–	–	–	–	65	74
Chemicals and synthetics	74	59	45	52	62	68	65	74
Forest, pulp and paper	56	55	43	50	65	84	77	72
Construction and building materials	13	18	17	28	32	65	66	71
Healthcare and pharmaceuticals	41	50	30	30	25	64	69	69
Transport and leisure	22	33	37	38	39	57	69	69
Metals, engineering and manufacturing	25	17	24	25	41	61	69	68
Trade and retail	11	7	15	22	26	52	62	58
Communication and media	7	16	20	29	47	74	75	–
Other services	5	4	6	18	36	53	–	–
Total companies in survey	**903**	**1,100**	**1,900**	**1,600**	**2,200**	**3,400**	**4,100**	**4,500**
Top 100 companies from each of n countries	**13**	**11**	**19**	**16**	**22**	**34**	**41**	**45**

Adapted from: Buhr et al., 2014; KPMG, 1996, 1999, 2002, 2005, 2008, 2011, 2013, 2015.

society and the environment than others publish more corporate responsibility-related information than those from less polluting sectors, such as the finance and service industries. Environmentally sensitive companies face stronger stakeholder pressure and public scrutiny, and hence become more involved in sustainability considerations along their production and supply chains, and intend to avoid possible future environmental regulations as well as future boycott and protest movements. Table 8.5 provides an overview of the sectoral developments of CRRep from 1996 until 2015. This overview shows that companies in 'polluting sectors', such as mining, utilities, electronics and computers, and automotive, tend to engage in CRRep more frequently than companies in such sectors as the finance, securities, insurance and service industries (and reflect a longer involvement in the topic). Another observation is that differences between sectors have diminished over time. This might partly be due to a growing number of sector-specific reporting guidelines (e.g. the GRI's sector supplements and the EMAS' 'Sectoral Reference Documents on Best Environmental Management Practices'). However, it should be stressed again that a high level of disclosure does not automatically correspond with high performance. For example, the finance sector was seen for a long time as a laggard in CRRep. A commonly cited reason for the non-disclosure of environmental and social information was that financial institutions would not generate substantial environmental and social impacts themselves. Ironically perhaps, the financial crisis brought about dramatic consequences for our economy and society only shortly after the sector caught up with other sectors regarding its CRRep intensity in 2008.

8.6 Case Study: The Global Reporting Initiative

The most generally accepted and universally applied CRRep framework is provided by the GRI. The GRI is an international, network-based non-profit organisation representing an international MSI involving businesses, civil societies, academia and public institutions worldwide. The GRI is well known for the development and issuance of their sustainability reporting guidelines. The advances in GRI guidelines that have gradually evolved since their first inception in 2000 are substantiated for a variety of reasons including the need to remove any ambiguity in interpretation of concepts and principles, to improve companies' understanding of material issues, to include additional disclosure requirements as gathered from the stakeholder consultative method, and to reach harmonisation with other major guidelines or initiatives related to CRRep. In essence, the GRI reporting guidelines attempt to simplify and standardise the reporting of companies' non-financial and economic impacts, make the information more comparable and consistent, and ensure the disclosure of relevant, useful and timely information that reflects the organisations' sustainability activities. Today, the GRI represents the leading initiative in providing voluntary reporting guidelines with 60 per cent of the top 100 companies in forty-five nations applying the GRI in 2015. For standalone corporate responsibility reports, the GRI application rate is at 74 per cent (KPMG, 2015). Due to being a common and widespread reference for the design of corporate responsibility reports, the GRI guidelines can be considered to be a de facto standard for CRRep. Hence, the GRI is often regarded as a standard-setter that plays a crucial role in inducing organisations to act in a more sustainable way and to pursue further objectives besides pure profit-seeking behaviour.

GRI's most recent reporting guidelines are called the G4 framework, consisting of two complementary documents, the reporting principles and standard disclosures and the implementation manual. The first document contains three components:

1) Reporting principles with respect to the content and quality of reports;
2) Standard disclosures, which can be classified into seven sections: strategy and analysis, organisational profile, identified material aspects and boundaries, stakeholder engagement, report profile, ethics and integrity, and governance; and
3) Specific standard disclosures, which are composed of four parts: disclosures on management approach, economic indicators, environmental indicators and social indicators (labour practices and decent work, human rights, society and product responsibility). With respect to the specific standard disclosures, the GRI also offers ten sector disclosure guidelines with distinct metrics for specific sectors.

The second document is the implementation manual which offers valuable guidance on how to apply the reporting principles, how to prepare report information, and how to interpret the reporting guidelines' concepts.

The main advances of the G4 guidelines encompass better user-friendliness and accessibility for first-time reporters, improved technical quality of the guidelines, increased harmonisation with other international standards, and guidance on linking sustainability reporting with integrated reporting. The most central change in the G4 guidelines is the enhanced focus on materiality. By providing assistance in identifying material issues, they encourage companies to solely report the environmental, social and economic impacts that are relevant to them and their stakeholders. Although the materiality principle is not a new development of the G4, it has been amended by introducing the concept of boundaries. Companies are now not only asked to determine the most material aspects but are also required to describe whether the impact, making an aspect material, occurs inside or outside the organisation and where the impact ends. Reporting companies need to delineate the reason for an aspect's materiality and outline how the material aspects are managed within the organisation in the 'Disclosure on Management Approach'. The materiality principle also determines the selection of the content for the 'Specific Standard Disclosures' and requires companies to more thoroughly report on how they manage the material impacts of their supply chains and publish a report on supply chain risk assessment and management (Cohen, 2013).

The new G4 guidelines, and their focus on materiality, create various opportunities and challenges for the reporting organisations as well as for their stakeholders. The move from 'put it all out there' to 'less is more' (Cox, Derks and LeFevre, 2013: 1) shall enable companies to emphasise what is essential for them and their key stakeholders. By concentrating on and limiting their reports to critical topics and key risk impacts, companies cannot only shorten their reports but also increase their clarity, relevance and credibility. This reduction in information redundancy is intended to foster enhanced transparency and understanding regarding the selection, prioritisation and management of core issues selected for the report. From a stakeholder perspective, stakeholders are assumed to better process and respond to fewer but more relevant CRRep. Thus, companies disclosing more material reporting in line with G4 might be more likely to engage with and receive feedback from stakeholders, as their reports are likely to become more meaningful and comprehensible to their stakeholders (Cohen, 2013).

Additional benefits arise from the process of defining material aspects. By justifying why certain information is included or excluded and how the impact boundaries for each material aspect are set, companies must reflect the importance assigned to sustainability in their organisation and rethink their sustainability structures. Hence, companies' sustainability and strategy departments are required to cooperate more intensively and to integrate sustainability into their corporate strategy. If companies comply with the requirements of the materiality principle properly, they may create and derive value from the reporting process.

Although materiality is generally regarded as a positive advancement of the G4, it also entails certain challenges. First, many companies face difficulties in identifying their material issues, especially large companies that operate in different industries and provide a broad range of products and services. As those companies applying previous versions of the GRI guidelines used to include as much information as possible in their reports, they now might have difficulties in identifying truly material issues and might be hesitant about excluding aspects not material but which they used to report on before. In addition, the institutional framework also impacts companies' perception of material aspects. Even though some information might not be relevant in every cultural context, companies might not exclude this information because they fear stakeholder criticism. Furthermore, companies might struggle finding a balance between concentrating on materiality and achieving positive evaluations in ratings such as the CDP and other sustainability indices, because these ratings require them to disclose as much sustainability information as possible. Finally, the underlying process used to assess materiality includes further deficits. The GRI's 'Materiality Disclosures Service' does not provide content-related audits and thus cannot guarantee the quality of the information disclosed for the different stakeholders. Hence, some critics foster the introduction of a CRRep evaluation procedure performed by the GRI as an external auditor.

Questions for Discussion

1. Do you think that the materiality principle leads to more clarity, relevance and credibility in companies' CRRep or creates more challenges with respect to CRRep?

2. Do you think that the GRI gives companies too much discretion when designing their corporate responsibility reports?
3. Do you believe that companies may misuse the GRI 'label' by arguing that the report meets GRI standards, while at the same time the reported information does not signal high degrees of responsibility?
4. Do you agree with critics who argue that the GRI should start evaluating the reports in order to guarantee the quality of the information disclosed? Why, or why not?
5. How can the GRI tackle the problem involved in the simultaneous focus on materiality and the fulfilment of rating objectives?

8.7 Chapter Summary

This chapter has outlined and discussed key developments in CRRep. We have shown that the nature of CRRep and its governance has been subject to some fundamental change. Companies have extended the scope of their reports in terms of content (multi-issue reporting of global reach) and changed or amended their reporting medium (e.g. new forms of reports and use of the Internet). These developments have been driven and guided by emerging frameworks for reporting and assurance, changes in standard-setting, and, most recently, a slowly maturing regulatory environment for mandatory CRRep.

There seems to be great interest by large and multinational companies, in particular, to engage in this agenda. As the foregoing has delineated, the number of corporate responsibility reports is increasing, both across countries and sectors, and differences between countries and sectors have diminished (e.g. with regard to reporting rates). By relying on some key theoretical lenses at the organisational and meso-level (e.g. stakeholder, legitimacy and institutional theories), we have attempted to shed light on how these involvements can be explained and how practices in CRRep can be evaluated.

It should also become clear from this chapter that criticism of a misuse of reporting for the self-interest of companies – commonly known as green- or bluewashing – has persisted. In fact, it has not changed much since CRRep's origins. The key problem of CRRep lies in its struggle to achieve a sufficient level of accountability to stakeholders and society at large. This problem has accompanied developments in reporting for a long time and is likely to do so in the future if rights to information and ways of empowering stakeholders and engaging them more meaningfully in corporate decision-making and reporting do not become more strongly institutionalised. Overall it seems that, although CRRep forms the basis of a constantly growing body of literature and enjoys wide attention in practice, much remains to be done to fully appreciate and realise the importance of transparency, accountability and the role CRRep can play within this context.

Chapter Questions

1. Why do you think that companies should or do engage with CRRep?
2. We discussed the advantages and disadvantages of voluntary and mandatory frameworks for CRRep. Which arguments do you find more difficult to follow than others? What in your view would be a reasonable approach to governing CRRep?
3. Choose a company that interests you, consult its website and search for its (electronic version of the) corporate responsibility report. You can also include other information provided on the website in your analysis. What do you learn about the way in which the company identifies and engages with its stakeholders? To what extent are stakeholders' views and expectations recognisable and considered by the company in its report?

FURTHER RESOURCES

Bebbington, J., Unerman, J. and O'Dwyer, B. (Eds.) (2014). *Sustainability Accounting and Accountability* (2nd ed.). New York, NY: Routledge.
This textbook provides probably the most comprehensive and contemporary account of the theory and practice of corporate responsibility reporting.

Gray, R. H., Adams, C. and Owen, D. (Eds.) (2014). *Accountability, Social Responsibility and Sustainability: Accounting for Society and the Environment*. Harlow, UK: Pearson Education Limited.
This textbook is aimed at students who want to gain comprehensive views on the developments in accountability, social responsibility and sustainability theories and practices. It represents a critical account of the tensions between the way in which organisations are controlled and the need for greater responsibility and accountability to society.

Hopwood, A., Unerman, J. and Fries, J. (Eds.) (2010). *Accounting for Sustainability. Practical Insights*. New York, NY: A. G. Carrick Limited.
This book provides rich insights into different tools and techniques that companies use to advance their engagement in the area of corporate responsibility and reporting. The book features case studies from eight organisations including HSBC, Sainsbury's, Novo Nordisk and BT.

Centre for Social and Environmental Accounting Research (CSEAR): https://www.st-andrews.ac.uk/csear/
CSEAR is an international membership-based network that generates and disseminates knowledge on social and environmental accounting and accountability. The website includes a rich database with respect to social and environmental accounting and shadow reporting, guidance documents

such as 'How to research a company' and 'Approaches to practice', and a range of key websites in this field of research. Access to most parts of the website is free.

CorporateRegister, www.corporateregister.com
This is probably the largest online directory of corporate responsibility reports, with more than 65,000 reports from more than 12,000 companies (once registered, accessible free of charge). Membership fees, however, are required for the use of the website's advanced search functions and when accessing the statistics sections.

Global Reporting Initiative (GRI), www.globalreporting.org
Besides the latest G4 Sustainability Reporting Guidelines, the website of the GRI is a rich source of additional supporting tools including a taxonomy, a content index tool, report templates, software and additional guidelines (e.g. on sector-specific reporting and 'how to' guidelines for SMEs). An extensive range of other publications elaborating, for example, on links between GRI and other social responsibility initiatives and standards can also be found on the website.

Integrated Reporting (IR), www.theiirc.org
Besides a detailed description of the IIRC, this website provides further information on integrated reporting and the IR framework. In addition, managerial and academic resources, including company case studies, on integrated reporting can be accessed and more information on integrated reporting networks can be found.

KPMG, www.kpmg.com
This website offers the latest findings from KPMG's international survey on corporate responsibility reporting. Interactive charts enable the users to compare reporting and assurance rates across countries and sectors. The website also offers access to further useful sources, including a guide to materiality assessment and studies into trends in voluntary and mandatory corporate responsibility reporting.

Sustainable Stock Exchanges Initiative (SSE), www.SSEinitiative.org
The website of the SSE initiative outlines its current activities aimed at fostering cooperation between stock exchanges and investors, regulators, and companies to improve corporate transparency. An overview of relevant reports and a collection of corporate responsibility reporting policies adopted around the world can be found here.

9

NGO Activism and CSR

FRANK G. A. DE BAKKER AND FRANK DEN HOND

Learning Objectives

- Understand the role of non-governmental organisation (NGO) activism in corporate social responsibility (CSR).
- Distinguish the characteristics of different types of activist NGOs, their tactics and (aspired) outcomes.
- Develop an overview of interactions between activist NGOs and firms.
- Apply these insights to a case study on activist NGO–business interactions.

9.1 Introduction: No Fracking Way!

A decade ago, few people would have heard about *fracking*, a technical process for the extraction of natural gas from rocky undergrounds that is based on creating fissures in the rock to allow for the extraction of the gas. The imminent depletion of more accessible natural gas supplies has made the technique an attractive supplement to more conventional extraction technologies. Yet, fracking has met with a lot of protest. In many countries, activist NGOs have pointed out the risks associated with the technology, including environmental pollution, occupational health hazards and earthquakes. They organised rallies, started petitions and took legal action; the targets being the companies that (intend to) use fracking technology and the authorities that issue the required licences. Not all protest was successful, but some projects were reconsidered and it surely sparked heated debate. Today, many people know about fracking.

This is just one example of the many issues on the agendas of activist NGOs. Many of their issues are about the conditions and consequences of corporate activities; think of climate change, child labour, workers' rights, product safety, or pollution. Whether activist NGOs seek to stop contested corporate practices or prefer to collaborate with industries and businesses in order to develop better alternatives, NGO activism has become a lasting element in the discourses and practices of CSR.

Understanding how NGO activism offers opportunities and poses challenges to firms is important to appreciate the broader question of what makes businesses more socially responsible. This chapter discusses NGO activism as a driver of CSR in the following way. We first provide an overview of what activist NGOs are. Next, we explore the various ways by which activist NGOs seek to influence corporate policies, ranging from collaboration and partnerships to contestation and protest. Then, we discuss which firms are more likely to encounter NGO activism, and how they may respond to it. At the end of this chapter, readers should be able to explain the role of NGO activism in CSR; to distinguish the characteristics of different types of activist NGOs and their tactics and (aspired) outcomes; and to develop an overview of types of interactions between activist NGOs and firms.

9.2 Activist NGOs: What Are They?

Over the last decades, interactions between firms and their organisational environments have attracted more and more attention. In these interactions activist NGOs have assumed an increasingly prominent position. Whereas previously they would typically have turned to governments in order to get their claims on businesses honoured through legislation or law enforcement, more recently activist NGOs have addressed their claims directly to businesses. This development is related to globalisation:

1. Policies of liberalisation and deregulation have made governments reluctant to directly regulate business, preferring other policy instruments such as self-regulation;
2. The unprecedented internationalisation of production and trade has changed the nature of their externalities from local to global, from isolated to interconnected; and
3. The availability and widespread adoption of information and communication technologies has facilitated the fast transfer of information across the globe.

For example, issues such as climate change and labour conditions in supply chains are highly complex, spread out across the boundaries of national and even regional authorities, and are rife with uncertainty. They have no easy solutions. Under such conditions, when climate change and other issues can no longer be effectively addressed by national policy-making only, many NGOs and businesses have come to realise that their involvement is needed. Some firms have taken proactive roles, out of perceived self-interest or because they believe they can contribute to addressing the issue. Others have been more sceptical and reluctant, only to experience pressure in public opinion and from activist NGOs to change their posture. Who are these activist NGOs? How can we define these groups that seek to influence firms' policies and practices? To define 'activist NGOs' we first need to define what NGOs are. That is not an easy task. In part, they are defined by what they are *not*: they are organisations, but not associated with the (national, regional or local) state structure, hence the label '*non-governmental*'. So are most business firms, but unlike firms, NGOs are not interested in making a profit; their *raison d'être* is in advancing some cause. When that cause is largely a private matter, such as (in many countries) the organisation of religion or sports, they are usually referred to as civil society organisations; when their cause is in advancing a common good or the interests of a third party (but not commercial or business-related), they are called NGOs. Often, a distinction is made between different types of NGOs: 'direct aid' NGOs aim to support those in need, 'empowerment' NGOs aim to strengthen local communities in achieving their objectives, and 'advocacy' NGOs attempt to influence the policy-making processes of governments and businesses. Of course, these categories are not mutually exclusive: some NGOs are of a mixed type, for instance when they combine (local) empowerment and international advocacy.

There are many organisations that operate independently from government and business and that are not driven by a profit motive. They vary according to whom they are accountable (if at all: members, constituents, donors, beneficiaries, etc.) and go by labels that emphasise some particular characteristic. We have civil society organisations, secondary stakeholders, social movement organisations, public interest groups and yet others. All of these labels are problematic as they are not mutually exclusive. Many actual organisations fit more than one label or are hybrids. For example, consumer leagues such as automobile clubs AA in the UK and ADAC in Germany are private interest groups, yet they not only advance the interests of their members but also (claim to) work for a common good; as not-for-profit organisations (NPOs) they nevertheless have substantial commercially profitable activities. Table 9.1 provides an overview of related terms and some examples.

In this chapter we narrow our focus to what we call 'activist NGOs' in order to emphasise, on the one hand, their willingness to organise collective action in the pursuit of their objectives, and on the other hand, their independence from state structures and commercial interests. They can also be referred to as NPOs, NGOs, INGOs (when they operate internationally), CSOs, secondary stakeholders and/or public interest groups. Some may consider them to be private interest groups; what is a 'public' and what is a 'private' interest can sometimes be debated and is ideologically laden. Activist NGOs not only lobby national, regional and/or local governments, but they also organise media campaigns to influence public opinion around the themes that they find important, and actively engage with others in collaborative and/or contentious ways in order to realise their objectives. In the context of this chapter, they muster supporters and resources which they use to help companies become more socially

Table 9.1 NGOs, activists and related organisational concepts

Label	Definition, characteristics, examples
Not-for-profit organisations (NPOs)	Organisations that do not have as their main objective the provision of income for their owners or shareholders.
Non-governmental organisations (NGOs)	Organisations that are not controlled by the state. Strictly speaking, business firms are NGOs when they are not state-owned, but usually business firms are not considered to be NGOs: the term is reserved for organisations that are neither a part of a government nor a conventional for-profit business. Often, a distinction is made between: • 'direct aid' NGOs, who seek to provide assistance to people in need: e.g. Red Cross, Médécins Sans Frontières (MSF) • 'empowerment' NGOs, who seek to stimulate emancipation of local communities and minorities: e.g. OXFAM • 'advocacy' NGOs, who seek to influence government or business policy: e.g. Greenpeace.
International non-governmental organisations (INGOs)	NGOs that operate in international arenas and have offices in several countries.
Civil society organisations (CSOs)	Organisations that do not operate in the realms of the state or the market. 'Civil society' is therefore considered the 'third' sector of society, associated with family and the private sphere, emphasising voluntary action, as distinguished from political and economic action. Examples include sports clubs, churches, neighbourhood committees, human rights organisations.
Secondary stakeholders	Organisations or groups upon whom a business firm does not in a direct way depend for its economic survival, such as media, communities and regulators.
Private interest groups	Organisations that seek to advance the private interests of its members, such as business associations, labour unions and consumer leagues.
Public interest groups	Organisations that seek to advance some public interest, or common good, beyond the private interests of its members.
Activist groups and social movement organisations (SMOs)	Organisations or groups of people that exhibit a propensity to mobilise and organise campaigns around themes they deem important, typically in opposition to some political, legal, cultural, religious or other kind of authority. The members of some activist groups are willing to run personal risks and to make certain sacrifices in order to reach their goals. Examples include Greenpeace, PETA, Friends of the Earth.

responsible (or less socially irresponsible). In the next sections we will examine these activist groups' activities in more detail.

9.3 NGO Activism: Some Characterisations

There are many possible grounds for comparison between different activist NGOs. Obviously, the objectives and focal areas of activist NGOs vary in topic and in scale: from environmental pollution to worker rights and child labour, from local to transnational. Rather than going into detail on all the varieties of activist objectives here, we introduce three important distinctions: preferred mode of operation, ideological position and tactical repertoire (den Hond and de Bakker, 2007).

First, regarding their preferred *mode of operation* we distinguish between collaboration and contention. Many activist NGOs engage in collaboration with corporations, enter in dialogue and agree to participate in corporate initiatives such as stakeholder engagement and cause-related marketing. A vast literature has developed on cross-sector partnerships and closely related concepts such as social alliances (cf. Seitanidi and Crane, 2014). This literature examines how actors from different backgrounds collaborate in order to establish some shared objectives, pool resources and develop joint standards or approaches to issues of shared concern, such as those relating to CSR. Collaboration can be an effective way for activist NGOs to influence corporate activities as joint projects and partnerships offer them the ability to steer corporate initiatives.

Other activist NGOs pursue more contentious engagements with corporations: they target corporations because they think collaboration is not an effective means to establish their goals of driving corporations towards greater levels of social responsibility. They are convinced that collaboration could jeopardise their independent position or their options to remain critical of corporate initiatives. Nevertheless, some activist NGOs entertain both collaborative and antagonistic relationships with the same corporations, depending on the topic or the geographical setting.

A second way to consider the different types of interactions between activist NGOs and businesses is by looking at the ideological position of the NGOs involved. We distinguish between radical and reformist NGO activist groups. Radical groups are the ones that 'offer a more comprehensive version of the problem and more drastic change as a solution' (Zald and McCarthy, 1980: 8). They strive for fundamental change in their area of concern and think that companies cannot be part of their envisaged solution, as in their view corporate 'success' is closely tied to the very problem they seek to address. On the other hand, reformist activist groups are inclined to work with business to evoke corporate social change. Although they see current business practices as part of the problem, they also think business can and should be part of the solution by reforming their ways of operating. Obviously, radical and reformist are the two poles of a spectrum and many intermediate positions are possible. Yet, to understand the different tactical approaches NGO activists use at the operational level, we build on this distinction.

A third way to characterise different activist NGOs is by looking at their tactical repertoire. Building on the work of della Porta and Diani, we suggest that three dimensions categorise the deployment of tactics by activist NGOs (della Porta and Diani, 1999). Their tactics can aim at inflicting damage or bringing gain, both of which can be symbolic or material. A boycott is an example of a tactic aimed at exerting pressure on a targeted firm or industry through inflicting material damage; a massive media campaign in support of an alternative practice is an example of a tactic aimed at establishing symbolic gain. Tactics aimed at a material impact directly affect the cost structure of a firm, either positively or negatively, whereas tactics with a symbolic impact affect the reputation of an organisation, again either positively or negatively. The first dimension is thus the nature of the intended effect on corporations.

Another dimension to categorise the deployment of tactics is in the amount of support that is needed to make some tactic effective. Some tactics only require a limited number of committed people in order to be effective. For example, maintaining a website to expose corporate misdoings only requires the efforts of a relatively small number of dedicated people. Similarly, preparing legal action can be done by a few highly competent individuals. In both examples the activists need specialised knowledge (and funds to finance their work). Other tactics rely on the participation of large numbers of people: a boycott can only succeed if enough people decide not to buy a certain product or service. As involving large numbers of participants in a tactic can be difficult to organise, activist NGOs will typically start off using tactics that require only a small number of dedicated participants. Staging a media campaign, negotiating collaboration and conducting research are some of the other tactics that can be thought of here.

Finally, there is also a time dimension to the deployment of tactics. When the use of some tactics turns out to be ineffective, there is a likelihood of escalation. Many activist NGOs initially choose tactics that require relatively small numbers of participants to be effective, but when these are to no avail they may seek to escalate. Escalation can be sought in various ways, such as moving from collaboration to confrontation, from tactics that require few participants to those that depend on large numbers of participants, from using 'carrots' (and 'sermons') to using 'sticks', or from inflicting symbolic to inflicting material damage. Radical and reformist activist groups are likely to differ in how they seek escalation, as their ultimate objectives and worldviews are very different. Diverging ideological positions imply different views on what is desirable, what is feasible, and how this should be accomplished. For example, radical activist NGOs are more likely to escalate towards tactics that increase material damage but are less likely to rely on large numbers of participants; reformist activist NGOs are more likely to escalate towards tactics that increase symbolic damage and that require large numbers of participants for their efficacy.

9.4 How NGO Activism Affects Corporations

There is a wide variety of tactics that activist NGOs deploy in their attempts to make businesses more socially responsible, or less irresponsible. Several studies have examined the tactical repertoires that NGO activists have at their disposal; in this chapter we group their tactics according to how they affect corporations. We specifically focus on tactics working through (corporate) governance, through financial means and through collaboration. Whereas these three sets of tactics imply direct engagement with firms, a fourth route works in an indirect manner, by creating alternatives to the provision of services and products by corporations.

9.4.1 Shareholder Activism

A distinction should be made between shareholder activism on social issues versus financial shareholder activism. The focus, here, is on shareholder activism on social issues. Both types of shareholder activism make use of the principal–agent relationship between a firm's owners and its management in order to influence privately held corporations, that is, they make use of the firm's corporate governance structure. For example, activist NGOs may find allies among a firm's shareholders who can voice their claims. Potential shareholder allies include large financial institutions such as banks, insurance companies, pension funds or social investment funds. Or, activist NGOs can become shareholders themselves and use the associated rights in shareholder meetings. Shareholder activism offers activist NGOs the option to exert influence through the threat of damage, either by generating negative publicity for the firm (i.e. symbolic damage) as shareholder meetings are typically well covered by financial media, or by stimulating institutional investors to invest in (or divest) the shares of particular companies, which is thought to increase (or decrease) the cost of capital for these companies (i.e. material gain/damage).

Shareholder activism in the form of **socially responsible investment (SRI)** was introduced by religious communities in the USA, such as the Quakers and Methodists. Early examples include their abstaining from investing in companies that undertake activities they disprove of for religious or moral reasons, such as making use of slave labour, the production and selling of tobacco, guns or alcohol, or gambling (Guay, Doh and Sinclair, 2004). Today, such negative screening is still a prevalent strategy, but it has been complemented by positive screening: investments are made solely in firms that meet certain criteria regarding their environmental, social and corporate governance (ESG) policies and performances. These criteria can be absolute or relative ('best in class', 'showing improvement'). Positive screening not only requires criteria, but also the production and processing of large amounts of verified data on how well various companies perform on these criteria; an entire industry has emerged around ESG reporting by companies, the verification of reported data, the rating of companies and the creation of a large number of subtly differentiated investment portfolios to meet the various preferences that are found in the market.

When investors use negative screening to inform their investment decision, they may feel little need to engage with a firm's management. However, when they use positive screening, there may be reasons for them to do so. For example, when a firm they have invested in (or that they would like to invest in) creates great value for its owners and almost meets their criteria for investment, they may wish to urge the firm's management to improve its performance on the wanting criteria. This mechanism, that a (major) shareholder uses its ownership rights to influence decisions of the company it has invested in, offers plenty of options to activist NGOs. When firms are publicly traded, NGO activists can use shareholder meetings to communicate their demands. Such meetings are attended by senior management, shareholders and the financial press. Attracting attention for one's cause at such events hence is one way to spread the NGO activists' demands among a wider audience; financial press covers these events, other shareholders may be triggered by the calls, while senior management may feel (or be, through voting) required to respond. This is certainly the case in the USA where 'proxy voting' has become the standard. Once a proposal had been submitted and met certain criteria, firm management has two options: either to reply to the proposal and put that resolution up for voting in the shareholder meeting, or to negotiate with the filers of the resolution. When an announced proposal is withdrawn this can be seen as a signal of success for the filers: apparently the need to put the proposal up for vote has disappeared because management has given in to their demands or because it has reached a compromise with the filers (Graves, Rehbein and Waddock, 2001). Similar pressures can be exerted in other jurisdictions, using the shareholder meeting and working through allies.

Although social shareholder activism is booming, the impact of this type of activism is difficult to determine and is sometimes seen as more procedural than substantial (Vogel, 2005). Furthermore, while this tactic may work with large firms that are listed on the stock market, it is less obvious how it would work vis-à-vis firms with different ownership structures, including many small and medium-sized enterprises (SMEs). Hence, it is important to look beyond these tactics to the other ways by which activist NGOs can exert influence on firms.

9.4.2 Operational Costs and Benefits

When we discussed shareholder activism we highlighted its potential influence on firms' cost of capital. Yet, there are more ways in which activist NGOs can impact the financial situation of a firm: they can try to influence its operational costs and benefits, both positively and negatively. There are two main routes to do so: directly through the marketplace and indirectly through the mobilisation of public opinion.

9.4.2.1 Marketplace Tactics

Our starting point to consider how activist NGOs can affect operational costs and benefits is in the field of 'political' or 'ethical' consumerism. The main tenet here is that consumption is fraught with ethical and political issues: buying a piece of clothing is not just to purchase some functionality, or to express adherence to some fashion, but also to financially support a firm that pollutes the environment and exploits workers, either directly or through its supply chains, and to contribute, when the piece of clothing is no longer worn, to the production of household waste. Political and ethical consumers seek to change firms, markets, industries and supply chains through their choice of products, services and producers (Micheletti, 2003). Which products, services or producers they select is informed by their evaluations of the supplier. Activist NGOs play important roles in developing and disseminating such evaluations, and in convincing firms that there is a demand worth catering for (Dubuisson-Quellier, 2013). Consumers can thus leverage activists' claims as they have a direct impact on a firm's sales: informed by activist NGOs' claims, consumers are politicised to use the marketplace as an arena for change.

Consumers' buying power is thus critical in political consumerism. By withholding their buying power, that is, by *not* buying certain products or services, consumers can exert influence over firms, provided they do so in sufficiently large numbers. After all, a boycott needs substantial numbers of participants to be effective and thus a problem of collective action needs to be overcome. Hence they need to make sure they reach and convince a fair amount of consumers. This requires considerable effort and has proven very difficult. Just as activist NGOs can call for a boycott to demonstrate that they disapprove of a certain issue, they can also call for a 'buycott': calling upon consumers to use their buying power in support of certain products or producers that are preferred for the values embedded in them.

Boycotts have been around for a long time. Well-known examples include the boycotts of multinationals that had invested in South Africa during the times of the Apartheid regime (from the 1960s to the mid-1990s), and the boycott of Shell in Germany over its plans to sink off the Brent

Spar oil rig in the mid-1990s. Examples of buycotts can be found in movements that seek to support local ('buy local'), fair trade and ecological products in the market. Beyond these, buycotts are more difficult to find, probably because they are less media savvy. One high profile example in the Netherlands is how the Dutch animal rights activist NGO 'Wakker Dier' introduced positive advertisements in its media campaigns against intensive animal husbandry, to praise those supermarket chains that made a significant step towards banning 'factory farmed meat' from their shelves. Of course, Wakker Dier also broadcast negative advertisements, in which it 'named and shamed' supermarket chains that had not done enough to ban 'factory farmed meat' from their shelves. These advertisements are examples of how activist NGOs may 'reward' or 'punish' companies through the market mechanism, by seeking to influence consumers' purchasing behaviour and thereby to shape markets.

Additionally, activist NGOs have been highly involved in advancing labels and standards as a way to influence 'value' and 'valuation' in the market. Through their involvement in standards and labels, activists can have an impact on what is considered a product or service that has been produced in an appropriate manner. The Marine Stewardship Council (MSC) for instance was established from the collaboration between a company (Unilever) and an NGO (World Wide Fund for Nature (WWF)). After the collapse of cod fishery in parts of the Atlantic Ocean, both had a joint interest: WWF was concerned about the loss of biodiversity whereas Unilever was concerned about its long-term supply of fish. Together they took the initiative to start the MSC which soon became independent of its founders. Nevertheless, this initiative is a clear example of collaboration between a firm and an activist NGO that worked through the marketplace, signalling to consumers that fish products that were labelled with the MSC logo had been produced in a well-managed, more sustainable way.

According to Micheletti, the use of boycotts, buycotts and labelling schemes has flourished since the 1990s, and their effect on firms' operational costs can make them successful (Micheletti, 2003). Yet, as these tactics require the participation of large numbers of consumers, they can be difficult and costly to organise. Hence, they are not among the tactics that activist NGOs initially select in their efforts to increase firms' CSR.

It is important to note that there is another set of tactics that can have the effect of increasing a firm's operational costs, although it may or may not be legal and is based on principles of non-violent action – that is, non-violent to people. Sabotage, obstruction of facilities, e.g. by the blocking of gates, and the hacking of computer networks are some of the tactics that more radical activist NGOs sometimes resort to. These tactics are not only highly visible in the media and thereby draw public opinion to the issue at stake (see next section), they can also be very disruptive for the daily operations in firms and thereby increase costs.

9.4.2.2 Public Opinion Tactics

A key factor for the success of boycotts and buycotts is the widespread dissemination of information regarding which ones are ongoing, why they are called for, and what their purposes are. Lists of current boycotts can be found on websites such as www.ethicalconsumer.org, and mobile apps have become available such as the one developed by buycott.com. Public opinion tactics, the use of mass media and social media to spread information and emotion on industries, firms, and their products and services, are very important to NGO activism that seeks to affect operational costs and benefits.

Mass media of course has the possibility to influence public opinion, and thereby to add to, or distract from, the reputation of those people, organisations or entities on which they shine the spotlight. Working through mass media offered a range of new means to NGO activists. They use media campaigns to support firms that work in line with their objectives, and to inflict symbolic damage on firms that do not. A firm's reputation is considered to influence its sales and market shares, and the overall attractiveness as an employer. Hence, reputation has become so important for many firms that they are eager to bolster or protect their reputations. Firms' heavy reliance on reputations thus gives activist NGOs a lever to gain influence: if their tactics support corporate reputations then that might be a selling point; if their tactics potentially harm these reputations then this strengthens activists' position vis-à-vis the firm. The advertisements by Wakker Dier, referred to above, are a point in case.

A wide variety of public opinion tactics communicate about corporate policies, plans and activities in an effort to influence both business and the general public. These tactics can be contentious, non-contentious or a mix of both. By endorsing certain firms, products or practices, NGO activists can provide symbolic gain to firms and strengthen their reputations; by engaging in negative publicity (in press, online or at meetings), NGO activists can exert pressure on firms and damage their reputations. One specific example of the latter tactic is 'culture jamming': corporate symbols and logos are taken out of context, transformed and released to the public. The subversion of well-known symbols or logos is supposed to disrupt the general public's positive attitude by raising questions and criticising the firm and its behaviour (e.g. adbusters.org). Rather than calling these people to action, this tactic causes negative publicity. As Bennett noted: 'unlike boycotts, many contemporary issue campaigns do not require consumer action at all; instead, the goal is to hold a corporate logo hostage in the media until shareholders or corporate managers regard the bad publicity as an independent threat to a carefully cultivated brand image' (Bennett, 2003: 152). Starting off as a threat of symbolic damage, such a tactic thus could well develop into one that inflicts material damage.

Over the last decade, several studies examined the impact of protest on market value. King and Soule found that the staging of protest did have a negative impact of stock price, but also that 'the most powerful feature of protest vis-à-vis stock price lies in its ability to upset image management, not in its ability to threaten direct costs to firms' (King and Soule, 2007: 38). Bartley and Child investigated the effects of anti-sweatshop campaigns on firms (Bartley and Child, 2011). They found 'compelling evidence' that only 'specialized and recognizable firms experienced notable declines in sales as they faced anti-sweatshop campaigns' (ibid.: 439). They also found a significant effect on stock price but only a limited effect on corporate reputation (ibid.: 445). Both studies were in the USA. These, and other studies, thus find mixed evidence of the impact of boycotts and campaigns. In individual cases, however, the impact may be substantial. That is of course what activist NGOs hope for, while the overall mixed evidence poses a dilemma to firms facing activism about whether and how to respond.

9.4.3 Partnerships

Yet another way for activist NGOs to exert influence over firms is to collaborate with a corporation, for example in the form of a partnership or alliance. Influence through collaboration is based on the 'giving and taking' between the parties that may be needed to develop common ground and shared objectives. Cross-sector collaborations have grown in prominence. Within the literature a whole range of partnerships is distinguished, ranging from social partnerships to cross-sector partnerships or social alliances. Although these partnerships differ in their exact focus and composition, they all involve a willingness to collaborate between different types of actors. According to Seitanidi and Crane, they can be characterised as 'the joining together of organisations from different sectors of society to tackle social problems' (Seitanidi and Crane, 2014: 1). Some of these partnerships involve the transfer of resources while others focus on establishing change in corporate policies and/or products. The development of standards and labels is one example (think of the MSC label mentioned earlier); collaboration on new products or services is another one. For example, several NGOs have teamed up with firms to increase the use of solar power. There also exist partnerships in which activists and firms collaborate to impact other firms, for example in the agri-food or clothing and shoes industries, in which firms and activist NGOs collaborate in helping other firms in the supply chain to reduce their environmental impact or to improve their labour conditions (e.g. McDonnell, 2016). In section 9.7 we present a detailed example of the different ways the NGO activist organisation Clean Clothes Campaign aims to impact firms in the garment industry.

Radical NGO activists are less likely than reformist groups to enter into partnerships with firms. After all, as they typically consider firms not to be part of their desired solution, they will not be much inclined to engage in partnerships. Reformist groups, on the other hand, will be willing to work with firms to try and change their behaviour, as reforming current practices is crucial in their worldview. For them, to enter a partnership may offer an effective way to induce change at a corporate level: their presence in the partnerships gives them influence. Many partnerships are presented as successful initiatives that create 'win-win situations'.

Yet, there is also criticism of the positive tone in which cross-sector partnerships are discussed. One could wonder what their actual contribution is: do partnerships really contribute to social change? Critics have argued that partnerships can be used, and indeed are used, by firms for window-dressing or greenwashing: they show off with a partnership but do not really change their operations or strategies. Finally, it is feared that NGOs jeopardise their independence when entering a partnership, by being co-opted. Co-option refers to processes by which authorities (e.g. government agencies, leadership teams or business firms) absorb critics into their policy or decision-making structures as a means of neutralising the threat that critics may pose to their stability or existence. For some activist NGOs, the risk of being co-opted is a reason for refraining from positive engagement with corporations. Notwithstanding such critique, partnerships can have far-reaching consequences in changing markets and organisations. Some standards and labels have led to the widespread adoption of new 'rules of the game' and therefore partnerships are likely to remain an important tactic for many activist NGOs.

9.4.4 New Business Systems

For some activist NGOs, partnerships are not a viable option. The more radical activist NGOs may well argue that entering into collaboration or negotiation with companies confers legitimacy to the entities whose very legitimacy they fundamentally contest. Others refrain from collaboration with firms because they feel that doing so would limit their ability to publicly criticise them. If, furthermore, their analysis is that protest is unlikely to fundamentally change the behaviour of companies, e.g. because the problems they seek to address are systemic and inherent to the prevailing corporate capitalist system, or if they would rather invest their energy in a positive way to create something new, they may turn away from engaging with firms. Instead, they may choose to contribute to developing some alternative economic order. Rather than challenging individual corporations, it is the institution of corporate capitalism that they challenge and that they seek to replace with one that, in their view, is not oppressive, exclusive, exploitative and polluting, but democratic, liberating, inclusive, respectful and sustainable. Such has been the thrust, e.g., of the Occupy and Alterglobalization movements.

There are many and widely diverging examples of initiatives that subscribe to such an agenda, including worker-owned factories and shops, local exchange trading systems and networks (LETS), such as time banks, food collectives, etc. Time banks, for example, are self-organising collectives, in which members exchange services of which the value is measured in units of time.

The common denominator of all these initiatives is a desire of their participants to become less dependent on the dominant corporate capitalist system. While there is the awareness that complete autarky is probably an ephemeral dream, participating in them is for many participants both an act of self-fulfilment and a way of showing that some alternative is possible. This is not a new idea. Whereas the idea and the term 'LETS' was coined in the early 1980s, various sorts of workers', consumers' and producers' cooperatives had already been set up in the mid-1800s to counter corporate power in areas such as agriculture, finance and retail, resulting in for instance cooperatively owned and managed sugar refineries, banks, supermarkets and – more recently – facilities for the production of wind power. The long and successful history of many such cooperatives suggests that multiple ways of organising economic exchange can be viable, and indeed can compete head on with more ideal-typical capitalist firms that are dominant in Western markets. Some of the alternative practices that cooperatives developed have been adopted by conventional firms: the organic agriculture movement has over time contributed to the mainstreaming of organic products in mainstream food markets. Yet, this development involves a risk as it might lead to crowding out organic producers by larger mainstream producers (Sikavica and Pozner, 2013).

Another form of new business systems is found in social enterprises. These organisations link their activities to a social mission and offer a business-like contrast to traditional non-profit organisations (Dart, 2004). In some of these enterprises, governments are heavily involved, whereas in others cooperation with existing firms is actively sought. Yet other social enterprises highlight the link with the local community in which they operate, such as the so-called community-enterprises that have become more prominent in the United Kingdom.

All in all, creating alternatives to current business systems provides the opportunity to establish new norms and standards that better fit the objectives of the activist group and that establish links between local communities and business initiatives, but the mainstreaming of these alternatives can also be a risk for the original initiatives.

9.5 Which Corporations are NGOs likely to target?

In a chapter highlighting NGO activism and CSR, it is also important to discuss which corporations are likely to encounter NGO activism. In the literature some attention has been given to the question of which factors increase the likelihood that firms are targeted by activists. These same factors may well be relevant as incentives or disincentives in explaining why NGOs select particular firms as partners.

According to Hendry, a firm is more likely to be targeted by NGO activism when (1) it is a proven, repetitive trespasser of social or legal norms, (2) it is visible to consumers in the value chain or through brands and is an important player in the industry, or (3) it operates in an industry that is under high levels of scrutiny by activist groups (Hendry, 2006). If a firm is a repeated wrong-doer, it will be easier to mobilise support for activism; if a firm operates in an advertising-intensive industry, reputational threats or support will provide leverage to the activist NGO; and if a firm is operating in an industry that is already considered socially or environmentally sensitive, it is more likely to be targeted by activist NGOs, either for collaboration or for contestation. Firm size might be another influential factor, although research is inconclusive on whether larger or smaller firms are most likely to respond positively to activists' calls for change.

Obviously, different activist NGOs will make different choices in targeting firms. They will be selective in picking their targets as campaigns require a lot of resources (money, time, energy) and hence they will try to select those targets that look most promising to help them reach their own objectives. Yet, as Rowley and Moldoveanu suggest, pursuing their interests is not always the sole reason for activist groups to target firms (Rowley and Moldoveanu, 2003). Strengthening their own position vis-à-vis their constituencies and reaffirming their social identity may be additional reasons: as targeting large, visible firms is more likely to attract media attention, activist NGOs may decide to do so, even if the chance of success in terms of change in firm behaviour is small.

In addition to pursuing interests and confirming its identity, its ideology will also be an important factor in targeting decisions, as suggested earlier, in section 9.3. Radical activist NGOs will select a different set of potential targets than reformist activist NGOs, because this fits in with their desired worldview: radical activists will be less inclined to collaborative interactions, whereas collaboration can be a fruitful tactic for more reformist activists, especially if the target firm is open to reassessing its CSR behaviour, or is performing better than its industry peers on the CSR issues at stake. Whereas reformist activist NGOs will be inclined to work with such leading firms, more radical activist NGOs will not.

Taking these considerations into account, it seems quite clear that certain firms are more likely to attract the attention of activist NGOs and to become a target, either for collaborative or for contentious interactions. Then how do firms respond?

9.6 Strategic Response or Taking Responsibility?

As the upheaval around fracking and many other examples show, business activities can be contested. Not everybody agrees that all activities undertaken by firms are legitimate. Following Suchman, business activities can be considered to lack moral legitimacy, in the sense that the activities themselves, or their consequences, violate some moral principle (Suchman, 1995). Think of paying bribes or the use of child labour, or of the Volkswagen scandal over its software manipulations to meet the norms in emission tests. Firms may also be considered to lack pragmatic legitimacy, in the sense that their activities, or their consequences, are against the interests of some of their stakeholders. Although many food companies are considered to have moral legitimacy, some of the products they offer have been scrutinised for possible health risks to consumers, which may affect these firms' pragmatic legitimacy with consumers.

Hence, even if a firm operates in such a way that its activities are legally permissible – it operates within the conditions set by law and regulation, it has obtained all the required licences and permits, and it adheres to their provisions – its activities, or the organisation as such, may still be contested. Legality and legitimacy are not the same. While being perfectly legal, some activities of the company might still be considered illegitimate by outsiders, for example because the activities or their consequences are associated with pressing social or environmental issues.

Activist NGOs have become main protagonists in articulating the social and environmental issues in which companies can be implicated, in mobilising people around the issues they find important, and in putting pressure on firms to effectively address these issues. The inability or unwillingness of national governments to directly regulate business activities has been a driver behind NGO activism towards firms, as we argued in section 9.2. Moreover, some of these issues, such as climate change, labour issues, upstream supply chains and poverty alleviation, are highly complex, involve radical uncertainty as to causes and consequences, and are infused with multiple and opposing values and interests to such an extent that they are beyond the capacity of governments and firms to resolve them. Many people have come to see NGOs as crucial agents in helping firms (and governments) to address these issues.

Many companies have experienced, or are likely to experience, NGO activism. As we have seen above, NGO activism may take various forms but always makes a claim on the firm. Most firms will not just sit and wait until they are approached and/or targeted by activist NGOs. A range of studies has examined the various ways in which firms can respond to, or anticipate, NGO activism. These responses vary from seeking allies and partnering with NGOs to defending their own positions and partnering with peers. Relevant questions for targeted firms include: which claims to respond to, and how to respond, if at all?

Building on stakeholder theory, Mitchell, Agle and Wood proposed a model to predict under what conditions a firm's management is more likely to respond to claims made by stakeholder groups such as activist NGOs (Mitchell, Agle and Wood, 1997). They argued that management is more likely to respond as the stakeholder's salience increases. Salience, in turn, is seen as a function of the urgency of the claim ('Do we, as a firm, need to respond swiftly?'), its legitimacy ('Is this a claim that is widely supported?') and the power of the claimant ('How potent are the means that the claimant can deploy to force us to respond?'). Rowley extended the notion of power by considering the position of the firm in the social network structure of its stakeholders (Rowley, 1997). Rowley argues that when the network of the firm's stakeholders is denser – i.e. the stakeholder has many allies – the firm faces a stronger claimant. However, when the firm's centrality is higher – i.e. there are several disconnected groups of stakeholders making claims on the firm – it has a stronger position, as it can 'play off' one group against another.

These two models start from the premise that firms have multiple stakeholders, including activist NGOs, each having different claims on the firm. Many of these are likely to be incompatible, or even contradictory. But even when the claims are not incompatible or contradictory, their sheer numbers may be such that the firm cannot attend to all of them; some prioritising will need to be done. Models such as these offer a way to think about how to prioritise among the variety of claims.

Having decided *which* claims to attend to, another question is *how* to respond. There is a considerable literature on 'response' to 'institutional pressures' which is relevant. As can be inferred from section 9.4, some of the tactics that activist NGOs deploy, such as public opinion tactics, are based on increasing the institutional pressure on firms. Moreover, NGO activism in itself can be seen as an expression of societal expectations about what companies should do. Much of this literature on how companies respond to institutional pressures builds on the framework developed by Oliver, whose framework was one of the earliest formulations of the idea that institutional pressures *can* be resisted (Oliver, 1991). Oliver's framework comprises five different response strategies that range from 'giving in' to 'resisting' institutional pressures. For example, acquiescence, or compliance, refers to a response in which companies accede to the claims posed upon them. Defiance, on the other hand, is a resisting response strategy in which claims are denied, dismissed, challenged or counter-attacked. Other response strategies on the continuum from acquiescence to defiance include compromise, avoidance and manipulation. Compromise is a response strategy that encompasses bargaining, negotiating or creatively working together to develop some solution that is acceptable both to the firm and the activist NGO. Avoidance is a strategy by which firms conceal their nonconformity, buffer themselves from NGO activism, or otherwise seek to escape from the claims upon them. To publish a CSR report that selectively highlights successes but does not mention failures or ongoing problems is an example of an avoidance strategy. Finally, manipulation is a response strategy in which firms seek to change or exert power over the content of the claims they face or over the activist NGOs that make these claims. Examples of manipulation strategies include co-opting activist NGOs, influencing public opinion, lobbying politicians and regulators, and seeking to prosecute activist NGOs by legal means.

While typologies such as these are helpful to classify and describe firms' responses to NGO activism, they can hardly be used as normative frames to guide how firms should deal with NGO activism. Their formulation and presentation seem to emphasise rationalised and instrumental self-interest on the part of the firm. They offer a set of highly instrumental frameworks for developing 'strategic response'. For example, they appeal to the 'bottom line' thinking, the economic calculus of costs and benefits, as well as the risk management approaches that are associated with the discourse of maximising shareholder value. But they do not easily open up to 'taking responsibility', because they disregard the values, and hence the morality, that are implied in the issues that NGOs seek to address.

For a firm to take responsibility implies that it moves beyond the defence of its own economic interests, to consider the questions of what kind of corporation the firm wishes to be, what role in society it aspires to fulfil, and how to relate to its various stakeholders. Despite all the talk of 'creating shared value' (Porter and Kramer, 2011) and 'win-win solutions', such opportunities remain rare events. Acquiescence may be a rational response strategy when it is inevitable that the firm has to address a societal demand as expressed or amplified in the claims by activist NGOs, or when the approach that the firm has developed to address a societal issue, perhaps in collaboration with activist NGOs, is going to strengthen its competitive position. But in many more instances, the issues at stake are far less unequivocal: there is disagreement about the causes, consequences and size of the issue, or there are multiple values and interests at stake. If this is the case, it might be appealing to consider the salience of the activist NGOs that bring the issue to the firm, and to wait and see if the NGOs salience increases to critical levels (instead of considering it as a weak signal of how the society in which the firm operates may change). It might be tempting to the firm to seek to defy, avoid or manipulate the claims from NGO activism in an effort to defend its own interests, because doing so is challenging the status quo. Yet, if the words and phrases such as 'responsibility', 'respect' and 'integration of economic, environmental and social considerations into business decision-making' that are often found in the 'core values', 'mission statements' and other expressions of a firm's purposes are to have any meaning, they imply an openness to other voices that may be dissonant with its talkings and doings. If the meaning and intent of a firm's CSR policies and practices are to be anything else than an instrument to the maximisation of shareholder value, they need to be open to the values and interests of its other stakeholders. Expressing such other voices, values and interests is what activist NGOs do. By shaping firms' views of potential alternative solutions, they might help in creating forms of CSR as **'aspirational talk'** (Christensen, Morsing, and Thyssen, 2013) that sets a more complete version of CSR in motion. Engaging with activist NGOs can be difficult, especially if there is hostility in how they approach the firm. Then again, sometimes contentious interactions can, in the end, lead to changes in practices. It will be the task of NGOs to ensure that these responses get beyond window-dressing and constitute real change.

9.7 Case Study: Clean Clothes Campaign

Over the past few decades, the garment and sportswear industries have become highly globalised due to extensive outsourcing of the labour-intensive parts of the production process to low-wage countries, such as in Central America and South and South-East Asia.[4] Brands and retailers have increasingly specialised in design, marketing and sales, and relegated production to an extensive and complex network of suppliers, contractors and subcontractors. In turn, many suppliers and subcontractors produce for multiple brands and retailers.

This move from integrated to outsourced production has enabled the brands and retailers in this industry to break away from traditional labour relations and to distance themselves socially from responsibility over large labour forces. The industry has become known for its abusive labour conditions and hazardous working conditions where workers – mostly women, sometimes children – are paid salaries below a level that allows them to support their families; they are forced to work exceptionally long hours, often without payment for over time; sexual harassment is not an uncommon phenomenon; work spaces are dark, dusty, noisy, without ventilation, and without adequate protection from dangerous machines and hazardous production processes such as dyeing, bleaching, stitching and sandblasting. The Bangladesh Rana Plaza collapse of 24 April 2013 hit the headlines in Western media, but factory collapses and fires regularly occur. Obviously, one would expect workers to organise under such conditions in order to demand better working conditions. However, labour organisation is often repressed, sometimes by intimidation or force, even when national law permits the workers to organise in independent labour unions – as opposed to those that are controlled by the firm's management.

In the late 1980s, the first reports of substandard labour conditions at supplier factories were published in Western media. Since then, a significant global anti-sweatshop social movement has emerged in North America and

---

[4] References have not been included in this section; they can be found in den Hond et al. (2014). *Mobilization*, 19(1), 83–111. Among the original references are:

Sluiter, L. (2009). *Clean Clothes. A Global Movement to End Sweatshops*. London, UK: Pluto Press.

Kryst, M. (2012). Coalitions of Labor Unions and NGOs: The Room for Maneuver of the German Clean Clothes Campaign. *Interface: A journal for and about social movements*, 4(2), 101–129.

Balsiger, P. (2010). Making political consumers: The tactical action repertoire of a campaign for clean clothes. *Social Movement Studies*, 9(3), 311–329.

Western Europe. One major constituent of the movement comprises individuals and organisations that are critical of the thoughtless, and thereby unethical, mass consumption in Western markets, as well as of the externalities of globalised mass production that emerged with the deregulation and liberation of international trade. Another major constituent of the movement is the international labour movement, comprising labour unions and their associations at industry, national and international levels.

The Clean Clothes Campaign (CCC) has become a central player in this movement. On its international website, CCC says that it is 'dedicated to improving [the] working conditions and supporting the empowerment of workers in the global garment and sportswear industries'. As of 2015, the CCC is an alliance of national coalitions of trade unions and NGOs from seventeen European countries, with an international secretariat in Amsterdam. Its members cover a 'broad spectrum of perspectives and interests, such as women's rights, consumer advocacy and poverty reduction'. Beyond the alliance that is CCC, it has built up a partner network of more than 250 organisations and unions in garment-producing countries, in order 'to identify local problems and objectives, and to help us develop campaign strategies to support workers in achieving their goals'. And there is extensive cooperation with like-minded alliances and organisations from the United States, Canada and Australia.

Regarding its activities, CCC says: 'We educate and mobilise consumers, lobby companies and governments, and offer direct solidarity support to workers as they fight for their rights and demand better working conditions.' According to CCC, responsibility for workers' rights and working conditions is not solely with the employers: the suppliers and subcontractors of the Western brands and retailers. The Western brands and retailers in the industry, in their search of profits, set the terms and conditions – such as price, quantity, quality and delivery times – for the contracts with their first-tier suppliers, and thereby for the entire production network. Very few of the supplier firms have sufficient bargaining power to resist and negotiate in any meaningful way with brands and retailers. In such situations, the terms of the supply contracts contain the seeds for the abusive labour conditions, as much as they can be the means to counter them.

Further, governments in producer countries are responsible for providing a legal basis for the protection of workers' rights and working conditions, and for ensuring their implementation. Meanwhile, governments in consumer countries – individually and collectively through their participation in international bodies such as the International Labour Organization (ILO), EU and North American Free Trade Agreement (NAFTA) – are implicated in creating, maintaining and furthering the legal frameworks and institutional conditions for international trade and production. Governments can thus be both targets and allies for CCC.

Finally, consumers in Western markets bear responsibility through their buying and voting decisions. Corporate profits depend on sales volumes, and the positions of Western governments in international political arenas are to some extent dependent on and related to election results. Buying and voting are related as both have moral dimensions that eventually reach the conditions under which garment workers earn their money.

This overview shows the complexities and inter-relatedness of the causal chains contributing to the abusive labour conditions in the garment and sportswear industries. Then how could CCC operate to make a real difference to the workers in the global garment and sportswear industries? Since its inception, CCC has developed various strategies and tactics to address the issues from multiple directions and, over time, discovered the potential synergies between them. Four strategies are analytically distinct but complementary and partly overlapping in their recombination of elements from the movement's repertoire of contention. The contentious strategy seeks to affect the reputations of brands and retailers through media campaigns; the collaborative strategy, as in multi-stakeholder initiatives (MSIs), involves working with brands and retailers on the formulation and implementation of labour standards that include certification, monitoring and verification mechanisms; the market-based strategy emphasises political consumerism; and the urgent appeal system is in direct support of workers in the industry.

9.7.1 Contentious

CCC was established in the aftermath of a protest event on 29 September 1988. That day, some fifty women – members of feminist groups, Third World solidarity groups, squatting communities and consumer organisations – picketed in front of a well-known department store in Amsterdam, to express their anger about the conditions under which the store produced clothes. Corporate campaigns such as this one are perhaps the oldest and most visible strategy in CCC's repertoire. Such protest is aimed at affecting the reputations of brands and retailers in Western markets, for example through the dissemination over the Internet and through mass media of images and information that associate brands and retailers with the labour conditions in their supply networks. Corporate marketing messages, brands, logos and symbols are 'subvertised' in order to disrupt, distort and satirise firms' reputations and their dominant positions in cultures of unrestricted and unreflective mass consumption. Additional tactics, such as celebrity endorsements, petitions, demonstrations and rallies, are used to further enhance the visibility of the campaign. It should be noted that boycotts have not been among the tactics used by CCC, because of the risk that it could rebound on the workers.

9.7.2 Collaborative

CCC quickly realised that it needed not only to express protest but also to propose some alternative. After long discussion and deliberation, both within and without the alliance, CCC presented its Code of Labour Practices in 1998. Its code offered an alternative to the corporate codes of conduct that many brands and retailers had adopted since Nike and Levi's pioneered them in the early 1990s, and which were rapidly seen as ineffective. But, to have a code is one thing; to have it implemented is yet another. CCC is a founding member of the Fair Wear Foundation (FWF), an MSI established in 1999 by various NGOs, labour unions and industry associations. Members of FWF agree on a code very similar to the one CCC developed on independent monitoring. As of 2015, FWF includes eighty member companies from seven European countries; FWF member companies represent more than 120 brands whose products are sold in over 20,000 retail outlets in more than eighty countries around the world. FWF is active in fifteen production countries in Asia, Europe and Africa. Through its heavy involvement in the FWF, CCC has been able to build a reputation of being a reliable partner, in addition to being a determined opponent, with many brands and retailers.

9.7.3 Market-based

Political, or ethical, consumerism refer to the movement's attempts to influence how consumers and institutional buyers select producers and products by encouraging them to take into account a broader set of valuation criteria. This strategy extends the contentious and collaborative strategies by politicising the market place. Sometimes, individual choice is emphasised; in other instances, collective forms such as boycotting and 'buycotting' are emphasised. Logos and labels, such as the FWF label, are important signifiers for political consumerism.

From 1999 onwards, so-called 'clean clothes communities' were founded to support local groups and communities in their demands on institutional buyers, such as public authorities, to buy workwear and uniforms from socially responsible suppliers only. As regular and large buyers, municipalities, police forces, fire services, hospitals, and the like might make a difference in setting specific procurement demands. CCC Switzerland took the political consumerism strategy to individual consumers by staging alternative fashion shows and printing booklets and maps to inform consumers where clean clothes might be purchased locally. According to some, the impact of this latter strategy might have less to do with actually changing consumer demand and more with signalling to firms that campaign claims are broadly shared.

9.7.4 Urgent Appeals

The previous three strategies are mainly intended to put pressure on brands and retailers and to stimulate and help them make their supply networks more responsible; they can only be expected to affect the workers in indirect ways and in the long term. Yet, infringements of labour rights can be acute. For that reason, CCC started to experiment with so-called 'urgent appeals'.

An urgent appeal is a request from a representative of garment workers, such as a (local) labour union or community organisation, addressed to CCC and its partners, to take action on a specific case of labour rights violations. If the request is taken up, CCC will demand that the factory management, the brands and retailers that source from this factory, and potentially other authorities redress the violations. If made public, an urgent appeal becomes a request for people to take action, usually in the form of sending protest letters and web-based petitioning. It thus directly connects workers and their organisations in the global garment production network to Western anti-sweatshop activists, and through them – when the urgent appeal is made public – to Western consumers. Since the late 1990s, well over 400 urgent appeals have been adopted. While their outcomes vary – in some instances, the workers' complaints are acknow-ledged and addressed; in others, nothing changes – urgent appeals are important for other reasons, too. The tactic highlights the pervasiveness of smaller, more local labour conflicts, beyond campaigns that focus on big scandals; it creates a bottom-up information flow from producer countries to CCC staff and volun-teers, as well as to the general public; and it provides international recognition to the affected workers, which may stimulate them to continue their struggles.

9.7.5 Conclusion

As this case on the CCC has shown, there is a wide variety of tactics that can be applied. The dilemma for an activist NGO then is how to balance these various tactics; the dilemma for targeted firms is in how to respond. Often a mix of contentious and collaborative tactics is applied, aimed both at firms and at consumers, and combining short-term goals with long-term aspirations of change on CSR. Selecting certain tactics, say more reformist ones, offers the option of more concerted effort but comes at a risk of losing some of the public support (of those constituents vying for more radical change). Likewise, working on short-term goals might result in losing track of the long-term objectives as focus shifts too often.

Questions for Discussion

1. Do you agree with CCC, that responsibility for workers' rights and working conditions in the supply chains is a responsibility of Western multinationals? To what extent? Why?

2. Do you believe that CCC can sustain its multi-strategy approach that combines collaboration and contention? To what extent? Why?
3. Do you, in your private life, consider political implications or ethical values when shopping? To what extent? Why?
4. Imagine that you are responsible for procurement in an internationally operating firm in the garment industry that is being challenged by the CCC. How would you respond? Why?
5. Imagine that you work for an activist NGO concerned with labour conditions in supply chains (such as, perhaps, the CCC). How would you balance the application of tactics that are orientated towards reaching structural, long-term results, versus those that aim for short-term results?

9.8 Chapter Summary

Starting from the premise that the wish of non-traditional stakeholders to engage with corporate policies, processes and outcomes is there to stay, the chapter has first sought to clarify some notions about how to talk about them. As noted, these actors have been conceptualised as NGOs, CSOs, social movements and several other terms. All of these terms have particular connotations that emphasise some of their traits and characteristics while downplaying others. We focused on 'activist NGOs' to highlight their willingness to organise collective action in the pursuit of their objectives and focus on their efforts to further their take on CSR.

Drawing on social movement literature, we argued that they can leverage their claims by showing that many people share them ('logic of numbers') or by using positive and negative incentives to make corporations change ('logic of damage'). Elaborating on these distinctions, we refined the idea of 'activism': we showed how collaboration and confrontation are often closely related, and how the most visible forms of activism typically have a longer history. Next, we discussed various ways by which NGO activism may knock on corporate doors. We focused on tactics working through (corporate) governance, through operational costs and benefits in direct and indirect ways, and through collaboration, as these are common routes NGO activists apply. These three sets of tactics were supplemented with a fourth one that does not imply direct engagement with firms: creating alternatives to the provision of services and products by firms.

Not all firms are equally susceptible to NGO activism. We reviewed literature that suggests which conditions increase the odds that a corporation will be facing NGO activism. Firm size, industry and visibility to consumers are important elements, as well as their historical record on CSR issues.

Furthermore, activist NGOs may also target firms to strengthen their own position vis-à-vis their constituencies by reaffirming their social identity or because doing so fits with their own ideological position.

Finally, we put the onus on corporations by suggesting that responding to NGO activism – or how to prevent it from popping up in the first place – involves corporate management and staff asking some tough questions about their identity, mission and values, policies and processes, and their role in – a globalised – society. Ultimately, these are questions of ethics. While it will be impossible to get rid of NGO activism, we suggested that considering the corporation not as a vehicle for maximising profit or shareholder value but as a means for shaping society for the better, will open up possibilities for constructive engagement with all sorts of ideas and preferences, including those held by activist NGOs.

Chapter Questions

1. How can the ongoing attention of activist NGOs for labour conditions in Chinese electronics factories be characterised in terms of the tactics they apply?
2. Sample a major newspaper for recent examples of different activist NGO tactics on issues of CSR.
3. Provide an overview of characteristics of activist NGO–business interactions.
4. Write a recommendation for a firm being targeted by activist NGOs, based on a worked real-life example.
5. Examine under which conditions partnerships between NGOs and firms may work out well.

FURTHER RESOURCES

Seitanidi, M. and Crane, A. (Eds.) (2014). *Social Partnerships and Responsible Business: A Research Handbook*. New York, Routledge. This edited volume presents a wide range of perspectives on cross-sector partnerships and critically examines the motivations for, processes within, and expected and actual outcomes of cross-sector partnerships from a variety of disciplines.

Soule, S. A. (2009). *Contention and Corporate Social Responsibility*. Cambridge: Cambridge University Press. This book presents a rich overview of anti-corporate activism over time, combining insights on social movements, private politics and their consequences.

Yaziji, M. and Doh, J. P. (2009). *NGOs and Corporations. Conflict and Cooperation*. Cambridge: Cambridge University Press.
These authors provide an overview of interactions between NGOs and corporations, both contentious and collaborative, illustrated with a range of examples.

SOMO, www.somo.nl/uk
SOMO is an independent, not-for-profit research and network organisation working on social, ecological and economic issues related to sustainable development. Since 1973, the organisation investigates multinational corporations and the consequences of their activities for people and the environment around the world. Their website provides a rich overview of research on CSR issues and activists' efforts to influence these issues.

The Clean Clothes Campaign, http://cleanclothes.org
The CCC is an activist NGO, dedicated to improving working conditions and supporting the empowerment of workers in the global garment and sportswear industries. Using a variety of tactics – as shown in the case study in this chapter – the organisation is an alliance of organisations in seventeen European countries, working with an extensive partner network of more than 250 organisations and unions in garment-producing countries.

Business for Social Responsibility, http://bsr.org
Business for Social Responsibility (BSR) is a global non-profit organisation that works with a large network of member companies to build a just and sustainable world by developing sustainable business strategies and solutions through consulting, research and cross-sector collaboration.

10

Government as a Regulator of CSR: Beyond Voluntarism

JETTE STEEN KNUDSEN

Learning Objectives

- Understand how and why boundaries are changing between public (government) and private (voluntary) regulation of corporate social responsibility (CSR).
- Identify different forms of government involvement in CSR.
- Explain why governments are increasingly regulating international CSR activities of home country firms.
- Evaluate strengths and weaknesses of government CSR regulation, focusing on regulatory efficiency and democratic legitimacy.

10.1 Introduction

Whereas many CSR formulations understandably focus on their position at the interface of business and society relations, this chapter shows how government is also part of the equation. The purpose of this chapter is to explore governmental roles in CSR more closely, particularly to illuminate the variety of issues that government regulation for CSR addresses and the range of forms that this regulation takes. This chapter also explores key issues in emerging CSR that government roles raise, including the international context for CSR and claims regarding the efficiency and legitimacy of CSR. The significance of government in the context of CSR is two-fold: first, that it is a *key CSR player*, as Chapter 2 demonstrates; and second, that its role is nonetheless *controversial*.

Governments are key players in CSR for two broad reasons: they provide a context for CSR and they also act to shape CSR, including through their

I would like to thank the editors for helpful comments on a previous version of this chapter. I also thank Samira Manzur for excellent research assistance. The usual disclaimers apply.

unique resources resulting from their monopoly of political authority within their respective territories (and sometimes even beyond). Governments provide an overall *legal context* for the corporate form and, by extension, for CSR. They provide a legal framework for civil society organisation and participation. Equally, governments are the focus of political participation, from lobbying to campaigning, as business and societal organisations seek to have their interests and values enshrined in law or supported by public recognition and financial resources. Business also looks to government to advance its collective interests (e.g. the provision of physical and social infrastructure) and to regulate its own collective action problems (e.g. in establishing and administering judicial and fiscal systems). Regarding CSR, governments have provided a broad context of rules and wider public provision which CSR complements, either by extending government policy (e.g. in funding higher education and research in the USA) or by filling governance gaps (e.g. in promoting tax transparency in contemporary remote resource extraction countries). In addition to contextualising CSR, governments have *actively supported* it for example through tax relief as illustrated in the English Charities Act 1601 and subsequent regulation providing tax relief for corporate giving in a variety of business systems from Denmark to Singapore. More recently, governments have acted to stimulate CSR in a variety of ways, ranging from the encouragement that the UK government under the premiership of Margaret Thatcher gave to CSR as a means of combating mass unemployment in the early 1980s, to the introduction of the Indian CSR tax, requiring companies over a certain size to allocate 2 per cent of their net profits to CSR spending.

The above examples highlight how governments engage with CSR over fairly mainstream issues. Yet the link between government and CSR, while now receiving more scholarly attention, has been the subject of disagreement and confusion. Presented with the above examples, some commentators might variously respond that these examples do not constitute CSR because they are not fully voluntary (a *definitional point*), or that they are inappropriate incursions into markets (a *normative point*).

The very thought of a relationship between CSR, broadly the responsibility of business to society, and government policies would seem counterintuitive to some. Traditionally CSR has been defined as *voluntary* (private) social and environmental activities by corporations (Vogel, 2008). Examples include philanthropy such as donations to a local school or art museum, but voluntary CSR has increasingly also come to mean private regulation that companies undertake to improve and protect labour rights and human rights in their global supply chains as they source from or operate in developing countries without adequate government regulation. From this perspective, activities which corporations might describe as CSR would simply be defined as public policy or regulation if these activities were either subsidised from public funds or reflected some regulatory requirements.

There is also a *normative* belief that government should not be involved in CSR: that CSR is best left to corporations to design and operate. The controversy has been illustrated in debates about the merits of the first and most recent CSR definitions of the European Commission. First, the European Commission in 2001 defined CSR as 'a concept whereby companies integrate social and environmental concerns in their business operations and in their interaction with their stakeholders on a voluntary basis' (Commission of the European Communities, 2002). Subsequently, in 2011 in recognition of the extent of government regulation for CSR, the word 'voluntary' was dropped in favour of a more encompassing – albeit vague and broad – CSR definition: 'the responsibility of enterprises for their impacts on society' (Commission of the European Communities, 2011). Whereas the initial definition was criticised by some civil society groups for overlooking business responsibilities in regulated areas of society, the 2011 definition was criticised by some business groups for its abandonment of the assumption of corporate discretion that they took to be axiomatic of CSR.

The key point underlying this chapter is that companies often develop their CSR initiatives in a close relationship with government policies and domestic policy-making traditions. Hence the way that a company develops its CSR programmes will to some extent reflect the political and economic institutions, traditions and policies where the company has its home base. The chapter proceeds in the following manner: section 10.2 offers an introduction to government involvement in CSR. Next, section 10.3 highlights government involvement in Europe and beyond, focusing on issues, regulatory examples and a typology of government CSR policies. Section 10.4 discusses CSR regulation along the public–private as well as the national–international dimensions, and highlights in particular the growing importance of government CSR regulation of international business. This section also discusses the emergence of public private partnerships as relevant for understanding CSR regulation. Furthermore, it illustrates the breadth of regulatory programmes for international CSR with a brief overview of initiatives to improve labour standards in the Bangladeshi ready-made garment sector. Section 10.5 examines the impact of public and private forms of CSR regulation with an emphasis on regulatory efficiency and democratic legitimacy. The chapter concludes in section 10.6 with a case study that explores government international CSR regulation of the extractive industry, focusing on enhancing tax transparency. The case highlights the UK and Norwegian governments' promotion of soft regulation in the form of a partnership called the Extractive Industries Transparency Initiative (the EITI) as well as mandatory regulation such as the US government's Dodd-Frank Act Section 1504 and the 2013 revision to the European Union Accounting Directive. The case illustrates that private regulation of an important CSR issue – tax transparency in extractives to combat corruption – can be closely linked to government regulation aimed at the same problem.

10.2 Government Involvement in CSR – An Overview

In recent years, governments have introduced policies which are directed at encouraging CSR (Knopf et al., 2010). National governments have become involved in new global governance initiatives for CSR, even sometimes contributing to their inception such as the UK government's role in the adoption of both the EITI as well as the Ethical Trading Initiative (ETI).

How does the domestic political and economic institutional environment affect a government's choice of CSR policies? While it is not possible to give a simple answer to this complex question, this chapter makes three points. First, liberal market economies such as the USA with less developed welfare states are more likely to foster private CSR *at home* to substitute for fewer public services than countries with extensive welfare states such as Denmark. Second, countries with large international corporations with extensive operations *abroad* in emerging markets or developing countries are more likely to promote CSR policies that strengthen the international competitiveness and/or minimise the business risks of these large corporations. For example, the UK has a large extractives sector with companies such as BP and Shell, and hence the government has promoted initiatives to make this sector more socially responsible including highlighting the need for greater tax transparency (see the case study below). Third, countries such as the USA with a strong tradition for pursuing solutions to regulatory problems through its legal system are more likely to prefer mandatory CSR regulation instead of partnership approaches such as multi-stakeholder initiatives (MSIs) such as the ETI. With a strong emphasis on solving business disputes through the courts in the US compared to in Europe, the US has developed a tradition for pursuing labour and environment initiatives through enforceable legislation (US companies also have a long tradition for undertaking voluntary philanthropic programmes to fill the voids left by a less extensive welfare state). UK firms are more likely to join MSIs compared to US firms, and in the UK MSIs are often supported by the government. MSIs reflect new forms of governance that often emphasise collaboration, learning and consensus-seeking about appropriate standards of business behaviour. They often cannot be enforced through the legal system and thus require participants to be willing to accept a process where initiatives and targets are developed jointly (Knudsen, 2017).

So far this chapter has focused on Western advanced industrialised countries and the role of governments in shaping CSR. However, governments in other parts of the world also develop CSR policies. Gond, Kang and Moon demonstrate how 'the kind of industrial paternalism and philanthropy shared by Western Europe and the USA in the nineteenth century can also be found in East Asian businesses (in Japan, South Korea, and more recently, China) in the twentieth century' (Gond, Kang and Moon, 2011: 656). These countries have stronger states, such as in the form of administrative guidance in Japan and South Korea and through state ownership and control in China. The 2006 revisions to Chinese company law include a requirement that companies 'comply with laws and administrative regulations, abide by social morals and business ethics, operate honestly and in a trustworthy manner, and accept supervision by the government and public to fulfil their social responsibilities' (Grayson, 2013). As a result, in 2008 the agency that controls the ownership of China's largest state-owned enterprises (SOEs) issued a CSR guidance for these enterprises. Social responsibility challenges include for example working practices, health and safety, collective bargaining rights, corruption, food safety and water usage. Since the largest 114 SOEs produce more than half of China's goods and services, this guidance has extensive reach. However, while the number of annual CSR reports in China has increased from 13 in 2005 to 1,337 in 2012 (Grayson, 2013), the effect on social and environmental outcomes remains uncertain. For China's government, corporate responsibility is strongly linked to economic development goals as described in the various five-year plans. Labour rights and human rights are seen as secondary to the goal of economic development (Hofman and Moon, 2015).

10.3 Government Involvement in CSR: Europe and Beyond

In recent years governments have introduced policies which are directed at encouraging CSR (Knopf et al., 2010). This section explores these, first with reference to a study of European government policies for CSR (Knudsen, Moon and Slager, 2015) and then more broadly with reference to the USA, Denmark and China.

In their study of European government regulation for CSR, 2000–2011, Knudsen et al. investigate the CSR issues to which European government regulation is addressed, the forms of regulation that are deployed to support CSR and the different approaches to regulating that the combined findings reveal (Knudsen et al., 2015).

Table 10.1 presents the findings of an analysis of the issue areas to which government regulation for CSR is addressed. This was conducted by identifying the different government ministries which had responsibility for CSR in twenty-two countries included in the study. Knudsen et al. explain that government ministries have been used as indicators of long-term trends in the issue focus of governments (ibid.). Although the table is not constructed to illustrate the chronological patterns, Knudsen et al. can report that in broad terms there was a shift from left to right on the table, from social (e.g. community, education) and environmental issues; through to economic and international issues (the CSR Ministry category clearly stands apart from this logic of issue

Table 10.1 Issue areas of European government regulation for CSR 2000–2011*

Ministry/country	Social	Education	Internal	Environment	Economy	Energy	Treasury	Foreign affairs	International development	CSR
Austria	X			X	X					X
Belgium	X				X	X				
Bulgaria	X									
Czech Republic				X						
Denmark	X	X		X	X	X		X	X	
Finland	X			X	X					
France	X			X	X			X		X
Germany	X	X	X	X	X			X		X
Greece	X		X							
Hungary	X			X		X				
Ireland				X		X	X	X		
Italy	X			X	X			X		
Luxembourg	X									
Netherlands				X	X		X			X
Poland	X			X	X					

Table 10.1 (*cont.*)

Ministry/country	Social	Education	Internal	Environment	Economy	Energy	Treasury	Foreign affairs	International development	CSR
Portugal	X									
Romania	X			X			X			
Slovakia	X			X						
Slovenia	X	X		X						
Spain	X									
Sweden				X				X	X	X
UK	X		X	X	X	X	X	X	X	X

Notes: *As indicated by Ministerial responsibilities

Ministries responsible for most government CSR policies are **in bold**.

There were other ministries assigned CSR responsibilities which we have not coded:

Germany: The Federal Ministry for Family Affairs, Senior Citizens, Women and Youth is involved in training initiatives related to diversity and equality.

The Netherlands: The Ministry of Justice and of Transport, Public Works and Water Management are involved in CSR-related policies.

Romania: The Ministry for Tourism is responsible for a tourism sustainable development project.

Source: Knudsen et al. 2015: 91.

focus) (ibid.). Thus, overall, there appears not to be a major area of public policy to which governments have *not* deployed CSR. However, some comparisons about issue range can be made. First and foremost, not all the countries have deployed CSR regulation for the full range of CSR issues. However, Denmark, France, Germany, Italy and the UK stand out as attaching CSR regulation to the broad range of issues as indicated by the CSR responsibilities assigned to social/ employment, environmental, economics, and foreign and development ministries. More generally, the breadth of the application of CSR to policy issues increases as one moves from the former Communist and the Mediterranean countries (Italy aside), to northern Europe, Scandinavia and the UK. Table 10.1 provides an overview of issue areas in European government regulation from 2000–2011.

The findings concerning the focus of CSR regulation on international CSR issues are somewhat counterintuitive in the light of, first, the literature on globalisation, which assumes that national governments are unable to regulate business in the international sphere (Stiglitz, 2002), and, second, the related CSR literature which assumes that in this light, corporations have assumed regulatory primacy in the context of MSIs (Scherer and Palazzo, 2011). These assumptions will be discussed in the light of the analysis of CSR and international business (below).

Turning to the ways in which European governments regulate CSR, Knudsen et al. (2015) adopted the framework of Fox, Ward and Howard (2002) to distinguish four types of government policy to encourage CSR: endorsement, facilitation, partnering and mandate (Table 10.2).

Governments can *endorse* CSR (e.g. by creating a ministerial portfolio in the area). Endorsement policy instruments raise awareness of CSR and promote good practices. Examples of endorsement policies include general information

Table 10.2 Forms of government CSR regulation

Type of regulation	Description
Endorse	Political support for CSR through general information campaigns and websites, political rhetoric, awards.
Facilitate	Incentives for companies to adopt CSR through subsidies or tax incentives; public procurement.
Partner	Collaboration of government organisations with business organisations to develop standards, guidelines etc. (Ethical Trading Initiative; Extractive Industries Transparency Initiative).
Mandate	Regulation of minimum standards for business performance (i.e. UK Anti-Bribery Act; mandatory non-financial reporting).

Source: Knudsen, Moon and Slager, 2015.

campaigns and websites, political rhetoric, awards and labelling schemes. Governments can also *facilitate* CSR by offering subsidies and tax expenditures (e.g. to companies or business associations) or by building CSR criteria into public procurement conditions. These policies include subsidies and tax expenditures for contributions to charities, the adoption of clean technologies, and the employment of disadvantaged workers in public procurement policies. Governments can support CSR *partnerships* by encouraging and joining business and other actors in CSR partnerships to deliver public goods, to ensure legitimacy or to raise business standards. Partnership approaches can assist in disseminating knowledge about CSR and sustainability issues, while sector-specific partnerships such as in garment or extractives often play a key role in the development of guidelines, standards or codes (see Chapter 7). Finally, governments can *mandate* CSR (e.g. mandatory non-financial reporting, which requires firms to disclose in their annual report which social and environmental activities they have been involved in). Policies that mandate behaviour involve the specification of some minimum standard for business performance embedded within the regulatory framework, such as requiring that companies submit a non-financial report outlining CSR activities (Fox et al., 2002). Mandating involves governments taking the most definitive role in CSR through regulations and decrees.

Knudsen et al. did not find that all European governments use the full range of regulatory forms (Knudsen et al., 2015). The Mediterranean countries tended mainly to use endorsement as their means of regulating CSR. This is a relatively weak regulatory form, mainly consisting of the imprimatur and legitimacy of government. At the other end of the spectrum, the countries which utilised a full range of endorsement, facilitation, partnership and mandate policies were most notably the UK, northern Europe and Scandinavia. Knudsen et al. therefore see these as embedding CSR most 'deeply' by virtue of this use of the full regulatory range (Knudsen et al., 2015). Together these regulatory forms reflect the fact that a range of legal (mandate), fiscal (facilitation) and organisational (partnership) are deployed for CSR government resources, along with those of the governmental imprimatur which goes with endorsement.

If the findings are combined for the issue focus and the regulatory forms selected for CSR policies, it is possible to present a typology of governmental CSR policies (see Table 10.3). The first dimension, the breadth of CSR policies, distinguishes partial (i.e. a narrow range of issues) and broad (i.e. a wide range of issues) addressed by CSR policies. The broader applications reflect a more systemic spread of CSR policies. The second dimension, the strength of CSR policies, distinguishes the regulatory forms in which endorsement is seen as relatively weak, facilitation and partnership as of medium strength, and mandate as strong for regulation policies. It is the mandate-type policies that are most likely to institutionalise CSR.

Knudsen et al. are therefore able to identify six broad approaches to CSR regulation by integrating the dimensions of strength of regulation and breadth

Table 10.3 A typology of government CSR policies

		Breadth of policy application	
		Partial	Broad
Strength of government policy	**Endorse**	Selective support	Systemic support
	Facilitate partner	Selective steering	Systemic steering
	Mandate	Selective institutionalisation	Systemic institutionalisation

Source: Knudsen et al., 2015: 94.

of issue range: 'selective support' for CSR; 'systemic support' for CSR; 'selective steering' of CSR; 'systemic steering' of CSR; 'selective institutionalisation' of CSR; and 'systemic institutionalisation' of CSR (Knudsen et al., 2015). Most governments started their regulation of CSR through 'selective support'. However, the governments of northern Europe, Scandinavia and the UK have all undergone a clear development towards 'systemic institutionalisation'. This chapter pays particular attention to Denmark and the UK because their governments were involved early on in shaping CSR programmes.

10.4 Public and Private Regulation of Business Activities

This section demonstrates that four different approaches exist regarding how CSR is explained that distinguish between the two dimensions of public and private regulation and between home and host country. Thus, along these two dimensions it is possible to distinguish between four CSR categories:

1. government regulation of CSR in a firm's home country;
2. private regulation of CSR in a firm's home country;
3. private regulation of CSR in a firm's host country; and
4. government regulation of CSR in a firm's host country.

10.4.1 Government Regulation of CSR in a Firm's Home Country

One approach focuses on governments' CSR regulation of home country companies and their activities in their home country. According to this perspective, government CSR regulation mirrors existing domestic political-economic structures and welfare services. For example, Campbell has argued that because government environmental regulation has traditionally been strong in Scandinavia, it is therefore not surprising that many Scandinavian companies voluntarily adopt ISO 14001 environmental management systems since they already meet strict environmental criteria (Campbell, 2007). The ISO 14000 family of standards provides practical tools for companies and organisations of all kinds looking to manage their environmental responsibilities. Furthermore, Scandinavian government support for active labour market policies, including skill upgrading, has traditionally been significant. When companies adopt programmes to recruit employees with problems other than unemployment (mental illness, physical disability, etc.), such private programmes are often financed by government subsidies at least during the first six months, and company interest in social inclusion thus mirrors welfare programmes. More generally, a growing literature has demonstrated that the domestic political and economic model of capitalism in a country will contribute to determining the priorities and extent of government regulation of CSR (Knudsen et al., 2015). However, while this approach views government regulation of CSR as important and sees the regulatory capability of the state as significant, the focus is on regulating home country firms' activities in their home country and not on government regulation of their activities abroad.

The next two approaches share the assumption that governments are too weak to regulate the CSR activities of corporations. While governments may be willing to regulate, they do not possess the resources required to offer and enforce social protection regulation. Reasons could include fiscal pressures at home or because governments lack the ability to enforce regulation in a host country context. New forms of private regulation have therefore emerged to fill such governance gaps. This chapter first considers private regulation that fills a governance void at home and next examines private regulation that fills a governance gap abroad.

10.4.2 Private Regulation of CSR in a Firm's Home Country

In contrast to Campbell's mirror thesis above where CSR initiatives complement existing government programmes, the so-called substitution thesis highlights the importance of government retrenchment of services such as vocational training, health and education in advanced industrialised countries. The substitution perspective interprets the emergence of CSR programmes as a way for companies to fill the governance gap in their home country (Matten and Moon, 2008). The literature on self-regulation sees regulation as a response to the problem of regulatory voids. Ayres and Braithwaite suggest that when no government regulator is available to monitor and enforce compliance, private parties can act as 'a proxy for the state' (Ayres and

Braithwaite, 1992: 32). The argument is that retrenchment of the welfare state in some cases means that private actors such as home country firms must step in to fill the governance void – inside the home country. For example, cutbacks in health care and education spending in the UK have resulted in companies stepping in to finance health care initiatives and offer stipends for students (Matten and Moon, 2008).

10.4.3 Private Regulation of CSR in a Firm's Host Country

The third view of CSR regulation is sometimes referred to as 'political CSR' (Scherer and Palazzo, 2011; see also Chapter 6). A key claim in the political CSR literature is that companies from advanced industrialised countries (the global North) increasingly have to act as political actors when they operate abroad in developing and emerging market contexts (the global South). Companies must provide social welfare because the state is no longer able to do so. Companies face a wide range of CSR demands from non-governmental organisations (NGOs), consumers and other stakeholders and therefore these companies have become political actors that seek to manage social and environmental challenges in global supply chains. The key rationale for these private international CSR regulatory initiatives is assumed to be their ability to fill a governance void that has become apparent as states are seen as unable to regulate international business that operates across national borders. However, this chapter demonstrates through a case study of international CSR – focusing on tax transparency regulation in extractives – that increasingly home country governments have begun to claim a 'governance space' by adopting a broad range of regulatory changes related to international CSR activities. Next, this chapter turns to government regulation of international CSR.

10.4.4 Government Regulation of CSR in a Firm's Host Country

In the course of the last decade or so, the focus of government CSR programmes has increasingly shifted from domestic to international challenges (Knudsen et al., 2015). As Western companies have become increasingly international and operate in emerging and developing countries, CSR challenges have come to include a wide range of social and environmental issues such as the protection of human and labour rights and preventing corruption. Stakeholders including consumers, investors and employees ask that multinational companies address these challenges in host countries. Home country governments have also begun to demand that home country firms improve their social and environmental performance in those subsidiaries and supplier firms that operate in host countries without adequate government regulation. The change from a domestic to an international government CSR focus is a general trend (Knudsen et al., 2015). Ministerial CSR responsibilities increasingly include foreign policy, international economic competitiveness and international development programmes aimed at company activities in host countries.

Government CSR regulation of company activities outside the home country is a surprising empirical development. With internationalisation of markets, many scholars and commentators have come to view governments as unable to regulate international business. Thomas Friedman, for example, famously argues that the world is 'flat' (Friedman, 2005). With the emergence of modern technology such as broadband connectivity around the world and undersea cables, as well as the growing use of email software and search engines such as Google, Friedman contends that intellectual work can increasingly be delivered from anywhere. According to this perspective, the regulatory capacity of governments is declining. This decline also applies to the ability of governments to regulate social and environmental activities. Because governments are perceived as weak regulators, many CSR experts have interpreted the CSR movement as private regulation by corporations that attempt to fill governance voids in developing countries where governments are weak (Locke, 2013). With these new communication technologies discussed above, Western consumers, NGOs, institutional investors and the media can more easily identify companies and their suppliers that do not live up to international human and labour rights standards and companies, therefore have to find ways to meet international social and environmental standards. Many governments in Europe for example have increasingly sought to regulate international CSR activities of their home country firms by linking public procurement to specific social and environmental performance criteria, including by international suppliers operating in developing and emerging market economies.

10.4.5 Public Private Partnerships

The discussion so far has focused on initiatives that are specifically labelled as CSR. However, other initiatives with different 'labels' are highly relevant to this chapter's discussion of public and private regulation of social welfare. One such example is public private partnerships (PPPs) that have grown tremendously in recent years and that can be defined as 'co-operation between public and private actors with a durable character in which actors develop mutual products and/or services and in which risk, costs, and benefits are shared' (Klijn and Teisman, 2010: 137). PPPs have existed since the Roman Empire, and examples include the construction of private toll roads and canals as well as the establishment of security forces. During the past thirty years, governments in the UK, Australia and the Netherlands in particular have pushed to develop infrastructure projects (ports, trains, roads, airports, telecommunications) as PPPs in order to reduce public finance costs as well as to leverage private sector expertise. PPPs can also include collaborations between a wider range of actors including business, government and civil society, aimed at addressing CSR challenges such as access to health, poverty alleviation, community capacity-building and environmental sustainability.

PPPs can be domestic (home country focus) or can cross borders (host country focus). As such, PPPs can be characterised according to the taxonomy used in this chapter as private regulation filling a governance void in both the home and host country of an internationally active firm. Here we focus on transnational PPPs and hence discuss PPPs as private regulation aimed at CSR challenges in a firm's host country. According to Andonova,

> Transnational partnerships involve voluntary agreements between states and a variety of non-state actors with cross-border activities such as NGOs, foundations, companies, research institutions, or transnational associations, on specific governance objectives and on means to advance them. Unlike intergovernmental institutions, which derive legal authority from intergovernmental delegation and operate through hierarchical bureaucratic structures, partnerships pool governance authority across the public and private spheres, typically via decentralised networks and have limited level of public legalisation. (Andonova, 2014: 402)

Even compared with private regulations that are typically managed by and for non-state actors in the shadow of the state (Bernstein and Cashore, 2007), partnerships entail more direct collaboration and a rearticulation of roles across state and society. Examples of partnerships in the CSR space include pharmaceutical companies collaborating with local government actors and civil society organisations to combat malaria, HIV/AIDS and tuberculosis. Another example is Brazil's agreement with the World Bank and the World Wide Fund for Nature (WWF) to conserve 10 per cent of the Brazilian Amazon. The agreement established a public–private partnership called the Amazon Regional Protected Areas with collaborative financing, management and implementation of conservation programmes.

10.4.6 Illustrative Example of CSR Regulation by Public and Private Actors: The Bangladeshi Ready-Made Garment Sector

A wide range of problems including violations of labour rights, factory fires and building collapses has plagued the Bangladeshi garment sector. Most notably, in April 2013 Rana Plaza, an eight-storey building collapsed, killing 1,129 garment workers and wounding approximately 2,500. The disaster led to a public outcry in Bangladesh as well as internationally, and to demands for initiatives to ensure that a similar tragedy would not happen again. Regulatory solutions included both mandatory government/European Union programmes as well as voluntary private sector programmes.

In 2013 two monitoring regimes establishing fire, electrical and building safety programmes emerged in the USA and the European Union: the business-dominated *Alliance* (USA-led) and the multi-stakeholder-orientated *Accord* (European Union-led). Union organisers and anti-sweatshop activists persuaded the big European brands such as H&M to sign an Accord to police safety conditions and allow access to trade unionists. The Accord's brands engage with more than 1,500 factories that employ more than 50 per cent of the Bangladeshi garment workers engaged in the export sector. The Accord has company and union representatives on its board, and a representative of the International Labour Organization (ILO) as board chair and tiebreaker. Nearly 200 garment corporations have signed the Accord from twenty countries in Europe, North America, Asia and Australia. Other signatories include two global trade unions, IndustriALL and UNI, and numerous Bangladeshi unions. The ILO acts as the independent chair and company signatories make a maximum annual contribution of $500,000 on a sliding scale basis relative to volume of sourcing from Bangladesh. The Bangladesh Accord for Fire and Building Safety is a legally binding agreement.

US retailers and brands would not sign the Accord due to liability fears. Instead a group of North American garment companies, retailers and brands led by Gap and Wal-Mart founded the Alliance for Bangladesh Worker Safety, an internally binding, five-year undertaking with the intent of improving safety in Bangladeshi garment factories. However this initiative has no union representation and the AFL-CIO has criticised the initiative for its lack of full engagement with the Accord. The Alliance has a governing board that consists of prominent leaders from major US brands. To date, Accord and Alliance factories do not appear to differ substantially in their occupational safety and health (OSH) performance (defined as fire safety, electrical safety and building safety). In fact Accord and Alliance factories share audit reports when they source from the same factories.

The European Union and the USA have also used trade policy to drive change. The European Union Commission is solely responsible for adopting external agreements on behalf of all EU member states. The EU promotes a policy of non-conditional trade access through its 'Everything But Arms' programme for Bangladesh – a duty-free, quota-free access programme. However, the EU monitors progress for labour rights in Bangladesh and has stated that lack of progress will lead to blocked trade access. The USA has a long tradition of using trade policy to promote social change in the exporting country. In 2013, President Obama adopted a foreign trade policy initiative, suspending Bangladesh's trade benefits under the Generalized System of Preferences (GSP) in view of insufficient progress by the government of

Bangladesh in granting Bangladeshi workers internationally recognised worker rights. That decision followed an extensive review under the GSP programme of worker rights and worker safety in Bangladesh during which the US government encouraged the government of Bangladesh to implement needed reforms. The AFL-CIO for violation of workers' rights and safety filed the GSP case against Bangladesh in 2007, to protest about unions being banned in Bangladesh during the 2006–2008 emergency rule. Furthermore, the USA raised issues of child labour and poor working conditions including in the shrimp industry. While US trade policy restrictions may only affect a minor share of Bangladeshi exports to the US, the significance of the termination of GSP should not be underestimated. Bangladeshi officials are concerned that the EU may follow suit and also limit trade access.

In sum, initiatives to promote better labour standards range from top-down hierarchical trade regulation to promote better labour standards (government regulation of CSR in a firm's host country) to bottom-up soft regulation in the form of MSIs (private regulation of CSR in a firm's host country) and business collaborations in the form of the Alliance. Table 10.4 provides an overview of the key regulatory initiatives to promote labour standards in the Bangladeshi garment sector and their relationship to the discussed modes of public and private CSR regulation.

10.5 Efficiency and Democratic Legitimacy – Differences between Public and Private CSR Regulation

The previous four sections have laid out how and why boundaries are changing between public and private CSR. The chapter has identified different forms of government involvement in CSR and explored why governments increasingly regulate international CSR. This section now turns to the question of how government CSR regulation differs from private regulation. Two key aspects of public and private CSR regulation need to be considered in this context: (1) their regulatory efficiency and (2) their democratic legitimacy. Regulatory efficiency refers to the regulatory strength and in particular the extent to which a regulation can be enforced. Democratic legitimacy refers to the extent to which CSR programmes represent the preferences of society or the preferences of business.

Some forms of regulation are efficient in the sense that they can be enforced through legal adjudication, while private forms of regulation such as company initiatives and many MSIs lack legal enforcement. An example of hard regulation is mandatory top-down hierarchical regulation (such as the Dodd-Frank Act Section 1504 and the European Union Accounting Directive). Mandatory public regulation can be enforced more effectively than soft regulation (public

Table 10.4 Four key regulatory initiatives to improve working conditions in the ready-made garment sector in Bangladesh

	Examples	Scope	Membership	Decision-making	Requirements
Business-only (no government role)	Alliance for Bangladeshi Worker Safety	Establish a standard for fire and safety	North American garment companies, retailers, brands (Gap; Wal-Mart)	Business-only initiative	Not legally binding
Private regulation of international CSR	Accord on Fire and Building Safety in Bangladesh	Establish a fire and building safety programme for five years – all suppliers	150+ garment companies from 20 countries in Europe and North America, two global unions, Bangladeshi unions and ILO	MSI	Legally binding (those who have been violated can take legal action against garment companies in the company home country)
Government regulation of international CSR	US trade agreement with Bangladesh	US trade access dependent on labour standards in Bangladesh	US government–Bangladeshi government	Bilateral trade	Legally binding (US imposes tariffs but not garment)
Government regulation of international CSR	EU trade agreement with Bangladesh	'Anything but arms'	EU 28 and Bangladeshi government	Bilateral trade	Legally binding (no trade restrictions have been imposed)

and private) because commitments are credible (Abbott and Snidal, 2000). However, mandatory government regulation can be difficult to agree on because clear and hard regulatory requirements require that actors are more willing to compromise than when they adopt soft regulation (Vogel, 2008). Soft regulation in the form of MSIs is often characterised by bottom-up consensus-seeking decision-making procedures. Examples include the EITI and many other initiatives such as the United Nations Global Compact, the Forest Stewardship Council (FSC), the Better Cotton Initiative (BCI), the Carbon Disclosure Project, the ETI and the Fair Labor Association (FLA). Companies and governments sometimes prefer softer forms of regulation such as individual company codes of conduct or MSIs to mandatory legally enforce-able regulations (some MSIs can be legally enforced, such as the Accord in Bangladesh, which was discussed above). For example, pre-empting more demanding public regulation can be a powerful incentive for the supply of private regulation (Vogel, 2008). Furthermore, MSIs can be flexible and open to change. They sometimes have the potential for mutual learning and collabor-ation as a way to deal with uncertainty and the possibility to facilitate com-promise. In short, while mandatory public regulation can be legally enforced, reaching agreement to adopt mandatory regulation can be difficult and there-fore private regulation may offer an alternative mode of regulation even if private regulation lacks legal enforcement.

Public and private CSR regulations also differ when it comes to democratic legitimacy (Reich, 1998). In the literature on private regulation, MSIs are often seen as more inclusive and hence more democratically legitimate than business-only CSR programmes (Bernstein and Cashore, 2007; Scherer and Palazzo, 2011). As Vogel succinctly puts it,

> underlying virtually every scholarly and popular discussion of global **civil regulation** is the claim that the global economy suffers from a democratic governance deficit, often attributed to the constraints posed by global competitive pressures on the willingness and capacity of states to effectively regulate both global and domestic firms. (Vogel, 2008: 266)

Private CSR initiatives are criticised for lacking democratic legitimacy because they are adopted by private entities and not by democratically elected public officials. Shamir argues that MSIs leave corporations to regulate social affairs in a manner that reflects business needs rather than democratic decision-making (Shamir, 2008). In short, according to Shamir, a shift from top-down regulation and juridical legitimacy to MSIs contributes to the development of a market-embedded morality in the form of CSR. According to Shamir, 'the means through which governmental authority is deployed, namely laws, rules and regulations, are partially replaced by a variety of "guidelines", "prin-ciples", "codes of conduct" and "standards" that do not necessarily enjoy the backing of the state' (Shamir, 2008: 7). While Shamir does not support the CSR movement and the private regulatory initiatives that constitute the bulk of the CSR agenda, he prefers governments to make decisions and for those decisions to be legally binding. According to this view, top-down hierarchical governmental authority – at least from a democratic representation perspec-tive – is preferable to private CSR programmes, whether individual company programmes or MSIs. Others have argued that MSIs can sometimes offer a voice to the interests and arguments of a wide range of constituencies that are affected by the activities of (multinational) corporations (Scherer and Palazzo, 2011). However, many MSIs are in fact not very inclusive. They might claim to be inclusive, but are often established by stakeholders from advanced industrialised countries with few representatives from less developed countries (Fransen and Kolk, 2007).

In short, regarding the strength of different forms of CSR regulation, mandatory public regulation is the strongest because it can be legally enforced. On the other hand, mandatory public regulation can be harder to adopt than other softer forms of public and private CSR regulation. Furthermore, public CSR regulation adopted in democratic countries has more democratic legitimacy than private initiatives including MSIs and company CSR programmes since it reflects the preferences of democratically elected public officials.

10.6 Case Study: Tax Transparency in the Extractive Sector

Extraction of oil, gas and mining resources can lead to economic growth and social development. However, poorly managed extraction has been known to lead to corruption and conflict. This phenomenon has come to be known as the 'resource curse': corruption, conflict and poor management of revenue in many resource-rich economies, and the use of commodity sales to finance violence and conflict. More openness around how a country manages its natural resource wealth is therefore seen as necessary to ensure that these resources can benefit all citizens. Transparent payment of taxes and charges by usually Western companies in the extractive sector to their host (usually developing) country governments is a long-standing issue in international business responsibility (Knudsen and Moon, forthcoming). The lack of accountability and transparency in revenues from oil, gas and mining can exacerbate poor governance and lead to corruption, conflict and poverty (Frynas, 2009). The aim of regulation is to increase transparency over payments by companies to host governments and government-linked entities, as well as transparency over revenues by those host country governments. This case examines two complementary types of CSR regulation of tax transparency in extractives:

1. A multi-stakeholder initiative called the EITI; and
2. Public regulation in the form of the US Dodd-Frank Act's Section 1504 as well as the European Union's revision of its Accounting Directive.

10.6.1 Private Regulation: The EITI

The UK government launched the EITI in 2003 (https://eiti.org/). The EITI regulates a sector of major importance to the British economy, including some of the world's largest extractive firms such as BP and Shell. The EITI is an

MSI, which is a collaborative form of CSR governance that involves stakeholders on a voluntary basis and crosses state/non-state and profit/non-profit boundaries. Stakeholders involved in the EITI include, for example, governments as well as extractive companies and civil society organisations such as Global Witness, the Publish What You Pay Coalition, Transparency International (TI) and Oxfam. Global Witness was a strong supporter for the EITI and in 1999 published a report on the lack of transparency and government accountability in the oil industry in Angola. The report highlighted how the Angolan civil war was financed by oil money and led to a successful campaign – 'Publish What You Pay'. The purpose behind the 'Publish What You Pay' campaign's emphasis on transparency was to make explicit how much each local mine paid in taxes as a way to empower local communities and their demands for public services. In February 2001 John Browne, then Chief Executive Officer of BP, responded to the campaign and committed to publish payments made to the government of Angola (Browne, 2010). In short, the campaign was successful.

The British government followed the lead from BP to enhance transparency, and then Prime Minister Tony Blair launched the EITI. The responsibility for launching and coordinating the initiative in its early years rested with the British Department For International Development. This included hosting a crucial EITI Conference in London, 2003, where initial signatories (national governments, companies, industry groups, international organisations, investors and NGOs) agreed on the basic principles. The UK government contributed £1 million at the outset for technical aspects related to developing the initiative. However, the EITI was very quickly internationalised with an endorsement by the 2004 G8 Summit, the 2005 Commission for Africa Report, the formation of an international board and the location of the international secretariat in Oslo in 2006, its adoption by an increasing number of countries (e.g. the USA in 2011), and its endorsement by over seventy major companies in the sector. The 100th EITI report was published in 2012 in which company and government reports of payments made are verified and reconciled (Extractive Industries Transparency Initiative, 2013 at https://eiti.org/eiti/history). As a result, the principles of transparency in payments by extractive industry multinational corporations (MNCs) to governments have been adopted by this wide international membership.

By launching the EITI, the UK government set in motion a process to 'level the playing field' for its significant extractive industry sector. If a country decides to become an EITI member then all companies operating in the country, including state-owned companies, are required to publish what they have paid to governments (taxes, royalties, etc.). The EITI requires a reconciliation of what a government discloses that it has received, as well as what companies say they have paid. Most importantly, the EITI establishes a mechanism for debate about the resources inside the host country, which includes the government, corporations and civil society organisations. In short, the EITI is not just about publishing the numbers, but also about creating a platform for dialogue and enhanced accountability in countries rich with natural resources. The EITI requires companies to report their payments to governments but also requires governments to report on revenues received. The intention is to ensure that discrepancies and inaccuracies are uncovered and acted upon. In Nigeria for example, US$5 billion in unpaid taxes was uncovered through their EITI process.

The EITI was a response to the fear that taxes, royalties and other payments, crucial for host country economic growth and social development, can, by virtue of poor accountability, lead to corruption, conflict and poverty. It is therefore a mechanism based around twelve principles (EITI, 2012) designed to hold host governments more accountable by holding corporations in this sector accountable as to their payments to those governments. Some companies and governments have gone a step further in terms of transparency: the Norwegian government has adopted legislation that makes it mandatory for Norwegian extractive firms to report on taxes paid for each project and by country. Institutional investors liked the idea because transparency was seen as a strong indicator of good management. EITI country members do not always meet the requirements. Although the EITI has quickly assumed the status of an international organisation reflecting a membership of national governments, companies, NGOs, investors and other international organisations, the role of the UK national government was critical in its initiation and its initial organisation and resourcing.

About 40 per cent of the EITI funding comes from national governments, particularly the UK, Denmark, Norway and Sweden. Responsibility for EITI implementation, including any relation to wider accounting regulation, is left to member national governments. From the initial interest of half a dozen countries, and the nine years it took for the first country, Azerbaijan, to become compliant, the EITI has mushroomed in terms of national membership and compliance, business associates and investor supporters. In 2016, forty-nine countries are implementing the EITI standard, thirty-one countries are deemed EITI compliant and forty-one countries have published revenue reports (even if not all are fully compliant). The remaining eighteen countries are described as 'EITI Candidates', meaning that they are at earlier stages of implementing the initiative (https://eiti.org/countries). A significant development in the growth of membership is the interest of developing countries with significant extractive sectors.

Regarding the regulatory strength of the EITI, a number of studies conclude that the EITI contributes to enhancing transparency because it includes local voices 'on the ground' where the problems exist. However, consensual decision-making bodies such as the EITI can be very slow, and accountability is lacking. For example, civil society actors argue that there is a need to better monitor how governments spend revenue raised from the extractive industries and that EITI outcomes should be made quantifiable (SARW and EITI, 2012). The EITI has no legal recourse to make countries comply with its requirements. However, if countries fail to comply even after repeated warnings, the EITI will suspend them. Two countries – the Central African Republic and Yemen – remain suspended at the time of writing (April 2016). A challenge has also been that the quality of EITI reporting varies greatly by country. Additionally, the EITI does not yet cover enough ground. For example while over thirty-five countries have adopted the EITI, a large company such as Shell operates in over ninety countries.

10.6.2 Public Regulation: Revision of the EU Accounting Directive and Dodd-Frank Section 1504

In addition to the EITI, the European Union and the US government have pursued mandatory regulation in order to promote tax transparency in the extractive sector. These regulatory initiatives are quite similar. The European Union in 2013 revised its 1978 Accounting Directive and now requires oil, gas, mining and logging companies to publicly disclose the payments they make to governments for the extraction of natural resources. The Accounting Directive requires large public companies incorporated in the EU to report such payments – the list of companies includes Shell, BP, Total, Anglo American and others. For example, since Shell is listed in the USA and in the EU, the new mandatory regulatory requirements will require a company such as Shell to provide information for payments to the US and EU authorities made in all ninety countries where it operates.

The US government sought to promote tax transparency by including new regulation in the form of Section 1504 of the Dodd-Frank Wall Street Reform and Consumer Protection Act. This Act focused on ensuring financial transparency, and with a focus on natural resource transparency, Section 1504 is unrelated to the US banking system. Section 1504 was adopted following a public outcry in the USA over conflict minerals in the Democratic Republic of Congo and requires publicly listed oil, natural gas and minerals companies to file reports to the Securities Exchange Commission on project-level payments to foreign governments. Some institutional investors (i.e. Calvert Investments) have argued that transparent companies attract more investors because disclosure clarifies investment risks (Kaufmann and Penciakova, 2011). Also, some large and internationally competitive companies such as Rio Tinto have supported implementation of the disclosure reforms, pointing out that such transparency can be a competitive advantage since firms can provide host governments with clear evidence of how they contribute to government revenues and to communities. Yet not all companies view such transparency reforms to be to their advantage. Some other large companies and industry associations that are opposed to the disclosure rule in Section 1504, such as Shell and the American Petroleum Institute (API), have suggested that project-level disclosure will be very costly, position publicly traded firms at a competitive disadvantage, and possibly lead to in-country discrimination in places with lack of disclosure.

The API, big oil and several other extractive industry companies lobbied heavily against rules that would require project-level disclosure and in favour of various exemptions, including the so-called 'tyrant veto', which would exempt companies from disclosing payments in countries where payment disclosure was prohibited by local law. The Securities and Exchange Commission (SEC) ruling rejected the 'tyrant veto' exemption and exemptions in cases where contracts stipulate secrecy. Further, the SEC also mandated that companies file disclosures, a significant mandate because the requirement to file enables investors to litigate in certain cases of false reporting. The SEC also specified that payments above $100,000 must be reported and disaggregated by category, rejecting the arguments put forth by the industry for a materiality approach or a threshold of $1 million. The US District Court of The District of Columbia vacated the rules on administrative law grounds. The SEC is not appealing this decision and is instead working on Section 1504 rules that will take into consideration the court's decision. At the time of writing, the SEC has not yet issued a new ruling.

Summing up, the EITI's main recourse is that it can expel members that do not follow the EITI requirements. In contrast, mandatory regulation that can be enforced through European or US courts offers more legal accountability. However, because 'hard law' is a stronger form of regulation, it is also harder to ensure political agreement to bring about regulatory change. The slow process of securing agreement in the USA about how to implement Section 1504 illustrates this point. The impact of these new regulations on host country societies remains unclear: do regulations contribute to improving social justice abroad for the populations in resource-rich countries, or do they simply reduce social and environmental risks for international firms from advanced industrialised countries that operate in the global South?

Questions for Discussion

1. What do you see as the advantages and drawbacks of respectively the EITI and the EU/US laws when trying to regulate tax transparency in the extractive industries?
2. Is it more efficient – and if so for whom – to adopt government regulation (such as the Dodd-Frank Act's Section 1504) instead of bottom-up MSIs (such as the EITI)?

3. Which kind of CSR strategy would you recommend for companies such as BP and Shell that operate in conflict-ridden states such as Nigeria and the Democratic Republic of Congo?

10.7 Chapter Summary

The purpose of this chapter is to explore governmental roles in CSR more closely and to show a variety of key issues that government regulation for CSR addresses and the range of forms that this regulation takes. The chapter also provides an overview of different approaches to CSR that highlight the public–private and domestic–international dimensions. It also considers PPPs for CSR. Using the example of labour standards in the ready-made garment sector in Bangladesh, it briefly points out different regulatory approaches in order to promote improvements on the factory floor. The chapter discusses the extent of regulatory efficiency and democratic legitimacy in government CSR regulations as well as in private CSR initiatives including MSIs and company regulation. The chapter provides a case study of public and private regulatory initiatives to enhance tax transparency in the extractives sector. It explores the UK government's promotion of the privately run EITI and mandatory regulation in the form of the US government's Dodd-Frank Act Section 1504, and the 2013 revision to the European Union Accounting Directive.

The discussion has highlighted that governments play a key role in shaping CSR through regulation of home country firms and their international activities, and thus that CSR is not only a series of voluntary initiatives undertaken by companies. Government regulatory forms vary, from the promotion of soft regulation such as the EITI to issuing hard law that can be enforced through the legal system. Furthermore, mandatory CSR regulation adopted in democratic advanced industrialised countries is seen by some to have more democratic legitimacy as it reflects the preferences of publicly elected officials, while the democratic legitimacy of private regulation depends on the extent to which stakeholders pursue inclusivity and these stakeholders are not democratically elected. It is, however, not yet clear how these different kinds of CSR regulation affect the communities where they are implemented.

Chapter Questions

1. Why have governments become interested in regulating (international) CSR?

2. Under what conditions are companies likely to oppose government regulation of CSR, and under what conditions are companies likely to favour it?

3. How do government CSR regulations in advanced industrialised countries compare to government CSR regulation in developing countries and in emerging market countries?

4. MSIs such as the EITI represent not just government interests but also the interests of business as well as civil society organisations in oil-producing countries. Would you consider MSIs to have more democratic legitimacy than traditional hierarchical government regulation (such as the Dodd-Frank Act's Section 1504)?

FURTHER RESOURCES

Abbott, K. W. and Snidal, D. (2000). Hard and Soft Law in International Governance. *International Organisation*, 54(3), 421–456.
This paper provides a general overview of different forms of regulation in international governance which frames this chapter. It is a reference point for much international relations and CSR literature.

Andonova, L. (2014). Boomerangs to Partnerships? Explaining State Participation in Transnational Partnerships for Sustainability. *Comparative Political Studies*, 47(3), 481–515.
This is one of the, still rare, contributions which recognise the significance of national governments for international sustainability agendas.

Bernstein, S. and Cashore, B. (2007). Can Non-State Global Governance be Legitimate? An Analytical Framework. *Regulation and Governance*, 1(4), 347–371.
This paper provides a framework for assessing the legitimacy that forms of private regulation can offer in addressing global social and environmental problems.

Frynas, J. G. (2009). *Beyond Corporate Social Responsibility: Oil Multinationals and Social Challenges*. Cambridge: Cambridge University Press.
This book – and various papers by Frynas – critically appraises international CSR initiatives with reference to their regulatory shortfalls.

Knudsen, J. S., Moon, J. and Slager, R. (2015). Government Policies for Corporate Social Responsibility in Europe: Support and Institutionalisation. *Policy and Politics*, 43(1), 81–99.
This paper presents a comparative analysis of government policies for CSR, focusing on their regulatory strength and their issue 'targets'.

Examples of government CSR websites

Denmark: http://csrcouncil.dk/ and http://csrgov.dk

EU: http://ec.europa.eu/growth/industry/corporate-social-responsibility/index_en.htm

Germany: www.bundesregierung.de/Webs/Breg/EN/Issues/Sustainability/_node.html

USA: www.state.gov/e/eb/eppd/csr/

Personal Reflection by *Clare Short*

The Regulatory Dynamics Underlying CSR

To be honest, I have always thought of corporate social responsibility (CSR) as consisting of fairly tokenistic gestures by companies to subsidise local community activities, or theatres or museums, in order to improve their image and reputation. And yet when in government I quite often sought out agreements with the corporate sector in order to achieve international development objectives. And since leaving the House of Commons in 2010 I have spent five years chairing the International Board of the Extractive Industries Transparency Initiative (EITI) which brings together governments, companies and civil society in order to bring transparency into the management of the extractive sector. The aim is to use transparency to counter the corruption for which the sector is notorious; and to improve accountability so that people derive real benefits from their natural resources. On reflection, the initiatives with which I was involved created a form of regulation which for me extends the concept of CSR in a most interesting and significant way. Perhaps my most helpful contribution here might be to describe the initiatives in which I was involved in a way that illustrates how and why such new regulatory arrangements arise.

The fair trade movement was gathering strength when I became Secretary of State for International Development in the UK in 1997. We were keen to encourage this movement because it guaranteed a fair price to poor coffee growers, cocoa farmers etc. so that they and their families had a better standard of living and more security. I provided funding to the fair trade headquarters and supported the movement's work in any way I could. The foundation carefully researched and then awarded the Fairtrade label to products that were procured in a way that guaranteed decent wages to suppliers of raw materials and encouraged ethical consumers to buy these products. With a similar objective but potentially larger impact, the Ethical Trading Initiative (ETI) was launched in 1998 to bring together companies, non-governmental

We decided to invite Clare Short for her reflections on the regulatory dynamics underlying CSR in view of her experience as a long-time business regulator, as a Member of the UK House of Commons (1983–2010). As UK Secretary of State for International Development (1997–2003), Ms Short was involved in the government support for the launch of the Ethical Trading Initiative (see Chapters 7 and 18) and of the Extractive Industries Transparency Initiative (EITI) (see Chapter 16). Later, she became the Chair of the EITI Board (2011–2016).

organisations (NGOs) and trade unions to protect workers' rights in global supply chains. Big UK companies such as Littlewoods, The Body Shop, Sainsbury's and Asda were early members of the ETI which works to try to enforce International Labour Organization (ILO) standards through the global supply chains. It now involves over seventy companies which collectively reach nearly ten million workers across the globe. I was involved from the beginning in supporting the initiative with some financial support, encouragement and help to sort out early tangles. There was no direct role in either of these initiatives for the UK government, but I was keen to support both movements in order to improve the working conditions of millions of poor workers across the globe.

By the year 2000 the HIV/AIDS pandemic was spreading across the world and a UN Special Session was to be held in June 2001 to mobilise international efforts to halt the spread and provide care to those already infected. Anti-retroviral drugs, which prolonged life for a disease that previously led to inevitable death, had recently become available. As a consequence there was a passionate and sometimes vitriolic campaign against the pharmaceutical companies, demanding that they provide the drugs at an affordable price for poor countries. The companies had inflamed international anger by taking legal action against the South African government, which had dared to pass a law to enable South Africa to import and manufacture cheaper generic HIV drugs (a right that was provided for in World Trade Organization (WTO) agreements when there was a national emergency). In early 2001 the legal action was withdrawn. *The Guardian* newspaper commented that the legal action 'will go down in history ... as one of the great corporate PR disasters of all time', and the 'hard lesson that the big pharmaceutical companies have been taught ... is that there can be no global marketplace without a world sense of right and wrong' (Denny and Meek, 2001).

The pharmaceutical companies were keen to find a way forward out of the mess they had got themselves into, and the Department for Foreign and International Development (DFID) was keen to reach agreement on an intelligent package of measures of cooperation. When reporting to the House of Commons, I explained:

> I certainly welcome the withdrawal of that court action, which was always ill advised, but it does not mean that we suddenly have an answer to the problem. Even at cost price, anti-retroviral drugs are more expensive than most African countries can afford. They might cost only $1 a day, but most countries in sub-Saharan Africa spend less than $5 a head per year on health care and most poor, infected people are not in touch with any health care system ... We need international co-operation between the pharmaceutical companies, the Governments of developing countries and the international community to put in place basic health care systems and deliver treatment for opportunistic

infections, such as TB, which is killing more people than many other illnesses. I hope now that the court case is out of the way, we can make progress . . .

I have had considerable talks with the pharmaceutical companies and their embarrassment about the court case may have been helpful. Those who call for an end to all intellectual property rules are not being helpful, as we need a global agreement to provide drugs and basic health care systems in the poorest countries. We can then provide drugs cheaply at cost or even less, but that has to be in return for a deal involving higher prices in developed countries so that pharmaceutical companies can get some return on their investment, particularly their massive research budgets. Otherwise, we will not get new cures for things like malaria and other diseases of poverty. I am therefore hopeful that we can get a global agreement . . . involving Governments, international financial institutions, purchasing funds, agreements on intellectual property and agreements that drugs that are provided cheaply to the poorest countries will not be exported to the richest, otherwise we will dry up the funding of research. I am hopeful that we will get there. (Short, 2001)

And we did go on to get such an agreement. This is another clear example of the way in which cooperation between the private sector, governments and multilateral institutions can achieve what none of the parties can achieve alone.

My third example is the EITI. Interestingly I was involved in government in the early days of bringing together extractive companies, governments and NGOs to see if agreement could be reached. Ten years later I went on to chair the organisation. A short description of this work helps to exemplify the challenge in working to reduce corruption in a major problematic sector and how an initiative bringing together companies, governments and civil society can establish a global regulatory standard.

It is only in the last twenty years that concern has been expressed about resource wealth feeding corruption and conflict, and the failure of vast oil and mineral resources to lead to sustainable development and the reduction of poverty. In the Cold War years, Western governments' major concern was security of supply, and companies shared that concern together with an anxiety to secure their profits and avoid nationalisation. The World Bank, and other banks and investment institutions, were focused on the return on investment and not on the wider governance and social consequences of their investments in this sector.

In fact, research evidence has been available since the founding of the Organization of the Petroleum Exporting Countries (OPEC) in the 1970s that, paradoxically, the discovery of oil and other natural resources tended to undermine and not improve poverty reduction and economic development. For a long time explanation focused on currency appreciation and fluctuations in revenues. But as early as 1975 Juan Pablo Pérez Alfonzo, the Venezuelan oil minister who was a co-founder of OPEC said, 'I call petroleum the Devil's excrement, it brings trouble ... waste, corruption ... public services falling apart. And debt, debt we shall have for many years.' (*The Economist,* 2003)

However from the mid-1990s onwards the perverse outcome of oil extraction in developing countries came into the spotlight. This was because research identified bad governance as the driver behind very dismal development in resource-rich countries. The research suggested that oil- and mineral-rich states in the developing world were more likely to suffer from lack of provision of basic public goods, corruption and civil war than comparable non-resource-rich countries, and also more likely to be poorer. These findings were generally referred to as 'the resource curse' which is a widespread reality. But countries such as Norway and the UK in the case of oil, and Canada and Australia in mining, are not so cursed. It is clear that the problem is governance, not the nature of the resources themselves, although it is true that fluctuating prices, resource depletion and the likelihood of currency appreciation do pose particular difficulties.

It is clear also that poor development outcomes were caused by the link between international and domestic factors, i.e. the interaction between multinational companies and their shareholders and investors, host governments and greedy elites. The work of Transparency International (TI) and the OECD Convention on Combating Bribery were important influences on public debate, as were Global Witness reports on egregious corruption in Angola. Global opinion turned against major companies, particularly oil companies, and denounced their behaviour. The old slogan that 'the business of business is business' was no longer acceptable.

The Publish What You Pay Coalition was formed initially from NGOs in the UK which has since spread to a worldwide movement. The idea behind the EITI is clear and simple: build a coalition of companies, governments and civil society at international and national level, and require companies to report what they paid to governments and governments to report what they receive, and publish the figures so that the public can hold governments to account. It took a little time to recruit a board with representatives of each sector, to establish a secretariat, to draw up reporting rules and procedures and a multi-donor trust fund in the World Bank to provide technical support. From 2006 on, the organisation grew quickly. There are now fifty countries implementing the EITI. Half are in Africa but the membership includes a wide range of countries ranging from Peru, Mongolia, Iraq, Trinidad and Tobago to Norway, the US and UK.

There is no doubt that the EITI got off to a good start. The number of countries that volunteered to sign up to the reporting requirements grew steadily, as did the supporting companies and members of the NGO network. It is interesting to reflect on why all these different entities decided to join. They came together but each sector had slightly different motivation. The countries tended to want an improved reputation so they could attract inward investment, the companies to prove that they did make payments to governments and the NGOs to try to ensure that the money was spent to help the poor.

There have been declarations of support from the G8, the G20 and the United Nations General Assembly among others. But a 2011 evaluation suggested that the simple pass/fail benchmark was inadequate as though reform was a simple matter of complying with basic EITI reporting rules and producing an EITI report. In addition academic commentators pointed out that a simple report of the amount of money paid by companies, and a reconciliation with government receipts, does not ensure that the original contract was fair, what was due to be paid was paid, that the money was properly spent, let alone that there are sensible plans to deal with price fluctuations and the economic consequences of exhaustion of resources. We must conclude that a vague commitment to transparency is not enough to ensure good governance, and we cannot assume that multi-stakeholder groups on their own will have the capacity to build adequate systems of political accountability.

This is the reason why EITI introduced more testing reporting requirements supported by all parts of the coalition at its conference in 2013 in Sydney. The new reporting Standard requires transparency across the value chain including licensing system, state-owned enterprises and production levels. It also encourages openness on contracts and as full as possible reporting on beneficial ownership. It requires an account of the overall context in each reporting country so that any concerned citizen could read the report and understand the importance of the sector and the challenge of managing it to the benefit of the future of their country. There is also a new emphasis on making government systems more transparent and robust, rather than requiring more and more elaborate EITI reports. The aim of the EITI must surely be to encourage member countries to put in place transparent and robust government systems and to develop more informed public debate in each country. Progress is being made but building strong and robust government systems and informed public debate takes time.

Multi-stakeholder governance is not for the fainthearted. Bringing together governments, companies and civil society in countries where they have rarely sat down together, can in very important ways help to build trust, dispel myths and focus on the real reforms needed to improve governance in the extractives sector. But on the International Board which has the same composition, campaigning northern NGOs tend to believe that the EITI should be used to discipline countries with imperfect systems, whereas those with development experience understand that reform takes place when local reformers want it and see the potential benefits. No doubt these arguments will continue for a considerable time but it means that meetings of the EITI International Board can be very fractious.

My conclusion is that CSR as a new form of international regulation is an intriguing and potentially powerful instrument for reform and progress. It enables companies to work with others to create real benefits and overcome the problem that competition can lower standards in a way that damages their reputation. But it is of course no panacea. More than ninety companies have signed up as EITI-supporting companies but little is demanded of them and some have poor reputations. Similarly the pharmaceutical companies did rise to the challenge on HIV/AIDS when they were under attack but that does not mean that the sector is ethical and no longer open to severe criticism. The ETI did not prevent the terrible collapse on 24 April 2013, of the Rana Plaza eight-storey garment factory supplying global brands, which killed 1,129 people and injured approximately 2,500. The poor construction standards and lack of oversight must surely have breached ILO standards. I conclude that CSR has become a very important instrument of global regulation that can bring real benefit to all parties, but that the detail of how such initiatives are constructed and implemented is crucial to ensuring effectiveness rather than tokenism and subsequent denunciation for false claims.

PART III

COMMUNICATION AND CSR

Introduction from the Editors

The third part of the book discusses corporate social responsibility **(CSR) communication** as a new area, reflecting the emerging CSR literature's responses to the increased demand on companies to be more explicit and transparent about their CSR activities. This selection of chapters introduces key concepts to understand the opportunities for business engagement in CSR communication, while it also unfolds the complexity and approaches to manoeuvre this complexity in the context of social media. CSR communication is most often linked to the way that companies present their CSR activities to external audiences in advertising, marketing campaigns or CSR reports. The basic idea is that the positive association of CSR will lend itself to improve the corporate image. However, in practice many companies have experienced such communication attracting attention from sceptical stakeholders who criticise the company for not doing enough or for doing the wrong things. All chapters in this part point to this 'double edge': CSR communication is necessary, yet it has reputational risks. CSR communication must be managed, yet it is often beyond the corporate control to do so. With the rise of social media, many different stakeholders take part in the conversation about companies' CSR. As such, the corporate messages from managers are only one among many other voices that come to influence the CSR communication and present managers with new challenges.

Mette Morsing (Chapter 11) introduces some of the key approaches to CSR communication. The discussion points out how CSR communication not only includes the strategically planned communication from managers but also the less planned and informal forms of communication. The chapter presents an overview of three CSR communication strategies and provides students with an insight into the main phases of the development of CSR communication. Tim Coombs (Chapter 12) builds on this overview by showing how crisis communication is centrally linked to CSR and reputation. Coombs takes the reader through the central modes of crisis communication exemplified by cases that illustrate the importance for companies in knowing how to respond when crises hit. Finally, Coombs recommends how to engage with CSR crisis communication.

Christopher Wickert and Joep Cornelissen (Chapter 13) pick up on Coombs' chapter, as they unfold the idea and challenges of CSR and reputation. They discuss the strategic importance of reputation as an intangible asset, and they place CSR as a central element for achieving a desirable reputation. They emphasise the difference between symbolic/substantial and rhetorical/material approaches in relation to managing CSR reputation.

The final chapter by Lars Thøger Christensen and Dennis Schoeneborn (Chapter 14) places the idea of transparency in the context of CSR. Drawing on communication theories, they argue that the conventional ideal of 'full transparency' is the exception rather than the norm, and that transparency is not neutral but rather *does* things by selecting and making some matters visual while downplaying or ignoring others. In contrast to conventional understandings, Christensen and Schoeneborn argue that this may actually be an advantage to businesses as well as to society and the advancement of CSR.

11

CSR Communication: What Is It? Why Is It Important?

METTE MORSING

Learning Objectives

- Explain why managers need to pay careful attention to corporate social responsibility (CSR) communication.
- Understand the role of morality for CSR communication.
- Understand the basic challenges of CSR communication, particularly in a digitalised world.
- Understand and apply different CSR communication strategies to meet those challenges.
- Explain phases in the development of CSR communication.

11.1 Introduction

Much CSR literature seems to assume that CSR communication is inferior to action and decoupled from influence, obligations and impact. CSR action is about 'doing' and CSR communication is 'just talking', it is said. This chapter challenges such assumptions. It argues that CSR communication matters strategically and importantly for business as well as for society. In CSR communication, CSR issues are raised, debated and challenged, and it is also in this communication that external and internal stakeholders develop their understandings of a company's contribution to society and hereby set a scene for directing future CSR action. CSR communication can be defined as a company's communication to internal and external stakeholders about its efforts to contribute to social, environmental and economic development of society. However, increasingly stakeholders participate and influence the conversation, and the definition of CSR communication accordingly comes to include how these stakeholders contribute to define a company's social and environmental responsibilities to society. In particular social media has given rise to conversations about companies' CSR communication without the respective companies being part of the conversation. Thus conventional ideas of CSR communication are challenged and the managerial role for engaging in CSR communication is changing.

The chapter builds on the notion that businesses operate in an environment where CSR is not defined once and for all but is rather a produce of ongoing change, dialogue and contestation, i.e. communication. Companies engage in CSR for a variety of reasons but the way they engage in *communication* about CSR is absolutely central for how they are perceived by others to contribute to society. CSR is generally seen as a desirable feature of a corporate strategy and as such it has become influential for achieving a high score in many business ranking systems (see Chapter 13), and many companies integrate CSR strategically into their brand communications. However, if a company is seen to communicate too much or too little about its CSR activities or to omit communicating about its critical CSR issues, this may have a negative impact on one of the company's most vulnerable and not easily repaired assets: the respect and trust it enjoys in the eyes of the public. Therefore managers must provide careful attention to how they communicatively engage in CSR.

In the following, you will be presented with some of the key dilemmas, strategies and phases, managers face when they deal with CSR communication. First, the chapter introduces the dilemma of CSR communication as both a desirable and risky phenomenon. Next the chapter explains how morality is one of the distinguishing features of CSR communication that includes expectations for the company to be societally orientated, sincere and transparent about its CSR engagement. Then you will be introduced to three CSR communication strategies that are frequently employed by companies in practice: information, response and engagement. Finally, three phases in the development of CSR communication are discussed: instrumental, political and network. While the CSR communication literature is predominantly positioned in the instrumental phase, the political and the network phases surface as some of the emerging areas of managerial attention when addressing CSR communication. CSR communication is not 'just' a matter of the corporate delivery of messages about 'corporate good-doing' but increasingly an area where corporate messages are seen to carry political messages and where (often unpredictable) networks of stakeholders are increasingly engaging in conversations carried by social technologies. The chapter concludes with a case study on how CSR communication was played out between Nestlé and Greenpeace on the issue of palm oil production in Indonesia.

11.2 A Key CSR Communication Dilemma: Desirable yet Risky

Let us start by reflecting on a central CSR communication dilemma for a moment and consider its strategic implications. Vattenfall is a Swedish state-owned company and one of Europe's biggest electricity providers, primarily generating power through coal and nuclear power plants but recently investing more in greener technologies. Since its establishment in 1909 the company has enjoyed a positive reputation in northern Europe. Since 2003 Vattenfall has produced an annual sustainability report, and in 2008 the company decided to more visibly show its dedication to the reduction of CO_2 emissions and launched a conspicuous CSR social media campaign: 'The Climate Manifesto – Consumers against climate change'. Employing a cyber-activism method Vattenfall set out to mobilise citizens across Europe to engage in a global dialogue to reduce CO_2 emissions (see reference to Vattenfall video (2009) at the end of the chapter). The idea was to ask citizens to help the company send a clear message to the politicians that 'the world needs structural changes to the system we are all a part of as individuals, consumers, and voters' (Vattenfall, 2009). By electronically signing the Climate Manifesto, people could show their support for development of (1) a global price on carbon dioxide emissions, (2) more support for climate-friendly technologies, and (3) implementation of climate requirements for products. This was in the early days of corporate online campaigns, and during a few months Vattenfall managed to collect what was then considered an impressive number of 244,192 signatures.

These were announced at the United Nation's Climate Change Conference in Poznan in 2008 and again presented three months later at the COP15 in Copenhagen where the world's leaders, regulators and climate negotiators met to negotiate environmental regulation and collaborative efforts. However, and to the surprise of Vattenfall's managers, despite what seemed an ambitious and successful CSR communication strategy in support of a greener world, Vattenfall received the 'Climate Greenwash Award' from Greenpeace for 'its mastery of spin on climate change, portraying itself as a climate champion, while lobbying to continue business as usual using coal, nuclear power, and pseudo-solutions such as agrofuels and carbon capture and storage (CCS)' (Greenpeace, 2009). Not only that, Vattenfall faced unprecedented critique in traditional as well as social media in the months that followed. A study of the social media debate during the campaign showed that neither Vattenfall nor their stakeholders appeared willing to listen to each other and engage in dialogue, but instead they repeated their respectively defensive arguments and negative accusations (Morsing and Eriksen, 2014). Ironically, decades of enjoying a positive reputation was seriously tarnished within a few months as an implication of the company's CSR communication.

11.2.1 The Dilemma: To Communicate or Not To Communicate ...

So, what is it about CSR communication that makes it so appealing and yet so risky for businesses to engage in? In The Bodyshop's first CSR report, CEO and founder, Anita Roddick, expressed the CSR communication dilemma rather bluntly: 'Damned if we do, damned if we don't' (Roddick, 1995: 3).

Companies are expected to communicate about their CSR activities, yet they are critiqued for 'greenwashing' or 'not doing enough' when they do it.

On the one hand, CSR is generally associated with 'good deeds' and some consumers are today willing to pay a premium price for 'CSR products'. Also, managers and employees take pride in the company's social and environmental responsibilities and are often themselves asked to explain and argue for the company's social engagement (Morsing, 2006). The marketing potential and employee identification are strong arguments for why corporate communication material is today burgeoning with statements about CSR ambitions, efforts and achievements, and why also more informal communication from managers and employees in networks, interviews and media appearances often involve CSR statements and comments about the company's role in society. The other strong argumentation for the increase of CSR communication is the political demand for corporate accountability. In the 'EU Commission Strategy on CSR', the Commission states that it will work for 'improving company disclosure of social and environmental information' (Commission of the European Communities, 2011), and national policy-makers in Europe applaud those companies that publish and publicly state their willingness to engage in addressing difficult social and environmental challenges (Crane, Matten and Moon, 2008). As a consequence, national regulation on CSR is emerging that leads companies to develop and publish CSR codes of conduct, strategies and policies and to produce performance measurements and CSR reporting (see Chapter 8).

On the other hand, CSR communication evokes critique. Consumers, policy-makers, investors and other stakeholders are also critical readers of corporate messages about 'good deeds'. They keep reminding companies that CSR means *doing* something for society, not just *talking* about it. CSR communication has been critiqued for being 'just marketing' or 'empty words', and CSR reports are critiqued for 'greenwashing' and to allow companies to show a 'pretty face' (Crook, 2005). Research has also pointed to how such critique may be based on a general scepticism towards corporate power; if a company focuses too intently on communicating CSR associations, it may be seen as trying to hide something (Brown and Dacin, 1997). In particular, companies that do not already enjoy a good reputation will be suspected of employing CSR communication as a cover-up (Morsing and Schultz, 2006). Moreover, those companies that communicate about their CSR efforts and challenges are also often those who will be the first targets of a critical media or non-governmental organisation (NGO) campaign. It seems that CSR communication not only informs but also triggers new questions on corporate behaviour, and a critical search for gaps between what is said and what is done become a main focus. When there is found to be a lack of consistency between a company's CSR promise and its CSR action, this is seen as an act of immorality and is often referred to as corporate hypocrisy. In the wake of a growing number of corporate scandals, this seems a fair critique of companies that have no intention of living up to their

CSR promises. The old saying, 'practise what you preach', seems to be particularly prevalent in the area of CSR.

CSR communication seems to have a 'double edge' (Morsing and Schultz, 2006) which is exactly what Anita Roddick referred to: you have to do it, yet you are likely to be criticised for it. And this challenge does not seem to go away. New communication technologies have added to the complexity. It is not just the company itself that communicates about its social responsibilities. Many other stakeholders engage in interactive online forums, where impressions, interpretations and images about corporate CSR behaviour are formed and changed – sometimes even without the participation of the company in question. A company's CSR actions may be seen as insufficient, failed or even illegitimate when authoritative NGOs manage to set a critical agenda on social media. As you will see in this chapter's case study, this was the situation facing Nestlé in 2010 when Greenpeace redefined the company's CSR agenda in a viral campaign from focusing on nutrition, water and rural development to focusing on what Greenpeace found the more important issue: namely Nestlé's sourcing of palm oil from Indonesia.

11.3 A Distinguishing Feature of CSR Communication: Corporate Morality

CSR communication may seem like most other types of corporate communication, where a company wants to or is expected to convey its activities to different audiences. However, unlike corporate communications that disseminate information about economic or technical issues, CSR communication is often seen to define a company's morality: to what extent does the company *really* care about society? Although it has systematically been argued that business profits and social progress depend on each other (see Chapter 2), it is often assumed that CSR communication rests on a profound CSR identity, i.e. that managers and employees *really* engage and support the CSR promises. While it is generally acknowledged that the content and the scope of the CSR communication may vary across industries, size and ownership structure, it is often expected that CSR communication reflects the company's morality. CSR communication is expected to mirror what managers and employees consider right and wrong corporate behaviour, and consequently, how they think they can improve both the company and importantly its environment.

The growing attention to the organisation 'behind' corporate messages was already the main idea in the book *Revealing the Corporation*, authored by two communication scholars (Balmer and Greyser, 2003). They argued that it is not an option but a necessity for companies to 'reveal' important identity traits to establish goodwill and legitimacy. In the same way, Corporate Responsibility Communication Director for the facilities management firm Sodexo, Johan Friedman says: 'Companies are recognizing that consumers are not interested in buying "responsible" products from companies that are not known for being "responsible" themselves' (Friedman, 2015). In this way CSR communication draws attention to the organisational identity and the way managers and employees behind the CSR messages themselves 'live' CSR. While corporate expressions of distinctive organisational identities are also part of many corporate brand campaigns, such as Ryanair's focus on being cheaper and Apple's concern for user-friendliness, CSR communication carries a promise of an ethical identity, such as Volvo's focus on safety. Volvo states: 'Our commitment is about re-thinking sustainability, and goes beyond our operations and our cars, and into society. It makes us think again every time we take decisions that affect the world and the lives of people.' (Volvo, 2016) CSR communication creates an expectation that extends beyond the company's products or services and also includes expectations to a moral mindset among its managers and employees. While Ryanair's promise is about an efficient organisation to secure a low price, and Apple's promise is about product design and service features to ease use for consumers, Volvo's CSR promise adds a moral dimension where managers and employees are expected to be responsible themselves. They are expected to be *societally orientated* and to be *sincere* about this commitment. As a consequence, companies are also expected to be *transparent* about their social responsibilities. Expectations to the corporate morality serve as a platform for managers and employees to develop their CSR communication strategies and for others to assess the corporate engagement.

11.3.1 Societal: Being Seen to Do Something to Improve Society

CSR communication is expected to reflect a contribution to the development of society. Whereas it was expected that CSR communication focused on corporate activities that extended beyond corporate interests in the early days of CSR communication, today the legitimacy of 'the business case for CSR' seems to have created an acceptance that CSR activities usually benefit the corporation itself. Corporate communication campaigns, advertisements and branding efforts, where companies promise to work to reduce poverty or CO_2 emissions, or show green certificates or fair trade labels, are often used as indicators of a CSR engagement. Corporate annual CSR reports often contain detailed accounts for how the contribution to society unfolds in practice, and many resources are invested not only in the report itself but also in collecting the information and data that give evidence of the CSR efforts. It is not enough to 'do' CSR, it is also important that the company is 'seen' to be a positive contributor to local and global communities. However, one central critique has pointed to how the 'social' (or the 'S') in CSR statements seems to lose prevalence to business economic rationales in current CSR communication (Aguilera, Rupp, Williams and Ganapathi, 2007; see also Chapter 3). Table 11.1 gives three examples of companies' CSR statements, where you will notice how companies engage in the balancing act of stating their mutual concern for corporate profits and societal progress. You may want to think

Table 11.1 Corporate CSR statements – examples from industry leaders

Nestlé Nestlé in society: Creating Shared Value and Meeting our Commitments (2014: 3)	'Creating Shared Value is the way we do business, and the way we connect with society. It's an approach based on respect for people, cultures and the natural environment.'
H&M Sustainability. About our commitments (2014) http://about.hm.com/en/About/sustainability/commitments/our-seven-commitments.html#cm-menu	'We believe in a better fashion future – one where you don't have to choose between something that looks good and something that does good too. That's what H&M Conscious is all about – it's our plan for making fashion sustainable and sustainability fashionable. To do this, we have to run our company in a way that's good for people, the environment and our business. That's where our seven commitments come in. We've sorted hundreds of actions under each of these commitments – what we call Conscious Actions – and they help us create a better fashion future.'
BP BP and Sustainability (2014) A letter from our group chief executive Bob Dudley www.bp.com/en/global/corporate/sustainability/bp-and-sustainability/a-letter-from-our-group-chief-executive.html	'Of course, as a business working in many countries we face challenges and choices. We are always learning but I believe that we can act as a positive force, aiming to set high standards in safety, employment practices, transparency and human rights. When challenged over our operations in a particular country, my acid test is to ask whether the community or country is likely to be better for our involvement. If the answer is yes, then I believe we are right to be there.'

about how these CSR statements are carefully articulated to show societal concern while at the same time retaining trust about profit generation from for example shareholders.

11.3.2 Sincere: Being Seen to Be Authentic about CSR

The second dimension takes a deeper step into the 'heart' of the organisation. It has to do with how managers and employees are expected not only to inform about its CSR engagement but also to 'mean it' and be sincere about it. Two prominent CSR scholars have put it this way:

> No matter which function is delivering the message or engaging the stakeholder group, what is important, however, is that the message that is being communicated is consistent, integrated deeply with the company's business practices, and based on authentic values and the actual strategy of the firm. Authentic means real, not just fluff, and truly not 'just' public relations. (Waddock and Googins, 2011: 37)

This adds an additional layer to CSR communication vis-à-vis other types of corporate communications. Not only is the company expected to present its 'business case' for CSR in strategic, technical and rational terms but it is also expected that managers and employees personally support and believe in it.

Many companies respond in their CSR communication to such expectations. For examples, real managers and employees rather than models have been used in CSR advertising and CSR brand campaigns for Shell, Vattenfall, American Apparel and Toyota, to show that the entire organisation stands behind the CSR promise. The CEO of Starbucks put it this way at the introduction of the annual Global Responsibility Report 2014: 'By staying true to our mission, values and guiding principles, I believe we've proven it is possible to build a world-class company with a conscience' (Starbucks, 2014). In the same way, CEO, Group President and family-owner of Grundfos, Niels Due Jensen, stated at the introduction of the company's CSR policy in 2002: 'Social responsibility is a natural part of this company's identity and fundamental values.' In the case of family businesses, CSR statements are closely tied to the founder and his family's values, and CSR communication hence becomes a personal matter tied to both family and top management (Spence, 2007). Support from family, managers and employees sends strong signals that the CSR claims are sincere and authentic and that the organisation can be trusted. Such CSR communication is crucial to convey that the company will not deviate from its promise to contribute to society in case of, for example, economic crises. Critical voices have argued that the idea of such 'true' and 'authentic' values are becoming a managerial means of unifying the organisation and oppressing managers and employees to conform, and that this may counterproductively work to silence critique and entrepreneurial voices that want to improve the status quo even more profoundly (Christensen, Morsing and Cheney, 2008).

11.3.3 Transparent: Being Perceived as Not Trying to Hide Anything

The third dimension that characterises CSR communication is the insistence on corporate transparency. Transparency means being open and willing to engage in dialogue on potentially critical issues. It is important for a company to be seen as not trying to hide anything in the dark. The quest for transparency implies in principle that a company also discloses its non-actions, i.e. why it has *not* taken action in areas where it would be expected to do so. A shipping company would for example be expected to be transparent about its action or omission to act on corruption or ship-wrecking, and a gold mining company to be transparent on child labour and working conditions, as these are 'normal' CSR challenges for those industries.

Transparency is not just about the product features (e.g., cars with fewer CO2 emissions when in use) but also about the context and the processes in which the product is sourced, produced and recycled (e.g., tomatoes grown with natural fertilisers). However, such CSR information is not immediately visible in a product and is often difficult to achieve. It is not physically evident if a gold ring is from a slave-free mining company or not, and if the tea leaves are picked by women earning a fair wage or not. It is a matter of trust and belief in the corporate claims (sometimes supported by third-party endorsed certifications) to reflect reality. Thus part of the corporate CSR communication effort is to convince audiences that the company is doing its best to provide honest information about its activities (Du, Bhattacharay and Sen, 2010). Some companies state transparency as one of their core values arguing: 'Transparency – because we must always be truthful, sincere and be able to justify our actions and decisions' (L'Oreal, 2015), and others relate honesty to their CSR reporting: 'We do it to be open and honest, and to show how we are contributing to sustainable development' (Shell, 2015). DNV, a provider of classification and technical assurance expert services, has the following recommendation to its business costumers: 'Sustainability Reporting. Go tell the people. Be honest.' (DNV, 2015). Critical voices have pointed at how corporate claims about transparency may simply be part of the 'marketing mix' and thereby they reduce transparency to a simulated openness, where companies are strategically honest about some issues while they remain silent on others (Christensen et al., 2008).

To sum up, what makes CSR communication distinct from other types of corporate communication is that it connects the corporate identity to a low or high degree of morality in terms of (1) how well the company is perceived as being concerned about society; (2) how well its managers and employees are seen to be sincere about this concern; and (3) how transparent it is about its activities and omissions, and problematic business influences on society.

We shall continue below by unfolding how managers engage in CSR communication in practice, and how they employ some key CSR communication strategies.

11.4 Managerial Strategies for CSR Communication

So, how do managers navigate the high and different expectations of CSR communication without disappointing some audiences? Because CSR is generally appreciated as socially desirable behaviour, it is easy for a manager to think that 'improved' CSR communication means 'more' CSR communication. However, in a context of corporate scandals and savvy stakeholders, such simple amplification of communicative strategies is likely to be penalised. Quite a few companies have experienced how their CSR communication efforts have attracted critique and disapproval rather than public support, as Vattenfall did in 2009. CEOs and boards of directors are among the least trusted societal actors according to the Edelman Trust Barometer (2016), and scepticism, doubt and distrust that corporate CSR communication reflects an intention to serve society are on the rise (Banerjee, 2008).

It is also important to understand that CSR communication is not just the well-designed and planned execution of a CSR campaign. CSR communication includes the less orchestrated encounters between business managers and their stakeholders, such as appearance in networks, newspapers, interviews, conferences and roundtables. Here managers are exposed to the public in contexts where 'on the spot' they have to argue, explain or perhaps even defend the company's CSR behaviour. Studies have shown that managers' willingness to engage in dialogue and confrontation, for example after criticism of their CSR communication, is no guarantee for reducing negative attention (Coombs, 2007). Vattenfall's communication director Marianne Reedtz Sparrevohn engaged in several public debates and press conferences to explain how Vattenfall's CSR campaign should be seen as only one of many steps towards cleaner and greener technologies, but this communication only stimulated more immediate critique and accusations about greenwashing. When managers express their concern and intention to improve corporate behaviour after an event where the company was seen to contribute negatively to society, in fact this may reinforce scepticism and stimulate only more criticism.

CSR communication – including the CSR apology – is a difficult communication genre. One of the most cited examples of this genre is BP's CEO Tony Hayward's statement after the disaster of the Deepwater Horizon oil spill in the Mexican Gulf. This is today considered the largest accidental oil spill in history (see also the BP case study in Chapter 13). It destroyed the livelihood of thousands of people and animals in the sea, and after two months of downplaying the scope of the disaster, CEO Hayward said:

> We're sorry for the massive disruption it's caused their lives. There's no one who wants this over more than I do. I'd like my life back. (Climatebrand, 2010; see also the YouTube video with CEO Tony Hayward listed at the end of this chapter)

While this statement was probably intended to show compassion with the victims, it was seen as a symbol of corporate narcissism and a big business's profound lack of empathy with the victims. The suspicion about BP's arrogant treatment of the catastrophe was reinforced a few days later, when BP's Chairman Carl-Henri Svanberg at a press conference in front of the White House said:

> [W]e care about the small people. I hear comments sometimes that large oil companies, or greedy companies, don't care. But that is not the case in BP, we care about the small people. (see reference to the video clip with Chairman Carl-Henri Svanberg at the end of the chapter)

The chairman's explicit positioning of 'the small people' as the families living at the Mexican Gulf who had lost their family members, jobs and livelihoods as a result of the oil spill, implicitly positioned 'the big people' to be found among BP management. Such condescending communication is not likely to be part of a planned communication strategy, but it came to be seen as part of the corporate mindset and morality. It was referenced in newspapers and shown on YouTube and other social media, and even TV journalists showed negative emotional reactions to the BP statements. The communication was only a few sentences but it became widely cited and reinforced public distrust in BP.

Although CSR communication is attractive, expected and even required, it is not a straightforward genre to manage, and there is no recipe to follow. Most important is for managers to understand that CSR communication extends the standard recommendation of corporate communication to 'show your best' by importantly including a self-critical distance to question your 'best' as well as your 'worst'. Below are presented three key CSR communication strategies that managers frequently employ to balance the many interests.

11.4.1 Three CSR Communication Strategies

Drawing on public relations theories, it has been suggested that CSR communication occurs either as a one-way process (from a sender to a receiver) or as a two-way process (an exchange between a receiver and a sender) (Morsing and Schultz, 2006). The following section draws on Morsing and Schultz's framework on how information, response and involvement are three central

Table 11.2 Three CSR communication strategies (adapted from Morsing and Schultz, 2006)

CSR communication ideal	Stakeholder information strategy	Stakeholder response strategy	Stakeholder involvement strategy
Direction of communication	One-way	Two-way asymmetric	Two-way symmetric
Corporate communication task	Design appealing CSR concept message	Identify relevant stakeholders	Build relationships on issues of shared concern
Managerial communication task	Inform about favourable corporate CSR action	Demonstrate integration of CSR concern	Establish proactive dialogue with stakeholders
Engagement of stakeholders	Unnecessary	Considered in surveys, rankings and opinion polls	Central involvement in development of corporate CSR

strategies for how companies communicate their CSR efforts to internal and external audiences. These CSR communication strategies are briefly summarised above in Table 11.2.

In the stakeholder information strategy, communication is basically viewed as 'telling, not listening'. The one-directional way of communication is dissemination with the purpose of informing primarily external stakeholders about the corporate action, and hence the corporate communication task is to design objective and appealing messages about the company's contribution to societal development. Managers are 'confident the company is doing the right thing, [and] believes the company just needs to inform the general public efficiently about what it is doing to build and maintain positive stakeholder support' (Morsing and Schultz, 2006: 327). Hence, there is no need to engage stakeholders because the source of trustworthy CSR communication originates from the corporate action. This communication strategy is typically seen in advertising, marketing and corporate branding campaigns. General Electric's Ecoimagination campaign in *The Economist* and Toyota's Zero Emission campaigns are examples of this strategy.

In the stakeholder response strategy, communication is two-way *asymmetric. This means that the company engages in dialogue (two-way) and listens to its stakeholders to understand their concerns. Based on this, managers design the corporate CSR messages (asymmetric) that are likely to be endorsed by stakeholders. This may lead to changes in corporate behaviour, but often 'the company attempts to change public attitudes and behaviour' of its stakeholders (Morsing and Schultz, 2006: 327). Hence a key communicative task becomes the identification of those stakeholders who are agenda-setters in contemporary society. This communication strategy is typically seen in CSR reports in response to surveys and CSR rankings and opinion polls, where companies respond to public assessment and critique. When insurance company TrygVesta discovered that the drop in the annual leadership survey was caused by a lower perception of the company's CSR profile, the CEO decided to focus on how to improve that dimension. This is a typical two-asymmetrical strategy, since the company responds to stakeholder perceptions with a focus on efforts to change it. Such efforts may include attempts to change organisational behaviour or public perceptions, or both.

The stakeholder involvement strategy suggests a two-way symmetric communication model, where interaction and exchange of concerns happen in an ongoing dialogue between the company and its stakeholders. Ideally, managers not only seek to influence but are themselves influenced by their stakeholders' local and global concerns, and accordingly they are willing to change their behaviours if alternative approaches are discussed and found appropriate. The stakeholder involvement occurs for example when companies engage in multi-stakeholder initiatives (MSIs) and partnerships with NGOs or public authorities, but it also more frequently and (perhaps less formally) occurs when companies engage locally with stakeholders. For example, confectionary producer TOMS Group, sourcing cocoa beans from Ghana, partnered with NGO IBIS to build schools in a destitute Ghanaian context, to serve the development of society and the next generation of cocoa producers. While this CSR involvement is not a conspicuous part of the company's product branding to consumers and it did not happen as an involvement between a company and its customers, the TOMS Group-IBIS partnership is a two-way communication strategy where TOMS Group involves IBIS in dialogue to understand how the company may improve its activities to serve society and eventually the company's brand. In the wake of strong international criticism of Western multinational chocolate producers' sourcing of cocoa and hence indirect exploitation of children, TOMS Group has experienced strong support for their CSR involvement strategy with IBIS from their own employees, as well as from the business press and local communities.

The three CSR communication strategies differ primarily in their perspective on how the company engages with its stakeholders, yet they all rest on an instrumental assumption about CSR communication being managed primarily from the corporate locus. Therefore they are referred to as managerial strategies. The 'involvement strategy' is the only strategy opening for what may be uncontrollable or unpredictable influence from stakeholders, as they are invited to have a say in the corporate CSR communication. Yet, the involvement strategy still rests on the assumption that the corporation is the locus of control of the CSR communication.

Below we shall see how CSR communication has developed in phases from more instrumental approaches to political and network orientated approaches, in which CSR communication is changing accordingly.

11.5 Three Phases in the Development of CSR Communication

In this section, three basic phases for understanding the development of CSR communication are unfolded: the instrumental, the political and the network phases of CSR communication. Drawing on the framework of CSR research developed by Schultz, Castello and Morsing (2013), the communication perspective is here developed as three phases of CSR communication. The instrumental perspective with its market-orientation to CSR communication assumes that a 'business case' approach to CSR is so far the most prevalent in CSR communication studies. However, the role of CSR communication has changed alongside, first, the new expectations to companies as political actors and, second, the new social technologies challenging the corporate-centric thinking in CSR communication.

Before we unfold the three phases in the development of CSR communication, they are presented below in Table 11.3. While these are presented as phases and hereby implicitly assume a progression from instrumental over political towards network, much CSR communication remains concentrated in the instrumental phase. Also, it is important to keep in mind that there is no assumption that one of these phases is better than the others. The idea is to provide an overview of how

Table 11.3 Three phases in the development of CSR communication (adapted from the CSR framework by Schultz, Castello and Morsing, 2013)

Phases of CSR communication	Instrumental phase	Political phase	Network phase
Institutional characteristics			
Central actor	The corporation	The corporation with its stakeholders	Networks
Company-social relations	Market mechanism: consumption	Societal development: deliberative processes	Networks: fluid, non-hierarchical relations
CSR Communication focus			
Corporate focus on CSR communication	Control-orientation	Consensus-orientation	Conflict-orientation
CSR communication is a:	… means to build favourable reputation	… means to enhance deliberative dialogue to improve action	… communicative action that mobilises new communicative actions
Manager communciation role	To inform commercially important stakeholders	To engage with politically influential stakeholders and build consensus	To engage and contribute to critical debate in socially alert networks

theory as well as practice have opened up the notion of CSR communication from being an issue of marketing and branding to include the complexity of communication when the company becomes seen as a political actor, and moreover as an actor that is just one among many others in a network, where the company is less in control of communications about its own CSR efforts than it used to be. Therefore, this section is a way of introducing you to CSR communication that includes but also extends beyond instrumental thinking.

11.5.1 The Instrumental Phase of CSR Communication

The instrumental phase of CSR communication is built on the ideological premise that corporations have a primary responsibility to maximise their profits. CSR is valued primarily as a means to increase corporate profits, and *CSR communication* is seen as an activity that serves to *inform* the relevant audiences about the corporate CSR activities. CSR communication means publishing the company's 'good activities' to relevant stakeholders in order to influence their perceptions of the company; it is seen as a dissemination activity in which information and messages are channelled from a sender to a receiver as neatly bracketed entities. The rise of social media is seen as an instrument that further enables the company to enhance its efficiency in amplifying and spreading the CSR messages faster and more broadly, reaching out to geographically dispersed stakeholders. This way of thinking about communication has been referred to as the 'transmission model' by communication scholars (Schoeneborn and Trittin, 2013). A key question for managers is how companies can communicate their CSR activities more effectively to gain market acceptance.

Ending an era of strategic low key public appearance, A.P. Møller – Maersk decided in 2009 to start communicating about the company's contribution to worldwide reduction of CO_2 emissions, as they acknowledged the need not only to *engage* in CSR activities but also to be *seen* by their business to business (B2B) customers as a socially engaged and legitimate provider of shipping services. This resulted in their first CSR report and a campaign that compared and contrasted the CO_2 emitted by carrying freight overseas in comparison to carrying freight by air. In the same way, DSB, the Danish railway system that had produced an annual environmental report since 1992, decided around 2010 to inform about their CSR more strategically to passengers, by for example reminding them on service litterbags and newsmagazines on board all trains how trains produce low emissions compared to car transportation. In both companies, the focus was not initially to improve the CSR actions but to improve the CSR communications to gain market acceptance.

CSR communication in the instrumental view is prevalent in research on marketing, branding, public relations and more generally in corporate communications (e.g. Du et al., 2010). It is seen as a strategic tool with a corporate-centric outlook, where CSR activities are assessed primarily based on their beneficial influence for the company. CSR communication is therefore seen as a way of improving the company's image and reputation (see also Chapter 13). Instrumental CSR communication is treated as an operational feature and a manageable resource that serves to provide pragmatic legitimacy to corporate actions. Pragmatic legitimacy has been defined as the 'organization's ability to instrumentally manipulate and deploy evocative symbols in order to gain societal support' (Suchman, 1995: 572). Pragmatic legitimacy relates to the business case of CSR (see Chapter 3) where the notion of 'shared value' is a central feature of the corporate message for the communication to be seen as successful. While instrumental CSR communication is about the corporate strategic attempts to produce a perception among stakeholders, it involves strong messages about how the company adds a positive contribution to society.

In 2014, the Nordic retailer COOP launched a series of food products called 'Savannah', with reference to the company's sourcing of products in sub-Saharan Africa for the production of milk, jam, coffee and chocolate for example. The campaign's main focus was how COOP supports development in Africa by sourcing products from the region, and how COOP by doing business with farmers contributes to improving human rights in Africa. The campaign highlighted how these farmers in sub-Saharan Africa will be empowered to invest in their children's education as a result of COOP's efforts. This is marketed to COOP consumers as a win-win-win situation: consumers will receive an enlarged variety of healthy and tasty products, African farmers will develop their society and COOP will increase their profits. In this sense, COOP's business motive to engage in Africa is business with additional benefits for local African communities.

To acknowledge the potential and challenges of the instrumental phase, it is important to understand that it rests on the assumption that a company's stakeholders perceive CSR as a positive corporate activity. Much consumer research and many surveys have supported this assumption, and demonstrated how efficient CSR communication can create desirable images about products and companies among consumers and hereby serve to improve reputation (see Chapter 13), support sales and increase the brand value of a firm (Du et al., 2010). However, studies have also shown growing consumer apathy and confusion about labels (see Chapter 7), and a growing number of corporate scandals and revelations of corporate hypocrisy have strengthened critical voices to point at the inefficacy of companies in solving global challenges such as poverty, corruption and climate change. They point at how corporations are profoundly driven by the profit motive, and therefore instrumental CSR communication will always be in the service of the corporate interests and is not to be trusted to serve the public good (Fleming and Jones, 2014).

11.5.2 The Political Phase of CSR Communication

The political phase of CSR communication is built on an ideological premise that companies exert a massive influence on society, not only in terms of their economic influence but importantly by setting norms and values that serve to define agendas for the broader development of society. Therefore the corporation is seen as a political actor (see also Chapter 6). The corporate articulation of CSR norms and values challenges the notion of the traditional role of business in society as a depoliticised profit-generator delivering politically neutral products and workplaces. As companies are engaging in social and environmental issues of public concern, they influence not only consumers (as emphasised by the instrumental perspective) but also the agendas of policy-makers, NGOs and civil society in general. CSR communication becomes an activity that contributes to *create* those norms and values that define the boundaries for the political role of companies. A key question for managers is how the company may engage in societal development without being perceived as wanting to co-opt political (and importantly democratic) processes, but rather to be seen as engaging positively in the development of society and thereby gain legitimacy.

In 2013, Starbucks CEO Howard Schultz decided to show how he disagreed with the highly politically charged right to 'open carry' firearms in public. On Starbucks' Facebook site he asked his 'Fellow Americans' to stop bringing guns into Starbucks' coffee shops based on what he described as 'increasingly uncivil and, in some cases, even threatening' behaviour. Schultz publicly announced that he still believed that gun policy should be addressed by government and enforced by law and not by Starbucks employees, whom he did not want to be put 'in the uncomfortable position of requiring customers to disarm or leave the stores'. Schultz said:

> Pro-gun activists have used our stores as a political stage for media events misleadingly called 'Starbucks Appreciation Days' that disingenuously portray Starbucks as a champion of 'open carry.' To be clear: we do not want these events in our stores. Some anti-gun activists have also played a role in ratcheting up the rhetoric and friction, including soliciting and confronting our customers and partners. For these reasons, today we are respectfully requesting that customers no longer bring firearms into our stores or outdoor seating areas—even in states where 'open carry' is permitted — unless they are authorized law enforcement personnel. (Schultz, 2013).

While Schultz insisted on this being an apolitical decision, this corporate communication challenged the moral legitimacy of US policy-makers pro 'open carry' policy and positioned Starbucks in one end of a polarised and sensitive US political debate.

The political phase has its roots in theories of sociology and political science with a macro-level orientation. CSR communication is often seen as the implicit way that companies set norms and aspirations. It brings an emphasis on how the power is shifting from state institutions to corporations and civil society actors on issues of public concern, such as for example to define standards for action and to determine the conditions under which social and environmental agendas can develop. As a result, corporations sometimes become embedded in highly complex situations in which they – intentionally or unintentionally – are seen as political actors supporting certain political agendas. In practice this was Starbucks' situation when they asked customers to leave their weapon outside the coffee shop. While such CSR communication may attract certain customers, it is likely to disenchant others. Such CSR communication not only shows that the company cares about its social contribution to society but it also shows what values (and hence political agenda) the company stands for. While Starbucks itself communicated its values on pro 'open carry', a corporate political stance may also be deduced from corporate behaviour such as trading with oppressive regimes.

The French oil extractor Total has witnessed ongoing critique of its engagement in Burma ever since oil extractions began in 1992. For example, under the banner of 'Totalitarian Oil: fuelling the oppression in Burma', a group of NGOs supported by exiled politician Aung San Suu Kyi demonstrated vehemently to stop Total from operating in Burma, as this was seen as an act of supporting the non-democratically elected government. Total has over the years responded by upgrading its CSR activities in Burma, arguing that it supports the country better in its democratic development by remaining and influencing the local Burmese society than withdrawing its activities. Willingly or not, Starbucks and Total have found themselves entangled in highly politicised situations that have questioned their apolitical intervention in society and forced them to relate their social responsibility to contested political issues. No matter how many good intentions corporations have to engage in improving society, their lack of democratic authority (i.e. companies are not democratically elected to represent the interests of the people) remains an overall democratic concern when engaging in CSR.

In Western societies, corporate norms and values are often related to capitalism where the corporate focus on values of commercialisation, efficiency and consumption is critically seen to permeate society as it influences the way individuals interact with one another. While these values are seen as sufficient to provide a pragmatic legitimacy (as emphasised by the market perspective), the political perspective points towards how these values may not be seen as sufficient to make a company seem a legitimate social actor today. To achieve a positive evaluation, the corporation needs to acquire a moral legitimacy.

Moral legitimacy refers to conscious moral judgements about an organisation's outputs, procedures, structures, leaders and impact (Suchman, 1995). The German philosopher Jürgen Habermas suggested that moral legitimacy can only be achieved through deliberative processes. According to the Habermasian framework of communicative rationality, deliberation assumes a dialogue with its cornerstone in the 'forceless force of the better argument' to serve as the rule that legitimises corporate action (Habermas, 1984). This means that stakeholders (including the company) voice their concerns and interests and listen to one another before a decision is made. Importantly, such a decision is grounded in 'the better argument'. This stands in sharp opposition to the notion of, for example, economic or hierarchical power as the defining rule to legitimise corporate action. Rather than manipulating the perceptions of stakeholders, companies will need to engage in a process of moral reasoning where it is initially not clear whether the corporation or other societal voices and expectations will win 'the better argument' and a new position will be created. *Communication* plays the role of *ideally* ensuring participation from relevant stakeholders. CSR becomes anchored in a corporate- and society-centric perspective, where CSR communication is a processual activity with the normative purpose of producing consensus across the participating 'voices' to ensure that not only companies but also society benefits. Corporate participation in partnerships or MSIs are examples of the corporate attempts to establish and be part of structures for such deliberative communication to occur (see Chapter 7).

Moreover, adding to the Habermasian idea of the corporate responsibility to engage in dialogue as a cornerstone of its political role, there is another dimension to the political phase of CSR communication. While most companies still argue that they hold a politically neutral position in their CSR communication and beyond, in practice many managers experience that their CSR engagement is seen as a political engagement. Hence, they develop a more explicit strategy that takes into account the political nature of their CSR engagement. It has been argued that CSR communication may imply that managers are moved out of their comfort zone because they are pushed into a non-commercial and political communication, that may have unexpected implications on the business (Chapter 6, see also Morsing and Roepstorff, 2015). This is what IKEA Denmark experienced when they launched a nationwide CSR campaign signalling respect for human rights with a focus on non-discrimination that depicted on large billboards young men with Sikh turbans and young women with Muslim headscarves. IKEA welcomed different people with different religious and ethnic backgrounds to apply for jobs in their stores in a national context of increasing political concern about what was perceived as a failed integration of Muslim immigrants. While this seemed a non-controversial action in the local context, IKEA's CSR communication became national centre stage in a heated political debate about religion and human rights, as the campaign coincided with the 9/11 terror attacks on the twin towers in New York. The Bush Administration perceived the event as a Muslim declaration of war on Western values of Christianity, and IKEA unexpectedly found itself being a target of accusations of supporting such values. IKEA customers came to the stores and cut their membership cards up in front of IKEA personnel, accusing them of supporting the wrong development of Danish society. Although he was seemingly overwhelmed by the political furore, IKEA's CEO decided to stand by his CSR commitment (Morsing and Roepstorff, 2015). The political phase of CSR communication reminds us that it is important to develop a managerial alertness to ongoing dialogue and to the ever-changing and unpredictable national and supra-national political events that may change the definition of companies' responsibilities to society.

11.5.3 The Network Phase of CSR Communication

The network phase of CSR communication is built on the premise that companies are embedded in society and are one among many agents that in network constellations influence societal development. This view rests on the observation that language plays a fundamental role for shaping social reality and that communication is a process that produces and reproduces social order. It emphasises that CSR communication is not a simple mechanism employed by organisations to convey their messages (as in the market perspective). Rather, CSR communication is a 'continuous process, through which social actors explore, construct, negotiate, and modify what it means to be a socially responsible organization' (Christensen and Cheney, 2011: 491).

In the network phase, it becomes central to understand that not just managers but also other participants have legitimate ideas and interests for what constitutes a company's CSR. The network phase differs most distinctly from the political phase in the appreciation of how the production and embracement of dissent is the normal modus operandi. In fact, such conflict is central for the actors to remain legitimate. A key challenging question for managers is how to engage (self-) critically in the ongoing communication processes in which the company's social responsibilities are challenged, defined and redefined.

In the 'Novo Nordisk CSR Report 2003' five ethical dilemmas were raised by Novo Nordisk from five critical voices that individually asked concerned questions on what they saw as key challenges for Novo Nordisk in their future operations to serve and cure diabetes patients (Novo Nordisk, 2003). The critical voices were representatives from hospitals, international organisations and NGOs, and although the dilemmas were clearly invited by Novo Nordisk and carefully responded to in the report by Novo Nordisk, this CSR communication showed an early and alternative way of inviting public self-critical inquiry into a company's CSR communication.

The network perspective on CSR communication builds on established constructivist perspectives with a descriptive ambition in which communication is defined as the 'ongoing process of making sense of the circumstances in which people collectively find themselves and of the events that affect them' (Taylor and van Every, 2000: 58). The pivotal role of communication is to constitute or *organise reality* (Weick, 1979). This communication view implies a different understanding of companies' social responsibilities and more fundamentally of *organisations*. If reality is communicatively constituted, organisations and their CSR activities cannot be understood as substantial unities or entities, but as constructs that emerge in communication. This idea, that organisations emerge in communication, has been developed further and argued in CCO theorising (Communication Constitutes Organizations) (e.g. Ashcraft, Kuhn and Cooren, 2009). Here a central observation is that organisations depend on many different and simultaneously occurring voices, and it is the continuous attempt to engage and manoeuvre among these many voices that define (and redefine) the company and its CSR engagement. The focus for CSR communication is not how the company defines and transmits its CSR engagement effectively to its stakeholders. Rather the focus of a company's CSR communication is that it is constantly challenged and modified, and accordingly CSR communication is characterised by a focus on dissensus.

So, when Starbucks decides to confront the pro 'open carry' movement and disagrees with such behaviour, it is in the disagreement itself and in that daring moment where Starbucks decides to disagree with this norm, that CSR definitions are pushed, challenged and redefined. Likewise, IKEA Denmark decided to make inclusion and non-discrimination the central dimension of their CSR communication strategy, and the company insisted on this in spite of strong public critique.

While the network phase of CSR communication is so far primarily an analytical framework, there have been attempts to test its strategic implications. Scholars have argued that if managers systematically appreciate dissensus and frequently invite critique and contestation (rather than the intuitive inclination to seek for agreement and consensus), this may serve as a vehicle for organisational development and improvement instead of constraining current and future experiences to focus on past definitions (Christensen, Morsing and Thyssen, 2015). Consensus, it is argued, leads to a 'discursive closure' (Deetz, 1992) in which past decisions rule future action and where assumptions taken for granted are not challenged. Dissensus, on the other hand, serves to 'keep the conversation alive' by focusing on alternatives and questioning the status quo. This is particularly important in highly volatile contexts with a high discretionary agency where there are no predefined modus operandi nor any firm legislation to refer to. In practice this is often the case with CSR where companies are addressing social and environmental issues that have not been previously attended to by corporations, and that therefore call for ethical assessment and ongoing interpretation and adjustment (Wijen, 2014).

In particular the rise of new social technologies have demonstrated how previously silent voices are now able to engage in critical conversations online about corporate social ir/responsibilities and challenge companies' 'licence to operate'. Social media have convincingly shown how a company's legitimacy is not only formed in communication between a company and its stakeholders within hierarchical orders of stable institutions or powerful rational elites, as Habermas (2001) argued, but is also co-constructed by 'networked publics' – sometimes without participation of the company itself (Arvidsson, 2010).

Facebook, Instagram, Skype and Twitter allow much faster and direct two-way-interaction than traditional sender-to-receiver campaigns, newspaper and surface mail correspondence, and social media networks invite dialogue and participation across geographically dispersed individuals to an extent that we have not previously witnessed. The communication is documented to increase the connectivity of individuals and organisations fundamentally (Schultz, Utz and Göritz, 2011). Scholars have suggested how this development results in a significantly more open, reflexive, self-organised and fluid public, but also in increasing network activism and new social movements (Bennett, 2003; see also Chapter 9), who can affect organisations dramatically. It may particularly empower individuals as recently seen in political movements around the Arab Spring starting in Egypt in 2011, and citizens have also raised their voices and influenced corporate behaviour as in the controversy between Greenpeace and Nestlé (which will be explored in the case study below). Importantly, it may also influence how citizens may become aware of systemic challenges, as witnessed by the leak of information in 2016 which showed how the bank sector and public investors have been intimately involved in tax avoidance activities in Panama. Through social media many more citizens have, in principle, the possibility of influencing the public discourse on companies' CSR communication and their CSR practices.

11.6 Case Study: Nestlé Meets Greenpeace in Social Media Campaign

In 2010, one of the world's largest food processing companies, Nestlé SA, found itself centre stage of a social media campaign that profoundly challenged its way of thinking about CSR communication. The environmental protection group Greenpeace International connected Nestlé's chocolate confectionery brand KitKat with the production of palm oil in Indonesia that leads to the destruction of rainforests and is known to cause large fires on degraded peatlands. This leads to considerable CO_2 emissions and destruction of local neighbourhoods. Palm oil is used as an ingredient in a broad variety of food products and is primarily grown in Indonesia, where the expansion of palm oil cultivation has led to destroying the home of many rare animals including proboscis monkeys and the primate species orang-utans. Greenpeace's social media campaign included a provocative video that was first published on their own Facebook and then followed by publication on Nestlé's own Facebook page. The video showed an office worker consuming a KitKat chocolate bar containing a bleeding finger of an orang-utan thereby linking the consumption of KitKat chocolate bars directly to the destruction of the natural habitat of the orang-utans in the rainforests in Indonesia. The KitKat logo was replaced by a

'Killer' logo. With this campaign Greenpeace put massive pressure on Nestlé to discontinue buying palm oil from its supplier Sinar Mas Group. The Sinar Mas Group is a major Indonesian conglomerate and the largest producer of palm oil in the country, and at that time alleged to have been involved in illegal rainforest clearance in Indonesia. The Greenpeace video was supported by other types of communication material from Greenpeace that all focused on Nestlé, involving demonstrations and protesters dressed up as orang-utans at the annual Nestlé shareholder meeting. Nestlé's immediate response was:

> We shared the deep concern about the serious environmental threat to rainforests and peat fields in South East Asia caused by the planting of palm oil plantations. The company recently announced its commitment to using only 'Certified Sustainable Palm Oil' by 2015, when sufficient quantities should be available.

However, as Greenpeace moved the YouTube video to the front of Nestlé's Facebook fanpage and the Nestlé fanpage was seen to stimulate many viewers to post the critical Killer-logo imitations of Kit Kat logos on their own Facebook pages, Nestlé responded with reference to the company's legal rights. Nestle argued that they considered the use of an altered logo a violation of property rights and they asked Facebook to remove the video while they posted a comment on their Facebook site:

> We welcome all comments but please don't post using an altered version of our logo as your profile pic. And please read our statement to answer many questions.

This response from Nestlé was received as a corporate attempt to censor a public debate and started a social media firestorm against Nestlé. 'You are committing social media suicide', as one comment prophetically stated. Another comment warned: 'Not sure you are going to win friends in the social media space with this sort of dogmatic approach. I understand that you're on your back-foot due to various issues not excluding palm oil but social media is about embracing your market and having a conversation rather than preaching!' To which Nestlé responded: 'Thanks for the lesson in manners. Consider yourself embraced. But it's our page, we set the rules, it was ever thus.' While online conversations about Nestlé increased 32 per cent during the following week, 93 per cent of this conversation was negative (Chaudhari and Purkayastha, 2011).

The pressure forced Nestle to clarify its strategy on palm oil sourcing and create a new strategy for its palm oil supply chain. Daniela Montalto, Forest Campaign Head at Greenpeace said:

> We had been asking Nestlé to stop buying products from rainforest destruction for two years before we launched our campaign. Nestlé cracked within just two months because the overwhelming public response made the company listen.

On 17 May 2010, Greenpeace stopped its campaign, as Nestlé announced that it had decided to profoundly change its strategy for palm oil sourcing. Importantly, Nestlé had made a partnership with The Forest Trust to help stop deforestation. Greenpeace thanked Nestlé on its Facebook site – and declared that they would follow Nestlé's progress closely.

This Nestlé–Greenpeace interaction has made many analysts and managers reconsider how companies should engage in CSR communication, and in particular wonder how to approach CSR communication in social media.

Questions for Discussion

1. What is the main problem with Nestlé's CSR communication strategy? Include in your discussion the legal versus moral forms of argument.
2. How would you recommend the CEO of Nestlé to prepare its CSR communication strategy for future similar incidents?
3. Is it better for a company to keep a low communication profile on its CSR activities than to engage visibly and proactively?

11.7 Chapter Summary

CSR communication is a many-headed beast. In its most basic definition, CSR communication is the company's communication about its CSR engagement to internal and external audiences. This communication includes formal and informal communications, planned and unplanned communications, but basically this type of communication originates and is controlled from the company. However, CSR communication is – like other types of corporate communications – only effective (seen from the corporate side) if stakeholders are influenced to think positively about the company. One central aspect of CSR communication is how it engages a conversation about its contributions to society, its sincerity to do so and its willingness to be transparent about its CSR efforts. These aspects converge into perceptions of the morality or amorality of the organisation behind the CSR messages. However, as this chapter has highlighted, social technologies have accelerated the complexity and even experienced managers in highly professional and internationally operating companies are challenged to develop new ways of engaging in the many expectations to CSR communication.

This chapter has introduced three CSR communication strategies: information, response and engagement strategies that are used by managers. It has also outlined three phases in the development of CSR communication: the instrumental, the political and the network phases; and while there is an idea of progression among these phases, much thinking and practice on CSR communication is still based in an instrumental way of imagining the purpose and results of CSR communication. The political and the network phases put new demands on CSR communication and seem to engage development of new types of two-way communications that will challenge companies but also open new roles and opportunities for them as they revisit their CSR role in society.

This chapter has emphasised the strategic importance of CSR communication, and how CSR communication is not necessarily inferior to action but rather a central dimension of CSR that is coupled to influence, obligations and impact. Understanding CSR communication is not only about understanding how managers become better at disseminating the corporate CSR engagement, but importantly also for managers and societal actors to play a significant role by collectively addressing and challenging important global challenges.

Chapter Questions

1. How would you describe the strategic role of CSR communication for business? What are the main tasks for managers accordingly? Do you think that all managers or only a few in an organisation should engage in CSR communication? What are the advantages and disadvantages?
2. Provide an overview of how companies engage in CSR communication. Find examples in newspapers, magazines, social media sites, etc.
3. To what extent should companies engage in two-way CSR communication strategies? Form an argument and examples from practice to support your argument, either for or against.
4. How would you characterise the main challenges and opportunities for companies in each of the three phases in the development of CSR communication?
5. How do you think social technologies will influence the development of CSR communication for companies?

FURTHER RESOURCES

May, S., Cheney, G. and Roper, J. (Eds.) (2007). *The Debate over Corporate Social Responsibility*. New York: Oxford University Press.
   This book is one of the first edited volumes emphasising the role of CSR communications. It critically deals with the many facets of CSR while introducing the reader to communication theories and their role for the definition of CSR.

Ihlen, Ø., Bartlett, J. L. and May, S. (Eds.) (2011). *The Handbook of Communication and Corporate Social Responsibility.* Sussex: Wiley-Blackwell.

This book is a collection of contributions from communication scholars ranging from marketing and public relations theories to organisational communication. It provides an extensive overview and has been influential in directing studies on CSR communication.

Crane, A. and Glozer, S. (2016). Researching Corporate Social Responsibility Communication: Themes, Opportunities and Challenges. *Journal of Management Studies*, DOI: 10.1111/joms.12196.

This article provides a review of the literature related to CSR communication and provides a useful conceptualisation of four different analytical approaches to CSR communication.

Christensen, L. T., Morsing, M. and Thyssen, O. (2013). CSR as Aspirational Talk, *Organisation*, 20(3), 372–393.

This article challenges mainstream assumptions that CSR communication must be aligned with CSR action. Instead it suggests that CSR aspirations, or CSR visions, that are relatively decoupled from practice may stimulate innovative ways of addressing CSR.

Vattenfall Climate Manifesto, www.youtube.com/watch?v=0Ubhr4MWbyo

This is Vattenfall's advertising video, mentioned at the beginning of the chapter, encouraging viewers to sign the petition. At the time it was seen as a very innovative and daring way for companies to communicate their CSR ambitions.

BP CEO Tony Hayward, BP on oil spill in Mexican Gulf, www.youtube.com/watch?v=EIA_sL4cSlo

This is CEO Tony Hayward's statement on Fox News shortly after the BP Oil spill in the Mexican Gulf.

BP Chairman Carl-Henri Svanberg, on the BP oil spill in the Mexican Gulf: www.veteranstoday.com/2010/06/17/bp-chairman-carl-henric-svanberg-we-care-about-the-small-people/

Nestlé–Greenpeace video, www.youtube.com/watch?v=1BCA8dQfGi0

This is the Greenpeace's YouTube video that was strategically used to point attention to the problem of deforestation and endangering of wildlife habitat supported by multinational companies sourcing palm oil in Indonesia. It is one in a series of YouTube films created by Greenpeace that has effectively contributed to draw attention to some of the global challenges caused by unsustainable practices.

12

CSR and Crisis Communication Strategies

TIM COOMBS

Learning Objectives

- Explain how corporate social responsibility (CSR) affects crisis communication.
- Differentiate CSR-based challenge crises from 'washing'.
- Apply the framework for evaluating threats and selecting a response to real-life cases of CSR-based challenge crises.
- Identify the role of reputation and social media in the fusion of CSR and crisis communication.

12.1 Introduction: CSR as a Crisis Risk

In July 2011, Greenpeace released a report online entitled 'Dirty Laundry' about the use of toxic chemicals in the garment industry, and formally requested that Nike and other major garment manufacturers agree to 'detox' by removing a specific chemical from their supply chains. Greenpeace was petitioning the firms for change. Nike declined the request from Greenpeace (as did all the other firms), resulting in the launch of the Detox campaign, an aggressive public communication campaign designed to pressure Nike and the other garment firms to detox. For the next three weeks Nike found itself awash with social media messages claiming their garment-making was irresponsible because it was poisoning employees and water supplies around the world. The first action was filming a dance protest in front of Nike stores at various locations around the globe, which was edited and placed on YouTube. Next came Twitter posts about the toxins found in Nike's clothes and the dangers those chemicals posed to people, animals and the environment, followed by a Nike logo redesign competition to reflect its toxic nature.

What would you do if you were Nike management?

This opening scenario illustrates the complex interrelationships that have evolved between reputations, CSR and crisis communication. CSR communication, from an instrumental perspective, can add value to a firm by enhancing its reputation, a valued asset. Stakeholders can now threaten a firm's reputation by redefining current firm practices as irresponsible. If other stakeholders accept the proposition that the firm is acting irresponsibly, the firm will suffer reputational damage and may even suffer what is called a reputational crisis.

This chapter explores the unintended consequences of CSR communication on crisis communication. A firm's commitment to CSR has implications far beyond just the CSR communication function. A public commitment to CSR creates opportunities and threats to other corporate communication functions such as crisis communication. By the end of this chapter, you will understand the links between CSR communication and crisis communication, the demands placed on organisations by a CSR-based challenge crisis, and the factors to consider when developing a firm's response to a CSR-based challenge crisis.

12.2 The Context for CSR-Based Challenge Crises

12.2.1 Increasing Importance of Reputation and CSR

If we return to the opening vignette, we find Nike is not the only major garment firm to agree to the Detox campaign. The list of firms agreeing to detox include Adidas, Puma, H&M, C&A, Zara and Li-Ning. How is it that some videos, Tweets and small in-store protests can create change when all these firms initially declined to detox? The answer can be found in a confluence of factors that are reshaping the landscape of strategic communication. The foundational element in this evolving strategic communication landscape is certification of reputation as a critical asset for firms. In the 1990s, managers and researchers were still debating whether the concept of reputation had any real value for firms. There was some early research linking reputation to investment but that was of rather limited benefit. The following decades witnessed a growing body of research that showed the multitude of benefits related to reputations, including improved employee morale and consumer interest in products and services (Coombs, 2015). While people might argue over what constitutes a reputation or how to measure it, there is widespread agreement as to the value of a favourable reputation to a firm.

Following a similar trajectory, CSR has become ingrained into the daily operations and strategic planning of firms. Again, there are debates over what constitutes CSR – it is a contested term – and questions remain on how to assess its effects on a firm and society. However, most managers would argue that CSR is an important consideration for modern firms. CSR involves expanding the scope of a firm's concerns beyond financial interests to social and environmental concerns. Essentially, it means that firms need to consider the interest of a wide array of stakes beyond the historical focus to financial stakes. There are still debates about what concerns should be addressed, the marginalisation of stakeholder interests, and even those who hold that CSR is a distraction, but the general direction of firms has been to integrate CSR into their operations and their strategic communication.

12.2.2 Linking CSR, Reputation and Crisis Communication

Business reputation has become intertwined with and inseparable from concepts of CSR in the modern business environment. The Reputation Institute estimates that over 40 per cent of a firm's reputation is a function of CSR (Smith, 2012). From an instrumental perspective, reputation is a critical benefit that corporate managers associate with CSR. While some might choose to challenge that assumption, an instrumental view regards CSR as a form of risk reduction for reputations. 'The threat of a loss of reputation and image is seen as a significant factor in encouraging companies to make a commitment to CSR' (Eisenegger and Schrang, 2011: 2006). CSR can be viewed as a form of risk management because it can prevent reputational threats. Reputation and CSR are not isomorphic but often demand to be considered in tandem with one another. Crisis communication is one of those areas where CSR and reputation are best viewed as inseparable. The growing importance of reputation as a firm's asset and the rising importance of CSR occurred simultaneously, with a shifting emphasis in crisis communication from operational to reputational crises. The operational–reputational shift is a critical contextual factor that requires greater explication.

A crisis occurs when organisations violate stakeholders' expectations, creating the potential for negative outcomes for the organisation and/or stakeholders (Coombs, 2015). Historically, crisis management and communication emphasised operational disruptions as the expectation violation. For instance, trains should not derail, a product should not make people ill, and chemical facilities should not release hazardous materials. All three of these violations involve a disruption to the regular operations of an organisation, but crises do not have to be limited to organisational disruptions.

A common refrain in the crisis communication literature is that a crisis threatens an organisation's reputation. Consider how organisational reputation is a primary outcome variable in image repair theory (IRT), corporate apologia and situational crisis communication theory (SCCT), the most commonly used theories in crisis communication research. The focus on reputation as an outcome is a limited view of crisis communication that reflects a firm-centric bias but is an accurate characterisation of the extant crisis communication literature. SCCT illustrates the focus on reputation as an outcome. It is driven by the attributions which stakeholders make about the firm's responsibility for a crisis, and emphasises the use of crisis communication to influence meaning. Crisis response strategies – the words and actions firms utilise when responding to a crisis – are intended to influence either perceptions of the crisis itself or perceptions (the reputation) of the firm involved in the crisis.

There are actually three broad categories of crisis responses strategies: (1) instructing information, (2) adjusting information and (3) reputation management. The first messages must present instructing information, followed by adjusting information, then reputation management. Obviously instructing and adjusting information do influence perceptions of reputations, but their focus is on public safety and welfare – the victims – and not the firm and its reputation. Crisis communication should begin with instructing information, telling people how to protect themselves physically from a crisis. Examples of instructing information are announcements about the recall of harmful products or warnings to evacuate an area because of a chemical release. Managers also need to provide adjusting information, helping people to cope psychologically with the crisis. Adjusting information can include explanations of why the crisis occurred, expressions of sympathy to crisis victims from management, trauma counselling for crisis victims, efforts to repair damage created by the crisis and details of what steps are being taken to prevent a repeat of the crisis; this is called corrective action (Coombs, 2015). Corrective action is critical because it helps to reduce the anxiety created by a crisis. If preventive measures have been taken, the dangerous event is less likely to reoccur in the future.

A core element of SCCT is the list of ten crisis response strategies intended to protect or repair the firm reputations–reputation management strategies. Table 12.1 provides a summary of the crisis response strategies for reputation management. SCCT groups the ten response strategies into four postures: (1) denial, (2) diminish, (3) rebuilding and (4) bolstering.

The denial posture seeks to disconnect the firm from any crisis responsibility and includes attacking the accuser, denial and scapegoating. If stakeholders accept the denial strategies, they believe the organisation has little or no responsibility for the crisis. Crisis responsibility creates the reputational damage from a crisis, hence, denial efforts protect the firm's reputation by separating the firm from the crisis. Attacking the accuser is a very aggressive response that seeks to prevent the accuser from disseminating information about the supposed crisis. Lawsuits, for example, have been used to silence critics of firms that are perceived to be creating a crisis for the firm. The denial approach means denying that the firm is involved in the crisis. Three major peanut butter producers in the US used denial when people wrongly thought the firms were involved in a peanut paste recall. The firms needed to reassure consumers there was nothing wrong with their products – they were not linked to the product harm crisis. Scapegoating is when the firm blames someone else for the crisis. When there was a concern about tyre blowouts in Ford Explore SUVs, Ford blamed Firestone (the tyre manufacturer) for the crisis. Shifting the blame mitigates crisis responsibility, thereby reducing the reputation threat

Table 12.1 SCCT crisis response strategies for reputation management

Denial posture	
Attacking the accuser	The crisis manager confronts the person or group that claims that a crisis exists. The response may include a threat to use force (e.g. a lawsuit) against the accuser.
Denial	The crisis manager states that no crisis exists. The response may include explaining why there is no crisis.
Scapegoating	Some other person or group outside the organisation is blamed for the crisis.
Diminishment posture	
Excusing	The crisis manager tries to minimise the organisation's responsibility for the crisis. The response can include denying any intention to do harm or claiming that the organisation had no control of the events that led to the crisis.
Justification	The crisis manager tries to minimise the perceived damage associated with the crisis. The response can include stating that there were no serious damages or injuries or claiming that the victims deserved what they received.
Rebuilding posture	
Compensation	The organisation provides money or other gifts to the victims.
Apology	The crisis manager publicly states that the organisation takes full responsibility for the crisis and asks forgiveness.
Bolstering posture	
Reminding	The organisation tells stakeholders about its past good works.
Ingratiation	The organisation praises stakeholders.
Victimage	The organisation explains how it too is a victim of the crisis.

posed by the crisis. The denial postures are the least accommodative because they deny responsibility for victims.

The diminish posture attempts to reduce the amount of crisis responsibility attributed to the firm. If crisis responsibility can be reduced, the reputational damage from the crisis is reduced. The excuse crisis response strategy denies any intention to do harm or any control over the events. The crisis is viewed more as a product of the circumstances than a result of the firm's actions or inactions. In one case, management of a firm emphasised the influence of a lightning strike on a chemical release – the organisation had little control over the strike and did not mean the chemicals to be released. Justification seeks to minimise perceptions of the damage created by the crisis. During the Exxon

Valdez crisis, management noted how the oil spill was not even in the top-ten spills in terms of volume. This was an attempt to reduce perceptions of the severity of the Exxon Valdez spill. The diminish posture is minimally accommodative because it recognises victims but downplays their situation.

The rebuilding posture seeks to enhance the damaged reputation and includes compensation and apology. Compensation involves giving victims money or gifts. After the Carnival Cruise ship Triumph's engine stranded people at sea in 2014, the firm provided the crisis victims with monetary compensation, hotel rooms and transportation. An apology is a public acceptance of responsibility for the crisis, often coupled with a request for forgiveness from the crisis victims. The rebuild strategies seek to create positive actions to offset the negatives being generated by the crisis. Moreover, the rebuild strategy is the most accommodative because it emphasises crisis victim concerns over concerns for the firm.

The bolstering posture is secondary and should only be used in combination with one of the other three postures. Bolstering strategies would look out of place if used as the only crisis response strategies. The bolstering posture tries to associate the firm with positive feeling. The reminder bolstering strategy tells people about the past good works of the firm. Firms might talk about their past community relations or CSR efforts, but this approach only works if the firm has performed good works in the past. The ingratiation strategy praises stakeholders for their support during the crisis. Toyota praised its customers and dealerships for their support during their brake crisis. The victimage strategy notes how the firm is a victim of the crisis as well. Johnson & Johnson indicated how the firm was a target of an external attack (a victim) during the first Tylenol tampering. The bolstering posture is rather neutral; it does not deny victims, but does little to address their concerns.

There is a strong connection between crisis communication and reputation. Prior reputation does impact the effectiveness of crisis communication efforts; in turn, crisis communication efforts can help to determine the amount of reputational damage inflicted by a crisis (Coombs, 2015). The link with reputation is a key point of connection between CSR and crisis communication, a focal point of this chapter. The perceived responsibility or irresponsibility of a firm shapes the effectiveness and selection of crisis response strategies. A responsible firm has added credibility and stakeholders are more likely to accept their crisis communication efforts. Crisis response strategies will not have the desired effect if stakeholders reject the messages (Coombs, 2015). For example, denial cannot severe the link between the organisation and a crisis if stakeholders do not accept the denial message. Similarly, an apology is ineffective if people reject the message. Irresponsible firms will find it much more difficult to win acceptance of their crisis communication messages.

Crisis response strategies should affect how responsible the firm is perceived to be by stakeholders during a crisis. In this case, responsibility does not mean crisis responsibility but reflects the moral character of the firm. Firms can enhance perceptions of 'being responsible' by focusing on the needs of the crisis victims. By providing, instructing and adjusting information along with accommodative reputation strategies, organisations should be perceived as 'being responsible' during a crisis. When Johnson & Johnson issued the recall during the first Tylenol poisoning crisis, their actions were hailed as caring for customers which enhanced perceptions that the firm was 'being responsible'. A crisis can provide an insight into a firm's soul. Does the firm respond by focusing on victims (a responsible manner), or by seeking to deny responsibility and expressing a callousness towards victims (an irresponsible manner)? It is possible for a firm to enhance how stakeholders perceive their reputation as socially responsible by how the firm responds to the crisis. SCCT places an emphasis on operational crises and firm reputations, but we also need to consider the implications presented by reputational crises.

12.2.3 Emergence of Reputational Crises

Operational disruptions cause reputational damage by creating the appearance of firm incompetence or malice. However, reputational damage is a potentially negative outcome for a firm that does not require disruption of operations. In fact, experts argue that reputational crises are a distinct form of crisis. Booth was among the first to articulate the idea of a reputational crisis, defining it as 'the loss of the common estimation of the good name attributed to an organization' (Booth, 2000: 197).

Sohn and Lariscy sought to refine the conceptualisation of a reputational crisis using the corporate association framework to distinguish between corporate ability (CA) reputational crisis and corporate social responsibility (CSR) reputational crises. For this chapter, the CSR reputational crisis is the most salient. A *CSR reputational crisis* is defined as 'a major event that poses a threat to reputation associated with norms and values cherished by society and socially expected obligation' (Sohn and Lariscy, 2014: 25). During a CSR reputational crisis, stakeholders begin to question the integrity of the firm. Based upon their research, Sohn and Lariscy argued for the 'importance of investing more resources in preventing a CSR crisis' (ibid.: 36). Not all crisis researchers or crisis managers accept the idea of a reputational crisis, and prefer to withhold the label 'crisis' for events related to potential or actual disruptions of operations. While there is some merit in this position, the rise of the importance of reputation and complications created by digital communication demand that we take the idea of reputational crises more seriously. However, the idea does demand further explication if it is to add to our understanding of strategic communication and CSR.

While useful in refining the conceptualisation of reputational crises, Sohn and Lariscy's work is constrained by a focus on crises as events. In other words, there is some specific event such as a fire or accident that marks the start of the crisis. Modern crises are no longer limited to simple events but can be a realisation by management that the firm is violating important stakeholder expectations. There is a growing realisation in crisis communication thinking that stakeholder perceptions play an essential role in a crisis. We should ask, 'Why should stakeholder perceptions be a significant factor in a potential crisis situation?' Reputational crises can also begin when management realises they are violating stakeholder expectations rather than with an event. The assumption is that when stakeholders perceive an organisation to be in crisis and respond to it, an organisation *is* in a crisis. How do you react to this assumption? What are the implications for modern managers when situations of differing perceptions arise, challenging managers to decide whether or not they agree a crisis exists (Coombs, 2015)? Booth's associational crisis and Lerbinger's challenge crisis are indicative of crises that are initiated by realisations rather than events (Booth, 2000; Lerbinger, 1997). An associational crisis occurs when the organisation is associated with 'some other activity, entity, or incident' (Booth, 2000: 197) rather than an existing crisis, while a challenge crisis occurs when stakeholders claim an organisation is acting immorally or irresponsibly (Lerbinger, 1997). Note the strong influence of stakeholder perceptions in both of these concepts.

12.2.4 Introducing the CSR-Based Challenge

The idea of stakeholder perceptions is at the heart of how CSR communication can become a crisis risk. When an organisation engages in CSR communication, it creates a general expectation that it values being perceived as socially responsible, whether or not it intends to do so. A violation of that expectation could create a reputational crisis. The organisation is now vulnerable to a CSR-based challenge – efforts by stakeholders to redefine current organisational practices as irresponsible. The act of CSR communication creates a risk that did not exist prior to its use. If an organisation never mentions CSR, a CSR-based challenge holds less merit. What does a manager care about claims or irresponsibility if the firm places no importance on being socially responsible? CSR is not an exposed value, therefore charges of social irresponsibility are less of a threat than to an organisation that places some value on CSR as part of its reputation. We can question the sustainability of ignoring CSR but some firms do not make CSR relevant to their reputations.

The position advanced in this chapter is that whenever an organisation engages in CSR and CSR communication, it creates a specific form of crisis risk. A crisis risk is a weakness that can develop into a crisis. CSR becomes a crisis risk when stakeholders publicly seek to redefine current organisational practices as irresponsible, labelled here as a CSR-based challenge. The claim of corporate irresponsibility creates a paracrisis, a crisis risk that is managed in public view (Coombs and Holladay, 2012). The appearance of a paracrisis leads people to term the situation a crisis, but the situation is about managing a crisis risk rather than managing an actual crisis. The distinction between a crisis and a crisis risk matters because it shapes how strategic communication can and should be used to resolve the situation.

The CSR-based challenge is a crisis risk because it can escalate into an actual reputational crisis. This can happen if other stakeholders accept the firm is acting irresponsibly. In turn, that perception can erode the corporate reputation and damage a valuable firm asset. The CSR-based challenge is premised on a series of links in a chain:

1. Managers value the firm's reputation because it is associated with numerous favourable outcomes.
2. CSR can be an important element in the construction of a reputation if a firm is engaged in CSR.
3. A crisis can develop when some stakeholders claim a firm is acting irresponsibly.
4. The potential crisis threatens the firm's reputational assets.

If an organisation makes no effort to be socially responsible, it is not at risk of a CSR-based challenge. Moreover, the greater an organisation's reliance on CSR for its reputation, the more vulnerable it would be to a CSR-based challenge. However, if a firm communicates about any of its CSR activities, it can be vulnerable to a CSR-based challenge because it has created the impression that the firm cares how it is perceived relative to social responsibility – CSR becomes an element in its reputation cultivation.

Online communication channels, epitomised by social media, provide voices for stakeholders seeking to challenge a firm's behaviour. Prior to the growth of the online environment, stakeholders relied heavily upon media advocacy to attract attention to their concerns. Media advocacy can produce mixed results because the media outlets are under no obligation to use publicity materials generated by stakeholders. Moreover, stakeholders that turn to extreme publicity tactics, such as protests, risk being framed in the media as marginal groups, with their cause largely ignored. Also, managers are much more likely to be used as sources by the news media than their stakeholders. The various social media and other online channels provide low-cost means to reach a potentially wide array of other stakeholders and to persuade them that the targeted behaviours are irresponsible and in need of reform. The key term here is 'potentially', because most of the original content posted online is never viewed by many people. However, when people are drawn to an online message, it can place pressure on firms. Consider how in the opening example Nike was defined as irresponsible through Twitter, YouTube and Greenpeace's own website. The Honey Maid case study included in this chapter provides additional insight into the role of social media in covering CSR communication into a crisis risk. Given that the CSR-based challenge is a paracrisis and not a crisis, the traditional crisis response strategies found in SCCT and IRT are not ideal response options (Coombs and Holladay, 2015). The next section elaborates on the CSR-based challenge in order to help develop a more fitting set of communicative response options.

12.3 Dynamics of the CSR-Based Challenge

A CSR-based challenge is qualitatively different from charges of 'washing' or exposing corporate hypocrisy involving its CSR claims. Washing is an exposé of an organisation's misrepresentation of its CSR efforts, while a CSR-based challenge seeks to redefine current organisational practices as irresponsible. There is no malice or hypocrisy on the part of the organisation. Rather, stakeholders want to redefine how the organisation behaves from responsible to irresponsible; behaviours that were unexamined are now questioned (Coombs and Holladay, 2015). This section explains the communicative mechanisms by which stakeholders seek to redefine a firm's behaviour and the strategic options firms have for responding to the CSR-based challenge. It begins by describing the redefinitional efforts, moves to a discussion of agitation and control, and concludes by viewing the process through the lens of the double interact.

12.3.1 Redefinitional Efforts

A CSR-based challenge attempts to redefine prevailing practices from acceptable to socially irresponsible. Consider how in the 1990s stakeholders redefined accepted labour practices in the garment industry, as sweatshop labour that was irresponsible and unacceptable. Definition can be a powerful force in shaping how stakeholders perceive a situation. Lange and Washburn developed an attribution theory-based model to explain how corporate actions become defined as irresponsible (Lange and Washburn, 2012). Their model can be supplemented with work from Den Hond and de Bakker's analysis of how activists attempt to pressure organisations about social issues (Den Hond and de Bakker, 2007). There are three components to Lange and Washburn's model:

1. Stakeholders realise there is an undesirable social outcome.
2. Stakeholders perceive the corporation to be responsible for the undesirable social outcome.
3. Stakeholders believe that the victims of the undesirable social outcome could not prevent the undesirable effect.

An undesirable social outcome is the starting point, and is a byproduct of socially irresponsible behaviour. If the organisation is responsible for an undesirable social outcome, it is involved in socially irresponsible behaviour.

Irresponsible behaviour indicates that an organisation has violated moral legitimacy by failing to promote societal welfare. More precisely, the focus is on the consequential aspect of moral legitimacy, based upon what the organisation does or does not do (Den Hond and de Bakker, 2007). An organisation is considered socially irresponsible if people attribute the cause of the undesirable social outcome to it. There must be some connection between the organisation and the undesirable social outcome. That link to the firm is weakened if people feel the victims of the undesirable social outcome are somehow complicit in creating their own problems (Lange and Washburn, 2012). A firm's behaviours can be redefined as irresponsible if they are linked to specific undesirable social outcomes with no extenuating circumstances involving the victims.

Another example from the garment industry can illustrate and clarify this dynamic. Sandblasting has been used to create a faded or distressed look, especially for denim. The problem is that the tiny sandblasting particles pose a threat to worker health because the dust can lead to the lung disease silicosis. We have an undesirable social outcome, lung disease among garment workers, and the garment firms are responsible because their practices result in the lung problems. If workers had been given proper protective equipment but chose not to use it, the workers would be responsible for their own problems, thereby eroding the firm's responsibility for the undesirable social outcome. In this case, the fine dust is extremely dangerous and the workers could have done nothing to prevent the undesirable social outcome.

If stakeholders successfully redefine current firm practices as irresponsible, a crisis risk now exists. If other stakeholders agree with this redefinition and perceive a firm as acting irresponsibly, the firm's reputation and its attendant benefits are eroded. The erosion is caused by a decrease in perception of CSR, a key driver in reputations. As discussed above, the CSR-based challenge is a form of paracrisis (events that mimic a crisis, frequently called social media crises). In reality, a paracrisis involves an organisation's effort to manage a crisis risk in public view of its stakeholders (Coombs and Holladay, 2012). In the earlier example, the sandblasting concern was a risk which companies such as Versace had to manage in public. CSR-based challenges represent a common type of paracrisis for modern organisations.

CSR-based challenges reflect the shifting nature of how activist stakeholders seek to alter corporate practices. Activist stakeholders have been moving away from issues management (attempts to influence corporations through government intervention) and embracing a concept known as private politics (King, 2011). The locus on constraint on corporate practices shifts from the government to the corporation itself, encouraged and compelled by activist stakeholders such as non-governmental organisations (NGOs) (Coombs and Holladay, 2015). Researchers have argued that activists are consciously shifting from the governmental to the private arena to achieve their goals. Private politics allow activists to avoid the time, costs and uncertainty of issues management efforts, and agitate directly for change. However, private politics does reflect the neoliberalism philosophy of allowing the marketplace rather than the government to regulate corporate practices (Coombs and Holladay, 2015).

12.3.2 Agitation: The Challenge

'To agitate' means to disturb or stir and frequently refers to actions designed to create public concern and spur people into action. In social movement studies, there is an analytic framework known as the rhetoric of agitation and control that examines how challenges from protesters (the agitation) lead to responses from the establishment (the control) (Bowers et al., 1992). As noted earlier, activist stakeholders use CSR-based challenges to agitate for change. Hence, the rhetoric of agitation and control can be used to illuminate further the communicative nature of the CSR-based challenge dynamic. More specifically, we can consider the CSR-based challenge and the firm's response through the lens of agitation and control.

Agitation begins with petition. Petition occurs when a groups asks an established power to change its policies or practices. A CSR-based challenge typically begins when the stakeholders ask the firm to change the behaviours it defines as socially irresponsible. For instance, in the opening example for this chapter, Greenpeace asked the major garment firms to stop using certain toxic materials in their supply chains. When this request was denied, Greenpeace initiated the Detox campaign to 'force' the garment companies to change (Coombs, 2014). A failure to petition can undermine the credibility of the challenging stakeholders because the firm can counterargue the changes would have been made had the stakeholders simply asked them to change. The stakeholders can then appear unreasonable and unfair in their attacks on the firm because the firm was never given the opportunity to change.

If petition fails, the next step is agitation, in which a group from outside the decision-making structure seeks to change that decision-making structure. In a CSR-based challenge, stakeholders from outside the firm try to change the decisions being made by the firm. Returning to the Detox example, Greenpeace sought to influence firms' decisions about what chemicals can and cannot be used in the supply chain. CSR-based challenges qualify as agitation because the stakeholders are not part of the firm's decision-making structure.

Stakeholders frequently utilise extra-institutional tactics to advance and enhance awareness of their concerns, and encourage other stakeholders to support their position – to enact promulgation (Bowers et al., 1992). Extra-institutional tactics are actions that seek to subvert conventional politics and bypass traditional inputs. CSR-based challenges regularly utilise extra-institutional tactics such as in-person protests and critical social media posts to pressure organisational decision-makers. Such actions are defined as promulgation because the objective is to create public awareness and support for the challenger's position; promulgation is leverage for those who are agitating.

If others are learning about the concern, there is pressure on authorities to decide how to respond to the agitation. The fear is that the issue will spread to other stakeholders and that these other stakeholders will support the agitation. 'Activist groups step forward to articulate societal preferences about the level and nature of corporate social change activities, and they challenge firms to comply with these preferences' (Den Hond and de Bakker, 2007: 917). Public awareness pushes firm managers to determine how they will respond to the CSR-based challenge; how firms respond to agitation is known as control.

12.3.3 Control: The Response

Following agitation, those in power must decide how to respond– engagement is what is termed 'control'. Control originates in studies of protests from the 1970s and uses the government as the establishment. The theory of agitation and control identifies four possible response strategies: (1) avoidance, ignore the situation; (2) suppression, seek to silence the protesters; (3) adjustment, make minor changes; and (4) capitulation, make all the requested demands (Bowers et al., 1992). Firms and governments have important differences, hence, control needs to be adapted to the organisational context. Den Hond and de Bakker argued that managers can respond to activists advancing social issues by ignoring the demands, refusing to make the changes or by modifying a firm's behaviours, a list that sounds very similar to the control strategies (Den Hond and de Bakker, 2007). Coombs and Holladay integrated the control strategies with Benoit's (1995) image repair strategies to form a more comprehensive list of response options for firms engaged in a CSR-based challenge (Coombs and Holladay, 2015). Benoit's work is relevant because it has been applied to efforts to repair firms' reputations following reputational threats but does not align perfectly with the paracrisis nature of the CSR-based challenge; hence, modifications were necessary utilising the control lens (Benoit, 1995). The six control responses managers might use when confronted with a CSR-based challenge are:

1. Refusal: management ignores the stakeholders and offers no comment on the situation.
2. Refutation: management presents its position for why it will not change.
3. Repression: management seeks to stop the challenge messages from spreading and to silence their critics.
4. Recognition/reception: management publicly recognises that a problem exists but does not offer to make changes.
5. Revision: management publicly makes some changes but not everything the stakeholders demanded.
6. Reform: management publicly makes the exact changes demanded by the stakeholders. (Coombs and Holladay, 2015)

The control strategies are arranged from least to most accommodative to the demands of the stakeholders. Refusal, for instance, ignores the challenge while reform embraces the changes specified in the challenge.

Three key variables tend to influence the managerial selection of a control response: (1) salience of the stakeholders, (2) material costs of requested changes, and (3) fit of the requested changes with a firm's strategy. Mitchell, Agle and Wood conceptualised stakeholder salience as a function of power (ability to influence behaviour of another), legitimacy (what is considered accepted and appropriate with social values) and urgency (time pressure and commitment to the concern) (Mitchell, Agle and Wood, 1997). In general, as stakeholder salience increases, the control response must become more accommodative to the demands of the stakeholders because the stakeholders have an increased capacity to harm the firm. Material costs refer to the financial price tag associated with the desired changes. Managers are unlikely to make changes that will cost them an exorbitant amount of money. Fit with strategy refers to whether or not the change is consistent with a firm's core strategy. The material costs and fit are what Den Hond and de Bakker would call pragmatic legitimacy, the desired change must be viable for managers to perform (Den Hond and de Bakker, 2007). Managers are unlikely to embrace changes that deviate greatly from the firm's core strategy and/or are too costly. Coombs and Holladay used the three key variables to create five recommendations about firm responses to CSR-based challenges (Coombs and Holladay, 2015). The recommendations are presented in Table 12.2.

The recommendations are an attempt to identify under what conditions the various strategic communication options are likely to be used by managers. The recommendations reflect the needs of management to balance stakeholder demands with firm priorities.

Recommendation 1 notes that refusal is a viable response option when the challenge is illegitimate because other stakeholders are unlikely to be attracted to the challenge and support it. Refusal is dangerous with legitimate challenges because the firm allows the challenge messages to stand unopposed. Recommendation 2 highlights the conditions that support the refute response options. There are times when firms must defend their current practices, including concerns over cost and strategy. Recommendation 3 warns of the dangers associated with the repress response option. Other stakeholders might be angered by a repression response unless the firm justifies it by identifying the false and damaging nature of the challenge. Recommendation 4 suggests that firms may simply recognise a problem but not take action on that problem due to certain constraints. Recommendation 5 identifies the circumstances under which firms will need to use the revise or reform response option. The need to change behaviours is largely a function of the salience of the challenger. Note that while the recommendations share similarities with those found in the crisis communication literature, the nature of the CSR-based challenge creates unique factors that require a different communicative approach that is found

Table 12.2 CSR-based challenge recommendations

1. Corporations should limit the use of the refusal strategy to situations when the challenge is illegitimate.

2. Corporations should limit the use of the refute strategy to situations where the challenge is factually wrong, illegitimate, is too costly or is contrary to corporate strategy.

3. Corporations should limit the use of the repress strategy to situations when the challenge spreads false and damaging information about the corporation.

4. Corporations should limit the use of the recognise response to situations when the challenger has legitimacy and power but the change is too expensive or contrary to corporate strategy.

5. Corporations should use the revise or reform strategies when the challenger has urgency, legitimacy, and power and the changes are consistent with corporate strategy.

Source: Coombs and Holladay, 2015.

in the traditional crisis communication literature. For instance, refusal (silence) is considered a poor choice in crisis communication, while there are no specific parallels in the crisis communication literature to refute and recognise (Coombs and Holladay, 2015).

12.3.4 Extending the CSR-Based Challenge: The Double Interact

The way in which Coombs and Holladay (2015) conceptualise the CSR-based challenge reflects the constructivist communication view of CSR (Schultz, Castello and Morsing, 2013). When stakeholders seek to redefine the firm's behaviour as irresponsible, they are using symbols to mediate a communication event. However, Coombs and Holladay stop after the agitation and the control response (Coombs and Holladay, 2015). In the language of Karl Weick, they have identified an interact composed on the challenge (act) and the firm's response (interact) (Weick, 1979). We will take the idea of the CSR-based challenge one step further, adding the reaction of the challengers to the response thereby creating a double interact, what we term the reconsideration step. Weick views the double interact as the building block of organisations because it facilitates organising (Weick, 1979). Similarly, the double interact can be viewed as a building block of or an episode within the stakeholder–firm relationship, and a CSR-based challenge can be an important episode in the relationship process.

The CSR-based challenge is a form of conflict within the stakeholder–firm relationship, and the firm's response can either escalate or de-escalate the conflict. In reconsideration, the challengers evaluate the response and decide on their next step. Reform, revision and recognition all have the potential to de-escalate the situation. In reform, the firm makes the requested changes. Groups such as Greenpeace often thank the firm when it makes the requested changes, and move on to the next concern. Another option is to monitor the firm to ensure that management fulfils the promise to change. Similarly, if the revision or recognition responses are close to what the challengers hoped to accomplish, the CSR-based challenge could be terminated. However, if stakeholders determine that revision or recognition is not enough, they can continue the challenge by reapplying pressure to the organisation. Refusal, refutation and repression are likely to escalate the conflict and stimulate renewed pressure on the organisation. The escalation can initiate another double interact, but this assumes that the challengers have the resources and desire to continue the CSR-based challenge. The stakeholders might lack the financial and human resources to continue the effort, or the stakeholders might lack a strong commitment to the issue (urgency in the terminology of stakeholder theory) and abandon the effort after the initial failure. A lack of resources or commitment to the cause will result in termination of the CSR-based challenge.

CSR-based challenges are often a series of double interacts, created when the challengers adjust their actions based upon the reactions of the challenged firm. For example, Green American has been engaged in a CSR-based challenge with Hershey since 2009 over the company's sourcing of cocoa from suppliers using child slave labour (Coombs, 2014). Initially, Hershey used the refusal response and refused to acknowledge the concern or challenge for over three years. Next, Hershey employed recognition by noting the problem of child slave labour in the cocoa supply chain in its annual CSR reports. Hershey also began using fair trade chocolate for some of its products, a form of revision. The fair trade line meant that some of Hershey's products were free of child slave labour. Hershey is now at the point of reform by stating it will verify that all its cocoa comes from non-child slave labour using suppliers by 2020 (Coombs, 2014). Green America still monitors Hershey to make sure it fulfils the promise.

12.4 Case Study: Honey Maid and Same-Sex Marriage

On 10 March 2014, the Honey Maid brand of graham crackers released an advertisement called 'This is Wholesome'. The advertisement featured a variety of families including mixed race and same-sex parents. The idea was to provide a broad range of the diverse families that are found in the US. The video was a very happy message, showing children and their parents having fun and eating graham crackers. The Honey Maid advertisement was placed online (it could be viewed through YouTube) with a post on Honey Maid's Facebook page, and also appeared on television.

People reacted to the 'This is Wholesome' campaign very quickly. Many people used digital media to complain about the use of a same-sex couple. Messages were posted asking people to boycott Honey Maid, and many people said they were going to throw away their Honey Maid graham crackers and never buy them again. Two conservative groups (One Million Moms and American Decency Association) in the US used their websites to call on the parent company Nabisco to remove the advertisements which included an online version on YouTube. (It should be noted that the true parent company is Mondelez International Inc. who owns the Nabisco brand.) The American Decency Association went as far as to claim that the advertisement was part of Satan's efforts to undermine American culture, while One Million Moms linked it to sin. There were thousands of online posts about the advertisement on the YouTube site and Honey Maid's own Facebook page. The traditional media soon began to report on the social postings about the message.

The Honey Maid brand is over ninety years old and traditionally has been associated with families. Graham crackers are a common snack for children in the US – children like graham crackers and the product is easy to carry and to store. The 'This is Wholesome' campaign was an attempt to modernise the brand and reinforce its connection to families. The variety of families in the messaging was designed to reflect the changing nature of families – the greater diversity among families in the US. At least in some sectors of the US public, the message had the opposite effect because it was considered to be anti-family due to the inclusion of a same-sex family.

Same-sex marriage is a polarising social issue in the US. Social issues have competing sides and tend to be divisive, but same-sex marriage is especially controversial in the US because there is a strong religious undertone to the debate. Conservative Christians tend to view same-sex marriage as a threat to marriage and traditional values. The push for same-sex marriage is frequently labelled as 'anti-family'. The idea is that people in a same-sex marriage are not a true couple, and their married status somehow harms traditional families. Firms that support same-sex marriage can be labelled as irresponsible because their efforts are deemed as harmful to society by some stakeholders. Clearly, not everyone agrees with this logic, but claiming a firm is irresponsible by supporting same-sex marriage is an argument that will be accepted by a certain percentage of stakeholders in the US. Similarly, those who support same-sex marriage pressure firms to support their position and expand the acceptance of same-sex marriage in the US. Many firms in the US have had to present and defend their positions on same-sex marriage, whether the firm is linked to pro or anti same-sex sentiments. Chick-fil-a, a US fast food chain, was drawn into the same-sex debate when the firm's founder noted he was against same-sex marriage in an interview that appeared in a religious publication. Some firms have even used their economic power to influence state policies related to same-sex marriage. Honey Maid purposely entered the discussion of same-sex marriage with the 'This is Wholesome' campaign.

On 3 April 2014, Honey Maid posted another video to YouTube. This video was called 'Love'. The video showed two female artists rolling up sheets of paper and placing them on the floor lengthwise. The sheets of paper were printed versions of comments from people about the advertisement. During the video, some of the negative comments about the advertisement were shown on the screen for people to read. The two artists used the rolled up negative comments to spell love on the floor. The video then noted that the company received ten times more positive comments than negative comments. The positive comments were then rolled up to form a background for the word love. The idea is that the negative comments were transformed into something favourable (love) and were surrounded by the overwhelming positive comments. There was a strong visual component to the response. Honey Maid stayed very positive by allowing some of the negative comments to be read and focusing on the positive ideas featured in the commercial. This was the primary public response Honey Maid provided to the critics of the 'This is Wholesome' campaign.

Prior to the 'This is Wholesome' campaign, Honey Maid was considered to be struggling to find a voice in its social media efforts. The brand had not found an effective way to engage its consumers. Some marketing experts felt that by embracing instead of avoiding a controversial issue, Honey Maid had found its social media voice. The logic holds that a firm can state a position on a controversial issue and then allow social media to spread that message. The social media discussion will stimulate engagement with the brand and the firm hopes that engagement will translate into brand loyalty and sales. This is a risky strategy because there is also the potential that the backlash from the controversial issue stance could damage the firm's and the brand's reputations. The firm is gambling that the social media reactions, which they cannot control, will help rather than hurt the brand. The statistics would suggest that Honey Maid was successful with the campaign. Google searches for Honey Maid increased 400 per cent after the video was posted. The searches indicate that people were showing a renewed interest in the brand. As of November 2015, the video has been viewed over 4.3 million times with over 53,500 likes and only 2,400 dislikes – a very strong 'favourable to unfavourable' ratio. The YouTube and Facebook posts demonstrated that stakeholders were engaging with the brand. Of course engagement is rather abstract and is meaningless unless it has some financial effects. In the summer months after the campaign, Honey Maid sales increased 7 per cent while the stock price of Mondelez International Inc. rose from 34.52 in March to 35.47 by the end of April, reaching over 38 by July. While the increases and sales and stock prices cannot be linked just to the 'This is Wholesome' campaign, Honey Maid did not seem to be suffering negative effects from the controversy.

Questions for Discussion

When answering these questions, consider how the 'This is Wholesome' campaign might be a paracrisis:

1. How could this situation be defined as a CSR-based challenge crisis?
2. What factors do you feel led Honey Maid to choose their response? How might management have evaluated the threat?
3. How do you think various stakeholders would react to the response and why would they respond in that way? What risks and rewards are associated with those responses?
4. What is the potential in this case for reconsideration resulting in an escalation of the challenge, and what is the rationale for that potential? Think about how the critics of 'This is Wholesome' might respond to the Love video.
5. Overall, how would you evaluate the effectiveness of Honey Maid's communicative response to the situation? Be sure to include how you have chosen to define 'effective' and what objective you think Honey Maid might have been pursuing with their communicative effort.

12.5 Chapter Summary

A variety of forces has made it difficult for a modern firm to ignore the gravitational pull of CSR. We can debate the merits of the drive to infuse firms with CSR and what actually constitutes CSR, but it is difficult to deny that CSR is now a part of a firm's practice. However, once a firm decides to engage in CSR communication, a new crisis risk is formed. CSR is frequently used to help bolster a firm's reputation, a valuable asset in the modern business world. When managers publicly indicate or signal that they value CSR and it becomes part of the firm's reputation, the firm can become vulnerable to CSR-based challenges. A CSR-based challenge can damage the firm's reputation and facilitate a crisis if stakeholders have redefined the firm's practices as irresponsible. Concerned stakeholders can utilise various online channels of communication to generate awareness about their redefinitional efforts and to increase the pressure on firms to change. If the redefinition argument is accepted by other stakeholders, the charges of corporate irresponsibility will erode a firm's reputation. Modern stakeholders hold expectations that firms will uphold select social and environmental concerns and frequently have both the means (through online channels) and desire to express those concerns in an effort to make a firm 'more' socially responsible. The value firms place on reputation and CSR, combined with easily accessible online communication channels, provides an environment where CSR-based challenges have the opportunity to flourish and demand the attention of crisis communicators.

CSR-based challenges have implications for the practice of crisis communication. Practitioners need to consider CSR-based challenges as part of the mitigation and preparation for a crisis (Coombs, 2015). Crisis managers must scan for emerging CSR-based challenges and consider how to evaluate and respond to the potential threats. We have just begun to understand the factors that create and shape a CSR-based challenge, and further research is required to expand our understanding of the variables that influence the double interact created by a CSR-based challenge and the emergence of a CSR-based challenge crisis, if we are to explain the phenomenon better and enhance managers' ability to handle this strategic communication concern.

The CSR-based challenge creates a richer and more nuanced connection between CSR communication and crisis communication. Extant research on washing charges (hypocrisy and CSR) and crisis research utilising CSR as a buffer to protect reputations during a crisis provide just a basic connection between the two strategic communication fields. Clearly when a firm is exposed for exaggerating or deceit involving its CSR messages, that revelation can create a crisis because the ethics of management is questioned. Similarly, a strong, positive reputation for CSR is an asset during a crisis because it can buffer a firm against the full damage the crisis might otherwise have inflicted. We need to appreciate the richness of the intersection of crises and CSR communication by moving beyond washing and CSR as potential assets in crisis communication. Managers must understand the full range of risks an organisation assumes when it publicly discusses its CSR efforts. The CSR-based challenge exposes the unintended consequences a firm's commitment to CSR can have on the firm's other strategic communication functions. Crisis communication must research the potential negative as well as the positive potential outcomes when organisations engage in CSR communication. We must develop a richer understanding of the bonds between CSR and crisis communication. Understanding the CSR-based challenge and the crises it may spawn are important steps in articulating a more nuanced understanding of the connections between CSR communication and crisis communication.

Chapter Questions

1. What role does reputation play in the development of the CSR-based challenge crisis?
2. How does a CSR-based challenge crisis differ from charges of 'washing'? What is the significance of those differences for communicators?

3. How does CSR become both an asset and a liability to crisis communicators?

4. In what ways do social media enhance efforts to redefine corporate behaviours as irresponsible? What challenges does that present for communicators?

5. How does a paracrisis differ from a crisis? Why should crisis communicators be concerned about those differences?

FURTHER RESOURCES

Coombs, W. T. (2010). Sustainability: A New and Complex 'Challenge' for Crisis Managers. *International Journal of Sustainable Strategic Management*, 2(1), 4–16.
> The article is the first articulation of the idea that CSR (sustainability) can be related to crises. This article considers a variety of ways that sustainability statements can be used against a firm, including the idea of the challenge of being unsustainable.

Coombs, T. and Holladay, S. (2015). CSR as Crisis Risk: Expanding how we Conceptualize the Relationship. *Corporate Communications: An International Journal*, 20(2), 144–162.
> This article explores the idea of CSR as a crisis risk. It explains the concept of a CSR-based challenge and how it centres on attempts to redefine current practices as irresponsible, discussing the conditions under which the responses are more or less effective in reducing the crisis risk.

Lange, D. and Washburn, N. T. (2012). Understanding attributions of corporate social irresponsibility. *Academy of Management Review*, 37(2), 300–326.
> A model of corporate social irresponsibility is developed based on attribution theory and provides in particular a discussion of how victims of a perceived undesirable effect have no responsibility for producing the undesirable effect.

The 'This is Wholesome' commercial, www.youtube.com/watch?v=cBC-pRFt9OM. Honey Maid 'Love' response, www.youtube.com/watch?v=cBC-pRFt9OM.

13

CSR and Reputation: Too Much of a Good Thing?

CHRISTOPHER WICKERT AND JOEP CORNELISSEN

Learning Objectives

- Learn why corporate reputation represents an important intangible asset and how to distinguish reputation from related constructs such as identity, image and legitimacy.
- Gain an understanding of how companies across industries manage their reputation in relation to corporate social responsibility (CSR).
- Gain an appreciation of how efforts to manage a reputation for CSR may be a double-edged sword; it may strengthen a company's reputation with stakeholders, yet it may also create increasing expectations about good conduct.
- Be able to critically reflect on, and analyse, more symbolic and rhetorical versus substantive and material approaches that companies take to manage their CSR reputation, that may create both opportunities and risks.

13.1 Introduction

When deciding to buy a product, what do people usually think of? Probably the price, the quality of the product, and maybe also whether they like the brand. Or would consumers also consider how well this company treats its employees, how ethical it is, and whether it shows environmental responsibility? As a matter of fact, most of us would probably relate to the former set of reasons (price and quality of the product and the brand). But, according to a recent study by the Reputation Institute (2015), people's willingness to buy, recommend, work for and invest in a company is driven about 60 per cent by their perception of the company – in other words by its reputation – and only about 40 per cent is driven by how people perceive the product itself or the price alone. Many firms, in particular global brands such as H&M, IKEA, Nike, Coca-Cola, McDonald's, Apple and the like often consider brand reputation their most important asset, besides other resources such as financial or human capital. For instance, H&M's reputation for being a fashionable but low-priced clothing brand has enabled the company to outperform its rivals for many years. Coca-Cola's reputation for being *the* global beverage of good taste and reliable quality has allowed the company to sustain its market share in the face of fierce competition.

13.2 Reputation and CSR

But what is corporate reputation? The Reputation Institute, a well-known consultancy and market research firm, identifies seven dimensions as constituting a reputation: workplace, governance, citizenship, financial performance, leadership, products and services, and innovation. On reflection, out of these seven, three can be directly related to CSR, namely citizenship (how a company behaves in relation to the natural environment and the local communities where it operates), workplace (how a company treats its own and its suppliers' employees), and governance (what a company does to ensure ethical conduct and prevent wrongdoing such as corruption). What the institute's analyses over the years have shown is that more than half of how people feel about a company (that is, the strength of the reputation of that firm) is based on their perceptions of a firm's CSR practices. According to Kasper Ulf Nielsen, executive partner at the Reputation Institute, 'CSR speaks to who the company is, what it believes in and how it is doing business,' which makes CSR a

> core element of reputation and [it] can be used to help establish trust and goodwill amongst stakeholders. [Almost half] of people's willingness to trust, admire, and feel good about a company is based on their perceptions of the company's CSR, so this is a key tool for companies to improve support from stakeholders like consumers, regulators, financial community, and employees. (Smith, 2013)

CSR thus seems to have moved centre stage as a key component of what makes a good corporate reputation. However, the rules of the 'reputation game' have become a bit trickier when looking at some of the companies that have recently scored high in reputation rankings. In 2013, the top spots went to Microsoft, The Walt Disney Company, Google and BMW. All of these companies, according to Reputation Institute's survey, are extremely proactive in terms of the dimensions that drive CSR reputation. But – critical voices may wonder – how can companies that have repeatedly been accused by non-governmental organisations (NGOs), industry analysts and governments of exploiting their monopolistic market position, of prohibiting employees to join labour unions and remunerating them with poor wages, of systematically engaging in tax avoidance strategies, or of selling products that pollute the environment, have a positive reputation for social, environmental or ethical responsibility? The question is whether reputation rankings accurately reflect the CSR efforts of companies, and if their performance in other areas (such as financial performance, or marketing and branding) may actually by association suggest to stakeholders that they make an equally sterling contribution in CSR terms. Interestingly, according to Mr Nielsen, reputation is not about a company's products or how they are produced, but about the company behind the products, and how people *perceive* this company. How then do stakeholders perceive and evaluate a company in terms of CSR? And what are companies doing to manage such perceptions of their stakeholders?

The picture becomes even more complicated when comparing those companies scoring high in reputation rankings, including the one issued by the Reputation Institute, but also other rankings such as *Fortune* magazine's CSR ranking. Nestlé, a well-known and highly reputed global brand, for instance made it in the top ten of the Fortune CSR reputation ranking, but has constantly been criticised by NGOs for acts of corporate social *ir*responsibility in relation to issues such as water and human rights, destruction of the rainforest and selling products that create massive amounts of hard-to-recycle waste. Surprisingly, in contrast to Nestlé's case, companies that are oftentimes applauded even by critical NGOs such as Greenpeace for their substantive efforts to make products and processes more sustainable, including Adidas, Unilever, or Marks & Spencer, score much lower and hence appear not to reap the benefits of having the best CSR reputation, despite their investments.

The overall question that emerges is the following: when is CSR reputation more a form of *symbolic impression management*, which is certainly done well by some companies, and when is it reflective of *substantive efforts* to promote social and environmental responsibility? What are the opportunities and advantages connected to building a reputation for CSR? And what are potential risks that arise when 'overstretching' one's reputation, or when not caring at all about building a good CSR reputation?

In order to answer these questions, in this chapter we will first explain the foundations of corporate reputation, delineate it from related concepts such as identity, image and legitimacy, and explain its relationship to CSR. Then, we will show how CSR management can be an opportunity to enhance reputation, but which – if poorly managed – can also present itself as a risk that might damage a company's reputation. We will propose that the effects of CSR on reputation can be better understood if examined against two key dimensions: first, whether a company is sincerely 'walking' CSR by substantially integrating socially and environmentally responsible business practices, or if a firm is rather 'talking' about CSR by engaging in symbolic impression management in order to construct an unsubstantiated façade of CSR. Second, whether CSR activities are aligned with a company's core business operations, or whether they remain at the periphery in non-core activities. These two dimensions together provide a framework that classifies different ways in which companies approach CSR, and how they use their CSR activities for reputation-building purposes. Furthermore, the framework sensitises us to advantages and pitfalls associated with each approach. We conclude the chapter by reflecting on some of the dynamics and controversies related to a company's CSR reputation. The case study of the 2010 Deepwater Horizon oil spill and the reputational disaster that oil giant BP suffered in the disaster's aftermath illustrates the importance of underscoring a reputation with substantive CSR commitments.

13.3 Defining Corporate Reputation

In one of Shakespeare's most famous plays, Othello bemoans that reputation is 'oft got without merit, and lost without deserving' (*Othello*: II, 3: 260). When we apply this insight to the corporate level, two important questions arise: how is reputation granted or built, and how can it be lost, or, perhaps less dramatically, damaged? These questions have brought considerable attention to the topic of corporate reputation, both among academics and practitioners. Studying reputation is theoretically meaningful because it contributes to our basic understanding of fundamental social processes and resources that are important to the corporate world, and it is practically important because reputations can also create substantial value for companies.

Most understandings of corporate reputation focus, broadly, on Shakespeare's *merit* part. They describe how reputation is built, and the benefits that having a good reputation entails. This includes gaining and sustaining competitive advantage, being able to charge a price premium on products, and attracting talent and investors. In general, reputation is conceived as the product of substantive and symbolic corporate actions over time, in which companies send information to external observers who use this information to form impressions of the company.

Scholars have not yet agreed on a commonly accepted definition of reputation, but the most basic understanding is that, as an important intangible asset, reputation refers to 'observers' collective judgments of a corporation based on assessments of the financial, social, and environmental impacts attributed to the corporation over time' (Barnett et al., 2006: 34). Reputation hence reflects 'that over time an organization can become well known, can accrue a generalized understanding in the minds of observers as to what it is known for, and can be judged favourably or unfavourably by its observers' (Lange et al., 2011: 154). Central to reputation in all definitions is that it implies an *evaluation* and *comparison* of organisations to determine reputation relative to one another. For any two organisations, they will either have the same reputation, or more likely, one will have a better reputation than the other. That is why a good reputation is perceived as an essential and distinctive competitive advantage for firms.

Seeing reputation as a source of competitive advantage in turn requires companies to behave and act consistent with their past performance and with the public's expectations. In this sense, reputation can be viewed as a solution for asymmetric information that market participants usually have about product quality, adequate pricing and, importantly, whether CSR messages of the company are symbolic or substantive. When faced with a lack of information on a product or on a firm's activities, stakeholders rely on the firm's reputation to judge its products or intentions. Reputation thus functions as a signal to external observers that allows them to grasp the firm's key characteristics. Assuming that for instance consumers make their buying decisions after scanning a firm based on its past behaviour and action, such as product quality, reputation provides assurance that the same firm will behave and act consistently in the future.

Accordingly, having a good reputation can be a considerable advantage to a company when dealing with its various stakeholders, such as consumers or investors. However, reputation is also often specific to issues and stakeholders. A company may have a particular, and potentially different, reputation for different issues, including its profitability, social and environmental responsibility, employee treatment, corporate governance and product quality. Goldman Sachs is a company that exemplifies this in its most extreme form, because it is both 'well loathed' and 'well loved' by stakeholders. It has an excellent reputation for profitability, but its ethics and CSR are considered very poor, or virtually non-existent. A corporation may also have a different reputation for each of its stakeholder groups. For example, while much of the general public is sceptical of Goldman Sachs' behaviour that reflects a particularly ruthless kind of capitalism, investors and clients may see the company in a much better light because it is able to deliver superior returns.

More generally, different stakeholder groups base their reputational judgements on a different set of outcomes. This means that for instance a company's reputation from the point of view of employees will be based primarily on workplace outcomes such as wages, career opportunities or healthcare benefits; that of consumers on product, service and marketing outcomes such as price, quality and branding; and that of investors on business and financial outcomes such as dividends or share price. Thus, members of each group would form their own specific evaluation of a certain company.

This issue and stakeholder specificity of corporate reputation may also explain the inconsistency that is oftentimes experienced in attempts to measure reputation, such as by the *Fortune Most Admired Companies* (http://fortune.com/worlds-most-admired-companies) ranking which represents probably the best-known reputation ranking in the world. However, the ranking is largely a self-assessment where managers of participating companies and financial analysts rate each other (except their own company). As such, the ranking reflects what *managers* think of a company, while other stakeholders, such as journalists or NGOs, do not directly participate and share their views. In short, what we have suggested so far is that reputation rests in the minds of its beholders and is a subjective concept, because it is essentially what different internal and external stakeholders believe about a company (Cornelissen, 2014).

The observation that reputation is socially constructed and based on the *perception* of stakeholders, and not factual or objectively provided by a 'neutral' party, renders it particularly likely for manipulation by those that aim to gain advantage by having a favourable reputation, including the company itself. To better account for manipulative efforts, we distinguish between symbolic commitments of companies in pursuit of a good reputation, and more substantive efforts around investments and resource commitments. To understand these counter-poles better, however, it is important to first delineate reputation from related concepts. We will then delve into the relationship between CSR and reputation and shed light on what companies do to manage their reputation.

13.3.1 Corporate Reputation and Related Concepts

Identity, image and legitimacy are concepts that are oftentimes seen as closely related to reputation. They share some of the same ground, but important differences remain. *Identity* describes the perception that employees and managers – those inside the firm – hold of the nature of their firm and which comprises the underlying core character of the firm. In other words, it relates to those features of the company that employees and managers believe are central, enduring and distinctive to their firm. Identity asks the question: 'Who/what do we believe we are as a company?' For instance, employees and managers can perceive their company as 'environmentally and socially responsible', or 'acting according to the highest ethical values'.

In contrast to identity, *image* is the perception that external observers, such as investors, consumers and the general public, have of a company. Image describes what comes to mind when one hears the name or sees the logo of a company, and hence refers to observers' general impressions of a particular firm. Image answers the question, 'What/who do we want others to think we are?' For instance, a company may want to create an image of being an environmentally responsible company, or being a very attractive investment for shareholders.

What becomes clear when comparing image and identity is that consistency in how a company sees itself and how others see the company is important when successfully managing reputation. This is because reputation is the aggregation of these perceptions of image and identity. Besides this, reputation also involves a more considered evaluation of a firm, whereas image is typically seen as a more immediate perception or response, for example to an advertising campaign. As such, where image may be more subject to change, and changes from moment to moment when impressions are formed, reputation is on the other hand more inert, and thus often more stable over time, as it involves a gradually built-up accumulation of experiences and impressions.

There are also many similarities between reputation and *legitimacy*, because both concepts result from similar social construction processes when stakeholders evaluate an organisation. However, while reputation is about a comparison among different organisations, legitimacy concerns the social acceptance resulting from adherence to social norms and expectations. For example, a company can have a superior reputation for delivering the highest quality products, or being the most environmentally friendly producer in its industry, but it may also have a reputation for poor labour relations or questionable ethical practices. In contrast, a company would be considered legitimate if it respects the law and fulfils the general purpose of what a business is and should do. Thus, it appears that a central element of legitimacy is meeting and adhering to the expectations of a society's norms, values, rules and meanings – in other words, conformity to a social category. Reputation, in contrast, is an evaluation of a firm by stakeholders in comparison to other firms. Based on this distinction, reputation is related to competitive advantage, whereas legitimacy is more like a 'hygiene factor', a necessary condition for long-term survival and the so-called social licence to operate. Having defined reputation more generally, we now turn to the question of what it means to have a 'CSR reputation', and how engaging in CSR may impact a company's overall reputation.

13.4 How CSR Impacts Reputation

Most people would probably agree that today we simply feel differently about the role of business in society than some generations before. Already more than a decade ago, Lewis reported that in the late 1970s, two-thirds of the British public agreed that the profits of large companies benefited society at large (Lewis, 2003). However, what became apparent in the early 2000s probably is even more evident today: the large majority of the public seems to disagree that society benefits if companies focus on nothing else than creating profits and maximising shareholder value (ibid.). This means that the trust of the general public in companies to look after society has gradually eroded. At the same time, the large majority of the public believes that companies have a moral obligation to society. Interestingly, many also believe that in particular large multinational companies 'do not really care' about the long-term environmental and social impact of their actions. In their perception, business falls short of paying proper attention to exactly those issues that are of increasing interest to the general public and society at large.

This observation reflects a broader trend that immediately speaks to the relationship between CSR and reputation. It underscores that out of the seven dimensions that constitute reputation as mentioned above, those that can be related to CSR are becoming increasingly important in the perception of stakeholders. For example, whereas in the past *the* major components that were necessary to gain and sustain a superior reputation were financial performance, good prices and high product quality, CSR issues have been receiving increasingly more salience recently. While the former components obviously are still very important, the social, environmental and ethical impacts of business moved centre stage. This process is fuelled by a more powerful civil society and NGOs such as Greenpeace or Amnesty International that use social media channels such as blogs, Twitter or Facebook to raise attention about how companies behave with regard to CSR. They even launch boycotts against companies, which can considerably impact their reputation. For example, the campaign that Greenpeace launched against Nestlé in 2010 to stop the unsustainable production of palm oil and the damage this caused to the habitat of endangered species had a massive impact on Nestlé's reputation, including among consumers (a drop in sales of the KitKat bars) and investors (Nestlé's plunging share price) (see case study in Chapter 11).

Stakeholders can now more easily find information online or in the media on how environmentally friendly the processes and products of a company are, for instance with regard to their CO2-emissions, water usage or toxic releases. Consumers are also more concerned, or at least more aware, about the social conditions such as workers' rights in supplier factories; by the same token, ethical breaches in the context of corruption or tax avoidance make it to the media much quicker than a few decades ago. However, consumers are not the only group to take CSR more into account when making reputational judgements about a firm. Prospective employees are also increasingly asking about the CSR activities of their future employers, and many do not want to work for a company that is regarded as unethical or irresponsible. Financial investors alike now see Socially Responsible Investing (SRI) as an important segment of the market, and include CSR issues in their stock evaluations. CSR can thus both be seen as an increasingly important *component* of reputation, and as something that increasingly influences the *overall* reputation of a firm.

While these examples seem to suggest that corporations can improve their reputation by paying close attention to CSR, cases also abound where reputation is threatened when companies do *not* pay sufficient attention to CSR. Likewise, reputation can be harmed when there is 'too much of a good thing' – in other words, a firm makes more symbolic than substantive commitments to CSR. We will therefore discuss CSR as an *opportunity* for enhancing reputation, as well as a *risk* that may damage reputation.

13.4.1 The Quest for CSR Reputations

Before we get into detail on how firms manage their CSR reputation, we will explain how individual stakeholders form the reputation of a firm, specifically in relation to its CSR activities. Reputation involves a considered evaluation of a firm vis-à-vis its rivals, where stakeholders consider its main and distinctive attributes (such as its profitability, the quality of services and products, and labour relations), which together make up a profile image. They in turn attribute that reputation to an organisation, and if asked, for instance in a survey, rate it accordingly. What is actually at the heart of these dynamics is the twin challenge for firms to be seen as doing the right things, and as doing things somewhat differently (and relatively better) from their competitors. Marketers, communication scholars and practitioners refer to this challenge as points of similarity and points of difference between a firm and its rivals on key aspects of its identity, image and reputation. Organisational sociologists and strategic management scholars use the more specific language of legitimacy (sameness) and reputation (distinction). As mentioned, legitimacy and reputation are distinct but closely related constructs in the context of CSR. Legitimacy refers to general norms and values in society that imply certain standards around what is acceptable behaviour of firms (or not). As far as CSR is concerned, it is clear from numerous studies that firms are

> transformed by new pressures to look like responsible actors. They are increasingly obligated, by law and public pressure, to take on expanded concerns such as environmental protection, corporate social responsibility and philanthropy, employee rights and job satisfaction, workplace diversity, community engagement, and consumer safety.
> (Bromley and Meyer, 2014: 7)

In other words, nowadays there are significant pressures on firms to meet public expectations and standards of legitimacy as far as its CSR engagement is concerned. Indeed, for many firms there is now something like a legitimacy baseline for CSR, in terms of what generally speaking is expected of them by their stakeholders. Such expectations may however vary depending on the size, visibility and sector of the company, but nonetheless the pressure for legitimacy is surely felt by many firms around the world. Reputation is distinct from legitimacy but builds on it in that, besides a baseline expectation, it is about what firms do differently specifically in terms of CSR, and what they are therefore known for, or rated more highly on, vis-à-vis their direct competitors.

One useful way of looking at this is to consider a firm as an individual actor, who needs to act responsibly towards its stakeholders and society at large and wants to build a specific reputation for its efforts. This kind of personification is one that is common in the communication, management and sociological literatures, where organisations are seen to have 'identities' and 'reputations' akin to human beings. In addition, research across marketing, consumer research, communication and organisational sociology confirms that stakeholders attribute a 'corporate identity' to an organisation, and also form a reputation of that organisation in ways that closely resemble how individuals form impressions of other human beings (Chun and Davies, 2006). As such, the responsible actor notion is not just a metaphor, as it resembles how stakeholders form reputations of firms.

While this particular perspective on reputation has been discussed at length elsewhere (see e.g. King et al., 2010 for more details), two specific implications arise when stakeholders attribute person-like images and reputations to organisations. First, stakeholders will relate the various direct encounters and impressions that they have of an organisation into a singular image or reputation, as if the various messages and actions of the members of the organisation actually came from a single embodied person. In other words, they integrate and compress different impressions into that of the actions of a single actor, who operates (and is seen to operate) in a particular environment where it attempts to differentiate itself from rival firms to gain reputation and legitimacy. As a result, stakeholders will think of a firm as a single unitary actor (rather than a loosely connected collective) and will, for example, refer to a particular bank or retailer as having taken a particular stance on a given issue, as having expressed certain opinions or as having done certain things.

Second, firms, like human agents, are seen to be capable of taking deliberate, reflective and goal-directed action. Stakeholders in effect attribute to firms the capacity of taking deliberate action, akin to how human beings have intentionality and agency. King et al. stress that such stakeholder attributions are commonplace, in part because firms have been legally and institutionally endowed with agency, and with individual rights and responsibilities (ibid.). The broader implication here is that in modern societies organisations are treated as if they are individuals, by law but also in the minds of stakeholders and the general public, and are granted analogous powers to act and assigned analogous responsibilities and rights.

The two implications together – the fact that stakeholders integrate their impressions into a single 'corporate' reputation and attribute intentions and actions to the firm – provide a useful starting point to consider how firms approach CSR, in their actions and communication, and how accordingly stakeholders form a reputation of that firm. Sticking with the image of the organisation as an actor (in the minds of its stakeholders), we make a distinction between a firm's CSR 'talk' and 'walk', which according to recent research accounts for differences in how firms practise CSR (see for instance Baumann-Pauly et al., 2013; Wickert et al., 2016).

CSR talk, akin to the kind of symbolic impression management tactics that we have sketched above, involves the various ways in which an organisation communicates with its external audiences such as customers. CSR talk by itself mirrors a form of advertising or 'a strategic variant of marketing aiming to promote a company's image and reputation ... as well as the sales of its products' (Eisenegger and Schranz, 2011: 6). In comparison, *CSR walk* encompasses substantive and behaviourally orientated activities inside a firm, such as adjusting production methods to mitigate environmental impacts, or improving working conditions across the firm's supply chain. Firms that 'walk' CSR invest in responsible business behaviour and implement CSR along core business processes in order to achieve measurable outcomes.

Together, 'walk' and 'talk' make up the overall profile of a firm in terms of its CSR engagement. They are obviously not mutually exclusive, as good behaviour (walk) will be broadcasted and reported by most firms (talk), and in some cases talk itself can be seen as a substantial investment (e.g. in stakeholder dialogue platforms addressing CSR standards and issues). Yet, we use this rough distinction here to develop a framework on CSR reputation management. In particular, when we see the two dimensions as separate but related scales, we can identify different approaches to CSR reputation management. For example, large and well-known multinational corporations may be overselling their CSR efforts (talking), by framing and spinning good stories about themselves and in a way that is not reflective of their actual investments and changes in behaviour (walk). In the literature, this phenomenon is termed as 'greenwashing'. Similarly, a firm may be actually making substantial progress on CSR targets internally, but without sufficiently broadcasting or communicating the results. This may be the case when firms are focused on CSR goals in themselves, and may as a result besides some basic reporting decide not to communicate much with their stakeholders about the real progress that they are making. The latter can be observed in particular among many small and family-owned firms (Wickert, 2016).

Obviously, an ideal state for firms is to be 'walking the talk', where they engage with their stakeholders, implement CSR activities, and transparently and collaboratively communicate about the results. In the following section, we sketch these different approaches, discussing when they are used and what the consequences may be in terms of a firm's CSR reputation – being an opportunity to enhance reputation or leading to a risk that may damage reputation.

13.5 Walking CSR: An Opportunity to Enhance Reputation

Broadly speaking, companies that aim to walk CSR attempt to seriously implement environmentally, socially and ethically responsible business practices as part of their core operations. This can create opportunities to enhance their reputation. What does existing research tell us about how companies should and in fact are walking CSR in order to improve their reputation?

Yoon et al. argue that the positive reputation effects of CSR with an important stakeholder group they analysed – consumers – are stronger if the motives for CSR are perceived as sincere; in other words, the company is able to show that it is indeed taking substantial steps towards integrating CSR in core business operations, rather than making symbolic commitments (Yoon et al., 2006). Consumers also tend to grant more reputation credits if they perceive a lower salience of firm-serving benefits from CSR activities. That means that the firm is seen to engage in CSR not only for instrumental reasons and because there might be a business case, resulting in higher profits, but also because paying attention to a particular CSR issue, such as child labour or climate change mitigation, is the right thing to do and does not depend on immediate payoffs. Yoon et al. further show that consumers consider CSR activities to be even more credible if they receive information about them from an independent, neutral source, rather than only from the company itself; for instance, through advertising or CSR reports (ibid.). For example, this means that sincere CSR walk further benefits a company's reputation if it is endorsed by certification organisations such as the Forest Stewardship Council (FSC) that stands for sustainable forestry, or the Fairtrade label which aims to ensure responsible sourcing of raw materials such as cocoa or coffee.

While research suggests that reputation effects are generally higher if companies manage to sincerely walk CSR, other studies also show that industry matters. Different sectors usually have different environmental and social impacts, which moderates reputation effects. While metals, mining, oil extraction and power generation for instance have a significant impact on soil, water, climate and other environmental aspects, textile production, food processing and agriculture often significantly violate labour and human rights of the involved workers, such as in factories or on plantations. By contrast, other industries (particularly the renewable energy industry, information and communication technology, and the service sector) are generally seen as causing much lower environmental and social impacts and are associated with fewer highly visible environmental issues.

Brammer and Pavelin argue that stakeholders such as local communities, regulators, the media and environmental pressure groups tend to observe those firms that create significant environmental externalities much closer, and they expect firms to reduce or make reparations for their impacts (Brammer and Pavelin, 2004). At the same time, 'good' environmental performance, in other words walking CSR, is more likely to contribute to enhanced reputation in those sectors where environmental or social impacts are present and if a company makes credible efforts to mitigate these impacts. What this also means is that companies are ill advised if they focus on CSR activities that are unrelated to the potentially harmful impact their operations have, assuming they aim to secure the positive reputation effects of CSR.

Examples abound both of companies that either fail to connect their social and environmental impacts to their CSR activities and thus find it difficult to reap the reputational benefits, and on the other hand companies that have managed to tackle those CSR issues that are material to their core business. For instance, supporting cultural events may be considered a social contribution by utility companies such as E.ON or GDF Suez, yet stakeholders are unlikely to grant significant reputation credits if these companies engaged in such CSR activities. Their carbon emissions, on the other hand, cause massive environmental impacts, and these companies are thus much better able to enhance their reputation by focusing on the development of climate change mitigation strategies or investing heavily in renewables. In contrast, for the textile industry and companies such as Inditex or H&M, carbon emissions are perhaps less salient, while CSR activities that are related to the improvement of working conditions in their supply chain may have a huge impact on workers' lives, thus providing a better lever to influence their reputation. Likewise, the AIDS pandemic in Africa may be a marginal social issue for a retailer such as Carrefour or Metro, but pharmaceutical companies such as Bayer or Novartis are much closer connected, as are mining companies such as Anglo American or DeBeers that depend on local labour supply for their operations.

Effectively managing CSR therefore also implies taking into account that if environmental or social impacts are less apparent, reputational benefits that are expected to result from CSR might be marginal, because stakeholders simply care about other things. If a company such as Shell provides recyclable paper cups on its oil platforms and exploration ships in the Arctic – a well-meant but also somewhat ironic attempt to be environmentally responsible – but simultaneously continues dangerous deep-water drilling in zones where endangered species are near extinction, few would be surprised that this did not significantly enhance their reputation as an environmentally conscious company. Rather, such behaviour makes the company even more likely to be accused of greenwashing. Moreover, there is also an administrative cost associated with those CSR activities that are peripheral to a firm's business operations and that do not fit with their real environmental and social impacts, which in turn may harm its financial performance and thus can even harm the reputation in the eyes of other stakeholders such as investors.

Research has also pointed to a positive correlation between corporate giving (making donations to charitable organisations such as childcare, culture or sports) and corporate reputation. In general, it is argued that companies who donate more enjoy a better reputation than those who donate less. However, other scholars have criticised these findings. They doubt whether such philanthropic activities are really beneficial to reputation and suggest that CSR activities need to be consistent with the company's overall strategy and attached to core business activities in order to have a positive effect on reputation (see for instance Becker-Olsen et al., 2006). At the same time, focusing on philanthropy as an instrument to enhance corporate reputation may not be a viable strategy in the future. As we have shown above, stakeholders and civil society in particular are increasingly distrustful of business, and shift their attention from corporate support of childcare, museums or festivals to more material issues such as working conditions, climate change mitigation or corruption. This basically means that stakeholders are paying more attention to how sustainable the actual value-creating activities are – 'how the money is made' – when evaluating CSR, and are less concerned about which charitable causes are allocated some percentages of profits – 'how the money is spent'. In turn, CSR activities that are largely unrelated to a firm's core business may no longer work to position oneself in a favourable light (see Chapter 3).

Besides the importance of ensuring that CSR activities focus on what stakeholders generally expect companies to do, scholars studying corporate reputation have also argued that walking CSR can help to protect a company's reputation from damage. While companies can use other means to improve their reputation, such as innovative products, engaging in CSR can also help create a buffer against reputation losses in times of scandals or when facing allegations of wrongdoing. Several authors argue that in situations of a reputational crisis, sincere CSR engagement offers protection against negative publicity in the media. Companies with credible CSR activities are thus exposed to lower reputational risks than those who are not perceived as sincerely walking CSR (Eisenegger and Schranz, 2011). This is because stakeholders are more likely to believe that the questionable issue at hand was rather a blip or an accident that can be resolved, instead of being a more systematic and fundamental part of how the company is doing business. Minor and Morgan for instance have studied the link between reputation and CSR among US firms over a period of fifteen years, and conclude that stock prices, used as a proxy for a company's reputation as perceived by investors, declined considerably less after an adverse event, such as a product recall, if a firm has been perceived as sincerely managing CSR (Minor and Morgan, 2011). We conclude that walking CSR, along core business operations and issues where social or environmental impacts are visible and substantially addressed, offers a significant opportunity for companies to both enhance and protect their reputation.

13.6 Talking CSR: Risking Reputational Damage

In contrast to walking CSR, companies that are not 'walking the talk' cannot be considered to seriously engage in CSR. Instead, an emphasis on only talking CSR involves unsubstantiated and symbolic impression management in order to create a façade of social, environmental and ethical responsibility that is however not connected to a firm's core business operations; in other words, to try washing business practices green in the eyes of stakeholders. However, this approach may backfire and therefore brings serious reputational risks. Cases abound where consumers have started to boycott a company if they find out that its CSR messages are not sincere. NGOs might launch campaigns and 'name and shame' particular firms, and social responsibility-orientated investors might withdraw their money. The oil company Shell had to withdraw an advertisement after being criticised for greenwashing by the Dutch and British governments, because it was showing an image of a smokestack with flowers sprouting from it (Lyon and Montgomery, 2015). Websites such as the 'Seven Sins of Greenwashing' (http://sinsofgreenwashing.com/) aim to make people aware of some of the worst forms of greenwashing among consumer products – and stop them from buying such products.

As we have shown above, companies face increasing stakeholder pressure to act in a socially and environmentally responsible manner, but at the same time having a good reputation is critical to success. This situation however confronts many corporations with a problem: while walking CSR is considered the 'better' choice in terms of long-term reputation-building, it is also very costly, while it is often difficult to directly measure outcomes and thus to evaluate short-term gains. Companies would have to roll out sophisticated CSR management schemes, policies and operating procedures, which could include installing expensive measures and monitoring processes in their operations, or rearranging supply chains in order to uphold adequate working conditions and pay fair wages. Focusing instead on talking CSR without corresponding integration of non-marginal CSR activities to core business operations, in contrast, is rather cheap, in particular for large multinational corporations, and as long as stakeholders do not discover the 'empty' CSR façade then companies may reap short-term reputational gains (Wickert et al., 2016). This brings about a fundamental dilemma for the relationship between corporate reputation and CSR.

Consider the case of an automotive company such as BMW and its CSR activities to become environmentally responsible. Dowling and Moran examine this case and pose the question: how should a company respond to environmental concerns when many of its operations, products and services can be easily construed as causing exactly this concern, such as pollution (Dowling and Moran, 2012)? They suggest that this is a dilemma with which major automobile, oil and other companies around the world have been struggling with, that 'the success of their business models makes the natural environment more congested and polluted' (ibid.: 30). Admittedly, most of these companies are well aware that many of their stakeholders are concerned about their environmental impacts. However, as Dowling and Moran assert, 'to date, the response to this dilemma has been to bolt-on some CSR activities, many of which are only marginally related to their core activities . . . [while] . . . these activities can easily be construed as a cynical attempt to deflect attention from the underlying problem.' (ibid.) The authors hence are very concerned that many CSR activities address rather marginal problems and are often aimed at directing attention away from more serious issues. According to a report by *The Guardian* in 2012, in the case of BMW this means that while the company makes attempts to offer environmentally 'friendly' electric and hybrid cars, it still lobbies heavily against stricter pollution regulations that would harm sales of its more polluting luxury cars which make up the majority of sales (Vaughan, 2012). Such behaviour can however be very risky in terms of long-term reputation effects.

Yoon et al. examine the effects of unsubstantiated and even hypocritical CSR talk and investigate the relationship between consumer perceptions about

CSR and a company's reputation (Yoon et al., 2006). While they suggest that CSR activities can enhance reputation if consumers perceive these activities as based on sincere motives, they also propose that CSR activities can be ineffective when the sincerity of motives is ambiguous, and that reputation can even be damaged if motives are perceived as insincere or misleading. This means that consumers might become suspicious as to whether the true motive behind a CSR activity is only meant to improve the company's reputation, or whether it reflects sincere efforts to improve important CSR issues that are related to a company's core business operations. If not, then such CSR talk may not only be inefficient in enhancing reputation, but it may actually backfire – in other words, leave the company with a more negative reputation than it would have had without talking about CSR at all.

Several examples show that poorly executed CSR campaigns can hurt reputation. The tobacco giant Philip Morris has been criticised by consumers and civil society groups for a CSR campaign to support youth smoking prevention. Stakeholders found this sort of CSR that Philip Morris was conducting cynical, in particular as it had no effect on the company's core business model: selling cigarettes that cause serious health effects. Not surprisingly, the hoped-for reputation gains backfired and probably left the company with a lower reputation in the eyes of its key stakeholders. Philip Morris' activities raised further scepticism that its motives were not sincere – if the company really cared about a particular issue, it would be better advised to change the business practice in question.

We conclude that a company that is not walking the talk can encounter significant reputational risks. What our discussion so far suggests is that two dimensions are important when making judgements about the effects of CSR activities on reputation. First, are these activities reflective of *substantive* efforts to promote social and environmental responsibility (CSR walk), or are they rather a form of *symbolic* impression management that aims to construct a façade of CSR without much substance (CSR talk)? Second, are CSR activities connected to a company's *core business* activities and address those areas of concern in its industry and in society that have considerable impacts, both positive when specific CSR activities are promoted, and negative when CSR activities are aimed to avoid or mitigate such impacts? Or are CSR activities only peripheral to a company's operations and can thus be considered a *non-core activity*? Table 13.1 summarises the relationship between these dimensions and indicates the expected reputation effects.

13.7 Reputational Dynamics: When 'Too Much of a Good Thing' Backfires

Most managers and researchers would probably agree that having a good reputation is beneficial for companies – it attracts consumers, investors and

Table 13.1 CSR and reputation effects

	Core business activity	Non-core activity
CSR walk: substantial efforts	Reputation effects: high opportunity to enhance reputation, and on a long-term basis.	Reputation effects: probably ineffective in the long run in enhancing reputation.
CSR talk: symbolic impression management	Reputation effects: risky, because no substance but high expectations (backfire).	Reputation effects: probably ineffective in protecting reputation from damage.

employees. However, some scholars have taken a closer look at reputation and asked whether there can be 'too much of a good thing'. For example, the ever-greater focus on reputation-building makes firms more vulnerable to the attacks of activist groups, such as critical NGOs like Greenpeace or Human Rights Watch (see Chapter 9). King and McDonnell argue that reputation can become an important liability for firms, a burden of being well-known (King and McDonnell, 2015). Once a good reputation is built, that firm is obliged to maintain it and the corresponding high expectations that it has created. From the perspective of activists, there is much to gain by forcing firms to defend their reputations. This is because negative events involving highly reputed, and so-called 'celebrity' firms are attractive for the media and generally garner higher stakeholder attention. Activists in turn depend on media attention if they want to influence public perception about a cause and the firms involved. They would select highly reputed firms as targets, even though these firms may not be solely responsible for a certain socially or environmentally harmful activity. This explains why companies such as Wal-Mart or Nestlé are commonly confronted with activist accusations about poor labour standards or human rights issues – this occurs in part because their fame helps activists to draw the public's attention to a cause. When Greenpeace attacked Nestlé for its unsustainable sourcing of palm oil from Southeast Asian rainforests, it made great sense from the activists' perspective to target this globally known multinational instead of the actual producer of the palm oil, the Indonesian company called Sinar Mas. The latter was unknown to most of the public and would have sparked very little media attention, let alone interest among Western consumers.

In effect, a closer look at some of the highly reputed firms and their CSR may show that these companies are not necessarily worse than other companies that are however largely unknown to the public. The Swiss mining company Glencore-Xstrata is a good example of a firm that has been accused of highly controversial social and environmental damages caused by its operations, but because few know about this company, they can 'fly under the radar' of media attention and are confronted with little public expectations to substantially invest in CSR (see Chapter 14).

13.8 Case Study: Beyond Control? Managing Reputation after the BP Deepwater Horizon Oil Spill

On 20 April 2010, one of the worst oil spills in the history of the petroleum industry began with the lethal explosion of the Deepwater Horizon offshore drilling platform in the Gulf of Mexico, about sixty miles off the coast of Louisiana. The accident resulted in the loss of eleven lives, the burning and sinking of the rig, and the spillage of approximately 750 million litres of oil into open waters that caused severe damage to the Gulf's ecosystem. The rig was operated by the company Transocean but owned by British-American multinational BP, one of the world's 'supermajor' oil and gas companies. The oil flowed for eighty-seven days and BP finally managed to seal the well on 19 September 2010.

Apart from the enormous environmental and economic damages, what happened in the summer of 2010 was also a reputational disaster. BP's share price crashed, and two months into the crisis the company's stock had lost nearly half its market value. US President Obama was outraged that BP started a US$50 million advertising campaign to try to save its reputation and had even announced a dividend to shareholders. BP, Obama insisted, should be spending its money on clean-up measures and repaying the victims of the spill. Tony Hayward, the then-CEO of BP, exacerbated public outrage as he infamously purported that the oil spill is 'relatively tiny' compared with the 'very big ocean'. This was accompanied by sales dropping between 10 and 40 per cent, causing some BP petrol stations even to cover their logos to avoid being associated with the BP brand.

The local and national governments and the media were also highly critical of BP: there had been no culture of safety, and BP more than the other involved companies, Transocean and Halliburton, was blamed for trying to avoid costly safety measures in their pursuit of operational efficiency. As *The Daily Telegraph* reported, a White House commission concluded that the spill resulted from 'systemic' root causes and was not a coincidence but foreseeable (Reuters, 2011). In response, BP was even temporarily banned from new federal contracts by the US administration over its lack of business integrity.

All in all, fines, clean-up costs and losses of revenue for BP amounted to approximately US$ 42 billion by 2013, which made the oil spill a disaster for the natural environment and also for BP's reputation. Not only did BP's share price drop considerably in the aftermath of the spill and until today remains at levels much lower than in the pre-spill period, but also the reputation of BP plunged to an all-time low. Shortly after the crisis, Covalence, a Swiss-based company that tracks ethical reputations of large companies for use by ethical investors, downgraded BP to level E, the lowest possible rank. According to Covalence, this was not only due to BP's poor reaction after the oil spill but included other factors such as deteriorating working conditions.

More bad news soon followed: almost a year after the oil spill, a survey released by Harris Interactive revealed that, among the sixty most visible US companies, BP was fifty-ninth – a dramatic drop from its much higher rankings in the years before the spill – and concluded that BP was still perceived as one of the companies with the worst reputations in the USA (Harris, 2011). It seems that whatever was left of the green image that BP had attempted to cultivate over the years, most notably by rebranding the company name from British Petroleum to 'beyond petroleum', completely dissolved in only a few weeks.

13.8.1 What Happened Before: Rebranding for CSR

BP was one of the first major oil and gas companies that publicly announced a turnaround in its stance towards sustainability. In May 1997, BP's CEO, John Browne, announced to the world both BP's decision to accept that climate change is occurring and also its intention to reduce greenhouse gas (GHG) emissions from all of its own business operations. This action attracted attention from politicians, environmentalists, the business press and consumers, and raised expectations regarding the actions of its direct competitors but also of BP itself as the company was proactively raising its own bar.

Following these announcements, BP undertook one of the largest and most successful green advertising campaigns, spending nearly US$ 200 million. In 2000, BP unveiled a new global brand with a fresh logo, a sunburst of green, yellow and white symbolising energy in all its forms. The letters 'BP' were to be interpreted as 'beyond petroleum', emphasising the company's wider perspective on other sources of energy besides crude oil and its thought leadership on addressing the greenhouse effect and its dedication to environmental stewardship. Together with the new brand symbolism, BP positioned itself as a company that in a responsible and sustainable way aims to meet the world's current and future energy needs. The campaign was highly successful: BP's brand awareness rose from below 10 per cent to more than 60 per cent, and BP consistently appeared as the most environmentally friendly oil company in US consumer surveys during the mid-2000s.

Under this new banner, BP took more steps towards addressing climate change. The company installed solar panels at its service stations, brought solar power to remote villages, promoted hydrogen-fuelled buses for public transportation, introduced new, cleaner types of motor fuel and published an annual CSR report. According to *Marketing Week*, by March 2008 BP had managed to position itself among the top ten green brands, holding place nine and surprisingly even one place ahead of Greenpeace.

However, the new image was not without criticism. Critics argued that despite these major rebranding efforts and the reconstruction of a reputation of being an environmentally aware company, almost all of BP's profits were still being generated from traditional oil and gas extraction, exploration and chemical production, including deep-water drilling. Only a tiny fraction of its investments and revenues were related to developing and commercialising alternative forms of energy. Environmental groups hence accused BP of greenwashing. Greenpeace commented: 'This is a triumph of style over substance. BP spent more on their logo this year than they did on renewable energy last year.' (BBC, 2000) Another NGO, Corpwatch, awarded BP its 'Greenwash Award' for being 'beyond preposterous' (Bruno, 2000). After all, while BP might have realised a relative 'green' advantage over its competitors such as ExxonMobil or Shell, critics accused BP that its changed reputation reflected at best an aspiration that was never really attainable, and 'divorced from reality' (Balmer, 2010: 97). In short, according to critics the image that BP had attempted to create was not underpinned by its identity, and largely reflected symbolic action rather than substantial efforts of organisational transformation to improve core business processes. As Balmer has argued, for BP this was ultimately disastrous, as the flawed notion that BP would live up to its environmental and green credentials, including a concern with sustainable energy sources and safety, backfired, and in a way that was probably more severe than if BP had not made such claims in the first place (ibid.).

13.8.2 Five Years later: Conceding Sustainability?

Some years after the oil spill, reports suggest that most of the environmental damage has been cleaned up, and the reputational damage also seemed to have ebbed away. While one might have expected an even more sincere commitment to sustainability by BP in response, and equally by its competitors that are exposed to similar risks, reality shows quite a different picture. In the last few years, reports mourned that BP, along with other oil and gas companies, has initiated large-scale divestments in renewable energies, marking a further step away from its former commitments to go 'beyond' petroleum. For instance, *Business Week* reported that in April 2013, BP announced that it was selling off its entire $3.1 billion wind energy business in the US as 'part of a continuing effort to become a more focused oil and gas company', according to a company spokesperson. Indeed, though it had famously rebranded itself 'Beyond Petroleum', BP also exited the solar energy business back in 2011. Today, its alternative energy investments are limited to biofuels and a lone wind farm in the Netherlands (Bakewell, 2013).

Questions for Discussion

1. What effect did the oil spill have on your personal perception of BP, your consumption of BP products and your general energy use?
2. Locate BP's behaviour in the reputation opportunity/risk matrix and explain possible reputation effects.
3. If BP were to invest in improving its CSR reputation, consider the costs and benefits of having a 'green' reputation for BP.

13.9 Chapter Summary

In this chapter we examined the relationship between CSR and corporate reputation. We have shown that social, environmental and ethical issues in business moved centre stage in the reputation landscape and make up an increasingly important component that influences the overall reputation of a company. The chapter started by introducing key terms, and with defining reputation alongside other related constructs such as identity, image and legitimacy. We then discussed investments in CSR as an important part of a company's reputation, and illustrated different ways in which companies invest in CSR to enhance and protect their reputation. Specifically, we distinguished between walking and talking about CSR, the first referring to substantive commitments and the latter involving symbolic public relations efforts. The two dimensions together provide a framework to position and analyse the CSR approaches of different companies, and to identify the potential risks and rewards for their reputation. Based on an overview of these risks and rewards, we generally advocate that companies 'walk the talk' and transparently communicate about and report on their commitments to, and progress on, substantial CSR activities such as reducing their carbon emissions and enhancing worker welfare.

Chapter Questions

1. Does CSR really have an effect on reputation? Think about the latest product you bought. What did you take into account other than price and general product quality? Did you think about any CSR-related aspects?
2. If you were a manager responsible for corporate reputation, to which stakeholder group(s) would you pay most attention? Why?
3. Assuming that walking CSR is costly, and talking CSR is cheap, why should companies 'walk the talk'?

4. Think of an industry and the different players within it; what are core versus peripheral CSR activities, and what approaches are companies in this sector taking in this respect?

FURTHER RESOURCES

Barnett, M. and Pollock, T. (2012). *The Oxford Handbook of Corporate Reputation*. Oxford: Oxford University Press.
This handbook provides a state-of-the-art overview of reputation research and is a valuable introductory reading for students who want to delve deeper into the topic of corporate reputation.

Cornelissen, J. (2014). *Corporate Communications. A Guide to Theory and Practice* (4th ed.). London: Sage.
This book is standard reading on corporate communications and provides valuable access to the topic on a theoretical level supported by numerous practical examples. Links between communication and reputation are explained.

Reputation Institute (2014). CSR RepTrak® 100 Report, www.reputationinstitute.com/thought-leadership/global-reptrak
Reputation Institute is a leading private sector institution that measures reputation and associated risks. This report will be interesting for those who want to gain a practical and hands-on perspective on the importance of corporate reputation.

Fortune magazine ranking of world's most admired companies, http://fortune.com/worlds-most-admired-companies/
Fortune magazine's ranking of the world's most admired companies gives an overview of those companies considered to have the best reputations worldwide, and gives insight into which criteria are considered to compile the ranking.

Forbes ranking of companies with the best CSR reputation, www.forbes.com/pictures/efkk45mmlm/the-10-companies-with-the-best-csr-reputations/
Forbes' ranking of companies with the best CSR reputation adds to the previous ranking by focusing specifically on CSR. This allows a comparison of companies who scored similarly/differently in the two rankings, and gives insight into which criteria are considered to compile this CSR-based ranking.

RepRisk, www.reprisk.com
RepRisk is a leading provider of dynamic business intelligence on environmental, social and governance risks for an unlimited universe of companies and projects.

14

The Corporate Construction of Transparency and (In)Transparency

LARS THØGER CHRISTENSEN AND DENNIS SCHOENEBORN

Learning Objectives

- Understand the notion of transparency and its relevance for the practice of corporate social responsibility.
- Discuss and illuminate possible limitations to organisational transparency.
- Explain why and how limits to transparency under certain conditions may be advantageous to corporate social responsibility (CSR).

14.1 Introduction

In this chapter, we discuss the role of transparency in the context of CSR governance. We elaborate on transparency's increasing importance in contemporary business corporations, emphasising that transparency is often associated with notions of accountability and good governance. Yet, although transparency is an important dimension of CSR, it is often easier to celebrate than to actually implement it. Even with the best intentions, organisations cannot reveal all matters about themselves, but need to select which types of information to disclose. Following these initial reflections, we unpack the notion of transparency, emphasising how conventional understandings of the term are often limited and presuppose simplistic notions of information and communication. With this background, we are able to demonstrate that organisational transparency practices do not always produce expected and desirable results. In fact, transparency may create new types of opacity. The thrust of our argument is that transparency is not neutral; it *does* things. By making certain organisational matters more visible to stakeholders, other dimensions are inevitably kept in the dark. Think, for example, of the leak of the 'Panama' papers in 2016. While these leaks obviously provide much information, they do not necessarily provide more knowledge or insight into matters of international taxation (cf. Roberts, 2012). Consequently, transparency practices do not always serve the interest of immediate stakeholder insight and knowledge. However, instead of condemning this trend altogether, we discuss how opacity may allow organisations to explore, inspire and encourage better practices in the CSR arena. More specifically, we argue that an initial condition of opacity may allow more organisations to talk themselves into better CSR practices – results that were not possible to achieve in contexts of full transparency where critics could detect and point out discrepancies between ideals and practice right away.

14.2 The Transparency Imperative

When corporations claim to be socially responsible – declaring, for example, that they treat their employees properly, are responsive to stakeholder needs, avoid harming the environment and eschew corruption – their audiences (consumers, citizens, non-governmental organisations (NGOs) and other stakeholders) might like to know that this is in fact the case, that the corporations are not just putting up façades of responsibility but are indeed living up to their own words. Often, however, such knowledge is not available and most audiences are therefore unable to judge whether corporate CSR talk reflects action. In such cases, a call for *transparency* seems appropriate and logical.

Today, transparency is a growing concern for organisations and institutions of various sorts. Hereby, we do not suggest that organisations are open or candid about everything they do; rather, that the *pressure for insight* from the surrounding world is rapidly increasing. Citizens, consumers, politicians, members of interest organisations, and other engaged individuals or institutions want to know, understand or perhaps even see for themselves that everything is fine and that they have no reason to suspect that illegitimate or immoral practices are taking place behind fronts of responsibility. And this is essentially the promise of transparency: to help the spectator move behind such fronts in order to provide *clarity* about corporate and political transactions so that *insight* can be increased and accountability improved (Christensen and Cheney, 2015).

Business corporations in particular but also governmental institutions and NGOs are expected to contribute to transparency around their core practices in order to make it possible for the surrounding world to judge what is going on. Procedures for transparency in these contexts include open meetings, financial disclosure statements, freedom of information legislation, budgetary reviews, reporting, audits, etc. The driving force behind such practices is the conviction that 'sunlight is the best disinfectant' (Brandeis, 1914: 92). This, in turn, is based on the assumption that commercial, political and other transactions will become more accountable when conducted in the full light of day. In the aftermath of corporate scandals and financial crises, this conviction is only growing stronger. At the same time, the spread of new communication technologies and social media – as well as the political and military leakages made possible through such technologies – is accentuating the belief that transparency is necessary and in fact possible to achieve in practice.

The transparency imperative has spread widely in today's society from politics over foreign aid, accounting and construction to medicine, tourism, fashion and many other arenas. Consider these examples from a variety of political, economic and social contexts: when US President Barack Obama took office in 2009, he publicised a memorandum on Transparency and Open Government in which he stated: 'My Administration is committed to creating an unprecedented level of openness in Government. We will work together to ensure the public trust and establish a system of transparency, public participation, and collaboration. Openness will strengthen our democracy and promote efficiency and effectiveness in Government.' While it has proven difficult for the Obama administration to fully live up to these statements, they continue to shape the expectations of key stakeholders inside and outside the political system. Driven by similar ideals, the European Commission has established a so-called 'Transparency Portal', dedicated to the task of providing direct access to information that will help European citizens be better informed about EU matters and, thus, better equipped to understand and participate in EU decision-making processes. Likewise, the Sunlight Foundation, a non-profit organisation that advocates for open government globally, uses technology to expand access to vital government information and, thus, make government more accountable and eventually stimulate equitable democratic participation.

In addition to these large-scale political initiatives, there is a sustained pursuit of transparency in a number of specialised areas. The International Monetary Fund, for example, strives for *fiscal* transparency, which entails being open to the public about the government's past, present, and future fiscal activities. Likewise, the International Aid Transparency Initiative (IATI), a multi-stakeholder initiative (MSI) that includes donors, partner countries and civil society organisations, strives to make information about *foreign aid spending* easier to access, use and understand. Similarly, CoST is a targeted initiative to improve the value for money spent on public infrastructure by increasing transparency in the delivery of *construction projects*. And, a growing number of public and private institutions construct *rankings* on a wealth of issues from mortality rates at hospitals to high school grading in order to help consumers make more informed choices (see, e.g. Etzioni, 2010).

The specialised transparency-orientated projects, however, go beyond such issues of economic spending and consumer choice. While Transparency International (TI), for example, publishes an annual Corruption Perceptions Index in order to put the issue of *corruption* on the international policy agenda, the Medicines Transparency Alliance (MeTA) brings together all stakeholders in the pharmaceuticals market to improve access, availability and affordability of *medicines* for the one-third of the world's population to whom access is currently denied. The ideal is also found in the *fashion* industry where transparency refers to knowledge about who actually makes the clothes as well as producer willingness to communicate such knowledge to customers, shareholders and staff.

Working across several specialised fields, the Transparency Policy Project at Harvard University seeks to understand and improve disclosure practices such as nutritional labelling, patient safety disclosure, toxic chemical reporting and financial accounting in order to protect the public against *risks* in these areas. And, focusing on the risks of transparency *itself*, a Canadian research centre called The New Transparency is dedicated to the study of *surveillance and social sorting* made possible by new communication technologies and large databases. As these diverse examples demonstrate, the transparency concern and pursuit permeates virtually all aspects of society today. Also, they illustrate that transparency is hugely important in the quest for increased fairness, participation, freedom of choice and many of the other ideals that characterise open, democratic societies.

14.3 What *Is* Transparency?

Given the growing number of transparency initiatives, it is interesting to observe that its meaning is all but clear. While the term is used extensively in the media and in political discussions, it is rarely defined or debated with precision and clarity outside the narrow circles of CSR experts and reporting specialists. Consequently, transparency is an ideal that is more often called upon than actually found in practice. There are several reasons why this is the case, including the difficulties of explaining and clarifying complicated material, the desire to conceal specific practices that will not stand the light of day, or the possibility that full transparency may prevent certain responsibility measures and initiatives from being taken in the first place. Whereas transparency suggests insight and clarity, there are always and inevitably dimensions of *opacity* at play when corporations enter the scene of transparency. And while this may be highly problematic in some contexts, it may be unavoidable and perhaps even necessary in others.

Transparency is usually employed simply as a vague synonym for common-sense understandings of 'openness', 'insight' or 'clarity'. The expectation seems to be that such qualities automatically make organisations more accountable to relevant stakeholders and, therefore, are the keys to better and more responsible governance. Moreover, by making organisations more open and visible to the critical gaze of stakeholders, transparency is expected to facilitate citizen participation and thus strengthen democratic practice. Such expectations, however, are rarely questioned or tested. As a consequence, transparency has become a widely celebrated, yet *un*questioned, stand-in for responsibility in the current business environment. In corporate and political practice, however, transparency is usually equated with *information generation and provision*.

Box 14.1	Transparency definitions

Free from guile; candid or open. Easily seen through or detected; obvious. (American Heritage Dictionary)

[Transparency is] a principle that allows those affected by administrative decisions, business transactions or charitable work to know not only the basic facts and figures but also the mechanisms and processes. (TI, cited in Oliver, 2004: 5).

[T]he extent to which the organisation provides relevant, timely, and reliable information, in written and verbal form, to investors, regulators, and market intermediaries. (Williams, 2005: 361)

Transparency is the deliberate attempt to make available all legally releasable information – whether positive or negative in nature – in a manner that is accurate, timely, balanced and unequivocal, for the purpose of enhancing the reasoning ability of publics and holding organisations accountable for their actions, policies, and practices . . . To be transparent, organisations should voluntarily share information that is inclusive, auditable (verifiable), complete, relevant, accurate, neutral, comparable, clear, timely, accessible, reliable, honest, and holds the organisation accountable. (Rawlins, 2009: 75, 79).

Given such understanding of the term, most calls for transparency manifest themselves as *demands for information*, even if information itself is not the ultimate goal. While disclosure of financial information has been regulated since the Great Depression of the 1930s, corporations of today are under growing pressure to make other types of information, including facts about their business conduct (including the larger value chains they are embedded in), sustainability practices, responsibility policies and programmes accessible and intelligible to all relevant stakeholders. As a consequence, huge amounts of information about organisational practices are piling up inside and outside organisations, giving the impression that the world of today is more transparent than ever before. The assumption seems to be that such information 'speaks for itself' and that the practice of providing it is a neutral act of responsibility *in and of itself*. Yet, such understanding of transparency is inherently problematic for several reasons, which we shall unfold in this chapter.

14.4 Managing Transparency

Transparency plays a particular role in business firms where the notion of responsible behaviour has expanded beyond shareholder value to include the interests of employees, unions, NGOs, the environment and the general public (Oliver, 2004). The growing demand for *organisational transparency* is essentially a result of new or newly engaged stakeholders calling for insight, accountability, trustworthiness and good governance. Some NGOs have been founded for the primary purpose of monitoring firms and their business conduct – and thus aiming to foster organisational transparency. One example is BankTrack, a network of NGOs that aims to serve a 'watchdog' function for the financial industry. They do so, for instance, by collecting and publishing data on 'dodgy deals', i.e. socially and environmentally harmful infrastructure projects (such as oil rigs or mining) that are rendered possible through credits by banks. Furthermore, the investments of large pension funds, for example, has attracted increased public, political and managerial attention and given rise to calls for greater scrutiny (Fung, Graham and Weil, 2007). Given the increasing exposure of corporate scandals, the calamitous consequences of financial crises and the spread of digital technologies, it is not surprising that these calls have intensified dramatically over the last decade and gradually proliferated in all types of organisational practice (e.g. Christensen and Cheney, 2015).

Exposed to the critical gaze of pressure groups, media, business analysts and other inquisitive stakeholders, organisations of today feel more transparent than ever before. Yet, transparency is not only an external condition facing contemporary organisations as an objective imperative they have to live up to; it is also, and increasingly so, a *strategic* practice through which they seek to handle the demand for transparency to their own advantage. Today's managers cannot ignore the transparency concern and need to consider how best to leverage the demand for more insight into their organisational practices. In order to understand what this means for the issue of transparency – and for society more generally – we need to consider the organisational limits to transparency.

For a number of practical reasons, including competitive concerns, organisations cannot simply open all 'gates' and make *all* facts and material available to *all* audiences. Organisations, therefore, do not passively break down all boundaries between themselves and their surroundings, and expose their presumed inner selves to the external world (see further below). Although the transparency imperative implies the ideal of full stakeholder insight, its practical implementation in the context of organisations inevitably implies thorough considerations and complex choices about what to disclose and what to keep confidential. Even with the best intentions of allowing maximum insight, thus, transparency involves careful *selection* of material. Below are listed some of the concerns that may shape such selections:

- *Regulation*: How is transparency measured, reported and controlled in society?
- *Expectations*: What types of transparency are expected in the industry in question?
- *Relevance*: What is relevant and what is irrelevant in each particular context?

- *Comprehension*: Which data can be understood or misunderstood by outsiders?
- *Credibility*: What types of transparency are convincing to relevant stakeholders?
- *Use*: In which ways can transparency efforts be misused by critical audiences?
- *Branding*: What types of transparency can help the organisation in its branding efforts?

How organisations handle the transparency imperative, including the question of which kinds of transparency practices to implement, is therefore not self-evident, but an important strategic issue that involves communication as an essential dimension. As it appears from the list above, transparency not only means to describe and expose the organisation as it 'is', free from guile and pretension. It also and simultaneously means to 'pose', including to display, to stage and to frame and perhaps even to hide – because to present something inevitably implies to conceal or downplay other matters (see also Hansen and Flyverbom, 2015). Before we elaborate on this observation, we need to take a closer look at the communicative assumptions implied in the notion of transparency.

14.5 The Implied Communication Model

Transparency is now a common synonym of good governance in all sectors and an umbrella term for information-provision practices in most organisations. Our commitment to organisational transparency rests, as Strathern puts it 'in the proposition that if procedures and methods are open to scrutiny, then the organisation is open to critique and ultimately to improvement' (Strathern, 2000: 313). This is a noble and sensible goal; however, to fully appreciate the complex nature of organisational transparency, its pursuit must be understood within the context of assumptions about and workings of communication.

The understanding of transparency as information provision assumes a simple, linear communication process through which organisational reality is described, conveyed and received. Yet, information does not 'travel' smoothly all by itself from an organisation to its various audiences; it is selected, presented, challenged, negotiated, reinterpreted or ignored at many levels in the process. Thus, from a communication perspective, the information-provision version of the transparency ideal described above is not realistic (Christensen and Cheney, 2015). If we take our point of departure in the basic dimensions of a communication process – the sender, the message and the receiver – we can begin to outline some of the most problematic assumptions surrounding the transparency ideal:

- *Senders*: Most understandings of transparency assume that sender organisations are capable of knowing and revealing themselves fully *and* willing to describe themselves in a manner that is comprehensive, balanced and unequivocal. This is hardly the case, however. Organisations have good reasons for partiality and perhaps even concealment, and may not know themselves well enough to deliver accurate descriptions on all significant matters.
- *Messages*: Transparency ideals tend to depict organisational reality as being accessible in a straightforward, simple and friction-free way, assuming that if everything is plainly revealed to us, the audience is able to see through all obstacles and clutter. However, this idealised notion tends to ignore the fact that most responsibility issues are far too complex to convey in a simple and straightforward language. Within the contexts of global governance, sustainability standards and CSR reporting, for example, the language of transparency is usually too esoteric for the layperson to be able to navigate and make sense. Moreover, even when complex matters – in the name of transparency – are conveyed in more easily consumable terms, there is a great danger that the insight offered is overly simplistic and one-sided, leaving more important and complex dimensions of the issue in the dark, thus, leading only to highly selective forms of transparency.
- *Receivers*: Transparency ideals tend to assume that receivers are generally involved, competent and willing to spend the resources necessary to understand the information provided. Yet, even if some stakeholders, like critical NGOs, are truly interested in transparency, most consumers and citizens are engaged in other matters and do not really care about what organisations say about themselves. Moreover, even if they do care, their reactions to the information provided may often not be as rational, relevant or predictable as assumed.

Put differently, the transparency ideal presupposes a communication process that unfolds smoothly and efficiently from the source to the receiver: a process in which senders willingly divulge information as required, in which the meaning of the released information is clear and self-evident, and in which the audience constitutes an informed public able to specify its own information needs and motivated to hold senders accountable on the basis of the information provided (Fenster, 2006). With these problematic and insufficiently complex assumptions about the nature of communication, the transparency ideal upholds unrealistic expectations about increased insight into the practices of corporations, institutions and governments (Drucker and Gumpert, 2007).

This observation is not brought forward to suggest that the ideal itself is wrong or misplaced. In fact, as we have indicated above, increased transparency is needed in most areas that involve organisational and political responsibility as well as good governance. In such cases, regimes of global visibility, comparability and legibility are highly important. Still, we want to stress the point that proponents of transparency need to replace naive expectations with a deeper understanding of its organisational and social implications. In order to increase transparency we need to understand in more depth its inherent weaknesses and ambiguities, including its often unintended consequences in the context of organisations and beyond. This topic will be further unfolded below.

14.6 Problematic Effects of Transparency

It is difficult to argue against transparency. After all, what is the alternative? Secrecy? Obscurity? Ignorance? In Western democratic societies, especially, where enlightenment is a founding value, progress and knowledge creation seem to presuppose a willingness and ability to reduce all types of opacities, including prejudices, myths, dogmas, conventions and other types of blind spots that stand between us and the truth.

In spite of this ideal, many organisational and institutional practices seem to defy or contradict the transparency ideal. Think of branding, as an initial example. Although consultants and marketing practitioners often talk about branding – and *corporate* branding in particular – as a way of presenting or selling the organisation *behind* the product (assuming that this is what the consumer wants), the general goal of branding is *not* to expose or make clear, but to add intangible dimensions to the offer in ways that obscure commonalities with similar products and thus protect the sender organisation from comparisons. Although rarely talked about in these terms, branding can in fact be thought of as an avoidance strategy designed to reduce effective transparency. To the extent that CSR practice holds elements of branding, this logic may apply to corporate responsibility messages as well.

But the transparency ideal is challenged by many other interests and concerns. After all, transparency is not the only pressure confronting contemporary organisations. In fact, it is rarely the primary concern when organisations manage information vis-à-vis its different audiences. No matter how open and responsible organisations are or desire to be, they simultaneously need to be efficient, profitable, flexible, innovative, etc. Such alternative concerns may be difficult to honour under conditions of 'full' transparency. Attempts to satisfy stakeholder demands for information and insight are, for example, often counteracted by privacy laws or doctrines of commercial confidentiality. Other examples include bargaining games, conflict resolutions, peaceful coexistence and security, where the need to withhold some information and protect identities or strategic positions may be predominant. Moreover, although managers may officially encourage open communication between and among their employees, there are numerous situations in which too much transparency may cause individuals to hold back or otherwise change behaviour; for example, when personnel matters and conflicts are involved, when new ideas are being tested or when identities and self-images are at play. In such cases, the willingness to share complete and accurate information may be limited and replaced by a desire to 'send the right signals' or make the right impressions. Even when transparency is enforced by rules and regulations, such as for example the implementation of open calendars or open meetings in some organisations, participants have a tendency to adjust and edit their behaviours in ways that conform to social norms and expectations (i.e. by creating a 'front').

Transparency practices, in other words, are never 'innocent' or neutral; they inevitably shape how people and organisations behave and how they account for their behaviour. Knowing that their words, decisions, plans and other behaviours are open for critical perusal, they may be less inclined to experiment, take chances, share ideas or talk freely about their accomplishments, ideals, assessments and aspirations. Increased transparency, accordingly, does not simply make an existing organisational reality more visible and legible, but dramatically shapes the communicative and behavioural landscape of business, government and public discourse.

14.7 Transparency Strategies

If we take a closer look at the strategies through which the transparency imperative are handled, what we might call transparency governance, it is even more obvious that organisations are ambiguous about the transparency ideal, even when they officially celebrate it. For instance, we know that organisations carefully select, simplify and summarise data before they are revealed, that they selectively disclose or leak information, for example through 'competitive signalling', and that they shrewdly manage the *timing* of disclosure, sometimes with the intention of deflecting critique or handling potential issues (Heil and Robertson, 1991). Moreover, it is well known that producers and custodians of data often shift the medium, the classification scheme or the level of comparisons when forced to share information that used to be confidential (Fenster, 2006). Think, for example, of open health records at hospitals. When doctors' comments about patients and their maladies are no longer confidential but available to the patients themselves (and perhaps also to their families), there is a great chance that the use of words and formulations will change. And while such change may protect the doctors against lawsuits, it may not always bring increased insight for patients. Similarly, it is not uncommon that employees and representatives of organisations handle imperatives for transparency by working around data requests in various ways, concealing as much as they make visible. Practices for doing that may include *strategic ambiguity*, where information is provided only in rather vague and imprecise terms, or *consistency policies*, where requests for transparency are handled by delivering

uniform corporate messages that present the organisation as coherent mono-
liths not to be questioned. These two practices are unfolded in the following.

In complex and turbulent environments with many different and sometimes
hostile audiences, it is often necessary for organisations and their communicators to cultivate ambiguity because it allows them to strike a balance between
being understood, maintaining a specific self-image and not offending others.
Strategic ambiguity refers to the practice of purposely using ambiguity to
accomplish strategic goals (Eisenberg, 1984). By making it possible for organisations to address several different audiences with the same message, the
strategic use of ambiguity helps organisations avoid revealing confidential
details while giving off the impression of openness and dialogue with internal
and external stakeholders. Strategic ambiguity, in other words, allows organisations to express *and* protect, reveal *and* conceal. And while this may sometimes be a deliberate strategy of power designed to keep critical stakeholders at
bay, it can also be a necessary approach when precise goals are unclear, when
new ideas are being explored or when management is trying to 'test the waters'
before new initiatives are implemented. In all such situations, 'full' transparency may slow down or even entirely inhibit processes of investigation and
learning, thus keeping organisations from finding new solutions and pushing
themselves towards different or innovative practices.

When transparency demands are imposed in spite of such difficulties, new
types of closure and opacity may arise, both as a reaction to the demand for
stakeholder insight and as a proactive mode of strategic protection. Many
contemporary organisations, for example, seek to handle the growing pressure
for transparency through *policies of consistency*, that is, by formalising and
integrating all communication flows and pursuing uniformity in everything they
say and do. Faced with critical media and journalists zealously looking for
gaps, contradictions and ambiguities in corporate messages, organisations and
institutions across sectors are focused on producing consistent messages for
both internal and external audiences. Although consistency may sound desirable, it simultaneously implies that certain voices, perspectives and accounts
are silenced or squeezed out. Organisations, thus, tend to use transparency
claims to discipline organisational messages and voices. While members of
political parties, for example, are expected to articulate only the official voice of
the party, corporations increasingly limit the voice to an official spokesperson,
especially in times of crisis, and then try to align all messaging throughout the
organisation. While it is understandable that organisations may want to present
themselves as coherent and rational entities that speak with more or less the
same voice, consistency policies do not necessarily serve to fulfil complex and
potentially contradictory stakeholder expectations and transparency demands.
Consequently, in the name of transparency, organisations produce new types of
closure and, eventually, opacity (Christensen and Langer, 2009).

It is tempting to conclude that organisations do not want transparency at all –
even when they officially celebrate it (as also illustrated by the glass façades of

corporate headquarters; Zyglidopoulos and Fleming, 2011). Yet, even when organisations have a sincere interest in delivering accurate descriptions of themselves, that is, even when the resultant opacity is unintentional, there is simply no neutral or purely objective way of (re)presenting an organisation; instead, there is always a perspective implied if not explicitly offered, for example in the selection of what counts as good, comprehensive or accurate information. Presenting is inevitably selecting, and any claim of delivering a true picture of an organisation is therefore met with suspicion: what is hidden behind what is made visible? As an imperative, thus, the transparency ideal puts regulators, policy-makers and corporate communicators in a bind where they risk pursuing the ideal in a way that undermines or at least circumvents itself.

14.8 Productive Effects of Transparency

The general premise in most discussions on transparency is that transparency serves – or rather *ought* to serve – as a tool to present organisations as they really 'are'. Transparency, in this view, is not supposed to *do* anything, except generate access and facilitate clarity through a more or less passive and 'neutral' conveyance of organisational facts.

However, communication itself is not passive – it inherently *does* things. To describe an organisation is simultaneously to *create* it in a number of significant ways. Speech act theory, for example, has taught us that utterances have performative qualities in the sense that they not only represent but also fundamentally (co-)create and shape social reality (Austin, 1962). For instance, an 'apology' is a typical form of a speech act: To say 'I want to apologise' is in fact to *do* it. Speech act theory is in line with philosophers of language who reminded us that words are not neutral, but have the capacity to direct our attention, shape our perception and engage us in new types of ideals and activities. Words tend to orientate their utterer as well as the audience towards certain dimensions of reality while downplaying or ignoring others. They shape what we see and what we are able to imagine. And since language carries within itself a source of light that helps illuminate certain dimensions of reality, it simultaneously and inevitably keeps other dimensions in the dark.

Drawing on these insights, contemporary scholars of communication have emphasised also that organisations are fundamentally constituted and formed by communication, for example, through the ways in which leaders and organisational members speak about and account for organisational decisions and activities. Organisations, in this view, are not given in advance of talk or seen to exist outside communicative practices, but are 'precarious accomplishments' realised *in* and *through* communication (Cooren, Kuhn, Cornelissen and Clark, 2011: 1150; see also Chapter 11). In other words, the ways organisations talk about themselves and their practices are never neutral undertakings but constitutive activities that contribute to the continuous creation of organisational realities through the articulation of ideals, values and horizons.

Following this line of thinking, we are able to acknowledge that transparency is not a passive conduit through which organisations simply convey the reality of corporate or institutional affairs to their surroundings. Rather, transparency is 'performative' in the sense that it influences the attention and behaviours of those who are subjected to it, altering their perceptions and predilections and shaping their preferred ways of describing and presenting themselves. This we see, for instance, when number-based transparency regimes, such as rankings and evaluations, are implemented. Such regimes do more than render qualitative phenomena countable and comparable. By working back on those who have to report on their behaviours and accomplishments in such regimes, rankings and evaluations impose a specific type of order on their activities, promoting certain types of behaviour while squeezing out others (Hansen, Christensen and Flyvebom, 2015). By determining what is important to inform stakeholders about – and what is not so important – transparency regimes not only increase insight but also and simultaneously produce organisations in a new shape.

Thus, there are many unexpected and sometimes highly problematic effects associated with transparency. Although transparency governance ostensibly serves the interest of increased social responsibility, the performative consequences of information disclosures are multiple, equivocal and often inconclusive for organisations and society. In particular, the tendency for transparency strategies to produce opacity as well as insight is significant and deserves further attention and elaboration. Before we can accomplish that, however, we need to take a closer look at corporate talk and its function in the process of making organisations more transparent and, eventually, more responsible.

14.9 Corporate Talk as Inspiration, Exploration and Aspiration

When asked to describe themselves in order to facilitate insight and transparency, social actors such as organisations first need to work out 'who' they are and how they can be described. Even when the intention of the communicator – which is often the manager – is to provide a precise rendition of the organisation, a desire for accuracy may not be the primary driver. When attempting to present the organisation 'as it is', the communicator seeks to recreate a collective understanding of the organisation in a way that makes sense in terms of how the organisation prefers to see itself and inspire further action. Acknowledging that the reality of organisation is always contested, Shotter writes: 'our talk is not about something which already actually exists, but is about what might be, what could be the case, or what something should be like' (Shotter, 1993: 153). Even though the situation in which many organisations find themselves is shaped by disorderly and incoherent events, managers must conjure up believable and inspiring images that can motivate personnel to improve daily practices and inspire top management to set new goals and standards. As a consequence, organisational self-descriptions are often shaped by *idealisation*. If such tendency is widespread and common, corporate talk may not be able to fully serve the interest of transparency.

Before we chastise such behaviour, however, it is important to recognise that information disclosures not only serve as communication to external audiences calling for more transparency and insight into corporate and political matters. In fact, external interest in specific disclosure messages may not be a widespread and common feature. Senders themselves, however, are usually highly involved in their own messages, using them to confirm and celebrate existing identities and preferred self-images, and to inspire themselves to embark on new and better practices. Such autocommunication is necessary to stimulate organisational coherence and membership engagement (Christensen, 1997). Organisations autocommunicate not because there is a widespread desire in the organisation to see and share precise descriptions of organisational reality, but because organisations want and need inspiring images of themselves – images that can help them to discover new avenues of action and seduce themselves to change and improve current practices.

In addition to such inspirational and explorational qualities of organisational information disclosures, self-descriptions also serve *aspirational* purposes. In describing themselves, organisations not only discover who they are, but also who they would like to *become*. With their notion of aspirational talk, understood as communication which current organisational practices cannot yet live up to, Christensen, Morsing and Thyssen argue that aspirations are important drivers of better practices, not the least in the areas of sustainability and CSR where precise standards and points of measurement are often missing (Christensen, Morsing and Thyssen, 2013). While accurate descriptions of organisational practices in these areas may satisfy some stakeholder demands for truth and insight, accurate descriptions may simultaneously demotivate organisational members and prevent better practices from being imagined, explored and implemented. The articulation of organisational ambitions in the area of CSR, the authors argue, is essential in stimulating new insight and moving organisations forward towards higher CSR standards and better practices. As Lundheim puts it:

> If you dress things up a little – that is, begin to tell the company's CSR story – it can affect, positively, how you feel and act. It can have other consequences as well. CSR communication can be deceptive and harmful, and it can be a magic, albeit misleading wand in the social

creation of reality. A tint of gloss and window-dressing is surely
guaranteed to make critics eager to peep through the curtains and soon,
more windows may be flung open than you could have imagined or
wished for. Yet, if you are sufficiently brave or cheeky to communicate
a few inches ahead of the actual state of affairs, as a CSR professional
you can help to assure that reality follows suit. If visionary leaders
hadn't had the nerve to dream and talk ahead of reality, many important
innovations would not have occurred. (Lundheim, 2005: 7)

The problem with aspirational talk, of course, is that corporate CSR aspirations do not unfold automatically or predictably into better CSR initiatives.
Talk, in other words, is not enough to trigger changes, no matter how ambitious
it may be. Constant pressure from critical media, stakeholders and NGOs is
needed to make sure that organisations do not simply use aspirational talk to
hold on to irresponsible practices. Yet, such talk – even if it defies the value of
accuracy and transparency – is nonetheless essential to instigate significant
changes. Corporate CSR aspirations, especially when announced in public
media of high status and authority, help define a collective 'horizon' of
excellence to which employees, NGOs and other stakeholders can hold the
organisation accountable.

If major organisations, out of fear of being caught in exaggerations, impre-
cisions and inconsistencies, abstain from articulating their CSR ambitions out
loud, then changes in that arena will most likely take place at a much slower
pace, if at all. From that perspective, the propensity of some critical audiences
to debunk virtually all corporate CSR talk a priori as 'greenwashing',
'window-dressing' or manipulative hypocrisy, because it does not provide
accurate descriptions of organisational reality and is not particularly constructive (Lundheim, 2005). While a critical attitude is essential in keeping corporate
communicators on their toes in terms of taking their own words seriously and,
thus, begin implementing practices that reflect those words, the area of CSR
stands to lose if major corporations keep their aspirations to themselves
because they are afraid of promising too much.

Let us consider an example: Livesey and Graham's study of Royal Dutch
Shell illustrates how corporate communication has the potential to influence an
organisation to change its behaviours to become more socially or environmentally responsible (Livesey and Graham, 2007). They claim that the talk of
large corporations may transform not only the perceptions but also the actual
practices of different social actors, including themselves: 'Corporate eco-talk
participates in (re)creating the firm and (re)constructing its relationship to
nature, while opening up novel possibilities of understanding and action at
the societal level' (ibid.: 336). Studying how eco-talk emerged in the Royal
Dutch/Shell Group after years of intense stakeholder criticism, Livesey and
Graham demonstrate how such talk became a creative force in pushing the
corporation towards more sustainable practices. Rather than seeing eco-talk

and other corporate initiatives in the area of sustainable development as simply public relations manoeuvres, the authors focus on the performative, pragmatic dimensions of language use and communication. For instance, by stimulating discursive shifts, changing social expectations and moving towards new environmental practice, Shell's adoption of a new way of talking about sustainability influenced the wider array of choices made by the corporation. The authors, thus, insist that what we think and say about sustainability and other dimensions of social responsibility – even when our utterances are occasionally contradictory or banal – matters in the process of shaping and adapting to new situations in our social and natural environments.

Although we should of course continue to demand transparency and be critical of what organisations say or do, especially with respect to topics such as social responsibility and sustainability, we may need to allow organisations to experiment with the ways they communicate about these and related issues. Such latitude not only allows them to find new solutions for themselves and their own organisational practices, but also help society at large discover new ideals, goals and healthy practices (see also Christensen et al., 2013).

14.10 The Function of Opacity

Our discussion so far has significant implications for our understanding of transparency and its potential role and value in stimulating socially responsible behaviours. On the one hand, one may argue that some sense of transparency is necessary to trigger self-evaluative steps among corporate actors. Knowing that the external world is watching and is able to follow and evaluate the organisation and its moves is likely to trigger some level of self-discipline among corporate actors. On the other hand, 'full' transparency is hard to accomplish in practice, as we have argued above. Furthermore, the transparency imperative may cause organisations to hold back on their ambitions. And while such restraint may provide some protection against blatantly self-celebratory corporate messages, it also means that fewer ideals and ambitions are going to be revealed and aired in the first place, thus leaving potentials for organisational and social change unused. In this regard, demands for corporate transparency may discourage or delay the development of new and better practices on the responsibility and sustainability arenas.

In line with this latter view, Haack and Schoeneborn argued, counter-intuitively, that opacity may under certain circumstances facilitate the development of *more* responsible practices (Haack and Schoeneborn, 2015). More specifically, the authors suggest that the implementation of CSR policies can be expected to be highest in an industry characterised by an initial state of (transitional) opacity (i.e. where external observers lack possibilities to fully assess whether CSR policies are adopted in actual business practices). If an initial state of opacity is followed by a *gradual* process towards increased transparency, it is more likely to ensure a deeply entrenched implementation of new CSR policies than an industry facing continuously high demands for transparency right from the start. This argument is based on the assumption that initial opacity lowers the bar for firms to engage with a CSR policy in the first place. As such, initial opacity increases the likelihood of reaching a critical mass of firms that allegedly adopt the policy. Moreover, and as we shall argue further below, these conditions tend to urge organisations to enter a communicative pathway towards stronger engagement with the policy. These theoretical considerations are informed by an earlier empirical case study by the same authors (see also the case study below on the 'Equator Principles' (EP)). More generally, these considerations have important implications for how to govern responsible business, as they suggest that a 'nurturant parent' model of governance is likely to be more effective than a 'strict father' model of transnational governance (see also Haack and Scherer, 2014). While the former allows governance-takers certain degrees of leeway and opacity, the latter implies a more thorough monitoring and sanctioning of governance-takers regarding their rule compliance. As such, the latter may inhibit firms from engaging in CSR activities to begin with.

In the following section, we illustrate these considerations by drawing on findings from an empirical study (Haack, Schoeneborn and Wickert, 2012) on the EP, a voluntary and self-regulatory CSR standard in the field of international project finance (IPF). IPF is a particular segment of the financial industry in which banks lend money to finance large infrastructure projects (e.g. building a river dam or a pipeline).

14.11 Case Study: The 'Equator Principles' Standard

The EP standard was established in 2003 by financial institutions operating in the IPF field (e.g. Credit Suisse, the Royal Bank of Scotland, and UniCredit) because these banks saw themselves under increasing pressure by societal observers (including the NGO network BankTrack) to legitimise their lending practices and to consider the actual social and environmental impact of the projects they are financing. Accordingly, the EP standard was introduced in an effort of industry self-regulation. The EP comprises a list of ten social and environmental criteria that EP-adopting banks need to follow whenever they lend money to a large infrastructure project.

The EP standard is generally seen as a 'success story' with regards to the *breadth* of the standard, i.e. its diffusion among financial institutions operating in the IPF field, given that (in 2008) more than 90 per cent of money-lending in the IPF field was executed in alignment with the EP criteria. This broad diffusion of the EP in the IPF field is also due to the special set-up of the standard: large infrastructure projects are typically financed by a *consortium* that involves several banks. Within each consortium, it only takes one EP-adopting bank to bring the CSR standard into effect (i.e. in this case, the money-lending will be contingent upon the project's compliance with the EP criteria).

However, at the same time, the EP standard has been criticised by societal observers (e.g. NGOs engaged in the BankTrack network) as being rather 'toothless' with regards to the *depth* of the standard, i.e. its actual implementation into concrete organisational practices and procedures. More specifically, critics point out that the EP standard makes it too easy for banks to *adopt* the standard (i.e. simply by proclaiming its adoption, e.g. in the form of a press release), while leaving it ultimately unclear and opaque for external observers (such as NGOs) to assess the degree to which the EP standard is substantially implemented in actual business practices.

In their empirical study, Haack et al. (2012) investigated the diffusion of the EP standards in the IPF field. Importantly, the findings of their study challenge the common assumption that a rigid and strictly enforced standard with high transparency requirements (what Haack and Scherer, 2014, called the 'strict father' model of governance) is best suited to make sure that firms 'walk the talk' in implementing CSR policies. To the contrary, the EP standard, at least in its initial set-up, can be seen as a rather soft standard with low transparency requirements (i.e. the 'nurturant parent' model of governance; see Haack and Scherer, 2014). Despite this character of the EP, the study by Haack et al. (2012) demonstrates that the banks operating in the IPF field nevertheless entered a pathway of communicative negotiations with NGOs and other critical observers (e.g. the media) that ultimately led them *step-by-step* towards a deeper implementation of the EP into organisational practices and procedures. Importantly, the authors argue that the initial conditions of a rather 'soft' standard with low transparency requirements was an essential precondition for this process to occur in the first place, as it allowed for low entry barriers to 'join the club' of EP-adopting banks. Within the growing club of EP adopters, some banks tried to differentiate themselves from their competitors by claiming in public statements to be the 'real' EP adopters, that is, the ones who *substantively* adopt the standard. In turn, by engaging in such public commitments (that typically took the form of promises of future in-depth EP implementation), these banks entered what Haack et al. (2012) called a process of 'creeping commitment'; in other words, the public expression of CSR ambitions created a situation where they can be held accountable for their promises and thus would need to live up to them at some point, if they want to retain their legitimacy.

To conclude, Haack et al.'s study (2012) implies that the EP standard's success was made possible exactly because the banks were (initially) able to operate under conditions of limited transparency – conditions that allowed them to communicatively explore the new reality of CSR practices without being forced into immediate implementation. In that sense, opacity was an important precondition for a process where banks 'talked themselves into' a new CSR reality. For managing CSR in practice, their study implies that CSR managers can make strategic use of public commitments to CSR ambitions in order to facilitate intra-organisational change towards in-depth CSR policy implementation (see also the notion of 'aspirational talk' by Christensen et al., 2013). For the practice of NGO activists, this research furthermore advises to 'cut firms some slack' at least in the beginning of CSR policy implementation processes, and slowly, steadily and carefully increase the demands for transparency.

Questions for Discussion

1. Should organisations always be forced to walk their talk? Why? Or why not?
2. Why may organisations experience a 'creeping commitment' to their own ideals and words?
3. What is the role of NGOs and CSR managers in this process?

14.12 Chapter Summary

In this chapter we have presented the mainstream idea of transparency as well as providing a more differentiated and sophisticated view on the role of transparency in the context of CSR governance and CSR communication. We are aware that our argumentation stands in contrast to conventional views that regard 'full transparency' as necessary to govern responsible business. Yet, while we sympathise with calls for transparency in general, our considerations in this chapter aim to show that the transparency imperative is problematic as soon as the detrimental effects of transparency regimes on corporate conduct are neglected or when transparency becomes an end in itself (Christensen and Cheney, 2015; Hansen and Flyverbom, 2015). Taking transparency seriously requires acknowledging that transparency is not a 'neutral' tool through which organisational practices simply become more visible and clear. Transparency practices are performative, in the sense that they *do* something, including changing the behaviours of the social actors subjected to it.

This change in perspective also yields important implications for 'governance-makers' and 'governance-takers' in practice (see terminology used in

Chapter 1). Studies (such as Haack et al., 2012) imply that 'governance-makers' (e.g. governments, NGOs, etc.), can best support an in-depth implementation of CSR practices in business firms by tolerating and encouraging experimentations that allow for mutual learning and dialogue, instead of unconditionally sanctioning firms for not 'walking the talk' as soon as the words are uttered (see also Haack and Scherer, 2014). For 'governance-takers' (e.g. CSR managers in business firms), studies such as Christensen et al. (2013) or Haack et al. (2012) imply that (intra)organisational change can be fostered by engaging in dialogues with NGOs and expressing aspirations and commitments in public forums because talk in such forums tend to bind organisational members to live up to the promises. In that regard, our considerations imply that CSR managers should embrace (rather than shut down) oppositional voices. Through the power of 'autocommunication' (Christensen, 1997), the public expression of corporate commitments provide the chance for facilitating organisational and societal transformations. Our focus on the promises and perils of transparency governance, thus, invite readers to acknowledge the constitutive and formative role of communication for the relations between organisations and society.

Chapter Questions

1. In which areas do *you* encounter the transparency ideal in practice?
2. How can organisations be urged to share more information with their stakeholders?
3. We have listed a number of issues that organisations need to consider before they share information with their stakeholders. Can you think of additional issues or concerns that need to be taken into consideration?
4. Do you share all information about yourself on social media? What are the limitations?
5. We may expect organisations to share information *more* openly than individuals. Why?

FURTHER RESOURCES

Florini, A. (2007). *The Right to Know. Transparency for an Open World*.
New York: Columbia University Press.
An introduction to the many different dimensions of transparency, including human rights, law making, financial institutions, security and sustainability.

Henriques, A. (2007). *Corporate Truth. The Limits to Transparency*. London: Earthscan.
A fascinating critique of transparency – including issues of ethics, reporting, taxation and corruption – written by a consultant.

Hood, C. and Heald, D. (Eds.) (2006). *Transparency. The Key to Better Governance?* Oxford, UK: Oxford University Press.
A collection of research papers that discuss the promises and perils of transparency in the context of governance.

Lord, K. M. (2006). *The Perils and Promise of Global Transparency*. Albany, NY: SUNY Press.
A discussion of transparency from a political theory perspective, focusing on issues such as peace, conflict and democracy.

Personal Reflection by *Daniel Mittler*

Changing Corporations the Greenpeace Way – And the Continuing Need for Global Regulation

Greenpeace started in the 1970s as a movement against nuclear weapons being tested by the US government in Alaska. But very soon after the birth of our movement, we became known not just for saving whales, but also for exposing corporate crimes and pollution. We dragged those companies dumping nuclear and toxic waste into the world's oceans into the public spotlight and ended this destructive business. In the 1990s, we fought the plan by Shell (and others) to use the North Sea as the dumping ground for oil platforms such as the Brent Spar – and achieved the prohibition of this practice.

Today, therefore, most people think of Greenpeace as a business adversary. Indeed, in some MBA courses, Greenpeace is referred to as a business risk. When it comes to destructive businesses, we take pride in being perceived that way. We absolutely do want to make destroying our children's future too risky to be worth thinking about. And we take that message to all who can make crucial investment decisions. For example, we show in detailed studies that Arctic drilling is unlikely to be a profitable proposition – at the same time as we take peaceful direct action e.g. against Shell icebreakers aiming to explore for oil in the Arctic. We inform investors how dwindling tuna stocks make firms such as Dongwon from South Korea a bad investment, while also taking direct, peaceful action at sea to disrupt destructive tuna practices in the Indian Ocean.

But while we are proud to disrupt destructive business, we also actively support the solutions the world needs. I am sometimes frustrated that this side of what we do is less well known. Indeed, at Greenpeace, *we never say no without offering an alternative!*

We invited to Daniel Mittler to reflect on the influence of communication in setting an agenda on CSR and engaging corporations in this dialogue. Mr Mittler is the Political Director of Greenpeace International. He has been an activist since his youth and has held positions in a number of non-governmental organisations (NGOs). Before joining Greenpeace International, he was Head of the Germany Programme at the European Climate Foundation where he helped to stop the construction of ten new coal plants.

That's why we have teamed up with the renewables industry to set out a plan to deliver clean energy for all and cut climate damaging gases – our so-called Energy Revolution scenario. This scenario has turned out to be the most accurate of all when it comes to predicting the recent boom in solar energy. We support communities from Papua New Guinea to Canada in managing their forests sustainably, not for short-term profits. And we back ecological farming practices that keep control over the food we eat in the hands of farmers, not the giant corporations that currently control over two-thirds of the world's agriculture trade.

We want governments to outlaw destructive practices, from dangerous chemicals to nuclear power. As a step in the right direction, we aim to make corporations fully liable for their social and environmental impacts, including the impacts of their supply chains. For example, we are asking the governments of India and Japan to uncap liability limits for the nuclear industry (making the industry pay for the full risks they impose on us all). We are also urging legal action against those corporations most responsible for the global climate crisis, such as the recent decision by the Commission on Human Rights in the Philippines to investigate fifty polluters for their role in creating destructive climate change.

We are so committed to getting the solutions the world needs adopted quickly, that we are willing to praise corporations that – as a whole – are still part of the problem, if they do take (some of) the right steps. We welcome it when supermarkets and giant food traders stop selling overfished fish species, eliminate pesticides or do without genetically modified crops. We do so even if their overall ecological impact remains negative and we continue to oppose their excessive power over small fisher people and farmers. We say 'well done' to Coca-Cola, for example, for eliminating climate-damaging refrigerants from their cooling equipment, because the benefits for our climate and future generations are significant and real. Or we praise Adidas or H&M when they eliminate toxic chemicals from the supply chains of their products, because that brings real benefits to the people dependent on the Chinese and Mexican rivers currently being poisoned for 'fast fashion'. But we always do so in the context of our demanding more fundamental change. We do so, as a step to the long-term goal: clean production, globally, enshrined by law.

Because protecting our future is popular, more and more corporations pretend to do the right thing. Greenpeace therefore also plays a role in helping consumers and citizens distinguish between the genuine steps forward some companies are taking and the shameful 'greenwash' which too many engage in every day. We can do so credibly because we will never endorse a brand as a whole and will never accept money from corporations (or governments).

Many, especially in business schools, try to understand and classify the 'Greenpeace corporate campaign method'. But our aim is to continuously innovate – and to surprise our opponents. Being unpredictable is indeed, at least as I see it, one key element of the 'Greenpeace method'.

Let me summarise my personal list characterising that method:

1. **Our work is visual.** Robert Hunter, one of the founders of Greenpeace, spoke of throwing (peaceful) 'mind bombs' and by doing so changing the conversation of society. That we do to this day. Pictures of pipes blowing out dirt or of heavy air pollution simply work better to wake up decision-makers and the public to the need for change than *only* learned analyses showing that there is a problem. The combination of 'killer facts' – facts that show the case for change without doubt – combined with visuals illustrating them is something we strive for.

2. **Fit for purpose.** Our principle is to deploy the best available tactics based on detailed research and analysis of the sector, company and issue we seek to influence. Planning a campaign to Green Apple or a campaign to stop the commercialisation of genetically engineered rice in China could not be more different in many ways. But they are the same, in the sense that you need to analyse your 'target' as accurately and effectively as you can. We sometimes spend years doing research before we find a 'lever' that we think can deliver real change. What effective levers are, depends on what you are trying to shift. In the case of Apple, for example, we realised that we needed to appeal to the Apple fanbase to effect change at Apple. Steve Jobs at the time of our 'Green My Apple' campaign was still making all the key decisions at Apple, and the Apple fanbase was the one community that could shift his mind. In contrast, when we were running a campaign on eliminating toxic ship paints, our target audience was often a very small number of technical magazines covering ship matters. It was (negative) coverage in those magazines that toxic paint producers were worried about because they directly influenced market decisions.

3. **Solutions.** Our commitment to solutions is the reason why so often our confrontations with businesses end in cooperation over time. The work *with* Coca-Cola to eliminate climate-damaging gases (so-called F gases) from cooling systems, for example, started as a *brand attack* on Coca-Cola who were providing the 'green Sydney Olympics' with cooling equipment that destroyed our climate. Similarly, a (successful) campaign asking Nestlé – via a viral campaign video linking KitKat with forest destruction – to cut its ties with Golden Agri Resources because of their destructive palm oil practices resulted in us – years later – working with palm oil producers in Indonesia to try and find a sustainable way forward.

4. **Integrity.** Some argue that they need to work in direct partnership with corporations as the only realistic way to achieve change and see it as only right and proper that business would fund such partnerships. Our experience is the opposite. When I talk of 'cooperation' with business in the previous paragraph, this working together never entails Greenpeace getting any money. And in my experience, it is this integrity that makes us

strong. We will never endorse a brand as a whole and will never accept money from corporations (or governments). Therefore, nobody can even *dream* of claiming that we only say something is good for people or the planet in order to receive corporate donations. Part of integrity is of course accuracy. Greenpeace has its own Science Unit and issue experts across the organisation, because we know we are only as strong as our claims are accurate.

5. **No permanent enemies, no permanent friends.** Fit for purpose strategies are the key to impact (see point 2 above). If you do the same thing again and again, that predictability will become your weakness (even if your execution of the campaign is excellent). The 'other' side will be prepared for your next move, or failing that, will be able – soon after you start your campaign – to decipher an effective counter-strategy based on previous experiences. That's why we are deliberately unpredictable. Just because we praise a corporation one day, does not mean that we will not attack it the next. Indeed, we always reserve the right to attack a company that we work with on one issue on another. When Coca-Cola opposes a much needed recycling scheme in Australia, for example, we run a harsh campaign criticising them for this stance – while continuing to work with them on eliminating climate-damaging coolants.

6. **Seeking fundamental change, not just 'a slightly greener product'.** Our strategies always aim for fundamental change. When we ask a toy company such as Mattel, for example, to change their packaging for Barbie dolls, our long-term aim is not (just) about Mattel, Barbie or more informed consumers, but to improve the pulp, paper and packaging sector as a whole (a process that is now underway). Whenever possible, we also link demands on individual corporations and demands for (better and better implemented) regulation. In Indonesia, for example, we identified that certain businesses were not just destructive in their operations but also preventing good forest protection laws. So exposing their individual bad practices was (and is) part and parcel of – at the same time – shifting power to allow for better, and more effective, forest legislation.

While many are pessimistic about the achievement of globally binding legislation, we at Greenpeace are campaigning for a future in which *binding legislation with teeth* will provide a long-term way to secure a safer future for us and the planet we depend on. *Our aim is a world in which governments ensure the rights of all to a decent environment by effectively regulating corporate behaviour.* And why should this be just a dream?

Global regulations with teeth are clearly possible – they exist! The World Trade Organization (WTO), for example, can impose punitive fines on countries that break its rules. In contrast, environmental institutions such as the UN Environment Programme (UNEP) can only plead, coach and build capacity.

But there is nothing inevitable about this. Institutions are created by people and so we, the people, can decide to create equally strong governance systems for the environment and social justice as we have created for trade. Only once we have such a global governance system ensuring that we operate within planetary boundaries, will Greenpeace campaigns attacking destructive business behaviour and forcing green solutions stop being necessary.

PART IV

THE GOVERNANCE OF TRANSNATIONAL ISSUES

Introduction from the Editors

The final part of this textbook looks at the underlying issues that corporations manage when addressing corporate social responsibility (CSR). Unlike other textbooks, which often focus mostly on CSR as a concept and its link to different stakeholder groups, we believe that emphasising real-life issues such as labour rights and corruption is critical. Without knowledge about such issue areas, it is hard to understand how CSR looks like in practice and how it is 'lived' in corporations.

Chapter 15 outlines the debate around business and human rights. Karin Buhmann and Florian Wettstein look at what human rights mean, both in general and in the particular context of corporations. Their chapter shows why non-state actors need to take human rights concerns seriously and how this debate relates to CSR. Most of all, they revisit a number of regulatory and policy frameworks that businesses need to be familiar with when managing for business and human rights, such as the United Nations Guiding Principles on Human Rights. Putting such a policy framework into action is still a challenge for many companies, as they often lack the capacity and the knowledge. The chapter shows how such challenges can be overcome.

The next chapter (16) by Hans Krause Hansen on corruption looks at one of the most neglected CSR topics. While much has been written about social and environmental problems, few people have made the link between CSR and corruption. Hansen starts by clarifying what corruption is and why it constitutes a problem for corporations and nation states. He then looks into different ways to fight corruption, ranging from state-based efforts (e.g. through extraterritorial law) to voluntary CSR-based initiatives (e.g. the Extractive Industries Transparency Initiative (EITI)). This chapter shows how widespread corruption still is and what companies can do to prevent it.

Chapter 17 by Stefano Ponte, René Toudal Poulsen and Jane Lister focuses on environmental problems. It shows the various challenges that businesses face when addressing the environmental impact of their activities (e.g. the global nature of value and supply chains). Ponte et al. discuss how far firms' environmental strategies may align with and/or clash with emerging environmental regulations on the national and international level. This discussion is important, as it reveals the difficulties of harmonising firms' CSR strategies and the policy-making by regulators. Finally, this chapter also identifies which factors influence the dissemination of environmental performance demands up and down the value chain.

The final chapter, by Dirk Ulrich Gilbert and Kristin Huber, revisits one of the 'hot' topics in CSR: the debate around labour rights in global supply chains. Driven by highly publicised scandals such as Nike in the 1990s and the Bangladesh Rana Plaza factory collapse in 2013, the authors outline what kind of labour rights violations are common in factories that supply global brand name companies. They discuss arguments that are usually raised for and against sweatshops. This debate is critical, as it shows that CSR problems can be evaluated from quite different moral points of view.

15

Business and Human Rights: Not Just Another CSR Issue?

KARIN BUHMANN AND FLORIAN WETTSTEIN

Learning Objectives

- Gain an understanding of the background, drivers, key actors and stakeholders, and key normative and guiding instruments of the business and human rights (BHR) regime.
- Gain an understanding of the philosophical and legal framework of human rights relevant to social expectations and regulatory developments of business responsibilities for human rights.
- Gain an understanding of what sets the BHR regime apart from general corporate social responsibility (CSR) due to its explicit normative guidance in international human rights law and explicit connection to public regulation of businesses through soft, hard and 'smart-mix' regulation.
- Gain an understanding of human rights due diligence (HRDD), enabling you to undertake a basic assessment of a human rights dilemma or conflict facing a business with regard to itself or its business relations in the value chain.
- Gain an understanding of remedy and accountability mechanisms related to business impact on human rights.
- Gain an understanding and competence to analyse and identify BHR issues, assess human rights dilemmas and conflicts in the value chain, and propose how to handle those in accordance with the United Nations Guiding Principles on Business and Human Rights (UNGPs).

15.1 Introduction

BHR may be regarded as part of CSR, or as a distinct current of corporate responsibility.

The idea that businesses should take responsibility for their impact on human rights or positively act to help the fulfilment of human rights is closely related to CSR and the moral underpinnings of business ethics, as well as the philosophical idea of human rights in their own right. Nevertheless, whether businesses have or should bear responsibility for human rights is contested and likely to remain so for some time. The international human rights regime, which was mainly developed in the twentieth century with a basis in international law, focuses on states as duty holders. The international economic regime, developed during the same period of time, has provided firms with considerable rights to make economic profits and few obligations in return. Since the mid-nineteenth century, civil society organisations have argued that businesses should take responsibility for their adverse impact on human rights. Evolving from movements against products made by slave labour or harming human life or health, civil society campaigns during the twentieth century came to argue that business should be responsible for taking action against production practices which harm employees' freedom of movement or health, or those in support of state-based institutionalised discrimination (such as the apartheid regime in South Africa or governmental endorsement of forced labour in Myanmar). Civil society organisations have also drawn attention to business impact on local communities' rights to access to land when an extractives firm desires to expand, and the human rights-related social impact of land-grabbing, frequently resulting from investment in biofuel. Some firms have agreed that business organisations have and should take responsibility for their impact on human rights. Others have insisted that if states are concerned with adverse business impact, they could put new or revised rules in place to regulate business conduct.

This chapter explores the business–human rights nexus and its tensions, challenges and opportunities. It provides an introduction to and overview of issues being discussed in regard to corporate human rights responsibility, guidance documents to help firms navigate social expectations on their human rights impact, and an increasing range of soft, hard and 'smart-mix' public regulation aiming to shape business conduct and impact on human rights. The chapter first looks at the idea and nature of human rights in general. It next reflects on the reasons – moral, managerial, political and legal – why human rights are relevant for business enterprises. Third, it explores the evolving international BHR regime as well as the concerns and initiatives that drive the BHR agenda, and moves on to introducing the UNGPs (UN, 2011) as a current key instrument offering human rights guidance for businesses. In this context, the chapter also discusses how the BHR regime is influencing broader CSR norms and guidance, followed by a section on operational issues and challenges that companies encounter. Finally, accountability and mechanisms for remedy are discussed, both on a state and business level. A case study is followed by a concluding summary and chapter questions.

15.2 What Are Human Rights?

Human rights are rights that derive from the inherent dignity of the human person. They are viewed to be unconditional, meaning that we have them merely by virtue of being human. This moral view underpins the international legal regime on human rights that has matured since the United Nations (UN) was established as an international organisation in 1945 with the protection and promotion of human rights as one of its core objectives (see Shelton, 2014: 7–13). This has resulted in a range of international declarations and treaties on human rights. The International Bill of Rights comprises the Universal Declaration of Human Rights (UDHR), adopted by the UN in 1948 (UN, 1948) and two international treaties, which set out the rights described by the UDHR in greater detail: the International Covenant on Economic, Social and Cultural Rights (ICESCR) (UN, 1966a) and the International Covenant on Civil and Political Rights (ICCPR) (UN, 1966b).

The UDHR has given rise to a number of other detailed international and regional legal instruments on human rights. Being developed by international organisations grounded in the state-centrist international law regime, these instruments typically create duties for states, but not for non-state actors such as private firms. Legally binding or hard law instruments typically include words such as 'treaty', 'convention' or 'covenant' in their title. Soft law instruments, which are not legally binding but are often perceived as morally or politically binding, typically include the word 'declaration', 'resolution', 'principle' or 'guideline' in their title. The principles set out in the International Labour Organization (ILO) *Declaration on Fundamental Principles and Rights at Work* (the 1998 ILO Declaration) (ILO, 1998) comprise freedom from discrimination, the right to collective bargaining and freedom of association (including freedom to form and belong to a trade union), the elimination of child labour, and the abolition of slavery, involuntary and forced labour. These freedoms and rights are considered *core labour rights*. The specific obligations of states and employers and rights of employees are described in details in eight treaties considered to be *ILO fundamental conventions*. The core labour rights are also mentioned in and covered by the International Bill of Rights. They are therefore considered human rights as well as labour rights. This illustrates the fact that human rights themselves and the international human rights instruments that set out the standards are both broad and deep. For example, the human right to the enjoyment of just and favourable conditions of work, which we find in Article 7 ICESCR, covers working standards in a broad sense and also specific issues that are set out in greater detail in the Covenant and ILO instruments, such as fair wages and equal remuneration, occupational health and safety, and reasonable limitation of working hours.

The UN Global Compact, which sets out ten principles for voluntary business conduct, refers to human rights in general in Principles 1 and 2, and the core labour rights in Principles 3–6.

Adopted in 2011, the UNGPs on Business and Human Rights understand human rights responsibilities of business enterprises as based on internationally recognised human rights. The UNGPs set out that business enterprises should, at a minimum, take account of the rights set forth in the International Bill of Rights and the 1998 ILO Declaration (ILO, 1998). Structured around the three 'pillars' of the state – duty to *protect*; the business responsibility to *respect*; access to *remedy* for victims – the UNGPs establish an inherent connection between the private and the public aspects of BHR. Along with their recommendations for a due diligence process to help business enterprises identify, prevent and mitigate adverse impact on human rights, the UNGPs have come to influence CSR normativity in a broader sense, as elaborated in the second half of this chapter after the detailed introduction to the UNGPs.

The legal regime is only a recent development in the long history of human rights, which evolved from moral, philosophical and political norms and thought developed in many nations and cultures. Modern human rights include elements that resonate with ideas of compassion and charity which chime with religious norms in many cultures around the world; with ideals on freedom from interference by powerful agents and opportunity to pursue ambitions and personal goals that were voiced by political philosophers such as Rousseau, Montesquieu and Hobbes; and with the ideal of freedom from want that resonates with socialist political philosophy. With human dignity at its core, the basic idea inherent in what we refer to as 'human rights' today is a global concern (see also Shelton, 2014: 1–44). Critique of human rights for being a Western construct belongs to the political value struggles of the late twentieth century, but do not reflect the multicultural participation in the group that drafted the UDHR.

We may distinguish between rights bearing the human rights 'label' and similar or related entitlements or claims found in philosophical or religious texts or currents. Understanding the human rights substance in terms of dignity, freedom from want and protection against abuse by powerful actors, rather than expecting human rights terminology, can help managers appreciate concerns of a human rights character and implement human rights in business practices in the context of a particular firm, sector and/or cultural background.

In the interface between philosophy and law, the roots of human rights can be found in the natural law tradition. This is a current within the philosophy of law, which holds that certain rights are naturally bestowed on human beings irrespective of what the actual law adopted by governments says. This can be somewhat confusing: how can a legal philosophy hold that certain rights overrule the adopted law? Yet, this is precisely the core of the idea of human rights: these rights are inherent, and persist even if regulators try to limit them through law.

Often, natural rights thinking had theological roots: natural rights were seen as pre-existing and to be 'discovered' by divine revelation. Modern natural rights thinking has been sceptical of such metaphysical justifications, and has replaced it with a reference to the human capacity to reason: human rights are thus not naturally bestowed, but are those rights that reasonable human beings ought to 'grant' to each other. Accordingly the term 'natural rights' is sometimes replaced with 'rational rights', referring to the idea that such rights derive from and can be discerned by appeal to human reason.

The idea of human rights as moral rights has always had its critics. Famously, the founder of utilitarianism, Jeremy Bentham, derided the thought as 'nonsense upon stilts'. 'From imaginary laws', as he proclaimed, 'come imaginary rights'; that is, only real laws can give rise to real rights. This position is echoed also by modern legal positivism. While it may endorse the idea of human rights as such, it rejects their quality as pre-legal, moral rights. Harvard philosopher and Nobel laureate Amartya Sen (2004) argues that beyond any legal stipulation of human rights, there is and must be also a philosophical justification. Human rights, as he argues, are 'quintessentially ethical articulations' which do not have to be legal claims at the same time. Again, this underscores that from the philosophical perspective human rights are inherent, whether or not they are accompanied by rights or claims established in law. The ideas and language of human rights gained strong ground in Japan after the country's opening to the world in the late nineteenth century and in pre-revolutionary China. Yet Confucianist ideals on exercise of power and provision of social goods had formed the ground (Buhmann, 2003).

Much of the origin of the modern notion of human rights is associated with the freedom from interference by a powerful agent. Human rights ideas played a key role in the struggle against absolutism in the seventeenth and eighteenth century. This is reflected in both the French revolution's Declaration of the Rights of Man (1789) and the American Declaration of Independence (1776). The writings of Karl Marx and the evolution of socialism added social and economic rights to civil and political rights. While the liberal human rights notion stressed freedom from interference, the socialist approach perceives human rights as claims held by individuals for specific goods to be provided by the state. This applies, for example, to rights to education, a decent standard of living and access to health services.

Traditionally, the state was seen to be the sole holder of obligations for human rights. This, too, is the approach that international human rights law and the International Bill of Rights have traditionally been seen to take. With globalisation and fast economic growth witnessed across the world, especially during the second half of the twentieth century and the early twenty-first century, firms – in particular multinational companies (MNCs) – extended their activities beyond the reach of the state and its powers to regulate. Non-state actors, and among them some companies, have become very powerful too. They may infringe on rights as well, and are increasingly subject to expectations to assume social responsibility or legal accountability commensurate to their economic and sometimes even political power.

Studies show that businesses are capable of infringing not only on the four core labour rights set out in the 1998 ILO Declaration, but on all human rights in the International Bill of Rights (UN, 2007). Accordingly, increasing attention has been given to potential human rights responsibilities of business enterprises in recent years. With human dignity as a core element, business responsibilities for human rights build on human rights developed in philosophy and law (Box 15.1).

15.3 Why Are Human Rights Relevant to Business?

The reasons why human rights matter to businesses include philosophically-based business ethics reasons; strategic, managerial, reputational and legal implications; as well as external political and governance reasons. The Rana Plaza collapse in 2013, which killed 1129 people and maimed many others, drew attention to the adverse human rights impacts of economic decisions to produce goods under cheap conditions which are unfortunately often substandard in terms of security, occupational health and safety, as well as salary, working hours and other working conditions. A fire in a Philippines shoe factory in May 2015, which killed around seventy people, underscored that business-caused human rights problems remain a pressing issue. The fact that those incidents are not rare but unfortunately common has called for critical assessments of decisions of certain firms (especially some multinational enterprises (MNEs)) to favour cheap production over safe working conditions. Often this is related to the existence of national 'governance gaps', which enable businesses to formally observe national rules and regulations but in reality operate under the radar of enforcement.

Recent decades have witnessed a surge in social expectations that businesses do not infringe on human rights of their employees and workers, neighbouring communities, suppliers or even customers. Reports on human rights problems may cause firms reputational problems, resulting in lost contracts with upstream buyers, delays in deliveries and disrupted relations with employees, suppliers and local communities (Ruggie, 2013). Allegations, proven responsibility or complicity in human rights infringements may cause investors to reduce their shares in the firm or to fully divest. Redressing such losses to the 'social licence to operate' may in turn require significant human and financial resources. Indeed, this forms an important reasoning of the UNGPs (Buhmann, 2015a).

As noted in the Introduction to this book, since the late twentieth century many of the world's largest economies are companies, rather than states. Such

| Box 15.1 | Overview of human rights in a business context |

Equality is a core idea in human rights philosophy and law, reflected in the general human rights principle of *non-discrimination*.[5] UDHR Article 1 spells out that 'all human beings are born free and equal in dignity and rights'. This has been carried over into detailed human rights instruments. Thus, there should be no distinction in the enjoyment of human rights on such grounds as race, colour, sex, language, religion, political or other opinion, national or social origin, property, birth or other status.

The rights to *life*, *liberty* and *security* are crucial for personal dignity and security. This includes the right to be *free from slavery, servitude, torture* or *cruel, inhumane or degrading treatment or punishment*. Several provisions in the UDHR deal with those rights, many of which are relevant to business operations and particularly to responsible supply chain management.

Rights protecting a person's *personal freedom* include privacy in matters relating to family, home, correspondence, reputation and honour, and freedom of movement. This matters to employers as rights of employees to be respected; and to firms in the IT sectors as rights that their products and services should not infringe upon. Personal freedom rights also include the *rights to seek asylum, to a nationality, to marry and found a family* and *to own property*, as well as *freedom of thought, conscience, religion, opinion* and *expression*. All of these may also be impacted by business practices, for example in relation to treatment of personal documents, resettlement as part of infrastructure development, employment practices influencing family life, and airlines' and other transport organisations' treatment of refugees.

Many aspects of the daily lives of people are concerns of *social, economic* and *cultural rights*, which form a large group. The right to *education* (including vocational training) is included in this group, as is the right to participate in the *cultural life* of the community, and to the protection of the *moral and material interests resulting from any scientific, literary or artistic production*. Among cultural rights, indigenous or other groups have a right to have their practices and special knowledge respected. This concerns, for example, knowledge of medicinal qualities of herbs that may be of interest to pharmaceutical companies for economic purposes. Such knowledge should be treated with respect and its usage rewarded.

While the right *to* work is a political aspiration, rights *in* work – working conditions – are economic and social rights of core relevance to business practices. These include equal pay for equal work and to just and favourable remuneration, ensuring for the worker and the worker's family an existence worthy of human dignity ('an adequate standard of living').

The right to form and join *trade unions*, the right to *rest and leisure*, reasonable limitations on *working hours* and periodic holidays with pay are other important work-related rights. The right to a *standard of living adequate for health and well-being, including food, clothing,*

---

[5] This overview of human rights partially draws on the UN Global Compact's broad presentation of human rights in a business context, based on the UDHR. Global Compact, 'Human Rights', https://www.unglobalcompact.org/AboutTheGC/TheTenPrinciples/humanRights.html, accessed 21 March 2015.

> *housing, and medical care* is of core relevance to employees and their families, and conse-
> quently to businesses and their supply chains. The right to (clean and safe) water has been
> interpreted to be encompassed in several other rights, including health rights and the right to
> an adequate standard of living.
>
> Rights to *social services* and *security* are human rights in their own rights, whose fulfilment
> may be influenced by working conditions, pay etc.

power comes with social expectations for actors to assume responsibility, based
in part on the idea that when firms start to rival states in terms of economic or
even political power, they should assume responsibilities commensurate to
those powers (Kobrin, 2009; Wettstein, 2009). Human rights, which as noted
are commonly viewed as a protection precisely from the abuse of power, are
chief among such expectations (Jägers, 2002; Ruggie, 2013).

Despite the moral imperative to respect human rights (Wettstein, 2012) and
the long-term costs of not respecting them, businesses sometimes focus on
short-term economic benefits from abusing human rights. *Strategic reasoning*
often deals with a so-called 'business case' for human rights responsibility,
which comes in two basic shapes. The negative business case stresses the
economic potential of respecting human rights. The argument is that this pays
off for the company because it reduces reputational risks or litigation risks. The
positive business case assumes that companies with proactive human rights
policies and initiatives benefit from enhanced reputation, from a better and
more motivated workforce, from decreasing staff fluctuation rates and so on.
In other words, managing human rights issues properly serves as risk and
opportunity management.

Political reasons for corporate human rights responsibility derive from the
increasingly challenging governance structure at the global level. The regulatory power of states is generally limited to their own territory, as a consequence
of the expansion of non-state actors such as companies beyond the borders of
the home state and tendencies of some MNCs to 'forum shop' to benefit from
or indeed exploit substandard protection of labour, environment, etc. Lack of
political will among states has been an obstacle for the international regulation
of businesses as regards human rights. Such governance gaps have fuelled
claims, often emerging in CSR contexts, that firms assume responsibility for
their impact and self-regulate (see Matten and Crane, 2005; Buhmann, 2006).

Legal aspects of BHR are more extensive than what is common for CSR, for
two reasons. First, BHR builds on a solid ground of normative guidance based
on international human rights law and sometimes also national law. Second,
the BHR regime – especially since the adoption of the UNGPs – makes an
explicit connection between the responsibility that companies have for human
rights, and the duty that states have to protect those rights. Recent years have
seen a surge in normative directives adopted by governments or international
organisations to promote CSR in firms. Whether in the form of guidance (soft

law), binding (hard law) or smart-mix forms of regulation (such as regulated self-regulation and incentives working through rewards rather than punishments), much of this public regulation aims at shaping business conduct in accordance with human rights (Buhmann, 2015a, 2015b).

A common way to regulate BHR between business partners is by integrating a code of conduct, containing requirements to respect human rights, into a contract with a business relation, or into a firm's contract with employees. Legal liability may arise if the business relation (e.g. a supplier) or employee does not observe the code of conduct, for example through neglect to exercise HRDD. A firm that incurs economic losses in its own value chain, for example due to reduced sales because a supplier violated a code of conduct prescribing respect for human rights, may be in a position to claim compensation in a national court. An employee, for example a manager of a local production unit, risks dismissal and claims for compensation if he or she breaks the code of conduct that was part of the employee's contract.

Public procurement and public contracting also shape business conduct. Governments across the globe are major buyers of a range of products used for their delivery of services. Examples include medical equipment such as operation gloves and medicines; office utensils and equipment such as pencils, papers, computers and printers; building and construction materials such as concrete, timber, bricks, marble and gravel; and services from operations to construction and private security services. This makes public procurement potentially a major economic factor to drive responsible production processes and supplies. Economic baseline criteria sometimes limit the options for public organisations to require socially responsible practices or products for potential bidders. The EU recently changed its public procurement directives to ease previous limitations on socially responsible procurement requirements.

Accountability is often seen as a reactive measure to disclose or punish actions after they occurred. But accountability may also carry proactive or 'prospective' aspects, by bringing attention to problems before they arise and thereby helping actors manage change, for example to avoid causing human rights abuse. In the human rights field, the saying that prevention is better than cure has strong standing. An arm lost in an occupational accident cannot be replaced, a childhood lost to child labour cannot be relived and a field contaminated by toxic emissions may take years to recover before it can supply its owners with a living.

Liability risks may carry a proactive effect too, as an impetus for companies to address their human rights impacts preventively (Schrempf and Wettstein, 2015). As a form of reactive accountability, legal liability may arise as a result of complaints by victims against a firm or group of firms. Court cases have been lodged in some countries whose legal systems allow the courts to handle cases on extraterritorial issues. These countries are especially the UK, the US and other common-law countries (Zerk, 2006; Ruggie, 2013). The US' Alien Tort Claims Act has drawn considerable attention in this respect (Box 15.2),

Box 15.2	The Alien Torts Claims Act

The US' Alien Tort Claims Act (ATCA, also referred to as the Alien Tort Statute (ATS)) dates from the late eighteenth century. It was originally passed to fight piracy but had a revival in the 1990s–2010s when it was applied to sue firms in American courts with the aim of claiming compensation for victims of business practices outside the US alleged to infringe human rights.

The US Supreme Court's 2013 ruling in the *Kiobel* v. *Shell* ATCA case, which involved oil companies alleged to have aided and abetted the Nigerian government in causing human rights abuse, resulted in a limitation to the application of the ATCA.

despite the somewhat overlooked fact that a connection to US-based companies always meant that this was not by default a global accountability mechanism. Most cases that were opened under this Act were settled before the final judgment. This suggests that firms prefer not to be seen as responsible for infringements on human rights or complicity in such action.

Mandatory non-financial disclosure is emerging as a regulatory modality to shape organisational practices, either from the outside through stakeholder responses (typically as a form of reactive accountability), from the inside though stimulating organisational change proactively (Gond and Herrbach, 2006) or as a form of regulated self-regulation (Buhmann, 2013). The US has introduced explicit human rights impact or sourcing disclosure, for example for conflict minerals. Inspired by the UNGPs, the EU has adopted new non-financial reporting requirements that include HRDD defined in accordance with the UNGPs. The EU Directive was partly modelled on mandatory CSR reporting introduced by Denmark in 2009 and later strengthened, based on the UNGPs, to include compulsory human rights reporting for certain firms (Buhmann, 2015b). Policy documents show that the original objective of the Danish reporting clause was to stimulate organisational learning and promote proactive accountability (Buhmann, 2013). Research and business applications have been more focused on compliance with the disclosure requirement (Gjerdrum Pedersen, Neergaard, Thusgaard Pedersen and Gwozdz, 2013), that is, the reactive approach. This suggests that more effort should be made by companies and governments to understand and communicate the significance of reporting as a proactive learning measure to prevent impact before it occurs (Buhmann, 2015d).

Legal issues related to BHR come in a range of forms, often applying hard or soft law (Box 15.3) in combination with an assumed power of the market to drive change in the company. These mean that a firm needs to comply not just with national law but also with the 'spirit' or intentions of the law. For example, a firm should not just simply observe minimal occupational health and safety standards or pay its employees the minimum salaries recognised in a sector or country, but go beyond those to offer employees better conditions.

Box 15.3	Examples of legal aspects of BHR

The legal aspect of BHR often works through combinations of legal instruments or forms of law. Some are enforceable in courts of law, but many others work in combination with market-based responses based on social expectations that firms observe human rights standards as expressions of morals. Examples include

- The soft law guidance offered by the UNGPs and their references to the standards in the International Bill of Rights and the ILO 1998 Declaration, which in turn refers to core labour rights: abolition of forced labour, elimination of child labour, freedom from discrimination and the right to form and join trade unions and engage in collective bargaining.
- Governmental guidance that help firms 'translate' the 'standards' or rights in the International Bill of Rights into application to business practices and in HRDD.
- Contractual requirements and codes of conduct.
- Disclosure requirements on firms' human rights policies, practices and applied guidance standards.

15.4 The BHR Regime

The emergent BHR regime is marked by efforts to establish codes or other guidelines, especially at the international level, and civil society initiatives, often centred on specific events, which testify to the connection between social needs and expectations, moral and legal arguments, political developments, and economic and strategic considerations, as discussed in the previous section.

The history of social expectations on business responsibility for human rights shows that for many practical purposes, BHR originated in CSR. Yet BHR is taking on a distinct and increasingly autonomous character. Increased focus on legal obligations of both businesses and states combines with distinct business responsibilities of ethical business conduct, which in turn are based in social expectations that business organisations respect human rights. Even though human rights law generally bestows obligations on states, societal actors expect firms not to violate international human rights, regardless of what the local law says or permits. This duality is reflected in the BHR regime that in its current form is institutionalised in the UNGPs.

The first major international attempt to formulate a code of conduct for transnational corporations began in the 1970s under a UN Commission on Transnational Corporations. It was abandoned at the beginning of the 1990s, however, partly due to Cold War legacies and divergence of investment-related interests, testifying to the inherent politicisation of the issue among states. The final draft text of the code had included formulated duties for transnational corporations (TNCs) to respect fundamental human rights, among other issues. The 1976 OECD Guidelines for Multinational Corporations and the 1977 ILO Tripartite Declaration of Principles concerning Multinational Enterprises and Social Policy referred to human rights at a rather general level. The OECD Guidelines were most recently revised in 2011 to ensure coherence with the UNGPs. They originated to provide directives for TNCs incorporated in OECD (Organisation for Economic Cooperation and Development) member states to govern their extraterritorial investment-related activities on a soft law basis. One of the important parts of ILO's Tripartite Declaration is to engage TNCs in respecting ILO Conventions and Recommendations even if these are not in force or enforced in the host state.

At the end of the 1980s and during the1990s, societal concern with business impact on the environment and complicity in human rights violations grew. This was spurred by specific incidents, such as oil companies' involvement in human rights violations and the 1984 gas leak in Bhopal in India in a plant run by American-owned Union Carbide Corporation, which caused the death of 15,000 individuals (Vogel, 2005: 140–144; Hennchen, 2015). 'Political consumerism' and ethical (or socially responsible) investment rose, along with concern about the prevalence of child labour, excessive working hours, dangerous working conditions, negative social and environmental impact of logging, and the discriminatory practices of the apartheid regime in South Africa.

Reports of substandard working conditions at supplier garment and textile facilities in Vietnam, Bangladesh and Indonesia led to consumer concerns and pressure on investors and states to cease activities that might support abusive regimes. Several multinational corporations, including Nike, Reebok, Nestlé and Shell, were the targets of boycott campaigns organised by non-governmental organisations (NGOs). Lawyers and NGOs began to lodge ATCA cases involving allegations of corporate complicity in authorities' human rights violations in relation to natural resource extraction in Asia or Africa by TNCs with a US connection.

In 1998, ILO adopted the Declaration on Fundamental Principles and Rights at Work, which refers to the four core labour rights. The Declaration states that all ILO member states – whether or not they ratified the ILO conventions on those principles – have an obligation arising from the very fact of their ILO membership. By implication, firms should respect those rights in all states in which they operate, whether or not they are enforced by that state.

The UN Global Compact was developed during 1999–2000 through a multi-stakeholder process (Buhmann, 2014) following business response to a speech delivered at the 1999 World Economic Forum by Kofi Annan, who was then Secretary-General of the UN. The speech emphasised that businesses had achieved many economic rights and few obligations for their social and environmental impact, and called on firms to support the UN in its environmental, human rights and labour objectives. The Global Compact comprises ten principles in four issue areas: human rights, labour, environment and anti-corruption. Participation in the Global Compact is voluntary and open to firms as well as civil society organisations and public institutions. Firms must submit an annual Communication of Progress (COP) report on how they implement the principles.

During 1998–2003, a group of human rights experts at the UN developed a document that is now known as the draft UN Norms on Human Rights Responsibilities of Transnational Corporations and other Business Enterprises (or sometimes the UN Norms). The 'draft Norms' were rejected by the UN Human Rights Council, in part due to corporate lobbying (Kinley and Nolan, 2008). However, the Council, which was composed of states representatives, had second thoughts and appointed a Special Representative of the Secretary-General (SRSG) on Business and Human Rights. The mandate was charged on Harvard Professor John Ruggie, who had previously worked with Kofi Annan to set up the Global Compact. As SRSG on BHR, Ruggie engaged in a multi-stakeholder process that in 2008 resulted in the UN Framework on Business and Human Rights (UN, 2008). The Framework set out the structure of the three pillars (mentioned above: state duty to protect, business responsibility to respect, and access to remedy), which form the basis of the UNGPs (Box 15.4). Through a series of consultations and arguments that emphasised the positive business case of respecting human rights, the processes leading to both instruments caused a shift in business attitudes to the idea of having responsibilities for human rights (Buhmann, 2012, 2014). The UN Framework and UNGPs are sometimes referred to as the 'Ruggie Framework' and 'Ruggie Principles'.

Box 15.4	The three pillars: protect, respect and remedy

As with the UN Framework which the UNGPs elaborate for practical application, the UNGPs are based on three pillars:

- Pillar 1: *The State Duty to Protect* is based on the idea of 'horizontal' human rights obligation of states. This means that they must protect individuals or communities against human rights abuses by third parties (such as companies). They should do so through policies, regulation, monitoring and enforcement.
- Pillar 2: *The Corporate Responsibility to Respect* is based on recognition that societies and stakeholders expect firms not only to comply with domestic law but, where it is inadequate or even conflicts with accepted human rights standards, to go beyond it by respecting international human rights law.
- Pillar 3: *(Greater) Access to Remedy* for victims of business-related human rights abuse. Remedy entails both a complaint- (or grievance-) handling institution and compensation, which must be culture- and context-specific. Remedies may be organised within a business context ('operational level') or state-based. Among state-based remedies, a distinction is made between judicial remedies (such as courts) and non-judicial (like National Contact Points under OECD's Guidelines).

The UNGPs are currently the most comprehensive and recent instrument to offer guidance on how businesses should respect human rights, what the obligations of states are to address governance gaps and develop rules, guidance and processes to ensure that firms respect human rights, and how both firms and states should offer remedy to those who perceive their human rights to be abused by firms. HRDD is a core element to help businesses identify and prevent or if necessary mitigate and remedy adverse human rights impacts caused by themselves or their business relations. Guidance for this process is a major part of the UNGPs' second Pillar.

The UNGPs and UN Framework have influenced several other CSR instruments, and others have been revised to enhance coherence. Thus, the UN Global Compact refers to the UNGPs and the UN Framework in its detailed guidance on human rights as an issue for businesses; the ISO 26000 Social Responsibility Guidance Standard was strongly influenced by the UN Framework and evolving UNGPs in regard to human rights, labour issues and due diligence; and OECD's Guidelines for Multinational Enterprises were revised in 2011 to ensure coherence with the UNGPs. Importantly, this led to the OECD Guidelines not only adopting the UNGP's due diligence process for human rights but expanding it to most of the Guidelines' CSR issues, including labour, environment and anti-corruption (Buhmann, 2015b).

In a 2011 Communication (policy document) on CSR, the EU revised its CSR definition to offer coherence with the UNGPs and the related 2011 revision of OECD's Guidelines. Significantly, under the influence of the smart-mix recommendations of the UNGPs and their elaboration of the inter-relationship between public and private CSR governance, the EU Communication changed its definition of CSR, to stop explicitly referring to voluntary action. The EU now simply defines CSR as 'the responsibility of enterprises for their impacts on society', adding that respect for applicable legislation and for collective agreements between social partners is a prerequisite for meeting that responsibility. In line with the UNGPs' due diligence approach, the Communication also notes that to fully meet their CSR, enterprises should have in place a process to integrate social, environmental, ethical, human rights and consumer concerns into their business operations and core strategy in close collaboration with their stakeholders. The new EU non-financial reporting requirements on CSR (effective from 2017) are a result of the new definition combined with the adoption of the smart-mix regulatory approach.

The revision of OECD's Guidelines to include due diligence across the Guidelines' CSR issues and the new EU definition and smart-mix approach demonstrate that the BHR regime through the UNGPs is having a significant impact on CSR in a much broader sense.

Indeed, the institutionalisation of business responsibilities for human rights in recent years has influenced governmental regulation of CSR beyond human rights to the extent that we may talk about CSR being significantly shaped by the BHR discourse and particularly the UNGPs (Buhmann, 2015a, 2015b).

At the time of writing, efforts are underway at the UN to create an international treaty on BHR, aiming to impose binding obligations on firms under international law. This would complement any legal obligations that firms have under national law in their countries of operation, as well as social expectations of consumers, investors and other business relations. The process of developing a treaty normally takes several years. A treaty and the UNGPs may coexist and be complementary. For these reasons, the UNGPs currently serve as the main normative and operational framework for BHR.

15.4.1 The Guiding Principles on BHR

The UNGPs guide businesses and other organisations in turning human rights issues into organisational practice. Doing so, however, requires insight into what human rights are, at some level of detail. For formal reasons, the UNGPs had to be limited to thirty pages. Additional guidance has been developed by the UN's Office of the High Commissioner for Human Rights (see UN, 2012).

The UNGPs establish HRDD as a core modality to identify risks of business-related adverse human rights impact, to prevent such impact, to mitigate impact that has already occurred, and to remedy damage done (Box 15.5).

By contrast to many other '**due diligence**' processes in firms, which aim to protect the firm against risk, HRDD focuses first and foremost on risks caused by the firm to society (individuals and communities): the primary objective is to protect society against risks caused by the firm. However, due to the reputational and other damage that the firm may suffer as a result of alleged or proven human rights abuse, HRDD may also serve as a form of risk management process for

Box 15.5	HRDD ('Human Rights Due Diligence')

Principles 17–21 of the UNGPs set out details on the due diligence process. An HRDD process should include steps to allow the firm to

- assess actual and potential human rights impacts;
- integrate and act upon the findings;
- track responses; and
- communicate how impacts are addressed.

Due diligence includes a policy commitment by the top management and integration throughout the firm. Experts and stakeholders, including in particular potential or actual victims, should be involved in the identification of human rights impacts and elaboration of steps to prevent abuse. If prevention is not possible (for example, because adverse impact has already occurred), impacts should be mitigated. Findings should feed into learning in order to reduce future risks. When abuse has occurred, culturally appropriate remedy should be available.

the firm, helping it preserve its social licence to operate. The process should start when a firm conceives a project idea and continue until the project is finished. For states, providing detailed guidance on due diligence or even requiring certain firms (such as those operating in weak governance conflict zones) to exercise due diligence is part of the state duty to protect. In line with the UNGP's 'do no harm' objective, the due diligence process ideally prevents human rights abuse, so that remedy is not necessary. When adverse human rights impact does occur, provision of remedy is also part of the cycle of due diligence.

The OECD has developed specific Due Diligence Guidance for Responsible Supply Chains of Minerals from Conflict-Affected and High-Risk Areas. Those guidelines have significance beyond the OECD because many OECD-based companies source from affected countries. But they also serve as source of norms more generally: China, which is not a member of OECD, in 2015 issued Guidelines for Chinese minerals and mining companies and their supply chains, which were developed so as to ensure consistency with OECD's Due Diligence Guidance. In order to assist the implementation of the UNGPs within Europe, the EU has developed guidance for firms in the IT and communication sectors, oil and gas sectors, and employment/recruitment services. Due diligence practices are an important element in all of these.

15.4.2 Critical Perspectives on the UNGPs

The UN Framework and the subsequent UNGPs have been broadly endorsed by companies, governments and civil society organisations, partly as a result of the multi-stakeholder process through which they were developed (Buhmann, 2014). However, there has also been a critical discourse since the publication of the UN Framework. Points of contention refer to the process of the UN mandate, as well as to the form and the content of the UNGPs (for an overview, see Wettstein, 2015).

The involvement of both business and civil society in addition to governments in the process towards the UNGPS has been associated with the UNGPs' broad legitimacy. Indeed, the mandate that was drafted by the UN Human Rights Commission explicitly asked the mandate holder to consult broadly with business. That point may well have been motivated by reflection on the process that led to the rejection of the draft Norms (Buhmann, 2014). However, the process has been criticised for giving too much voice to businesses and marginalising the victims of human rights violations.

Some business ethicists have criticised the UNGPs for a lack of normative grounding and for an outlook on corporate human rights responsibility that emphasises reputational aspects over moral obligations (Arnold, 2010; Cragg, 2012; Wettstein, 2012b). Business ethicists also critiqued the separation and distribution of responsibility as being unclear. Some have called for a more extensive approach, which includes not only a 'do no harm' provision but also positive duties in the realm of protecting and fulfilling human rights (Wettstein, 2012b; Wood, 2012).

It is worth keeping in mind, however, that the UN Framework and UNGPs were never intended to be the absolute solutions but rather breathe life into a process that had been dealt a fatal blow with the rejection of the UN Norms. The immediate need was to achieve a breakthrough that was politically viable in the broad set of stakeholders with strong and often competing interests, in order to start to reduce the number of victims of business-caused human rights abuse (Ruggie, 2013; see also Sanders, 2015).

Against the backdrop of the critique, one may observe that the UNGPs were a breakthrough in bringing about multi-stakeholder-based agreement on international guidance on business responsibilities for human rights, and through this paved the way for the treaty process. Moreover, while the UNGPs are soft law without their own enforcement and remedy mechanism, as noted above they have influenced other CSR instruments to adopt the due diligence process approach and even spread it across CSR more generally, and they have led the EU and states to require CSR disclosure. The UNGPs strategically 'piggy-back' on to other CSR instruments such as ISO's 26000 Social Responsibility and OECD's Guidelines for implementation and enforcement (Buhmann, 2015c).

15.5 Operational Aspects: Managing Human Rights

15.5.1 Human Rights and Responsibility Management

The UNGPs recommend that firms have a policy commitment, integrate it into business processes, and measure, assess and continually approve accord with empirical findings on effective CSR management in general, especially that responsible business hinges on a vision which establishes meaning and purpose (see e.g. Waddock and Rasche, 2012). In line with this, corporations can and ought to integrate their commitment to human rights into their vision and mission and, as the UNGPs point out explicitly, adopt a formal human rights policy statement which consistently and coherently guides and coordinates their respective efforts and activities across all functions and divisions.

Until now, such human rights policy statements have especially been adopted by large firms. They cover a range of issues such as relations with suppliers, strategic partners or local communities, commitment to human rights standards, and applying due diligence and/or human rights impact assessments. However, human rights are equally important for small and medium-sized enterprises (SMEs), and should be integrated into supply chain management in order to contribute to human rights throughout a firm's business relations.

As with CSR in general, human rights responsibility must become engrained into the day-to-day operations and routines. This will often follow the approach of the HRDD process, and should be done in such a way as to provide for active, bottom-up participation of affected individuals and communities. It may be desirable for an extractive company operating in the global South to engage in community projects and support the maintenance of local infrastructure on a philanthropic basis, but its core human rights responsibility is to assess the impact of their operations on people, communities and environment, to reduce pollution (which may affect peoples' health and therefore their human rights), maintain stable and safe employment, pay fair wages and adequate royalties (recognising the knowledge that they make use of) and taxes (to enable governments to deliver in order to fulfil human rights claims by their inhabitants), as well as to consult and integrate local communities into their decision-making processes.

Finally, the impact of responsible business activity must be measured, assessed and continuously improved. The development of adequate qualitative accounting and reporting systems, internal and external evaluation, and monitoring and certification systems is an important precondition for adequate management of human rights responsibility.

When human rights are at stake, there is a danger of reducing responsibility to a mere compliance issue. Human rights responsibility may then be approached as a checklist exercise handled by the legal departments or CSR communication departments with little or no transformational impact on the organisation itself (Wettstein, 2016). A lasting improvement of companies' human rights conduct hinges primarily on their adopting a learning approach to transform their culture (Gond and Herrbach, 2006).

15.5.2 Human Rights, Human Resources and Labour, and Supply Chain Management

Human rights issues often occur in the context of human resource management. The UNGPs refer explicitly to core labour rights, but other human rights are also relevant to human resources. Core labour rights are also referred to in UN Global Compact's labour principles (Principles 3–6).

Working hours, salaries, conditions and cost of accommodation and food as part of the remuneration, and occupational health and safety are major human rights issues facing human resource management in a firm or its supply chain. In many states, statutes may accord with international human rights law or ILO standards, but implementation or enforcement on the ground fails, or information is lacking so that local subsidiaries or suppliers fail to respect the rights. In such situations, firms need to understand the requirements in order to cover the gap between the formal and the deficient factual protection offered by the state. Similarly, a common practice of an employer retaining an employee's passport or ID is a violation of human rights. It keeps the employee from freely leaving the place of work (thus entailing forced or involuntary labour) and often also from accessing social rights such as health services (meaning a violation of other

Table 15.1 Minimum age for admission to employment or work

Developed countries		Developing countries	
Light work	13 years	Light work	12 years
Regular work	15 years	Regular work	14 years
Hazardous work	18 years	Hazardous work	18 years

ILO Convention No. 182 requires governments to give priority to eliminating the worst forms of child labour undertaken by all children under the age of 18 years. They are defined as:

- **All forms of slavery** – including the trafficking of children, debt bondage, forced and compulsory labour, and the use of children in armed conflict.
- The use, procuring or offering of a child for **prostitution**, for the production of **pornography** or for **pornographic performances**.
- The use, procuring or offering of a child for **illicit activities**, in particular the **production and trafficking of drugs**.
- Work which is likely to **harm the health, safety or morals** of the child as a consequence of its nature or the circumstances under which it is carried out.

Source: UN Global Compact website, UNGC principle 5, available at www.unglobalcompact.org/what-is-gc/mission/principles/principle-5 (accessed 4 April 2016).

pertinent human rights). Conversely, firms may contribute to fulfilling human rights by offering on-the-job training or health services. To avoid employing children in violation of minimum age requirements, firms should respect ILO conventions 138 and 182 as set out in Table 15.1.

Respecting human rights is an important element in responsible supply chain management. Where products are sourced, there is a risk that the process has adverse human rights impacts. Labour rights abuse risk is particularly prone in low-wage countries with weak protection of labour rights. Several supplier codes of conduct include human rights with a view to reducing human rights risks. Firms may include HRDD requirements in their contracts with suppliers.

The UNGPs draw particular attention to the duty of firms' home states to require HRDD of firms' operations in conflict zones, such as the regions where many rare earth mineral uses in the IT industry are sourced. Table 15.2 provides a brief overview of a number of relevant guidance instruments in regard to corporations' supply chain and labour rights responsibilities.

15.6 Remedy

Access to remedy offers a grievance mechanism to an individual or community who perceive one or more of their human rights to have been violated, which ideally should bring clarity, dialogue and learning to avoid similar occurrences in the future, and reparation in case a violation is found to have occurred. It is

Table 15.2 Examples of guidance texts

Public or public-private guidance instruments	UN Guiding Principles on Business and Human Rights (www.ohchr.org/Documents/Publications/GuidingPrinciplesBusinessHR_EN.pdf)
	International Bill of Rights: Universal Declaration on Human Rights, www.un.org/Overview/rights.html International Covenant on Economic, Social and Cultural Rights, www.ohchr.org/EN/ProfessionalInterest/Pages/CESCR.aspx International Covenant on Civil and Political Rights, www.ohchr.org/Documents/ProfessionalInterest/ccpr.pdf ILO fundamental labour standards: see references listed below at ILO 1998 Declaration and core labour conventions.
	UN Global Compact (www.unglobalcompact.org) Global Compact Principles 1 and 2: Human Rights (refer also to explanatory sites) Global Compact Principles 3–6: Labour Rights (refer also to explanatory sites)
	OECD's Guidelines for Multinational Enterprises (http://mneguidelines.oecd.org/text/)
	ISO 26000 Social Responsibility Guidance Standard (www.iso.org/iso/catalogue_detail?csnumber=42546 – the standard text is available for purchase)
	ILO 1998 Declaration and core labour conventions ILO 1998 Declaration: ILO Declaration of Fundamental Principles and Rights at Work www.ilo.org/public/english/standards/decl/declaration/text/ ILO Core labour conventions (accessible at ILO's website: www.ilo.org/dyn/normlex/en/f?p=1000:12000:0::NO:::) Freedom of Association, Right to Organise; Collective bargaining: Convention No. 87 (1949), Convention No. 98 (1949) Forced labour: Convention No. 29 (1930), Convention No. 105 (1957) Non-discrimination and equal remuneration: Convention No. 100 (1951), Convention No. 111 (1958) Child labour: minimum age for employment; worst forms of child labour: Convention No. 138 (1973), Convention No. 182 (1999)
Private guidance instruments	SA8000 (www.sai.org)
	Forest Stewardship Council/FSE (www.fsc.org)
	Fair Labor Association (www.fairlabor.org)
Sector-specific initiatives	International Code of Conduct for Private Security Service Providers (www.geneva-academy.ch/docs/publications/briefing4_web_final.pdf)
	Global Network Initiative (www.globalnetworkinitiative.org)
	Accord on Fire and Building Safety in Bangladesh (http://bangladeshaccord.org/)/ Alliance for Bangladesh Worker Safety (www.bangladeshworkersafety.org/)
	The Voluntary Standard on Security and Human Rights (extractives) (www.voluntaryprinciples.org/)

important to note that remedy procedures and reparation are often culturally sensitive. Both should be designed to be culturally appropriate and adequate. Monetary compensation is expected and/or adequate in some circumstances but may be inadequate without an apology in others, or if administered without understanding of the specific context of the victims.

15.6.1 Reputational Damage and Accountability

Several companies have experienced the backlash that transgressions in regard to human rights can have on their reputation. Nestlé's baby formula marketing disaster in the 1970s, for example, still affects their reputation and image today. Similarly, Shell's role in Nigeria or the revelation of Nike's reliance on child labour and sweatshops in the 1990s are still present in many people's minds today. Not coincidentally, these companies have invested much in improving their human rights records after they experienced the serious public relations repercussions such incidents can cause. Holding companies to account for their human rights impact presupposes accountability standards by which the impact can be assessed.

15.6.2 Business Mechanisms: Operational level remedy

The UNGPs recommend that firms establish remedial mechanisms. Such mechanisms offer an opportunity for victims to bring human rights impact to the attention of the firm directly rather than having to rely only on court procedures that are often expensive and lengthy. Ideally, operational level remedy mechanisms enable the firms and the victims to identify and handle a problem before it escalates, and provide a forum for learning for the management to know more about human rights concerns and risks in the country, region and/or sector of operation so that they may better identify and prevent those in future. Operational level modalities include, for example, whistle-blower systems or operational ombudsmen at firm level.

For operational level mechanisms to be effective, trust is highly important. In addition, as with state-based remedies they should be legitimate, accessible, predicable, equitable, transparent, rights-compatible, a source of continuous learning and based on engagement and dialogue. The UNGPs elaborate this in principle 31.

15.6.3 State-Based Remedies: Judicial (Courts) and Non-Judicial

The possibility of applying human rights litigation to sue companies for liability for causing or being complicit in human rights abuse varies between countries. Liability cases may be lodged in most countries, but are normally limited to companies or torts linked to or occurring within that state. The statutes of some nation states, especially in the US, UK, Canada and Australia, allow for courts to handle cases of extraterritorial damage under certain circumstances. While the US Supreme Court decision on the *Kiobel* v. *Shell* case (see Box 15.2) has reduced such opportunities, particularly related to US-related firms.

National Contact Points (NCPs) are a remedial and complaints mechanism established at the state level under OECD's MNE Guidelines. NCPs are state-based, but non-judicial: they do not issue judgments. The territorial scope of the Guidelines – being recommendations from governments to MNEs operating *in* or *from* adhering countries[6] – means that companies may be subjected to grievances before home state NCPs for actions committed in another state without an NCP, and therefore to reputational damage that may result from such a case. Addressing both parent companies and local entities within a MNE, the Guidelines provide non-binding principles for enterprises with the aim of promoting positive contributions by enterprises to economic, social and environmental progress. The main focus of NCPs is mediation and conflict resolution, but statements may be issued if mediation is not possible and/or the infringement is serious. Some National Human Rights Institutions (NHRIs) have somewhat similar functions.

15.7 Case Study: Lundbeck's Pentobarbital Human Rights Dilemma

Lundbeck is a global pharmaceutical company based in Denmark which specialises in drugs for the treatment of different brain-related diseases.[7] The company has 6000 employees of which 2000 are based in Denmark, and has products registered in 100 different countries around the globe.

In early 2011, media reports, especially in the US, had drawn attention to the fact that a particular medical product owned by Lundbeck was one of the three substances included in a lethal cocktail used by US prison authorities to execute prisoners sentenced to the death penalty. The drug – pentobarbital – was produced in the US by a subsidiary of Lundbeck and sold under the brand name Nembutal. The drug was approved and marketed as a treatment for

---

[6] Besides OECD countries, some non-OECD countries, including Argentina, Brazil and Egypt, adhere to the Guidelines.
[7] This case study is a summarised version of 'Lundbeck's pentobarbital human-rights dilemma, or when good intentions turn lethal'. The full version of this case (for students) with teaching note (for instructors) and a different set of questions are available through The Case Centre (www.thecasecentre.org).

particularly strong seizures suffered by some epileptics. As such, it was an important and potentially life-saving treatment when used according to the manufacturer's intention. However, unintended use of the drug to carry out the death penalty had the exact opposite effect, resulting in death rather than continued life. At the time, Lundbeck and the management team were unaware that the product was being used by US prison authorities.

As of 2011, the US had not acceded to international human rights instruments banning the death penalty. Although some federal states did not allow the death penalty, capital punishment could be legally executed in more than thirty states. The most common method of execution was lethal injection. The lethal injection consisted of three drugs, each with a specific function: an anaesthetic/sedative, a drug to paralyze the inmate and a drug to stop the heart. Up to 2011, the US-based pharmaceutical firm Hospira Inc. manufactured and sold the drug Pentothal which was used as a sedative for executing the death penalty in the US. However, in 2011, Hospira moved its production to Italy, and the Italian government banned the use of Pentothal for executions. Hospira therefore ceased production of Pentothal as it was unable to guarantee that the drug would not be used in executions. As a consequence, US prison authorities shifted to new sedatives that had not been formally tested for use in the lethal cocktail. This was why Lundbeck's Nembutal was introduced into the lethal cocktail for executing death penalty prisoners.

Civil society organisations and the media were concerned with the human rights implications of the use of Nembutal to carry out the death penalty. In response to the initial media reports, Lundbeck referred to its UN Global Compact participation and its CSR policy. However, the media were highly critical of Lundbeck, and the firm's response to the situation led to more critique of the corporation for not paying sufficient attention to the pertinent and potential CSR issues and the firm's human rights responsibilities in relation to its products. Human rights groups and civil society demanded that Lundbeck stop making the product available to US prison authorities, possibly by simply stopping sales of the product in the US. In particular, the UK-based civil society organisation Reprieve actively engaged in a campaign aimed at forcing Lundbeck to discontinue making the drug accessible to US prison authorities. Withdrawing the product from the market might save Lundbeck from complicity in causing the death of inmates, but it might also cost the lives of patients for whom the drug was intended.

Because Lundbeck's Nembutal was manufactured and distributed by a subsidiary in the US, the Danish headquarters neither produced the drug nor shipped it to the US. Lundbeck had acquired Nembutal in a portfolio of drugs it obtained through the acquisition of the American pharmaceutical company Ovation in 2009. The American subsidiary sold approximately 50,000 doses of the drug per year. Nembutal was insignificant from the perspective of the Lundbeck brand as well as in terms of the drug's contribution to the firm's revenue (Nembutal accounted for less than 1 per cent of the company's sales).

It was also not strategically significant as Lundbeck's core business focused on treatments for diseases such as depression, Alzheimer's, Parkinson's and schizophrenia.

Following the initial media reports, Lundbeck's US subsidiary sent letters to the Departments of Correction (prison authorities) in Arizona, Oklahoma and Ohio asking them to discontinue using the product for purposes other than those intended. They received no response. Some weeks later, some of Lundbeck's management team met representatives of Reprieve and invited the Danish division of Amnesty International to participate in the dialogue. Possible solutions were discussed, but none were adopted as there was no fundamental agreement between the company and the NGOs on the issue or the preferred approach. Following the meeting, the Danish newspaper *Politiken* as well as Reprieve featured articles criticising Lundbeck for refusing to put measures in place that would prevent the use of its products for executions. In addition, Reprieve publicly stated that Lundbeck had not done enough to stop the use of Nembutal for executions.

Questions for Discussion

1. What are the human rights issues at stake?
2. Where could Lundbeck look for guidance for handling the human rights problems?
3. Why would civil society expect Lundbeck to be prepared for the human rights dilemma? Consider both the business context and the timing.
4. What would you advise Lundbeck to do to solve the dilemma? Consider the economic issues and options to address the human rights issues.
5. What should Lundbeck do to avoid another human rights problem in the future? Your answer should be based on the UNGPs.

15.8 Chapter Summary

This chapter introduced the background to the idea that businesses hold responsibility for their impact on society. We explained the philosophical and legal background to the modern perception of human rights, and the moral, managerial, political and legal reasons why human rights are relevant for business enterprises. We showed that there is often an intimate connection between such aspects of a business-related human rights issue, and explained that an appreciation of this interdependence helps the business manager to make well-informed decisions in relation to human rights issues. We explained that the legal aspects of BHR are not just related to requirements that may be enforced in court such as private contractual or public legal requirements, but also very much to soft guidance and smart-mix regulation such as non-financial reporting requirements, as well as incentives promoted through public procurement opportunities. We explained the evolution of the BHR regime and the course towards the UNGPs that currently serve as advanced guidance for businesses as well as states, with a point of departure in the International Bill of Human Rights. We discussed critique that has been levelled against the UNGPs and the current process towards a treaty on business responsibilities for human rights.

The chapter explained that BHR is closely related to CSR, but differs by being grounded in an explicit set of detailed norms of conduct and through a more explicit connection between public regulation and private self-regulation than what is common in CSR. We offered examples showing the influence that the BHR regime has come to have on CSR, in particular through the broad adoption of the due diligence approach aimed at identifying, preventing, mitigating and remedying a firm's adverse social impact. In sum, we showed that while BHR emerges from and has much in common with CSR, it is not simply 'another CSR' issue, but increasingly an autonomous set of norms of responsible business conduct that is even beginning to shape CSR.

Chapter Questions

1. Your boss asks you to provide a list of human rights of relevance to business operations. Where do you find such a list – and is there just one list?
2. What are the moral arguments for firms to assume responsibility for their impact on human rights?
3. The UNGPs, as a soft law initiative, are not legally binding for businesses. Does this make them irrelevant?
4. What is so special about HRDD?
5. Human rights have been defined as obligations for states. If a firm complies with the law in its country of operation, why should it care about human rights?

FURTHER RESOURCES

Buhmann, K. (2015). Public Regulators and CSR: The 'Social Licence to Operate' in Recent United Nations Instruments on Business and Human

Rights and the Juridification of CSR. *Journal of Business Ethics*, DOI
10.1007/s10551-015-2869-9
Overview of public regulatory governance in relation to the juridification
of CSR. Engaging analysis of public regulation which transcends
territorial and jurisdictional boundaries of public law.

Buhmann, K. (2006). Corporate Social Responsibility – What Role for law?
Some Legal Aspects of CSR. *Corporate Governance – The International
Journal of Business in Society* 6(2), 188–202.
Discussion of the function of law for CSR. This dynamic is explored with
specific attention to the role of CSR as informal law.

Ramasastry, A. (2015). From Corporate Social Responsibility to Business and
Human Rights: Putting Law into the Equation. *Journal of Human Rights*
14(2), 237–259.
Informative exploration of the differences between the CSR and BHR
narratives.

Wettstein, F. (2012). CSR and the Debate on Business and Human Rights:
Bridging the Great Divide. *Business Ethics Quarterly* 22(4), 739–770.
Interesting article which helps explain the divide between CSR and
Human Rights and, moreover, connects and identifies possibilities for
coordination between the two debates.

Wettstein, F. (2016). From Side Show to Main Act: Can Business and Human
Rights Save Corporate Responsibility? In: Baumann-Pauly, D. and Nolan,
J. (Eds.), *Business and Human Rights: From Principles to Practice*.
London; New York: Routledge.
Specific focus on the challenges and opportunities for BHR that emerge
from working within a CSR context.

16

Anti-Corruption Governance and Global Business

HANS KRAUSE HANSEN

Learning Objectives

- Analyse and discuss the complex nature of the problem of corruption as it manifests itself at the beginning of the twenty-first century.
- Analyse and discuss the multifaceted characteristics of contemporary anti-corruption efforts, including the central actors involved, the major techniques deployed and the key challenges facing anti-corruption efforts.
- Analyse and discuss the growing and ambiguous role of corporations and industries in the governance of corruption, including the drivers behind and main obstacles to corporate anti-corruption efforts.
- Analyse and discuss the relationship between anti-corruption efforts undertaken by corporate actors and other issues of corporate social responsibility (CSR).

16.1 Introduction

Only a few decades ago it was commonplace to regard corruption as mainly existing in the global South. By the 1990s this understanding began to change. Researchers and policy-makers increasingly acknowledged that corruption is much more complex and deeply intertwined with globalisation and wider shifts in legal and social norms across the world. Corruption affects economic development negatively, weakens the legitimacy of public institutions and the rule of law, and, not least, it undermines the credibility of international business involved in corrupt transactions. From 2000 onwards, anti-corruption became a global discourse with initiatives created to address the risks that corruption poses, often in conjunction with other initiatives aimed at tackling the illegal production of drugs, money laundering, human right violations, and so on.

Corruption has also emerged as a CSR issue, as companies have moved from regarding corruption as a business expense and simply blaming 'a few bad apples', as US President George W. Bush described the Enron scandal

(*The Economist*, 2002). An increasing number of companies attempt to manage their 'corruption risk' and have even collaborated in efforts to agree standards of probity. The most high profile indication of this new item on the CSR agenda was the UN Global Compact's adoption of an additional, tenth, anti-corruption principle in 2004: 'Businesses should work against corruption in all its forms, including extortion and bribery'. Prior to this, however, a number of businesses had recognised that 'corruption' posed a number of reputational as well as financial risks, and had worked with Transparency International (TI). Today, more than a hundred companies are 'official supporters' of the Extractive Industries Transparency Initiative (EITI), many of whom signal this as an indicator of their CSR. The risks to business of corruption were further magnified by the opprobrium following the 2007 financial crisis; by the 2008 Siemens US $1.6 billion out of court settlement with the US and European authorities for routine corruption offences; and by the UK Bribery Act 2011. Prior to some of these state-driven legal initiatives, a number of voluntary anti-corruption initiatives had emerged, such as the TI's 'Business Principles Against Corruption' (2013) and the World Economic Forum's Partnership Against Corruption Initiative (PACI).

How and why did all these changes happen? This chapter sets out to investigate the phenomenon of corruption and particularly the key institutional shifts and mechanisms, which have put corruption on the global agenda. Section 16.2 reviews some of the main challenges of defining corruption and understanding its ramifications. It suggests the need to move beyond simple models and instead regard corruption in contextual terms. Section 16.3 analyses the contemporary scope and scale of 'corruption governance'. This concept captures key actors, regulations and techniques in contemporary anti-corruption efforts, and thus highlights the intersections of traditional and new regulatory forms emerging on a transnational scale with localised company risk management practices. To further illustrate some of the characteristics of corrupt transactions and corruption governance, section 16.4 examines a recent corruption scandal. The protagonist – German multinational giant Siemens AG –actively contributed to various forms of corruption in remote corners of the world, but it also, once the systematic misuse was discovered, engaged itself in the development of compliance programmes aimed at detecting and preventing future corruption. Finally, section 16.5 concludes and discusses these findings, putting them into perspective.

16.2 Corruption

Social scientists have debated how corruption can be understood for decades (Johnston, 2005). A common but controversial definition of corruption depicts the phenomenon as *the misuse of public power for private gain*. According to this definition, corruption takes the shape of monetary and other symbolic exchanges that violate standards framed in legal or wider moral-ethical terms. The simplicity of this definition has made it a powerful communicative tool among mainstream Western economists, political scientists and journalists, and international institutions such as the World Bank. But it also raises a number of problems.

For one thing, it lumps together rather distinct forms of social practice into one category, leaving aside important nuances and theoretical problems relating to each of them (Haller and Shore, 2005). For example, under this definition corruption can be taken to refer to practices as diverse as gift-giving and facilitation payment, also known as the 'speed money' or 'grease' paid by a citizen to a public servant to make him or her do his duty. It can also refer to bribery, the money paid to a public official to make him violate legal rules to the benefit of the bribe payer and himself, or to nepotism and favouritism, where public sector jobs or benefits are illegally channelled to family, friends or acquaintances. Integral to such exchanges are the informal, personalised and moreorless reciprocal networks, in which material services offered by a patron are exchanged for the personal loyalty shown to him by a client, a phenomenon also known as patron-clientelism. Illicit financing of political parties, as well as state capture, i.e. the efforts of corporations to tweak the laws, policies, and regulations of the state to their own advantage by providing illegal private benefits to public officials, are also practices that typically fall within the broad definition of corruption. Each of these practices can appear to various degrees in different contexts, and each of them can have a variety of rather specific causes and consequences. Depending on theoretical and disciplinary perspectives, they can be analysed as instruments of influence or power, the result of strong socio-economic inequalities or the prevalence of cultural norms that are at odds with the rules of the modern state. They can also be viewed as a consequence of the lack of democratic rule, or the product of particular informal organisational cultures that clash with the rise or consolidation of formalised bureaucratic rules and institutions (Ashforth et al., 2008). Some of these factors can be said to be particularly manifest in areas of limited statehood, i.e. where the state is relatively weak and hence unable to enforce collectively binding decisions concerning public goods, ultimately through its monopoly over the means of violence (Börzel and Risse, 2010).

The diverse causes of corruption have often also led scholars to assess its consequences differently. For example, some researchers have argued that widespread corruption can bring considerable political and economic benefits to a society. Political elites can buy political support, co-opting other elites and/ or violent critics, all of which produces some kind of societal peace and consensus. Companies can bribe public officials to break through bureaucratic bottlenecks and get relevant business permissions and contracts. By paying bribes, ordinary citizens urgently in need of social and educational assistance might get easier access to public goods officially provided by the state. Other research has come to converge on the opposite stance, namely that the economic, political and social costs of corruption clearly outweigh its potential benefits. Buying off political enemies or favouring economic elites and giving them 'special treat' undermine democratic rules. The erosion of trust in such rules increases the risk of conflict and war. Business paying bribes to win public contracts annuls fair competition, prompts incompetence and inefficiency, and puts corporate reputation at high risk if discovered. Speed money paid to public officials in order to have them do the work they are supposed to anyway will not get rid of bureaucratic red tape but rather communicate to other officials that they too can earn a little money by dragging their feet. Accepting corruption creates ripple effects (Nichols, 2012). Corruption can be functional or dysfunctional.

While a general definition such as the one above may be apt as a starting point for reflection and analysis, its usefulness in concrete studies of the manifestations of corruption, their causes and consequences obviously depends on further refinement and critical review. This becomes even more evident as we consider how the definition regards 'misuse' and the distinction between 'public' and 'private' as concepts which are universally understood. As such, the definition represents a normative and Western-biased view of corruption, in which the phenomenon is defined as crime. While all of the practices mentioned above involve exchanges of material and symbolic resources between people who act in different roles, the contextual meanings and significance of the processes going on differ across time and space (Blundo and De Sardan, 2006). In some local understandings, gift-giving or facilitation payments between citizens and office holders has little to do with what outsiders deem as 'corrupt', just as the favourable treatment of relatives by office holders might be seen as natural and legitimate. Conversely, even though formal legal rules almost everywhere on the planet generally have come to prohibit the use of bribes, it does not necessarily follow that such rules and ensuing procedures are 'morally acceptable' under any circumstance. It is easy to imagine situations, typically in authoritarian systems or war zones, where the payment of a bribe can appear to be more 'ethical' than obeying official rules and procedures that establish such payment as unlawful. More generally, the risk of concentrating too much on an etic perspective on the matter, i.e. an external normative view in which corruption is defined as crime, is the sacrifice of an emic perspective, which would seek to understand the meanings of activities, exchanges and roles from within. A classic but still valid critique of much theorising about corruption is exactly that it neglects the task of thoroughly understanding the meanings of complex social and contextual dynamics (Haller and Shore, 2005).

Perhaps part of the reason for this omission is that many of the exchanges and activities are extremely difficult to investigate from an emic perspective. They are generally hidden or secret. Even though this is not always the case, as studies from organisations and societies with systemic corruption have shown

(Blundo and De Sardan, 2006), the topic is generally surrounded with taboos and often puts researchers at risk. This is particularly the case where corruption is part of organised crime activity and functions as an instrument which ensures that criminal activity can take place. For example, in states that have been captured by economic elites, there is often a symbiosis between organised criminals and politicians. Criminal groups provide help and money to mobilise support for politicians. In turn, politicians provide information, protection and de facto support for the criminals. In such settings, organised crime and specifically the use of corruption can best be understood, paraphrasing Clausewitz, as 'the continuation of business by other means'.

The failure to consider the contextual meanings of corruption, irrespective of methodological challenges, is also related to the theoretical frameworks being applied to understand deviant or norm-breaking behaviour. These are often based on theoretical assumptions about rational economic behaviour in a principal–agent model, with self-interested 'perpetrators' – agents – pursuing utility maximisation in the light of inadequate regulatory and sanction systems set up by principals. But purely rationalist accounts of corruption typically fall short of explaining the social processes that have come to define what constitutes corruption in the first place, including the wider social process and relations in which corruption is embedded. Also, by generally locating corruption as a problem of the public sector, with public officials as the main perpetrators, many contemporary approaches to the phenomenon have neglected the role of non-state actors such as business as complicit social actors.

The reason for the insistent focus on public sector wrongdoing appears to be largely ideological. When in the 1990s the 'war against corruption' was waged by the World Bank and other influential actors, it coincided with the predominance of visions and policies praising the market economy and criticising the state and public bureaucracies (Bukovansky, 2006). It was expected that downsizing government would eventually reduce corruption. But comprehensive privatisation and deregulation undertaken in emerging markets and developing countries did not reduce corruption. While mainstream corruption theorising now differentiates between the demand-side of corruption – government and bureaucracy – and the supply-side – e.g. corporations – it is still a challenge to conceptualise corruption in a way that highlights the centrality of non-state actors for corruption to take place.

The definition of corruption as the *misuse of entrusted power for private benefit*, originally developed by the international non-governmental organisation (NGO) TI, opens up a broader space for considering the role of non-state actors in the production corruption. The term 'entrusted power' expands misuse 'beyond the state' and includes 'private-to-private' relations as well. 'Private benefit' does not mean that the benefits derived from corruption are always pocketed by private individuals, but can be and often are distributed among larger groups, organisations or sectors. Thus, it is useful to speak of organisational or institutional benefit as well. When studying corruption from such a vantage point, however, there is still a risk of oversimplification as the definition highlights the processes from a principal–agent model mainly, and fails to draw attention to the ambiguity of activities taking place inside and outside the law, and on its boundaries, so to speak. Yet it allows for more nuances in the analysis of specific cases of corruption, and also for better understanding key aspects of contemporary efforts to govern corruption, which go well beyond the state. After all, the study of corruption and corruption governance should provide us with insights into the norms and rules that shape conduct, to the practices and instances where such norms and rules are violated, and not least to how different actors react to these.

16.3. Corruption Governance

The project of governing corruption has become an increasingly important issue on the global agenda since the early 1990s. It has moved beyond national concerns and now entangles a much broader set of actors, relations and activities across borders. While the growing focus on corruption and its control can also be related to recent developments in media technologies and public perceptions, in large part shaped by the constant bombardment of corruption scandals featuring prominent politicians, bureaucrats and business people, it is worth asking whether this attention also reflects important changes in the phenomenon of corruption itself (De Sousa et al., 2009). For example, it is well documented that multinational corporations (MNCs) are often enmeshed in dense networks of agents, intermediaries, local state officials and political leaders, through whom monetary and immaterial services are exchanged for deals and concessions. Growing economic activity across borders has intensified the opportunities for misusing public office and other forms of entrusted power for private and organisational benefit. Also, the sheer diversity of actors involved in corrupt exchanges today, the complexity of the exchanges themselves, the dynamics in the social networks through which exchanges are carried out, and importantly, the sophistication of the mechanisms used to facilitate obscure illegal or illegitimate transactions, all suggest changes in the phenomenon itself. To date, however, we have few reliable indicators showing that all this is really the case. Evidence is impressionistic, relying on press reports, investigative journalism of single cases, crime and other forms of proxy statistics, including perception indices.

    In the following I use the term 'corruption governance' to refer to the complex process of detecting, curbing and preventing, within and beyond national space, the misuse of public office and other forms of entrusted power for private or organisational benefit (Hansen, 2010). The focus here is mostly on attempts to govern corruption in the exchanges between Western businesses and public sector agencies in different regions of the world. The key feature of corruption governance is not that it acts directly on such transactions, but rather that it seeks to shape the conduct of the categories of actors that purportedly are engaged in or affected by them: industries, corporations, intermediaries, public sector agencies, international organisations, and so on.

Conceptually, corruption governance can be approached in different ways. One way is to draw inspiration from literatures on global governance and regulation and focus on the actors and modes of regulation involved (e.g. Haufler, 2006; Börzel and Risse, 2010). From this vantage point governance is multi-layered and pluralistic, involving states and non-state actors, but with national governments operating as strategic sites for tying together these various networks of governance, and importantly, for legitimising regulation beyond the state. This approach leaves scope for considering how state and non-state actors develop and deploy various 'hard' and 'soft' regulatory systems to contribute to the detection, curbing and prevention of various problems, such as corruption. A slightly different way to approach corruption governance is to explore how corruption has come to be discursively constructed as a problem to be acted upon, and how this is being done in everyday governance practices. From this perspective, which draws on insights from Foucauldian studies of governmentality, 'governing' always takes a very practical form and is irreducible to the state, suggesting the existence of multiple beliefs and tools of governing, as well as a wide range of sites from which government may emanate, such as corporations, industries, systems of education, etc. (Larner and Walters, 2004; Hansen, 2011).

The two approaches have much in common as they contest state-centrism in the analysis of corruption governance. But they also differ (Hansen, 2010). The first position tends to study various forms of regulation of predefined issue areas and on different scales, struggling with questions relating to the fate of sovereignty, who rules, and the distinctions between the public and private, the national and international. The second position tries to steer clear of the institutional or functional accounts of the state, which are often implied in the first position. Instead, the focus is on specific rationalities and technologies of governing located in a wide variety of sites and performed many times by actors whose location on the public and private, national and international continuum cannot always easily be defined in advance. How is corruption understood and how is it tackled, if at all? In practice, the exercise of power in this regard is not so much a matter of imposing sovereign will as it is a process of enrolling actors into particular projects addressing various risks and opportunities. Networks and centres of power that exercise government at a distance play an important role, shaping the conduct of social actors vis-à-vis one another and equipping them with dispositions and instruments for self-regulation as they face various risks and opportunities.

In the following section, insights from both positions are used. First, an overview of corruption governance in terms of main actors and modes of governance is provided. This is followed by an examination of the rise of corruption risks, i.e. the rationalities and technologies of corruption governance as mainly seen from the perspective of business. The case of Siemens AG briefly highlights the central role of corruption governance in practice. It demonstrates how a company was targeted by multiple actors and regulations, how it adapted to emerging anti-corruption norms, and how it aligned itself to corruption risk management practices. However, the case study also prompts questions about how efficient corruption risk management is and can ever be.

16.3.1 Multiple Actors and Hard and Soft Regulations

Corruption governance targets and involves business through *traditional regulation*, developed and enforced by sovereign governments acting on their own or together with other governments through international cooperation. It also takes place through *industry self-regulation* based on best practices and codes of conduct developed in the private sector. Finally, corruption governance is also about *multi-stakeholder regulation*.

The first building block of global corruption governance was in fact laid by a traditional and national regulatory initiative: the passage of the US Foreign Corrupt Practices Act (FCPA) in 1977. The FCPA criminalises bribery on the part of US citizens and firms conducting business overseas, and on the part of companies based elsewhere in the world but listed in the US. It thus sets standards for combating corruption based on an extraterritoriality principle. It also introduces mandatory company self-regulation by requiring corporations to set up internal control mechanisms and improve their accounting practices. During the 1980s, US corporations lobbied the US government to seek international cooperation in suppressing bribes with a view to creating a level playing field, and by the 1990s the Organisation for Economic and Cooperative Development (OECD) was increasingly being used as a platform for extending the principles of the FCPA to the international business community. The 1990s mark the emergence of international conventions against corruption. The OECD Convention on Combating Bribery of Foreign Public Officials in International Business Transactions (OECD Convention) in 1997 drew heavily on the FCPA. Bribing a foreign public official is now a punishable crime in all OECD countries. Nor can bribes any longer be written off as tax deduction. The OECD Convention seeks to ensure enforcement of legal requirements through a comprehensive monitoring system based on peer-reviewing. Another example of an inter-state arrangement is The Group of States against Corruption (GRECO), established in 1999 by the Council of Europe to monitor its member states' compliance with evolving anti-corruption standards. However, the United Nations Convention against Corruption (UNCAC) from 2003 is the most comprehensive anti-corruption instrument to date by including initiatives concerning asset recovery. But it has less to offer in terms of implementation and monitoring. The same goes for regional initiatives such as the Organization of American States Inter-American Convention Against Corruption, which is in fact the first binding multilateral agreement on corruption, signed in 1996.

Existent legal frameworks have come to be complemented by other legally based arrangements. Official anti-corruption agencies have been established in a wide range of countries in the global North and South (De Sousa et al., 2009), and national legislations with extraterritorial reach have proliferated across the globe (Nichols, 2012). Importantly, the UK Bribery Act 2011, like the FCPA, draws on the extraterritorial principle. It regards the failure to prevent bribery as a corporate offence, and facilitation payments are prohibited. Noteworthy is also the US Dodd-Frank Wall Street Reform and Consumer Protection Act (DFCPA), signed into law by the US Congress in July 2010. This Act requires extractive companies registered with the US Securities and Exchange Commission to make public their payments to governments for access to the exploration of natural resources.

Since the early 2000s, US authorities have increased the number of FCPA cases against corporations for criminal conduct occurring within and outside the US. Convicted corporations are now rewarded with a reduction in sanctions if they cooperate with the authorities and take steps to develop and implement anti-corruption programmes. The UK Bribery Act has spurred initiatives and campaigns on the part of governments, consultants and NGOs to inform business about the need for assessing corruption risks, planning for anti-corruption systems and policies, monitoring implementation, reporting to stakeholders and seeking external assurance that anti-bribery systems are effective.

But corruption governance includes more than the traditional forms of regulation. Industry self-regulation, for example, can emerge when international regulation is absent, partial or ineffective, or as a response to international governmental strategies to steer corporate conduct towards public goals without appearing to interfere directly or too much in corporate autonomy. In corruption governance, both forms can be found in the emergence of standards, best practices and codes of conduct, which are developed by business associations, echoing existing international anti-corruption activities and legislation while pointing to the need of reshaping these efforts. One example is the International Chamber of Commerce (ICC), which has developed rules that encourage business to confront issues of extortion and bribery and provides it with the input to engage international initiatives in anti-corruption. Also business-driven is the PACI, organised under the World Economic Forum (WEF), whose mission is to develop industry principles and practices in order to establish a competitive level playing field, with fairness and ethical conduct.

Finally, the Maritime Anti-Corruption Network (MACN) represents an interesting voluntary anti-corruption initiative driven by business. In 2010, Maersk Line sought to convince industry competitors that all industry players would gain from cooperating on anti-corruption efforts, especially in the light of growing FCPA enforcement and the launch of the UK Bribery Act. In 2011 an informal network between major global shipping industry players was set up, aiming to map the challenging countries and locations to do business with and through. It was decided to investigate industry issues relating to corruption and geographical 'hot spots' more systematically. The initiative attracted the attention of local and national authorities, international organisations and NGOs, specifically customers and port agents in a number of countries, the United Nations Development Programme (UNDP) and TI. MACN was officially born in 2012, which also marked the beginning of external communications efforts. Members began to refer to the network on their websites and at official meetings and conferences, capturing further interest from customers, local authorities and suppliers. The cooperation with the UNDP was further strengthened. By 2013, an online platform had been established and in-person meetings annually stated as the norm. Together, online communication and annual meetings are believed to provide a foundation for sharing best practice and raising issues with improper demands. The same year, a pilot project in Nigeria began in cooperation with the UNDP and the United Nations Office for Drugs and Crime (UNODC). By September 2015, MACN had forty regular and seventeen associate members. Regular members are companies or incorporated organisations for whom ownership and/or operation of commercial vessels for business purposes constitute a significant business activity. Associate members are companies or incorporated organisations in the maritime industry, such as ports, terminal operators, shipping agents, freight forwarders, associations and others who do not fulfil the criteria for regular membership.

A third category of business regulation includes multi-stakeholder regulation. Here different actors – public, private, NGOs and grassroots, national and international – set out to develop regulatory frameworks, to establish standards and goals, frameworks for decision-making, and procedures for achieving the standards. One recent example of this is the ISO standard 37001 for anti-bribery systems, which was developed and launched by the International Standard Organization (ISO) in 2016. It provides general guidelines for establishing, implementing, maintaining, reviewing and improving anti-bribery management systems in organisations worldwide. Two equally important examples of stakeholder regulation in corruption governance are the UN Global Compact and its Principle 10 against corruption, which was adopted by the Compact in 2004 and since then has served as one of the progress yardsticks on which participant companies have to report, and not least the EITI, which emerged in 2002–2003. EITI is a cross-sectoral arrangement, involving governments, companies, civil society groups, investors and international organisations. EITI is related to another initiative, Publish What You Pay (PWYP), a coalition of NGOs which campaigns for the mandatory disclosure of taxes, royalties and other payments by oil, gas and mining companies to governments and public agencies. Designed to organise governments, business and civil society at both the global and national levels, the formal governance structure of EITI was established in 2006, with a board consisting of members from governments, companies and civil society. The participation of civil society organisations is regarded as central.

EITI was founded on the idea that transparency in the financial flows between on the one hand companies, who pay royalties and taxes to governments, and on the other hand the governments receiving these revenues, will curb the opportunities for rulers and officials to pocket the money for their own use, and for companies to engage in related corrupt practices. The challenge is how to turn this ideal into practice. Here, EITI aims to set a voluntary standard for how the disclosure of these flows should be constructed. It is therefore different from an international convention where reporting of royalties and revenues would typically be mandatory and non-compliant subject to legal sanctioning. By early 2015, EITI had forty-eight countries implementing the standard, of which thirty-one are *compliant* countries and seventeen *candidate* countries. The majority of implementing countries are from the African continent and central Asia. There are only four Latin America countries, even though many countries of that continent are among the world's richest in terms of resources. The UK, the US and Norway are the only countries from the global North that have signed up to the initiative. Absent from the list are thus major resource-rich countries from North America (Canada and Mexico), Asia (e.g. Russia) and the Middle East (e.g. Saudi Arabia).

However, by early 2015 EITI had also developed a supporting stakeholder base consisting of:

1. seventeen governments of Western, industrialised countries supporting the initiative financially and politically, the only formal requirement being that a supporting country makes a clear public endorsement of the initiative;
2. 110 of the largest oil, gas and mining companies in the world, the requirement being here that the company publicly supports EITI and helps to promote the standard internationally and in countries where it operates;
3. eight large civil society organisations, including PWYP, The Open Institute, TI and the Revenue Watch Institute;
4. eleven partner organisations, including international organisations such as the OECD, G20, G8 and business associations such as the American Petroleum Institute; and
5. ninety-four global investment institutions that together manage over US$19 trillion and have signed a supportive document.

EITI focuses on only one aspect of transparency in the value chain, namely on revenue collection. Important aspects, such as transparency in the awarding of procurement, the monitoring of operations, transparency in the distribution of revenues and the public expenditure stemming from the extractive industry revenues, are not covered by the initiative. Thus, the benefits described at best refer to a very limited part of the process. Further, and importantly, the increasing amount of information to the public domain that the initiative is supposed to deliver is highly technical and extremely complex, and uneven from country to country due to differentiated access to financial data and standards of communication. As such, the initiative is based on a model of communication characteristic of the transparency movement that anticipates that the disclosed information makes sense in the receiving end, which so far has not been very much the case. More generally, EITI has no effective sanction mechanisms to governments nor to companies for not complying with the standard of disclosure set up, however limited it is, except from being excommunicated from an arrangement, which is basically voluntary. Much like the UN Global Compact and its Principle 10 on anti-corruption, EITI represents a soft, 'light touch' approach to regulation, testifying to what some scholars have portrayed as the emergence of transparency as an international norm relying on specific techniques of representation and assumptions of what constitutes true knowledge (Gillies, 2010).

Finally, an important social force in multi-stakeholder forms of regulation is TI, an NGO founded in 1993 by former World Bank officers, aid experts, diplomats and businessmen, who convinced the World Bank to place anti-corruption on the top of its agenda, including to develop a public blacklist of companies involved in corrupt activity in development projects supported by the Bank (Hansen, 2012). Since then, TI has been deeply involved in the development of anti-corruption programmes and projects through international organisations. TI cooperates closely with and receives funding from international business through its national chapters, and has been the pioneer behind the continuous aggregation, in collaboration with research institutions, of corruption perception indices (CPI) and maps that measure and locate corruption by the proxy of perceptions and identify methods for preventing and tackling it. TI is the setter of standards and principles of transparency, and the impact of TI's practices in terms of making visible a phenomenon traditionally understood as hidden, elusive, uncontrollable and politically sensitive is hard to overestimate. TI's early work came to feed into the aggregated governance indices to be developed by international organisations such as the World Bank. Over the years, CPIs of various sorts have been widely publicised in global media and have shaped decision-making processes concerning significant financial and political matters, including the investment decisions of corporations and the allocation of development aid by government agencies. However, they have also spurred many controversies among experts and triggered protests from lower ranking countries finding themselves trapped in processes of 'naming and shaming' (Hansen, 2012).

As we have seen, the governance of corruption today can be analysed as driven by a multiplicity of actors – state, non-state and hybrid in-betweens – and a variety of regulatory arrangements spanning traditional to new forms of regulation on a continuum from hard to soft law. We now turn to a more focused analysis of how corruption has come to be constituted as a risk, and how measures taken against it are designed and enacted from the perspective of corporate actors.

16.3.2 Corruption Risk Management

When an individual or organisation describe something as a 'risk', it has two immediate consequences. First, it makes the depicted risk visible, which is a precondition for governing it. Second, framing something in terms of risk raises questions about what to do, as well as wider expectations about management and actor responsibility. Uncertainties become risks when they enter into management systems for their identification, assessment and management (Power, 2007). Risk assessment and risk management in business precede the contemporary concern with risk proliferation on a global scale (the risk society thesis), but is not unconnected to it. Societies and organisations are deeply concerned with anticipating and avoiding risks, such as events that in fact have not happened.

In recent years, corporations' focus on risk has come to tie in with concerns about making explicit and visible the ethical and unethical conduct of organisations. Business responds more actively to an altered global commercial landscape shaped by a multiplicity of political, juridical and social dynamics (O'Callaghan, 2007). At the same time, the phenomenon of reputation in its various forms has come to be seen as an increasingly valuable corporate asset. Risk management incorporates various concerns about reputation loss, for instance as a consequence of corporate entanglement in corruption scandals. Badly managed risks can potentially destroy a corporation's ability to operate and seriously damage its standing in a community and beyond. In turn, by demonstrating that it has moved into the area of responsible risk management, a company can convert risks into opportunities.

The process of making corruption risk visible and of assigning responsibility to the private sector in terms acting anticipatorily upon this risk, has been contingent upon multiple state and non-state forces depicted above. Against this backdrop, corporations have begun to develop and use corruption risk technologies of various sorts. Before the rise of anti-corruption and its ensuing governance mechanisms, Western companies seldom problematised doing business in environments regarded as pervaded by corruption, although there are examples of the opposite. The view of corruption as being standard business practice prevailed in international business, indicating that corruption was rarely considered a risk to be proactively countered but rather as one among a wide range of uncertainties. In many Western countries this view was de facto officially supported until the late 1990s by the continuance of governmental tax regulation that allowed deductibility of bribes.

But the efforts by organisations such as TI and World Bank at making the problem of corruption visible to global publics and decision-makers from the mid-1990s pioneer the de facto construction of corruption as a risk object. Such efforts have later been complemented by consultancies and law firms conducting surveys to measure the degree of corruption risk awareness among corporations, including their awareness of changes in international national legislation (Hansen, 2011). More and more companies claim to be aware of anti-corruption legislation and corruption risks, and more and more companies have anti-corruption systems in place. A constant feature emphasised is the risk posed to corporate reputation by engaging in corruption, and the potential business opportunities derived from having corruption risk management systems in place.

The process of making corruption risk visible and framing private sector responsibilities has been accompanied by considerable efforts at introducing specific corruption risk technologies. Preventive instruments include codes of conduct, communication to and the training of management and employees. While also having long-term preventive purposes, detecting instruments embrace various forms of investigating business partners, auditing and monitoring, some of which entail public disclosure. The proliferation of such technologies and their deployment by private actors points to the regulatory and organisational complexity at stake in this field. The use of these instruments enables various forms of governing at a distance by linking the management of corporations to its employees, intermediaries, partners and suppliers in geographically remote areas. For example, following the exposure of payment of bribes to Iranian officials in 2002–2003 and later legal prosecution in Norway and the US, Norwegian StatoilHydro began to invest heavily in training programmes for its management and exposed employee groups in relation to matters of anti-corruption compliance. Drawing on outside consultancy, an e-learning programme reaching thousands of employees around the globe was rolled out in 2008, not only to direct employees' attention to the company's codes of conduct, but also to help them in identifying and managing the operational risk that corruption poses (Hansen, 2011).

The use among corporations of various forms of detection instruments has also been scaled up. One example is the growing attention to whistle-blowing, i.e. former or current employees going public with criticism of illegal or immoral practices. Whistle-blowing is becoming systematically organised, that is, turned into an internal risk instrument at the service of management. This risk instrument is sometimes called an employee hotline or helpline. Another corruption risk instrument in the realm of detection is due diligence, which refers to the steps taken by corporations when they go through the histories of their potential partners before closing a deal. It includes the verification and evaluation of financial facts about a business or individual, and the check of the existence of any violations, previous legal disputes or illicit activities. The legal core of due diligence has been complemented significantly over the years with other facets, illustrated by terms such as human and cultural due diligence, as well as integrity due diligence (Hansen and Tang-Jensen, 2015). Implicit here is the claim that corporations can no longer argue that they have no legal or moral responsibility if local partners or agents pay bribes without their direct knowledge or approval. Consequently, to protect their own interest corporations have to monitor what local partners do in their name by investigating their partners' potential family relationships to key bureaucrats, politicians and competing companies, etc.

Many corporations no longer react passively to the challenges posed by corruption in a host country. Increasingly, corporations seek to shape and alter the properties of business systems in which they are embedded through their own practices. Corporations are enrolling clients, agents and other actors on foreign markets into wider networks in which anti-corruption values are being articulated. To the extent that business engagement in anti-corruption suggests a connection between its competitiveness aspirations and wider political projects of economic liberalisation, it is a linkage that stretches well into the foreign territories where these companies operate.

Corruption risk has been conveyed so far in terms of corruption avoidance, if not elimination. However, managing risk is also about making the most of its positive potential. In other words, risk and its management also embrace logics of opportunity, enterprise and value creation (Hansen, 2011). Such logics involve commercial and non-commercial actors developing risk management designs and software. For example, the development of e-learning programmes about business ethics and anti-corruption, whistle-blowing technologies, and the conduct of due diligence rely on expertise that many corporations have to purchase from outside legal professionals, consultancies and risk management service providers, profit or non-profit. Examples include the Big Four accounting firms (Deloitte, PwC, EY, and KPMG) and more specialised consultancies such as TRACE International. Often, such knowledge producers are linked to centres of expertise at universities and public agencies. More generally, corruption governance seems to have prompted the emergence of a global anti-corruption industry consisting of an overlapping network of public and private actors, which uses the newest digital technologies and promotes its various services online, at on-site anti-corruption conferences, workshops and seminars, and in educational programmes at universities and business schools (Hansen and Tang-Jensen, 2015). Technological developments have made it possible for large and small companies to gain access to basic due diligence tools at no or little cost at anti-corruption portals, typically sponsored by governments in the North, international organisations and large corporations. Examples include the Copenhagen-based GAN Integrity Solutions.

Computerisation increasingly allows for the routine processing and analysis of data relating to due diligence investigations and, importantly, often enables the dissemination of findings to wider publics. In fact, conducting due diligence involves the mobilisation and enrolment of a comprehensive network of actors, including credit rating agencies, multilateral financial institutions with political clout, public and private export credit agencies, business intelligence services and other organisational forms. Credit ratings concerning the potential partner in question must be checked, including for bankruptcy, and so must the blacklists developed and made public by organisations such as the World Bank (Hansen, 2012). The growing focus on international money laundering and terrorist financing since 2001 has spurred the proliferation of databases with Know Your Costumer services. Developed by governmental agencies, private companies and organisations, such databases inform about government sanctions, regulatory warnings, civil litigation, and criminal indictments and about suspected individuals. In 2011, Dow Jones Risk and Compliance launched an anti-corruption Portal, which provides companies with advanced risk identification and monitoring capabilities for anti-corruption compliance with regulations including the FCPA and the UK Bribery Act. This tool makes it possible for compliance professionals to screen all business partners against Dow Jones Risk and Compliance's database, as well as the Factiva archive of global business news and information.

Commercial database applications including the introduction of so-called big data analytics in the field of anti-corruption may make information-gathering and analysis more efficient, but they also raise new challenges. The likelihood that unacceptable methods are being used to obtain information poses the risk that companies compromise their own standards in the process of trying to prove that they are being met. Put differently, risk instruments are themselves risky. One of the responses to such situations has been a growing introduction of new forms of integrated risk management instruments, most notably Enterprise Risk Management (ERM). Such systems seek to identify, assess and respond to external risks on an ongoing basis while continuously screening the production of new risks in the risk management process itself (Power, 2007). Business analysts have emphasised a number of advantages inherent to ERM, such as identifying opportunities, and their associated risks and rewards, creating greater transparency both internally and externally, and improving communication with shareholders and other external stakeholders. In this trend towards exposure and visibility, the ranking and benchmarking of company performance by various commercial actors also becomes of increasing importance. A commercial actor specialising in this is the FTSE Index Company, owned by *The Financial Times* and the London Stock Exchange. Devoted to the development of indices with a view to generating business information for consultants, asset owners and managers, investment banks, stock exchanges and brokers, the company highlights the standards within different areas and the risks that, if unwisely handled, can have damaging effects on a company's brand values. An FTSE4Good Index Series has been designed to measure the performance of corporations in terms of corporate responsibility standards, including an additional set of criteria covering the issue of bribery based on the *Business Principles for Countering Bribery* published by TI in 2003 (Hansen, 2011). Such benchmarking of corporate corruption control, developed and performed by a private actor with a view to generating market information, is a selective and comparative technique that links up those organisations understood to have value according to the indicators designed. Becoming part of such schemes requires company self-optimization according to the stipulated standards.

In summary, the construction of corruption as risk has created commercial opportunities for business concerned with various forms of business intelligence, information and surveillance systems, corporate ranking and benchmarking. Such processes place corporations in the limelight of industrial competitors and investors, and in a wider sense, of governments and NGOs. The continuous circulation of standards for corruption risk management through techniques of ranking and benchmarking can create isomorphic pressures, in this case on corporations, to comply with these models. Such pressures obviously do not imply that corporations will no longer engage in bribery, but non-compliance with evolving standards in the field can have negative reputational consequences for corporations.

16.4 Case Study: Siemens AG

In November 2006, several offices of Munich based Siemens AG, one of the world's largest corporations with around 475,000 employees, operating in most countries on the planet and a participant of the UN Global Compact since 2003, were raided by the Munich authorities. The dramatic activities followed allegations that company employees and managers had made corrupt payments to public officials in various countries within and outside Europe, purportedly to win lucrative business contracts for the company.

On 15 December 2008, following more than two years of investigation, the US Department of Justice (US DOJ) announced that Siemens AG had pleaded guilty to violations of the FCPA. According to US authorities, the German corporation had been engaged in a 'systematic and widespread effort to make and to hide hundreds of millions of dollars in bribe payments across the globe'. The techniques used included 'slush fund accounts and shell companies to facilitate bribes', 'removable post-it notes so as to hide the identity of executives who had authorized illicit payoffs', as well as 'suitcases filled with cash' at 'cash-desks' in the corporation's offices (US DOJ, 2008). However, by confessing all wrongdoing and cooperating with the US authorities, the company allegedly avoided being debarred from future business with the US government, suggesting that the considerable fine imposed on the company was less important than the possibility of being blacklisted.

At first, key Siemens executives played down the November 2006 raid at the Siemens office, repeatedly denying awareness and involvement. After all, wasn't this what many other company leaders had done over the years? However, during the months that followed, this all changed. The raid was followed up by internal investigations initiated by the company itself, and by external experts. The company decided to hire the law firm Debevoise and Plimpton LLT and the accounting firm Deloitte and Touche GmBH. These investigations took place alongside the criminal investigations conducted by the Munich prosecutor. In addition to this, the US DOJ and the US Securities and Exchange Commission (SEC) began their own investigations, just as other jurisdictions, including Liechtenstein, Austria and Switzerland, which in various ways were entangled in the emerging affair. Along the process, the US DOJ and SEC cooperated closely with the Munich Public Prosecutor's Office, sharing information and evidence through the use of the mutual legal assistance provisions of the OECD Convention (US DOJ, 2008).

The new compliance system that gradually emerged in Siemens in the wake of the 2006 raid was not only the result of the depth and thoroughness of the investigations conducted, but also reflected the swift change of company leadership and structure. The question was this: would it be possible to root out corruption without changing the company and its leadership fundamentally, and without bringing in outside expertise? The answer was a no.

First, the company cooperated with a wide range of authorities and experts in the conduct of investigations. This taught the company's management about the techniques and procedures of the bribery schemes deployed, and thus informed the construction of a comprehensive system to prevent this happening in the future. Until 1999, the year in which Germany implemented the OECD Convention, German law did not prohibit the payment of foreign bribes to secure business, and in fact such payments had been tax-deductible. However, in spite of the change of the law and being listed on the New York Stock Exchange in 2001, which made Siemens subject to the FCPA, greater efforts had in fact been taken by the company to conceal such payments by diverting slush funds to a network of shell corporations and accounts. Among other things, Siemens had hired local, outside consultants to help win contracts, and set up business consultant agreements that paid the 'commissions' of the consultants, all of which had been implicitly condoned by the company's managers. Now the situation was turned around: Siemens had to bring in people who had not been attached to the company before.

Second, a new CEO, Peter Löscher, was hired in July 2007 as the first CEO to be recruited from outside Siemens since its foundation in 1847. Löscher had previously served at Hoechst, GE and Merck. He considered the Siemens bribery scandal to be the result of severe and long-standing leadership failure in a company shaped by a corruption culture. Hence the idea was not only to clean up the bribery affair in cooperation with the authorities, but also to draw on the opportunities that come from a deep crisis: 'The scandal created a sense of urgency without which change would have been more difficult to achieve, regardless of who was CEO' (Löscher, 2012: 40). Among the steps taken under the new CEO was the replacement of a range of senior managers who appeared to be involved in bribery schemes, the implementation of a 'new tone at the top', as well as the establishment of an amnesty programme for former and current employees. The idea was to protect employees fully cooperative with the investigations undertaken.

During this process, Siemens also hired more than 500 full-time compliance officers worldwide. It set up a compliance investigation unit, and a new position for legal counsel and compliance was to be filled by Peter Solmssen with whom Löscher had worked in GE. The company began to systematically train its global workforce in anti-corruption and business ethics, and it renewed guidelines and handbooks on these matters. An online 24-hours compliance hotline was set up, and an external ombudsman was institutionalised. Other internal reporting systems were tightened up, and control systems focusing on funds, banks accounts and ongoing payments were established. But organisational innovations did not stop with initiatives relating directly to the clean-up process. A number of changes were introduced to streamline the organisation and reduce bureaucracy, such as changing the company's complex matrix structure, which had allowed entire divisions to run themselves; dividing its operating groups into three sectors – industry, healthcare and energy; and grouping the 190 countries in which Siemens operated into twenty clusters.

The scale of the Siemens case is underscored by the enormous costs and fines associated with the investigations and the final settlement, as well as its transnational extension. The company paid US$1.6 billion in fines and profit disgorgements to German and US authorities, as well as US$850 million for internal investigations conducted by around 200 lawyers and 1300 forensic investigators from external law and consultancy firms. Finally and in addition, Siemens, as part of its settlement with the World Bank in the wake of its acknowledged past misconduct in development projects in which the Bank had been a key partner, agreed to pay US$100 million to support anti-corruption work. In this way, only one Siemens subsidiary ended up on the World Bank's list of debarred companies, and Siemens AG avoided being debarred from one of its major markets, the US (Hansen, 2012).

If the Siemens case is unusual in terms of the scale of costs and fines, other aspects of it are less unusual when compared to other examples of corporate engagement in corruption.

For one thing, as in many other companies, bribery was a standard procedure in Siemens, and this in spite of the existence since at least 1991 of various written codes and rules of conduct in the company prohibiting the use of bribery. The payment of bribes was not limited to specific operating groups or business activity that Siemens carried out, but was pervasive across the company. Second, and also similar to many other companies, Siemens had developed highly sophisticated schemes to disguise the objective and ultimate targets of illicit payments. Third, as has also been the pattern in many other cases, the company's senior management were deeply involved in these procedures and efforts at disguising what was going on.

Even when the regulatory web began to tighten by the late 1990s and early 2000s, the practice of paying bribes to public officials abroad persisted, as illuminated in three cases involving Siemens subsidiaries operating in Argentina, Venezuela and Bangladesh. In the case of Argentina where the company was involved in a project to create national identity cards, the Siemens subsidiary paid millions of Euros to Argentine government members as well as third-party agents and consultants to facilitate these payments. In Venezuela and Bangladesh, local Siemens subsidiaries paid millions to consultants and third-party agents with the understanding that some of this money would be passed to public officials with the purpose of retaining major infrastructure projects; in the first case, two major transit projects and in the second case, mobile phone network (Siemens, 2008: 9). It seemed that the company's aggressive growth strategy combined with its managers' attempts at reaching challenging performance targets by means of illegal payments was well anchored in a corporate culture tolerant of, if not actively encouraging, corruption.

However, from 2008 onwards, and as part of the restructuring process, the company decided to establish compliance as one of the key parameters of the compensations paid to its top management. In 2012, Siemens was included in the FTSE4Good Index Series as a result of the company's efforts at making considerable changes to its governance and anti-corruption compliance systems.

Questions for Discussion

1. Why did Siemens become the target of external corruption investigations?
2. How did Siemens respond to these investigations and what became the major characteristics of the compliance system that was set up?
3. Discuss the potential benefits and challenges of company anti-corruption compliance and risk management programmes, including their wider ramifications.

16.5 Chapter Summary

The aim of this chapter was to investigate the phenomenon of corruption and specifically the processes that have placed anti-corruption on the global policy and corporate agendas.

It first demonstrated how corruption covers a wide range of social practices, whose dynamics, meanings and significance today can only be comprehended by taking into account the social and cultural contexts in which they are unfolding – hence the need for a conception of corruption that is critically sensitive to its Western bias while being attuned to understand the role of social context, and state and non-state actors, in the production of the various practices depicted by the term.

To understand the rise of anti-corruption as a global policy and corporate issue, the chapter then highlighted the most significant hard and soft modes of corruption governance mechanisms and technologies. These range from national legal arrangements of a mandatory nature with extraterritorial reach, to voluntary multi-stakeholder arrangements, business-driven initiatives and activities by NGOs. The emergence of more specific corruption risk technologies, including organised whistle-blowing, due diligence and employee training programmes, is associated with company concerns with legal breaches, reputation and social responsibility management. It is driven by a proliferating anti-corruption industry, made up of public, private and hybrid organisations, profits and non-profits, providing knowledge in increasingly refined ways. This suggests how corporations have come to rely on corruption risk technologies, as well as on a wide variety of experts on the matter, including the multiple and interconnected agencies and organisations doing the rating, ranking and benchmarking that constitute risk management, today clearly a key characteristic of corruption governance.

Many of these complex processes were illustrated through a case study of Siemens, which became the target of a major corruption scandal in 2006. The firm restructured its organisation and introduced a comprehensive compliance programme, following massive external investigations by multiple legal authorities and consultancies, and subsequent punishment in terms of enormous fines and costs.

Corporate anti-corruption is often seen as a source of business innovation and opportunity, if not competitive advantage. From this perspective, business should be proactive in the field of anti-corruption, recognising that a transparent business environment based on a level playing field will work to its favour: the high cost of pursuing anti-corruption practices and compliance will pay off in the long run (Nichols, 2012). While potentially providing constructive input to business strategising, this line of thought may leave the impression that corruption risk management is a 'neutral tool' that unproblematically helps to bring along a more democratic and socially responsible social order. A few things should be kept in mind, however. Corruption risk management is embedded in relations of power, and, if effective, provides mechanisms of inclusion and exclusion that determine who is part of the global networks of actors involved in business. The assumptions and knowledge on the basis of which decisions are made concerning investment targets – countries – are likely to impinge on the countries in which companies subscribing to anti-corruption operate, their people and their institutions. There is some relevant future research to be done as regards the acceptance of or resistance towards anti-corruption activities deployed by Western corporations as they operate in non-Western markets.

Chapter Questions

1. Is corruption unequivocally a bad thing? Discuss the different perspectives that can be taken to answer this question.

2. What is corruption governance? Identify and discuss the different analytical positions that can be taken to answer this question.

3. How have national governments sought to limit and eradicate corruption since the 1970s? Give examples and explain the focus of the initiatives.

4. How and why have companies and the private sector more generally become engaged in anti-corruption?

5. What is corruption risk, and how is it related to issues of reputation?

6. What are the major techniques deployed by corporations in the fight against corruption today? Do these techniques appear realistic, given the magnitude of the problem?

FURTHER RESOURCES

Hansen, H. K., Christensen, L. T. and Flyverbom, M. (2015). Logics of Transparency in Late Modernity, special issue of *European Journal of Social Theory* 18(2), 1–114.

This special issue provides a critical analysis of the transparency debates and movements so central to current anti-corruption efforts.

Healy, P. and Djordjija, P. (2012). *Fighting Corruption at Siemens*. Harvard Business School Multimedia/Video Case, March 2012.

This multimedia case study provides more details on the Siemens scandal.

These links provide more information on anti-corruption in practice:

GAN Integrity Solutions, www.ganintegrity.com

TRACE International, www.traceinternational.org

Transparency International – the Global Coalition Against Corruption, www.transparency.org

17 Business and Transnational Environmental Governance

STEFANO PONTE, RENÉ TOUDAL POULSEN AND JANE LISTER

Learning Objectives

- Understand the challenges businesses face in addressing the environmental impact of their activities.
- Appreciate how business environmental strategy may align and/or clash with international, regional and national regulation.
- Understand the potential and limitations of self-regulation and multi-stakeholder voluntary initiatives on environmental governance.
- Identify the push and pull factors that may facilitate the transmission of environmental performance demands up and down the value chain.

17.1 Introduction

Increased consumer awareness of the environmental impact of production and transportation of goods, numerous campaigns and direct action by non-governmental organisations (NGOs) and other civil society groups, and emerging national and international regulation are leading business to assess and address the environmental impact of activities linked to its products, also beyond those carried in-house (Dauvergne and Lister, 2012).

Business can do much in reducing the environmental footprint of its own operations. But the fact that production is increasingly fragmented in geographical and organisational terms poses specific challenges in transmitting environmental demands to other supply chain actors. The many scandals that have touched branded companies in particular have led them to devise environmental strategies for their own operations and for those of their suppliers to avoid reputational risk, and to increasingly participate in multi-stakeholder initiatives addressing sustainability issues in supply chains (Nadvi, 2008; Vurro et al., 2010; Wahl and Bull, 2014).

Environmental improvements that business can implement on its own include those affecting production, processing, distribution, consumption and disposal or recycling. Sometimes, these processes lead to net cost reductions for operators due to, for example, increased efficiency or reduced energy consumption. Other times, they lead to net value addition, for example through the creation and certification of new environmental qualities that become embedded in products selling at a premium price. But they can also impose net costs. If net costs of environmental improvements in the short term are recouped in the long term, there is still a business case to carry them out. If net additional costs are permanent, firms will carry out environmental improvement only if all competitors do so, either through regulation or through industry-wide voluntary standards (Orsato, 2011).

However, many environmental impacts, such as the greenhouse effect caused by excessive CO2 emissions, have global dimensions and require global governance. They may also be non-tangible and have time-delayed effects, as in the case of greenhouse gas (GHG) emissions. Therefore, they provide specific challenges that can be fairly distinct from more narrowly defined corporate social responsibility (CSR). In these cases, national regulation, even in key polluting countries, can only provide partial solutions. At the same time, truly global environmental governance is very hard to attain through international legally binding agreements. International organisations and agencies, such as United Nations Environment Programme (UNEP), and Multilateral Environmental Agreements (MEAs) have important roles to play. MEAs with a relatively narrow focus, such as the Convention on International Trade in Endangered Species, the Stockholm Convention on Persistent Organic Pollutants, and International Stratospheric Ozone Regime (1987 Montreal Protocol) have been relatively successful. But broader multilateral negotiations, such as the 1992 UN Framework Convention on Climate Change (UNFCCC) are prone to deadlock. While the 1997 Kyoto Protocol took only two years to negotiate (with rules of implementation finalised in 2001), the negotiations to replace it have been very complex and time-consuming, finally leading to the Paris Agreement of 2015.

A number of hybrid governance solutions have also emerged alongside national regulation, MEAs and voluntary business actions. These include the UN Global Compact, many forms of public–private partnerships, and an increasing number of multi-stakeholder initiatives (MSIs) for the environmental sustainability of agro-food and forestry products, mining operations, chemicals, electronics, etc. In other words, environmental governance is taking *transnational* features – it includes components of intergovernmental negotiation, private initiative and hybrid public-private-civil society interaction.

In this chapter, we aim at: (1) recognising the various private, public and hybrid instruments that come together to constitute transnational environmental governance; (2) examine the ways in which national governments and international organisations 'orchestrate' this variety of initiatives to achieve collective environmental improvements; and (3) delineate the potential but also the limits of these initiatives. First, we examine the main categories of available instruments of environmental governance. Second, we provide the analytical and theoretical tools that can be helpful in making sense of the complexity and overlaps of these instruments: transnational environmental governance (TEG), **orchestration**, and **global value chain (GVC) analysis**. Third, we apply these tools frameworks to examine the case study of maritime shipping. Finally, we draw lessons from the case study to highlight the complexity of TEG and the potential and limitations of its orchestration.

17.2 Instruments of Environmental Governance

17.2.1 Regulation

Direct environmental regulation expanded dramatically in the 1970s, organised around an environmental target (such as a limit to emissions of a pollutant), the specification of measurement indicators and technological instruments, and a series of penalties if the target was not met. Direct regulation usually includes a system based on standards of reference and related permits and licences that allow individual firms to pollute up to a certain level. The advantages of this system are that its obligations and penalties are relatively clear and precise, and it is effective in curbing pollution when firms are easily identifiable. Conversely, it can be difficult to apply to mobile or remote firms, and on sources of pollution that are transferred from e.g. land to water; it can be inflexible if measurement technology does not keep up with changes in production systems; it requires comprehensive information on the industry regulated; it can be costly, complex and difficult to implement; and it lacks incentives for firms to go beyond the minimum standards required in regulation (Gunningham, Grabosky and Sinclair, 1998).

To partly address these limitations, a number of regulatory innovations have been developed in the past few decades: more flexibility to allow site-specific adjustments; better information flows and participation from communities affected by pollutants; accreditation of good performers to lighten the regulatory burden; long-term negotiated agreements between governments and industry on target reduction plans; and systems-based management (hazard and risk assessment, risk control) to wholly or partly substitute for ex post measurement (ibid.).

Governments and international organisations have also developed more indirect forms of regulation, such as systems of tradable pollution rights or tradable resource rights. Public authority in this case determines the overall level of accepted pollutants based on the total capacity of a specific environment, then allocates tradable rights or quotas up to that level. This allows firms to decide whether it is more expensive to take action in their operations, or to pay for the 'right to pollute'. This means that regulators do not need to know much about the individual circumstances in which firms operate, thus cutting out complexity and costs of enforcement. However, regulators also face challenges in finding appropriate ways to allocate permits (on the basis of history, equity or plant capacity), in avoiding uncompetitive behaviour in trading rights (e.g. hoarding), and in ensuring that the price for the 'right to pollute' does not become so low that it encourages firms not to abate their emissions (which is what happened in the EU emission trading system).

Finally, public authorities can also govern the environmental behaviour of firms (and of consumers) through other indirect instruments, such as: taxation systems adjusted to the amount of polluting activity (such as emission and effluent charges); financial subsidies (such as tax deductions related to energy efficiency); other financial instruments (soft loans, green investment funds); imposing civil liability; and setting minimum mandates (such as the EU mandate on a minimum level of biofuel to be blended in gasoline) (Gunningham et al. 1998).

17.2.2 International Negotiations and MEAs

While regulatory instruments can be useful and effective in shaping the behaviour of firms to localised environmental externalities, international regulation is necessary for trans-boundary and global environmental issues, such as CO_2 emissions. For this reason, many negotiations have taken place in intergovernmental institutions in the past few decades, and a number of MEAs have been concluded. Yet, great challenges face these multilateral negotiations.

Within the World Trade Organization (WTO), for example, the Doha Ministerial Declaration of 2001 mandated the members of the WTO to negotiate the reduction or elimination of barriers to trade in environmental goods and services (EGS). The Doha mandate, however, did not specify what constitutes an environmental good or service, nor the desirable extent of liberalisation. As a result, countries have been struggling since its adoption to come up with a list of EGS for liberalisation. This initiative is a good example of the ways in which the multilateral trade system could deliver on environmental outcomes, but is also an example of how negotiations can proceed very slowly. Fortunately, the prior experience of other MEAs provide some level of optimism in relation to trade-related instruments, at least in fairly specific and focused environmental areas. The Convention on International Trade in Endangered Species (CITES), signed in 1973, provides an example of how countries can work with a set of criteria to define a list of environmental goods for trade liberalisation, and regularly update it to maintain its environmental soundness. CITES has been in force for more than three decades, has global membership, and is considered one of the most effective environmental treaties regulating trade in more than 5,000 fauna and 28,000 flora species. Other more recent

MEAs, such as the Rotterdam Convention on Prior Informed Consent (the PIC Convention, dealing with the trade of hazardous chemicals) and the Stockholm Convention on Persistent Organic Pollutants (the POPs Convention) also provide important examples on how to manage listed goods for special treatment in trade (Cosbey, Aguilar, Ashton and Ponte, 2010).

Another example of the challenges faced in MEA formation is the case of climate change negotiations. Climate change came into the political agenda towards the end of the 1980s, following mounting evidence of global warming. The successful conclusion of the 1987 Montreal Protocol on Substances that Deplete the Ozone Layer (and the 1990 London amendments of the same) provided the momentum that led to the signing of the UNFCCC by over a hundred states at the 1992 Rio Earth Summit. The expectation was that the model used to address the ozone problem could also be transferred successfully to broader climate change negotiations – a model based on a global and binding agreement, a framework convention followed by specific protocols, and differentiated response depending on national levels of economic development. But various disagreements on whether and how to bind GHG emissions, and the extent to which developing countries should take differentiated responsibilities, led to a relatively weak framework convention. The following 1997 Kyoto Protocol required an average 5 per cent of emission reductions for industrialised countries, below 1990 levels, to be achieved by 2008–2012. No targets were set for developing countries. In order to enter into force, at least fifty-five countries that are responsible for at least 55 per cent of emissions were to ratify the agreement. The US eventually withdrew from the protocol, which came finally into force in 2005. Under the protocol, several Emission Trading Schemes were developed, as well as the Clean Development Mechanism, which finances climate projects such as the REDD+ schemes. Since the Bali Conference of the Parties in 2007, negotiations have focused on what would take the place of the Kyoto Protocol upon its expiration in 2012. Expectations for this to happen at the Copenhagen Conference of the Parties in 2009 failed spectacularly (Blowfield, 2013). An agreement was finally reached in Paris in 2015, seeking to limit global average temperatures to 'well below' 2°C above pre-industrial levels. It went into effect in November 2016.

17.2.3 Self-Regulation and Corporate Environmental Responsibility (CER)

Partly as a result of the complexity of direct regulation and MEA formation, and partly because of the changed political climate starting in the 1980s towards deregulation, self-regulation has emerged strongly in the environmental field. There are many variations of self-regulation: *pure* self-regulation is when specific behaviour is recommended by an organised group (often a business association) to its members, through the stipulation of codes of conduct, best practices and, sometimes, externally audited standards; *mandated* self-regulation takes place when public authority mandates an industry to regulate its own behaviour; and *hybrid* self-regulation takes place when public authority sets the framework conditions for self-regulation, but leaves much of the detail to be specified by industry associations (Gunningham et al., 1998).

Self-regulation can be less expensive, can promote improvements beyond minimum standards, and generally offers more flexibility than direct regulation. At the same time, it can also be used to narrowly serve industry interests, can lead to weak standards, and can lack credibility. It works best when there is alignment between industry self-interest and wider public interest, for example when it leads to reduced energy use and thus costs; it also works best when noncompliant behaviour has clear consequences (e.g. in terms of reputation through 'name and shame' lists or de-registration from an association).

Differently from self-regulation, CER is based on individual firms taking steps on a voluntary, unilateral basis. CER can include: wholly individual initiatives at the firm level to address environmental externalities beyond what is mandated in regulation; being part of industry-level initiatives without coercion; entering in initiatives with public authority, but where the latter only plays a coordinating or facilitating role; producing environmental reports; voluntary releasing of relevant information to affected communities and the public more generally; and signing up to international initiatives such as the UN Global Compact. CER has the benefit of being non-interventionist, has high industry acceptability and flexibility, and can promote environmental stewardship. It can also be used to build a 'green' brand or firm reputation (see below). At the same time, it can also be used to promote misleading or false environmental claims due to lack of proper oversight (Gunningham et al., 1998).

17.2.4 Environmental Strategies and Value Chain Transmission Mechanisms

Environmental improvements in business operations can take place through strategic choices that respond to push factors, pull factors or a combination of the two. Push factors are at play when firms choose to be proactive in their environmental improvements. Pull factors in this context occur when firms react to demands placed by the buyers of their products and services (in addition to public regulation and civil society pressure).

Companies can employ *push factors*, fostering environmental innovation proactively, in several different ways, both in-house and in placing demands on their immediate suppliers. They can benefit from environmental improvements when they improve their competitiveness, open a new market for their products, decrease costs, and/or improve the commitment and productivity of their workforces. Four environmental innovation strategies are commonly identified among firms, which combine two sources of competitive advantage (lower cost; or differentiation) and two competitive foci (on organisation and procedures; or on products and services) (Orsato, 2011):

1. *Eco-efficiency* is based on lowering costs through organisational and procedural improvements (e.g. lowering energy costs by allowing natural lights into stores);
2. *Environmental cost leadership* is based on lowering costs while improving the environmental qualities of products or services (e.g. using cheaper but more environmentally friendly materials, or lighter packaging);
3. *Beyond compliance leadership* is based on differentiation through organisational and procedural improvements (e.g. building brand or company reputation for environmental excellence, even though it increases operational costs); and
4. *Eco-branding* is based on differentiating the products and services offered to customers (e.g. through environmental certification or a 'green' brand).

Pull factors are those that are placed on suppliers by their own buyers, also travelling further along value chains. Given that outsourcing and offshoring have become common ways of organising business operations, environmental improvements in-house are often not sufficient to improve the environmental footprint of products and services in their complete lifecycle. Firms have to shape the behaviour of their suppliers too, and increasingly of the suppliers of their suppliers. But how do environmental demands travel along value chains? We highlight two possible drivers (De Marchi, Di Maria and Ponte, 2013):

(1) In *standard-driven greening*, lead 'buyers' identify the main environmental impacts to be reduced, decide how to deal with them and embed such information into standards that suppliers have to comply with. These standards may affect both the supplier selection process and the relation between lead firms and existing suppliers. When standards can be complied with through established third-party certifications that suppliers can handle, buyers can stimulate environmental upgrading in a relatively hands-off manner. However, when certifications are not available and/or supplier capacity to meet these standards is lacking, they are enforced through stronger monitoring and control efforts, which often involve knowledge transfer in a relatively top-down manner and the provision of other supporting tools. Standard-driven greening seems to work best with environmental improvements that are linked to eco-efficiency or to other production processes.

(2) In *mentoring-driven greening*, personal relations between buyers and suppliers are of key importance. Transactions are complex and handled through trust, reputation and face-to-face interactions. Actors tend to be mutually dependent on knowledge and skills: buyers tend to exert leadership on environmental knowledge, while suppliers tend to lead on

technical knowledge. Environmental problems and their solutions are considered on a case-by-case basis and do not necessarily need to fit easy-to-measure metrics. The main tools used by buyers to green the value chain tend to be design and product specifications, which enable suppliers to improve their environmental performance even if they have a low environmental awareness to begin with (De Marchi et al., 2013).

17.2.5 MSIs and Market-Based Instruments

In-house business decisions and demands placed on suppliers are important factors in handling environmental externalities. Yet, the complexity of the problems at hand, and of the instruments available to tackle them, can be too high or expensive for individual firms to handle. As a result, in the past few decades, a large number of environmental standards and certifications have been developed not only by industry associations (see section on self-regulation above), but also through MSIs involving industry associations, individual firms, NGOs, communities and in some cases the public sector as well. Some of these initiatives develop product certification systems, some manage 'award schemes' to publicise environmental excellence, while others develop codes of conduct and publicise 'best practices'. In this section, we explore those that have developed market-based solutions, especially consumer-facing labels backed up by third-party certifications – with a focus on the agro-food sector. We briefly highlight their general features, some of the main trends that are unfolding in this field, and the limitations which MSIs encounter in terms of participation and democratic process, and in terms of achieving actual environmental outcomes.

MSIs in the agro-food sector are often 'voluntary' only in the sense that they are not demanded by direct regulation or mandated self-regulation. But they are de facto mandatory for firms that seek to supply the increasing number of large processors and retailers (such as Unilever or Walmart) that demand certified 'sustainable' products, such as palm oil or seafood. Many of these MSIs have taken the form of 'stewardship councils' and 'sustainability roundtables', and some have developed consumer-facing labels. They include the Forest Stewardship Council (FSC, established in 1993), the Marine Stewardship Council (MSC, 1999), the Roundtable on Sustainable Palm Oil (RSPO, 2004), the Roundtable on Responsible Soy (RTRS, 2006), the Roundtable on Sustainable Biomaterials (RSB, 2009), the Aquaculture Stewardship Council (ASC, 2010) and the Sustainable Beef Roundtable (SBR, under way). Other MSIs take a 'Better' nomenclature, such as Bonsucro (formerly the Better Sugar Cane Initiative, 2008) and the Better Cotton Initiative (BCI, 2009). In addition to these, we find a host of other MSIs, including those that were developed in the coffee sector and then expanded to other commodities, such as Fairtrade (1989/ 1998), Rainforest Alliance (1993), Utz (2002), and 4C (2006).

These initiatives showcase their multi-stakeholder elements explicitly, either from their very inception or soon after the basic design of the standard and certification system is set in place, usually by a small group of initiators. They are increasingly built around a common set of 'must have' institutional features and procedural elements. Institutional features usually include an executive board or a board of directors; an assembly or council, often with specific chambers that represent different stakeholder interests; technical advisory committees of appointed experts; and an executive director with support staff that handle the day-by-day operations (Ponte, 2014).

Procedural elements include a set of what are now considered 'best practices' in standard-setting, certification and accreditation, and impact evaluation, which are built around the concepts of transparency, inclusiveness, consensus and accountability. These best practices are inherited and adapted largely from the experience of the FSC model and have been subsequently codified by the International Social and Environmental Labelling Alliance (ISEAL). ISEAL is an association whose members are social and environmental standard-setting and accreditation organisations. It aims at developing guidance for and strengthening the effectiveness and impact of these standards. ISEAL has developed three 'Codes of Good Practice' for setting, assessing and assuring compliance with social and environmental standards.

The governance set-up of MSIs is meant to signal (if not ensure) a degree of professionalisation, participation of relevant stakeholders in key decision-making processes and transparency. As a result, they are becoming ever more sophisticated in how they facilitate formal participation of relevant stakeholders, manage deliberation and use technologies that ensure *some* provision of input even from more marginalised actors. A particular set of institutional features is thus used by these initiatives to establish a legitimate presence as a governance instrument, to showcase supposed democratic and inclusive processes, fend off possible criticism, and to 'sell' their systems to potential users of certifications and labels (branded processors, retailers and ultimately consumers) (Ponte, 2014).

The FSC was the first established initiative of this kind (in 1993) and has developed perhaps the most democratic governance structures. But because this meant a long inception period and complex deliberations, other forestry sustainability initiatives that were less inclusive and democratic, and had a much more industry-driven agenda (such as the Programme for the Endorsement of Forest Certification, PEFC) adopted quicker and more commercially-orientated procedures, and ended up taking a major share of the sustainability certification market. In time, however, PEFC gradually took on some multi-stakeholder features itself, thus FSC can be said to have had a positive overall influence on the overall depth and breadth of the sustainability certification market, in what the literature calls the 'ratcheting up' of standards (Cashore, 2002; Overdevest and Zeitlin, 2014). More worryingly, forest certification has had only limited effect in halting deforestation, due to its predominant application in the global North.

The experience of the MSC points to a different trajectory. Although generally inspired by FSC, MSC was designed around a much more corporate and top-down structure, a less inclusive process and a much more aggressive commercial strategy. It was able to capitalise on first-mover advantage and has held dominant position in the certification of capture fisheries and sale of 'sustainable fish'. This means that MSC did not have to face 'watering down' pressures from competing certification systems (Gulbrandsen, 2014). So far, MSC has been able to create and dominate the market for 'sustainable fish', but success has also been accompanied by serious challenges: first, MSC has so far failed to convincingly show that its certification system has positive environmental impacts; and second, it has marginalised fisheries in the global South, especially in low-income countries. This has resulted in a peculiar configuration of the 'sustainable fish market', where we have a dearth of information on whether it is actually 'sustainable' and where a large majority of MSC-certified fish is captured in northern fisheries despite the fact that around half of total global exports of fish originate in the global South (Ponte, 2012).

The more recent ASC has returned to a much more open and participatory process in comparison to MSC, especially when the participation of southern stakeholders is concerned. Its creation came after a long gestation process that took place through twelve Aquaculture Dialogues (ADs) established by World Wide Fund for Nature (WWF) and focused on specific species. However, ASC faces sharp competition from existing schemes, especially in North America, where the commercially-orientated Aquaculture Certification Council (ACC) has a strong presence.

The experience of these certification systems suggests overall that the more complex, transparent and participatory an MSI, the smaller its share of the sustainability certification market. But these dynamics are also confounded by first-mover advantage and by the restraints of a small market size for sustainable products. The case study of sustainability certification in biofuels, however, can provide some additional insights. It is particularly instructive as mandatory biofuel sustainability certification in the EU was initiated following the adoption of the Renewable Energy Directive (RED) in 2009. Under this scheme, in order to receive government support or count towards mandatory national renewable energy targets, all biofuels used in the EU (whether locally produced or imported) have to comply with sustainability criteria. This means that RED has created a captive market for sustainability – and one where all certification systems could apply for recognition from the EU at the same time (Ponte, 2014).

One of the first certification systems to be recognised, the RSB, attempted to go back to the original spirit of FSC by going through a long, complex and highly participatory process of multi-stakeholder consultation, the development of strict standards and the setting up of transparent procedures.

But differently from FSC, it had to face commercially aggressive and lean competitors from the beginning, including International Sustainability and Carbon Certification (ISCC). The RED directive does not differentiate between different certification systems beyond its minimum set of standards, in relation to how inclusive, equitable and transparent their governance structures are. In the case of biofuel, regulation played a function of level-field formation in the sustainability market, but with a low-level sustainability bar. National-level direct or indirect government support went behind selected private certifications (in Germany first, then in France, the Netherlands and the UK). The fastest and most aggressive mover in this context, ISCC was able to establish a substantial presence in the market and thus close off the expansion of a far more inclusive and transparent RSB.

It is unlikely that RSB will be able to ride the normative wave that helped FSC to remain commercially relevant and that led to improvements in the features of its competitors. RSB did not enjoy the FSC's head-start over competitors, biofuels are mixed with regular fuel – making consumer boycotts difficult to carry out – and social movements and NGOs are generally against sustainability certification for biofuels. RSB is therefore in a much weaker position in terms of mobilising the normative push that it would need (Ponte, 2014).

In sum, these experiences suggest that more complex, transparent, democratic and participatory initiatives tend to be less successful in establishing a sizeable presence in the market. This is because they compete in the market for sustainability standards over: securing enough suppliers that can meet the requirements of certification; finding a retail market for certified products; and securing support from, and alliances with, influential NGOs, other civil society groups, and if applicable, the public sector. At the same time, the forestry industry experience also suggests that these MSIs can lead to normative pressure (originating from NGOs and transmitted by major retailers) on commercially driven sustainability initiatives to improve their standards further. Yet, in the cases highlighted here, the actual impact of certification on sustainability outcomes is at best limited and contingent, if not unknown. These experiences also indicate that often MSIs have problematic distributional effects in terms of the geographical spread of existing certifications, especially in relation to North–South dynamics.

Finally, it should be kept in mind that even though many MSIs do not include governments in their stakeholders, the role of state engagement is very important for their success. First, during the agenda-setting and negotiation of standards, governments can provide expertise, and technical and financial support; they also influence the agenda through direct regulation. Second, they can be important in the certification implementation stage through public procurement and state-controlled operations. And third, monitoring and enforcement of standards is often dependent on effective and supportive regulation and the availability of public research results (Gulbrandsen, 2014).

17.3 Theoretical and Analytical Tools: TEG, Orchestration, and GVC Analysis

In the previous section, we briefly examined the widening portfolio of environmental governance instruments that have emerged in the past few decades, and their successes and challenges. In this section, we provide the theoretical and analytical tools that can help to make sense of this complexity in order to highlight what role public authority (national and international) can play in steering environmental governance towards wished-for collective goals. To do so, we explain the main features of: TEG, orchestration and GVC analysis. Common to all three is a focus on the *transnational* features of economic, social and environmental governance. This is in recognition that important aspects of regulation take place beyond the nation state, outside the venues of international agreement formation, and that regulatory processes rarely reach truly global dimensions. In other words, we strive to make sense of how collective and individual actors from different national contexts engage in cross-border rule-making, implementation and enforcement activities.

All three also highlight the *hybrid*, rather than simply private or public, features of transnational governance – business, civil society and public actors interact at different levels, in parallel and intersecting arenas, and in contexts where private and civil society actors can be subject to domestic and intergovernmental legal orders. These are dynamics that cannot be neatly characterised as private-driven or public-driven, but are indeed hybrid.

One of the main tenets of the literature on TEG is that actors and institutions involved in it are constantly seeking to assert political and rule-making authority – the decision-making power over particular environmental issues that is accepted as legitimate from specific audiences (Cashore, 2002; Fransen, 2012). This is because they cannot rely on the exclusive authority of the state or a global institution. TEG discussions also indicate that the emergence of private authority has not led to a wholesale retreat of the state, but to new overlaps between public and private spheres. While the literature shows that private authority has been on the rise, it also argues that it may actually apply to areas that were never regulated by the state to begin with; when private authority addresses transnational problems, it can actually enhance state capacity by allowing the state to escape innate constraints placed by territorial borders and to focus more effectively on other areas of regulation; and, private authority often needs public authority to establish legitimacy, thus making it difficult to disentangle the two. This suggests that what is normally conceived as private authority in contrast to public authority actually has salient hybrid features.

The literature shows that while these hybrid dynamics can facilitate self-interest for individual actors to achieve particularistic goals, TEG can also provide alternative and more flexible venues to solve environmental problems – including the transnational experiments and entrepreneurial governance initiatives that are being carried out by industry associations and individual corporations, international and local NGOs, and other non-state actors (Bäckstrand, 2008; Andonova, Betsill and Bulkeley, 2009; Hoffman, 2011). TEG can also overcome two of the main problems that have plagued intergovernmental treaty formation: path dependency and institutional inertia. Finally, the literature shows that state capacity and intergovernmental action are still crucial in facilitating the emergence, implementation and enforcement of environmental governance – and indeed successful public support (national and international) is more likely to happen when norms, objectives, and interests align between the public and private spheres (Guldbrandsen, 2014).

One of the main concerns in discussions on TEG, however, is how to create some coherence in the fragmentation of governance instruments in the environmental field (Zelli and van Asselt, 2013). Thus, much attention is now being dedicated to the possible mechanisms and strategies that nation states and international organisations can use to shape environmental outcomes. The concept of orchestration provides a useful tool to address the perceived transnational governance deficit. Orchestration refers to a wide set of mechanisms, some of which are 'directive' and others 'facilitative'. *Directive* orchestration relies on the authority of the state and seeks to incorporate private initiatives into its regulatory framework, for example through mandating principles, transparency and codes of conduct. *Facilitative* orchestration relies on softer instruments, such as the provision of material and ideational support, in order to kick-start new initiatives and/or further shape and support them (Abbott and Snidal, 2009; Schleifer, 2013; Hale and Rogers, 2014; Abbott, Genschel, Snidal and Zangl, 2015).

Thus, orchestration happens when states or intergovernmental organisations initiate, guide, broaden, and/or strengthen transnational governance by non-state and/or sub-state actors. It can combine a variety of instruments, including: (1) intermediation, when a governor uses intermediary actors to achieve governance goals (soft instruments, indirect influence) (Abbott et al., 2015); (2) regulatory hierarchy (hard instruments, direct influence); (3) collaboration (soft instrument, direct influence); and (4) delegation (hard instruments, indirect influence) (Green, 2014). Orchestrators may thus combine straight regulation (or the threat of future/stronger regulation) with collaboration, delegation, intermediation and other hybrid mechanisms, such as placing their own representatives in key positions in intermediary organisations.

The literature on orchestration shows that the likelihood of successful public orchestration in the environmental field can be linked to four dimensions: regulatory fragmentation and uncertainty; issue visibility; interest alignment; and issue scope (Lister et al., 2015).

- On *regulatory fragmentation and uncertainty*, the conditions for orchestration are more difficult in situations when public regulation of environmental concerns is fragmented and uncertain, and when relevant private or hybrid initiatives are multiple and diverse.

- On *issue visibility*, there is more potential for orchestration if the industry involved, and the related set of environmental issues, are clearly visible to the general public and to consumers.
- On *interest alignment*, there are better orchestration possibilities if there is substantial overlap between public and private interests, and relative cohesion internally within each sphere.
- On *issue scope*, orchestration is more likely to succeed when addressing a narrower, more specialised set of issues, rather than a more comprehensive set.

Finally, GVC analysis is also relevant for examining TEG. As indicated in the previous section, 'pull factors' are important in determining environmental improvements, and usually operate when firms react to demands placed by the buyers of their products and services (in addition to public regulation and civil society pressure). GVC analysis explains how outsourcing and offshoring of production are 'driven' by the strategies and decisions of 'lead firms' in value chains. These groups of firms define the terms of supply chain membership, incorporate or exclude other actors, and allocate where, when and by whom value is added (Ponte and Sturgeon, 2014). The GVC literature distinguishes between: *'unipolar'* value chains, where lead firms occupying one specific functional position in the chain play a dominant role in shaping it; *'bipolar'* value chains, where two sets of actors in different functional positions both govern the chain, albeit in different ways; and *'multipolar'* chains, which are different from 'markets' as they are strongly shaped by the explicit strategic actions of powerful actors (both inside and outside the chain). The GVC literature also shows that levels of 'driving' are likely to be higher in unipolar chains, where power is concentrated, than in multipolar chains, where power is more dispersed. These distinctions are important for the case of (container) shipping below, where two sets of very powerful actors (shipping companies and cargo-owners) suggest the presence of 'bipolar' governance, and thus only partial leverage from cargo-owners in transmitting pressures for environmental improvement on to shipping companies (Ponte and Sturgeon, 2014).

In the next section, we apply these three theoretical frameworks to the analysis of 'sustainable shipping'.

17.4 Case Study: Sustainable Shipping

17.4.1 Background

Maritime shipping is the oldest transnational business and the transmission belt of global production, trade and consumption – as 90 per cent of international trade travels by ocean vessel. Yet, shipping lags well behind other global industries in its environmental performance. Over 3 per cent of global carbon emissions are from ships, and without change this is expected to reach 18 per cent by 2050. Furthermore, with a reliance on burning low-grade bunker fuel, ships and ports are major air polluters. Concerns regarding spills, noise and invasive species from ballast water discharge have gained public attention.

State-led regulatory initiatives to reduce impacts on air, land and water as well as private standards to improve environmental practices, accountability and transparency across maritime shipping value chains are emerging. Table 17.1 shows that the resulting TEG is a complex hybrid of public and private actors, institutions and standards across multiple transnational, regional, national and local levels (Poulsen et al. 2016).

Ships by definition are mobile, and ship registration, which defines a ship's nationality, is highly flexible. These factors shape industry practice and make shipping particularly 'footloose' (DeSombre, 2006). In 2013, an estimated 73 per cent of the world fleet was registered under 'flags of convenience' open registers, which provide freedom from stricter labour, tax and environmental regulation. As a consequence, regulatory intervention has been difficult and, in the case of environmental standards, lagging and minimal.

The main *internal drivers* of environmental improvements within shipping companies have been fuel savings and energy prices. CO2 emissions are linearly related to fuel consumption, and up to a certain level, energy efficiency enhancement represents a win-win for business and the environment. However *external drivers* of environmental improvement are also emerging: tightening regulation; various forms of cooperation (business to business as well as of multi-stakeholder nature); and value chain demands – specifically, the emerging sustainability requirements posed by cargo-owners (such as brewers or car manufacturers) to their shipping companies.

17.4.2 Regulation

The standards for maritime safety and environmental protection are formulated and adopted by United Nations' IMO, and subsequently implemented by flag-states in national legislation. The IMO's International Convention for the Prevention of Pollution from Ships (MARPOL) represents the main body of the international regulatory framework for marine pollution from international shipping.

In 2013, the IMO introduced two new measures to stimulate environmental improvements in international shipping through the reduction of CO2 emissions: the Energy Efficiency Design Index (EEDI) and the Ship Energy Efficiency Management Plan (SEEMP). EEDI aims at reducing CO2 emissions relative to the transport work performed. SEEMP is a mandatory plan for all ships, aimed at reducing fuel consumption in the daily ship operation. The EU

Table 17.1 Main aspects and sources of possible environmental improvements in container shipping

Issues	Regulatory tools	Industry initiatives and MSIs	Buyer-driven measures
CO_2 emission-reduction and improved fuel efficiency	IMO MARPOL Convention	Clean Cargo Working Group (CCWG)	A handful of cargo-owners are including environmental performance on fuel efficiency and CO_2 emissions in their pricing models when buying shipping services.
	IMO's Energy Efficiency Design Index (EEDI)	Sustainable Shipping Initiative (SSI)	A small number of cargo-owners use these indicators for procurement decisions (volume allocation).
	IMO's Ship Energy Efficiency Management Plan (SEEMP)	A variety of 'green shipping' rating schemes	A larger, but still small in absolute terms, number of cargo-owners are starting to collect data on suppliers' fuel efficiency and CO_2 emission performance.
	EU mandatory scheme for monitoring, reporting and verification of CO_2 emissions from shipping (MRV) (under discussion)	Carbon Disclosure Project (CDP)	
SO_x and NO_x emission-reduction	IMO MARPOL Convention: Regional regulation fuel-sulphur content (SECA) for the Baltic and North Sea and North American coastal waters	A variety of 'green shipping' rating schemes; Trident Alliance of ship-owners lobby for strong enforcement of SECA	None
	IMO MARPOL Convention: Global reduction of fuel-sulphur content (2020 or 2025)		
	IMO MARPOL Convention: Regional limits to NO_x emissions (NECA) in North American coastal waters (2016)		
Invasive species	IMO Ballast Water Management Convention (different regional rules)	None	None

has implemented a mandatory scheme for monitoring, reporting and verification (MRV) of CO2 emissions from shipping, but it is still uncertain whether a global MRV scheme will come into existence under the IMO. The problem is that these measures will in any case only slow down growth in CO2 emissions, but not achieve actual reductions due to the expected growth in demand for maritime shipping (Poulsen et al., 2016).

Reducing emissions of sulphur oxides (SOx) and nitrogen oxides (NOx) are also means of achieving environmental upgrading sources of major concern due to their effects on human health and marine environments, in particular close to densely populated areas such as port cities. To reduce SOx emissions, regional regulations for the Baltic and North Sea, and US coastal waters have entered into force in 2015. A global reduction of fuel-sulphur content is planned in 2020, but may be postponed for five years subject to the availability of such fuel. NOx emissions are addressed in the IMO MARPOL Convention, and regional limits to NOx emissions have entered into force in 2016 (Poulsen et al., 2016).

Other environmental problems are caused by invasive marine species. Non-native species, transported in ships' ballast water tanks and on the outside of ship hulls, can cause great damage to marine ecosystems. In order to avoid further damage by invasive species, the IMO has adopted the Ballast Water Management Convention in 2004. The US, however, has a different set of regional rules, which also cause uncertainty in the regulatory framework.

17.4.3 Voluntary 'Green Shipping' Standards and Rating Schemes

With the knowledge of growing regulatory pressure but an absence of regulatory certainty, shipping companies are increasingly participating in MSIs on 'green shipping' and in the development and adoption of industry-led, voluntary standards (Lister, Poulsen and Ponte, 2015).

Table 17.2 shows that groups such as the CCWG and the SSI have formed to provide collaborative forums and to develop performance metrics to rank and reward companies for better performance. CCWG was formed in 2003 by an industry-led NGO, Business for Social Responsibility (BSR), and aims at improving the transparency and environmental performance of container ships and shipping companies through standardised measures and what they identify as best practices. The SSI is more of a 'lighthouse' providing a vision and future direction for sustainable shipping efforts, and seeks to influence policy-makers in advancing greener shipping practices. It also seeks to create coherence between the many green shipping rating schemes that have emerged.

Hybrid, quasi-private port authorities have also been active in the rating scheme field. For example, the World Ports Climate Initiative (WPCI) has established a benchmarking tool which measures reduced air emissions as required by current IMO regulation. On this basis, the best performing vessels

Table 17.2 Green shipping rating schemes

	Audience	Ship-types	# ships	Environmental issues covered	Scoring framework	Membership fee	Data source
Clean Cargo Working Group (CCWG)	Cargo-owners	Container	2,300	CO_2, SO_x, PM, NO_x, water and waste; chemical use	Yes (based on NO_x, SO_x, CO_2 and access to shore power in port)	Fee for all members	Partly performance data received from ship-owners; partly vessel design specification
Clean Shipping Index (CSI)	Cargo-owners	Container, dry bulk, ro/ro, cruise	2,000	CO_2, SO_x, NO_x, water and waste; chemical use; hull-fouling	Yes (based on CO_2, NO_x, SO_x, chemical and water use/waste)	Free for cargo-owners; costs for ship-owners for data verification	Partly performance data received from ship-owners; partly vessel design specification
Environmental Ship Index (ESI)	Ports	Container, dry bulk, general cargo, ro/ro, cruise	>2,000	CO_2, SO_x, PM, NO_x	Step rating (with four levels); for CO_2 the scheme only asks if emissions are calculated or not (Yes/No)	Information not available	Partly performance data received from ship-owners; partly vessel design specification

Green Award	Ports	Dry bulk, tankers, inland barges and LNG	>1.500	CO_2, SO_x, PM2, NO_x, water and waste, anti-fouling paint	Information not available	Ship-owner fee	Information not available
RightShip	Charterers	Container, dry bulk, tankers, general cargo, ro/ro, cruise	60,000	CO_2	Step rating (with seven steps)	Subscription fee for detailed data sets	Based on vessel design specifications
Shipping Efficiency.Org	Charterers	Container, dry bulk, tanker, general cargo, ro/ro, cruise	60,000	CO_2	Step rating (with seven steps)	Subscription fee for detailed data sets	Based on vessel design specifications
Triple-E	Ship-owner	Container, dry bulk, tankers, general cargo, ro/ro, cruise	33	CO_2, SO_x, PM, NO_x, water and wastewater; chemical use	Step rating (with four levels)	One time fee for ship-owners when rating is issued	Partly based on vessel design specifications; partly based on performance data

with the lowest emission levels are granted a reduction in port dues by some port authorities.

Shipping companies are interested in, but also have major reservations about, these green rating schemes, given their wide variety, lack of standardisation and verification of measures, inconsistency of data collection methodology and ranking, and the inherent difficulty of shaping uniform measures across a very diverse industry. Coordination, not just among the many private initiatives but also between public and private regulatory efforts, is thus a mounting dilemma in view of ensuring environmental progress.

17.4.4 Value Chain Drivers of Environmental Improvements

In addition to an uncertain regulatory framework and a multiple set of industry and stakeholder initiatives, shipping companies are also increasingly under pressure from cargo-owners (their clients, such as retailers, manufacturers or processors) to improve selected elements of environmental performance, especially in the container shipping sector, which transports goods that are much closer to the end consumer than dry bulk or tanker vessels.

In recent years, in response to growing consumer environmental concerns as well as increasing costs and reduced demand with the global financial crisis, brand companies have embraced environmental improvement as a new business strategy to reduce risk, gain value chain control and increase sales. They have introduced aspirational company commitments including zero carbon, zero waste and 100 per cent renewable energy, not just in their own operations but also with their suppliers and along the entire value chain.

To assess the extent to which brand companies are implementing and demonstrating environmental upgrading in maritime shipping, Table 17.3 summarises the commitments of the top-ten US container import customers (Poulsen, Ponte and Lister, 2015). It shows that nine out of ten companies reported a corporate commitment to reductions in GHG emissions, with transport as a specific target within their overall reduction goal. With respect to transport, the focus for the most part is on improving fuel efficiency in trucking and on CO_2 reduction. Only four out of ten addressed maritime shipping – two of these (Dole Food and Chiquita) own their own vessels, while the other two (Heineken and Philips Electronics) are members of CCWG. Walmart is also a member of CCWG but did not report on any carbon reduction commitments or efforts related to maritime shipping (which they contract out). Other environmental upgrading issues related to maritime shipping discussed earlier (such as SOx, NOx and invasive species) are not specifically addressed in company CSR/sustainability reports.

In sum, while in other industries we observe 'buyer-driven' environmental improvements, in the case of shipping, cargo-owners have not (yet) developed sophisticated environmental demands – nor have they placed them at the core of

Table 17.3 US container importer commitment to sustainable maritime transport

Top ocean container importers to US	TEU 2012*	Carbon commitment?	Address transport?	Address maritime shipping?
Walmart[1,2]	720,000	YES	YES	X
Target[2]	496,200	YES	YES	X
Home Depot[2]	315,400	YES	YES	X
Dole Food	235,000	YES	YES	YES
Lowe's[2]	229,000	YES	YES	X
Sears Holding[2]	201,500	Under development	X	X
Chiquita	149,400	YES	YES	YES
LG Group	147,300	YES	YES	X
Heineken[1,2]	144,800	YES	YES	YES
Philips Elec[1,2,3]	124,700	YES	YES	YES
% Commitment		90%	90%	40%

*Source: *Journal of Commerce* (2012).
[1] *Members of the CCWG.*
[2] *Report GHG emissions to the Carbon Disclosure Project (CDP).*
[3] *Also report Scope 3 GHG emissions to CDP.*

negotiations regarding the procurement of shipping services. This is attributable to relatively balanced power relations between cargo-owners and shipping companies – with the latter mainly interested, for the time being, in environmental measures that lead to cost-savings (mainly, lower fuel consumption).

17.4.5 Lessons for Orchestrating TEG in Shipping

Addressing the environmental impacts of shipping is an essential and pressing governance issue. In this case study, we highlighted the complexities of TEG in shipping, which includes a combination of international agreements, national and regional regulation, an increasing number of MSIs and benchmarking processes, and an early and tentative set of private demands from cargo-owners to improve selected environmental concerns.

We have shown that shipping is characterised by: high regulatory fragmentation and uncertainty; low issue visibility (with the partial exception of container shipping); low interest alignment; and wide issue scope, with some problems that can be alleviated simultaneously, but others that are difficult to address together (e.g. ballast water treatment increases energy consumption). This means that environmental improvements are particularly challenging. This is even more so as cargo-owners are only partially able to push environmental demands upstream to (container) shipping companies, given the 'bipolar' governance feature of the shipping value chain. Although cargo-owners can exert substantial power, the container shipping industry is highly concentrated and also powerful, with five major shipping companies accounting for the majority of cargo transported. Therefore, cargo-owners are limited to wielding their environmental upgrading influence by threatening to shift volume from one carrier to another rather than dropping shipping companies for poor performance. Cargo-owners' efforts have just started, and their focus is so far mainly on CO2 emission and fuel efficiency, largely ignoring other significant environmental problems. However, expectations among container lines and branded retailers and manufacturers are that environmental demands will continue to develop, strengthen and expand. At the same time, better alignment of voluntary initiatives with regulatory requirements is essential to improve the situation (Lister et al., 2015).

It is thus essential for the IMO to act as a successful orchestrator by: (1) redoubling its efforts to minimise regulatory uncertainty and fold regional regulatory initiatives under its global mantle; (2) ensuring that green shipping initiatives align in their objectives, also by granting them consultative status at IMO; and (3) supporting independent audits of data sets in green rating schemes to improve the quality of data available to business operators. IMO efforts should thus be directed to empower private and hybrid efforts as complementary, not surrogate, to regulation, and thus encourage beyond compliance innovation under the shadow of public authority.

Questions for Discussion

1. Why has shipping fallen behind other sectors in improving its environmental footprint?
2. Why do governments have a limited role in shaping the TEG of shipping?
3. What can business and civil society groups do to improve the environmental impact of shipping?
4. What aspects of existing green shipping initiatives are helping to achieve this? What aspects are hampering further improvements?
5. How can the IMO act as a successful orchestrator?

17.5 Chapter Summary

National regulation is no longer sufficient to ensure environmental protection, especially when trans-boundary and global environmental issues are at stake.

At the same time, intergovernmental treaty formation has been slow and often inconclusive; private and hybrid forms of environmental governance have multiplied – involving industry associations, individual firms, MSIs, international and local NGOs, and other non-state actors; and value chain demands for environmental improvements only work in specific circumstances.

More generally, public sector capacity and intergovernmental action remain crucial in addressing the fragmentation of governance instruments and the resultant governance deficit, not only in the environmental field, but also in other global governance arenas. Thus, nation states and international organisations need to actively orchestrate transnational governance to facilitate the achievement of collective objectives. They can do so by combining regulation (or the threat of future/stronger regulation), the incorporation of private and hybrid initiatives into their regulatory framework; and the provision of material and ideational support to initiatives that align with public goals, environmental and otherwise.

Chapter Questions

1. Why should international organisations and national governments get involved in orchestrating TEG?
2. Should they not use their limited means to conclude and enforce global environmental agreements?
3. Why are firms and industry associations getting involved in MSIs on sustainability, which they can only partly shape and control?
4. Should they not focus on environmental strategies that help their bottom line or lobby for smarter regulation?
5. Would it not be more efficient to achieve global environmental governance by setting up a world environmental organisation?

FURTHER RESOURCES

Blowfield, M. (2013). *Business and Sustainability.* Oxford: Oxford University Press.
    An accessible and comprehensive introduction on the role of business in fostering sustainability, both within the firm and in its relations with the external environment.

Green, J. F. (2014). *Rethinking Private Authority: Agents and Entrepreneurs in Global Environmental Governance.* Princeton: Princeton University Press.
    An in-depth examination of the role of non-state actors in global environmental politics, with specific attention to the delegation of authority to private actors.

Gunningham, N., Grabosky, P. N. and Sinclair, D. (1998). *Smart Regulation: Designing Environmental Policy*. Oxford: Clarendon Press.
A classic text on environmental policy design, covering all its main aspects at different geographic scales (local, national, transnational, global).

Hoffmann, M. J. (2011). *Climate Governance at the Crossroads*. Oxford: Oxford University Press.
A comprehensive overview of climate governance tools and of recent innovative instruments, partnerships and entrepreneurial initiatives.

18 Labour Rights in Global Supply Chains

DIRK ULRICH GILBERT AND KRISTIN HUBER

Learning Objectives

- Name the core labour standards of the International Labour Organization (ILO).
- Describe cases of labour rights violations that commonly occur in global supply chains.
- Evaluate the arguments for and against sweatshop labour.
- Identify institutional responses at different levels to improve working conditions in global supply chains.

18.1 Introduction: Globalisation and Global Supply Chains

Globalisation is often defined as a process of increasing economic, social, political and cultural interconnectedness. While globalisation is certainly not a new phenomenon, as international trade has always been part of human history, the speed and scope of globalisation has increased substantially in recent years. Over the past two decades, globalisation has particularly manifested itself in the spread of global supply chains. The income generated in global supply chains has nearly doubled over the past fifteen years. Successive rounds of trade liberalisation, advances in information and communication technology (ICT) as well as the liberalisation of the global financial system and capital markets have substantially reduced trade and coordination costs and have been important drivers for the increase in global trade and the related growth of global supply chains.

Today, countries at all stages of development, ranging from low-income countries to the most advanced, are involved in global supply chains. The expansion of supply chains has also led to a growing specialisation of countries and firms in specific activities or stages in the value chain. Multinational Corporations (MNCs) increasingly outsource activities from industrialised countries to international networks of contractors in both developed and less developed countries. As a consequence, many industries today are characterised by a clear division of labour. In the footwear, garment or electronics industry, for example, MNCs mainly concentrate on value chain activities such as research and development, product design and marketing while thousands of independent contractors in developing countries and emerging economies focus on the often labour-intensive production of goods. These contractors cobble shoes, sew shirts or assemble mobile phones according to exact specifications of MNCs, and are required to deliver high-quality products often according to very tight delivery schedules. International production networks therefore reach over many national and cultural borders and are affected by multiple jurisdictions and different cultural norms and values. While the participation in global supply chains provides many developing countries with the chance to enhance economic growth and generate new income opportunities for the population, as will be highlighted in this chapter, the working conditions for many workers in local production facilities are frequently abysmal.

In this chapter we are particularly interested in the contracting arrangements of MNCs with suppliers in less developed countries which have been labelled as 'sweatshops'. Critical stakeholders from civil society such as labour and human rights activists, trade unions and non-governmental organisations (NGOs) have charged that large MNCs exploit workers in sweatshops by failing to pay a living wage, tolerating child labour and disregarding basic labour rights.

This chapter proceeds as follows: in the next section we provide a brief overview of the labour rights frequently affected by the contracts between MNCs and their suppliers before we discuss a number of examples for violations of these labour rights in global supply chains. We offer a definition of sweatshops and then continue to critically evaluate the pros and cons of sweatshop labour. Based on these insights we briefly review opportunities at different levels and by different actors to regulate and improve working conditions in global supply chains. In particular, we discuss the role of MNCs, industry-led initiatives, multi-stakeholder-initiatives (MSIs) and governments in improving labour rights in global supply chains. Finally, a case study addresses the collapse of the Rana Plaza factory complex in Bangladesh in April 2013, which killed 1,129 textile workers and left approximately 2,500 injured. This case study provides both the opportunity to better understand the manifold problems associated with labour rights in sweatshops and to review different initiatives intended to improve working conditions.

18.2 Labour Rights

Working and having a job is central to people's well-being all over the world. Work not only provides income but also paves the way for social and economic advancement of individuals, their families and the communities they live in.

Throughout history, workers have tried to express their interests and claim their rights. After World War I, based on the insight that social peace is a crucial prerequisite for peace and economic growth, the ILO was established in 1919. The ILO is a key player in the arena of labour rights and has developed a system of international labour standards. It promotes opportunities for workers to obtain productive and decent work in conditions of freedom, equality, security and most importantly, dignity (ILO, 2015). In 1946 the ILO became a specialised agency of the newly formed United Nations (UN). The UN also backed workers' interests by incorporating some key labour rights into Articles 23 and 24 of the United Nations Declaration of Human Rights.

The goal of both the UN and the ILO is to introduce globally applicable and acceptable minimum standards to protect employees' rights. The labour standards are, however, only legally binding once a member state has ratified them. Since its inception, the ILO has issued 189 conventions on labour rights (as of 2014), of which eight are considered as the 'core labour standards' being recognised internationally and claiming validity for all countries. The core labour standards are the following:

- Freedom of association and the effective recognition of the right to collective bargaining (Convention No. 87 and No. 98);
- The elimination of all forms of forced and compulsory labour (Convention No. 29 and No. 105);
- The effective abolition of child labour (Convention No. 138 and No. 182);
- The elimination of discrimination in respect of employment and occupation (Convention No. 100 and No. 111).

The UN and the ILO are only two of a large number of stakeholders (e.g. consumers, governments, NGOs) who are interested in labour rights, and the core labour standards mentioned above represent only a small fraction of the multitude of labour rights which are possibly at stake. The list of these labour rights is long and covers for example the right to a living wage based on a regular working week that does not exceed forty-eight hours, or a safe and healthy workplace free from violence and harassment. We focus mainly on the role of MNCs in regard to labour rights, showing that labour rights violations are commonplace in global supply chains and mostly happen in the plants of local contractors, the so-called sweatshops.

18.3 Violations of Labour Rights: Sweatshop Labour in Global Supply Chains

The definitions of 'sweatshops' vary in the literature. The US General Accounting Office (1988) defines sweatshops as production sites employing workers at low wages, for long hours and under poor conditions. Arnold and Hartman define the term 'sweatshop' as

> any workplace in which workers are typically subject to two or more of the following conditions: income for a 48 hour workweek less than the overall poverty rate for that country; systematic forced overtime; systematic health and safety risks due to negligence or the wilful disregard of employee welfare; coercion; systematic deception that places workers at risk; and underpayment of earnings. (Arnold and Hartman, 2006: 677)

Other authors believe that defining a sweatshop only by referring to different aspects of working conditions is hampering a substantive debate over the morality of sweatshop labour by definition. They propose to define sweatshops more broadly as industries which violate labour rights in a way which makes their actions prima facie wrong (Zwolinski, 2007). Following this definition, sweatshops exist throughout the world in both developed and less developed countries. The critical discussion of sweatshops in the public and in the academic literature has nevertheless primarily focused on developing countries. These sweatshops are usually legally independent firms that have become part of the global supply chains of large MNCs.

The critical discussion concerning sweatshops mainly focuses on the violation of labour rights and the moral status of sweatshop labour. It is important to note that violations of labour rights are widespread and often happen with the implicit approval of local authorities. In Bangladesh, for example, factory owners have in the past been accused of colluding with state institutions and bribing government officials to defy regulations and building codes. Moreover, factory owners are among the wealthiest people in the country, occupying around 10 per cent of the seats in the Bangladeshi parliament (Zaman, 2014). Table 18.1 provides only a few examples of such labour rights violations to exemplarily illustrate the magnitude of the problems related to the global contracting arrangements of MNCs.

Violations of labour rights can be found in almost all industries and in nearly every part of the globe. As Table 18.1 indicates, each industry faces particular challenges. Nonetheless, there are a number of labour rights issues that cut across industries and countries. Health and safety issues, freedom of association as well as wages range at the top of the most common labour rights violations worldwide. The worst breaches against labour rights are usually recorded at subcontracting workshops (i.e. second- or third-tier suppliers) as these are much harder to control than those factories which directly supply MNCs. These examples highlight that although jobs in international supply networks may be better than other available alternatives in developing countries, the working conditions often are hazardous.

Table 18.1 Common labour rights violations in global supply chains

Form of labour right violation	Example
Child labour The ILO estimates that around the world approximately 168 million children are working instead of going to school. 60% of child labour occurs in the agricultural sector (e.g. in the production of cocoa, tea, cotton, palm oil). Most child labourers face 'hazardous' work environments that are harmful in physical and mental terms (ILRF, 2015, ILO, 2015).	**Cocoa industry, Côte d'Ivoire** Côte d'Ivoire accounts for much of the world's supply in cocoa. While cocoa is lucrative to international traders, farmers in West Africa often receive very low wages. Farmers often cannot hire labourers to harvest, but draw their children out of school to perform this arduous task. According to the US Department of Labor, in the harvest season of 2008–2009, in Côte d'Ivoire, roughly 820,000 children aged between 5 and 17 were working in the cocoa sector, 10% of which were victims of child trafficking and forced labour. Children working on cocoa plantations are exposed to chemicals and long working hours. Child labour often leads to low educational access and attendance which again traps families in a vicious cycle of poverty (US Department of Labor, 2013).
Forced labour In 2014, the ILO recorded around 21 million people as victims of forced labour. The sectors most afflicted with forced labour are domestic work, agriculture, construction, manufacturing and entertainment. Besides women and girls, indigenous people and migrant workers are particularly vulnerable to being forced into labour (ILO, 2015).	**Electronics industry, Malaysia** A recent study by the human rights NGO Vérité found that working conditions in the Malaysian electronics sector, particularly for migrant workers, are prone to result in forced labour. 28% of workers, both female and male, were found to be in situations of forced labour. High recruitment fees and the debt that workers often incur to pay those fees, leave workers vulnerable to exploitation. A common practice in the Malaysian electronics sector is the retention of passports. As the study reports, for 71% of foreign workers it was either difficult or impossible to receive their passport back when they asked for it (Vérité, 2014).
Living wages In many countries of the world, a considerable gap exists between the wages that workers earn and the cost of their basic needs. While ILO has set standards on regular payment of wages, and minimum wage levels, often wages are either not paid out or workers are paid in manufactured goods or alcohol. Some governments have also set the legal minimum wage below the actual cost of living, in order to attract	**Garment industry, Cambodia** Cambodian garment factories produce for the whole of the global fashion industry. The lion's share (80%) of workers in the Cambodian garment industry is made up of women aged 18–35. Due to high inflation rates, the minimum wage in Cambodia does not cover the costs for basic needs. Factory workers in Cambodia are only consuming half of the calories recommended for a grown-up person, with the result that many workers are experiencing health issues due to underweight. While the Cambodian minimum

Table 18.1 (*cont.*)

Form of labour right violation	Example
foreign investment. With a living wage workers should not only be able to satisfy their basic needs but also be able to e.g. pay for education of their children and transportation (ILO, 2015; ILRF, 2015).	wage was recently set at US$100/month, the Asia Floor Wage Alliance suggests that in order to provide a living for a family, a wage would need to be set at US$283/month (CCC, 2015).
Freedom of association In many countries, workers are hindered to collectively organise. Intimidations and acts of violence are often used to stop workers from collective action. To undermine unionisation, workers are fired, imprisoned or replaced with migrant workers or children who are often even less able to claim their rights (ILRF, 2015).	**Electronics industry, China** China is the largest manufacturer of consumer electronics, producing goods for MNCs such as Microsoft and IBM. In China the only union allowed is the non-democratic 'All-China Federation of Trade Unions' (ACFTU). However, Chinese workers are often unaware of its existence or its mandate. As an audit by the Fair Labor Association at the Apple subcontractor Foxconn brought to light, the majority of the members of the union committee were nominated by the management team and while there were elections, the candidates were often supervisors (SOMO, 2012).
Health and Safety The ILO reports that every year about 2.3 million people die from work-related accidents or diseases, while a further 160 million people suffer from diseases related to their occupations. Non-fatal accidents amount to 313 million per year. Most of these accidents are preventable (ILO, 2015).	**Garment industry, Bangladesh** – see also case study In 2013, the Bangladeshi garment sector was struck by the worst industrial accident in the country's history. The building complex Rana Plaza, hosting five garment factories, collapsed, burying under it thousands of mostly female garment workers. After the incident, 29 global brands were identified as having placed orders at the factories within Rana Plaza and were accused of having been complicit in creating or maintaining a deadly work environment (CCC, 2015).

References

CCC (2015). Clean Clothes Campaign. Retrieved 20 September 2015 from www.cleanclothes.org/

ILO (2015). International Labour Organization. Retrieved 20 September 2015 from www.ilo.org/global/lang–en/index.htm

ILRF (2015). International Labor Rights Forum. Retrieved 21 September 2015 from www.laborrights.org/

SOMO (2012). Freedom of association in the electronics industry. Retrieved 17 November 2015 from www.somo.nl/publications-en/Publication_3804

US Department of Labor (2013). Cote d'Ivoire. Retrieved 25 June 2015 from www.dol.gov/ilab/reports/child-labor/findings/2013TDA/cotedivoire.pdf

Vérité (2014). Forced Labour in the Production of Electronic Goods in Malaysia. A Comprehensive Study of Scope and Characteristics. Retrieved 22 September 2015 from www.verite.org/sites/default/files/images/VeriteForcedLaborMalaysianElectronics2014.pdf.

18.4 The Sweatshop Labour Debate

There is a lively debate in the disciplines of philosophy, economics, politics, sociology and business ethics whether and to what extent sweatshop labour is coercive and exploitative. This heated debate around the already negatively connoted term 'sweatshop' has not only received a tremendous amount of attention from theory, but also from NGOs, governments, consumers and MNCs. The question of whether sweatshop labour leads to desirable or undesirable consequences heavily depends on the theoretical perspective one adopts. A large body of critical and positive literature in regard to sweatshops can be found, and we note that the discussion has evolved beyond the superficial objections to sweatshops in the 1990s. Proponents of sweatshop labour mainly argue from an economic point of view (e.g. neoclassical theory) to justify sweatshop labour. Opponents of sweatshop labour usually apply ethical theories (e.g. Kantian ethics) to frame the debate in terms of the moral status of sweatshop labour. Both parties have strong arguments and the debate over what to do about sweatshops is far from being resolved. Drawing the line between right or wrong in terms of sweatshop labour is difficult and basically a matter of balancing economic and moral arguments against each other.

18.4.1 Pros of Sweatshop Labour

Proponents of sweatshop labour usually start from the assumption that individuals who work in a sweatshop freely choose to do so. The choice to accept a job in a sweatshop is an exercise of autonomy even if it is not a fully autonomous one. For workers accepting the (bad) conditions of a sweatshop, this is probably their most preferred option among a very restricted set of options. Furthermore, sweatshop workers usually do not accept difficult labour conditions in order to gain an extra income for luxuries, but work to survive and escape the misery of poverty (Zwolinski, 2007; Powell and Zwolinski, 2012). According to the proponents, choices to work in a sweatshop, when they are made autonomously, deserve respect and generate a claim against interventions of NGOs, MNCs, governments and other stakeholders trying to fight or even prohibit sweatshop labour. Although workers' rights may be violated in a sweatshop environment, the abuse of peoples' rights is only a consequence of the autonomy of their own choice and not an objection to it (Zwolinski, 2007: 692–693). Proponents also argue that workers are aware of the difficult working conditions and have much more local knowledge of the particular situation in host countries than first-world scholars and activists. Claims by opponents of sweatshops that workers are somehow irrational and will not choose the option which is in their best self-interest would, hence, require considerable empirical evidence which so far cannot be found (Powell and Zwolinski, 2012).

Based on these assumptions, it would be wrong to deprive workers of the option to choose to work in a sweatshop because it would be a violation of the worker's autonomy. All else being equal, sweatshops make their workers better off even if the conditions are unfair. Sweatshop labour might not be the first choice but this kind of labour is preferred by most of the workers to any other alternative. The salary earned in sweatshops is typically higher than that paid by alternative sources of employment and better than being unemployed (Zwolinski, 2007). Workers living in poverty often have only a very small list of viable options to improve their living conditions. These options often range from prostitution or theft to sweatshop labour, and removing one option from this very short list, often the most preferred one, would not be any better for the worker. A comparison of wages paid by sweatshops with those earned through non-sweatshop jobs (e.g. working as a nanny or waiter) even shows that sweatshop jobs seem to outpay the other domestic rivals significantly (Zwolinski, 2007: 703–704). A study by Powell and Skarbek found that sweatshop wages in the Dominican Republic, Haiti, Honduras or Nicaragua were three to seven times higher than wages paid elsewhere in the domestic economy, regardless of whether the salaries were paid by MNCs or local subcontractors (Powell and Skarbek, 2006). Even if the salary is meagre, the money earned in a sweatshop may still help workers to educate their children, feed their families, pay their rents and improve their living conditions. Workers thus seem to be better off than they would have been without sweatshop labour. In light of these arguments it is not beneficial to prohibit sweatshop labour because it does not make a contribution to solving problems such as poverty. On the contrary, without sweatshops developing countries such as Bangladesh or Cambodia would lose a significant amount of their gross domestic product (GDP) and tax revenues that MNCs bring to those countries. The range of currently available options to fight poverty would be even more reduced, and governments typically worry that an increase in the cost of running sweatshops could lead MNCs to leave or stay away (Zwolinski, 2007: 697).

Following this argument, one can conclude that not only MNCs but also workers benefit from sweatshop labour because they are both better off than without this form of work. The wages paid by MNCs to workers help to increase their standard of living, even if the gain from sweatshop labour does not seem to be fairly distributed among both parties. The argument of proponents is that MNCs outsourcing to sweatshops at least do *something* and this is better than doing *nothing* to make workers in developing countries better off. MNCs not outsourcing their labour to sweatshops and producing under higher standards in their home countries do not benefit those workers at all. Zwolinski argues that it would be odd to blame MNCs for helping *some* workers while most other firms and individuals are helping *none* (Zwolinski, 2012). This does not necessarily mean that MNCs in their global supply chains are doing as much as they *should* be doing – from a moral point of view – to improve the living of sweatshop workers. Nonetheless, relative to offering no job alternatives, a job with low labour standards and low wages might be the best option available to most of the workers.

A closer look at the labour rights affected by sweatshop labour reveals that wages and other standards, regarding e.g. health and safety, workers' rights to collective bargaining or forced labour, must be treated as different kinds of labour rights. The arguments in favour of sweatshops mainly focus on wages and have shown that although sweatshop wages may not be high enough to lift workers out of poverty, sweatshops can make a significant contribution to improve the standard of living in developing countries. From a moral point of view, nevertheless, concerns over other labour rights may be distinct from concerns over wages (Zwolinski, 2012). Morally, critics may hold that forced labour or unsafe working conditions violate workers' rights in a way that low wages do not. In practice, however, issues such as low wages and other labour standards are inextricably linked, and proponents of sweatshop labour usually argue that improvements in both areas lead to an increase in total cost of production. For MNCs and the sweatshops in their global supply chains the overall costs of a transaction matter, and often an increase in worker safety may come at the expense of other forms of compensation (e.g. wage or overtime bonus). This leads to the paradoxical situation that workers themselves are not willing to sacrifice any wages in order to receive e.g. higher health and safety standards. A recent survey found that only very few Guatemalan sweatshop workers were actually willing to trade any wages for more health and safety standards (Zwolinski, 2012: 164). Nearly 65 per cent of the employees approached in this survey responded that they were not willing to sacrifice any wages for an improvement of their labour standards. Following this argument one can conclude that both parties affected, the sweatshop and the workers, do not want to put their competitive advantage at risk and implement measures to improve labour standards. However, based on this (purely economic) rationale, it would even make sense to further reduce labour standards to achieve an 'improved' cost position and with it an even greater competitive advantage. From an economic point of view, a profit-maximising firm is indifferent to compensating workers with money or with other benefits (e.g. health, safety, leisure) because the firm only cares about the overall cost of the total compensation package.

Powell and Zwolinski argue that workers think differently because they actually care about the mix of compensation they receive (Powell and Zwolinski, 2012). Economic theory suggests that the higher the overall compensation, the more likely workers are to desire non-monetary benefits. Unfortunately, many sweatshop workers only receive low wages because their productivity is low and hence, their compensation level is also low. Accordingly, and as indicated above, workers demand most of their compensation in wages and only little in improvements of labour conditions such as health and safety. This leads to a problem for the opponents of sweatshop labour, who want to separate the discussion about wages from safety and other working conditions. Workers and firms are limited by the same factor, the worker's marginal revenue product. And if activists only demand to improve safety in sweatshops, then they either are pushing for a reduction in wages (which workers do not seem to prefer) or they will unemploy workers by raising their package of total compensation more than their marginal productivity. Powell and Zwolinski refer to empirical studies providing (only weak) evidence that an increase of the minimum wage leads to an increase in unemployment (ibid.). However, the literature on this important question provides mixed results and does not produce clear implications for policy-makers.

18.4.2 Cons of Sweatshop Labour

Contrary to the proponents of sweatshops, opponents claim that sweatshop labour is wrongfully coercive and exploitative. The economists' standard response to this criticism is that sweatshop labour can be mutually beneficial for the worker and the firm, although it may be coercive and exploitative. In this response lies the core of a first problem which opponents of sweatshop labour criticise. From their point of view, it is a mistake to narrowly focus on the interaction between a worker and the company running a sweatshop and to only focus on the *economic* benefit to the worker relative to which he or she stood prior to the employment. The choice to accept a job in a sweatshop may be an inevitable move for a worker to improve his or her standard of living, but this does not *morally* justify the unjust conditions that lie in the background of the specific interaction. People only choose to work in a sweatshop because their situation presumably is desperate and they live in an environment characterised by injustice of political and economic institutions. We can expect that the more desperate a worker's situation is, the greater is his or her motivation to accept any job in a sweatshop that helps him or her to improve it. Kates proposes that even if workers personally choose to work in sweatshops, third parties should interfere with this choice through banning or regulating sweatshop labour, since sweatshop workers are trapped in a collective action problem (Kates, 2015). A collective action problem is characterised by a conflict of interest of a single sweatshop worker and the interests of the entire group of sweatshop workers. The trouble is that labour usually is an abundant factor in developing countries, such that a single complaining worker can easily be replaced by a worker who accepts the conditions of a sweatshop, although they are not in his or her interest. Sweatshop workers are only able to give effect to their autonomous choices through collective action, which can however only come into effect with the help of the law. Hence, Kates concludes that, paradoxically, in order to respect the autonomy of sweatshop workers, it is necessary to regulate sweatshops (ibid.).

Critics further argue that a firm which takes advantage of such structural injustice fails to give the worker the appropriate respect which he or she deserves. Based on Kantian ethics, Arnold and Bowie argue that both managers of MNCs and sweatshops have the duty to guarantee the dignity of workers and not to coerce and exploit them (Arnold and Bowie, 2007). Both individuals and firms who contribute to unjust social processes bear a moral responsibility for the processes themselves and the results they produce. These duties may include paying workers a living wage, meeting health and safety standards, and adhering to local labour laws. Arnold and Bowie claim that workers as human beings with autonomy and dignity are ends in themselves and should not be treated only as means (ibid.). Coercion and exploitation are wrong, simply because subjects are turned into mere tools and objects lacking the ability to choose for themselves how they want to act. From a Kantian perspective we have an obligation to respect the dignity of both ourselves and others. Hence, any form of exploitation, e.g. wages below a living wage or forced labour, is inherently disrespectful and fails to meet the moral principle of the categorical imperative. Take the example of the abuse and exploitation of girls and women workers in the South Indian textile industry. A study by two international NGOs, published in 2014, found that many girls and women working in the Indian textile industry suffer from forced and bonded labour (SOMO and ICN, 2014). Recruiters convince parents to send their daughters to spinning mills or other sweatshops by promising a well-paid job, accommodation and education as well as a lump payment at the end of three years. In reality, however, the girls have only very limited freedom of movement, face long hours of work, do not get any form of education and only rarely receive the lump payment promised to them.

According to the categorical imperative, managers of MNCs and their suppliers would have a moral obligation to pay adequate wages for the hard work in sweatshops to ensure that workers do not live under conditions of forced labour and poverty. From this moral point of view, the cost of respecting workers must be regarded as a necessary condition of running a business. An 'adequate' wage thereby is the minimum wage required by law or the wage which is necessary to live above the poverty line. Contrary to the arguments discussed above, opponents of sweatshop labour even argue that MNCs usually have a certain degree of latitude when it comes to wages, such that they should be able to voluntarily raise wages in sweatshops without inevitably causing unemployment.

Arnold and Bowie are convinced that managers of MNCs and sweatshops should not be seen as subject to overwhelming economic forces who must inevitably lay off workers when they increase wages (Arnold and Bowie, 2007). On the contrary, competent managers should be able to find ways to increase wages on the one hand and to absorb additional costs on the other hand, by means of internal cost-cutting elsewhere in the value chain or by reducing executive compensation. Interestingly, a study in the Indonesian garment and footwear industry found that a voluntary increase in wages after massive anti-sweatshop campaigns actually did not lead to an increase in unemployment (Harrison and Scorse, 2006). Rather, the increased wage costs in relation to the total costs of the MNCs were so small that the firms seemed to be able to compensate this investment easily somewhere else in the value chain, and that these costs could be successfully passed on to the consumer. In the footwear industry where companies such as Nike, Adidas and Puma heavily compete, labour costs in Indonesia typically account for less than 5 per cent of the sales price of a sport shoe. MNCs sell those shoes in New York or London in many cases for US$100–200. An increase in labour costs of for example 50 cents per hour is not likely to have a dramatic impact on the profitability of an MNC, but it has a noticeably positive effect on the sweatshop worker (Harrison and Scorse, 2006). The authors of this study even found that not only wages increased in Indonesia over a longer period of time but also employment. A reason for this could be that the increase in costs is often cushioned by the fact that product demand is also growing.

Proponents of sweatshop labour emphasise that MNCs who employ contracting arrangements with suppliers in less developed countries have only a limited responsibility for the problems associated with sweatshops, because these production sites belong to legally independent companies. MNCs when outsourcing their activities often draw on indirect sourcing via purchasing agents. These agents take over responsibility for handling the purchasing contracts and further subcontract the work, often to a number of different factories. As a result, the sourcing process becomes more and more opaque. Nevertheless, critics of sweatshop labour argue that it is the MNC's responsibility to know the conditions under which their products are being made, and that they do have leverage to influence their value chains (Phillips and Caldwell, 2005). Firms such as Adidas, Nike or H&M benefit from international production networks and hence have to shoulder more responsibility for the externalities caused by these value chain activities. Moreover, MNCs have distinct duties regarding the workers of their contract factories because of the power and the substantial resources they have at their disposal. MNCs typically dictate the terms and conditions of their orders such as price, quantity or date of delivery to their supplier network. Increasingly, standards related to health and safety and environmental protection become part of those terms. MNCs consequently have the ability to foster labour rights and fair working conditions in their supply chain (Arnold and Bowie, 2007). Even in cases when a firm is too small to use all of a supplier's capacity and only places orders representing a small percentage of the supplier's total turnover, it is partly responsible for the working conditions in a sweatshop. Although in such cases a single firm cannot directly exert influence over the supplier, a firm which is genuinely interested in respecting labour rights could collaborate with other buyers to develop and ensure acceptable standards.

18.5 Regulation and Improvement of Working Conditions in Global Supply Chains

Different actors at various levels and through diverse institutional arrangements, ranging from voluntary approaches to hard law, are addressing working conditions in global supply chains. We draw a distinction between measures to regulate and improve working conditions on the company level, the industry level, the multi-stakeholder level and the governmental level.

18.5.1 Company Level

MNCs have good reasons to actively deal with low labour standards in their supply chains; ignoring such issues may put them at risk of a bad corporate reputation and thus at risk of losing corporate legitimacy and their licence to operate. In the 1990s, Nike became the poster child of the anti-sweatshop movement when the working conditions at its overseas suppliers came to light (Zadek, 2004). As a response to these allegations, Nike, and soon after many other sportswear brands as well as MNCs from other industries, drew up a code of conduct. A code of conduct can be defined as a set of standards, guidelines or rules for ethical behaviour which firms impose on their suppliers as a prerequisite for entering into contract with them. The formulated standards and procedures of a code can come in a variety of forms. Codes of conduct can be formal or informal, contain a lot of detail or be rather broad in their application. In its code of conduct, Nike, for example, outlines the minimum standards it expects each supplier factory to meet. Suppliers of Nike are among others expected to refrain from using forced labour, employing workers that are at least sixteen years of age or older, paying their workers promptly as well as at least the minimum wage required by country law (Nike, 2010). Since the 1990s, codes of conduct have become a standard of operation for dealing with labour conditions in global supply chains (Jenkins, Pearson and Seyfang, 2002). In order to check whether suppliers actually abide by a certain code, MNCs usually monitor and audit compliance. Such audits are either performed internally (also referred to as first party monitoring), i.e. by the firms themselves, or externally through second or third parties. Second party monitoring means that an auditing company is commissioned and paid to oversee compliance with a company code. Third-party monitoring means that an independent party, usually an NGO that does not have any business relation with the firm, checks the compliance with a certain code.

Supplier codes of conduct and the associated monitoring, auditing and reporting practices have received intense criticism. O'Rourke, for example, through an analysis of the monitoring methods of PricewaterhouseCoopers (PwC), a large private auditing company, found that their approach to monitoring exhibited serious flaws: it consisted of very brief factory-walk-throughs, used the managers as key information sources, and failed to effectively gather information from workers. Often, audits were preannounced so that factories were able to mimic compliance with a certain code without actually doing so (O'Rourke, 2002).

While monitoring practices can be improved, e.g. through unannounced random visits and sophisticated information-gathering techniques such as interviewing workers outside the factory or gathering information from organisations that workers trust, in practice MNCs alone will never be able to completely monitor their global supply chains. Only a more collaborative approach of governance of global production, including MNCs and their suppliers but also other stakeholders such as NGOs, national governments, trade unions and local communities, can provide realistic insights into local working conditions and improve them. Only when MNCs critically review their purchasing practices and pay higher prices to their suppliers, can sweatshop owners afford to pay higher wages. Another prerequisite to improve supplier–MNC relationships is to increase transparency and to establish long-term partnerships and commitments to source from specific suppliers. The garment and sports company PUMA has recently started to offer such long-term partnerships to suppliers that perform well on economic, environmental and social criteria (Baumann-Pauly, Scherer and Palazzo, 2015). The rationale behind this long-term strategy is to educate and convince both suppliers and internal stakeholders of the firm (such as the managers of the sourcing department) that sustainability in general and social standards in particular can be improved through true partnerships. Suppliers seem to make improvements on environmental and social aspects of their business voluntarily, because they start to realise that this not only has a positive impact on their workers but also pays off economically as they are rewarded from brands with long-term sourcing commitments (Baumann-Pauly et al., 2015). In order to support such long-term partnerships, MNCs need to invest in capacity development at the local level and should not expect the supplier to shoulder all of the costs of compliance with existing codes of conduct.

18.5.2 Industry Level

Besides the efforts of individual companies, issues of labour rights and supply chain transparency are also being addressed at the industry level. In this case MNCs cooperate with other firms in their respective industry in order to commit themselves to industry-specific standards and articulate guidelines for appropriate conduct. Examples include the Electronics Industry Citizenship Coalition, which aims at creating industry-wide standards regarding social, environmental and ethical issues in the electronics industry supply chain, or the recently formed Alliance for Bangladesh Worker Safety. The Alliance was set up by a group of mainly North American brands, retailers and companies of the garment industry as a response to the collapse of the factory building in Bangladesh in April 2013, with the aim to improve safety in Bangladeshi garment factories (see case study below). The benefit of industry codes and standards is that they take the pressure from suppliers to comply with different, and sometimes conflicting, codes of conduct and reduce the burden of multiple inspections. However, industry initiatives are often criticised for the lack of inclusion of other stakeholders, particularly trade unions, at the governance level, since the governing bodies or executive organs of industry initiatives are usually entirely comprised of business representatives. In contrast to industry initiatives, MSIs, which will be outlined in the next section, aim at a more substantive engagement of different stakeholders from different spheres of society.

18.5.3 Multi-Stakeholder Level

Over the last two decades there has been an increase in MSIs. The majority of MSIs generate voluntary corporate social responsibility (CSR) standards that are intended to provide MNCs and their respective stakeholders with ways to systematically assess, measure and communicate their social and environmental performance. Many MSIs directly or indirectly address working conditions in global supply chains and try to make a contribution to improve labour rights on a global level. The difference between MSIs and the above-mentioned industry-led initiatives mainly lies in the groups of stakeholders involved in the process of fostering accountability. MSIs typically include not only MNCs and associations directly linked to the respective industry but also many other stakeholders (e.g. NGOs, unions, government actors, investors, or at times also consumers). Examples for such MSIs are the UN Global Compact, SA 8000, the Global Reporting Initiative or ISO 26000 (see Chapter 7).

The proliferation of MSIs can mainly be attributed to the lack of a unified system of transnational regulation for social and environmental issues. MSIs generally aim at filling the omnipresent governance voids related to the manifold activities of MNCs by issuing standards, which define voluntary rules of appropriate conduct (see Chapter 7). This is why such standards are also often referred to as soft law, since they are not legally binding (Abbott and Snidal, 2000). The standards produced by MSIs are usually regarded as having more legitimacy than those of industry initiatives since MSIs bring a more diverse set of stakeholders to the table. Research has however indicated that MSIs also have limits when it comes to improving working conditions. For example, in an analysis of the impact of the Ethical Trading Initiative (ETI) on workers' rights, Barrientos and Smith found that while slight improvements could be registered in terms of outcome standards, i.e. tangible issues such as minimum wage and working hours or health and safety standards, no improvements had become evident in terms of process rights, i.e. freedom of association and protection against discrimination (Barrientos and Smith, 2007).

18.5.4 Governmental Level

Both the proponents and opponents of sweatshop labour emphasise the importance of governmental regulation when reforming working conditions and addressing labour rights. Legal institutions within countries facing labour rights issues are often either weak or absent, or in the worst case exploitative. A primary solution to the problem of sweatshop labour hence lies in a stronger (or at least different) regulation by states and a more successful implementation of labour laws. Responses at the governmental level can come in three main forms. First, developing country governments can pass laws and regulations regarding, e.g. health and safety standards or minimum wages or improve on the enactment of existing laws. Bangladesh, for example, has very elaborate building regulations on the book, but those laws have often been disregarded in the past. Second, wealthier countries can adopt laws relating to wages and working standards, to regulate the import of products made in factories abroad, or can pass laws to hold 'national' MNCs accountable for human rights violations occurring at their subsidiaries and suppliers abroad. In France, Germany and Switzerland, public debates have sparked around whether a corporate responsibility to respect human rights should and can be turned into a legal liability through extraterritorial regulation in the future. Finally, at the inter-governmental level, a number of organisations such as the European Union (EU), United Nations (UN) or the ILO, whose members are national governments, engage in efforts to regulate labour rights in the global economy. Yet, in the absence of coercive institutions at the international level, intergovernmental organisations also rely on voluntary compliance by states.

Regulation at the governmental level becomes particularly important when MNCs are unwilling to address labour rights issues and improve the working conditions on a voluntary basis. In this case, laws may help to improve safe and healthy working conditions and minimum wages for sweatshop workers. However, even if the regulation of labour rights at the governmental level would be ideal, governments are usually slow-moving or exposed to conflicting interests. For example, developing country governments often refrain from stricter regulations, fearing that it might hamper international investments. High levels of corruption in many of the export-orientated developing countries also prevent the effective implementation of regulatory approaches. In India, for instance, labour regulation has been used by government officials to extort businesses instead of protecting the rights of workers. Even if developing countries are willing to improve the situation for workers, they are often unable to finance substantive changes due to budgetary constraints. The drawbacks of regulation at the governmental level again highlight the importance of soft law approaches and voluntary agreements by MNCs to improving labour rights.

18.6 Case Study: Labour Rights in the Garment Supply Chain – The Rana Plaza Factory Collapse

When cracks appeared on the walls of the factory complex Rana Plaza, some of the workers became scared. Rana Plaza, situated in Savar near Dhaka, the capital city of Bangladesh, was an eight-storey commercial building containing five clothing factories in which about 5000 people, mostly female garment workers, were employed. The workers told their supervisors about the worrying cracks and some even left the building. After hasty inspections the supervisors told them not to worry: these were just simple cracks, and the workers should go back up to their floors of the building. Even more so, they beat some of the scared workers and threatened that they would cut their wages if they did not return immediately. On the morning of the next day, 24 April 2013, there was a power cut – a frequent nuisance in the capital region of Dhaka. Survivors of the disaster later reported that shortly after the generators on the roof of the building had been cranked, the whole building started to shake and suddenly the ceiling came down. The building collapsed. The search for survivors lasted over seventeen days. More than 1100 people were found dead, while about 2400 were evacuated. Many of the survivors were left with lifelong injuries. With its death toll, Rana Plaza takes the debate on sweatshops to a new level and begs the question of who is responsible for workplace conditions and safety issues in global supply chains.

At Rana Plaza, construction regulations had been ignored. The owner of Rana Plaza had illegally added several stories to the building. Yet, government officials had approved the construction of the building, although these officials never visited the site to check whether the building plan had been kept. About forty people, among them the owner of Rana Plaza, owners of individual factories within the building as well as a number of government officials, have to answer in court in Bangladesh for their role in the tragedy. Yet, can the issue be considered as solved with the court ruling?

The disaster at Rana Plaza only constitutes the peak of a series of tragic events that have struck the garment industry of Bangladesh over the preceding years. Since 2005, hundreds of workers have died in Bangladesh in garment factory incidents. The garment industry has turned into Bangladesh's most important industry sector, making up 13 per cent of its GDP and approximately 80 per cent of its exports. About 60 per cent of these exports go to Europe and approximately 25 per cent to the US. Bangladesh is the second biggest clothing manufacturer in the world behind China. Around 3.5 million people are employed in the garment industry in Bangladesh – the majority (approximately 80 per cent) are young women (World Bank, 2013). With 152 million inhabitants, Bangladesh counts as the eighth most populous country in the world. While Bangladesh has experienced considerable GDP growth over the past thirty years, with about 47 million people living in poverty it still is one of South Asia's poorest countries (World Bank, 2013). International investors are drawn to Bangladesh due to its low-cost manufacturing opportunities. Wages in Bangladesh are only half those in India and Vietnam, and only one-fifth of China's. While the wages in the garment sector hardly provide for a comfortable living, the jobs in the garment sector, for many Bangladeshis and particularly for women, remain better than most of the alternatives.

Twenty-nine Western MNCs, among them Primark, J.C. Penney, Benetton, Wal-mart and Carrefour, were found to have been linked with factories in the Rana Plaza building at the time of the disaster (CCC, 2015). The distressing images of Rana Plaza have put international garment brands and retailers under pressure to act. The industry responded to the disaster with the instalment of two initiatives, the 'Alliance for Bangladesh Worker Safety' as well as the 'Accord on Fire and Building Safety in Bangladesh'. The Alliance represents an industry initiative, i.e. a company-developed and company-controlled programme, and was mainly endorsed by North American garment companies, most prominently by Wal-mart and Gap. The Accord, on the other hand, was initiated by a number of international NGOs, and signed by MNCs and worker representatives, thus constituting an MSI. By now, 150 garment corporations, mostly from Europe and including H&M, Inditex, C&A and Primark, and two global unions (IndustriALL, UNI Global), as well as a number of local Bangladeshi unions, form part of the Accord. While the Accord represents a legally binding agreement, the Alliance remains voluntary. The goal and programme of both initiatives is however similar. Both aim to improve fire and structural safety in Bangladeshi factories through safety inspections and the provision of low-cost capital funding to factory owners to fund the necessary improvements. Yet, while the Alliance has been criticised for not having engaged with unions and not providing independent assessments of their inspection results, the Accord in turn does not engage with factory owners at its steering level, and has been criticised for remaining vague on who should fund required factory upgrades as well as who should compensate workers in case a factory has to suspend operations due to safety concerns. A number of brands see the primary responsibility for safety improvements with the factory owners, who however often claim that they do not have the necessary resources to pay for renovations, let alone keep paying workers during renovation periods. Who should be responsible for funding the factory upgrades?

While the speed and scope of the inspections of both the Accord and the Alliance are impressive, it is questionable whether factory audits are adequate to address the structural causes of the Rana Plaza disaster and to sustainably transform the Bangladeshi garment industry. The collapse of Rana Plaza itself tragically highlights the weakness of an audit-focused model of CSR. Two of the five factories in the Rana Plaza building had been audited against the code of conduct of the Business Social Compliance Initiative (BSCI), and both factories had been approved (CCC, 2015). The BSCI audits however only focused on particular factories within the building and thus failed to identify the safety issues related to the construction of the overall building. Given the inherent flaws of audit systems, it remains questionable whether the factory audits of the Accord and Alliance will be able to prevent future tragedies. As in the case of Rana Plaza, many safety problems relate to the use of power generators, which are needed due to a lack of a reliable energy infrastructure in Bangladesh. Solving this issue requires substantial infrastructure investments. Should and can international brands and retailers also be held responsible for such investments?

Taken together, 1,800 factories fall under the auspices of the Accord and the Alliance, as both initiatives are mainly concerned with top-tier suppliers. While there is controversy about the total number of factories in the garment sector in Bangladesh, some estimates suggest that overall about 5,000 factories exist (CCC, 2015). These numbers indicate that the industry goes well beyond the purview of the Accord and the Alliance and point to the issue of subcontracting. In the aftermath of Rana Plaza, a number of MNCs could not tell with certainty whether or not their products were affiliated with one of the factories in the building. While MNCs tend to know their first-tier suppliers and pledge those to abide by some code of conduct, lower-tier factories further down the chain are frequently not known. In the Bangladeshi garment sector, however, subcontracting is endemic. The current system of subcontracting is evoked through the industries' focus on fast fashion. Fast fashion exerts enormous pressure on suppliers due to unpredictable production schedules, tight deadlines and budgets, and late changes. Often suppliers need to subcontract part of the work to other factories to be able to meet the requirements of MNCs. To address the issue of subcontracting, international brands and retailers would need to alter their purchasing practices. They, however, argue that their hands are tied, since they need to respond to the high and rising demand of consumers in Western countries for cheap clothing and the latest fashion.

The factory numbers above imply that the government of Bangladesh has to take responsibility for the remainder of the factories not covered by the Accord or the Alliance. Whether the government will be capable of inspecting and fixing unsafe factories remains to be seen. Given the record of past negligence, it is however highly questionable. At any rate, the government of Bangladesh, together with representatives of the Bangladesh employers' and workers' organisations, instituted a tripartite 'National Plan of Action on Fire Safety and Structural Integrity' for the garment sector. In relation to this action plan, the government also reformed and upgraded its Labour Inspectorate. It is projected that the government will employ 575 labour inspectors, while there were only 55 at the time of the Rana Plaza disaster. Moreover, after heavy protests from workers, the government of Bangladesh also conceded to reform a number of its labour laws, including the rise of the minimum wage.

The industry and governmental responses that have been triggered by the collapse of Rana Plaza remain limited to the garment sector in Bangladesh. If a similar disaster is to be prevented in the future, these collaborative efforts need to be extended to other industry sectors and exporting countries such as Cambodia, Pakistan or India, which exhibit similar structural conditions and challenges as Bangladesh.

Questions for Discussion

1. The Rana Plaza incident involved a large number of different actors in Bangladesh and abroad. Who are they, and who do you think is responsible for improving working conditions in Bangladeshi factories?
2. Two initiatives (the Accord on Fire and Building Safety and the Alliance for Bangladesh Worker Safety) resulted from the disaster at Rana Plaza. Which of the two do you consider more legitimate? Why? Do you consider the response of the industry as adequate?
3. What role does the consumer play in this case?

18.7 Chapter Summary

Globalisation has primarily manifested itself in the growth and spread of global supply chains. The increased outsourcing of value chain activities of MNCs to developing countries has raised concerns about the working conditions of millions of workers within global supply chains. The ILO core labour standards form an internationally accepted baseline when it comes to protecting workers rights. Nonetheless, labour rights are frequently violated, e.g. in the food, consumer electronics or garment supply chain. Violations pertain to inadequate pay and long working hours, forced and child labour, health and safety breaches or freedom of association, among others. Throughout different disciplines, a fierce debate has emerged whether and to what extent work in so-called sweatshops is exploitative. Arguments in favour of sweatshops have mainly been voiced by neoclassical economists, proposing that sweatshops are mutually beneficial arrangements between workers and a factory, and that taking away the option of working in a sweatshop would disregard the autonomous choice of workers. Arguments against sweatshops largely stem from business ethicists and philosophers who, often based on Kantian ethics, argue that sweatshops fail to respect the dignity of workers and that MNCs have a moral duty to ensure adequate working standards. Attempts to improve working conditions in global supply chains can be found at different levels and involving different actors. In this chapter we have drawn a distinction between efforts at the company, industry, multi-stakeholder and governmental level.

Chapter Questions

1. Are MNCs benefiting the poor when outsourcing value chain activities to developing countries?
2. Can the choice of women working in Indian spinning mills be considered a free one?
3. If it were possible, would you recommend shutting down all sweatshops at once?
4. Should MNCs be held liable in their home countries for the working conditions at their local contractors in developing countries?
5. Can labour rights be effectively addressed through self-regulation?
6. Does the setting of social and environmental standards of MNCs for suppliers represent a form of cultural colonialisation?

FURTHER RESOURCES

O'Rourke, D. (2006). Multi-Stakeholder Regulation: Privatizing or Socializing Global Labor Standards? *World Development* 34(5), 899–918.
Assesses and evaluates multi-stakeholder labour regulation initiatives with a view to their effectiveness, achievements, failures and challenges.

Barrientos, S. and Smith, S. (2007). Do Workers Benefit from Ethical Trade? Assessing Codes of Labour Practice in Global Production Systems. *Third World Quarterly* 28(4), 713–729.
Empirical study which addresses the impact of codes of labour practice on improving labour standards in supply chains.

Rasche, A. (2010). The Limits of Corporate Responsibility Standards. *Business Ethics: A European Review* 19(3), 280–291.
Critically assesses the limits of addressing labour rights through corporate responsibility standards. This article suggests that there are inherent limitations to a standardisation approach.

International Labour Organization (ILO) (2013). Marking Progress against Child Labour: Global Estimates and Trends 2000–2012, www.ilo.org/wcmsp5/groups/public/–ed_norm/–ipec/documents/publication/wcms_221513.pdf

A report in which the ILO takes stock of the progress achieved in reducing global child labour since the year 2000. It presents estimates that 168 million children worldwide are still in labour, accounting for almost 11 per cent of the worldwide child population.

Three Reasons Why Sweatshops Are Good for the Poor (2012), https://m.youtube.com/watch?v=NxBzKkWo0mo
In this short video, Zwolinski outlines his arguments in defence of sweatshops.

The Dark Side of Chocolate (2010), www.youtube.com/watch?v=BeJy3dA4Ahk
This documentary investigates the exploitation of children in the cocoa industry of Côte d'Ivoire.

ILO video on forced labour (2014), www.ilo.org/global/topics/forced-labour/lang–en/index.htm
In a short animated video, the ILO raises awareness of modern-day forms of forced labour.

Sweatshop – Deadly Fashion (2014), www.huffingtonpost.com/2015/01/28/sweatshop-reality-show_n_6555436.html
Three Norwegian fashion bloggers are sent to Cambodia to live as sweatshop workers in a month-long reality TV show. Article about the TV show with link to video in Norwegian.

Accord on Fire and Building Safety in Bangladesh, www.bangladeshaccord.org/

Alliance for Bangladesh Worker Safety, www.bangladeshworkersafety.org/

International Labor Rights Forum (ILRF), www.laborrights.org/
ILRF is a human rights organisation that advocates for workers globally.

The Centre for Research on Multinational Corporations (SOMO), www.somo.nl/
SOMO is a not-for-profit research organisation investigating the role of multinational corporations and the consequences of their activities for people and the environment. It regularly publishes reports on labour-related issues.

Business and Human Rights Resource Centre, http://business-humanrights.org/en
The Resource Centre is an independent non-profit organisation dedicated to tracking the human rights performance of companies.

Clean Clothes Campaign (CCC), www.cleanclothes.org/
The CCC is an alliance of organisations including trade unions and NGOs. The aim of CCC is to improve working conditions of workers in the global garment and sportswear industries.

Online Debate: Can Global Brands Create Just Supply Chains? http://bostonreview.net/forum/can-global-brands-create-just-supply-chains-richard-locke
Richard M. Locke, political science professor at MIT, debates the issue with other leading scholars from different disciplines.

Personal Reflection by *Mark Moody-Stuart*

The Governance of Transnational Issues

The late twentieth century and the early years of the twenty-first century were characterised by a battle between those (mainly civil society organisations) who sought some kind of global legally binding regulation of the activities of businesses and those who opposed such a concept (mainly the businesses targeted). The battle was brought to an end, or perhaps just to a lengthy truce, by the work of the UN Secretary-General's Special Rapporteur on Business and Human Rights, John Ruggie, with the publication and acceptance in 2011 of the Guiding Principles on Business and Human Rights. The Guiding Principles, published after several years of extensive consultation, placed the responsibility to protect human rights firmly on national governments, and at the same time placed the responsibility to respect human rights equally firmly on businesses, with both governments and businesses being responsible for providing access to remedies where human rights had been infringed.

The quest for globally binding legislation has always been somewhat quixotic. This is not just because such efforts would have tied the UN into fruitless arguments for decades, as among other things many countries of the South would see this as a potentially protectionist move by the North. It is also because, had such a global charter been achieved, it would ultimately have depended, in the absence of a global police force, on implementation by the nation states who are signatories. This is true of the Universal Declaration of Human Rights, which although signed by almost every country, often fails because of weak national supporting legislation or enforcement within individual states. This is not to say that governments who are hosts to companies active in other jurisdictions should not enact legislation to allow people in those jurisdiction access to remedies in their own courts, but to emphasise that universal protection of rights and access to justice ultimately depends on the laws and governance of the state in which the acts occur.

We decided to invite Mark Moody-Stuart for his reflections on the governance of transnational issues in view, first, of his long experience as a leader of international corporations (e.g. Managing Director and Chairman of the Royal Dutch/Shell Group; Chairman of Anglo American). In addition, he has been involved in several major international CSR multi-stakeholder initiatives (e.g. Vice Chairman of the UN Global Compact Board). His extended reflections on these issues are presented in *Responsible Leadership* (2014).

So does this mean that provided a company respects human rights and obligations such as those covered by the ten principles of the United Nations Global Compact – respect for the environment, proper working conditions, anti-corruption and so on – a company's responsibility ends? That may or may not be the case, but it is certainly true that even where a company has acted responsibly in line with the Principles of the UN Global Compact (UNGC) and the Guiding Principles (UNGP) in its own operations, in countries where after many years of poor governance little wider benefit can be seen from the economic activities, there will be a strong tendency to blame the company, even if the failure was one of government. So a poor or weak government, or one guilty of oppressive behaviour, can certainly be damaging to responsible companies operating in that country, even if they are not directly complicit in any improper activities.

Individual efforts by a company or even by a group of companies to address such a situation may not be either effective or desirable, but one of the most encouraging movements in the last twenty to thirty years has been the growth of alliances between businesses and civil society to address very specific issues. These efforts began in the field of traded goods with such initiatives as the Forest Stewardship Council (FSC) looking to make sure that the supply of timber products came from sustainable forests, or World Wide Fund for Nature (WWF) and Unilever working together on the Sustainable Fisheries so that fish was sourced from sustainable sources and was not destroying fisheries. Both of these examples are discussed elsewhere in preceding chapters. The idea spread to issues outside trade, such as the Kimberley Process working to eliminate conflict diamonds from the supply chain or the Extractive Industries Transparency Initiative (EITI), also described elsewhere, which sets out to reduce corruption in the extractive industries.

The UN Global Compact is by far the largest of such corporate responsibility alliances, and often supports and promotes such initiatives through its own issue platforms – whether they be on water through the CEO Water Mandate, or the Caring for Climate initiative, the Women's Empowerment Principles or the Supply Chain Working Group. Although voluntary, such standards become incorporated into the World Bank and IFC Performance Standards. Banks which are signatories to the Equator Principles will only finance projects which apply these sort of standards. The UNGC has come a long way in the fifteen years since its founding in response to a challenge by the then Secretary-General of the UN, Kofi Annan. Some forty companies responded to that challenge. Since then, under the leadership and encouragement of Secretary-General Ban Ki-Moon, the initiative now has over 8000 active business signatories in countries all over the world.

If business is to work hand in hand with civil society, it is essential to build trust, and this is the third differentiating feature. The best way for businesses to build trust is by being transparent and open about what we are doing and how we are doing it. This means reporting on all activities – not just on the very good parts, but also on those areas where we have challenges. This is why the UNGC insists on regular 'Communications on Progress' against the ten principles, and delists companies who persistently fail to report. It is encouraging that many stock exchanges are mandating more open reporting on environmental, social and governance issues and are joining another spin off of the UNGC, the Sustainable Stock Exchanges Initiative (SSE).

Some years ago, a frequently heard complaint from leaders of major corporations doing excellent work in the field of sustainability and responsible business was that while they and the people in the company were very engaged and committed, little interest was shown by their shareholders. That has changed, and the UNGC has been part of that change. Together with the UN Environmental Programme's Finance Initiative, the UNGC developed the Principles for Responsible Investment (PRI) which commit investors to incorporate environmental, sustainability and governance factors into their investment process and to encourage transparent reporting on these issues. The PRI now has some 1400 signatories, many of them long-term investors such as pension funds, who collectively manage some US$55 trillion of investment.

Apart from addressing the investment end, the UNGC has also promoted the Principles of Sustainable Management Education (PRME). This is to ensure that young business people do not just learn analysis in business schools but also learn the importance of embedding the principles of the UNGC, sustainability and responsible business during their management education. This includes programmes on the steps that need to be taken to avoid corruption and other challenges which businesses may face, both within their own countries of domicile and also as they expand into overseas markets. This initiative now has the involvement of over 500 business schools from countries all around the world including in China, Japan and Korea. PRME signatories and supporters can exchange teaching cases and also do academic research on the benefits of responsible business.

The PRI and PRME are just two of the spin-offs from the UNGC into other sectors which interact with and impinge on business. There are numerous issue platforms which various businesses find of interest to exchange experience or to hold learning events on, or from which best practice guidance notes can be developed. These cover climate, water, human rights, the empowerment of women, supply chains, anti-corruption and so on. Each of these has a core group of businesses which find a particular aspect of particular interest to their day-to-day business.

One of the great strengths of the UN Global Compact is its local networks. It is not enough for the Global Compact to engage only in New York or Geneva, or indeed for global companies to operate and engage only in their home markets or countries of domicile. To achieve a more sustainable world and to promote sound governance and sound regulatory frameworks, businesses of all sizes, both international and national, need to be engaged. For this reason

Global Compact local networks exist, or are in the process of development and formalisation, in almost a hundred countries.

These networks are the only way to bring together companies of all sizes, from small or medium-sized enterprises (SMEs) to larger national and international companies and the local affiliates of global companies. At the same time, in line with the philosophy of the Global Compact, the local networks also involve local civil society organisations and labour organisations, forming a basis for the alliances between civil society and business.

The local networks focus on national priorities and issues, whether they be human rights, working conditions, the environment or corruption. They do so in a national context but informed by the global principles of the Compact. This allows the Principles to be implemented in a culturally sensitive way. It provides a golden opportunity for the local affiliates of major global corporations to learn from the practices of responsible national companies, many of which have been applying responsible business practices for many years in a way that has developed in line with local culture. This is a two-way process as national companies can also learn from the experience of global companies and review and develop their own practices in the light of ideas from elsewhere in the world.

Both global and national companies benefit from the involvement of SMEs, providing opportunities for shared value approaches in the development of local supply chains. The discussion in a local network can and does also lead to alliances to address local issues in a practical way, taking into account political or cultural sensitivities. The networks and the involvement of civil society provide a great source of intelligence on national issues and allow a major company to become more embedded in local society and communicate much more effectively with its national customers and suppliers, as well indeed as with its own people.

These local networks provide an avenue for the formation of alliances between civil society and business which can be a positive influence on national governments without the risk of any one section of society becoming overly dominant. Governments sometimes shrink from taking the necessary steps to put in place the necessary frameworks to protect the interests of society at large – whether this be in the areas of working conditions, environmental or building regulations, or other necessary regulation, for example pricing externalities such as carbon. This is because of business' fears that such regulations will render national business internationally uncompetitive, or a similar backlash from society that prices will go up. Working together as an alliance, different sectors can more readily come to an agreed practical solution which meets the needs of society, overrides special pleading by vested interests and can support a government in taking necessary steps in the interests of society as a whole.

Looking forward, perhaps we are beginning to see the first instances of responsible businesses being supported while working in poorly governed societies, as opposed to coming under pressure to withdraw their operations. Since its inception, the UN Global Compact has promoted the role of business in building peaceful societies. Early work concentrated on the need for companies to avoid exacerbating situations in conflict-sensitive areas, and one of the very first 'learning workshops' involved companies working with civil society organisations and unions on the topic of operating in 'conflict sensitive areas'. Later work with investor signatories of the Principles for Responsible Investment and human rights organisations developed 'Guidelines for Companies Operating in Conflict Sensitive Zones', published in 2010. This was the result of workshops in many countries including Sudan, Japan and Latin America which looked at the more positive contributions of livelihood and employment generation in conflict sensitive areas.

This led in 2014 to the launch of a UNGC platform called 'Business for Peace'. A strong initial driver for this was the need perceived by UNGC local networks to re-integrate former militias into society in such post-conflict countries as Sri Lanka, Colombia and Sudan. Other networks focus more on addressing tensions within their societies; for example in Indonesia, working to regularise marriages in order to ensure that the children are properly registered so that they can be accepted in schools. Progress may also be made simply by maintaining workplaces where men and women of different religions or ethnicity can work together harmoniously to achieve corporate goals in a non-discriminatory environment. Yet others work across national boundaries which are politically fraught such as that between Sudan and the new country of South Sudan.

The Korean example of the Gaesong Industrial Zone is an imaginative example of this concept, which was actually started more than ten years ago, well before the formation of the Business for Peace initiative. The zone is an enclave in North Korea where companies from South Korea have made investments in manufacturing facilities of a high standard, where decent work is provided to some 55,000 citizens of North Korea who enter the zone for work every day. This means that citizens of the two countries interact in a cooperative way, delivering commercial and livelihood benefits and breaking down barriers. Thanks to the Korean Network, my wife and I had the opportunity to visit the Gaesong Industrial Zone earlier this year and we were very impressed by what we saw, although the operation faces challenges and is controversial in some areas such as the handling of wages for work by the North Korean workers. A few months before, at the first Business for Peace Annual meeting held in Istanbul, I was given a gift of some of the ceramic and textile products from the Zone. My wife and I were very moved when we returned home to see that the label on one item of clothing did not say Made in the Republic of Korea or North Korea, but it simply said 'Made in Peace'. That I think sums up the spirit and drive behind this imaginative venture. There is perhaps an opportunity in future for the UNGC local networks to contribute further to the building of more robust societies in difficult and contentious areas.

Epilogue

JONAS HAERTLE

Change does not happen by itself. It must be pursued with vigor, and by all of society. The sustainable journey that we need to take is in everybody's best interest. Nobody benefits from catastrophic climate change or rampant unemployment and the social unrest that comes with it. Prosperous, stable societies and a healthy planet are the bedrock of political stability, economic growth and flourishing new markets. Everyone has a role to play... The UN Global Compact has brought business to the table as a key partner. We have seen that responsible business practices combined with innovation and collaboration can bring about powerful change. Now, we need more companies around the world to commit to sustainability, and take shared responsibility for achieving a better world.

Ban Ki-moon, Secretary-General, United Nations

When reflecting on this quote by Ban Ki-moon, the Secretary-General of the United Nations from 2007 to 2016, who was my former boss, as well as on the content of this book, it occurs to me that the chapters you have studied contain answers to many of the questions I raised myself and to others almost twenty years ago. At that time, I had to decide what academic subject to study after graduating from a *Gymnasium* (high school) in Germany and later, what professional career to pursue. I had already lived and worked for a while in Germany, the United States of America and Mexico, and I considered myself interested in politics and governance. At the end of the 1990s, the term *globalisation* began to make its rounds in public discourse. A political science degree seemed to be the right subject for me since I believed it would give me answers to my questions. However, I quickly discovered that the political sciences core curriculum at universities was not aligned with the popular perception surrounding the increased economic and *political* power of businesses. Rather, the primary focus of many courses seemed to be the role of state actors, such as governments, or, at most, about the declining power of governmental actors, without outlining alternative actors or scenarios. The perception

---

We decided to invite Jonas Haertle for some final reflections on this book in view of his significant experience as a leading figure and influencer in the area of responsible management education. Since 2010, Mr Haertle has been Head of the Principles for Responsible Management Education (PRME) secretariat of the United Nations Global Compact Office. The PRME is the world's largest network of business schools committed to embedding social and environmental issues into their teaching and research activities.

I had from following the public discourse made me wonder: what should the role and responsibilities of multinational corporations be? The annual gathering of leaders from businesses at the World Economic Forum (WEF) in Davos, Switzerland began to be seen as an important contender in the search for answers to global governance questions. This did not go unnoticed by many non-governmental organisations, which increasingly began to organise across national borders and at a global level, and began to criticise corporations for their perceived lack of responsibility.

I didn't know it at that time, but in 1999, the then Secretary-General of the United Nations, Kofi Annan, gave a policy speech addressing world and business leaders at the WEF in which he called on business leaders to accept their responsibilities beyond mere considerations for their companies' financial bottom line. Kofi Annan argued that social and environmental factors needed to be taken into account by companies as well. It almost appears as if Kofi Annan's speech, which was entitled *A Global Compact on Human Rights, Labour, and Environment*, provides the backdrop for this book and the many advances in the field that the chapters reflect on. The chapters explore what I see now as the responsibilities and the changing role of business in a global society, which is reflected in the title of this book.

If you read this book from a student's perspective, let me give you some evidence, and hopefully confidence, that corporate responsibility and sustainability practices are here to stay and that the subject is an exciting one for you to pursue, both academically and in practice (i.e. should you choose to pursue a career in business or other organisations, including non-governmental and governmental ones). Through engagement with this book's content, a deeper understanding of the essential issues facing society can be developed, and this can help you to identify important answers to global governance challenges *and* the role of business. Incorporating these themes into research, coursework and business practice can give us hope for the future we want as the role of business matures in our global society.

First, corporate social responsibility (CSR) practices and theory building are advancing in academia. Across the globe, we have witnessed an increase in the number of corporate responsibility-themed courses taught, degrees offered, and commitments made by higher education institutions. This is true of business and management degrees, both at the undergraduate and graduate level, across the globe. This shift reflects a two-fold demand: from businesses wishing to hire sustainability literate graduates, and from students seeking an education that enables them to become responsible leaders. Both of these forces demonstrate the advancement of CSR from a supplemental practice to a core, value-adding business strategy. As this understanding evolves, the world will continue to face a paradigm shift in the importance of implementing responsible business practices.

By understanding the practices outlined in the book as a benchmark, and in some cases as a vision of where to reach to, the reader is able to reflect on how far businesses have come and how far they still should go. Progressing through the chapters, the underpinnings of CSR and responsible business define and encapsulate our present understanding and governance. In particular, 'Part IV: The Governance of Transnational Issues' scores the essential need for CSR practices to be rooted in their respective contexts, as well as the need to refer to human rights, anti-corruption, ecology and labour rights.

Not only do these topics reflect global issues that the next generation of business leaders will continue to face as they make decisions and develop strategy, but they also reflect elements of individual Sustainable Development Goals (SDGs), which are part of the ambitious Agenda 2030 agreed upon by all 193 United Nations member states to guide us to the world we want by 2030, including ending poverty and living within the planet's ecological limits. By tying in the issues highlighted by the SDGs, students are able to connect with these pressing topics and identify their own role in the narrative of Agenda 2030. This can be accomplished via several approaches throughout industry, such as voluntary corporate responsibility platforms like the UN Global Compact, which is the world's largest initiative in this area, with over 8000 businesses in over 100 countries worldwide. The UN Global Compact's work covers most of the issues addressed by the SDGs. Further, the UN Global Compact aims to make advances in these issues through special initiatives, including the Principles for Responsible Management Education (PRME) and the Principles for Responsible Investing (PRI). In the context of education, particular attention should be brought to the PRME initiative (www.unprme .org). PRME aims to 'inspire and champion responsible management education, research and thought leadership globally'. This mission clearly aligns with the issues discussed throughout these chapters. The initiative serves as a bridge and platform for responsible research and progressive dialogue on CSR throughout higher education.

As the global economy is a large and complex system comprising a myriad of actors, institutions, rules and mind-sets, it is assumed that systemic change is needed in order to achieve the vision outlined in Agenda 2030.

I hope you have found this book – as I did – engaging and thought-provoking. As the worldview on global governance and the role of businesses continues to evolve across different global and local contexts, I encourage you to stay attuned to the debate and practices. This is certainly a landmark time to be studying CSR, as it may see more progress and international attention than any other topic in formalised higher education and specifically business degrees. Understanding and committing to a formalised education in CSR gives you a competitive advantage in the globalised economy. As higher education and global entities, such as the United Nations, continue to take strides towards creating a more sustainable world, I encourage you to promote these practices in your own life and to leverage your new understanding of CSR as you excel into the roles of tomorrow's business leaders. Now is the time for you to engage.

Glossary on CSR and Related Concepts

Activism: Activism has its origins in politically conscious citizens protesting against the elite in the quest for social change. Activism within CSR entails efforts to promote and direct social, environmental and economic change in order to correct companies taking advantage of social injustice and exploitation of the natural environment. Examples of activism are boycotts, political campaigning and economic activism such as consumer boycotts. Social media is a demonstrably forceful vehicle for mobilising activists in global dissent to persuade companies to support social change. Activists have successfully used social media to change corporate behaviour, and more recently, companies have been seen – albeit with some challenges – to try to create the image of online grassroot movements to mobilise the same kind of legitimacy.

Aspirational talk: Aspirational talk refers to expressing future CSR ambitions. As a supplement to the conventional notion that managers must 'walk their talk', it is suggested that managers must also 'talk their walk' (Weick, 1979). This implies attention to the transformative potential of differences between organisational reality and aspirational talk (Christensen, Morsing and Thyssen, 2013). This is particularly relevant in the context of CSR, where problems are ever-changing, challenges are long-term and sustainable solutions cannot be predefined.

Business case: The business case for CSR is concerned with how businesses benefit in tangible ways from engaging in CSR. It describes the business rationale for accepting social and environmental responsibility. This business rationale is usually expressed in financial terms, arguing that there is a positive relationship between a firm's social and environmental performance as well as its financial performance. This makes CSR a 'value driver' in the corporate context. The business case for CSR can relate to, for instance: improved growth for the company (e.g. new products and markets), efficiency gains (e.g. energy efficiency) and reduced risk (e.g. reputational risk). The business case can be measured in financial (e.g. return on investment) and non-financial (e.g. employee motivation, reputation) terms. The business case is usually distinguished from the 'moral case' for CSR, which is entailed in business ethics.

Business ethics: Business ethics focuses on moral judgements and is concerned with questions of 'right' and 'wrong' in the context of business situations (Crane and Matten, 2007: 5). Business ethics can be seen as a framework to examine business situations where values are in conflict and ethical dilemmas occur as a result. While CSR focuses on the corporate policies and

management practices that allow firms
to live up to societal expectations,
business ethics reflects on the values
that underlie business decisions.
Normative business ethics looks at
whether an action is morally right or
wrong (mostly based on philosophical
thinking), while descriptive business
ethics analyses how individuals make
ethical decisions (Crane and Matten,
2008: 53–59).

Civil regulation: Unlike self-regulation,
civil regulation involves multiple
parties from different societal domains
(e.g. business, civil society,
government) into the design,
implementation and enforcement of
general societal expectations, standards
and rules. CSR standards, which are
designed as multi-stakeholder
initiatives, are a practical example of
civil regulation. Civil regulation
usually enjoys higher degrees of input
legitimacy when compared to self-
regulation, as it includes collaboration
and deliberation between different
parties.

Civil society organisation (CSO): Civil
society is seen as the public space for
collective action that exists between
market and government. CSOs refer to
a diverse set of organisations that are
committed to democratic principles and
work on a non-profit and non-
governmental basis, including:
community groups, NGOs, faith-based
organisations, foundations, labour
unions, professional associations and
charitable organisations. Unlike NGOs,
not all CSOs are designed to advance a
common cause or to profit third parties.
For instance, most associations are
designed as 'clubs', which only work
for their members' interests and values.

Code of conduct: A code of conduct is a
formal (and in most cases written)
statement that is supposed to guide the

behaviour of individuals or
organisations on a voluntary basis.
Codes of conduct are designed for
compliance purposes, and breaching
the code is sanctioned. While CSR
standards are applicable to firms from
different sectors and countries, codes of
conduct are usually designed to fit the
specific needs of a particular company.
Some codes are designed to regulate
the behaviour of a company's
employees (e.g. with regard to
accepting gifts from third parties),
while other codes are designed to
regulate the behaviour of a firm's
suppliers (e.g. with regard to work
conditions). Codes of conduct were
originally designed by and for
individual companies, but they have
increasingly been derived from codes
of MSIs and other CSR standards.

Compliance: Compliance can be
understood as individuals' or
organisations' conformity with pre-
given rules. It is usually seen as a
certain minimum standard that needs to
be fulfilled. Compliance can refer to the
law (legal compliance) as well as non-
legal rule specifications (e.g. standards
or policies). Compliance occurs in
different contexts. Some firms have
developed internal codes of conduct
and require employees to comply with
the relevant rules. Other firms have
signed up to CSR standards and are
therefore expected to comply with the
rules of this standard. Compliance
usually involves auditing and
controlling.

Corporate accountability: Giving 'an
account' refers to the need for
individual or collective actors to
explain and justify their actions.
Corporate accountability is about a
firm's ability to be answerable to
society, regulators and the firm's other
stakeholders for its actions and

omissions. Corporate accountability can be achieved through various means, such as CSR reporting, the creation of complaint and response mechanisms, and participatory models of corporate governance. Corporate accountability shows how firms have enacted their CSR policies.

Corporate citizenship (CC): Corporate citizenship stresses corporations' membership of societies and associated political responsibilities. It focuses on how corporate roles do or should reflect theories of citizenship, and by constitutional provisions for corporations (e.g. the US right to free speech; the German requirement for labour representation on boards). Crane et al. (2008) identify three CC roles: (1) corporations acting alongside human citizens (e.g. in corporate community involvement); (2) corporations acting alongside or in place of governments in order to administer rights or provide public goods (e.g. in delegated government authority or filling governmental voids); and (3) by enabling citizenship (e.g. empowering stakeholders and wider society members in business–NGO partnerships).

Corporate governance: Corporate governance refers to the interplay of rules, relations and mechanisms by which a certain firm is directed and controlled. Corporate governance is different from socio-economic governance (as related to in global governance) in that it exclusively focuses on how corporations are governed. The discussion of corporate governance looks at the rights and responsibilities of different interest groups within the corporations (e.g. the Board of Directors, management, shareholders and other stakeholders). Corporate governance can set the frame for CSR activities within a corporation (e.g. when the Board of Directors approves a firm's strategic direction).

Corporate social performance (CSP): Wood (1991: 693) defines CSP as 'a business organization's configuration of principles of social responsibility, processes of social responsiveness, and ... observable outcomes as they relate to the firm's societal relationships'. The idea behind CSP is that if firms can be assessed based on their economic performance, the same should be possible for their social performance (which also includes environmental and ethical issues). A company's CSP can thus be evaluated by looking at whether and how a corporation's CSR policies are translated into specific business processes that motivate measurable outcomes.

Corporate social responsibility (CSR): CSR refers to the responsibilities of corporations towards society. Discussions around CSR are part and parcel of the broader debate about businesses' role in and impact on (global) society. There are many different perspectives on what CSR is and what it is not. In this book, we refer to CSR as the integration of an enterprise's social, environmental, ethical and philanthropic responsibilities towards society into its operations, processes and core business strategy in cooperation with relevant stakeholders.

Corporate social responsibility (CSR) standards: CSR standards is an umbrella term to describe those forms of soft law that promulgate predefined rules and/or procedures to guide, assess, measure, verify and/or communicate the social and environmental performance of firms. There are four different types of CSR standards: (1) standards that reflect broad principles; (2) standards that contain certification mechanisms to independently assess corporate performance; (3) standards that regulate the disclosure of non-financial information; and finally (4) standards that outline management processes and guidance with regard to CSR. While codes of conduct are developed by individual companies and hence are only applicable within the scope of a firm's activities, most CSR standards are based on the input of a number of different stakeholders and are thus governed as multi-stakeholder initiatives (MSIs).

Corporate sustainability: This refers to the intersection between corporate resilience and wider social, economic and environmental sustainability. CSR is a contribution to corporate sustainability by which business can both contribute to sustainable development and business performance (Moon, 2007). The language of sustainability enables corporations to engage engineering and scientific staff in their CSR agendas. However, the relationship between corporate interest and value, and sustainable development is often vague (e.g. used as a synonym for CSR or environmental responsibility).

Creating shared value (CSV): Popularised by Michael Porter and Mark Kramer, who define CSV as 'policies and operating practices that enhance the competitiveness of a company while simultaneously advancing the economic and social conditions in the communities in which it operates' (Porter and Kramer, 2011: 66). Companies are supposed to embrace CSV by reconceiving products and markets, redefining productivity in the value chain and enabling local cluster development.

CSR communication: CSR communication is defined as a company's communication to internal and external stakeholders about its contributions to society, the environment and economic development. In the digital era, stakeholders are increasingly participating in and influencing this conversation. This challenges conventional ideas of CSR communication originating *from* the company *to* external stakeholders (one-way communication) and introduces the influence of external stakeholders on the CSR communication (two-way communication) (Morsing and Schultz, 2006). While two-way communication – or dialogue – is a central ideal in CSR literature and practice, it is highly contested to what extent social media furthers or restricts such dialogue on CSR.

CSR reporting: Firms' disclosure of non-financial information to their stakeholders is usually referred to as sustainability or CSR reporting. CSR reporting focuses on the communication of environmental, social and governance (ESG) information. The content of sustainability reports is increasingly standardised and comparable, as firms are asked to follow internationally accepted CSR standards such as the Global Reporting Initiative (GRI). CSR reporting is legally required in some countries, at least for publicly listed firms and/or companies exceeding a certain size. Especially larger corporations have their report content externally verified in order to avoid greenwashing allegations. CSR reporting is usually seen as a way to enhance corporate transparency and work towards better corporate accountability.

Deliberation: Deliberation can be understood as a process of argument and debate between equal citizens. Deliberative democracy refers to an understanding of democracy 'whose affairs are governed by the public deliberation of its members' (Cohen, 1989: 17). While other understandings of democracy rest on strategic compromise between competing interests, deliberative democracy emphasises the public expression of reasons (Brassett and Smith, 2007). In the CSR context, deliberation is often used to discuss how corporations legitimise themselves by engaging in communicative networks (e.g. MSIs).

Due diligence: Due diligence refers to an in-depth analysis of a company, organisation or project. It can be a legal requirement (e.g. in regard to compliance with the US-based Foreign Corrupt Practices Act) or it can be performed on a voluntary basis. Often, due diligence is exercised prior to major business transactions (e.g. a merger or an acquisition). In the CSR context, due diligence is especially used in the context of human rights. The UN Guiding Principles for Business and Human Rights understand due diligence as a process by which a firm can understand, monitor and mitigate its impact on human rights. Human Rights Due Diligence (HRDD) is a process that protects society from risks caused by a particular firm and which also protects the firm against risk exposure (e.g. reputational risk).

Extraterritorial regulation: Extraterritorial regulation describes the ability of countries to extend the impact of their national legal regulation beyond their own territory. The ability of states to regulate actors 'abroad' via hard law is often seen as a potential way to close existing global governance gaps. Examples of extraterritorial regulation relevant to the CSR context include the US Foreign Corrupt Practices Act, the UK Bribery Act and the US Alien Tort Claims Act. Extraterritorial regulation is particularly used in areas where the misconduct of 'home country' businesses happens in other countries (e.g. when paying a bribe to foreign officials). It is necessary to distinguish the exercise of direct extraterritorial regulation, which was designed for that purpose, from domestic regulation with extraterritorial implications.

Global governance: Global governance, or transnational governance, aims at the worldwide achievement of order by issuing and enforcing rules that deal with problems relevant to more than one nation (e.g. climate change and trade). It is necessary in areas where 'global governance gaps' create social, environmental and economic problems. Global governance cannot rest on the authority of governments alone. Organisations such as the United Nations and the World Bank exercise global governance, but their enforcement capacity remains restricted. That is why global governance often rests on the voluntary interplay of state and non-state actors through civil regulation (e.g. in multi-stakeholder initiatives (MSIs)).

Global value chain (GVC) analysis: GVC analysis explains how the outsourcing and offshoring of production are 'driven' by strategies and decisions of 'lead firms' in value chains. These groups of firms define the terms of supply chain membership, incorporate or exclude other actors, and allocate where, when and by whom value is added (Ponte and Sturgeon, 2014).

Governance: Governance refers to the 'processes and institutions, both formal and informal, that guide and restrain the collective activities of a group' (Keohane and Nye, 2000: 12). Governance is about influencing the behaviour of actors, such as individuals, groups, organisations or nation states (e.g. via different types of regulation). Governance can be exercised through different modes. For example, governments, networks or also single organisations can exercise governance. Global governance is usually perceived as a challenge, as it is hard to consistently steer the behaviour of actors across nation states in the absence of a 'world government'. Companies are also governed through corporate governance.

Greenwashing: Greenwashing is an application of the term 'whitewashing' to exaggerated environmental claims by organisations. More precisely, it refers to the simultaneous existence of two firm behaviours: poor CSR performance and positive communication about this performance (Delmas and Burbano, 2011: 65). Greenwashing is used to create a misleading impression of an organisation's CSR performance in the eyes of consumers, investors, governmental actors and other stakeholders. Firms can greenwash in different ways, for instance by overstating CSR achievements or downplaying corporate misconduct. Firms who have misled the public about their performance in the UN Global Compact are often referred to as being engaged in 'bluewashing' – that is, to wrap their 'dirty' corporate image in the 'clean' UN flag.

Integrated reporting (IR): IR aims at combining elements of financial and non-financial reporting in order to offer a more comprehensive perspective on corporate performance and value creation. IR was set up in order to account for the fact that different factors determine the value of an organisation. IR looks at these factors in an integrated way in order to understand interaction effects between financial and non-financial value drivers. The International Integrated Reporting Council (IIRC) launched an IR Framework in 2013.

Legitimacy: Organisational legitimacy refers to the 'perception or assumption that the actions of an entity are desirable, proper, or appropriate within some socially constructed system of norms, values, beliefs, and definitions' (Suchman, 1995: 574). There are two different forms of legitimacy relevant to the study of CSR. Input legitimacy refers to whether an organisation's decisions reflect the preferences of those that are being governed by this decision (Mayntz, 2010). In other words, input legitimacy deals with questions of accountability and representation of relevant stakeholders in decision-making. Output legitimacy deals with an organisation's ability to provide an effective solution to the policy issues that are being addressed (e.g. whether or not its rules are enforced).

Materiality: A CSR issue is described as being material if it impacts a company's long-term success and survival. Material CSR issues are those issues that are (1) judged as being of high importance to a firm's stakeholders, and (2) judged as having a significant influence on a firm's strategic positioning. Which CSR issues are considered material depends on the context in which a firm operates. For instance, the materiality of CSR issues can be influenced by a firm's sector, size and geographic location.

Multi-Stakeholder Initiatives (MSIs): MSIs are means of addressing specific global governance problems and therefore have broader aims than do partnerships. MSIs reflect a particular way of governing CSR standards. Within MSIs the authority for designing and enforcing relevant rules is shared between different interest groups, which, as a whole, cross the state/non-state and profit/non-profit boundaries (Rasche, 2012: 683). Typical stakeholder groups that participate in MSIs are: businesses, NGOs, governments, academics and professionals, and unions.

Non-governmental Organisation (NGO): NGOs are organisations that are not associated with any state structure and do not primarily exist to make a profit. NGOs are designed to advance the common good or the interests of a third party, but not in a commercial or business-related way. Some NGOs are focused on advocacy (e.g. through campaigning), while others concentrate on the provision of services to those in need (e.g. through NGO-business partnerships). NGOs have different sources of income. They are usually funded by governments, foundations, businesses, private people and also their own activities (e.g. income through research).

Orchestration: Orchestration happens when states or intergovernmental organisations initiate, guide, broaden and/or strengthen transnational governance by non-state and/or sub-state actors. Orchestration refers to a wide set of mechanisms, some of which are 'directive' and others 'facilitative'. *Directive* orchestration relies on the authority of the state and seeks to incorporate private initiatives into its regulatory framework, for example through mandating principles,

transparency, and codes of conduct. *Facilitative* orchestration relies on softer instruments, such as the provision of material and ideational support, in order to kick-start new initiatives and/or further shape and support them.

Partnerships: Partnerships have emerged as a common mode for CSR. These can include: (1) Public–private partnerships (PPPs) which imply an agreement between a public sector authority and a company to address or solve a challenge of public concern. As such, the private party provides its financial, technical or social skills to provide a service or a project. (2) NGO-business partnerships include a collaboration between one or more NGOs and one or more companies. They can be used for philanthropic purposes (including charitable donations) and/or for the exchange of complementary resources (including transfer of skills and knowledge about new markets). (3) Tripartite partnerships bring together the resources of business, (inter-)governmental actors and NGOs. In contrast, MSIs define and enforce rules that companies can sign up to.

Paternalism: Paternalism, meaning a 'fatherly attitude', is a term that was applied to nineteenth-century models of responsible business. It has also been subsequently deployed to distinguish cases of modern CSR where it is assumed that the beneficiaries, usually employees, are either unaware of their own interests or do not possess the required resources to pursue them. The corollary is that the business owners and leaders, or the corporations, possess appropriate knowledge and resources, and volunteer to devote these to the service of the beneficiaries (e.g. in the form of employee housing, community education or 'appropriate' recreational facilities). It has been argued that there may be a business case for paternalism (e.g. a stable, motivated and compliant workforce). Critics point to the restrictions that some forms of paternalism impose (e.g. some Quaker-owned businesses did not provide pubs in their housing schemes).

Philanthropy: Philanthropy, originating from Greek, means 'love for humanity' in the sense of caring and helping people in need. In the CSR context, philanthropy refers to charitable donations by corporations (either financially or in-kind). Although traditional philanthropy can be viewed as part of CSR, it is not at its core, as philanthropic activities do not directly relate to a corporation's value and supply chain. Philanthropy is about how profits are used, not about how they are made. Often, philanthropy is used by businesses to create better relationships to the local communities around them (e.g. by giving money to local clubs). Some companies endeavour to use their philanthropy in strategic ways (e.g. in alignment with employee volunteering).

Political corporate social responsibility: The political perspective on CSR looks at how corporations are turned into political actors 'by engaging in public deliberations, collective decisions, and the provision of public goods or the restrictions of public bads in cases where public authorities are unable or unwilling to fulfill this role' (Scherer et al., 2016: 276). It analyses corporations' contributions to (global) governance, such as, but not limited to, firms' engagement in multi-stakeholder initiatives (MSIs). Political CSR is closely related to the concept of corporate citizenship.

Private regulation: Private regulation is an umbrella term used for regulatory activities exercised by non-state actors. Unlike legal regulation, which is based on legally enforceable standards, private regulation is based on actors' voluntary commitments. Private regulation can be exercised by single organisations (as in the case of self-regulation or regulation in supply chains) or it can be carried out in a collaborative manner (as in the case of civil regulation). Private regulation is not designed to replace legal, state-based regulation but may precede it. Often, it supplements legal regulation in cases where the latter does not exist.

Self-regulation: Self-regulation means that a firm monitors its own adherence to pre-given standards on a voluntary basis. A firm may use a code of conduct to monitor its own compliance with the standard. Self-regulation implies that there is no external and hence independent party that monitors adherence to standards. Industry self-regulation can also happen on a collective level, such as when a group of firms decide to follow a certain standard on a voluntary basis without using external verification mechanisms. Self-regulation can cause a conflict of interest, as firms are asked to police themselves.

Socially responsible investment (SRI): SRI (also known as sustainable, green or ethical investing) refers to investment practices that try to achieve good financial returns while simultaneously maintaining high social, environmental and governance (ESG) standards. Some investors perform negative screenings – that is, they exclude firms from certain sectors (e.g. tobacco, gambling) and firms with a weak ESG performance from their investment activities. In some cases investors also perform direct divestments by removing stocks with a weak ESG performance from their portfolio. Positive investing (also called impact investing) refers to investment activities in firms that show a particularly good ESG performance. Shareholder activism is also seen as an SRI strategy. Such activism refers to individuals or organisations using their rights as a shareholder in a publicly traded company to put pressure on the company's management to improve the firm's ESG performance. SRI was institutionalised through performance indexes (e.g. FTSE4Good) and investor principles (e.g. Equator Principles).

Soft law: Soft law and hard law operate on a continuum; they are not dichotomous. Soft law differs from hard law in three ways: (1) it refers to regulation that is not legally binding and hence contains lower levels of obligation to relevant rules and non-legal punishment for failure to comply with them; (2) it is less precisely formulated (while hard law usually unambiguously defines required conduct); and (3) it can rest on the delegation of authority to non-state actors (e.g. NGOs) to make and enforce relevant rules (Abbott et al., 2000: 401–402). While soft law can appear in a variety of different contexts, it is especially relevant for CSR. Private regulation of CSR activities (e.g. through self-regulation or civil regulation) can be described as soft law.

Stakeholders: The classic notion of stakeholders as 'any group or individual who can affect or is affected by the achievement of the organization's objectives' (Freeman, 1984: 46) is a general and encompassing conceptualisation (including virtual stakeholders).

Freeman argues that there are ethical and strategic reasons for engaging with stakeholders. Early discussions have pointed out the importance of distinguishing between primary (e.g. employees, investors, customers) and secondary (e.g. communities, media, NGOs) stakeholders. In the era of digitalisation, managers have become even more aware of how the company is not centre stage but rather one stakeholder entangled in webs of many stakeholders where importance is often unpredictable.

Strategic corporate social responsibility: Related to the discussion of the business case, strategic CSR implies that there is an economic motivation for engaging in responsible business activities. Strategic CSR assumes that there is no intrinsic (i.e. moral) motivation to design and implement relevant business practices. Rather, CSR is seen as a way to achieve a competitive advantage and to better position a firm in its market environment. Strategic CSR relates to and overlaps with the concepts of CSV, CSP and stakeholder management.

Sustainable development: The World Commission on Economic Development (WCED) defined sustainable development as meeting 'the needs of the present without compromising the ability of future generations to meet their own needs' (World Commission on Environment and Development, 1987: 54). The definition emphasises that there are certain limitations to socio-economic development, which are imposed by the environment's capacity to satisfy present and future needs. As a concept, sustainable development is focused on the development of (global) society, while corporate sustainability highlights the contribution of individual corporations to sustainable development.

Sweatshop: The term was originally coined to describe British garment factories in the mid-nineteenth century. A sweatshop is a production site (e.g. a factory or a farm) in which workers are employed under poor working conditions, such as, but not limited to: low or illegal wages, exposure of workers to health and safety risks, overtime work (in some cases forced and unpaid), employment of underage workers, restrictions to collective bargaining and harassment of workers based on gender, religion and sexual orientation. Although sweatshops also exist in Western countries, most of the discussion is now focused on their existence in developing and emerging nations.

Transparency: Conventional notions of transparency suggest insight and clarity, that we can 'see through' all activities: nothing is hidden from view. Transparency is expected to enable corporate accountability, specifically for the disclosure of information relevant to compliance with socially accepted norms and rules. However, communication scholars have pointed to how this ideal may be somewhat illusory because such communicative processes about transparency can be strategically designed to obscure important activities in the interest of, for example, power or profit (Christensen, Morsing and Cheney, 2008), and as such, lead to production of new areas of opacity and greenwashing.

Triple bottom line: The triple bottom line concept relates to discussions around corporate sustainability and sustainable development. It captures the fact that organisations create value in three interrelated dimensions: social, environmental and economic. Triple bottom line thinking aims at moving corporations beyond the consideration of a single bottom line (i.e. the financial one).

References

A.P. Møller – Mærsk A/S (2015).
Sustainability Report 2014. Retrieved
on 23 November 2015 from www
.maersk.com/en/the-maersk-group/
press-room/press-release-archive/
2015/2/press-release-sustainability-
report-2014.

Aakhus, M. and Bzdak, M. (2012).
Revisiting the Role of 'Shared Value'
in the Business-Society Relationship.
*Business and Professional Ethics
Journal*, 31(2), 231–246.

Abbott, K. W., Keohane, R. O., Moravcsik,
A., Slaughter, A.-M. and Snidal, D.
(2000). The Concept of Legalization.
International Organization, 54(3),
401–419.

Abbott, K. W. and Snidal, D. (2000).
Hard and Soft Law in International
Governance. *International
Organization*, 54(3), 421–456.

Abbott, K. W., Genschel, P., Snidal, D. and
Zangl, B. (Eds.) (2015). *International
Organizations as Orchestrators*.
Cambridge: Cambridge University
Press.

(2009). The Governance Triangle:
Regulatory Standards Institutions and
the Shadow of the State. In W. Mattli
and N. Woods (Eds.), *The Politics of
Global Regulation* (pp. 44–88).
Princeton: Princeton University Press.

Adams, C. A. (2004). The Ethical, Social and
Environmental Reporting-Performance
Portrayal Gap. *Accounting, Auditing
and Accountability Journal*, 17(5),
731–757.

Adams, C. and Narayanan, V. (2007).
The Standardization of Sustainability
Reporting. In J. Bebbington, J.
Unerman, and B. O'Dwyer. (Eds.),
*Sustainability Accounting and
Accountability* (pp. 70–85). New York,
NY: Routledge.

Aguilera, R. V., Rupp, D. E., Williams, C. A.
and Ganapathi, J. (2007). Putting
the 'S' back in Corporate Social
Responsibility: A Multilevel Theory
of Social Change in Organizations.
Academy of Management Review,
32(3), 836–863.

Ahrne, G. and Brunsson, N. (2011).
Organization Outside Organizations:
The Significance of Partial
Organization. *Organization*, 18(1),
83–104.

Alliance for Bangladesh Worker Safety
(2016). Retrieved 27 June 2014 from
www.bangladeshworkersafety.org/
who-we-are/about-the-alliance.

Alvesson, M. (1993). Organizations as
Rhetoric: Knowledge-Intensive Firms
and the Struggle with Ambiguity.
Journal of Management Studies, 30(6),
997–1021.

(1996). *Communication, Power and
Organization*. Berlin: Walter de
Gruyter.

Andersson, I., Shivarajan, S. and Blau, G.
(2005). Enacting Ecological
Sustainability in the MNC: A Test of
an Adapted Value-Belief-Norm
Framework. *Journal of Business Ethics*,
59(3), 295–305.

Andonova, L. (2014). Boomerangs to Partnerships? Explaining State Participation in Transnational Partnerships for Sustainability. *Comparative Political Studies*, 47(3), 481–515.

Andonova, L. B., Betsill, M. and Bulkeley, H. (2009). Transnational Climate Governance. *Global Environmental Politics*, 9(2), 52–73.

Annandale, D., Morrison-Saunders, A. and Bouna, G. (2004). The Impact of Voluntary Environmental Protection Instruments on Company Environmental Performance. *Business Strategy and the Environment*, 13(1): 1–12.

Aragon-Correa, J., Martin-Tapia, I. and Hurtado-Torres, N. (2013). Proactive Environmental Strategies and Employee Inclusion: The Positive Effects of Information Sharing and Promoting Collaboration and the Influence of Uncertainty. *Organization and Environment*, 26(2), 139–161.

Arnold, D. G. and Bowie, N. E. (2007). Respect for Workers in Global Supply Chains. *Business Ethics Quarterly*, 17(1), 135–145.

Arnold, D. G. (2010). Transnational Corporations and the Duty to Respect Basic Human Rights. *Business Ethics Quarterly*, 20(3): 371–399.

Arnold, D. G., and Hartman, L. P. (2006). Worker Rights and Low Wage Industrialization: How to Avoid Sweatshops. *Human Rights Quarterly*, 28(3), 676–700.

Arvidsson, S. (2010). Communication of Corporate Social Responsibility: A Study of the Views of Management Teams in Large Companies. *Journal of Business Ethics*, 96(3), 339–354.

Asariotis, R. and Benamara, H. (2012). *Maritime Transport and the Climate Change Challenge*. New York, NY: Earthscan.

Ashcraft, K. L., Kuhn, T. R. and Cooren, F. (2009). Constitutional Amendments: 'Materializing' Organizational Communication. *The Academy of Management Annals*, 3(1), 1–64.

Ashforth, B. E., Goia, D. A., Robinson, S. L. and Trevino, L. K. (2008). Re-viewing Organizational Corruption. *Academy of Management Review*, 33(3), 670–683.

Auld, G. (2014). Confronting Trade-offs and Interactive Effects in the Choice of Policy Focus: Specialized versus Comprehensive Private Governance. *Regulation and Governance*, 8(1), 126–148.

Austin, J. L. (1962). *How to Do Things with Words*. Oxford, UK: Oxford University Press.

Avi-Yonah, R. (2005). The Cyclical Transformations of the Corporate Form: A Historical Perspective on Corporate Social Responsibility. *Delaware Journal of Corporate Law*, 30(3), 767–818.

Axelrod, L. (1984). Balancing Personal Needs with Environmental Preservation: Identifying Values that Guide Decisions in Ecological Dilemmas. *Journal of Social Issues*, 50(3), 85–104.

Ayres, I., and Braithwaite, J. (1992). *Responsive Regulation: Transcending the Deregulation Debate*. Oxford: Oxford University Press.

Bakan, J. (2004). *The Corporation: The Pathological Pursuit of Profit and Power*. London: Constable and Robinson.

Baker, S. (2007). Sustainable Development as Symbolic Commitment: Declaratory Politics and the Seductive Appeal of Ecological Modernisation in the European Union. *Environmental Politics*, 16(2), 297–317.

Bakewell, S. (2013). BP to Sell U.S. Wind Business in Retreat to Fossil Fuels. Retrieved on 13 February 2015 from

www.bloomberg.com/news/articles/
2013-04-03/bp-to-sell-u-s-wind-
buiness-in-retreat-to-fossil-fuels.

Balmer, J. T. and Greyser, S. A. (2003).
*Revealing the Corporation: Perspectives
on Identity, Image, Reputation,
Corporate Branding, and Corporate-
level Marketing: an Anthology.* New
York: Psychology Press.

Balmer, M. (2010). The BP Deepwater
Horizon Débâcle and Corporate Brand
Exuberance. *Journal of Brand
Management*, 18(2), 97–104.

Banerjee, S. B. (2003). Who Sustains
Whose Development? Sustainable
Development and the Reinvention of
Nature. *Organization Studies*, 24(1),
143–180.

(2008). Corporate Social Responsibility:
The Good, the Bad and the Ugly.
Critical Sociology, 34(1), 51–79.

(2008). Necrocapitalism. *Organization
Studies*, 29(12), 1541–1563.

(2012). A Climate for Change? Critical
Reflections on the Durban United
Nations Climate Change Conference.
Organization Studies, 33(12),
1761–1786.

B. Ki-Moon, (2013) Opening remarks at
Global Compact Leaders Summit:
'Architects of a Better World'.
Retrieved on 13 April 2016 from
www.un.org/apps/news/infocus/
sgspeeches/print_full.asp?statID=1976.

Bansal, P. (2005). Evolving Sustainably:
A Longitudinal Study of Corporate
Sustainable Development. *Strategic
Management Journal*, 26(3), 197–218.

Barnett, M., Jermier, J. and Lafferty, B.
(2006). Corporate Reputation: The
Definitional Landscape. *Corporate
Reputation Review*, 9(1), 26–38.

Baron, D. P. (2001). Private Politics,
Corporate Social Responsibility and
Integrated Strategy. *Journal of
Economics and Management Strategy*,
10(1), 7–45.

Barrientos, S. and Smith, S. (2007). Do
Workers Benefit from Ethical Trade?
Assessing Codes of Labour Practice in
Global Production Systems. *Third
World Quarterly*, 28(4), 713–729.

Bartley, T. and Child, C. (2011). Movements,
Markets and Fields: The Effects of Anti-
Sweatshop Campaigns on U.S. firms,
1993–2000. *Social Forces*, 90(2),
425–451.

Baumann-Pauly, D., Scherer, A. G. and
Palazzo, G. (2015). Managing
Institutional Complexity.
A Longitudinal Study of Legitimacy
Strategies at a Sportswear Brand
Company. *Journal of Business Ethics*,
January 2015, 1–21.

Baumann-Pauly, D., Wickert, C., Spence, L.
and Scherer, A. (2013). Organizing
Corporate Social Responsibility in
Small and Large Firms: Size Matters.
Journal of Business Ethics, 115(4),
693–705.

BBC (2000). *BP goes green*. Retrieved
on 16 February 2015 from http://
news.bbc.co.uk/2/hi/business/
849475.stm.

BBMG, GlobeScan and SustainAbility
(2013). *RE:Thinking Consumption:
Consumers and the Future of
Sustainability.* New York, NY: BBMG.

Bebbington, J. (2001). Sustainable
Development: A Review of the
International Development, Business
and Accounting Literature. *Accounting
Forum*, 25(2), 128–157.

Becker-Olsen, K., Cudmore, B. and Hill, R.
(2006). The Impact of Perceived
Corporate Social Responsibility on
Consumer Behaviour. *Journal of
Business Research*, 59(1), 46–53.

Beddewela, E. and Herzig, C. (2013).
Corporate Social Reporting by MNCs'
subsidiaries in Sri Lanka. *Accounting
Forum*, 37(2), 135–149.

Benn, S., Dunphy, D. and Griffiths, A.
(2014). *Organizational Change for*

Corporate Sustainability. London, UK: Routledge.

Bennett, W. (2003). Communicating Global Activism. *Information, Communication and Society,* 6(2), 143–168.

——— (2003). *New Media Power: The Internet and Global Activism.* Oxford: Rowman and Littlefield.

Benoit, W. L. (1995). *Accounts, Excuses, and Apologies: A theory of Image Restoration.* Albany: State University of New York Press.

Benz, A. (Ed.). (2004). *Governance – Regieren in komplexen Regelsystemen.* Wiesbaden: VS Verlag für Sozialwissenschaften.

Berle, A. and Means, G. (1932). *The Modern Corporation and Private Property.* New York: MacMillan.

Bernstein, S. and Cashore, B. (2007). Can Non-State Global Governance be Legitimate? An Analytical Framework. *Regulation and Governance,* 1(4), 347–371.

Bertini, M. and Gourville, J. T. (2012). Pricing to Create Shared Value. *Harvard Business Review,* 90(6), 96–104.

Blowfield, M. (2013). *Business and Sustainability.* Oxford: Oxford University Press.

Blundo, G. and Olivier de Sardan, J. P. (2006). *Everyday Corruption and the State: Citizens and Public Opinion in Africa,* London: Zed Books.

Blythe, I. (2011). *From Philanthropy to Essential Business Investment – the Evolution of CSR at Boots UK* (PDF document). Retrieved on 19 April 2016 from www.jpf.org.uk/images/newsfiles/1311777104JapanFoundation CSRpresnIDBJuly2011v1.pdf.

Boiral, O. (2007). Corporate Greening Through ISO 14001: A Rational Myth? *Organization Science,* 18(1), 127–146.

Bonini, S. (2011). *The Business of Sustainability.* Silicon Valley, CA: McKinsey & Company.

Booth, S. A. (2000). How Can Organisations Prepare for Reputational Crises? *Journal of Contingencies and Crisis Management,* 8(4), 197–207.

Boström, M. (2006). Regulatory Credibility and Authority through Inclusiveness: Standardization Organizations in Cases of Eco-Labelling. *Organization,* 13(3), 345–367.

Boswell, J. (1983). The Informal Social Control of Business in Britain: 1880–1939. *Business History Review,* 57(2), 237–257.

Bowen, H. R. (1953). *Social Responsibilities of the Businessman.* New York: Harper&Row.

Bowers, J. W., Ochs, D. J., Jensen, R. J. and Schulz, D. P. (2009). *The Rhetoric of Agitation and Control.* Chicago: Waveland Press.

Brammer, S. and Pavelin, S. (2004). Building a Good Reputation. *European Management Journal,* 22(6), 704–713.

Brandeis, L. D. (1914). *Other People's Money and How Bankers Use It.* New York: Stokes. Retrieved on 6 April 2016 from https://archive.org/details/otherpeoplesmone00bran.

Brassett, J. and Smith, W. (2007). *Deliberation and Global Governance: Liberal, Cosmopolitan and Critical perspectives (GARNET Working Paper No.25/07).* Coventry, UK: University of Warwick.

Bromley, P. and Meyer, J. (2014). 'They are all organizations': The Cultural Roots of Blurring between the Nonprofit, Business, and Government Sectors. *Administration and Society,* 4, 1–28.

Brown, J. and Fraser, M. (2006). Approaches and Perspectives in Social and Environmental Accounting: An Overview of the Conceptual Landscape. *Business Strategy and the Environment,* 15(2), 103–117.

Brown, T. J. and Dacin, P. A. (1997). The Company and the Product: Corporate

Associations and Consumer Product Responses. *Journal of Marketing*, 61(1), 68–84.

Browne, J. (2010). *Beyond Business: An Inspirational Memoir From a Visionary Leader*. London: Weidenfeld and Nicolson.

Bruno, K. (2000). BP: Beyond Petroleum or Beyond Preposterous? *CorpWatch*. Retrieved on 4 April 2016 from www .corpwatch.org/article.php?id=219.

Brunsson, N., Rasche, A. and Seidl, D. (2012). The Dynamics of Standardization: Three Perspectives on Standards in Organization Studies. *Organization Studies*, 33(5–6), 613–632.

Buhmann, K. (2003). Reforms of Administrative Law in the PRC and Vietnam: The Possible Role of the Legal Tradition. *Nordic Journal of International Law*, 72(2), 253–290.

(2006). Corporate Social Responsibility – What Role for Law? Some Legal Aspects of CSR. *Corporate Governance – The International Journal of Business in Society*, 6(2), 188–202.

(2012). Business and Human Rights: Analysing Discursive Articulation of Stakeholder Interests to Explain the Consensus-Based Construction of the 'Protect, Respect, Remedy UN Framework'. *International Law Research*, 1(1), 88–101.

(2013). The Danish CSR Reporting Requirement as Reflexive Law: Employing CSR as a Modality to Promote Public Policy. *European Business Law Review*, 24(2), 187–216.

(2014). *Normative Discourses and Public-Private Regulatory Strategies for Construction of CSR Normativity: Towards a Method for Above-National Public-Private Regulation of Business Social Responsibilities*. Copenhagen: Multivers publishing.

(2015a). Public regulators and CSR: The 'Social Licence to Operate' in recent United Nations Instruments on Business and Human Rights and the juridification of CSR. *Journal of Business Ethics*, DOI 10.1007/s10551-015–2869-9.

(2015b). Juridifying Corporate Social Responsibility in Public Law: Assessing Coherence and Inconsistencies against UN Guidance on Business and Human Rights. *International and Comparative Corporate Law Journal*, 11(3), 194–228.

(2015c). Business and Human Rights: Understanding the UN Guiding Principles from the Perspective of Transnational Business Governance Interactions. *Transnational Legal Theory*, 6(1), DOI 10.1080/ 20414005.2015.1073516.

(2015d). Introducing Legal Method when Teaching Stakeholder Theory: Enhancing the Understanding of Stakeholder Expectations in relation to Human Rights and CSR Reporting. *Journal of Business Ethics Education*, 12 (Special Issue), 4–42.

Buhr, N., Gray, R. and Milne, M. (2014). Histories, Rationales, Voluntary Standards and Future Prospects for Sustainability Reporting: CSR, GRI, IIRC and Beyond. In J. Bebbington, J. Unerman and B. O'Dwyer (Eds.), *Sustainability Accounting and Accountability* (pp. 51–71). New York, NY: Routledge.

Bukovansky, M. (2006). The Hollowness of Anti-Corruption Discourse. *Review of International Political Economy*, 13(2),181–209.

Bunge, J. (2015). Monsanto Shareholder Meeting gets Heated. *Wall Street Journal*, 30 January. Retrieved 30 January 2015 from http:// blogs.wsj.com/corporate-intelligence/ 2015/01/30/monsanto-shareholder- meeting-gets-heated/.

Bäckstrand, K. (2008). Accountability of Networked Climate Governance:

The Rise of Transnational Climate Partnerships. *Global Environmental Politics*, 8(3), 74–102.

Börzel, T. and Risse, T. (2010). Governance Without a State: Can it Work? *Regulation and Governance*, 4(2), 113–134.

Campbell, J. L. (2006). Institutional Analysis and the Paradox of Corporate Social Responsibility. *American Behavioral Scientist*, 49(7), 925–938.

(2007). Why Would Corporations Behave in Socially Responsible Ways? An Institutional Theory of Corporate Social Responsibility. *Academy of Management Review*, 32(3), 946–967.

Cantó-Milà, N. and Lozano, J. M. (2009). The Spanish Discourse on Corporate Social Responsibility. *Journal of Business Ethics*, 87(1, Supplement), 157–171.

Carroll, A. B. (1979). A Three-Dimensional Conceptual Model of Corporate Performance. *Academy of Management Review*, 4(4), 497–505.

(1991). The Pyramid of Corporate Social Responsibility: Toward the Moral Management of Organizational Stakeholders. *Business Horizons*, 34(4), 39–48.

Carroll, A. B, Lipartito, K. J., Post, J. E. and Werhane, P. H. (2012). *Corporate Responsibility: the American Experience*. Cambridge: Cambridge University Press.

Carroll, A. B. and Shabana, K. M. (2010.) The Business Case for Corporate Social Responsibility: A Review of Concepts, Research and Practice. *International Journal of Management Reviews*, 12(1), 85–105.

Carson, R. (1962). *Silent Spring*. Boston: Houghton Mifflin.

Carvalho, G. (2001). Sustainable Development: Is it Achievable within the Existing International Political Economy Context? *Sustainable Development*, 9(2), 61–73.

Case, P. (2013). March against Monsanto planned for UK cities. *Farmers Weekly*, 159(22), 83. Web version published online 23 May 2013. Retrieved 5 January 2016 from www.fwi.co.uk/arable/march-against-monsanto-planned-for-uk-cities.htm#.Uc-v3jvVC1w.

Cashore, B. (2002). Legitimacy and the Privatization of Environmental Governance: How Non-State Market-Driven (NSMD) Governance Systems Gain Rule-Making Authority. *Governance*, 15(4), 503–529.

Castello, I., Etter, M. and Nielsen, F. A. (2016). Strategies of Legitimacy through Social Media: The Networked Strategy. *Journal of Management Studies*, 53, 402–432.

Castells, M. (2000). *The Information Age: Economy, Society and Culture* (2nd ed., Vol. I), *The Rise of the Network Society*. Oxford: Blackwell.

Caulfield, P. A. (2013). The Evolution of Strategic Corporate Social Responsibility. *EuroMed Journal of Business*, 8(3), 220–242.

CCC (2015). Clean Clothes Campaign. Retrieved on 20 September 2015 from www.cleanclothes.org/.

Chandler, A. D. (1984). The Emergence of Managerial Capitalism. *Business History Review*, 58(04), 473–503.

Chapple, W., Moon, J., Pouryousefi, S. and Herzig, C. (forthcoming). A Conceptual Framework for Corporate Sustainability Impact Assessment and Management. In A. Martinuzzi and P. Hardi (Eds.) (forthcoming), *A Corporate Sustainability and Impact Assessment and Management of the Evaluating Sustainable Development Series* (Vol. 5). Cheltenham: Edward Elgar.

Chaudhari, A. and Purkayastha, D. (2011). Greenpeace, Nestle and the Palm Oil Controversy: Social Media Driving Change? *IBS Center for Management Research*, case no. 911-010-1.

Christensen, L. T. (1997). Marketing as Auto-Communication. *Consumption, Markets and Culture*, 1(3), 197–227.

Christensen, L. T. and Cheney, G. (2011). Interrogating the Communicative Dimensions of Corporate Social Responsibility. In Ø. Ihlen, S. May and J. Bartlett, *Handbook of Communication and Corporate Social Responsibility* (Eds.) (pp. 491–504). Malden, MA: Wiley-Blackwell.

(2015). Peering into Transparency: Challenging Ideals, Proxies and Organizational Practices. *Communication Theory*, 25(1), 70–90.

Christensen, L. T. and Langer, R. (2009). Public Relations and the Strategic Use of Transparency. Consistency, Hypocrisy and Corporate Change. In R. L. Heath, E. Toth and D. Waymer (Eds.), *Rhetorical and Critical Approaches to Public Relations* (Vol. II), (pp. 129–153). Hillsdale, NY: Routledge.

Christensen, L. T., Morsing, M. and Cheney, G. (2008). *Corporate Communications: Convention, Challenge, Complexity*. London: Sage Publications.

Christensen, L. T., Morsing, M. and Thyssen, O. (2013). CSR as Aspirational Talk. *Organization*, 20(3), 372–393.

(2015). Discursive Closure and Discursive Openings of Sustainability. *Management Communication Quarterly*, 29(1), 135–144.

Christmann, P. and Taylor, G. (2006). Firm Self-Regulation through International Certifiable Standards: Determinants of Symbolic versus Substantive Implementation. *Journal of International Business Studies*, 37(6): 863–878.

Chun, R. and Davies, G. (2006). The Influence of Corporate Character on Customers and Employees: Exploring Similarities and Differences. *Journal of the Academy of Marketing Science*, 34(2), 138–146.

Ciulla, J. B. (2005). Integrating Leadership with Ethics: Is Good Leadership contrary to Human Nature? In J. P. Doh and S. Stumpf (Eds.), *Handbook on Responsible Leadership and Governance in Global Business* (pp. 159–179). Cheltenham, UK: Edward Elgar.

Clark, J. M. (1916). The Changing Basis of Economic Responsibility. *The Journal of Political Economy*, 24, 209–229.

climatebrad (2010). *BP CEO Tony Hayward: 'I'd Like My Life Back'*. Online Video, 31 March. Retrieved on 1 March 2016 from www.youtube.com/watch?v=MTdKa9eWNFw.

Cohen, J. (1989). Deliberation and Democratic Legitimacy. In A. Hamlin and P. Pettit (Eds.), *The Good Polity: Narrative Analysis of the State* (pp. 17–34). New York, NY: Basil Blackwell.

Cohen, E. (2013). *Understanding G4: The Concise Guide to Next Generation Sustainability Reporting*. Oxford: DōShorts, Dō Sustainability.

Commission of the European Communities. (2002). 'Corporate Social Responsibility: A Business Contribution to Sustainable Development', Brussels, 2.7.2002 COM(2002) 347 final.

(2006). 'Implementing the Partnership for Growth and Jobs: Making Europe a Pole of Excellence on Corporate Social Responsibility', Brussels, 22.3.2006 COM(2006) 136 final.

(2011). 'Communication from the Commission to the European Parliament, the Council, the European Economic and Social Committee of the Regions: A Renewed EU Strategy 2011–14 for Corporate Social Responsibility', Brussels, 25.10.2011 COM(2011) 681 final.

Coombs, W. T. (2007). Protecting Organization Reputations During a Crisis: The Development and Application of Situational Crisis Communication Theory. *Corporate Reputation Review*, 10(3), 163–176.

(2010). Sustainability: A New and Complex 'Challenge' for Crisis Managers. *International Journal of Sustainable Strategic Management* 2(1), 4–16.

(2014). *Applied Crisis Communication and Crisis Management*. Thousand Oaks: Sage Publications.

(2015). *Ongoing Crisis Communication: Planning, Managing, and Responding* (4th ed.). Thousand Oaks: Sage Publications.

Coombs, W. T. and Holladay, S. J. (2012). The Paracrisis: The Challenges Created by Publicity Managing Crisis Prevention. *Public Relations Review*, 38 (3), 408–415.

(2015). CSR as Crisis Risk: Expanding how We Conceptualize the Relationship. *Corporate Communications: An International Journal*, 20(2), 144–162.

Cooper, S. M. and Owen, D. L. (2007). Corporate Social Reporting and Stakeholder Accountability: The Missing Link. *Accounting, Organizations and Society*, 32(7–8), 649–67.

Cooren, F., Kuhn, T., Cornelissen, J. P. and Clark, T. (2011). Communication, Organizing, and Organization: An Overview and Introduction to the Special Issue. *Organisation Studies*, 32(9), 1149–1170.

Cornelissen, J. (2014). *Corporate Communications. A Guide to Theory and Practice* (4th ed.). London: Sage.

Cosbey, A., Aguilar, S., Ashton, M. and Ponte, S. (2010). *Environmental Goods and Services Negotiations at the WTO: Lessons from Multilateral Environmental Agreements and Ecolabels for Breaking the Impasse*. Winnipeg: International Institute for Sustainable Development.

Cowan, S. and Gadenne, D. (2005). Australian Corporate Environmental Reporting: A Comparative Analysis of Disclosure Practices across Voluntary and Mandatory Disclosure Systems. *Journal of Accounting and Organizational Change*, 1(2), 165–179.

Cox, M., Derks, C. and LeFevre, K. (2013). *The Fourth Generation of GRI, Guideline Changes You Need to Know*. Kansas City, MO: Burns & McDonnell.

Cragg, W. (2012). Ethics, Enlightened Self-Interest and the Corporate Responsibility to Respect Human Rights. *Business Ethics Quarterly*, 22(1), 9–36.

Crane, A. and Matten, D. (2007). *Business Ethics: Managing Corporate Citizenship and Sustainability in the Age of Globalization*. Oxford: Oxford University Press.

(2008). Business Ethics. In W. Visser, D. Matten, M. Pohl and N. Tolhurst (Eds.), *The A to Z of Corporate Social Responsibility* (pp. 52–59). Chichester: John Wiley.

Crane, A., Matten, D. and Moon, J. (2008). *Corporations and Citizenship*. Cambridge: Cambridge University Press.

Crane, A., Palazzo, G., Spence, L. J. and Matten, D. (2014). Contesting the Value of 'Creating Shared Value'. *California Management Review*, 56(2), 130–149.

Cremer, A. and Bergin, T. (2015). Fear and Respect: VW's Culture under Winterkorn. Retrieved on 31 March 2016 from www.reuters.com/article/us-volkswagen-emissions-culture-idUSKCN0S40MT20151010.

Crook, C. (2005). A Survey of Corporate Social Responsibility. *The Economist*, 22 January, p. 2.

Cuervo-Cazurra, A. (2006). Who Cares about Corruption? *Journal of International Business Studies*, 37(6), 807–822.

Dart, R. (2004). The Legitimacy of Social Enterprise. *Nonprofit Management and Leadership*, 14(4), 411–424.

Dauvergne, P. and Lister, J. (2012). Big Brand Sustainability: Governance Prospects and Environmental Limits, *Global Environmental Change*, 22(1), 36–45.

Davis, G. F. (2009). The Rise and Fall of Finance and the End of the Society of Organizations. *Academy of Management Perspectives*, 23(3), 27–44.

Davis, K. (1960). Can Business Afford to Ignore Social Responsibilities? *California Management Review*, 2(3), 70–76.
    (1973). The Case For and Against Business Assumption of Social Responsibilities. *Academy of Management Journal*, 16(2), 312–322.

De Marchi, V., Di Maria, E. and Ponte, S. (2013). The Greening of Global Value Chains: Insights from the Furniture Industry. *Competition and Change*, 17(4), 299–318.

De Sousa, L., Larmour, P. and Hindess, B. (Eds.) (2009). *Governments, NGOs and Anti-Corruption: The New Integrity Warriors*. London: Routledge.

Deegan, C. (2014). An Overview of Legitimacy Theory as applied within the Social and Environmental Accounting Literature. In J. Unerman, J. Bebbington and B. O'Dwyer (Eds.), *Sustainability Accounting and Accountability* (pp. 248–272). New York, NY: Routledge.

Deetz, S. (1992). *Democracy in an Age of Corporate Colonization: Developments in Communication and the Politics of Everyday Life*. Albany: State University of New York.

della Porta, D. and Diani, M. (1999). *Social Movements: An Introduction*. Oxford: Blackwell.

Delmas, M. A. and Burbano, V. C. (2011). The Drivers of Greenwashing. *California Management Review*, 54(1), 64–87.

Dembek, K., Singh, P. and Bhakoo, V. (2015). Literature Review of Shared Value: A Theoretical Concept or a Management Buzzword? *Journal of Business Ethics*, DOI 10.1007/s10551-015-2554-z.

den Hond, F. and de Bakker, F. G. A. (2007). Ideologically Motivated Activism. How Activist Groups Influence Corporate Social Change. *Academy of Management Review*, 32(3), 901–924.

Denny, C. and Meek J. (2001) Drug Giants made to Swallow Bitter Pill. *The Guardian*, 18 April 2001. Retrieved on 17 January 2016 from www .theguardian.com/world/2001/apr/19/ highereducation.aids.

DeSombre, E. R. (2006). *Flagging Standards: Globalization and Environmental, Safety, and Labor Regulations at Sea*. Cambridge, MA: The MIT Press.

Dey, C. (2007). Developing Silent and Shadow Accounts. In J. Unerman, J. Bebbington and B. O'Dwyer (Eds.), *Sustainability Accounting and Accountability* (pp. 307–327). New York, NY: Routledge.

Dey, C., Russell, S. and Thomson, I. (2011). Exploring the Potential of Shadow Accounts in Problematising Institutional Conduct. In S. Osbourne and A. Ball (Eds.), *Social Accounting and Public Management: Accountability for the Public Good* (pp. 64–75). New York, NY: Routledge.

Djelic, M. L. and Sahlin-Andersson, K. (Eds.) (2006). Transnational Governance: Institutional Dynamics of Regulation. Cambridge: Cambridge University Press.

DNV (2015). *Sustainability Reporting. Go tell the people. And be honest.* Retrieved on 5 May 2016 from www.dnvusa.com/focus/srm/services/sustainability_reporting.asp.

Donaldson, T. and Walsh, J. P. (2015). Toward a Theory of Business. *Research in Organizational Behavior*, 35, 181–207.

Dowling, G. and Moran, P. (2012). Corporate Reputations: Built in or Bolted on? *California Management Review*, 54(2), 25–42.

Driver, M. (2012). An Interview with Michael Porter: Social Entrepreneurship and the Transformation of Capitalism. *Academy of Management Learning and Education*, 11(3), 421–431.

Drucker, S. J. and Gumpert, G. (2007). Through the Looking Glass: Illusions of Transparency and the Cult of Information. *Journal of Management Development*, 26(5), 493–498.

Du, S., Bhattacharya, C. B. and Sen, S. (2010). Maximizing Business Returns to Corporate Social Responsibility (CSR): The Role of CSR Communication. *International Journal of Management Reviews*, 12(1), 8–19.

Dubuisson-Quellier, S. (2013). A Market Mediation Strategy: How Social Movements seek to Change Firms' Practices by Promoting New Principles of Product Valuation. *Organization Studies*, 34(5–6), 683–703.

Dunham, L., Freeman, R. E. and Liedtka, J. (2006). Enhancing Stakeholder Practice: A Particularized Exploration of Community. *Business Ethics Quarterly*, 16(1), 23–42.

Edelman Trust Barometer (2016). *Trust Barometer 2016*. Retrieved on 5 May 2016 from www.edelman.com/insights/intellectual-property/2016-edelman-trust-barometer/global-results/.

Eggers, D. (2013). *The Circle*. Kindle edition: Penguin.

Eisenberg, E. M. (1984). Ambiguity as Strategy in Organizational Communication. *Communication Monographs*, 51(3), 227–242.

Eisenegger, M. and Schranz, M. (2011). Reputation Management and Corporate Social Responsibility. In O. Ihlen, J. Bartlett and S. May. (Eds), *Handbook of Communication and Corporate Social Responsibility* (pp.128–146). Oxford: Wiley-Blackwell.

EITI (2012). The EITI Principles. Retrieved on 5 May 2013 from http://eiti.org/eiti/principles.

(2016). History of EITI. Retrieved on 15 January 2016 from https://eiti.org/eiti/history.

Elman, A. and Barry, M. (2012). *The key lessons from the Plan A business case.* September 2012. Retrieved on 19 April 2016 from https://corporate.marksandspencer.com/documents/plan-a-our-approach/key-lessons-from-the-plana-business-case-september2012.pdf.

Ernst and Young, and Boston College Center for Corporate Citizenship (BCCCC) (2013). *Value of Sustainability Reporting.* London, UK: Ernst and Young.

Ethical Corporation (2009). *How to Embed Corporate Responsibility across Different Parts of your Company.* London, UK: Ethical Corporation.

(2014). *South Asia Briefing: India's Companies Act – The 2% solution.* 9 June. Retrieved on 31 March 2016 from www.ethicalcorp.com/stakeholder-engagement/south-asia-briefing-indias-companies-act-2-solution.

Etzion, D. and Ferraro, F. (2010). The Role of Analogy in the Institutionalisation of Sustainability Reporting. *Organization Science*, 21(5), 1092–1107.

Etzioni, A. (2010). Is Transparency the best Disinfectant? *The Journal of Political Philosophy*, 18(4), 389–404.

European Commission (2016). 'Corporate
Social Responsibility: EU Multi
Stakeholder Forum on Corporate Social
Responsibility.' Retrieved on 5 May
2016 from http://ec.europa.eu/growth/
industry/corporate-social-responsibility/
index_en.htm.

European Parliament, and European Council
(2004). *Directive 2004/109/EC of the
European Parliament and of the
European Council as of 15 December
2004*. Brussels, Belgium: European
Parliament and European Council.

(2014). *Directive 2014/95/EU of the
European Parliament and of the
Council as of 22 October 2014*.
Brussels, Belgium: European
Parliament and European Council.

FDA. (2000). *Guidance for Industry
Voluntary Labeling Indicating Whether
Foods Have or Have Not Been
Developed Using Bioengineering,
Draft Guidance*. Retrieved on
1 January 2016 from www.fda.gov/
OHRMS/DOCKETS/98fr/
001598gd.pdf.

Fenster, M. (2006). The Opacity of
Transparency. *Iowa Law Review*, 91,
885–949.

Fergus, A. and Rowney, J. (2005).
Sustainable Development: Lost
Meaning and Opportunity? *Journal of
Business Ethics*, 60(1), 17–27.

Fifka, M. S. (2013). Corporate Responsibility
Reporting and its Determinants in
Comparative Perspective – A Review of
the Empirical Literature and a Meta-
analysis. *Business Strategy and the
Environment*, 22(1), 1–35.

Fleming, P. and Jones, M. T. (2014). *The End
of Corporate Social Responsibility*.
London: Sage.

Fox, T., Ward, H. and Howard, B. (2002).
*The Public Sector Roles in
Strengthening Corporate Social
Responsibility: A Baseline Study*.
Washington, DC: World Bank.

Fransen, L. (2012). Multi-Stakeholder
Governance and Voluntary Programme
Interactions: Legitimation Politics in the
Institutional Design of Corporate Social
Responsibility. *Socio-Economic Review*,
10(1), 163–192.

Fransen, L. W. and Kolk, A. (2007). Global
Rule-Setting for Business: A Critical
Analysis of Multi-Stakeholder Standards.
Organization, 14(5), 667–684.

Frederick, W. C. (1978/1994). From CSR_1 to
CSR_2 – The Maturing of Business-and-
Society Thought. *Business and Society*,
33(2), 150–164.

(2006). Corporation Be Good! The Story
of Corporate Social Responsibility.
USA: Dog Ear Publishing.

Freeman, R. E. (1984). *Stakeholder
Management: Framework and
Philosophy*. Mansfield, MA: Pitman
Publishing.

(1984). *Strategic Management:
A Stakeholder Approach*. Boston, MA:
Pitman Publishing.

(2008). Managing for Stakeholders. In
T. L. Beauchamp, N. E. Bowie and
D. G. Arnold (Eds.), *Ethical Theory
and Business* (8th ed.) (pp. 56–68).
Upper Saddle River, NJ: Pearson
Prentice Hall.

Freeman, R. E., Harrison, J. S., Wicks, A. C.,
Palmar, B. L. and de Colle, S. (2010).
*Stakeholder Theory: The State of the
Art*. New York: Cambridge University
Press.

Friedman, F. (2015). *Corporate Social
Responsibility: the Ultimate Marketing
Tool*. Retrieved on 5 May 2016 from
www.europeanceo.com/home/
corporate-social-responsibility-the-
ultimate-marketing-tool/.

Friedman, M. (1970). The Social
Responsibility of Business is to Increase
its Profits. *The New York Times
Magazine*, 13 September.

(1987). The Social Responsibility of
Business Is to Increase Its Profits

(reprinted from 13 September 1970, *New York Times Magazine*). In D. Poff and W. Waluchow (Eds.), *Business Ethics in Canada* (pp. 7–11). Scarborough, ON: Prentice Hall Canada.

Friedman, T. L. (2005). *The World Is Flat: A Brief History of The Twenty-First Century*. New York, NY: Farrar, Straus and Giroux.

Fromm, T., Hägler, M. and Ott, K. (2015). VW-Topmanager schwer belastet, Retrieved on 31 March 2016 from www.sueddeutsche.de/politik/abgas-affaere-vw-topmanager-schwer-belastet-1.2669920.

Frynas, J. (2009). *Beyond Corporate Social Responsibility*. Cambridge: Cambridge University Press.

Frynas, J. G. and Stephens, S. (2014). Political Corporate Social Responsibility: Reviewing Theories and Setting New Agendas. *International Journal of Management Reviews*, DOI. 10.1111/ijmr.12049.

Fung, A., Graham, M. and Weil, D. (2007). *Full Disclosure: The Perils and Promise of Transparency*. Cambridge, UK: Cambridge University Press.

Garriga, E. and Melé, D. (2004). Corporate Social Responsibility Theories: Mapping the Territory. *Journal of Business Ethics*, 53(1/2), 51–71.

George, B. (2004). *Authentic Leadership*. San Francisco, CA: Jossey Bass, Inc.

Ghoshal, S. (2005). Bad Management Theories are Destroying Good Management Practices. *Academy of Management Learning and Education*, 4(1), 75–91.

Gil de Zúñiga, H. (2013). Social Media Use for News and Individuals' social Capital, Civic Engagement and Political Participation. *Journal of Computer-Mediated Communication*, 17(3), 319–336.

Gilbert, D. U., Rasche, A. and Waddock, S. (2011). Accountability in a Global Economy: The Emergence of International Accountability Standards. *Business Ethics Quarterly*, 21(1), 23–44.

Gilbert, L. and Jeweler, S. (2014). *All-seeing Google lacks Transparency*. Retrieved 13 March 2015 from http://thehill.com/blogs/congress-blog/technology/204292-all-seeing-google-lacks-transparency.

Gillies, A. (2010). Reputational Concerns and the Emergence of Oil Sector Transparency as an International Norm. *International Studies Quarterly* 54(1), 103–26.

Gjerdrum Pedersen, E. R., Neergaard, P., Thusgaard Pedersen, J. and Gwozdz, W. (2013). Conformance and Deviance: Company Responses to Institutional Pressures for Corporate Social Responsibility Reporting, *Business Strategy and the Environment*, 22(6), 357–373.

Gladwin, T. N., Kennelly, J. and Krause, T. S. (1995). Shifting Paradigms for Sustainable Development: Implications for Management Theory and Research. *Academy of Management Review*, 20(4), 874–907.

Gond, J. P., Grubnic, S., Herzig, C. and Moon, J. (2012). Configuring Management Control Systems: Theorizing the Integration of Strategy and Sustainability. *Management Accounting Research*, 23(3), 205–223.

Gond, J.-P. and Herrbach, O. (2006). Social Reporting as an Organisational Learning Tool? A Theoretical Framework. *Journal of Business Ethics* 65(4), 359–371.

Gond, J-P., Kang. N. and Moon, J. (2011). The Government of Self-Regulation: on the Comparative Dynamics of Corporate Social Responsibility. *Economy and Society*, 40(4), 640–671.

Gond, J.-P. and Moon, J. (2011). Corporate Social Responsibility in Retrospect and

Prospect: Exploring the Life-cycle of an Essentially Contested Concept. In J.-P. Gond and J. Moon (Eds.), *Corporate Social Responsibility: A Reader. Critical Perspectives in Business and Management* (Vol. 1) (pp. 1–28). New York, NY: Routledge. (Reprinted in *ICCSR Working Paper 59–2011*. Nottingham: Nottingham University Business School.)

Graves, S. B., Rehbein, K. and Waddock, S. (2001). Fad and Fashion in Shareholder Activism: The Landscape of Shareholder Resolutions, 1988–1998. *Business and Society Review*, 106(4), 293–314.

Gray, R. (2006). Does Sustainability Reporting Improve Corporate Behaviour?: Wrong question? Right time? *Accounting and Business Research*, 36(supp. 1), 65–88.

Gray, R. H., Adams, C. and Owen, D. (Eds.) (2014). *Accountability, Social Responsibility and sustainability: Accounting for society and the Environment*. Harlow, UK: Pearson Education Limited.

Grayson, D. (2013). Essay: Corporate Responsibility with Chinese Characteristics. *Ethical Corporation*. Retrieved 11 July 2015 from www.ethicalcorp.com/business-strategy/essay-corporate-responsibility-chinese-characteristics.

Grayson D. and Nelson J. (2013). *Corporate Responsibility Coalitions: The Past, Present, and Future of Alliances for Sustainable Capitalism*. Stanford, California: Stanford University Press.

Green, J. F. (2014). *Rethinking Private Authority: Agents and Entrepreneurs in Global Environmental Governance*. Princeton: Princeton University Press.

Greenpeace (2009). Climate Greenwash Awards 2009. Retrieved on 5 May 2016 from www.climategreenwash.org.

Guay, T., Doh, J. P. and Sinclair, G. (2004). Non-governmental Organizations, Shareholder Activism, and Socially Responsible Investments: Ethical, Strategic, and Governance Implications. *Journal of Business Ethics*, 52(1), 125–139.

Gulbrandsen, L. H. (2012). *Transnational Environmental Governance: The Emergence and Effects of the Certification of Forests and Fisheries*. Cheltenham: Edward Elgar.

(2014). Dynamic Governance Interactions: Evolutionary Effects of State Responses to Non-State Certification Programs. *Regulation and Governance*, 8 (1), 74–92.

Gunningham, N., Grabosky, P. N. and Sinclair, D. (1998). *Smart Regulation: Designing Environmental Policy*. Oxford: Clarendon Press.

Guthey, E. and Morsing, M. (2014). CSR and the Mediated Emergence of Strategic Ambiguity. *Journal of Business Ethics*, 120(4), 555–569.

Habermas, J. (1984). *The Theory of Communicative Action: Vol. 1. Reasons and the Rationalization of Society*. Boston, MA: Bacon Press.

(1998). *Die postnationale Konstellation: Politische Essays*. Frankfurt: Main Suhrkamp.

(2001). *The Postnational Constellation: Political essays*. Cambridge, MA: MIT Press.

Hale, T. and Roger, C. (2014). Orchestration and Transnational Climate Governance. *Review of International Organizations*, 9(1), 59–82.

Haller, D. and Shore, C. (Eds.) (2005). *Corruption. Anthropological Perspectives*. London: Pluto Press.

Hamed, B. (2013). 'The Top 8 Things We Learned from Marks & Spencer's 2013 Plan A Report.' Retrieved on 20 April 2016 from www.sustainablebrands.com/news_and_views/communications/8-most-important-things-we-learned-marks-spencers-2013-plan-report.

Hansen, H. K. (2010). Governing Corruption through the Global Corporation. In M. Ougaard and A. Leander (Eds.), *Business in Global Governance* (pp. 118–137). London: Routledge.

(2011). Managing Corruption Risk. *Review of International Political Economy*, 18(2), 251–275.

(2012). The Power of Performance Indices in the Global Politics of Anti-Corruption. *Journal of International Relations and Development*, 15(4), 506–531.

Hansen, H. K., Christensen, L. T. and Flyverbom, M. (2015). Logics of Transparency in Late Modernity: Metaphors, Power and Paradoxes. *European Journal of Social Theory*, 18(2), 117–131.

Hansen, H. K. and Flyverbom, M. (2015). The Politics of Transparency and the Calibration of Knowledge in the Digital Age. *Organization*, 22(6), 872–889.

Hansen, H. K. and Tang-Jensen, M. H. (2015). Making up Corruption Control: Conducting Due Diligence in a Danish Law Firm. *Ephemera Theory and Politics in Organization*, 15(2), 365–385.

Harris Interactive (2011) *Annual RQ Summary Report*. New York, NY: Harris Interactive. Retrieved on 12 February 2015 from www.rankingthebrands.com.

Harrison, A. and Scorse, J. (2006). Improving the Conditions of Workers? Minimum Wage Legislation and Anti-Sweatshop Activism. *California Management Review*, 48(2), 144–160.

Hart, S. L. (2005). *Capitalism at the Crossroads: The Unlimited Business Opportunities in Solving the World's Most Difficult Problems*. Upper Saddle River, NJ: Wharton School.

Hart, S. L. and Sharma, S. (2004). Engaging Fringe Stakeholders for Competitive Imagination. *Academy of Management Executive*, 18(1), 7–18.

Hartman, L. P. and Werhane, P. H. (2013). Proposition: Shared Value as an Incomplete Mental Model. *Business Ethics Journal Review*, 1(6), 36–43.

Haufler, V. (2006). Global Governance in the Private Sector. In C. May (ed.), *Global Corporate Power* (pp. 85–103). Boulder, CO: Lynne Rienner Publishers.

Haugh, H. and Talwar, A. (2010). How do Corporations embed Sustainability across the Organization? *Academy of Management Learning and Education*, 9(3), 384–396.

Hawken, P. (2007). *Blessed Unrest*. London: Penguin Books.

Heald, M. (1970). *The Social Responsibilities of Business: Company and Community 1900–1960*. Cleveland, OH: The Press of Case Western Reserve University.

Heil, O. and Robertson, T. S. (1991). Toward a Theory of Competitive Marketing Signaling: A Research Agenda. *Strategic Management Journal*, 12(6), 403–418.

Helper, S. and Henderson, R. (2014). *Management Practices, Relational Contracts and the Decline of General Motors*. Working paper, Harvard Business School, 14–062. Retrieved on 5 January 2016 from www.hbs.edu/faculty/Publication%20Files/14-062_29ad7901-c306-44fa-88df-31e97a17cbbf.pdf.

Hendry, J. R. (2006). Taking Aim at Business: What Factors lead Environmental Non-governmental Organizations to Target Particular Firms? *Business and Society*, 45(1), 47–86.

Hennchen, E. (2015). Royal Dutch Shell in Nigeria: Where Do Responsibilities

End? *Journal of Business Ethics*, 129(1), 1–25.

Herzig, C. and Ghosh, B. (2014). Sustainability Reporting. In P. Moltan-Hill (Eds.), *The Business Student's Guide to Sustainable Management: Principles and Practice* (pp. 84–119). Sheffield: Greenleaf.

Herzig, C. and Moon, J. (2013). The Financial Sector, Economic Crisis and Recession: Discourses on Corporate Social Ir/Responsibility. *Journal of Business Research*, 66, 1870–1880.

Herzig, C. and Schaltegger, S. (2011). Corporate Sustainability Reporting. In J. Godemann and G. Michelsen (Eds.), *Sustainability Communication – Interdisciplinary Perspectives and Theoretical Foundations* (pp. 151–169). Heidelberg, Berlin: Springer.

Higgins, C. and Larrinaga, C. (2014). Sustainability Reporting: Insights from Institutional Theory. In J. Bebbington, J. Unerman and B. O'Dwyer (Eds.), *Sustainability Accounting and Accountability* (pp. 273–285). New York, NY: Routledge.

Hoffman, A. (2003). Linking Social Systems Analysis to the Industrial Ecology framework. *Organization and Environment*, 16(1), 66–86.

Hoffman, A. and Sandelands, L. E. (2005). Getting Right with Nature: Anthropocentrism, ecocentrism, and Theocentrism. *Organization and Environment*, 18(2), 141–162.

Hoffmann, M. J. (2011). *Climate Governance at the Crossroads*. Oxford: Oxford University Press.

Hofman, P. S. and Moon, J. with Wu, B. (2015.) *Corporate Social Responsibility under Authoritarian Capitalism: Dynamics and Prospects of State-led and Society-driven CSR, Business and Society*, DOI: 10.1177/0007650315623014.

Holliday, C., Schmidheiny, S. and Watts, S. (2002). *Walking the Talk: The Business Case for Sustainable Development*. Paper presented at the World Business Council for Sustainable Development, Geneva, Switzerland.

Husted, B. W. (2015). Corporate Social Responsibility Practice from 1800–1914: Past Initiatives and Current Debates. *Business Ethics Quarterly*, 25(1), 125–141.

Haack, P. and Scherer, A. G. (2014). Why Sparing the Rod does not spoil the Child: A critique of the 'strict father' model in Transnational Governance. *Journal of Business Ethics*, 122(2), 225–240.

Haack, P. and Schoeneborn, D. (2015). Exploring the Institutionalization of Corporate Responsibility: A Formal Modeling Approach. *Academy of Management Best Paper Proceedings*, 62, 1–7.

Haack, P., Schoeneborn, D. and Wickert, C. (2012). Talking the Talk, Moral Entrapment, Creeping Commitment? Exploring Narrative Dynamics in Corporate Responsibility Standardization. *Organization Studies* 33(5–6): 815–845.

ILO (1998). *Declaration of Fundamental Principles and Rights at Work*. Retrieved on 13 April 2016 from www.ilo.org/public/english/standards/decl/declaration/text/.
(2015). *International Labour Organization*. Retrieved on 20 September 2015 from www.ilo.org/global/lang–en/index.htm.

Indeed. (2015). *The Indeed website*. Retrieved on 1 May 2015 from www.indeed.com/cmp/Monsanto/reviews?fcountry=USandstart=20.

International Integrated Reporting Council (IIRC) (2013). *The International IR Framework*. London, UK: International Integrated Reporting Council.

Isidore, C. (2015). *Volkswagen sold 3,060 diesels in the U.S. last month before scandal*. Retrieved on 31 March 2016 from http://money.cnn.com/2015/10/01/news/companies/volkswagen-emission-scandal-sales/.

Jenkins, R., Pearson, R. and Seyfang, G. (2002). Introduction. In R. O. Jenkins, R. Pearson and G. Seyfang (Eds.), *Corporate Responsibility and Labour rights: Codes of Conduct in the Global Economy* (pp. 1–10). London: Sterling, VA: Earthscan.

Johnston, M. (2005). *Syndromes of Corruption. Wealth, Power, and Democracy*. Cambridge, US: Cambridge University Press.

Jones, T. M. (1991). Ethical Decision Making by Individuals in Organizations: An Issue-Contingent Model. *Academy of Management Review*, 16(2), 366–395.

Jägers, N. (2002). *Corporate Human Rights Obligations: In Search of Accountability*. Antwerp: Intersentia.

Kaplan, R. (2015). Who has been Regulating Whom, Business or Society? The Mid-20th-century Institutionalization of 'Corporate Responsibility' in the USA. *Socio-Economic Review*, 13(1), 125–155.

Kates, M. (2015). The Ethics of Sweatshops and the Limits of Choice. *Business Ethics Quarterly*, 25(2), 191–212.

Kaufmann, D. and Penciakova, V. (2011). Transparency, Conflict Minerals and Natural Resources: Debating Sections 1502 and 1504 of the Dodd-Frank Act. *The Brookings Institution*. Retrieved on 8 November from www.brookings.edu/research/opinions/2011/12/20-debating-dodd-frank-kaufmann.

Keohane, R. O. and Nye, J. S. (2000). Introduction. In J. S. Nye and J. D. Donahue (Eds.), *Governance in a Globalizing World* (pp. 1–44).

Washington, DC: Brookings Institution Press.

Kim, R. C. and Moon, J. (2015). Dynamics of Corporate Social Responsibility in Asia: Knowledge and Norms. *Asian Business and Management*, 14 (5), 349–382.

King, B. and McDonnell, M.-H. (2015). Good Firms, Good Targets: The Relationship between Corporate Social Responsibility, Reputation, and Activist Targeting. In: K. Tsutsui and A. Lim, (Eds), *Corporate Social Responsibility in a Globalizing World* (pp. 430–454). Cambridge, UK: Cambridge University Press.

King, B., Felin, T. and Whetten, D. (2010). Finding the Organization in Organizational Theory: A Meta-Theory of the Organization as a Social Actor. *Organization Science*, 21(1), 290–305.

King, B. and Weber, K. (2014). Corporate Activism Yesterday, Today, and Tomorrow. *KellogInsight*. Retrieved on 9 May 2016 from http://insight.kellogg.northwestern.edu/article/corporate_activism_yesterday_today_and_tomorrow.

King, B. G. (2011). The Tactical Disruptiveness of Social Movements: Sources of Market and Mediated Disruption in Corporate Boycotts. *Social Problems*, 58(4), 491–517.

King, B. G. and Soule, S. A. (2007). Social Movements as Extra-Institutional Entrepreneurs: The Effect of Protests on Stock Price Returns. *Administrative Science Quarterly*, 52(3), 413–442.

Kinley, D. and Nolan, J. (2008). Trading and Aiding Human Rights in the Global Economy, *Nordic Journal of Human Rights*, 7(4), 353–377.

Klijn, H. E. and Teisman, G. R. (2010). Institutional and Strategic Barriers to Public–Private Partnership: An Analysis of Dutch Cases. *Public Money and Management*, 23(3), 137–146.

Klostermann, J. and Cramer, J. (2006). The Contextual Meaning of Sustainable Development: The Case of the Dutch Drinking Water Sector. *Sustainable Development*, 14(4), 268–276.

Knopf, J., Kahlenborn, W., Hajduk, T., Weiss, D., Moira, F. and Romy, K. (2010). *Corporate Social Responsibility: National Public Policies in the European Union. European Commission*. Berlin: Adelphi.

Knudsen, J. S. (2017). 'How Does Government Regulation Drive Corporate Social Responsibility (CSR) in Large International US and UK Firms?' *Global Policy* (forthcoming).

Knudsen, J. S. and Moon, J. W. (2017). *Visible Hands: Government Regulation of Corporate Social Responsibility in Global Business*. Cambridge: Cambridge University Press.

Knudsen, J. S., Moon, J. and Slager, R. (2015). Government Policies for Corporate Social Responsibility in Europe: Support and Institutionalization. *Policy and Politics*, 43(1), 81–99.

Kobrin, S. J. (2009). Private Political Authority and Public Responsibility: Transnational Politics, Transnational Firms and Human Rights. *Business Ethics Quarterly*, 19(3), 349–374.

Kolk, A. (2004). A Decade of Sustainability Reporting: Developments and Significance. *International Journal for Environmental and Sustainable Development*, 3(1), 51–64.

Kollewe, J. (2015). *VW chief promises 'ruthless' crackdown on culprits of emissions scandal*. Retrieved on 31 March 2016 from www.theguardian.com/business/2015/oct/28/volkswagen-posts-first-quarterly-loss-in-15-years.

Kotchen, M. and Moon, J. J. (2012). Corporate Social Responsibility for Irresponsibility. *The B. E. Journal of Economic Analysis and Policy*, 12(1), Article 55.

KPMG (1993–2013). Various international surveys of corporate responsibility reporting. Retrieved from https://www.kpmg.com/.

(2008). *KPMG International Survey of Corporate Responsibility Reporting 2008*, Vol. 2009. Amsterdam, The Netherlands: KPMG.

(2011). *KPMG International Survey of Corporate Responsibility Reporting 2011*. Amsterdam, The Netherlands: KPMG.

(2015). *Currents of Change: The KPMG Survey of Corporate Responsibility Reporting 2015*. Amsterdam, The Netherlands: KPMG.

Kramer, M. R. and Pfitzer, M. W. (2016). The Ecosystem of Shared Value. *Harvard Business Review*, October. Retrieved on 1 October 2016 from https://hbr.org/2016/10/the-ecosystem-of-shared-value.

Kurylko, D. T. and Crate, J. R. (2006). 'The Lopez affair'. *Automotive News Europe*, 20 February. Retrieved on 5 January 2015 from http://europe.autonews.com/article/20060220/ANE/60310010/the-lopez-affair.

L'Oreal (2015). *Our Values and Ethical Principles*. Retrieved on 5 May 2016 from www.loreal.com/group/who-we-are/our-values-and-ethical-principles.

Lacy, P., Cooper, T., Haywood, R. and Neuberger, L. (2010). *A New Era of Sustainability: UN Global Compact-Accenture CEO Study*. New York: UN Global Compact-Accenture.

Lange, D., Lee, P. and Dai, Y. (2011). Organizational Reputation: A review. *Journal of Management*, 37(1), 153–184.

Lange, D. and Washburn, N. T. (2012). Understanding Attributions of Corporate Social Irresponsibility. *Academy of Management Review*, 37(2), 300–326.

Larner, W. and Walters, W. (Eds). (2004). *Global Governmentality. Governing International Spaces*. London: Routledge.

Larrinaga, C., Carrasco, F., Correa, C., Llena, F. and Moneva, J. M. (2002). Accountability and Accounting Regulation: The case of the Spanish Environmental Disclosure Standard. *European Accounting Review*, 11(4), 723–740.

Lawton, T., McGuire, S. and Rajwani, T. (2012). Corporate Political Activity: A Literature Review and Research Agenda. *International Journal of Management Reviews*, 15(1), 86–105.

Leopold, A. (1970). *A Sand Country almanac with essays on conservation from Round River*. New York: Ballantine.

Lerbinger, O. (1997). *The Crisis Manager: Facing Risk and Responsibility*. Mahwah, NJ: Lawrence Erlbaum.

Levin, K., Cashore, B. and Koppell, J. (2009). Can Non-State Certification Systems Bolster State-Centered Efforts to Promote Sustainable Development through the Clean Development Mechanism? *Wake Forest Law Review*, 44(3), 777–798.

Levy, D. L. (2008). Political Contestation in Global Production Networks. *Academy of Management Review*, 33(4), 943–963.

Levy, D. L. and Egan, D. (1998). Capital Contests: National and Transnational channels of Corporate Influence on the Climate Change Negotiations. *Politics and Society*, 26(3), 337–361.

Lewis, S. (2003). Reputation and Corporate Responsibility. *Journal of Communication Management*, 7, 356–366.

Lister, J., Poulsen, R. T. and Ponte, S. (2015). Orchestrating Transnational Environmental Governance in Maritime Shipping. *Global Environmental Change*, 34 (September), 185–195.

Livesey, S. (2002). Global Warming Wars: Rhetorical and Discourse Analytic Approaches to ExxonMobil's Corporate Public Discourse. *The Journal of Business Communication*, 39(1), 117–148.

Livesey, S. M. and Graham, J. (2007). Greening of Corporations? Eco-talk and the Emerging Social Imagery of Sustainable Development. In S. May, G. Cheney and J. Roper (Eds.), *The Debate over Corporate Social Responsibility* (pp. 336–350). Oxford, UK: Oxford University Press.

Locke, R. M. (2013). *The Promise and Limits of Private Power: Promoting Labor Standards in a Global Economy*. Cambridge: Cambridge University Press.

Lockett, A., Moon, J. and Visser, W. (2006). Corporate Social Responsibility in Management Research: Focus, Nature, Salience and sources of Influence. *Journal of Management Studies*, 43(1), 115–136.

Lohr, S. (2011). First, Make Money. Also, Do Good. *New York Times*, 13 August.

Loureiro, M. L. and Lotade, J. (2005). Do Fair Trade and Eco-Labels in Coffee Wake up the Consumer Conscience? *Ecological Economics*, 53(1), 129–138.

Lunheim, R. (2005). Confessions of a Corporate Window-Dresser. *Leading Perspectives*, Summer, 6–7.

Lynn, L. E. J. (2010). Has Governance Eclipsed Government? In R. F. Durant (Ed.), *The Oxford Handbook of American Bureaucracy* (pp. 669–690). Oxford: Oxford University Press.

Lyon, T. and Montgomery, A. (2015). The Means and End of Greenwash. *Organization and Environment*, 28(2), 223–249.

Löhr, J. (2015). *Two-thirds of Germans still trust Volkswagen after Emissions Scandal*. Retrieved on 31 March 2016

from www.theguardian.com/business/
2015/oct/20/two-thirds-of-germans-
still-trust-volkswagen-after-emissions-
scandal.

Löscher, P. (2012). How I did it . . . The CEO
of Siemens on Using a Scandal to Drive
Change. *Harvard Business Review*,
November, 39–42.

Macalister, T. (2015). BP dropped Green
Energy Projects worth Billions to focus
on Fossil Fuels. *The Guardian*, 16
April.

Mahon, J. F. and Waddock, S. A. (1992).
Strategic Issues Management: An
Integration of Issue Life. . . *Business
and Society*, 31(1), 19–32.

Marks & Spencer Company Archive (2016a).
A Short History of Marks & Spencer.
Retrieved on 20 April 2016 from https://
marksintime.marksandspencer.com/
download?id=996.

Marks & Spencer (2016b). *Key Facts*.
Retrieved on 19 April 2016 from https://
corporate.marksandspencer
.com/aboutus/key-facts.

  (2016c). *Delivering Plan A*. Retrieved on
  19 April 2016 from https://corporate
  .marksandspencer.com/plan-a/our-
  approach/delivering-plan-a.

  (2016d). *The Challenges*. Retrieved on
  19 April 2016 from http://challenges
  .marksandspencer.com/.

  (2016e). *Our approach*. Retrieved on
  19 April 2016 from https://corporate
  .marksandspencer.com/plan-a/our-
  approach.

Matten, D. and Crane, A. (2005). Corporate
Citizenship: Toward an Extended
Theoretical Conceptualization.
Academy of Management Review,
30(1), 166–179.

Matten, D. and Moon, J. (2008). 'Implicit'
and 'Explicit' CSR: A Conceptual
Framework for a Comparative
Understanding of Corporate Social
Responsibility. *Academy of
Management Review*, 33(2), 404–424.

Mayer-Schönberger, V. and Cukier, K.
(2013). *Big Data: A Revolution that will
Transform how we Live, Work and
Think*. London: John Murray.

Mayntz, R. (2010). *Legitimacy and
Compliance in Transnational
Governance* (Working Paper 10/5).
Cologne: Max Planck Institute for the
Study of Societies.

McDonnell, M. H. (2015). Radical
Repertoires: The Incidence and Impact
of Corporate-Sponsored Social
Activism. *Organization Science*, 27(1):
53–71.

  (2016). Radical Repertoires: The
  Incidence and Impact of Corporate-
  Sponsored Social Activism.
  Organization Science 27(1): 53–71.
  Retrieved on 1 October 2016 from
  http://dx.doi.org/10.1287/
  orsc.2015.1017.

McGee, P. and Wright, R. (2016). *VW
management back in scandal spotlight*.
Retrieved on 31 March 2016 from
www.ft.com/cms/s/0/ef00293c-e0f1-
11e5-8d9b-e88a2a889797.html.

McVea, J. F. and Freeman, R. E. (2005).
A Names-and-faces Approach to
Stakeholder Management. How
Focusing on Stakeholders as
Individuals can bring Ethics and
Entrepreneurial Strategy Together.
Journal of Management Inquiry, 14(1),
57–69.

McWilliams, A. and Siegel, D. (2001).
Corporate Social Responsibility:
A Theory of the Firm Perspective.
Academy of Management Review,
26(1), 117–127.

  (2011). Creating and Capturing Value:
  Strategic Corporate Social
  Responsibility, Resource-Based
  Theory, and Sustainable Competitive
  Advantage. *Journal of Management*,
  37(5), 1480–95.

Mena, S. and Palazzo, G. (2012).
Input and Output Legitimacy of

Multi-Stakeholder Initiatives. *Business Ethics Quarterly*, 22(3), 527–556.

Messner, M. (2009). The Limits of Accountability. *Accounting, Organizations and Society*, 34(8), 918–938.

Micheletti, M. (2003). *Political Virtue and Shopping: Individuals, Consumerism, and Collective Action*. New York: Palgrave Macmillan.

Milanez, B. and Buhrs, T. (2007). Marrying Strands of Ecological Modernisation: A Proposed Framework. *Environmental Politics*, 16(4), 565–583.

Minor, D., and Morgan, J. (2011). CSR as Reputation Insurance: Primum non nocere. *California Management Review*, 53(3), 40–59.

Mitchell, R. K., Agle, B. R. and Wood, D. J. (1997). Toward a Theory of Stakeholder Identification and Salience: Defining the Principle of Who and What Really Counts. *Academy of Management Review*, 22(4), 853–886.

Mol, A. and Spaargaren, G. (2000). Ecological Modernisation Theory in Debate: A review. *Environmental Politics*, 9(1), 17–49.

Monsanto (2015a). *Monsanto website*. Retrieved on 1 May, 2015 from http://news.monsanto.com/recognition.

(2015b). *Monsanto website*. Retrieved on 1 May 2015 from http://sustainability.monsanto.com/commitments/stakeholder-engagement.

(2015c). 2011 Corporate Responsibility and Sustainability Reports. *Monsanto website*. Retrieved on 1 May 2015 from www.monsanto.com/whoweare/Pages/corporate-sustainability-report.aspx and www.monsanto.com/SiteCollectionDocuments/CSR_Reports/2011-csr.pdf.

Montiel, I. (2008). Corporate Social Responsibility and Corporate Sustainability, Separate Pasts, Common Futures. *Organization and Environment*, 21(3), 245–269.

Moody-Stuart, M. (2014). *Responsible Leadership- Lessons From the Front Line of Sustainability and Ethics Personal Reflection*. Sheffield, UK: Greenleaf.

Moog, S., Spicer, A. and Bohm, S. (2014). The Politics of Multi-Stakeholder Initiatives: The Crisis of the Forest Stewardship Council. *Journal of Business Ethics*, DOI 10.1007/s10551-013–2033-3.

Moon, J. (2001). Business Social Responsibility as a Source of Social Capital. *Reason and Practice: the Journal of Philosophy and Management*, 1(3), 35–45.

(2002). Business Social Responsibility and New Governance. *Government and Opposition*, 37(3), 385–408.

(2007). The Contribution of Corporate Social Responsibility to Sustainable Development. *Sustainable Development*, 15(5), 275–327.

(2014). *Corporate Social Responsibility: A Very Short Introduction*. Oxford: Oxford University Press.

Moon, J., Crane, A. and Matten, D. (2004). Can Corporations be Citizens? Corporate Citizenship as a Metaphor for Business Participation in Society. *Business Ethics Quarterly*, 15(3), 429–454.

Moon, J., Kang, N. and Gond, J. P. (2010). Corporate Social Responsibility and Government. *Oxford Handbook of Business and Government* (pp. 512–543). Oxford: Oxford University Press.

Moon, J. and Richardson J. J. (1985). *Unemployment in the UK: Politics and Policies*. Aldershot, UK: Gower.

Morsing, M. (2003). CSR – a Religion with too many Priests. *European Business Forum*, Autumn (15), 41–42.

(2006). CSR as Strategic Auto-Communication: On the role of External

Stakeholders for Member Identification. *Business Ethics: A European Review*, 15(2), 171–182.

Morsing, M. and Eriksen, R. A. (2014). *Online Company-stakeholder Communication: Lessons from Vattenfall's Social Media Campaign on Climate Change*. Paper presented at EBEN European Business Ethics Network Conference, Berlin.

Morsing, M. and Roepstorff, A. (2015). CSR as Corporate Political Activity. Observations on IKEA's CSR Identity-Image Dynamics. *Journal of Business Ethics*, 128(2), 395–409.

Morsing, M. and Schultz, M. (2006). Corporate Social Responsibility Communication: Stakeholder Information, Response and Involvement Strategies. *Business Ethics: A European Review*, 15(4), 323–338.

Nadvi, K. (2008). Global Standards, Global Governance and the Organization of Global Value Chains. *Journal of Economic Geography*, 8(3), 323–343.

Nichols, P. (2012). The Business Case for Complying with Bribery Laws. *American Business Law Journal*, 48(2), 325–368.

Nike (2010). Nike, Inc. Code of Conduct. Retrieved on 17 November 2015 from www.nikeresponsibility.com/report/ uploads/files/Nike_Code_of_Conduct .pdf.

Novo Nordisk (2003). *Sustainability Report 2003*. Retrieved on 5 May 2016 from www.novonordisk.com/content/dam/ Denmark/HQ/Sustainability/documents/ Novo_SustainabilityReport_2003_ UK.pdf.

(2011). *The Triple Bottom Line—our way of doing business*. Presentation by Susanne Stormer, Vice President, Global Triple Bottom Line Management. 16 June. Novo Nordisk, Bagsværd, Denmark.

Opensource-solar (2015). *Opensource-solar website*. Retrieved on 1 May 2015 from www.opensource-solar.org/.

O'Callaghan, T. (2007). Disciplining Multinational Enterprises: The Regulatory Power of Reputation Risk, *Global Society*, 21(1), 95–117.

Odum, E. (1975). *Ecology: The Link between the Natural and the Social Sciences*. New York, NY: Hold, Rinehart and Winston.

OECD (2011). OECD Guidelines for Multinational Enterprises. Paris: OECD. Retrieved on 9 May 2016 from www.oecd.org/investment/mne/ 1922428.pdf.

Oliver, C. (1991). Strategic Responses to Institutional Processes. *Academy of Management Review*, 16(1), 145–179.

Oliver, R. W. (2004). *What is Transparency?* New York, NY: McGraw-Hill.

O'Rourke, D. (2002). Monitoring the Monitors: A Critique of Third-Party Labour Monitoring. In R. O. Jenkins, R. Pearson and G. Seyfang (Eds.), *Corporate Responsibility and Labour Rights: Codes of Conduct in the Global Economy* (pp. 196–208). London: Sterling, VA: Earthscan.

Orsato, R. (2011). *Sustainability Strategies: When Does It Pay to Be Green?* Basingstoke: Palgrave MacMillan.

Overdevest, C. and Zeitlin, J. (2014). Assembling an Experimentalist Regime: Transnational Governance Interactions in the Forest Sector. *Regulation and Governance*, 8(1), 22–48.

Owen, D. and O'Dwyer, B. (2008). Corporate Social Responsibility. The Reporting and Assurance Dimension. In J. Crane, A. McWilliams, D. Matten, J. Moon and D. Siegel (Eds.), *The Oxford Handbook of Corporate Social Responsibility* (pp. 384–409). New York: Oxford University Press.

Paine, L. S. (2000). Does Ethics Pay? *Business Ethics Quarterly*, 10(1), 319–330.

Peloza, J. (2009). The Challenge of Measuring Financial Impacts from Investments in Corporate Social Performance. *Journal of Management*, 35(6), 1518–1541.

Perella, M. (2014). Marks and Spencer Outlines Challenges for Plan A Global Scale-up. *Edie News*, 5 June. Retrieved on 19 April 2016 from www.edie.net/news/6/Marks—Spencer-outlines-challenges-for-Plan-A-global-scale-up/.

Perrini, F., Russo, A., Tencati, A. and Vurro, C. (2011). Deconstructing the Relationship Between Corporate Social and Financial Performance. *Journal of Business Ethics*, 102(Supplement 1), 59–76.

Perrow, C. (1991). A Society Of Organizations. *Theory and Society*, 20, 725–762.

Pfitzer, M., Bockstette, V. and Stamp, M. (2012). Innovating for Shared Value. *Harvard Business Review*, 91, 100–107.

Phillips, R. (2003). *Stakeholder Theory and Organizational Ethics*. San Francisco, CA: Berret-Koehler Publishers.

Phillips, R. and Caldwell, C. B. (2005). Value Chain Responsibility: A Farewell to Arm's Length. *Business and Society Review*, 110(4), 345–370.

Ponte, S. (2012). The Marine Stewardship Council (MSC) and the Making of a Market for 'Sustainable Fish'. *Journal of Agrarian Change*, 12(2–3), 300–315.

(2014). 'Roundtabling' Sustainability: Lessons from the Biofuel Industry. *Geoforum*, 54(July), 261–271.

Ponte, S. and Sturgeon, T. (2014). Explaining Governance in Global Value Chains: A Modular Theory-Building Effort. *Review of International Political Economy*, 21(1), 195–223.

Pope Francis (2015). *Encyclical Letter 'Laudato Si' Of The Holy Father Francis On Care For Our Common Home*. Retrieved on 8 April 2016 from http://w2.vatican.va/content/francesco/en/encyclicals/documents/papa-francesco_20150524_enciclica-laudato-si.html.

Porsche (2014). *Porsche Annual Report 2014*. Retrieved on 5 May 2016 from https://newsroom.porsche.com/download/?id=945c3b38-b038-4fb0-b28f-6904c4a5f461andlang=en.

Porter, M. E. and Kramer, M. R. (2002). The Competitive Advantage of Corporate Philanthropy. *Harvard Business Review*, December issue, 5–16.

(2006). Strategy and Society: The Link Between Competitive Advantage and Corporate Social Responsibility. *Harvard Business Review*, 84(12), 78–92.

(2011). Creating Shared Value. *Harvard Business Review*, 89(1/2), 62–77.

(2014). A Response to Andrew Crane et al.'s article by Michael E. Porter and Mark R. Kramer. *California Management Review*, 56(2), 149–51.

Potoski, M. and Prakash, A. (2013). Do Voluntary Programs Reduce Pollution? Examining ISO 14001's Effectiveness across Countries. *Policy Studies Journal*, 41(2), 273–294.

Poulsen, R. T., Ponte, S. and Lister, J. (2016). Buyer-driven Greening? Cargo-owners and Environmental Upgrading in Maritime Shipping. *Geoforum*, 68, 57–68.

Powell, B. and Skarbek, D. (2006). Sweatshops and Third World Living Standards: Are the Jobs Worth the Sweat? *Journal of Labor Research*, 27(2), 263–274.

Powell, B. and Zwolinski, M. (2012). The Ethical and Economic Case Against Sweatshop Labor: A Critical Assessment. *Journal of Business Ethics*, 107(4), 449–472.

Power, M. (2007). *Organized Uncertainty. Designing a World of Risk Management*. Oxford: Oxford University Press.

PR Newswire (2014). '2014 Annual Automotive OEM-Supplier Relations Study Shows Toyota and Honda on top; Nissan displacing Ford in the middle; Chrysler and GM falling behind.' *The Business Journals website*, 12 May. Retrieved on 5 January 2016 from www.bizjournals.com/prnewswire/press_releases/2014/05/12/DE23932.

Prahalad, C. K. and Hart, S. L. (2002). The Fortune at the Bottom of the Pyramid. *Strategy+business*, 226, 1–14.

Prakash, A. and Potoski, M. (2007). Investing Up : FDI and the Cross-Country Diffusion of ISO 14001 Management Systems. *International Studies Quarterly*, 51(3), 723–744.

Preston, L .E. and Post, J. E. (1981). Private Management and Public Policy. *California Management Review*, 23(3), 56–63.

Purser, R. E., Park, C. and Montuori, A. (1995). Limits to Anthropocentrism: Toward an Ecocentric Organization Paradigm? *Academy of Management Review*, 20(4), 1053–1089.

Quelch, J. A. and Rodriguez, M. L. (2014a). Rana Plaza: Workplace Safety in Bangladesh. *Harvard Business School Case*, 514–034.
   (2014b). Rana Plaza: Workplace Safety in Bangladesh. *Harvard Business School Supplement*, 514–035.

Rao, H. (2009). Market Rebels and Radical Innovation. *The McKinsey Quarterly*. Silicon Valley, CA: McKinsey & Company.

Rasche, A. (2008). *The Paradoxical Foundation of Strategic Management*. Heidelberg/New York: Springer.
   (2009). 'A Necessary Supplement': What the United Nations Global Compact Is and Is Not. *Business and Society*, 48(4), 511–537.
   (2012). Global Policies and Local Practice: Loose and Tight Couplings in Multi-Stakeholder Initiatives. *Business Ethics Quarterly*, 22(4), 679–708.
   (2014). The Corporation as a Political Actor – European and North American Perspectives. *European Management Journal*, 33(1), 4–8.

Rasche, A., de Bakker, F. G. A. and Moon, J. (2013). Complete and Partial Organizing for Corporate Social Responsibility. *Journal of Business Ethics*, 115, 651–663.

Rawhouser, H., Cummings, M. and Crane, A., (2015). Benefit Corporation Legislation and the Emergence of a Social Hybrid Category. *California Management Review*, 57(3), 13–35.

Rawlins, B. (2009). Give the Emperor a Mirror. Toward Developing a Stakeholder Measurement of Organizational Transparency. *Journal of Public Relations Research*, 21(1), 71–99.

Ray, D. E., Berman, S. L., Johnson-Cramer, M. E. and Van Buren III, H. J. (2014). Refining Normative Stakeholder Theory: Insights from Judaism, Christianity, and Islam. *Journal of Management, Spirituality and Religion*, 11(4), 331–356.

Reich, R. B. (1998). The New Meaning of Corporate Social Responsibility. *California Management Review*, 40(2), 8–17.

Reinecke, J., Manning, S. and von Hagen, O. (2012). The Emergence of a Standards Market: Multiplicity of Sustainability Standards in the Global Coffee Industry. *Organization Studies*, 33(5/6), 791–814.

Reputation Institute (2015). *Global CSR RepTrak ranking*. Retrieved on 15 February 2015 from www.reputationinstitute.com/thought-leadership/csr-reptrak-100.

Reuters. (2011). Obama Oil Spill Commission's Final Report Blames Disaster on Cost-cutting by BP and Partners. *The Telegraph*, 5 January. Retrieved on 12 February 2015 from www.telegraph.co.uk/finance/ newsbysector/energy/oilandgas/ 8242557/Obama-oil-spill-commissions-final-report-blames-disaster-on-cost-cutting-by-BP-and-partners.html.

Rhenman, E. (1968). *Industrial Democracy and Industrial Management*. London: Tavistock.

Rhodes, T. (1999). 'Bitter Harvest. The Real Story of Monsanto and GM food.' *The Sunday Times*, 22 August (London).

Rinaldi, L., Unerman, J. and Tilt, C. (2014). The Role of Stakeholder Engagement and Dialogue within the Sustainability Accounting and Reporting Process. In J. Bebbington, J. Unerman and B. O'Dwyer. (Eds.), *Sustainability Accounting and Accountability* (pp. 86–107). New York, NY: Routledge.

Rising, D. and Sopke, K. (2015). *Volkswagen Employees began Working on Emissions in 2005 as Firm Sought to Expand in US*. Retrieved on 31 March 2016 from www.usnews .com/news/business/articles/2015/12/ 10/vw-indicates-investigation-wont-spare-top-managers.

Rivoli, P. and Waddock, S. (2011). 'First They Ignore You . . .': The Time-Context Dynamic and Corporate Responsibility. *California Management Review*, 53(2), 87–104.

Roberts, A. (2012). WikiLeaks: the illusion of transparency. *International Review of Administrative Sciences*, 78(1), 116–133.

Roberts, J. (2003). The Manufacture of Corporate Social Responsibility: Constructing Corporate Sensibility. *Organization*, 10(2), 249–265.

Roddick, A. (1995). *Values Report 1995*. London: The Body Shop.

Rosen, L. D., Whaling, K., Rab, S., Carrier, L. M. and Cheever, N. A. (2013). Is Facebook creating "iDisorders"? The Link between Clinical Symptoms of Psychiatric Disorders and Technology Use, Attitudes and Anxiety. *Computers in Human Behavior*, 29(3), 1243–1254.

Rosenau, J. (1990) *Turbulence in World Politics: A theory of Change and Continuity*. Princeton, NJ: Princeton University Press.

Rothkopf, D. (2012). *Power, Inc. – The Epic Rivalry between Big Business and Government – and the Reckoning that lies ahead*. New York: Farrar, Straus and Giroux.

Rowley, T. J. (1997). Moving beyond Dyadic Ties: A Network Theory of Stakeholder Influences. *Academy of Management Review*, 22(4), 887–910.

Rowley, T. J. and Moldoveanu, M. (2003). When will Stakeholder Groups Act? An Interest-and Identity-Based Model of Stakeholder Group Mobilization. *Academy of Management Review*, 28(2), 204–219.

Ruddick, G. (2015). *Volkswagen Scandal: US chief says carmaker 'totally screwed up'*. Retrieved on 31 March 2016 from www.theguardian.com/business/2015/ sep/22/volkswagen-scandal-us-chief-carmaker-totally-screwed-up-michael-horn.

Ruggie, J. G. (2008). *Protect, Respect and Remedy: A Framework for Business and Human Rights*. Report of the Special Representative of the Secretary-General on the Issue of Human Rights and Transnational Corporations and Other Business Enterprises, U.N. Doc A/HRC/8/5 (7 April 2008).

(2013). *Just Business*. Boston, MA: Norton Publishers.

Samuelson J. and Birchard, B. (2003). The Voice of the Stakeholder. Is Sustainability Sustainable? Twelve works argue there is value in 'corporate values'. *Strategy+business*, 32. Retrieved on 5 January 2016 from www.strategy-business.com/article/03311?gko=201aa.

Sanders, A. (2015). The Impact of the 'Ruggie Framework' and the 'United Nations Guiding Principles on Business and Human Rights' on Transnational Human Rights Litigation. In J. Martin and K. E. Bravo, (Eds.), *The Business and Human Rights Landscape: Moving Forward, Looking Back* (pp. 288–315). Cambridge: Cambridge University Press.

Santayana, G. (1905). *Reason in Common Sense: Volume One of 'The Life of Reason'*. New York, NY: Dover Publications.

SARW and EITI. (2012). *Impact of the Extractive Industries Transparency Initiative (EITI) on the Promotion of Transparency and Accountability in Southern and East Africa. Cape Town.* Retrieved on 9 May 2016 from www.osisa.org/sites/default/files/eiti_openforum_meeting_report.pdf.

Scharpf, F. W. (2009). Legitimacy in the Multilevel European Polity. *European Political Science Review*, 1(02), 173–204.

Scherer, A. G. and Palazzo, G. (2007). Toward a Political Conception of Corporate Responsibility: Business and Society seen from a Habermasian Perspective. *Academy of Management Review*, 32(4), 1096–1120.

(2008a). Globalization and Corporate Social Responsibility. In A. Crane, A. McWilliams, D. Matten, J. Moon and D. S. Siegel (Eds.), *The Oxford Handbook of Corporate Social Responsibility* (pp. 413–431). Oxford: Oxford University Press.

(2008b). Corporate Social Responsibility, Democracy and the Politicization of the Corporation. *Academy of Management Review*, 33(3), 773–775.

(2011). The New Political role of Business in a Globalized world: A Review of a New perspective on CSR and its Implications for the Firm, Governance, and Democracy. *Journal of Management Studies*, 48(4), 899–931.

Scherer, A. G., Rasche, A., Palazzo, G. and Spicer, A. (2016). Managing for Political Corporate Social Responsibility: New Challenges and Directions for PCSR 2.0. *Journal of Management Studies*, 53(3), 273–298.

Schleifer, P. (2013). Orchestrating Sustainability: The case of European Union Biofuel Governance. *Regulation and Governance*, 7(4), 533–546.

Schoeneborn, D. and Trittin, H. (2013). Transcending Transmission. Towards a Constitutive Perspective on CSR Communication. *Corporate Communications: An International Journal*, 18(2), 193–211.

Schouten, G., Leroy, P. and Glasbergen, P. (2012). On the Deliberative Capacity of Private Multi-Stakeholder Governance: The Roundtables on Responsible Soy and Sustainable Palm Oil. *Ecological Economics*, 83, 42–50.

Schrempf, J. and Wettstein F. (2015). *Beyond Guilty Verdicts: Human Rights Litigation and Its Impact on Corporations' Human Rights Policies.* Journal of Business Ethics, DOI 10.1007/s10551-015–2889-5.

Schultz, F., Castello, I. and Morsing, M. (2013). The Construction of Corporate Social Responsibility in Network Society: A Communication View. *Journal of Business Ethics*, 115(4), 681–692.

Schultz, F., Utz, S. and Göritz, A. (2011) Is the Medium the Message? Perceptions of and Reactions to Crisis Communication via Twitter, Blogs and Traditional Media. *Public Relations Review*, 37(1), 20–27.

Schultz, H. (2013). *An Open Letter from Howard Schultz, ceo of Starbucks Coffee Company*. Retrieved on 10 May 2016 from www.starbucks.com/blog/an-open-letter-from-howard-schultz/1268.

Seitanidi, M. and Crane, A. (Eds.) (2014). *Social Partnerships and Responsible Business: A Research Handbook*. New York: Routledge.

Seitanidi, M. M. and Crane, A. (2009) Implementing CSR Through Partnerships: Understanding the Selection, Design and Institutionalization of Nonprofit-Business Partnerships. *Journal of Business Ethics*, 85(Supplement 2), 413–429.

Sen, A. (2004). Elements of a Theory of Human Rights. *Philosophy and Public Affairs*, 32:4, 315–356.

Shamir, R. (2008). The Age of Responsibilization: On Market-Embedded Morality. *Economy and Society*, 37(1), 1–19.

Shared Value Initiative. (2016). *About the Initiative*. Retrieved on 19 April 2016 from https://www.sharedvalue.org/about-initiative.

Sharma, S. and Henriques, I. (2005). Stakeholder Influences on Sustainability Practices in the Canadian Forest Products Industry. *Strategic Management Journal*, 26(2), 159–180.

Sharma, S. and Vredenburg, H. (1998). Proactive corporate Environmental Strategy and the Development of Competitively Valuable Organizational Capabilities. *Strategic Management Journal*, 19(8), 729–753.

Sharman, A. and Brunsden, J. (2015). *New problem with 800,000 vehicles, including some petrol cars*. Retrieved on 31 March 2016 from www.ft.com/cms/s/0/15cb2940-8305-11e5-8095-ed1a37d1e096.html.

Shell (2015). *Sustainability Report 2015*. Retrieved on 5 May 2016 from www.shell.com/sustainability/sustainability-reporting-and-performance-data/sustainability-reports.html.

Shelton, D. L. (2014). *Advanced Introduction to International Human Rights Law*. Cheltenham, UK; Northampton, MA: Edward Elgar.

Short, C. (2001) Speech in House of Commons (UK). Hansard (Parliamentary Debates), 25 April 2001, Col 157643.

Shotter, J. (1993). *Conversational Realities: Constructing Life through Language*. London: Sage.

Shrivastava, P. (1994). Castrated Environment: Greening organizational Studies. *Organization Studies*, 15(5), 705–726.

(1995). Ecocentric Management for a Risk Society. *Academy of Management Review*, 20(1), 118–137.

(1995). The Role of Corporations in Achieving Ecological Sustainability. *Academy of Management Review*, 20(4), 936–960.

Siemens (2008). Statement of Siemens Aktiengesellschaft: Investigation and Summary of Findings with respect to the Proceedings in Munich and the US. Press Release, Munich, Germany, 15 December 2008. Retrieved 19 October 2015 from www.siemens.com/press/pool/de/events/2008-12-PK/summary-e.pdf.

Sikavica, K. and Pozner, J.-E. (2013). Paradise Sold: Resource Partitioning and the Organic Movement in the US

Farming Industry. *Organization Studies*, 34(5–6): 623–651.

Smith, C. (2015). *The Problem with those who Cheat*. Retrieved on 31 March 2016 from www.ft.com/cms/s/2/32689e6c-6c3e-11e5-8171-ba1968cf791a.html.

Smith J. (2012). *The Companies with the best CSR reputations*. Retrieved on 18 April 2016 from www.forbes.com/sites/jacquelynsmith/2012/12/10/the-companies-with-the-best-csr-reputations/.

Smith, J. (2013). *The Companies with the best CSR Reputations*. Retrieved on 13 February 2015 from www.forbes.com/sites/jacquelynsmith/2013/10/02/the-companies-with-the-best-csr-reputations-2/2/.

Smith, N. C. (2003). Corporate Social Responsibility: Whether or How? *California Management Review*, 45(4), 52–76.

Sohn, Y. J., and Lariscy, R. W. (2014). Understanding Reputational Crisis: Definition, Properties, and Consequences. *Journal of Public Relations Research*, 26(1), 23–43.

SOMO and ICN (2014). *Flawed Fabrics. The Abuse of Girls and Women Workers in the South Indian Textile Industry*. Retrieved on 23 March 2015 from www.indianet.nl/pdf/FlawedFabrics.pdf.

sonsofliberty2009. (2010). *BP chairman Like Obama, we care about the 'small people'*. Online video, 16 June. Retrieved on 1 March 2016 from www.youtube.com/watch?v=HIvcljZiN9o.

Spence, L. (2007). CSR and Small Business in a European Policy Context: The Five 'C's of CSR and Small Business Research Agenda 2007. *Business and Society Review*, 112(4), 533–552.

Spence, L. and Rutherford, R. (2003). Small Business and Empirical Perspectives in

Business Ethics: Editoral. *Journal of Business Ethics*, 47(1), 1–5.

Starbucks (2014). *What is the Role and Responsibility of a For-Profit Public Company?* Retrieved on 5 May 2016 from www.starbucks.com/responsibility/global-report.

Starik, M. and Rands, G. (1995). Weaving an Integrated Web: Multilevel and Multisystem Perspectives of Ecologically Sustainable Organizations. *Academy of Management Review*, 20(4), 908–935.

Statista (2016). *Marks & Spencer share of the clothing and footwear market in the United Kingdom (UK) as of financial year 2014/15, by market segment*. Retrieved on 19 April 2016 from www.statista.com/statistics/413641/clothing-market-share-marks-and-spencer-mands-united-kingdom-uk-by-segment/.

Steering Committee of the State-of-Knowledge Assessment of Standards and Certification (2012). *Towards Sustainability: The Roles and Limitations of Certification*. Washington, DC: Resolve, Inc.

Stiglitz, J. (2002) *Globalization and Its Discontents*. New York: W. W. Norton and Company.

Stout, L. (2012). *The Shareholder Value Myth: How Putting Shareholders First Harms Investors, Corporations and the Public*. San Francisco, CA: Berrett-Koehler Publishers.

Strand, R. and Freeman, E. (2015). Scandinavian Cooperative Advantage: The Theory and Practice of Stakeholder Engagement in Scandinavia. *Journal of Business Ethics*, 127(1), 65–85.

Strand, R., Freeman, R. E. and Hockerts, K. (2015). Corporate Social Responsibility and Sustainability in Scandinavia: An Overview. *Journal of Business Ethics*, 127(1), 1–15.

Strathern, M. (2000). The Tyranny of Transparency. *British Educational Research Journal*, 26(3), 309–321.

Strike, V. M., Gao, J. and Bansal, P. (2006). Being Good while Being Bad: Social Responsibility and the International Diversification of US Firms. *Journal of International Business Studies*, 37(6), 850–862.

Stubbs, W. and Cocklin, C. (2008). Conceptualizing a 'Sustainability Business Model'. *Organization and Environment*, 21(2), 103–127.

Suchman, M. C. (1995). Managing Legitimacy: Strategic and Institutional Approaches. *Academy of Management Review*, 20(3), 571–610.

Sustainable Stock Exchanges Initiative (SSE) (2014). *Sustainable Stock Exchanges. Report on progress 2014.* New York, NY: SSE.

Tata Sons Ltd. (2008, March). *The Quotable Jamsetji Tata.* Retrieved on 19 April 2016 from www.tata.com/aboutus/articlesinside/The-quotable-Jamsetji-Tata.

(2015). *Our Heritage.* Retrieved on 19 April 2016 from www.tata.com/htm/heritage/HeritageOption1.html.

(2016a). *About Tata Sustainability Group.* Retrieved on 19 April 2016 from www.tatasustainability.com/aboutTSG.aspx.

(2016b). *Sustainability at Tata.* Retrieved on 19 April 2016 from www.tata.com/sustainability/articlesinside/sustainability-at-tata.

Taylor, J. R. and Van Every, E. J. (2000). *The Emergent Organization: Communication as Its Site and Surface.* Mahwah, NJ: Lawrence Erlbaum Associates.

Teisl, M. E., Peavey, S., Newman, F., Buono, J. and Hermann, M. (2002). Consumer Reactions to Environmental Labels for Forest Products: A Preliminary Look. *Forest Products Journal*, 52(1), 44–50.

The Boots Company PLC (2015a). *Boots History.* Retrieved on 19 April 2016 from www.boots-uk.com/About_Boots/Boots_Heritage/Boots_History.aspx.

(2015b). *Our Approach.* Retrieved on 19 April 2016 from www.boots-uk.com/corporate_social_responsibility/our-approach.aspx.

(2016). *Corporate Social Responsibility.* Retrieved on 19 April 2016 from www.boots-uk.com/corporate_social_responsibility/.

The Economist (2002). *Corporate malfeasance is on the verge of becoming a big political issue—even though the public hardly cares about it yet.* 4 July. Retrieved on 22 February 2016 from www.economist.com/node/1217728.

(2003). *The Devil's Excrement: is oil wealth a curse or a blessing.* 22 May. Retrieved on 17 January 2016 from www.economist.com/node/1795921.

The Hauser Institute for Civil Society (2014). *Corporate Social Responsibility Disclosure Efforts by National Governments and Stock Exchanges.* Cambridge, MA: The Hauser Institute for Civil Society – Harvard Kennedy School.

The Hofstede Centre. (2016). *The Hofstede Centre website.* Retrieved on 1 March 2016 from http://geert-hofstede.com/sweden.html.

Tophman, G., Clarke, S., Levett, C., Scruton, P. and Fidler, M. (2015). *The Volkswagen emissions scandal explained.* Retrieved on 31 March 2016 from www.theguardian.com/business/ng-interactive/2015/sep/23/volkswagen-emissions-scandal-explained-diesel-cars.

UN Global Compact, and Principles for Responsible Investment. (2013). *A Tool for Communicating the Business Value of Sustainability.* New York, NY: UN Global Compact Office.

UN (1948). *Universal Declaration on Human Rights*. Retrieved on 18 April, 2016 from www.un.org/Overview/rights.html.

——— (1966a). *International Covenant on Economic, Social and Cultural Rights*. Retrieved on 18 April 2016 from www.ohchr.org/EN/Professional Interest/Pages/CESCR.aspx.

——— (1966b). *International Covenant on Civil and Political Rights*. Retrieved on 18 April 2016 from www.ohchr.org/Documents/ProfessionalInterest/ccpr.pdf.

——— (2007). *Business and Human Rights: Mapping International Standards of Responsibility and Accountability for Corporate Acts. Report of the Special Representative of the Secretary-General on the issue of human rights and transnational corporations and other business enterprises*, UN Doc. A/HRC/4/35, 9 February 2007.

——— (2008). *Protect, respect and remedy: A framework for business and human rights. Report of the Special Representative of the Secretary-General on the issue of human rights and transnational corporations and other business enterprises*, John Ruggie, UN Doc. A/HRC/8/5 (2008), 7 April 2008.

——— (2011). *Guiding Principles on Business and Human Rights: Implementing the United Nations 'Protect, Respect, Remedy' Framework. Report of the Special Representative of the Secretary-General on the issue of human rights and transnational corporations and other business enterprises*, UN Doc. A/HRC/17/31, 21 March 2011.

——— (2012). *The Corporate Responsibility to Respect Human Rights: An Interpretive Guide*. New York and Geneva: Office of the High Commissioner for Human Rights.

United Nations Environmental Programme (UNEP), KPMG Advisory, Global Reporting Initiative (GRI), and Unit for Corporate Governance in Africa (2013). *Carrots and Sticks. Sustainability Reporting Policies Worldwide – Today's Best Practice, Tomorrow's Trends*. Nairobi: UNEP, KPMG Advisory, GRI and Unit for Corporate Governance in Africa.

US Department of Justice (2008). *Siemens AG and Three Subsidiaries Plead Guilty to Foreign Corrupt Practices Act Violations and Agree to Pay $450 Million in Combined Criminal Fines*. Press release, 15 December 2008. Retrieved on 19 October 2015 from www.justice.gov/archive/opa/pr/2008/December/08-crm-1105.html.

US General Accounting Office. (1988). *'SWEATSHOPS'. IN THE U.S. Opinions on Their Sweatshops in the U.S.: Opinions on Their Extent and Possible Enforcement Options*. Washington DC.

USDA (2014). Adoption of genetically engineered crops by U.S. farmers has increased steadily for over 15 years. *The Economic Research Service at the United States Department of Agriculture website*, 4 March. Retrieved on 5 January 2016 from www.ers.usda.gov/amber-waves/2014-march/adoption-of-genetically-engineered-crops-by-us-farmers-has-increased-steadily-for-over-15-years.aspx#.Vo1LUflsPb1.

Utiger, T. (2013). NZ urged to remain GE-free zone. *Taranaki Daily News online*, 21 May. Retrieved on 5 January 2016 from www.stuff.co.nz/taranaki-daily-news/news/8696022/NZ-urged-to-remain-GE-free-zone.

Utting, P. (2008). The Struggle for Corporate Accountability. *Development and Change*, 39(6), 959–975.

Valente, M. (2012). Theorizing Firm Adoption of Sustaincentrism. *Organization Studies*, 33(4), 563–591.

Vallentin, S. (2015). Instrumental and Political Currents in the CSR Debate: On the Demise and (Possible) Resurgence of 'ethics'. In A. Pullen and C. Rhodes (Eds.), *The Routledge Companion to Ethics, Politics and Organizations* (pp. 13–31). London: Routledge.

Van der Merwe, L. F., Pitt, L. P. and Abratt, R. (2005). Stakeholder Strength: PR Survival Strategies in the Internet Age. *Public Relations Quarterly*, 50(1), 39–48.

Van Riel, C. and Balmer J. (1997). Corporate Identity: The Concept, its Measurement and Management. *European Journal of Marketing*, 31(5/6), 340–355.

Vanhamme, J. and Grobben, B. (2009). 'Too Good to be True!' The Effectiveness of CSR History in Countering Negative Publicity. *Journal of Business Ethics*, 85(2), 273–283.

Vattenfall (2009). *Vattenfall Climate Manifesto*. Online video, 10 June. Retrieved on 5 May 2016 from www.youtube.com/watch?v= 0Ubhr4MWbyo.

Vaughan, A. (2012). BMW accused of hypocrisy over opposition to European car targets. *The Guardian*, 9 July. Retrieved on 13 February 2015 from www.theguardian.com/environment/ 2012/jul/09/bmw-hypocrisy-european-car-targets.

Villiers, C. de, Rinaldi, L. and Unerman, J. (2014). Integrated Reporting: Insights, Gaps, and an Agenda for Future Research. *Accounting, Auditing and Accountability Journal*, 27, 1042–1067.

Vogel, D. (2005). *The Market for Virtue. The Potential and Limits of Corporate Social Responsibility*. Washington, DC: Brookings Institution Press.

(2008). Private Global Business Regulation. *Annual Review of Political Science*, 11, 261–282.

Volkswagen A. G. (2015a). Statement of Prof Dr Martin Winterkorn, CEO of Volkswagen AG, 20 September 2015. Retrieved on 31 March 2016 from www.volkswagenag.com/content/ vwcorp/info_center/en/news/2015/09/ statement_ceo_of_volkswagen_ag.html.

(2015b). Dissemination of an Ad hoc announcement according to §15 WpHG: Statement by Prof Dr Winterkorn. Retrieved on 31 March 2016 from www.volkswagenag.com/ content/vwcorp/info_center/en/news/ 2015/09/VW_ad_hoc_Erklaerung .html.

Volvo (2016). *Sustainability*. Retrieved on 5 May 2016 from www.volvocars.com/ intl/about/our-company/sustainability.

Vurro, C., Russo, A. and Perrini, F. (2010). Shaping Sustainable Value Chains: Network Determinants of Supply Chain Governance Models. *Journal of Business Ethics*, 90 (Supplement 4), 607–621.

Waddock, S. A. and McIntosh, M. (2009). Beyond Corporate Responsibility: Implications for Management Development. *Business and Society Review*, 114(3), 295–325.

Waddock, S. and Googins, B. (2011). The Paradoxes of Communicating Corporate Social Responsibility. In Ø. Ihlen, J. L. Bartlett and S. May (Eds.), *The Handbook of Communication and Corporate Social Responsibility* (pp. 23–44). Sussex: Wiley-Blackwell.

Waddock, S. A. and Rasche A. (2012). *Building the Responsible Enterprise. Where Vision and Values Add Value*. Stanford, CA: Stanford University Press.

Wahl, A. and Bull, G. Q. (2014). Mapping Research Topics and Theories in Private Regulation for Sustainability in Global

Value Chains, *Journal of Business Ethics*, 124(4), 585–608.

WardsAuto (2015). U.S. vehicle sales market share by company, 1961–2014. *The WardsAuto website*, 19 January. Retrieved on 1 May 2015 from http://wardsauto.com/keydata/historical/UsaSa28summary.

Weick, K. E. (1979). *The Social Psychology of Organizing* (2nd. ed.). New York, NY: McGraw-Hill.

Wettstein, F. (2009). *Multinational Corporations and Global Justice. Human Rights Obligations of a Quasi-Governmental Institution*. Stanford, CA: Stanford University Press.

(2012a). Human Rights as a Critique of Instrumental CSR: Corporate Responsibility Beyond the Business Case. *Notizie di POLITEIA*, 28 (106), 18–33.

(2012b). CSR and the Debate on Business and Human Rights: Bridging the Great Divide. *Business Ethics Quarterly*, 22(4), 739–770.

(2015). From Side Show to Main Act: Can Business and Human Rights Save Corporate Responsibility? In D. Baumann-Pauly and J. Nolan (Eds.), *Business and Human Rights: From Principles to Practice*. Abingdon, UK and New York, NY: Routledge.

Whelan, G. (2012). The Political Perspective of Corporate Social Responsibility: A Critical Research Agenda. *Business Ethics Quarterly*, 22(4), 709–737.

Whelan, G., Moon, J. and Grant, B. (2013). Corporations and Citizenship Arenas in the Age of Social Media. *Journal of Business Ethics*, 118(4), 777–790.

Wickert, C. (2016). 'Political' Corporate Social Responsibility in Small- and Medium-sized Enterprises: A Conceptual Framework. *Business and Society*, 55(6), 792–824.

Wickert, C., Scherer, A. and Spence, L. (2016). Walking and Talking Corporate Social Responsibility: Implications of Firm Size and Organizational Cost. *Journal of Management Studies*, 53, 1169–1196.

Wiersema, A. (2013). The GOP sees the world through Google Glass. *ABC News*, 15 May. Retrieved on 13 March 2015, from http://abcnews.go.com/blogs/politics/2013/05/the-gop-sees-the-world-through-google-glass/.

Wijen, Frank. (2014). Means versus Ends in Opaque Institutional Fields: Trading off Compliance and Achievement in Sustainability Standard Adoption. *Academy of Management Review*, 39(3), 302–323.

Willard, B. (2009). *The Sustainability Champion's Guidebook*. Gabriola Island, BC: New Society Publishers.

Williams, C. C. (2005). Trust Diffusion: The Effect of Interpersonal Trust on Structure, Function, and Organizational Transparency. *Business and Society*, 44 (3), 357–368.

Wood, D. J. (1991). Corporate Social Performance Revisited. *Academy of Management Review*, 16(4), 691–718.

Wood, S. (2012). The Case for Leverage-Based Corporate Human Rights Responsibility. *Business Ethics Quarterly*, 22(1), 63–98.

World Bank (2013). *Bangladesh Poverty Assessment. Assessing a Decade of Progress in Reducing Poverty, 2000–2010*. Retrieved on 17 April 2014 from www.worldbank.org/en/news/feature/2013/06/20/bangladesh-poverty-assessment-a-decade-of-progress-in-reducing-poverty-2000–2010.

World Commission on Environment and Development (WCED) (1987). *Report of the World Commission on Environment and Development (UN General Assembly A/42/427, 4 August 1987)*. New York, NY: United Nations.

Yoon, Y., Gürhan-Canli, Z. and Schwarz, N. (2006). The Effect of Corporate Social Responsibility (CSR) Activities on Companies With Bad Reputations. *Journal of Consumer Psychology*, 16(4), 377–390.

Yun, O. (2005). Profile of William S. Knowles. *Proceedings of the National Academy of Sciences*, 102(47), 16913–16915.

Zadek, S. (2004). The Path to Corporate Responsibility. *Harvard Business Review*, 82, 125–132.

Zald, M. N. and McCarthy, J. D. (1980). Social Movement Industries: Cooperation and Conflict amongst Social Movement Organizations. *Research in Social Movements, Conflicts and Change*, 3, 1–20.

Zaman, I. (2014). *Corruption rampant a year after Bangladesh factory collapse*. Retrieved on 18 November 2015 from http://blogs.ft.com/beyond-brics/2014/04/24/guest-post-corruption-rampant-a-year-after-bangladesh-factory-fire/.

Zelli, F., and van Asselt, H. (2013). The Institutional Fragmentation of Global Environmental Governance: Causes, Consequences, and Responses. *Global Environmental Politics*, 13(3), 1–1.

Zerk, J. A. (2010). *Extraterritorial Jurisdiction: Lessons for the Business and Human Rights Sphere from Six Regulatory Areas* (Corporate Social Responsibility Initiative Working Paper No. 59.). Cambridge, MA: Harvard Kennedy School of Government.

(2006). *Multinationals and Corporate Social Responsibility: Limitations and Opportunities in International Law*. Cambridge: Cambridge University Press.

Zwolinski, M. (2007). Sweatshops, Choice, and Exploitation. *Business Ethics Quarterly*, 17(4), 689–727.

(2012). Structural Exploitation. *Social Philosophy and Policy*, 29(1), 154–179.

Zyglidopoulos, S. and Fleming, P. (2011). Corporate Accountability and the Politics of Visibility in 'Late Modernity'. *Organization*, 18(5), 691–706.

Name Index

Subject Index